Reginald Pole
Prince & Prophet

THOMAS F. MAYER

CAMBRIDGE
UNIVERSITY PRESS

CAMBRIDGE UNIVERSITY PRESS
Cambridge, New York, Melbourne, Madrid, Cape Town, Singapore, São Paulo

Cambridge University Press
The Edinburgh Building, Cambridge CB2 8RU, UK

Published in the United States of America by Cambridge University Press, New York

www.cambridge.org
Information on this title: www.cambridge.org/9780521371889

First published 2000
This digitally printed version 2007

A catalogue record for this publication is available from the British Library

ISBN 978-0-521-37188-9 hardback
ISBN 978-0-521-03869-0 paperback

Contents

[v]

Tables

Illustrations

List of illustrations

Acknowledgments

This book was John Guy's idea and I am deeply grateful to him. It was fitting that he made his pitch after I had read a paper in Sir Geoffrey Elton's seminar, because Elton stood as godfather to the project. I regret that he did not live to see it completed, although perhaps this is as well given his emphatic 'good!' after I had expressed reservations, since revised, about Pole. Neither Guy nor Elton would have approved of the time it took to complete the book, a delay of almost Polian dimensions, and I must therefore thank William Davies for his inexhaustible patience and commitment to editing as both science and art.

Generous material support of the kind Pole usually lacked came from the Andrew W. Mellon Foundation through both Harvard University and St Louis University; the National Endowment for the Humanities and I Tatti: The Harvard University Center for the Study of the Italian Renaissance; the Gladys Krieble Delmas Foundation; the American Council of Learned Societies; the American Philosophical Society; and the Augustana Research Foundation and Faculty Research Committee.

An earlier version of chapter 1 appeared in 'Nursery of resistance: Reginald Pole and his friends', in Paul A. Fideler and T. F. Mayer, eds., *Political thought and the Tudor commonwealth: deep structure, discourse and disguise* (London: Routledge, 1992), pp. 50–74 and I am grateful for permission to rework the material.

A truly humbling number of people and institutions facilitated my research. The original Pole was a collective effort, and so is this simulacrum. I hesitate to draw invidious distinctions, but a few old friends and counsellors have been especially helpful. Although out of alphabetical order, Diana Robin must head this list, along with Elisabeth Gleason, S. E. Lehmberg, Thomas McCoog, Daniel Woolf, and Price Zimmermann. Fred Conrad, Dermot Fenlon, Gigliola Fragnito, my former student John Frymire, Steven Gunn, Bill Hudon, Charles Knighton, John Marmion (who lent both his own thesis and Noëlle Marie Egretier's on Pole), Sergio Pagano, Eletto Ramacci, Richard Rex, Marcello

Simonetta, Susan Wabuda, Breifne V. Walker, Jonathan Woolfson, and Fabiano T. Fagliari Zeni Buccichio have been generous with their time and information. Thomas F. Dunn made me a gift of his extensive collection of materials on Pole, including copies of all the manuscripts of *De unitate*, on which he had been set to work by George Parks. Such are the subterranean traditions of scholarship. My colleague Thomas Banks checked some of my translations from Latin. From Leonard Barkan I learned a great deal about art history, as from Celeste Brusati, and from two other members of Barkan's NEH seminar, Michael Kissane and Julie McGee, as well as at a later date from Elizabeth Pilliod. Ken Bartlett contributed much, not least well-timed social occasions. Newer friends have lent their encouragement and occasionally their labour, especially Bill Connell and Ken Gouwens, the second of whom organized a speaking tour for me which covered many of the subjects of this book and provided the occasion in a Burger King in North Carolina for me to resolve its central methodological dilemma. At I Tatti in addition to Connell, I profited especially from conversations with Patricia Rubin, Stephen Kolsky and Clare Robertson, who has continued to be unfailingly helpful. Paolo Prodi at Trent and Giuseppe Alberigo and Alberto Melloni at Bologna gave me an especially important opportunity to air some of chapter 5. Melanie Barber, Deputy Librarian and Archivist, Lambeth Palace Library, saved me from a multitude of mistakes.

Without access to manuscripts and printed sources, there would have been no book, and I offer a regrettably formulaic thanks to the staff of the following institutions: Accademia dei Concordi, Rovigo; Archivio della Congregazione per la Dottrina della Fede, especially the prefect of the Congregation, Josef Cardinal Ratzinger, the secretary, Mons. Alberto Bovone, and the archive's director, Mons. Alejandro Cifres; Archivii di stato of Florence, Mantua, Modena, Parma (especially its director Marzio Dall'Acqua), Trent, Venice, and Verona; Archivio storico comunale, Trent; Augustana College Library, especially Inter-library Loan; Biblioteca apostolica vaticana and Archivio segreto vaticano; Biblioteca civica, Bergamo; Biblioteca civica, Brescia, especially Rosa Zilioli and Paolo Galimberti; Biblioteca comunale, Trent; Biblioteca comunale degli Ardenti, Viterbo, especially Nello De Santis; Biblioteche del seminario, Modena and Padua; Biblioteca Estense, Modena; Biblioteca nazionale Marciana, Venice; Biblioteca palatina, Parma; Bibliothèque municipale de Douai, especially its director Michelle Demarcy; the Biblioteche universitarie of Bologna and Padua; Bodleian Library; British Library; Cambridge University Library; Canterbury Cathedral Archives, especially its director Michael Stansfield; Photographic Section of the Courtauld Institute of Art, especially Sarah Wimbush; Institute of Historical Research in the University of London and the University Library; Istituto storico italo-germanico, Trent; Istituto per le scienze religiosi, Bologna; Kunsthistorisches Institut, Florence; M. Camilleri, director of the National Library of Malta; National Portrait Gallery Archives, above all Jill Springall who greatly facilitated my work on site and has continued to assist promptly thereafter; the National Trust; Public Record Office, London, especially Hillary Jones; Manuscript and Prints Departments of Sotheby's, London; the University of Iowa; the University of Minnesota; and perhaps most important of all, the Vatican Microfilm Library, St Louis University, especially Charles Ermatinger and Barbara Channell. This book would have taken twice as long without that collection and their help.

A number of others have aided me, and to all I am very grateful: Josef Altholz; Thomas Amos; Paul Ayris; Adrian Blunt; Brendan Bradshaw; Toby Bridge; Mrs G. Cannell of the Parker Library, Corpus Christi College, Cambridge; Francesco Cesareo; David Dean; Andrew Gow; James Hankins; Robert Klein and DiAnn Kilburg at the Loras College Library; Nicholas Orme; Jonathan Reid; Larry Rhu; Sharon Strocchia and several of her research assistants; Ronnie Terpening; Pamela Tudor-Craig, Lady Wedgwood; Benjamin Watson; Donald Weinstein; and Jo North, who copy-edited a long and complex text efficiently and accurately.

Finally, my colleagues in the history department at Augustana have consistently supported my work and I am grateful to them. My students have put up with it, and even affected to find it interesting.

I am certain I have failed to note other assistance, and I apologize for the oversight.

Three people own this book almost as much as I do. The first is my former student Peter Starenko, who was my research assistant and nanny for a year in Italy doing yeoman work on both scores, as well as putting up with me and Pole. Peter had that last assignment for only a year. I dedicate this book to my wife Jan Popehn and daughter Molly who have had to do this, Molly for as long as she has been alive, Jan for almost as long as she has known me. A book is a poor reward for such tolerance.

Thomas F. Mayer
Moline, Illinois

Abbreviations

Archives and libraries

ASAS: Biblioteca Civica 'Angelo Mai', Archivio Stella in Archivio Silvestri, Bergamo

AS (BCAV): Archivio storico (Biblioteca comunale degli Ardenti), Viterbo

ASF: Archivio di stato, Florence
    ASF:CC: Carte Cerviniane
    ASF:AMP: Archivio mediceo del principato

ASM: Archivio di stato, Mantua
    ASM:AG: Archivio Gonzaga
    ASM:CEG: Copialettere Ercole Gonzaga

ASMod: Archivio di stato, Modena

ACDFSO: Archivio della Congregazione per la Dottrina della Fede, Sanctum officium

ASP: Archivio di stato, Parma

ASV: Archivio segreto Vaticano

ASVe:APR: Archivio di stato, Venice, Archivio Proprio Roma

BAV: Biblioteca apostolica vaticana

BCQ: Biblioteca civica 'Queriniana', Brescia

BL: British Library

BNM: Biblioteca Nazionale Marciana, Venice

BNN: Biblioteca Nazionale 'Vittorio Emmanuele III', Naples

BMD: Bibliothèque municipale, Douai

BPP: Biblioteca palatina, Parma

CCA, Dcc: Canterbury Cathedral Archives, Dean and chapter

CCCC: The Parker Library, Corpus Christi College, Cambridge

LPL: Lambeth Palace Library

PRO: Public Record Office

Single manuscripts

BMIC24/25   Bodleian Library, Oxford, MS Ital. C 24 or 25

Books

Alumbrados Massimo Firpo, *Tra alumbrados e 'spirituali'. Studi su Juan de Valdés e il valdesianesimo nella crisi religiosa del '500 italiano* (Florence: Olschki, 1990)

Bonelli Giuseppe Bonelli, 'Un archivio privato del Cinquecento: Le Carte Stella', *Archivio storico Lombardo*, 34 (1907), pp. 332–86

Carranza y Pole J. I. Tellechea Idigoras, *Fray Bartolomé Carranza y el Cardenal Pole. Un Navarro en la restauración católica (1554–1558)* (Pamplona: CIES, 1977)

CPM Thomas F. Mayer, 'A reluctant author: Cardinal Pole and his manuscripts,' *Transactions of the American Philosophical Society*, 89:4 (1999)

CPRPM Calender of patent rolls, Philip and Mary (London: HMSO, 1936–39; 4 vols.)

CRP The correspondence of Reginald Pole, ed. Thomas F. Mayer (Aldershot: Ashgate Publishing, to appear beginning in 2002)

CSPDom Robert Lemon and Mary A. E. Green, eds., *Calendar of state papers domestic, 1547–1625* (London: Longman, Brown and Green, 1856–72; 12 vols.)

[xiv]

CSPDomR C. S. Knighton, ed., *Calendar of state papers domestic series of the reign of Mary I, 1553–1558, revised* (London: PRO, 1998)

CSPFor W. H. Turnbull, ed., *Calendar of state papers foreign series of the reign of Mary, 1553–1558* (London: Longman, Green, Longman and Roberts, 1861)

CSPSp Gustav A. Bergenroth et al., eds., *Calendar of letters, despatches and state papers, relating to the negotiations between England and Spain* (London: Longman et al., 1862–1954)

CSPV Rawdon Brown, ed., *Calendar of state papers and manuscripts, relating to English affairs in the archives and collections of Venice* (London: Longman et al., 1864–98; 9 vols.)

CT Concilii Tridentini, ed. Sebastian Merkle, Stephan Ehses, Gottfried Buschbell et al., 1, 2, 4, 5, 6, 8–12 (Freiburg: Herder, 1901–66)

DBI A. M. Ghisalberti, ed., *Dizionario biografico degli italiani* (Rome: Istituto dell'enciclopedia italiana, 1960–)

Doc. hist. J. I. Tellechea Idigoras, ed., *Fray Bartolomé Carranza. Documentos historicos* (Madrid: Real Academia de la Historia, 1962–1981; 6 vols.)

ERP Angelo Maria Querini, ed., *Epistolarum Reginaldi Poli* [*libri*] (Brescia: Rizzardi, 1744–57; 5 vols.)

Evan. ital. Paolo Simoncelli, *Evangelismo italiano del cinquecento. Questione religiosa e nicodemismo politico* (Rome: Edizioni di Storia e Letteratura, 1979)

Fenlon Dermot Fenlon, *Heresy and obedience in Tridentine Italy: cardinal Pole and the counter reformation* (Cambridge: Cambridge University Press, 1972)

Hallé Marie Hallé (writing as Martin Haile), *Life of Reginald Pole* (London: Pitman, 1911; 2nd ed.)

Höllger Christoph Höllger, 'Reginald Pole and the legations of 1537 and 1539; diplomatic and polemical responses to the break with Rome', University of Oxford, DPhil thesis, 1989

Inq. rom. Massimo Firpo, *Inquisizione romana e Controriforma. Studi sul Cardinal Giovanni Morone e il suo processo d'eresia* (Bologna: Il Mulino, 1992)

L&P J. S. Brewer, James Gairdner and R. H. Brodie, eds., *Letters and papers, foreign and domestic of the reign of Henry VIII* (London: HMSO, 1862–1932; 29 vols.)

NB, 15 Heinrich Lutz, ed., *Nuntiaturberichte aus Deutschland. Erste Abteilung 1533–1559*, 15, *Friedenslegation des Reginald Pole zu Kaiser Karl V. und König Heinrich II. (1553–1556)* (Tübingen: Niemeyer, 1981)

MMB G. B. Morandi, ed., *Monumenti di varia letteratura* (Bologna: Istituto per le scienze, 1797–1804; 2 vols.)

PC Giacomo Manzoni, ed., 'Il processo Carnesecchi', *Miscellanea di storia italiana*, 10 (1870), pp. 189–573

PM Massimo Firpo and Dario Marcatto, eds., *Il processo inquisitoriale del Cardinal Giovanni Morone* (Rome, 1981–96; 6 vols.)

Pogson R. H. Pogson, 'Cardinal Pole – Papal Legate to England in Mary Tudor's Reign', University of Cambridge, PhD dissertation, 1972

Schenk Wilhelm Schenk, *Reginald Pole, cardinal of England* (London: Longmans, Green and Co., 1950)

Simoncelli, *Caso* Paolo Simoncelli, *Il caso Reginald Pole: eresia e santità nelle polemiche religiose del cinquecento* (Rome: Edizioni di Storia e Letteratura, 1977)

Weiss Charles Weiss, *Papiers d'Etat du Cardinal de Granvelle*, 4 (Paris: Imprimerie royale, 1843)

Journals

ARG: *Archiv für Reformationsgeschichte*
RSLR: *Rivista di storia e letteratura religiosa*
SCJ: *Sixteenth century journal*

NB All quotations have been modernized.

Introduction

IN THE SEVENTEENTH century William Joyner had doubts about offering the first work in English devoted to Reginald Pole (1500–58), likening praise of him to recommending Scipio in Carthage or Hannibal in Rome.[1] At least Joyner expected that Pole would be known in England. Fifty years ago, the author of the last serious life displayed less optimism. 'Cardinal Pole . . . is little known in his native country', sighed Wilhelm Schenk.[2] In between Edmund Lodge put his finger on a major reason that Pole the man has not been understood anywhere: 'it is rather his *character* than his history that has been transmitted to posterity'.[3] Lodge then went on to produce the same kind of sketch, reinforcing an approach that has dominated writing about Pole ever since the first two lives were composed shortly after his death in 1558. One historian thought the situation virtually irretrievable from the power of Pole's 'myth of sanctity'.[4]

Things are not so bleak, although still not easy. In Italy over the last twenty years Pole and his circles have received much attention, especially from Massimo Firpo and Dario Marcatto, Paolo Simoncelli, and Gigliola Fragnito, even if the last important English-language scholarship is ten years older. Despite his standing as cousin of Henry VIII, cardinal and archbishop of Canterbury, mainstay of the Italian reformation, and reconciler of England, making him one of the most important international figures of the mid-

---

[1] William Joyner, *Some observations upon the life of Reginaldus Polus cardinal of the royal blood of England. Sent in a pacquet out of Wales, by G. L. gentleman and servant to the late majesty of Henrietta Maria* (London: Matthew Turner, 1686), p. 8.

[2] Schenk, p. vii.

[3] Edmund Lodge, *Portraits of illustrious personages of Great Britain, with biographical and historical memoirs of their lives and actions* (London: Henry Bohn, 1849; 8 vols.), 1, p. 253, emphasis added.

[4] Simoncelli, *Caso*, ch. 3, *passim*.

sixteenth century, as well as the first well-known anti-Machiavellian, Pole remains an enigma. He seems a classic instance of the adage *inglese italianato, diavolo incarnato* ('italianate Englishman, devil incarnate'), first fastened on him by Matthew Parker. Pietro Carnesecchi pointed to a central difficulty for any biographer of Pole in his summary judgment of his former ally. 'He has been very unfortunate . . . being considered a Lutheran in Rome, in Germany a papist, in the [imperial] court of Flanders French, and in that of France, imperial.'[5] Even if we simplify Carnesecchi's matrix to the more usual two aspects of Pole's career and attend only to his time in England and Italy, those periods remain as disjointed as Carnesecchi's French were from the Imperialists.

The nature of the evidence causes another difficulty. While it might have appeared in the past that there was too little to go on, in fact there is too much. It is of three types. First and most impenetrable, Pole threw up around himself a smoke-screen of writings, many in his increasingly wretched scrawl as well as a sorry state of conservation. This poses two separate sub-problems, one technical, palaeographical and codicological, the other analytical, of deciphering the content and then the meaning of the texts contained in the manuscripts. The second proved more difficult than the first, but taking the complete corpus of Pole's work into account helped with both.[6] Second, Pole's correspondence amounts to more than 2,000 items, many of them previously unknown.[7] Finally, Italian archives yield a staggering amount of ancillary material, especially but not exclusively for the conclave of Julius III (see the list of repositories above).

Evidence by itself is not history. Another more serious stumbling-block in the way of a convincing Pole is the failure to recognize that like most Renaissance literate people, his life was constructed through the medium of texts and rhetoric. The 'myth of sanctity' obscuring the 'real' Pole was ineluctably rhetorical, intended to serve persuasive purposes. 'Pole' arose through a process in which its author tried on in writing a series of identities, often several at once, until the original Pole (so to say) established a consistent image and maybe even a consistent personality. To judge from the sway he (or they) established over those closest to him, Pole and 'Pole' enjoyed success. This was not a one-way street. 'Pole' and his sway depended on collaborative effort, again as in the case of most Renaissance individuals.[8] This holds literally true of

---

[5] *PC*, p. 301.
[6] For the manuscripts, see *CPM*.
[7] Forthcoming in *CRP*.

[8] As was argued in the session 'Collective individualism' at the Renaissance Society of America meeting, New York, 1995.

his writings, most of them composed by a team, and his (auto)biographies arose in similar fashion, with similarly rhetorical purposes.[9] Thus Pole always existed in two phases, the life as lived and the life as written. Almost without exception, the second has been taken as equivalent to the first. This will no longer do. The container (the texts) is not the contained (the life).[10]

In this book I shall pursue a method like that attempted in my study of Pole's satellite Thomas Starkey.[11] It involves uncovering intentions in texts through close reading, the motives behind them, and after establishing a dialectic between these two, placing both in tension with their contexts. Only by allowing text and life equal time can we understand either or both. This does not guarantee recovery of the 'real' Pole, but holding in tension what Pole and his friends said he did with what Pole did as established by historical criticism should bring us closer. In addition, I have drawn on the inspiration if not necessarily the specifics of Stephen Greenblatt's theory of 'Renaissance self-fashioning', which explains how and why men like Pole remade their *personae* (almost literally 'masks') through literary means, as well as the approach in terms of 'tensions and contradictions' adopted in William Bouwsma's *John Calvin*.[12]

It would be as well to admit immediately that limitations of space have made it impossible to execute this approach quite as I would have liked.[13] Context has had to be pretty tightly drawn around Pole, and wider events at best sketched. More seriously limiting, a prosopographical approach has been abandoned almost entirely. One of the greatest losses is nearly all the literary milieu around Pole, especially the poetry written by many of his intimates.[14] I intend to return

---

[9] See for now Thomas F. Mayer, 'A sticking-plaster saint? Autobiography and hagiography in the making of Reginald Pole' in T. F. Mayer and D. R. Woolf, eds., *The rhetorics of life-writing in early modern Europe: forms of biography from Cassandra Fedele to Louis XIV* (Ann Arbor: University of Michigan Press, 1995), pp. 205–22.

[10] Kenneth Burke, *A grammar of motives* (Berkeley: University of California Press, 1969), ch. 1 and *passim*.

[11] Thomas F. Mayer, *Thomas Starkey and the commonweal: humanist politics and religion in the reign of Henry VIII* (Cambridge: Cambridge University Press, 1989).

[12] Stephen Greenblatt, *Renaissance self-fashioning, from More to Shakespeare* (Chicago: University of Chicago Press, 1980); William J. Bouwsma, *John Calvin: a sixteenth century portrait* (Berkeley: University of California Press, 1988), quotation on p. 5.

[13] Other consequences of length limits are that I have usually not given the original of passages translated in the text, and there is no bibliography.

[14] For a suggestion about the importance of 'literary' phenomena for cultural history, see Lino Pertile, 'Appollonio Merenda, segretario del Bembo, e ventidue lettere di Trifone Gabriele', *Studi e problemi di critica testuale*, no. 34 (April, 1987), pp. 9–48, p. 36.

to it and them in the future.[15] One other vital area left largely untouched concerns Pole's use of the Greek fathers. Jonathan Woolfson recently suggests their importance, and a casual read through Pole's works confirms the necessity of further research.[16] The at least sixteen manuscripts of John Chrysostom in his library crudely indicates the scale of his interest.[17]

Pole's career is easily encapsulated as a contest for authority. On a personal level, Pole struggled throughout his life with the consequences of writing 'Pole', that is, with being an author and the authority that identity conveyed. His era witnessed a major change in the notion of authorship as the possibilities of print slowly took hold. Yet Pole tried hard to avoid admitting that he was a writer, despite the fact that he *was* one in a sense more profound than nearly any of his contemporaries, with the possible exception of Erasmus.[18] He admitted that writing gave him pleasure, and acknowledged its therapeutic value, but at almost the same time he insisted that 'I do not place myself in the number of writers, [since] when I write something, I never write it with the intention to publish'.[19] Pole's stance was typical, given the 'stigma of print' and the protracted transition from manuscript to print culture.[20] So also were the serious troubles the more general nature of authority gave Pole. Beginning with the conflicted prose of *De unitate* and continuing right through to his forthright

---

[15] Some of them dropped away simply because too little is known. A persuasive reason to omit the others is that a new edition of the *processo* against Pietro Carnesecchi is under way but will not be completed for at least several years, and Massimo Firpo kindly tells me that it contains a great deal more information than *PC*. The first volume has just appeared: Massimo Firpo and Dario Marcatto, eds., *I processi inquisitoriali di Pietro Carnesecchi (1557–1567)*, 1, *I processi sotto Paolo IV e Pio IV (1557–1561)* (Vatican City: Archivio Segreto Vaticano, 1998).

[16] Jonathan Woolfson, *Padua and the Tudors: English students in Italy, 1485–1603* (Toronto: University of Toronto Press, 1998), p. 112.

[17] I. Hutter, 'Cardinal Pole's Greek manuscripts in Oxford', in A. C. de la Mare and B. C. Barker-Benfield, eds.,

Manuscripts in Oxford: an exhibition in memory of Richard William Hunt (Oxford: Bodleian Library, 1980), pp. 108–14, p. 112. Pole's library is recorded in Bodleian Library, MS Broxbourne 84.11, printed in Alessandro Pastore, 'Due biblioteche umanistiche del Cinquecento (I libri del cardinal Pole e di Marcantonio Flaminio)', *Rinascimento*, ser. 2, 19 (1979), pp. 269–90.

[18] Lisa Jardine, *Erasmus, man of letters* (Princeton: Princeton University Press, 1995).

[19] *MMB*, pp. 350–1 and quotation from *CRP*, no. 636.

[20] Wendy Wall, *The imprint of gender: authorship and publication in the English renaissance* (Ithaca: Cornell University Press, 1993), p. x and David R. Carlson, *English humanist books: writers and patrons, manuscript and print, 1475–1525* (Toronto: University of Toronto Press, 1992), *passim*.

criticisms of Paul IV, Pole remained uncomfortably suspended between competing notions of authority. His reluctance to accept the dictates of pope or emperor points to the same problem. The possibilities that Pole's struggles were in part genetic in a grandson of George, Duke of Clarence, two of whose brothers paid dearly for a similar inability to control themselves, as well as connected to the death of his father at a very young age immediately suggest themselves, but Pole did not take the route that certain kinds of psychological analysis might predict and cast about constantly for father substitutes.[21] With the possible exception of Gasparo Contarini, who was in any case only a half-generation older, Pole did not seek for mentors. Or rather, whenever he did, he sooner or later turned on them, with the likely exception of Contarini. Henry VIII and Gianpietro Carafa, his two greatest antagonists, make obvious instances. Even his painful acceptance of the necessity of obedience, about which he had to write over and over again as much to himself as to his audiences, did not finally settle the issue. This unresolved issue helps to account for Pole's predilection for the life as written and his characteristic use of *personae* to mask his conflicts.

A permanent tension between ambition and self-abnegation shaped Pole's lives into two basic *personae*, prince and prophet, as well as a variant of the second, martyr.[22] These were precariously synthesized in the last stage of Pole's life. Pole's *personae* were dearly won creations, their standing always in doubt. Hence his eagerness to affirm them over and over again in writing in an attempt to convince himself of their reality. A combination of social position and Italian experience provided the external framework of Pole's life as lived. Historical and literary criticism makes its first phase straightforward. Until the age of thirty, Pole sought to recover his rightful place as a younger son of the highest nobility, especially one who had lost the princely position his royal blood deserved and found himself entirely dependent on Henry VIII's favour. Having

---

21 Peter S. Donaldson, 'Machiavelli and Antichrist: prophetic typology in Reginald Pole's *De unitate* and *Apologia ad Carolum quintum*', in *Machiavelli and mystery of state* (Cambridge: Cambridge University Press, 1989), pp. 1–35 offers some suggestions about how Pole's relation to his father affected some of his writing. For Sir Richard see Hazel Pierce, 'The king's cousin: the life, career and Welsh connection of Sir Richard Pole, 1458–1504', *Welsh history review*, 19 (1998), pp. 187–225 and for two of his brothers, Sir Henry and Sir Geoffrey, my articles in H. C. G. Matthew, ed., *New dictionary of national biography* (Oxford: Oxford University Press, forthcoming).

22 For Pole as prophet, see the suggestions of Noëlle-Marie Egretier, ed. and trans., Reginald Pole, *Défense de l'unité de l'église* (Paris: J. Vrin, 1967), pp. 34 and 41 and Donaldson, for martyr, see W. F. Hook, *Lives of the archbishops of Canterbury*, 8 (London: Richard Bentley, 1869; 2nd ed. 1884).

gambled in 1530–1 that he could dissuade Henry from getting rid of Katherine and failed, Pole slowly turned his back over the next five or six years on aspirations to secular preferment. A drawn-out religious conversion helps to account in part for the appearance of Pole's second *persona* in *De unitate* (1536). In that work, Pole cast himself as prophet-cum-martyr calling Henry to repentance and defending ecclesiastical authority. Simultaneously, instead of self-assertion, Pole adopted the self-denying belief that human effort could contribute nothing to salvation.

In moments of crisis, the passivity first seen during his legation of 1537 overcame Pole. His behaviour during the papal conclave of 1550 offers a clue to the meaning of this self-denial. Although coming within one vote of election, Pole stoutly refused to campaign, spending his time instead writing a refined version of his martyr self, a Christ-like *persona*, coupled slightly later with an image of himself as the ass which bore Christ into Jerusalem. Thus it might be said that Pole's inaction resulted from his self-image, although the point could as well be put the other way around. However phrased, Pole's preference for deflecting conflict through writing is one of the most important constants in his career, incorrectly called in the past a preference for withdrawal. Rather, Benjamin Pye, eighteenth-century translator of Ludovico Beccadelli's life of Pole, tritely if exactly understood that 'his PEN was his SWORD, and they against whom he drew it always found it a very smart and vindictive weapon'.[23] It is equally important to realize that Pole and his supporters meant 'his' writing, however motivated and violent, as an aesthetic object, exactly parallel to the graphic image created for Pole beginning in 1546. He and his life were to be a thing of beauty.

The last phase of Pole's career back in England after 1554 as legate and then archbishop of Canterbury is relatively the best studied. During this time Pole's two principal *personae*, perhaps through long practice almost become modes of being rather than seeming, coalesced into the identity of prince of both church and realm (figuratively, anyway). Nor was the *persona* of Christ forgotten, as Rex Pogson first observed.[24] Pole and his new synthesis were not seriously threatened until Paul IV, moving by fits and starts, tried to destroy Pole, his party, and his identity. The pope thereby unwittingly provided the impetus to impress on later historiography Pole's self-image as martyr. The power of his

---

[23] *The life of Cardinal Reginald Pole, written originally by Lodovico Beccadelli . . . translated by Benjamin Pye* (London: Bathurst, 1766), pp. 156–7.

[24] Pogson, p. 39.

pen had finally given Pole a stable and satisfactory *persona*. This book is about the process through which that mask arose and then transcended its original context.

My view has changed considerably over the twenty years I have worked on Pole. I argued earlier that Pole was a weathercock who trimmed his opinions in a consistently inconsistent fashion. I still maintain that as a good rhetorician he could accommodate his message to any audience, although he did not always try, often with unfortunate consequences. Much to my surprise, I discovered that major elements of his message were more nearly unified than I had thought. Putting the two halves of Pole's life together, the English and Italian, aided that discovery. Far from the ambiguous, ambivalent, even confused figure of most recent historiography, even a 'Hamlet', Pole laid out his basic theological positions in *De unitate* and refused to back down on any significant point thereafter, including the necessity of justification by faith.[25] He did, however, drift in the direction of a steadily more mystical religion, which may have appealed to him as a solution to the problem of authority. While both points may amount to endorsing the constant Pole of hagiographical tradition, steadiness of ideas does not equal steadiness of existence. One of the major arguments of this book is how active Pole's life was, even as he led much of it in writing.

Having said that Pole stuck to his theological guns, I must confess that this book is not much about theology as a technical subject. It is, however, very much about what might be called the political history of religion and the role of ideas within it, as practised by Firpo, Simoncelli, and Paolo Prodi. One standard category in work like Firpo's and Simoncelli's I have found unhelpful: the assessment of orthodoxy vs. heterodoxy. Once glaringly obvious, this judgment is now often implicit, especially in newer studies of the Inquisition, despite the slowly dawning awareness that there was no such thing even as theoretical orthodoxy before Trent and not for a long time thereafter in practice.[26] Instead of positing

---

[25] Simoncelli attacked Hubert Jedin's thesis of Pole's *confusione teologica* as *apologetica e politica*. *Evan. ital.*, p. 177 n102. Firpo especially emphasizes Pole's confusion, *e.g.*, *PM*, 1, p. 141. Cf. also Fenlon, p. 248 and most recently Adriano Prosperi, 'Evangelismo di Seripando', in Antonio Cestaro, ed., *Geronimo Seripando e la chiesa del suo tempo nel V centenario della nascita* (Rome: Edizioni di storia e letteratura, 1997), pp. 33–49, who contrasts the 'Hamletic' Pole's 'reserve and mystery' to

Seripando's straightforwardness (p. 47). See chapter 4 for evidence against this antithesis.

[26] See most recently, Gigliola Fragnito, *La Bibbia al rogo: la censura ecclesiastica e i volgarizzamenti della Scrittura (1471–1605)* (Bologna: Il Mulino, 1997) and Giuseppe Alberigo, 'Dinamiche religiose del Cinquecento italiano tra riforma, riforma cattolica, controriforma', *Cristianesimo nella storia*, 6 (1985), pp. 543–60.

a binary opposition, I have taken a dialectical approach, substituting for the prevailing model of good guys (the *spirituali*, to whom we shall return in a moment) and obvious bad guys, the *intransigenti* or plain old 'intransigents', the idea of a 'reform tendency' embracing nearly all the characters in this story.[27] Constantly shifting, realigning, metamorphosing, anything but a party, this tendency includes all those who expressed allegiance to reform and who usually cooperated with one another until driven apart by personality or politics, *not* in the first instance religious differences.[28] Rather than reading the story backwards as one of division from the first, I have followed the evidence which shows that the reform tendency broke down very gradually and that Pole played a key role in its decline. If Pole was a victim, he helped to victimize himself.

The last paragraph raises a problem of definition. What to call Pole and his allies? Delio Cantimori, dean of historians of reform in Italy, identified the problem: their position arose from individual psychological experience, and doctrine therefore meant comparatively little.[29] While there may be more social and political regularities behind the phenomenon than Cantimori allowed, complex varieties of religious experience flourished across Italy in the early sixteenth century, often to be grasped at a level little above individuals. This complexity has often been read as ambiguity, but in Pole's case if not more generally, ambiguity is a function not so much of the individual as of his situation, caught in the middle between opposites that increasingly demanded clear and unambiguous answers. As the landscape changed, so apparently did Pole's opinions. His never fully resolved difficulties with authority contributed to further cloud his image, since they have not been acknowledged in recent work. Nevertheless, individuality and complexity hold for Pole, the more so as he got older, against the prevailing view. We shall see this particularly from a study of his 'De reformatione ecclesiae'. Taking full account of all the difficulties inherent in labels and this one in particular, Pole and his allies must still be called something, and I shall continue to use *spirituali*. Labels for the phenomenon

---

[27] I here borrow in part from Dominic Baker-Smith's stimulating suggestion. 'Florens Wilson: A distant prospect', in Janet Hadley Williams, ed., *Stewart style 1513–1542: essays on the court of James V* (East Linton, Scotland: Tuckwell Press, 1996), pp. 1–14, pp. 6–7, 11.

[28] Paul Grendler has recently highlighted the difficulties of classifying sixteenth-century Italian religious history. 'The Adages of Paolo Manuzio: Erasmus and the Roman censors', in James V. Mehl, ed., *In laudem Caroli: Renaissance and reformation studies for Charles G. Nauert* (Kirksville, MO: Thomas Jefferson University Press, 1998), pp. 1–21, p. 21.

[29] Delio Cantimori, *Eretici italiani del Cinquecento. Ricerche storiche* (Florence: Sansoni, 1977; reprint of 1939 edition), pp. 24–5.

cause more discomfort, and rightly so.[30] I submit that reform tendency alleviates this difficulty.

Elisabeth Gleason some years ago offered the best characterization of the *spirituali* (while identifying the phenomenon as *evangelismo*).[31] According to her, their central theological belief, justification by faith, arose from another vaguely defined 'movement', *paulinismo preluterano* ('pre-Lutheran Paulinism'), intensified by the coming of the reformations. Reform of the church came high on the agenda, usually but not necessarily cast in institutional terms, and preaching was a vital tool. I would also emphasize the degree to which politics contributed both opportunities for the growth of '*evangelismo*', most obviously in Pole's falling out with Henry, and also the means for it to effect its ends, however much the *spirituali* pretended to ride above the fray.

The allegedly painful process by which the *spirituali* chose to remain within the Roman church, despite their affinity for Protestant theology, has attracted much attention. Here, too, Pole's consistency suggests an easier and less wrenching solution. He never regarded papal obedience in a juridical or political sense as essential, not in *De unitate*, not even as papal legate for the restoration of England, no matter how much Pole protested to the contrary. His notion of the papacy was profoundly charismatic, not monarchical, and the church he envisioned was much less hierarchical and hieratic than has been thought. Certainly his enemies feared that he intended to subvert the institutional church. It is only with hindsight that historians have created a problem of allegiance when contemporaries could have had no way of knowing that Paul IV's reassertion of papal 'absolutism' (for lack of a better term) was not an aberration. Before that Paul III and Julius III (and probably Marcellus II had he lived) operated much more by consensus and the balancing of contending forces than through the imposition of their will by bureaucratic means, especially the Inquisition, as Paul IV habitually did.[32] Pole was simply not as prescient as historians would have liked. In any case, the claim that the reformation was much more about ecclesiology than about theology holds true for him.[33]

---

[30] See especially Firpo's review of Marcantonio Flaminio, *Lettere*, ed. Alessandro Pastore in *Rivista storica italiana*, 91 (1979), pp. 653–62.

[31] Elisabeth G. Gleason, 'On the nature of sixteenth century Italian evangelism: scholarship, 1953–1978', *SCJ*, 9 (1978), pp. 3–25.

[32] Gigliola Fragnito, 'Evangelismo e intransigenti nei difficili equilibri del pontificato farnesiano', *RSLR*, 25 (1989), pp. 20–47.

[33] Heinz Scheible, 'Reform, reformation, revolution: Grundsätze zur Beurteilung der Flugschriften', *ARG*, 65 (1974), pp. 108–33, pp. 117–19.

Two other prevailing and related interpretations of Pole must also be questioned and one rejected. From Francesco Negri's and Pier Paolo Vergerio's attacks forward, Pole was identified as one who knew the truth and yet refused to embrace it publicly. Vergerio not very covertly derided Pole's dictum that 'it is necessary to be prudent, and await occasion and the opportune moment'.[34] He was a Nicodemite, as John Calvin branded such cowards.[35] This label continues to stick to Pole, even as its meaning becomes problematic.[36] The debate takes two positions. One sees Nicodemism as a coherent theory of dissimulation, and the other as a practice derived from circumstances. Recently, a middle ground has been staked out and Nicodemism construed as arising from practice, while rooted in ethical considerations, above all the importance of prudence.[37] This formulation might fit Pole up to a point, and he did figure as a hero to Italians who probably were Nicodemites.[38] Many of his writings concerned themselves with prudence, and we shall repeatedly see that his retrospective interpretations skated in prudential fashion around the literal truth. He took as his motto the verse from Matthew 10:16 'Estote prudentes sicut serpentes, et simplices sicut columbae' ('Be as wise as serpents, and as simple as doves') or a version of it and had it painted on a window in his new wing of Lambeth Palace as well as on his tomb.[39] Yet there is reason for hesitation before labelling Pole a Nicodemite. He often regarded prudence as synonymous with 'human prudence', the opposite of divine wisdom and one of if not the most serious threats, and, as for his practice, reluctance to act does not amount to dissimulation. If, as I shall demonstrate, Pole was not confused, especially not about justification, and really did believe that only words separated him from Trent's decree on it, this points directly to

---

[34] Salvatore Caponetto, ed., *Il 'beneficio di Cristo' con le versione del secolo XVI, documenti e testimonianze* (Florence, DeKalb, IL and Chicago: Sansoni, Northern Illinois University Press and The Newberry Library, 1972), p. 444.

[35] Simoncelli, *Caso, passim* and Carlos M. N. Eire, 'Calvin and nicodemism: a reappraisal', *SCJ*, 10 (1979), pp. 45–70.

[36] Manfred Welti, for example, describes Pole as 'a born Nicodemite, taciturn by nature'. *Breve storia della riforma italiana* (Casale Monferrato: Marietti, 1985), trans. Armido Rizzi, p. 34.

[37] John Martin, *Venice's hidden enemies. Italian heretics in a renaissance city* (Berkeley: University of California Press, 1993), ch. 5.

Martin has recently taken his argument in a somewhat different direction in 'Inventing sincerity, refashioning prudence: the discovery of the individual in Renaissance Europe', *American historical review*, 102 (1997), pp. 1309–42. He maintains that the discourses of prudence and sincerity served to foster the development of a new kind of essentially secular self that both made agency and dissent easier and also 'the expression of one's feelings and passions' (p. 1340). This might apply to Pole, except for two points. First, Pole rejected prudence in Martin's definition, and his sense of self remained rooted in religion.

[38] Fenlon, p. 248.

[39] See pp. 322 and 349 below.

the root of his 'Nicodemite' behaviour in rhetoric, not ethics. His ethics might be perfectly consistent and his behaviour much less so, since the demands of persuasion always meant paying close attention to circumstances and adjusting one's words to fit the occasion. Playful, humanist theology could not match the serious-minded, scholastic demand for consistency. The irony is not that Pole concealed his opinions out of necessity or pusillanimity, but that he steadfastly refused to identify himself as an author and take the consequences.

The second interpretation provides the theoretical grounding for Pole the Nicodemite. This traces his distinctive theological views to Juan de Valdés. To a degree, this book makes the problem of origins moot by its stress on how Pole used his ideas, not where he got them, another element in the unproductive debate over orthodoxy. Yet I shall engage this argument to the degree of demonstrating that the ideas allegedly peculiar to Valdés which showed up in Pole were common currency (see chapter 2). Carlo Ginzburg and Adriano Prosperi are almost certainly right that Valdés's religion acted as a catalyst of a more general disquiet, rather than the source of every religious idea in Italy.[40] It seems useful to adopt A. D. Wright's and Carlo Ossola's argument that the real 'substratum' of Italian (and European) religious ferment after Luther was a revival of Augustine.[41]

It may be as well to get my religious opinions on record at the start. Christopher Haigh recently felt required to do that in the preface to his study of the English reformations, and his subject matter, although sensitive, was less of a lightning rod than Pole. I am a devout agnostic, and I hope I have brought a detached attitude to this work. Pole stands for no particular religious position that I defend. I do not claim that I have entirely managed to escape the spell cast by his situations and the fascination of any human being trying to deal with them. Religious sympathies I hope do not enter into my interpretation; human ones may.

It would also be well to stress that this is not the definitive life of Reginald Pole. It may come closer than its predecessors because of the amount of information incorporated, but it is still not it. For one thing, it has become commonplace to regard biography as fictional, even more so than 'straight' history, and therefore to exclude by definition the possibility of definitiveness. For another, as the talk of dialectics above may have indicated, the particular kind of

---

[40] Carlo Ginzburg and Adriano Prosperi, *Giochi di pazienza. Un seminario sul 'Beneficio di Cristo'* (Turin: Einaudi, 1975), p. 147.

[41] A. D. Wright, *The counter-reformation.* *Catholic Europe and the non-Christian world* (New York: St Martin's Press, 1982), introduction, and Juan de Valdés, *Lo evangelio di san Matteo*, ed. Carlo Ossola (Rome: Bulzoni, 1985), pp. 27 and 29.

fiction I prefer is not the teleological variety that makes for definitive work. Instead I aspire to meet the challenge thrown down by Paul Valéry: 'I don't know if anyone has ever tried to write a biography and attempted at each instant of it to know as little of the following moment as the hero of the work knew himself at the corresponding instant of his career. This would be to restore chance in each instant, rather than putting together a series that admits of a neat summary and a causality that can be described in a formula.'[42]

A few more words about the approach taken here will help in the reading. First, some of the organization is thematic, rather than chronological, especially in the first chapter. Second, I have not constantly either cited or criticized earlier work, in part because I have preferred to go to the sources and in part for reasons of space. I have especially not referred much to the first lives by Beccadelli and Andras Dudic, since they contributed so much to Pole's 'myth of sanctity' and only rarely contain information not to be had elsewhere. They are, however, invaluable to any discussion of Pole's image.[43] I have thus usually rejected the old reporter's adage – and too often rule of thumb in scholarship on Pole – 'when the legend deviates from fact, print the legend'.

---

[42] Paul Valéry, *Tel quel II* (Paris, 1943), p. 349, quoted in Georges Gusdorf, 'Conditions and limits of autobiography', trans. James Olney, in James Olney, ed., *Autobiography: essays theoretical and critical* (Princeton: Princeton University Press, 1980), pp. 28–48, p. 41.

[43] See chapter 9 below and my forthcoming critical edition to be published by Medieval and Renaissance Texts and Studies.

1

A book and a life

R EGINALD POLE WAS one of those authors whose first book makes his reputation. As often in such cases, he does not deserve it, either for good or for bad.
For one thing, the book was not his. A large number of people involved themselves in the composition and even Erasmus in Basel knew about it.[1] For another,
the work does not qualify as a book, nor did Pole give it the title by which it has
come to be known, *Reginaldi Poli ad Henricum octavum Britanniae regem, pro
ecclesiasticae unitatis defensione*, abbreviated as *De unitate*.[2] The version sent to
Henry VIII has no title and begins like a letter, except that it lacks a salutation.[3]
The informal manner of address bears out the interpretation of *De unitate* as a
letter, as does Pole's insistence that the work was for the king's eyes only. However
characterized and by whomever written between September 1535 and March
1536 when its principal author was just turning thirty-six, it immediately generated great demand and great anxieties, on the part of both author and readers.

The letter/book created both Pole and its original target Henry, making
images of each that have proven coeval with subsequent historiography. Marie
Hallé was typical in her dogmatic assertion that Pole told the truth and nothing
but the truth in *De unitate* to such a degree that he could be implicitly believed in
anything he said.[4] While few working historians would endorse this hermeneutic, now or ever, the equally sweeping contention that the work defended papal
primacy against all comers has served as a fulcrum from which to survey not only
Pole's career, but also large tracts of the history of both the English and continental reformations. At the risk of immediately descending to fatuity, the story is not
so simple. Henry the ogre is in as large measure Pole's fiction as is Pole the speak-

---

[1] *OEE*, 11, no. 3076.
[2] For the text of *De unitate*, see *CPM*, catalogue no. 1. I cite the Blado printed edition of 1539 which runs very close to the best MS in so far as one can tell, given its sad state.
[3] PRO, SP 1/104, pp. 1–280.
[4] Hallé, p. 72.

er of truth. *De unitate* contains at least as many ideas at odds with the sort of papal monarchy Pole has been taken to defend as it does crudely hieratic statements. Pole did not reveal the literal truth, or at least not all of it, when he quickly told Henry that the issue was his opinion 'about the power of the Roman pontiff and this your new and now for the first time usurped honour by which you have arrogated the title and right of supreme head of the church of England'. Pole *did*, however, reveal the literal truth when even before this passage he exactly described his attitude not only then, but throughout his life. As he told Henry, many things were happening 'that render my soul *suspensum, dubium* and poor (*inopem*) of all counsel' (fo. Ir). The rest of Pole's career makes sense when considered as the working out of the consequences of such a 'suspension' in the face of a congeries of pieties and authorities, not just Henry. Pole's first text, especially when read as a text and not an oracle's utterance, becomes a conflicted story.[5]

One point stands out. It is a story of resistance. Characterizing *De unitate* in this way is not new, but the nature of its resistances has been little explored, and it has been overlooked that they were not aimed exclusively at Henry. The pope and the church came in for almost as much attention. Pole exhibited a number of resistances on both scores, but undoubtedly the most important was the adoption of a set of *personae*, in almost the original sense of masks, a range of identities that made it almost impossible to strike at 'Pole himself'. Throughout he experimented with literary forms through which to resist cultural and political hegemony. The work's superficial design of bringing the errant Henry back into the church by the shortest, epic path frequently falls victim to romance interludes. This literary sophistication together with Pole's ambivalent attitude and its consequences – above all the masks he wore – have made it nearly impossible to decide just what he was.

Although *De unitate* represented a major change in Pole's itinerary, he did not turn his back on his education for royal service. He claimed that the work repaid Henry for 'all the years I have spent in the labor of my studies [which] you supported'. Since these studies were overtly political as we shall see and Pole treated this motive as distinct from 'the confession of Christ's name', he meant that *De unitate* was to be read in part as a political tract.[6] Pole first identified his compe-

---

[5] Of earlier interpretations of *De unitate*, only a few go beyond reportage. About the best previous reading is Breifne V. Walker, 'Cardinal Reginald Pole, papal primacy and church unity 1529–1536', University College, Dublin, MA thesis, 1972.

[6] Adriano Prosperi, 'Evangelismo di

Seripando', in Antonio Cestaro, ed., *Geronimo Seripando e la chiesa del suo tempo nel V centenario della nascita* (Rome: Edizioni di storia e letteratura, 1997), pp. 33–49, p. 48 brings out the coalescence of political and religious in Seripando.

tence as 'sicknesses of the soul', and physician to Henry's soul became one of the roles Pole most frequently adopted.[7] He reached this specialty only after he had already drawn the standard analogy between corporal and mystical bodies (fo. IIr–v), and when he 'entered the argument', he compared the church and the *civitas* (fo. IIIIr) in a common political analysis. Thus the soul was political, as were the acts which it caused, especially Henry's, and so were family relationships. On fo. IIv Pole passed directly from calling himself Henry's mother to assuring the king that he would never have wished to be subject to any other *imperium*. Pole often characterized Henry's crimes against the church in political terms, especially *seditio* (fos. XXVIIIr; LXXIIIv–LXXIIIIr).

Pole immediately also claimed skill in letters and their political use (fos. IIIv, VIIr), and just as immediately made plain the intensity of his text's political resistance. He told Henry that he knew the truth about the respective powers of pope and king or about the headship did not interest the king. Pole attacked on these two fronts, arguing from scripture and ancient history, the grounds Henry and his propagandists had chosen, rather than human reason or the power of example (although both put in numerous appearances; fos. Vv–VIr). Unable to agree with Henry's claim, Pole could see no option but to write and make himself guilty of treason and, worse, ingratitude. This would be the height of imprudence. As Sallust said, it was 'extreme madness' to act in such a way as to arouse hatred. A quotation – the first in the book – from a classical author well-known for his republican sympathies was probably not accidental. Whether drawn from Sallust or from many other sources, a discussion of the nature of true prudence became one of the work's major arguments (fo. Ir–v), closely paralleled by discussion of true foolishness (*stultitia*). Much of the strategy of *De unitate* turned on such resistance by definition. This in turn depended on resistance by unmasking dissimulation, the highest form of political prudence.[8]

Pole prescribed a simple remedy for the twin causes of Henry's illness (fo. XCVIIr), the love of a prostitute and 'diversity of opinions' about religion, but its meaning is not so straightforward. The king had to repent and do penance in order to re-enter the church, his mother. Quite apart from the wildly spiralling family romances Pole constructed around Henry's 'mother' Pole defined the church differently than his hagiographers have argued. He did indeed defend

---

[7] This could have been a legacy from Galen. Cf. F. W. Conrad, 'A preservative against tyranny: the political theology of Sir Thomas Elyot', Johns Hopkins University Ph.D. thesis, 1988, p. 48.

[8] P. S. Donaldson, 'Machiavelli and antichrist: prophetic typology in Reginald Pole's *De unitate* and *Apologia ad Carolum quintum*', in *Machiavelli and mystery of state* (New York: Cambridge University Press, 1989), pp. 1–35.

papal power, but as the mere title of the printed version of his work must have reminded his learned readers, not necessarily at the expense of the rest of the hierarchy, particularly the bishops. The title probably raised strong overtones of Cyprian's most famous treatise, *De ecclesiae catholicae unitate*. Although sometimes read as an unequivocally papalist statement, Cyprian actually defended a collective leadership of the church.[9] Pole's tortuous and partial reading of Cyprian's letter to Cornelius could not hide the fact that it did not support his interpretation of it as a defence of Roman primacy (fo. LXIIr–v).[10] His difficulties with Cyprian may well have arisen because Pole, too, at several points defended episcopal authority. In his attack on Henry's argument from classical Christian precedent, Pole claimed that Constantine had intervened in the Council of Nicaea only to shame the bishops into behaving themselves. This cleared the way for the council to gain the same authority as the apostles (fo. XIXr). More importantly, when explaining Peter's primacy Pole identified the church which never differed from Peter as the succession of the bishops 'who rule it' (fo. XXXIIIv). Later Pole went so far as to define the church, along with Ockham, as 'the multitude of believers' (fo. LXVIv).

The bishops, 'the successors of the apostles', might not individually always meet the apostolic standard, but this did not reduce the dignity of their office, any more than unworthy occupants did the papal or royal dignities. Peter was important, but not singular even after he had undergone a metamorphosis produced by divine revelation of his new status. He was not even the only rock, a label Pole applied to all Christians (fo. XLVIIIv). Peter did stand out in 'dignity and degree of excellence, nor did all get the same place of nobility in this building [of the church]' (fo. XLVIIIv), but earlier Pole defended divine right episcopacy (fo. XXr). Even in the heat of a protracted insistence on Peter's power, Pole both allowed that the other apostles might have had the same power, if not dignity, and also pointed to the example of Moses and the seventy elders to illustrate that neither he nor the pope had their powers diminished by sharing them.

A short and cryptic statement may tell most about Pole's attitude to papal

---

[9] G. S. M. Walker, *The churchmanship of St Cyprian* (Richmond: John Knox Press, 1969), p. 26. The only examples Walker cites of the work's use by Catholics are very late (p. 61).

[10] Pole quoted Cyprian's letter to Pope Cornelius, but partially and misleadingly (fos. LXIIv–LXIIIr). He included the phrase 'Petri cathedram, atque ecclesiam principalem, unde unitas sacerdotalis exorta est', but stopped short of the rest of the passage 'eos esse Romanos quorum fides apostolo praedicante laudata est'. Wilhelm Hartel, ed., *S. Thasci Caecili Cypriani Opera Omnia* (Wolfenbüttel: Herzog August Bibliothek, 1872), pp. 673–4.

primacy. Should the pope not feed Christ's sheep, as Pole earlier admitted had happened, 'remedies are not lacking, by which the church can easily cure this evil' (fos. XXXIIIv–IVr and CIr). Although Pole hurried on to talk of unity, he did so by turning to the Council of Florence in order to refute Henry's claim that the Greeks did not recognize papal headship. His mere reference to the council is distinctive, since very little was known about it even after it occasionally inspired fierce debate at Trent.[11] Pole's mind easily ran from remedies to councils. He offered a more pointed criticism of the papacy when using the myth of Hercules and Cacus against Henry's apologist Richard Sampson. Did Sampson think he could get away with stealing from the pope, as Cacus tried to do while Hercules slept? No, 'the lord of sheep does not sleep, but he sees you, and sees you from the heaven' (fo. LVIIIv). If the pope missed what Sampson was up to, God would not.

Pole was anything but a high papalist in other important ways, for example, making good use of the distinction between man and office, which eventually became that between man and Christ (fo. Cv). Did Henry and his propagandists not know that they owed honour not to the occupant, but to Christ (fo. XXXVIIIr)? The pope's role as successor of Peter meant only that he must 'bear the burden of the church' (fo. XLIXv). Feeding Christ's sheep, another of the proof-texts behind the primacy, did mean that a single man had to be the head of the 'multitude' in the church which would otherwise dissolve (fo. LIv), and that man had been Peter, according to 'the most learned and most holy' Chrysostom (fo. LVv). Nevertheless, Christ established Peter in order to suppress competition for the headship (fo. LIIIr–v). The principal requirement of the head of the church was lack of ambition (and contrariwise, this was one of Henry's principal faults; fo. XIXr–v). Christ had repressed 'contention over the

---

[11] Pole very likely learned of the manuscript of the Greek acts of Florence which Gregorio Cortese found in the Biblioteca San Marco in Venice either directly from Cortese or through Giovanni Battista Egnazio who was co-operating with him. *Gregorii Cortesii monachi casinatis S. R. E. cardinalis omnia quae huc usque colligi potuerunt, sive ab eo scripta, sive ad illum spectantia* (Padua: Giuseppe Comino, 1774; 2 vols.), 1, p. 114. For the scarce knowledge of Florence otherwise, see, e.g., ASP, Carteggio Farnese Estero, Venezia, 509, 83/1, nuncio to Venice-Alessandro Farnese, 23 November 1542, or Marcello Cervini's hush-hush inquiry to the librarian of the Biblioteca apostolica in 1546 in connection with the discussion of the canon of scripture. *CT*, 1, p. 399. Vittorio Peri, *Ricerche sull'editio princeps degli atti greci del Concilio di Firenze* (Vatican City: Biblioteca Apostolica Vaticana, 1975), p. 6 says there was no further search for the acts until the 1560s. Peri notes that Bernardino Scotti owned a MS, so it may also have been through him that Pole knew the council's proceedings. Pole could also have known the Latin acts which had been printed at least once in 1526 by Antonio Blado.

principate [the papal office]' as 'most foreign to those who should rule the church of God, where humility, not ambition . . . should have the first place'. Christ, 'since he was the lord of all, excelled everyone in humility, and ministered to all' (fo. LIIIv). These statements posed a resistance of the first order to the direction in which papal government had evolved since at least the thirteenth century. Even stronger was Pole's claim that superiors in the church did not rule 'as dominators . . . but as servants', thereby pointing to Gregory the Great's famous description of himself as 'the servant of the servants of God' quoted on fo. LXIIr. Pole continued that 'the house of God is ruled by charity' quickly qualified as 'inflamed by the spirit of God', which meant that no inferior should ever hesitate to correct an erring superior (fo. LXXr).

In the final book of *De unitate* Pole spelled out a dangerous implication he had raised earlier. He contrasted the early days 'in which the sons of the church abounded in the gifts of the holy spirit' with 'these same most corrupt times in which many judge that knowledge which is had through divine light to be almost extinct in men' (fo. CXXVv). The same held true for secular history, the countless examples of which could only be understood in the light of spiritual illumination. Since the test of successful illumination was consistency, both the church and secular power had to return to their original state. This set a tough standard, offering equally strong resistance on both ecclesiastical and secular fronts. Pole's rooting of the present church in its primitive ancestor dictated very limited claims about the papacy. Not only did he stress its lowly social status, but he also thought that not even the apostles collectively, much less Peter alone, had been its entire leadership. This included 'the others who [had] first fruits of the power of God's spirit', a less than hierocratic statement (fo. XVr). Pole again quoted Chrysostom, a father of great importance to him and his circles, to the effect that 'bondman (?) of Jesus Christ was to be preferred as a title of honour not only to the name of king, but even to the very apostles, even to the very angels and archangels' (fo. XVv).[12] Pole played the Augustinian card about the difference between Christ's 'doctrine' and the 'domination' of rulership to prove that Christ, and therefore the church, did not claim coercive authority (fo. XVIv). Christ had come in part to sort out the confusion between the two powers (fo. XIVv). The clerical office, however, remained superior to the king's, since priests had responsibility for souls (fo. XIIIIr), dealt with divine things (fo. XXr), and knew a higher form of wisdom than

---

[12] Pole's word was *vinctus*, which Joseph G. Dwyer rendered as prisoner. *Pole's defense of the unity of the church* (Westminster, MD: The Newman Press, 1965), p. 38.

human prudence (fo. XXIr). Their superiority and the entirety of their office consisted in prayer for those things above human powers (fos. XXIIIv; XXVr). This duty, like everything else touching the clergy, all priests had in common (fos XXIIIIrff.). Likening praying priests to 'legates sent by everyone' to God was scarcely a hierocratic move, either (fo. XXVr at length). Later Pole contradicted himself by adding that priests 'stood above' kings who merely commanded and could 'prescribe what ought to be done in the royal office' (fo. XXVIr). Eventually he came to describe the church in terms of a hierarchy composed of lower orders, priests, bishops, archbishops, and 'he who bears the *persona* of God' (but no cardinals; fo. XXXVIIIr). In short, the leadership of the church was oligarchical, rather than monarchical, just as it was for his client Thomas Starkey and friend and possible teacher in Padua, Marco Mantova.[13] Pole breathed hardly any word of the papacy as a judicial institution, and none at all of papal monarchy. The sole reference which suggests a jurisprudential reading of the papacy occurred when Pole wrote of the controversy between Peter and Paul over the limits of Peter's *ditio*, a very ambiguous word frequently employed in a sense close to territorial jurisdiction. That Pole probably did not intend this meaning emerges from the fact that he used it of Christ, who had no earthly authority (fo. LXIXr).[14]

It would have been strange if Pole had thought He had, since ultimately he rested his case for the clergy on prophetic authority (fo. XLIIv). He adopted a number of prophetic *personae* of great importance for his identity, from David (fo. Xr; cf. fo. CXIXv) to Moses, to Isaiah, the most frequently cited.[15] Pole often supported his points with one prophet or another speaking 'in the *persona* of God' (e.g., fo. XXXVIr) and several times made his own prophecies. One of the most threatening came at the end of book I when Pole foretold Henry's destruction. The martial opening of book II heightened the threat (fo. XXXr–v). Immediately after his exhortation to Charles V to invade England,

---

[13] Thomas F. Mayer, 'Thomas Starkey, an unknown conciliarist at the court of Henry VIII', *Journal of the history of ideas*, 49 (1988), pp. 207–27 and 'Marco Mantova, a bronze age conciliarist', *Annuarium historiae conciliorum*, 14 (1984), pp. 385–408.

[14] Thomas F. Mayer, 'Tournai and tyranny: imperial kingship and critical humanism', *HJ*, 34 (1991), pp. 257–77 together with the critique by C. S. L. Davies, 'Tournai and the English crown, 1513–1519', *HJ*, 41 (1998), pp. 1–26.

[15] Donaldson, pp. 21–30 first drew attention to how the prophets functioned in Pole's argument, and how he identified with them. There are thirty citations to Isaiah in the index to Noëlle-Marie Egretier, ed. and trans., Reginald Pole, *Défense de l'unité de l'église* (Paris: J. Vrin, 1967) as against seven for Ezekiel.

Pole effaced the *persona* of prophet and claimed that the Old Testament prophets spoke through him (fo. CXIIIIv).[16] He called himself Elijah, the only man left after the deaths of John Fisher and Thomas More (fo. XXVIIIv; cf. fo. LXXIIIIv). Moses frequently appeared, at least once as Pole's alter ego in a discussion of the significance of Moses's prophetic powers to government (fo. XXI–IIIV; cf. e.g., fos. XXIIIIr, XLIIr, Lr–v). As this instance indicates, Moses's status as a type of the secular ruler gave rise to some peculiar overtones on what Pole thought of his own position. Pole applied to himself Isaiah's words 'Raise your voice like a trumpet' (Isa. 58:1, quoted from memory). Ezekiel, from a walk-on (fo. CVIr), became a starring *persona* when his voice spoke through Pole to tell Henry that God can deceive prophets (fo. CXIVv).[17] Given how importantly dissimulation and its exposure figured in Pole's argument, Ezekiel's words resonated loudly. The last quotation in the work comes from Ezekiel telling Henry not to let 'your iniquity be your ruin' (fo. CXXXVIr; Ez. 18:30, quoted from memory).

When Pole came to his final exhortation to Henry, he turned to Isaiah. He asked the king whether he heard Isaiah's voice, after raising the likelihood that Francis I would attack Henry (fo. CIXr). He cited Isaiah's judgment of Sardanapalus as a prophecy of Henry's tomb (fo. CXVIIIr; Isa. 14:18–20 according to Dwyer). More important, he introduced Isaiah's definition of a true teacher at the end of a discussion of faith and reason to endorse the claims of faith (fo. CXXIIv; Isa. 30:19–21). Nearing the climax, Pole advised Henry to consult Isaiah about what he should do to save himself (fo. CXXXr; Isa. 58:1), a passage which reflects the typological nature of Pole's argument, since everyone in it was assigned an Old Testament role.

The church's dependence on prophecy and revelation ran right to the very top. Peter owed his position to revelation and he alone knew it because only he had direct, personal, testimony from God (fo. XLVr; cf. fo. XLIXr). This claim both here and earlier (fos. XLIIv–IIIv) was closely linked to a defence of ecclesiastical custom. Pole quickly explained that such divine revelation had nothing to do with flesh and blood (fo. XLVIr–v). Pole maintained that the church only

---

[16] In 'Nursery of resistance: Reginald Pole and his friends', in Paul A. Fideler and T. F. Mayer, eds., *Political thought and the Tudor commonwealth: deep structure, discourse and disguise* (London: Routledge, 1992), pp. 50–74, I said that this passage had been cut from the presentation copy, misinterpreting

Thomas F. Dunn, 'The development of the text of Pole's *De unitate ecclesiae*', *Papers of the bibliographical society of America*, 70 (1976), pp. 455–68, p. 463.

[17] The reference is Ezekiel 14:4,5 according to Dwyer, p. 280. This seems doubtful, but I have found no closer quotation.

knew God's will thanks to 'the light of the Holy Spirit' (fo. CIIv). Nor did his church require much institutional structure; it was not, after all, a physical building, even though composed of a multitude of men (fo. XLIXv).

The church did, however, need nobility, and Pole made a contest over Peter's true nobility the central point (fo. XLVIIIv). Just as Pole thereby resisted both secular and ecclesiastical 'absolutism', so insisting on the status of the English nobility and of himself as one noble in particular furthered the same end. At first, it might have seemed that Pole was merely establishing another claim to be heard when he reminded Henry of how the king had singled him out, 'one out of all the English nobility' (fo. IIIv; cf. fo. CXXr). When he turned to how Henry had thrown the succession into doubt, Pole greatly magnified his own standing in a transparently threatening way (fo. LXXXv) by justifying on grounds of scripture the innocence of his uncle, the earl of Warwick whom Henry VII had quietly executed (fo. LXXXIr). Pole also warned Henry that he would never get away with repudiating Mary. Amongst 'such a number of most noble families' any disruption of the succession would certainly lead to sedition. That is, unless Henry did away with all the nobility (fo. LXXXIv). Thus when Pole shortly after this reminded Henry of his educational benefits to him by suggesting an analogy for what Henry had done to the church, he did not randomly choose a republic (*civitas*) undergoing a change from rule by the privileged classes (*populus*) to rule by one. 'Consult the histories of all republics, and you will find that those republics which were constituted by the rule of the people (*populus*) suffered no greater injury than when they were reduced under the power of one' (fo. IIIIv). Only after this resoundingly aristocratic statement did Pole allow that rule by one was the 'best state' of a republic.

Pole then hurried on to note the dangers in any alteration to the *status* of a country (fo. IIIIr), and to insist that no single head could behave to the church as Henry had, as an 'emperor' who had conquered territory and could dispose of it as he wished. Pole knew Henry's more extreme claims. He reproduced the basic one that 'in a republic the cases of all citizens are referred to the king, as to the supreme head of the body politic' (fo. XVIr). He obliquely referred to another when he applied language to Henry which echoed the famous legal maxim 'the king is an emperor in his own kingdom' (fo. LXr). Henry had made similar noises, probably ventriloquizing his French predecessors, since early in his reign.[18] Later Pole compared Henry to the Great Turk, stressing the role of consent in England. The realm now had no more than 'a memory of its pristine liberty',

---

[18] Mayer, 'Tournai and tyranny', *passim*.

despite its best men's efforts (fo. CIv). Pole asserted that the king's office consisted in only two things: domestic justice and defence against attack.

Kings ruled by human prudence, which Pole set parallel in the earthly kingdom to 'the spirit of God, the spirit of Christ that rules the church' (fo. XLIIr),
and to the prophet's word in the church (fo. XLIIv). 'Human prudence alone'
could maintain civil concord, even if the greater hope the priests could offer was
also needed (fo. XXIr–v). Human prudence, like the king, belonged to the order
of nature, and was therefore subordinate to that of supernature, the realm of
Christ and his representatives (e.g., fos. XIv–XIIr). Put another way, the end of
the *civitas* was a matter of the flesh, that of the church of the soul and the spirit,
and finally Christ and God. The blessings which Moses promised the *civitas*
that observed the laws of nature would be dwarfed by those coming to the community that kept God's laws (fo. XLIIr). But it must be emphasized that Pole
stressed the value of human prudence throughout the work.

The problem of its status, like that of the separation of roles between king and
clergy, and like the larger line of demarcation between church and civil society,
could have been made clearer in what Pole finally admitted was a *mysterium*, likening himself attempting to explicate it to Moses hidden in a cloud (fo. XXIVv).
Although Pole harshly criticized English apologists for confusing political society with the church and insisted 'as much as the sky is distant from the earth, so
much [space] is there between civil and ecclesiastical power' (fo. XVIr–v), he
never managed to keep the two societies distinct, and compounded the problem
by recasting both on the parallel lines of a new kind of spiritual politics. In a passage of ekphrasis, he simultaneously drew parallels and distinctions between
ecclesiastical and secular government. In order to explain the nature of rule by
one, Pole imagined 'a shadow or as if a picture' like that a good artist could make
of a 'real body'. Although he cautioned that continuing the metaphor would
confuse the issue of their differences, he did just this. A *civitas* was 'a multitude
of men joined by right [*iure*] and laws' under the rule of one. The same
definition applied to the church, imagined 'in the mind's eye'. The only
difference lay in the source of the two communities' laws, one human, the other
divine. In terms of structure, they were identical.

In theory, Pole pursued the line opened up in the quest for origins when he set
the church above civil society because of its unique role in salvation, but even
there he slipped. At one point, for example, he paraphrased Cicero as saying
kings made citizens 'blessed' (fo. XXIIr; repeated on fo. XXIVv). He granted
that distinguishing clergy and king was difficult, since the clergy were also part
of the *populus* and should therefore apparently be subject like the rest of it to the
king (fo. XXIIv). The usual solution was to examine origins, but this would not
work in the case of the first priest Melchisedech, since he had neither father nor

mother (fo. XXIIIr). In terms of dignity or nobility the problem was easily solved. Since everything came from God, priests were required to deal with 'the things of the people' before God, which made them superior to kings. Without 'heavenly favor' all things would be frustrated (fo. XXIIIv).[19] As Pole concluded, 'if it is more superior to deal with God than with men', then the priests had to have the upper hand. Their 'end' of salvation was more important than the king's 'end', as even Plato knew (fo. XXIVv).

This is perhaps the clearest traditional hieratic statement in the work, going back at least to Pope Gelasius in the fourth century, and consequently one of the points to which Henry might have objected most strongly. It turned out that Pole caused himself most trouble in the long run by implying that 'the people' could reverse the decision by which they had constituted a single head for themselves (fos. XIIr, XXIIr).[20] Arguing from origins Pole concluded that 'therefore on account of the people, the king, not the people on account of the king' (fo. XXIIr). Many nations managed entirely without kings, including the Jews. When they finally got theirs, God granted Saul 'not as a benefit, but rather for punishment' (fos. XXIIIv, XXXVv). Pole also adduced the Romans getting rid of their kings, allegedly as an example of the consequences of removing an institution because of a bad man wielding its power, but he failed to draw any negative conclusions (fo. XXXVIIr). By talking about this transference of power in terms of the *lex regia*, Pole entered into the ongoing debate over the origins not only of royal but also of imperial power (fo. LXr). The *lex regia* by which the Romans had supposedly transferred all their power to the emperor had been one of the proof-texts medieval lawyers and political writers had used to resist various earlier moves in the direction of absolutism.[21] Pole's description of the modelling of secular society on the hierarchy of the universe further carefully made room for two layers of magistrates between the 'lowest common people' and 'the command [*imperium*] of one supreme [head]' (fo. XXXIIr), an analogy immediately applied to the church, once more violating the absolute distinction between church and civil society that Pole had posited. Worse, German Lutherans had begun to use the same argument to justify resistance by the lesser magistrates to Charles's religious policy, as Pole almost certainly knew.[22]

---

[19] Pole also deployed the classical terminology of *numen* throughout this passage.

[20] Pole did not write about a 'pact' between king and people, as Dwyer, p. 56 mistranslated *quo pacto* rather than 'how'.

[21] H. Morel, 'La place de la *lex regia* dans l'histoire des idées politiques', in *Etudes*

offertes à J. Macqueron (Aix-en-Provence: Faculté de Droit et des Sciences Economiques, 1970), pp. 545–56.

[22] Quentin Skinner, *Foundations of modern political thought*, 2, *The reformation* (Cambridge: Cambridge University Press, 1978; 2 vols.), pp. 195–208.

At the very least, a king had to listen to his counsellors and friends, among whom Pole ranked himself high (fo. VIIr). Fisher and More should have been Henry's best friends. They certainly were Pole's, a point repeated often (e.g., fo. XXXr). Denuded of all his friends, Henry was at the mercy of flatterers and self-servers among his advisers, worse than those of any earlier king, Sampson above all (fos. Vr–v; XIXv; CXVIIIv–CXIXr). Pole engaged in one of the favourite forms of noble behaviour in his confrontation with Sampson, casting most of the first two books of *De unitate* as a duel with Henry's champion. Sampson was like Goliath, pushing ahead of him an enormous spear and sword, the proem to his book. Pole returned to play on Sampson and Goliath, refusing to call Sampson by his biblical namesake's name (fo. Xv). Then he was a gladiator, prematurely basking in the glory showered on him by the crowd (fos. VIIIv–IXr). Sampson mistakenly not only thought he had won, but also played with a serious matter, or worse, deliberately deluded the English people (fo. Xr).

Knowing when to play and when to be serious comes close to the meaning of prudence. That Pole could draw the distinction might have been another reason why he deserved to replace Sampson among Henry's counsellors. His pristine record of opposition to Henry's fatal politics assuredly qualified him. Here Pole offered resistance through autobiography, especially when rewriting the story of his role in Henry's consultation of the university of Paris about his divorce (see below). Pole's account may have saved his face, but it represented another kind of truth than what happened in the first place. Pole also rewrote other kinds of history. One of the odder bits concerned the tale of the unwavering allegiance shown by the kings of France to the pope. Philip the Fair, to name only one of Francis's predecessors, had been erased (fo. CVIIIv).

Some of Pole's attack on Sampson is clearly playful, even if he accused Sampson of trying to force him to play (fo. Xr), and some of it is perhaps humorous. Like the high noble he was, Pole could not joke at length about the serious matter of duels. One of the central conceits of the work makes it a combat with Henry, not merely Sampson (announced already on fo. VIIr). Pole even offered a challenge to 'single combat' (*singulare certamen*) to any who would defend Henry. Honour, the value duels defended, was also one of Pole's central values, and he insisted that he was not attacking Henry's.[23] In fact, it was his only con-

---

[23] As Mervyn James said, Pole 'systematized' the language of crusade with its emphasis on honour as a means of resisting Henry. See 'English politics and the concept of honour 1485–1642', *Past and present*, supplement 3 (1978), p. 37 reprinted in *Society, politics and culture: studies in early modern England* (Cambridge: Cambridge University Press, 1986), pp. 308–415. See also W. A. Sessions, 'Surrey's Wyatt: autumn 1542 and the new poet', in Peter C. Herman, ed., *Rethinking the Henrician era: essays on early Tudor texts and contexts* (Urbana and Chicago: University of Illinois Press, 1994), pp. 168–92.

cern, and he promised the king that if he came back to the church, Christ would give him more than any other king (fo. VIIv). Nonetheless, attack he would, at least on the metaphoric level (fo. VIIIr). Like David tending his sheep, Pole had no experience of arms (although he had carried them as a student in Venice, a fact he ignored), but this would not prevent the outcome of his duel from being like David's with Goliath, since he had 'God's army' on his side (fo. Xv).[24] Pole hastened to add that God did not conquer with swords and spears, but this did not prevent him from carrying through the metaphor of a duel.

In thus framing his work, the play was the thing to Pole. He deployed a multitude of *personae* together with a great range of other literary devices, especially dramatic metaphors. One of Pole's best strategies was rhetorical criticism both of Sampson's book and of Henry's actions which became 'tragedies' in Pole's representation. A marginal note pithily summed up this line of attack: 'Sampson plays Goliath' (fo. Xv). Near the beginning of book II, Pole replied at length to Sampson's rhetorical device of having Peter criticize his unworthy successors as pope. Dramatic metaphors litter this passage, above all *personae* (fos. XXXIIrff.). Despite a long discussion of the dangers of rhetoric, Pole objected most strongly to Sampson not that he had created characters but that he violated verisimilitude in them. Sampson was a *bad* rhetorician who offended both against the 'laws of rhetors' and 'ordinary, vulgar prudence' (fo. XXXIIIr). When explicating the equivalence of Peter and the rock on which Christ had founded his church, Pole offered a lesson in how to read metaphors (fos. XLVIIrff.). Indeed, his entire case for Peter's superior nobility rested on a *similitudo*, a metaphor, that of the mystical body of the church (fo. XLVIIIv; cf. fo. XIVv where Pole appealed to the growth of the mystical body as proof that Christ must have left a visible head behind). Similarly, like the good humanist Pole was, he termed his method an exercise in putting examples (fo. IIr).

At one of the book's climaxes, Pole drew an extended theatrical analogy between the reaction of the Athenian *populus* to Socrates's death and how Londoners had taken More's execution. The Athenians had performed 'as if reciting words in a theatre', imitating 'some tragedy'. The Londoners, with juster cause for indignation, had not confined their rage to 'your [Henry's] theatre', but spread it throughout the Christian world. While the Athenians might have been playing, the Londoners were 'more than serious'. How could Henry have missed the implied sequel in the fate of Socrates's prosecutors, murdered by their enraged fellow citizens (fo. XCIIIIv)?

---

[24] Jonathan Woolfson, *Padua and the Tudors: English students in Italy, 1485–1603* (Toronto: University of Toronto Press, 1998), p. 190 for his licence to bear arms in 1523.

Pole leaned very heavily on the deaths of Fisher and More.[25] They had brought him to write, and taught him as much as he had learned in years of study (fo. Iv). Pole identified himself with them through the device of assigning both them and him the *persona* of physician of Henry's soul (fo. IIr). Even an identification of More with Socrates was insufficient. More would ultimately become a Christ-figure combating Henry's Antichrist and sacrificing himself for the king (fos. XCr and XCIIv). By then, Pole had already identified himself with Christ, beginning on fo. IIIr where he said that God had made his voice Christ's and given it the power to raise the dead. Pole began by telling the king that 'your intelligence [*ingenio*], learning, prudence and finally experience' could never be compared to Fisher's and More's, a point that later grew into several eulogies of More's prudence and political acumen (e.g., fos. LXXXIXrff.).[26] Even if Henry had superior endowments, he still lacked the one thing needful, 'the spirit of Christ', which had allowed Fisher and More to understand scriptural metaphors (*figurae*) (fos. LXXIIv–LXXIIIr). Overtly political resistance had its place, but as in the case of the papacy, Pole found a charismatic defence more appealing. This did not mean that he neglected the bluntly physical. Among the other uses to which Pole put Fisher and More, he emphasized the brutality done to their bodies, and dwelt on the ignominious manner of their deaths and the fate of their (and the other martyrs') bodies (fos. IIr and LXXXIIIvff.). Pole could not resist several horrid puns on heads, including the rhetorical question 'can we doubt whose church's head [he means Satan's] cut off those heads' (fo. LXXXIIIIr)? Pole repeatedly said he was crying while writing, but it seems he must also have been laughing, however grimly.

More and Fisher had stood up to Henry by 'the present help of God and present virtue of Christ' (fo. Cr), and physical presence and bodies, especially Christ's, figured in Pole's case for Petrine supremacy. One of his justifications rested on Christ's dual nature as God and man, which meant that he had to leave a human successor. 'If Christ was equally God and man, and is head, then it necessarily follows that either Peter or someone else of the number of those who are mere men, should hold the place of head after Christ' (fo. LIr). Christ had established the 'form' of the church with a head to its multitude. Did it make sense to think that because he had left 'the presence of the body' the form would dissolve (fo. LIv)? He had established a successor while present in the flesh (fo.

---

[25] He put less stress on the other martyrs, but they too appeared, e.g., on fo. CIIIv. For Pole's martyrological notion of papal primacy, see below chapter 5.

[26] Pole cut this passage on Contarini's objections. Dunn, pp. 462–3.

LVIv). Christ promised that even though 'I will certainly not be present in the body', the spirit will sustain the church (fo. LVIIv).

Very shortly after his deadly serious treatment of Fisher and More Pole veered well out of the epic, even cosmic, path he had set himself. In order to remind Henry of how far he had already fallen, Pole recalled the high expectations early in Henry's reign for 'a golden age'. 'What did your outstanding virtues not promise, which shone in you especially in the first years of your reign?' Further, Henry's father had added to his education 'the care of letters, as streams pouring into a well-planted garden, by which, like waters, your virtues were irrigated, so that they might grow better and spread themselves more like the branches of a tree'. Making his favourite move, Pole then quoted the prophet Ezekiel to compare Henry to a tree in the Garden of Eden! This simile held above all because Henry's tree united in itself the contenders for the throne and thus brought the faction fights of the fifteenth century to an end. (Can Pole have been unconscious of the overlap between his garden metaphor, the genealogical one of a family tree, and the horticulturally labelled Wars of the Roses?) Henry had begun as part of a deliberately created garden, but was fated to become twisted epic. Quoting Isaiah, Pole warned that God had promised to destroy his vineyard, a proleptic move out of the idyll of Henry's early years into the current tragedy (fo. LXXIXv).

Pole's ultimate move against Henry returned to Christ's passion. Here Pole claimed to advert to the hermeneutic he had proposed very early in the work, according to which the king as interpreter should pay attention 'not so much to the words, but rather penetrate into the sense', always assuming that any words could support the king's case (fo. VIr; cf. XLIIIIv). Many people knew what the 'sign' meant, but only a few, like Peter, could know a higher sense (fo. XLVIr–v). Finding it required divine inspiration, which produced the allegorical interpretation Pole preferred.[27] 'The whole of this mystery is contained in Christ's passion', Pole told Henry. Only one who had 'eyes so illuminated by faith' could understand that Christ was 'the son of God, author of our felicity, and teacher of the same' (cf. fo. LXXIIIr). Christ's bodily death set the pattern for all his 'members', who also had to suffer crucifixion of their bodies if they wished salvation. Such 'living books' revealed God's will as no written books could, even those dictated by the Spirit. 'These books that were written in the blood of the martyrs are to be preferred to all others. These were archetypical books, in which the sole finger of God appears' (cf. fo. CIIIv). Pole pushed his anti-intellectual stance by

---

[27] As suggested by Egretier, p. 40. On fo. LVIr Pole described his effort to get at the 'inner sense' through allegory. The word was like the body, its true meaning like the spirit.

continuing that any books, even divinely inspired ones, were subject to interpretation and therefore distortion, even deliberate invention, 'while those written in the blood of martyrs cannot be adulterated', a significantly physical term
(fos. XCVv–XCVIr).

Combining both martyrology and its original, Christ's passion, Pole developed the metaphor of legation which he had earlier applied to priests as emissaries to God. Before offering this (perhaps) metaphorical solution to Henry's
problems, Pole assured the king that he was not 'playing seriously' (fo. XCVIIv).
Metaphors had at least two edges. Pole tried to guard against being cut by one of
them by a pre-emptive strike on his reader. Of course, the emissaries were to be
Fisher, More, and the monks, for all of whom Pole once more presented credentials in the form of capsule biographies, along with himself. Pole quickly got
back to his argument against learned pretension and in favour of the ability of
any 'simple Christian' to understand what he meant with the aid of revelation
(fo. CIIv). This Erasmian-sounding theme occurs frequently. Pole provided the
idiota, the unlearned common person, with a long oration to Henry, summed up
simply as 'we do not listen to your words'. Pole's unlearned speaker concluded
with his own major point: 'we will no more listen to words, but now we will look
at things written by the finger of God, that is, the holy martyrs' (fo. CIIIr). As
for Henry, all should pray that God would not only send him good counsellors,
but that 'he might hear good counsellors'. Having suggested a wide range of
possible resistances, Pole left ordinary Christians only prayer (fo. CVr).

This was not the only option for him. A prince and prophet could appeal to
the bluntest strategy of resistance and call on Francis I and Charles V to attack
England. Isaiah unmasked 'your [Henry's] counsels', but Pole claimed that no
one really needed a prophet to see what the king was doing (fo. CIXr–v).
Charles above all could hardly miss it, given Henry's private injury to Charles's
aunt Katherine and the much more serious public one done to the church. Since
Charles had just then scored a major victory over the church's external enemies
in the battle of Tunis, he was fully prepared to deal with Henry (fo. CXv). If
Charles had somehow missed Henry's devilry, Pole told him about it. A set oration followed, designed to shame Charles into dealing with the most serious
'danger to the republic' (fos. CXIr–CXIIIIr, continued on CXVIvf). Among
the incentives he offered Charles, Pole included an English fifth column of
'whole legions, lurking [*latent*] in England' (fo. CXIIv). In addition to military
attack, Pole proposed economic warfare. What would England do if its trade
with the continent were cut off (fo. CXVIIr–v)?

Pole then turned his back on such plans and on both powers in favour of faith.
One of Pole's most determined later antagonists, Bernardo Fresneda, thought

De unitate was about justification by faith, and he was right.[28] The only certain source of knowledge, faith was both the light and the fire 'through which light we believe and know [*cognovimus*] that Jesus is Christ'. 'The spirit . . . in that faith which is the gift of God . . . gives . . . firm and stable knowledge.' Pole defined faith as 'supernatural light' which gave form to unformed human belief (fo. CXXVIIr). 'True faith', as the marginal note had it, was 'the only way to be given entry to knowledge of the divine mysteries'. This meant, 'unless you believe, you will not understand'. Everything of any value in earthly bodies came from 'the image of faith' that Pole now called Henry to contemplate. The examples of Sennacherib and Sodom and Gomorrah showed what happens to people who trust in their own powers rather than faith (fos. CXXVIIv–CXXVIIIr). Pole offered a quasi-scholastic disquisition on the nature of faith as an 'accident in the mind of man' (fo. LXVIv).

This was not the sort of faith Pole had in mind. He meant faith that led to felicity 'and that kingdom with God which raises us an infinite distance above our nature'. Transcendence to the maximum degree became the final resistance. 'And here is that spirit, which in that faith which is the gift of God, gives *cognitio* and firm and stable knowledge above what can be thought by man' (fo. CXXVIIr). This was the faith with which Pole hoped to 'ravish' Henry, the faith which meant believing before understanding, as the prophet said (fo. CXXVIIv). Sounding a great deal like Erasmus, Pole offered this escape, as he had before, as appealing because 'it easily persuades the wise both to hold in contempt their wisdom and to be least offended to take themselves as fools' (fo. CXXVIIIv).[29] Pole had introduced the dyad *stultus/imprudens* when he first turned to Sampson's work (fo. IXv), and had called himself foolish almost immediately because of his hope for Henry's salvation (fo. IIv). Usually Pole appeared simply to reverse the valence on his opponents' use of these terms. What Sampson thought wisdom (*sapientia*) was really foolishness, and vice versa, a point which also allowed Pole once again to contrast seriousness and playfulness, smiles and tears (fo. Xr).[30] But his fondness for *serio ludere* immediately gives reason for pause. Pole's handling of wise/foolish is reminiscent of their treatment in Erasmus's *Moriae encomium*, including the final escape into *afflatus*.[31] Pole

---

[28] *Doc. hist.*, 2, pp. 563–4. Walker (pp. 245–6) was the first to note the importance of justification by faith to *De unitate*.

[29] M. A. Screech, *Erasmus: ecstasy and the praise of folly* (London: Duckworth, 1980).

[30] The possibility that these binary oppositions are really disguised dialectics will be discussed in the next chapter.

[31] Screech, chs. 4–6.

certainly had a high opinion of Erasmus.[32] He defended him stoutly against Sampson's misreading, assuring Sampson that Erasmus was a good supporter of the pope. Pole praised his knowledge in letters, his productivity, and above all his edition of Jerome, than whom there was no worthier or holier ancient. The edition proved that Erasmus had recognized no church but Rome.

Probably this judgment is true, in something like the sense of church that Pole developed in *De unitate*.[33] Pole unquestionably saw no alternative to it. Basing himself on Paul's apostrophe of divine light's transforming powers, Pole inserted his faith within the church, outside of which there could be no light of Christ (fo. CXXIXr). The conclusion that Henry had no choice but to do penance and submit to ecclesiastical authority automatically followed Pole's belated introduction of the church's laws, combined with a short argument that the scriptures owed their authority to the church, by which he meant the patristic interpreters (fos. CXXXIv and XXXIr). Both points may have responded to the difficulty raised by Pole's demonstration of the power of unmediated faith. Faith yes, but only within the church. Yet this solution did not hold for very long. Pole quickly returned to the necessity and power of revelation, concluding his 'oration' with the hope expressed by Ezekiel that 'your iniquity will not be your ruin' (fos. CXXXIIv–CXXXVIr).

Pole's emphasis on faith and his formulation and perhaps potentially unstable resolution of the apparent dilemma which confronted those who shared his view at the same time as they were determined to stay within the Roman church immediately identifies him as already a member of the 'Italian (or latterly English) evangelicals' or *spirituali*.[34] Some key elements of the vocabulary of *De unitate* reinforce Pole's allegiance. One of the most important of these was *beneficium*, especially in its most famous form of the *Beneficio di Cristo*.[35] In *De unitate*, Pole frequently used the word, sometimes in a political sense that would have come naturally to him as a noble, more often and much more importantly

---

[32] He owned copies of eight of Erasmus's works, including the New Testament. Bodleian Library, MS Broxbourne 84.11, unfoliated, printed in Alessandro Pastore, 'Due biblioteche umanistiche del Cinquecento (I libri del cardinal Pole e di Marcantonio Flaminio)', *Rinascimento*, ser. 2, 19 (1979), pp. 269–90, pp. 279–80.

[33] Brian Gogan, *The common corps of Christendom: ecclesiological themes in the*

writing of Sir Thomas More (Leiden: Brill, 1982), p. 326.

[34] J. F. Davis, 'Lollardy and the reformation in England', *ARG*, 73 (1982), pp. 217–37, p. 232. Davis does not mention Pole.

[35] Carlo Ossola called *beneficio* the 'leitmotiv, a suggello e compendio dell'intero messaggio valdesiano'. Juan de Valdés, *Lo evangelio di san Matteo*, ed. Carlo Ossola (Rome: Bulzoni, 1985), p. 30.

with a meaning very close to the *Beneficio*'s of Christ's sacrifice, and at the grand finale, in a combination of the two.[36] In the narrow meaning, he criticized Henry's belief that the headship was a *beneficium* rather than an injury (fo. IIIIv) and sarcastically asked whether the king's attack on the nobility was his *beneficium*. Pole moved very close to the *Beneficio*'s understanding in a long passage on Simon bar Jonah's recognition of Christ. This he could do only through revelation, 'such that afterwards, liberated, and made blessed, he rather recognized his liberator's *beneficium*' (cf. fo. XLIXr). It had come 'not from works, nor from any other thing that should be subject to the senses, but rather he received this knowledge of God infused into his soul'. As a result, Simon took the name Peter to signify that he was a new man, not like 'his first parent' Adam (fos. XLVr–XLVv). Pole glossed 'Tu es Petrus', the verse of Matthew which provided the principal foundation of papal primacy, to mean 'You who by nature are a son of death, son of hell, completely surrounded by shadows; who drew nothing from your father Jonah except sin, shadows and death, now by this knowledge [*cognitione*] of the creator and liberator are made blessed, free from misery, from sin and death . . . .You, who by nature are miserable, are a slave, are the son of Jonah, bear the form of a [the?] son of God.'[37] As Pole concluded, this *beneficium patris* was eternal life (fo. XLVIv). It is of great importance that Pole depended on Pauline soteriology, including as a commentary on the primacy. This would not have left that much distance between Pole and Sampson, who had glossed the 'rock' as faith, not Peter and been severely castigated by Pole as a result (fo. LXVIv).[38]

Beneficium did not derive solely from Christ's action. The martyrs' deaths could also produce *beneficia* (fo. LXXXIIIIr), above all for England, but only through Christ. Pole offered an apostrophe to *Anglia* urging it to recognize 'the greatest benefit of Christ to you' in the martyrs. If England did this, it could have the honour of saving Germany by *Christi beneficio* (fo. CIIIIv). Most important, Pole's own action could contribute to the *beneficium* of saving Henry.

---

[36] For the language of benefits in the political realm, see David Harris Sacks, 'The countervailing of benefits: monopoly, liberty, and benevolence in Tudor England' in Dale Hoak, ed., *Tudor political culture* (Cambridge: Cambridge University Press, 1995), pp. 272–91.

[37] 'Tu qui natura es filius mortis, filius gehennae, totus tenebris circunfusus; qui ex patre tuo Iona nihil hausisti praeter peccatum, tenebras, & mortem, iam hac cognitione creatoris & liberatoris tui factus es beatus, liber a miseria, liber a peccato & morte' (fo. XLVIv).

[38] Pole reinterpreted Nicholas of Lyra, Sampson's preferred exegete, to have written that the rock stood for 'faithful Peter' not Peter's faith.

In exchange for the many *beneficia* Henry had given Pole, Pole would return to him the *beneficium* of doing penance (or repenting; it is impossible to be sure of Pole's meaning), a gift that he had from Christ's hands. This was 'the privilege conceded to men by Christ's merit, through which we are called from death to life' (fo. CXXr–v). Pauline soteriology again, this time with political implications. Religion and politics were inseparable.

In full-blown 'spiritual' terminology, *beneficium* produced *consolatio* against fear and death, as it did for the humanists, and it did in *De unitate* as well.[39] Pole concluded a section on fos. XCIIIr–XCIIIIr about More's death with praise of 'the greatest power of divine consolation. Oh you, Christ, the sole consoler of souls' and 'leader and *exemplar* of our life'. If Christ, then Peter, whom Pole identified as peculiarly the consoler, like Christ, rather than assigning that duty to all Christians as he said Henry's proponents did (fo. LIXr). Leading up to his peroration, Pole noted that although he had promised *consolatio*, he had delivered only tears. Now he pointed to the 'pact' (*foedus*) that God offered any believer, implicitly calling it *consolatio* (fo. CIIr). Those who received *beneficium* became new men and 'sharers and participants [*consortes & participes*] of his glory' (fo. XIV). Henry, too, were he to be converted, would be 'His [Christ's] participant' and transformed into the image of Christ's face (fo. CXXIXr). All of this recurs in the *Beneficio*.

The source of this language, together with Pole's great emphasis on faith, has been disputed. Recently, a link has been posited between Juan de Valdés and Pole, through the means of a deliberate plan executed by Marcantonio Flaminio in 1541.[40] The centrality to *De unitate* of *beneficium, fides,* and the illuminationist soteriology behind them has gone unremarked. As a matter of chronology, it is perhaps not a coincidence that while writing *De unitate* Pole was studying with Jan van Kampen, the man who formulated the 'scientific' version of the *beneficium Christi* in his *Commentariolus . . . in duas divi Pauli epistolas, sed argumenti eiusdem, alteram ad Romanos, alteram ad Galatas* (Cracow: Matthias

---

[39] For *consolatio* as a marker of Valdesian sympathies, see *Inq. rom.*, pp. 146–50 and for the humanists, George W. McClure, *Sorrow and consolation in Italian humanism* (Princeton: Princeton University Press, 1991). It is almost as hard to be certain of the significance of the use of *consolatio* as of *beneficio*. At least later in the century, virtually anyone could use it in an insignificant sense to mean relief. See the numerous instances in the Carafa family correspondence in BAV, Barberini latini, e.g., 5709, fo. 92; 5710, fo. 18r–v, Cardinal Durante reporting that the appointment of his nephew as coadjutor of the see of Brescia consoled him; and 5711, in letters from Scipione Rebiba to Cardinal Carafa, often over something quite trivial, e.g., fo. 63r a letter.

[40] *Alumbrados*, pp. 135–6.

Scharfenberg, 1534).[41] The phrase may have come from Melanchthon.[42] Whatever its derivation, Kampen's little book makes much of it, but it did more, including deploying *consolatio*.[43] Further, Pole had no need to wait for Flaminio or Valdés to theorize the problem of concealing one's real views by the practice of Nicodemism characteristic of many of the 'spirituals'. He had already done this in *De unitate* as well, specifically on the same pedagogical grounds of protecting the weak as Valdés put forward. He even called it prudent to dispense the Word in this fashion, while acknowledging that success depended on 'God's highest providence', thereby introducing another constant of 'spiritual' terminology and Pole's personal sheet anchor (fos. LXIXv–LXXr).

The most important human action in Paul's soteriology was conversion, laying aside the old Adam and putting on the new man in Christ. To judge from the number of identities Pole tried on in *De unitate*, he was ripe for conversion.[44] He discussed the concept at length when explaining Peter's status as head of the visible church. God had built man in the first place as his dwelling, but sin had ruined the original construction. In the words of Ecclesiastes, man had been made just, that is, 'he converted [*convertit*] himself completely to the archetype in whose image and likeness [*similitudinem*] he was made'. Had he subordinated his will to God's, he would have remained just. As Jeremiah put it, the establishment of man had been meant 'to remove sins, and to convert his whole will to the divine will'. This happened to a believer in the church, who 'after the remission of sins . . . converts his whole will from himself to God' (fo. XLVIIv). The effect of conversion, sanctification, also crops up, once more as an argument for Peter's headship (fo. LIr).

---

41 For Kampen, see Henry de Vocht, *History of the foundation and rise of the Collegium trilingue lovaniense* (Louvain: Bibliothèque de l'Université, 1951–5; 3 vols.) *ad indices*; *John Dantiscus and his Netherlandish friends as revealed by their correspondence 1522–1546* (Louvain: F. Vandermeulen, 1961), *passim*; and Thomas F. Mayer, *Thomas Starkey and the commonweal: humanist politics and religion in the reign of Henry VIII* (Cambridge: Cambridge University Press, 1989), pp. 191–4. Priuli studied with van Kampen the Old Testament, perhaps including Isaiah and perhaps in Hebrew. *CRP*, no. 88.

42 Schenk, p. 45. *Evan. ital.*, pp. 66–8,

including an oblique but unmistakable comparison of Kampen's ideas to the *Beneficio di Christo*. Simoncelli further traces the phrase to Melanchthon, as Kampen did not explicitly do.

43 Sigs Bv, Diiiiv, Dvv.

44 Woolfson (p. 112) suggests the same point on the evidence of Pole's purchases of patristic, especially Greek, manuscripts in the 1520s. Woolfson's case supporting the date of these purchases is weak (the only evidence he cites is one manuscript datable to 1533) and he is probably wrong that Pole's 'ambivalence towards the king was almost certainly older than Henry's matrimonial difficulties'.

1 Priuli barca, *Treville.*

The writing of *De unitate*

De unitate was thus an amalgam of political analysis and religious belief, shot through with literary turns, and dressed up with all manner of classical and scriptural allusions. It was not at all the kind of thing for which Henry had asked, neither in substance nor in length. Pole, then in the environs of Padua, probably either at Alvise Priuli's villa at Treville (illus. 1) or at a farm belonging to Santa Giustina now called the Villa Ottavia in Rovolon (illus. 2), began writing in response to repeated requests from the king for his opinion on the divorce and supreme headship.[45] The first came in February 1535, via Starkey.[46] In another letter probably about a month later, Starkey suggested that Pole consult 'Master Gasparo' and the bishop of Chieti, framing Pole between two of the principal exponents of the reform tendency, Contarini and Gianpietro Carafa.[47]

---

[45] Pole was in Treville and Rovolon in June and July 1536. He frequently stayed at Priuli's villa and had been a guest at Rovolon in 1524. *CRP*, nos. 99, 109 and 17.

[46] *CRP*, no. 73.
[47] *CRP*, no. 74.

2 Villa Ottavia, Rovolon.

Probably in June, Starkey wrote yet again, acknowledging Pole's promise to write and expounding the case against papal primacy at greater length. Starkey closed with further urgings to Pole from the king, Thomas Cromwell, and Andrew Baynton, a member of the privy chamber, to get on with his writing and gave him a deadline of two months. All expected him to give up his retirement and return to England.[48] On 3 June Pole declared that he was ready to begin, drawing only on scripture. Starkey was certain that Pole's careful consideration of scripture and history would lead him to see that 'Christ's doctrine determines no one kind of policy [polity]'. Starkey suggested that Pole read Marsilio of Padua, who, despite his crude style, made useful points from scripture and philosophy. Not even were the newly promoted Cardinal Contarini to become pope would England restore unity with the papacy, Starkey told Pole. He thought Pole had been remiss in not writing a summary of his opinion to Cromwell, but Cromwell was not much offended and continued to favour Pole.[49]

At almost precisely the time Pole began to write *De unitate*, he approached Charles. First, Contarini recommended him and his efforts to remedy the

---

[48] *CRP*, no. 76.   [49] *CRP*, no. 78.

schism Henry had caused.[50] Then, allegedly at the urging of the Spanish consul in Venice, Martin de Çornoça, Pole wrote Charles superficially offering a peaceful solution to England's problems. Pole emphasized several times that Charles had to try peace before arms, but this was not the sequence envisioned by either of his sponsors, Çornoça or his ally Eustace Chapuys, the imperial ambassador in London. As is unfortunately usual from now on, Pole's precise designs would be put before the emperor by the bearer of his letter, 'his gentleman' Edmund Harvel.[51] That Harvel carefully covered his tracks, putting out the story that he had gone to Sicily – where the emperor was – to buy grain and wind up his business affairs, must raise suspicions about his mission's purpose. He had been with Pole in Padua before his departure, and knew something about Pole's writing.[52] Charles replied to Pole from Palermo, and Harvel carried the letter.[53] Harvel's role is murky in the extreme, since he was also at least acquiescing in various efforts to gain him Cromwell's favour (although he may have been playing a stalling game like Michael Throckmorton's in 1537).[54] It is possible that he thought he was acting in England's interest by trying to prevent war with the emperor, at the same time sharing Pole's belief that there was no reason for a rupture with Henry, if the king would simply listen to Pole. Pole took sufficient pride in this initiative to have it recorded in his first biography. He also took credit for telling Charles what would likely befall Katherine.[55] Çornoça first outlined Pole's value in August 1534, and Charles very quickly asked Chapuys to substantiate Çornoça's report.[56] Considering the extent of Chapuys's involvement with the domestic opposition to Henry in 1534 and 1535, Pole had entered into a dangerous commerce.[57]

Nor could he have been as innocent as he claimed about his actions. Çornoça's first letter contained details of Pole's lineage, his wide connections, his reasons for leaving England, and the potential trouble he could cause. Even more, it included a summary of his opinion on the divorce that Çornoça could

[50] BL, Add. MS 28,587, fo. 323v (*CSPSp*, 5:1, no. 172).

[51] *CRP*, no. 77. Robert Barrington, 'Two houses both alike in dignity: Reginald Pole and Edmund Harvel', *Historical journal*, 39 (1996), pp. 895–913 seriously mistakes Harvel's involvement in *De unitate* as he does the nature of Pole's household in general. I shall return to this point in the future.

[52] *CRP*, nos 79 and 77.

[53] *CRP*, no. 81.

[54] *L&P*, 8, no. 373; no. 511 (BL, Nero B VII, fo. 116r); no. 535 (*ibid.*, fo. 122r); and no. 874 (*ibid.*, fo. 107r–v).

[55] *MMB*, 1:2, p. 330.

[56] BL, Add. MS 28,587, fos. 7v-9v (*CSPSp*, 5:1, no. 80; a shorter resume in *L&P*, 7, no. 1040) and *CSPSp*, 5:1, no. 109.

[57] See the sketch of Chapuys's contacts in J.-P. Moreau, *Rome ou l'Angleterre? Les réactions politiques des catholiques anglais au moment du schisme, 1529–1553* (Paris: PUF, 1984), pp. 90–4, 226–36.

probably only have had from Pole himself. The consul claimed that he did not know what Pole thought of his machinations, and Pole later confirmed that Çornoça had originally approached the emperor without his knowledge.[58] This story smacks of collusion, especially in light of Pole's twin assertions that he was living in retirement in Venice and that Çornoça had to tell him about the situation in England. The second point is a lie, unmasked by Starkey's correspondence. If the first allegation were true, how could Pole have known Çornoça? If he did not, how did Çornoça get his detailed information? Pole had also likely contacted the emperor before June. On 6 February 1535, Charles wrote Chapuys that he was waiting for a communication from 'Reynard' (so named in the calendar summary) living near Venice, and he must by then have given Çornoça the go-ahead to encourage Pole.[59] Not that Charles the Dilatory acted on Pole's response, but he might have.

It took Pole another three months to set pen to paper. Ill health, especially an attack of what may have been impetigo or pink eye, or perhaps a sign of more serious cardio-vascular illness, may have slowed him down.[60] Towards the end of September he wrote Priuli that he could not accept his summons, because he had been writing for twenty days and had just reached the heart of the book, 'the defense of Peter's boat'.[61] Pole's resolve soon wilted and he gave in to Priuli's blandishments and went to visit him in Padua.[62] For another three months there is no further word until John Friar's mysterious report to Starkey, written in Greek, to the effect that Pole was studying divinity and 'meteorology' (a pun, playing on Pole's penchant for predicting storms and tempests as metaphors of trouble?) and turning his back on human and earthly things. Friar said Pole was going through a major transformation, substituting God for man.[63] It may be this to which Pole referred when he said of *De unitate* that if God could put

---

[58] BL, Add. MS 28,587, fo. 9v and *CRP*, no. 77.

[59] *CSPSp*, 5:1, 133. For the date, see Mayer, *Starkey*, p. 216, note 64. Chapuys had talked up Pole's prospects already in 1532 (*CSPSp*, 4:2, no. 888).

[60] For Pole's treatment by the physician Giovanni Battista Opizo of Pavia, see BL, Nero B VI, fo. 55 (*L&P*, 8, 542); fo. 109r (*L&P*, 8, 875); and Nero B VII, fo. 111v. Trouble with his eye bothered Pole again in 1542 when it prevented him both from going to Rome and also from attending mass. BMIC25, fos. 190r–2r. My thanks to

my colleague Robert Tallitsch for discussions of Pole's symptoms.

[61] *CRP*, no. 80. Pole may have begun work earlier, if his reference to writing in an undated letter to Priuli of summer 1536 is to *De unitate* (*CRP*, no. 79).

[62] BL, Nero B VII, fo. 111v (*L&P*, 9, no. 512).

[63] PRO, SP 1/99, fo. 124r–v, 1 December 1535 (*L&P*, 9, no. 917, where Pole is incorrectly said to have turned to man, not God). Frair's reference to the emperor's trip to Rome confirms the year date.

penance in his heart, He could do this for Henry.[64] His penance may have involved a change in his opinion of papal authority, which Henry Cole later said Pole had thought when he began to write an indifferent thing until the Holy Spirit taught him otherwise.[65] The king tried to sway Pole by ordering Sampson's *Oratio, qua docet . . . Anglos regiae dignitati cum primis ut obediant . . .* sent. It had been followed by Stephen Gardiner's *De vera obedientia*, which Pole thought the more important book. The two made it impossible for him to remain silent, and he sent Gardiner's book to Contarini.[66] Harvel informed Starkey twice in December that Pole was writing, keeping it to himself, since he wished the next reader to be the king.[67]

Pole continued to work through January, promising to send Contarini the section about the pope. Before he did this Contarini wrote back with his opinion of Gardiner's work, beginning a collaboration that would have a major impact on the form of *De unitate* as sent to England. Contarini had thought Gardiner's book 'written not without the greatest artifice, but composed of the lightest arguments', and Pole completely agreed. It reminded him of the proverb about the dicer: the better he is, the worse. Revealing the reversal of valences which figured so largely in *De unitate*, Pole called Gardiner a traitor whose book forced him to write in order to make the church's opinion plain to the *populus*, an assertion that raises questions about Pole's intended audience. He repeated that he would send the section on the primacy by the next messenger and hoped to have the whole book finished soon.[68] The messenger was Priuli, who did not leave for Rome until February, carrying the opening, another section next to that which Contarini had already read. Together they formed a continuous text missing only the conclusion.[69] Pole realized that his reply to Sampson (books I and II) was too long-winded, and asked Contarini to prune it since he could not stop himself from writing too much. He had been encouraged to appeal to Contarini by the Theatine Bernardino, probably Scotti, who had assured Pole the cause was Christ's, not his.[70] By thus urging Pole to consult Contarini,

---

[64] *CRP*, no. 91.
[65] S. J. Herrtage, *England in the reign of Henry VIII*, 1, *Starkey's life and letters* (EETS extra ser., 32, 1878), pp. xxxiv–xxxviii.
[66] *CRP*, no. 85.
[67] BL, Nero B VII, fo. 120r, 6 December (*L&P*, 9, no. 927) and Nero B VI, fo. 139r–v, 22 December (*L&P*, 9, no. 1029). Harvel's next bulletin of 18 January reported that Pole was still hard at it, and would be done within a month. Nero B VII, fos. 114r–15r (*L&P*, 10, no. 124).
[68] *CRP*, no. 88.
[69] BL, Nero B VII, fos. 114r–15r (*L&P*, 10, no. 124) and fo. 125r (*L&P*, 10, no. 479).
[70] Scotti had then asked Pole's 'butler' Bernardino Sandro to help him correct *otto orationi* of Gregory Nazianzenus for the press. BL, Nero B VII, fo. 125r–v (*L&P*, 10, no. 479).

Scotti played almost as important a role at this juncture as Contarini and Priuli, and would be almost as important in later stages of Pole's career.

Pole once more told Contarini that he was writing to the king, to his opponents, and even more to the *populus*, which accounted in part for his verbosity since the English were not as clever as Cicero said the Athenians were, and needed things spelled out at greater length.[71] Contarini's positive opinion of the manner in which Pole treated the primacy encouraged Pole, an opinion that Pole had also heard from Matteo Dandolo, yet another member of Contarini's circle involved in the discussions.[72] Pole accepted Contarini's opinion that he had dealt too harshly with Henry, but he felt compelled to do this in order to overcome the flattery at the root of the problem. It is therefore somewhat ironic to hear Pole describe the Cassinese Benedictine abbot Gregorio Cortese as 'the image of Contarini', and to have Cortese return the fulsome compliment, naming Pole instead as Contarini's 'living image'. This exchange highlights in a graphic way Contarini's importance to Pole during the writing of *De unitate*, as does Pole's concern to have a miniature portrait of him.[73] Whoever was the real image, they both consoled one another, according to Cortese. Pole showed Cortese his writing as well. Cortese praised both style and substance, and noted that Pole had thought of having it published before he decided that would not help Henry. In Cortese's opinion, the opening and those passages treating the deaths of Fisher and More needed to be softened, lest the king reject the work out of hand.[74] But neither Cortese, Contarini, nor Priuli made much headway in trying to tone down Pole's vehemence, nor could Contarini persuade Pole that he should come to Rome in order to prepare for action against England.[75]

As Pole neared completion of the final section about penance, he took a brief break in Padua with the young Cosmo Gheri, with whom he also intended to spend Easter in Priuli's house there.[76] Pole was tired and worried that there might be a reconciliation with England. Henry's ambassador to Venice had

---

[71] Pole repeated this point in stronger terms in a letter to Priuli, calling the *populus* his real audience. He also covered most of his other replies to Contarini's objections, which Priuli seems to have shared. Despite his larger claims about audience, Pole asked Priuli to show the manuscript to no one other than Contarini and his secretary, Ludovico Beccadelli. *CRP*, no. 90.

[72] *Ibid.* He and his brother hosted Pole at their villa in the summer. *CRP*, no. 112.

[73] *CRP*, no. 91.

[74] *CRP*, no. 89 and two letters from Cortese to Contarini in *Omnia scripta*, 1, pp. 104 (partially translated in Hallé, p. 151n) and 110–11. Dunn, p. 459 said the letters are to Pole.

[75] *CRP*, no. 90.

[76] *CRP*, nos. 91–2.

gone to Rome, and Pole feared that his opinion would be ignored.[77] He wrote it at length to Priuli in late March, as well as another defence of the manner of *De unitate*. Their cause was Christ's, began Pole. Whatever was of value in the work, was Christ's, not his. Pole at two points reported disturbing news from England, but saved his special outrage for a report from Naples that had Katherine died at the right time, Henry would have been excommunicated. Is the church thus to hang on the 'little soul of one woman?', he asked, and demanded that Contarini show the emperor what rewards came from the defence of the church. The book was done, and Pole now called its point the need to get rid of the root of heresy, 'which I call confidence in human reason'. He had tried to remove this, confirm obedience to the church, and underscore the necessity of penance. He again approved Contarini's judgment that he needed to rework the parts which would make him 'hateful and rather suspect', and promised to add a peroration on papal authority. He did not. The courier's delay had allowed him to finish, and he sent the final three quartos, asking again for Contarini's and Priuli's judgment of the bad parts, his work. The rest was from God.[78] Carafa may have been allowed to read part of the work, although exactly when is unknown.[79]

The conclusion of writing coincided with the emperor's arrival in Rome, and Pole tried to capitalize on it. He urged Priuli to break up an accord that would prevent Charles from acting against England, and intended to send his own messenger, who would perhaps again be Çornoça.[80] Pole was disappointed to learn that the emperor had chosen war above religion, meaning an attack on France instead of England. He offered a list of questions to the emperor as a draft for Priuli's use. If this did not work, Pole cast Contarini as Ambrose upbraiding Theodosius. This might not be prudent, but Contarini had nothing to do with prudence. Pole referred to Bernard's actions in a similar case and ended by throwing himself 'completely on Christ' and hoping to have Contarini's opinion of his book soon.[81] Unfortunately, that opinion does not survive except in the form of Contarini's editing on the manuscript in the Marciana, most of which is unimportant. Contarini wished Pole to cut the sections on Anne Boleyn, Pole's Plantagenet ancestry, and the effect of Henry's actions on the succession, the second two of which may have raised objections for their immodesty, the first perhaps for its salaciousness.[82] Contarini's suggestions, incorporated in a

---

[77] *CRP*, no. 91.
[78] *CRP*, no. 92.
[79] *CRP*, no. 636.
[80] *CRP*, no. 93.

[81] *CRP*, no. 94.
[82] Dunn, p. 463. The longest deletion falls in the Blado edition at fos. LXXIIIvff.

manuscript he had written out, had not been enough to stop Pole, and Contarini had to stoop to purloining several quires of the work.[83]

Having ignored most of Contarini's comments, Pole dispatched *De unitate* to Henry on 27 May probably in Throckmorton's hands without waiting for Contarini's final views.[84] He may have done this simply because he did not regard the work as finished. Pole had a habit of working over texts that had been in one way or another 'published' and his friends sent reactions throughout the summer.[85] Pole gave Throckmorton detailed instructions, which in part responded to the criticism levelled by Contarini and others. He was to tell the king that Pole's only object was the truth. Pole called Henry one of God's elect who might yet be saved, especially since God had sent him a prophet as he once did in order to save David. The king should ignore the book's 'vehemency', since God knew what he had intended. Given its length, it would be best for the king to appoint a learned man to make an abstract, and Pole recommended Cuthbert Tunstall. Pole affirmed that he had wished to keep the book secret, as he had done with his earlier writing on the divorce (see below), but his security had been breached. Anne's death gave Henry a perfect opportunity to return to the church. He must either obey the general council being clamoured for, or risk defending his case before it.[86]

Pole sent his book in post and Cromwell replied in the same way. The king ordered Pole to return immediately. Pole refused, telling Contarini that to obey Cromwell would cost his soul.[87] Cromwell may have shared Pole's grim view, but not everyone did. Henry (or Cromwell in a different mood, perhaps) took Pole's advice about how to digest his massive book, and went one better than Pole, apparently at Starkey's initiative.[88] Instead of Tunstall alone, whom Pole called his friend and to whom he wrote in mid-June, the committee Starkey suggested was appointed, composed of him and Richard Morison and probably of John Stokesley.[89] Starkey's reaction was remarkably temperate, both now and in a later letter, nor did his career suffer from association with Pole.[90] Morison made an abstract of *De unitate* that glossed over the most incendiary passages

---

[83] I assign Contarini a more active role in the production of the manuscript than Dunn did because BNM, Ms. Lat. IV, 114 (2304), fos. 1r–171v is written out continuously, except for a break at the point where Contarini's second, very long deletion occurs, as if he were instructing the copyist. For the missing sections, cf. *CRP*, nos. 110 and 112.

[84] *CRP*, nos. 96 and 100.
[85] *CRP*, nos. 99 and 109.
[86] *CRP*, no. 97.
[87] *CRP*, no. 98.
[88] Pole seemed to think he could trust Starkey, whom he had obliquely called to witness to his gentle character in *De unitate*, fo. CXXr.
[89] *CRP*, no. 99.
[90] Mayer, *Starkey*, pp. 232–4.

(perhaps meaning that Henry never knew of them), and he too wrote Pole a restrained letter of criticism.[91] To take one example from his résumé almost at random, Morison laconically summarized Pole's treatment of More and Fisher by saying that Pole wrote that they 'were taught by the Holy Ghost, and that they leaned not to their opinion, neither stood by man's wisdom'.[92] Newly returned from Italy and much more careerist than Starkey, Morison might have been expected to trim his sails to any anti-Pole winds blowing through the court. The fact that he did not strongly suggests that the air was moving at much less than gale force. It was probably now that Cole averred that Pole's notion of papal authority was new. As a recent article of belief, it might yet be reversed.

Tunstall wrote Pole in mid-July with the first official response.[93] Although critical, it was temperate, and Tunstall promised that he would try to have Pole's 'plain fashion of writing . . . taken in the best part'. Tunstall faulted Pole primarily for stirring up trouble without proposing solutions and for having risked *De unitate* in the hands of a single messenger. He, like the others who engaged Pole, was deeply worried that Pole might publish. Instead, Tunstall told Pole that he should burn the book, along with the missing quires once he had found them. Tunstall sketched a rejoinder in defence of the proposition that Henry was restoring the church to its primitive state. Appeals to general councils and Nicholas of Cusa's *De concordantia catholica* served to prove that there was then no papal monarchy such as presently claimed. Tunstall closed with an appeal to Pole's feelings for king, country and family, and assured Pole that when he found the truth, the king would take him back.

The air was not moving at all in the heat of Italy, and Pole was unwell. Neither deterred him from continuing to write, pouring out letters and plans. In June, Pole responded enthusiastically to 'the German opportunity' as likely to help England.[94] Contarini asked his opinion, and Pole replied that he thought things were looking up on the basis of the king's recent actions. Unity with the vicar of Christ was still required to preserve dogma, however. Pole complained that while English matters might have improved, his own danger had never been greater.[95] He heightened it in mid-July by refusing Henry's orders to return.[96] Although he would welcome the chance to explain his book, it needed no gloss. In any case, the Act of Supremacy threatened Pole with the penalties of treason and prevented him from speaking to Henry. He offered a short summary of his book as both sharp and loving, which it had to be because of the lack of

[91] *CRP*, no. 116.
[92] PRO, SP 1/104, fos. 57r–61v (*L&P*, 10, no. 975.2), fo. 60v.
[93] *CRP*, no. 101.
[94] *CRP*, no. 99.
[95] *CRP*, no. 117.
[96] *CRP*, no. 102.

physicians who could cure Henry's festering wounds. Pole repeated the topical-ly political point that Anne's death opened the way for Henry to resume his early promise. At the same time, Pole wrote his mother reminding her that she had surrendered him entirely to God and telling her not to worry about him.[97] Instead, Pole turned to Priuli, still in Rome, wondering where his letters were which ought to console Pole and provoke him to console in return?[98] In their absence, Pole drew divine comfort from his *sodales*, whom he likened to Enoch and Elijah, probably meaning Cortese and Marco da Cremona.[99] He hoped Gheri could join them.[100] The reference to Enoch and Elijah, the major commonality between whom was their 'assumption' into heaven without dying, suggests that Pole had his own death on his mind and hoped it to be as painless as possible. As Contarini had written the emperor, Pole hoped for martyr-dom.[101] He put himself very high in God's favour by hoping for such a mercy, as well, perhaps, as stressing the quality of his faith, which according to *Hebrews* (11:5–6) was what earned Enoch his reward.

Pole told Priuli he had renounced his country, and shortly thereafter Contarini wrote several times to tell him that the pope wanted him in Rome to consult about the general council and England. Contarini promised Pole that he would be safer in Rome than in Venice and have lodgings in the papal palace.[102] On 19 July, Paul III officially summoned Pole, and he accepted a few weeks later.[103] Perhaps because his mind was now being made up for him, Pole had an epiphany in his reply to Tunstall. Although most of the letter repeats *De unitate* (especially its medical metaphors) and rebuts Tunstall's case, at one moment Pole realized that the two were talking past one another. He rushed on to note that the Boleyn marriage had been a defeat for his party and that Henry's new wife had not improved matters, and neither would the general council. Nevertheless, Pole still insisted on the strength of his 'bond' to Henry.[104] Tunstall's reply in September rehearsed many familiar arguments, while contin-uing to insist on how much he was Pole's friend.[105]

As the time to leave for Rome approached, Pole wrote Contarini frequently, consulting about his case in particular and about English affairs in general. Pole rendered a generally favourable judgment of the Act of Ten Articles, except for the headship, and assigned credit for it to the *plebs* who had forced Henry back to the faith.[106] His intention to go to Rome elicited a stronger response in

---

[97] *CRP*, nos. 103 and 112.

[98] *CRP*, no. 104.

[99] *CRP*, no. 112.

[100] *CRP*, no. 109.

[101] *CSPSp*, 5:1, no. 172.

[102] *CRP*, nos. 1046 and 108.

[103] *CRP*, nos. 107 and 111.

[104] *CRP*, no. 110.

[105] *CRP*, no. 118.

[106] *CRP*, no. 117.

England than *De unitate* had. Both Pole's brother Lord Montagu and his mother sent letters denouncing his plan, and threatening to write him off. Both stressed how he was violating his duty to his prince, and his mother added how upset he had made her. She closed her letter by saying that she would pray God to lead Pole to serve his prince or call Pole to Him.[107] Pole had already left for Rome, in company with Gianmatteo Giberti, bishop of Verona. He had tried to pay Pole to visit him the previous year, and Pole had solicited his opinion about the call to Rome.[108] Carafa and Flaminio joined the party.[109] It went via Tuscany, intending to stop at the remote monasteries of Vallombrosa and Camaldoli.

The trip was not easy, at least not mentally for Pole. Not only was he caught between the two strong personalities of Giberti and Carafa, like Mercury constantly pulled back and forth between Saturn and Mars, as Cortese put it, but also the consequences of his opening breach with England began to appear.[110] For one thing, he would be left without resources. From Florence Flaminio fired off a letter to Contarini telling him to do all he could for Pole, who had 'neither house, nor means of support'.[111] For another, his family did not back his decision. When Pole received his mother's and brother's letters before leaving Verona, he almost changed his mind about continuing, since he could not see how to go to Rome without destroying his closest relationships. Both Giberti and Carafa had refused to hear of Pole abandoning his trip. They persuaded him that it was better 'for the manifesting of Christ's glory and the utility of my [Pole's] citizens' for Pole to defend his opinion about papal authority, all that he had written 'in that prolix volume'. Obedience to the vicar of Christ overrode ties of nature. Pole thought he heard Christ speaking through the two. He had sent brief replies to England from Bologna, saying that no human threats would sway him.[112]

Pole arrived in Rome probably in October, and next month joined the commission for reform that Contarini had been assembling.[113] Its other members included his two travelling companions, plus Cortese and Federico Fregoso, along with Tommaso Badia, Jacopo Sadoleto, and Girolamo Aleandro. Even though nearly all of these had close ties to Contarini and all qualified as

---

[107] *CRP*, nos. 120–1.

[108] BL, Nero B VII, fo. 111v (*L&P*, 9, no. 512) and *CRP*, no. 98.

[109] *CRP*, no. 117.

[110] *Omnia scripta*, 1, pp. 115–16.

[111] Marcantonio Flaminio, *Lettere*, ed. Alessandro Pastore (Rome: Ateneo & Bizzarri, 1978), no. 8, p. 40.

[112] *CRP*, no. 122.

[113] Best summary treatment in Elisabeth G. Gleason, *Gasparo Contarini: Venice, Rome and reform* (Berkeley: University of California Press, 1993), pp. 141–3.

members of the reform tendency, things did not go smoothly. Sadoleto opened with a stinging attack on corruption in the church, and Cortese wrote Pole a guarded letter of advice about tactics intended for Contarini's eyes, which made clear that sharp debates had ensued.[114] Unfortunately, practically nothing else is known of the commission's deliberations.

Nor is there any point in trying to assign responsibility for its final product, the *Consilium de emendanda ecclesia*. Its general view of the church and particularly the papal office is striking, and not incompatible with the charismatic theory Pole developed in *De unitate*.[115] The prophetic, even apocalyptic mode in which it is cast would have appealed to him (p. 85). It analysed problems in medical terms, and laid the root of the pope's difficulties to flattery, in particular the interpretation according to which the pope was lord of all benefices and his will was law (p. 86), all elements of Pole's analysis in Henry's case. The framers would have severely curtailed the pope's financial prerogatives, especially by emphasizing that benefices existed for the cure of souls (pp. 88–92), and by restricting his right to issue lucrative dispensations (pp. 96–8), both of which flouted the law, which should always be observed to the maximum degree possible, as Aristotle had said (p. 87). The cardinals were to become the pope's assistants, and were all to receive equal stipends. The bishops were to reside and both were to set good examples to their flocks (pp. 92–4). Monastic observance had to be improved, the university curriculum pruned of 'impiety', the printing of books regulated (Erasmus's *Colloquies* were singled out), and Roman morals overhauled (pp. 94–9). It has been well said that the *Consilium* represented a Venetian view of the papacy and the church.[116] Had its provisions been implemented, the course of papal monarchy might well have come screeching to a halt.

With the exception of the attack on Erasmus, Pole would have embraced the *Consilium*. Shortly after the commission began to write, Pole, along with Sadoleto, Carafa, and Aleandro became cardinals. Pole later claimed to have been instrumental in overcoming Paul III's reservations about Carafa.[117] According to Beccadelli, Pole accepted promotion reluctantly, fearing for his family, but was finally persuaded to acquiesce in it after the imperial

---

[114] *CT*, 4, pp. 108–19 and *CRP*, no. 123.

[115] *CT*, 12, pp. 131–45. References are to the English translation by Elisabeth Gleason in *Reform thought in sixteenth-century Italy* (Chico, CA: Scholars Press, 1981), pp. 85–100. For a summary, see Gleason, *Contarini*, pp. 143–9.

[116] Luigi Donvito meant that judgment as a criticism of patrician reform for confining itself to 'arid prescriptiveness'. 'La "religione cittadina" e le nuove prospettive sul Cinquecento religioso italiano', *RSLR*, 19 (1983), pp. 431–74, pp. 451 and 442–3.

[117] *CRP*, no. 2076, fo. 406v.

ambassadors led the pope to refuse to change his mind.[118] Beccadelli may have embroidered a little here on two points. First, Pole hastily wrote Georges de Selve and perhaps also Vittoria Colonna to assure them that his promotion was not due to ambition.[119] Second, from Count Cifuentes's dispatch the day after the nominations it does not sound as if he lobbied very hard on Pole's behalf, although he did close by advising Charles to endorse Pole's selection as a sincere Imperialist, since the emperor had been offered no others.[120] Then again, Pole told the same story in a letter to Charles's right-hand man Nicholas Perrenot de Granvelle in 1539.[121] This development did not please the English. Even the mild Starkey warned Pole that accepting the cardinalate would only worsen the schism.[122] Pole's conversion, although still not complete, had made progress as he began to turn his back on his intended career first in *De unitate* and even more in its aftermath.

An education fit for a king

Very near the beginning of *De unitate* Pole offered his status as Henry's *alumnus* as one of his reasons for writing. Henry had singled Pole out of all the English nobility and given him an education in letters. Near the end of the work he thanked the king again for having privileged him above the rest of the nobility and paid for his education. Pole likened himself to the crown prince for whom the king could not have done more (CXXr). In between, Pole assured the king that 'I had directed the purposes and counsels of my life from boyhood' towards royal service (VIIv). The least he could do was offer his first work in praise of the king. As his correspondents in England reminded him, he should have been grateful and should have served Henry. Until at least 1535, there was no hint that Pole would do anything else, and on at least one occasion, Pole successfully executed an important assignment from the king.

Pole was predestined to become Henry's client by the troubles of his grandfather, George, duke of Clarence, brother of Edward IV. This august ancestry meant that in the eyes of a Yorkist, Reginald's oldest brother Henry had a better claim to the throne than Henry VIII.[123] Still, even to a Yorkist partisan the relations of 'false, fleeting, perjured Clarence' would have borne watching. Despite

---

118 *MMB*, 1:2, p. 292.
119 This is an inference drawn from *CRP*, no. 130.
120 *CSPSp*, 5:2, no. 126.
121 *CRP*, no. 258.

122 *CRP*, no. 142.
123 It is often said that Pole had a better claim to the throne than Henry's heirs, but this is to overlook his older brother.

uncertain loyalties and close connection to the monarchy, Henry VII and even more his son restored the family of Clarence's daughter and Pole's mother Margaret, who became countess of Salisbury.

There is little information about Pole's early education beyond what his biographers say, except for one indication that he had some training at Christ Church, Canterbury. In one of its schoolbooks now in the British Library occurs the signature 'Reynoldus Polus'.[124] According to Beccadelli, Pole was educated first at home, and then at the Charterhouse at Sheen.[125] He went up to Oxford at a relatively early age, perhaps first to the Carmelite house, the king paying a stipend beginning in 1512 and arranging another in the following year.[126] Some of the rest of his doings – not including the forty-day disputation Beccadelli claims he made – can be documented. He was a member of Magdalen College, where he may have lodged with the president John Claymond, and had the shadowy William Latimer as his tutor.[127] Probably between 1518 and 1520 Thomas Linacre also taught Pole.[128] During his time at Oxford Pole made one potentially important friend, More. They met some time before 1518, when More thanked Pole both for sending advice on how to deal with the sweating sickness and for having his mother take care of the prescription for him.[129] They stayed in touch, and Pole's tutor in Padua wrote More that Pole was one of his principal propagandists.[130]

Pole's exposure to John Colet was now considerably more significant than contact with More.[131] Colet's Pauline soteriology and Neoplatonic cosmology and psychology closely resembled Pole's, as did his ideas about church reform encapsulated in his famous Convocation sermon.[132] He argued that the clergy's

---

[124] Hallé, p. 7 cited BL, Harl. MS 1587, fo. 208, improving upon the exceedingly vague reference given by F. A. Gasquet in an untitled article in *Downside review*, 10 (1891), pp. 31–45, p. 45.

[125] *MMB*, 1:2, p. 281.

[126] Schenk, p. 3 and Anthony à Wood, *Athenae oxonienses*, ed. Philip Bliss (London: F. C. and J. Rivington, *et al.*, 1815; originally published in 1668), 1, col. 279.

[127] Hallé, p. 9; Schenk, p. 6; *MMB*, 1:2, p. 281.

[128] *OEE*, 6, no. 1595 and Dudic, *ERP*, 1, p. 5. Woolfson, p. 83 suggests the time and the possible significance of Linacre's tuition, while Schenk, p. 3 raises cautions about how extensive it could have been.

[129] *CRP*, no. 2.

[130] E. F. Rogers, ed., *The correspondence of Sir Thomas More* (Princeton: Princeton University Press, 1947), pp. 301 and 303.

[131] Mayer, *Starkey*, pp. 30–5. There is a little uncertainty about the nature and timing of Pole's contacts with Colet. In Beccadelli's own manuscript of his life of Pole, he deleted his original claim that Pole had lived with Colet as a young man. BPP, MS Pal. 973/3, fo. 7r.

[132] Christopher Harper-Bill, 'Dean Colet's convocation sermon and the pre-reformation church in England', *History*, 32 (1988), pp. 191–210.

refusal to follow Paul's example lay at the root of the church's troubles, as they could not but set a poor example to their flock.[133] At its heart Colet's reform depended on administrative change.[134] However good Colet may have been at putting forward reform programmes, he remained deeply anti-intellectual, stressing faith over reason, which could have been one of his most important legacies to Pole.[135] Similarly, his emphasis on the necessity of spiritual understanding of scripture 'which requires the spirit of prophecy' is almost identical to Pole's attitude, as is the corollary that only some people would ever know God's *arcana*.[136] Pole's method of exegesis would be every bit as homiletic as Colet's.[137] The criticism of Colet's sermons as too spiritual might well apply to Pole's.[138] For what it is worth, Colet shared Pole's esteem for Bernard, the only author later than Gregory the Great cited in his sermon. Thus some of Pole's reforming ideas had native roots.[139] But as has been observed, those roots grew out of Petrarch's world.[140]

This was Pole's next stop, both geographically and intellectually. The plan to get him the best foreign education may have come from Henry, but Pole had to beg both king and Cardinal Wolsey for its implementation. He also had to guarantee results in the form of practical experience gained (*peritiam atque usum rerum*).[141] Pole headed to Padua first perhaps in 1519 and certainly in 1521.[142] He spent a good deal of time elsewhere in Italy. He was away from Padua for much of the first eight months of 1524, for example, and again in 1525; these extended absences must raise some question about how much he could have learned even from his tutor Niccolò Leonico, much less at the University. He stayed in Italy until July 1526, when he went to France and shortly thereafter to England where he is known to have been in November 1528.[143] In October of the following year he left for Paris (see below). Back in England in mid-1530,

---

[133] J. H. Lupton, *A life of John Colet* (London: George Bell and Sons, 1909), pp. 294 and 295.

[134] Peter Iver Kaufman, *Augustinian piety and catholic reform: Augustine, Colet and Erasmus* (Macon, Ga.: Mercer University Press, 1982), pp. 102–3 labelled Colet a reactionary reformer who looked forward to the withering away of the church.

[135] John B. Gleason, *John Colet* (Berkeley: University of California Press, 1989), p. 131.

[136] Gleason, *Colet*, pp. 137 and quotation 149–51.

[137] Gleason, *Colet*, p. 133.

[138] Gleason, *Colet*, p. 179. For Pole's preaching, see pp. 246–51.

[139] One thing Pole could not have learned from Colet was his approach to scripture, which remained resolutely traditional. Gleason, *Colet*, pp. 94, 114, 117 and chapters 6 and 7.

[140] Cf. Gleason, *Colet*, p. 200.

[141] *CRP*, nos. 3 and 5.

[142] See *CRP*, no. 5 for discussion.

[143] *CRP*, nos. 16–24, 28, 43, 46.

Pole stayed there, for at least some of the time in Colet's house in the precincts of Sheen, until he once more set out for Italy in January or February 1532 (see below).[144] After a six-month stop in Avignon and Carpentras with Sadoleto, he headed via Verona for Padua where he arrived before the end of October.[145] He mainly kept to its vicinity until his call to Rome in July 1536.

The opinions of his friends in Italy substantiate the claim that Pole's studies pointed toward royal service. As Christophe Longueil put it early in the 1520s, Pole eagerly scrutinized the governors of his native land, looking for 'that quality you would like to see in the majority of all responsible men these days, a talent perfectly suited to the running of affairs of state'.[146] Leonico has recently been singled out as an example of the 'profound fusion of Aristotelian philosophy and Venetian political principles' created by Venetian and Paduan humanists, as well as an 'Erasmian' in religion.[147] What is more, Donato Giannotti not only recommended Leonico's political expertise at the end of *Della repubblica de' Veneziani*, but also further intended to use him as the main speaker in another work on the general principles of republicanism.[148] It is very likely that Giannotti's work reflects political discussions in Pole's circles in the same way that Contarini's *De magistratibus et republica venetorum* probably does.[149] It also indicates how close Pole was to the Florentine exiles in Padua and Venice, among them Antonio Brucioli who cast Pole in the role of tutor to one of his clients in the dialogue 'Della providentia divina'.[150] Brucioli was a strong proponent of Machiavelli, and could perhaps have contributed to Pole's knowledge of him.[151] Francesco

---

[144] Mayer, *Starkey*, p. 97. Beccadelli (*MMB*, 1:2, p. 284) said Pole had taken over Colet's house and later (p. 285) referred to his 'usual residence' at the Charterhouse. Some of his things were still there six years later. PRO, SP 1/129, fos. 204r–5r (*L&P*, 13:1, no. 422).

[145] *CRP*, nos. 63 and 65.

[146] *CRP*, no. 13.

[147] M. L. King, *Venetian humanism in an age of patrician dominance* (Princeton: Princeton University Press, 1986), p. 182 and Luca D'Ascia, 'Un erasmiano italiano? Note sulla filosofia della religione di Niccolò Leonico Tomeo', *RSLR*, 26 (1990), pp. 242–64.

[148] Mayer, *Starkey*, p. 50.

[149] Gigliola Fragnito, 'Cultura umanistica e riforma religiosa: Il "De officio viri boni ac probi episcopi"', *Studi veneziani*, 9 (1969), pp. 75–189, p. 114n. Giannotti was in Venice from June 1525 until November 1526, and then again for six months in 1527. Randolph Starn, *Donato Giannotti and his epistolae* (Geneva: Droz, 1968), p. 20. Mayer, *Starkey*, pp. 67–70 for the marked similarities between Starkey and Giannotti.

[150] Aldo Landi, ed., *Antonio Brucioli, Dialogi* (Naples-Chicago: Prismi-The Newberry Library, 1982). Pole also appeared in 'Della virtù'.

[151] For Brucioli and Machiavelli and what little is known of Brucioli's possible ties to Pole and his circle, see Mayer, *Starkey*, pp. 56–7 and see ch. 2 *passim* for more on Pole's likely Paduan circles and their politics.

Robortello later claimed that the apparently apolitical Lazzaro Bonamico, another of Pole's tutors, lectured on *respublica administranda*.[152]

The Venetian Signory treated Pole as a person of consequence (which helped to cause him financial problems) and made sure that he had a proper residence, Palazzo Roccabonella in via San Francesco (illus. 3), built at the end of the fifteenth century by the physician Pietro Roccabonella.[153] Pole quickly gained entrée to the most important humanist in Padua, Pietro Bembo, formerly Leo X's secretary and one of the dominant literary figures of the first half of the sixteenth century.[154] Padua's exalted reputation attracted students from all over Europe.[155] Pole knew many of them who later played key roles in his career, including the future cardinals Rodolfo Pio, Otto Truchsess, Stanislaus Hosius, Cristoforo Madruzzo, and Giovanni Morone.[156] Bembo and Leonico provided Pole with numerous introductions in Padua and Venice. Bembo opened doors for Pole in Rome, too, especially to Sadoleto, Bembo's former colleague in the papal secretariate, who became a close friend. Similarly, Bembo put Pole in touch with one of the most powerful men in the papal court, Giberti, formerly datary to Clement VII and in effect his chief minister.[157] Through Giberti Pole met Carafa. After their first conversation, Carafa wrote Giberti that he could not understand Pole because Pole would not let himself be understood.[158] This did not prevent Pole and his familiars from having the highest opinion of Carafa.[159]

---

[152] William McCuaig, *Carlo Sigonio. The changing world of the late renaissance* (Princeton: Princeton University Press), p. 46.

[153] *CRP*, no. 1100. Beccadelli (*MMB*, 1:2, p. 282) said that Pole 'presa casa honoreuole con honesta famiglia', which sounds as if the Signory did not put the palace entirely at his disposal. For Palazzo Roccabonella, begun in 1498, see Giovanni Lorenzoni in Lionello Puppi and Fulvio Zuliani, eds., *Padova, case e palazzi* (Vicenza: Neri Pozza, 1977), pp. 66–8.

[154] *CRP*, no. 8.

[155] For law, see Biagio Brugi, 'L'università dei giuristi in Padova nel cinquecento', *Archivio veneto-tridentino* (1922), pp. 1–92 and Peter J. van Kessel, 'The denominational pluriformity of the German nation at Padua and the problem of intolerance in the 16th century', *ARG*, 75 (1984), pp. 256–76 for a start on the others.

[156] Ernesto Travi, ed., Pietro Bembo, *Lettere* (Bologna: Commissione per i Testi di Lingua, 1987–93; 4 vols.), no. 652; *CRP*, no. 312; and Friedrich Zoepfl, *Das Bistum Augsburg und seine Bischöfe im Reformationsjahrhundert* (Munich: Schnell & Steiner, 1969), pp. 177–8. Pole and Morone were not close in Padua, but they moved in the same circles. Cf. Travi, no. 2323.

[157] *CRP*, no. 25; Adriano Prosperi, *Tra evangelismo e controriforma: G. M. Giberti (1495–1543)* (Rome: Edizioni di Storia e Letteratura, 1969), pp. 111–12.

[158] Carafa to Giberti, 1 January 1533, cited in *Evan. ital.*, p. 169.

[159] Marcantonio Flaminio, for example, tried to join Carafa's Theatines at almost the same time as Carafa and Pole met, but was refused. *Ibid.* No doubt Carafa's stinging rebuke of 1535 at least modified Flaminio's opinion. *Ibid.*, pp. 48 and 170.

3 Palazzo Roccabonella, Padua.

The two would compete for leadership of the reform tendency for the rest of their lives.[160] Among others Pole knew were some of his fellow students, however secluded his own instruction as a high-ranking noble might have been. These included Pier Paolo Vergerio the younger, Pietro Martire Vermigli (Peter Martyr), and Vettor Soranzo, like Pole a student or satellite of Trifone Gabriele.[161] Vergerio, later to be one of Pole's nastiest antagonists, had studied in Padua and taught there until at least 1527. Until 1540 at the earliest he counted himself a member of the *scuola* of Contarini, Pole, Bembo, and Fregoso.[162] Vermigli's sixteenth-century biographer called Pole 'sometime a special friend', probably through Bembo, and other Lateran canons knew Pole well; one of them claimed that he had frequented their houses in Padua and Verona.[163] Perhaps more important to Pole were Flaminio and Pole's life-long companion Priuli.[164] Pole's biographers gave their own lists of his friends, divided into two groups according to degree of intimacy. The 'B' list named Bembo, Gabriele, Marcantonio de Genova, a philosopher, Benedetto Lampridio, and Bonamico, both of whom were living in Pole's household in late 1535. Those closer to Pole were Gheri, 'Marco the monk of Cremona', and Priuli.[165] We may take Beccadelli's word for it that these two groups held different places in Pole's heart, but not for the reason Beccadelli gave: all of them, with the possible exception of Bonamico, shared religious beliefs like Pole's.[166]

---

[160] Still the only decent sketch of Carafa's career is Gennaro Maria Monti, *Studi sulla riforma cattolica e sul papato nei secoli XVI–XVII* (Trani: Vecchi & Co., 1941), pp. 53–88. The most important recent contribution is Alberto Aubert, *Paolo IV Carafa nel guidizio della età della controriforma* (Città di Castello: Tiferno Grafica, 1990).

[161] Philip McNair, *Peter Martyr in Italy: an anatomy of apostasy* (Oxford: Clarendon Press, 1967), pp. 99–100 for Vergerio (who left Padua in 1522) and Vermigli, probably according to Vermigli's own testimony (p. xv); Lino Pertile, 'Vettore Soranzo e le *Annotationi nel Dante* di Trifon Gabriele', *Quaderni veneti*, 16 (1992), pp. 37–58, *passim*, esp. pp. 47–8.

[162] A. J. Schutte, *Pier Paolo Vergerio, the making of an Italian reformer* (Geneva: Droz, 1977), ch. 1, especially pp. 36–8. Cf. Ermanno Ferrero and Giuseppe Müller,

eds., *Vittoria Colonna, Marchesa di Pescara, Carteggio* (Turin: Hermanno Loescher, 1892), no. CXV.

[163] McNair, pp. 97–8 and 100 and *PM*, 4, pp. 330–3.

[164] Fenlon, p. 25 and Alessandro Pastore, *Marcantonio Flaminio. Fortune e sfortune di un chierico nell'Italia del Cinquecento* (Milan: Franco Angeli, 1981), pp. 37–8.

[165] *MMB*, 1:2, pp. 287–8. Fenlon, p. 31 misread Querini's confusing Latin identifying Marco, and I followed his lead in *Starkey*, p. 194. For him see Collett, pp. 48–9 and 111–12.

[166] Paolo Simoncelli, 'Pietro Bembo e l'evangelismo italiano', *Critica storica*, 15 (1978), pp. 1–63; *Starkey*, pp. 194 and 196 and *Alumbrados*, p. 170 on Lampridio; Rino Avesani, 'Bonamico, Lazaro', *DBI*; E. L. Hirsh, 'George Lily', pp. 3 and xxi; and for Gheri see below. It must also be noticed that Beccadelli and Dudic

Leonico's successor Bonamico is perhaps the first personality we see through Pole's eyes. Pole called him the master and 'quasi-tutor' of his youth.[167] More important, Pole's relation to Bonamico stands as a marker of his later religious evolution, further reflected in two disagreements with Sadoleto. Both turned on education. Pole read Sadoleto's *De liberis recte instituendis* on his way to Padua in 1532, and quickly sent Sadoleto his opinion that a student had to go beyond philosophy to divine things.[168] Sadoleto defended himself in two ways, arguing that philosophy included theology, and, besides, no one should study theology before age twenty-five and his book concerned only the education of youth.[169] The dispute dragged on into 1533, and led almost directly into a further disagreement over Bonamico.[170] Should Bonamico remain a mere grammarian, or turn to more serious philosophical and ethical pursuits? According to Pole, Bonamico's continued fondness for his (and Contarini's) old teacher Pietro Pomponazzi should have meant that he would teach philosophy and cease merely to pursue rhetoric, as Sadoleto advised. Bonamico had to see that he should concentrate on the philosophy which 'deals with the precepts of life . . . [rather] than remaining among the orators and poets, repeating the precepts for forming an oration from Cicero, or of tilling a field from Vergil'.[171] And Pole was not really suggesting that Bonamico become a mere philosopher, either. Philosophy served to demonstrate that humans could know nothing, and therefore had to escape the senses in order to contemplate truth, which became an act of faith. Pole described his letter as a search for 'consolation'.[172]

Sadoleto took Bonamico's side, offering another defence of the relations of philosophy and theology and the necessity of cultivating all branches of learning. Since the Christian faith was very simple, contained in only a few books, there was plenty of time to study the liberal arts. Bonamico should not therefore become a philosopher. Sadoleto's opinion defeated Pole (as it probably did in the case of a similar dispute over Gheri's education).[173] Pole lost graciously, and declared himself eager to read Sadoleto's new book on philosophy, *Hortensius*, in the midst of writing *De unitate*.[174] Bonamico would have made a much different theologian from Pole in any case. Not only did he believe in the rationality of the universe, like the Thomist Contarini and unlike the Pyrrhonist Pole, but he also

---

telescoped time by combining people like Bembo whom Pole met almost immediately with those like Lampridio whom he probably met only perhaps as much as a decade later.
[167] *CRP*, no. 70. For the date at which they met, see *CRP*, no. 59.

[168] *CRP*, no. 64.
[169] *CRP*, no. 65.
[170] *CRP*, nos. 66 and 68.
[171] *ERP*, 1, pp. 411–13.
[172] *CRP*, no. 70.
[173] *CRP*, no. 71.
[174] *CRP*, no. 17.

recommended meditating on the classics as the means to solve the church's problems.[175]

Royal servant

Sufficiently prepared after about five years in Padua, Pole returned home. Writing his 'Dialogue' shortly thereafter, probably some time in late 1528 or early 1529, Starkey cast his patron as the character Longueil had, an authority on the commonwealth. More than this, Starkey intended to take advantage of the opportunity he saw lying before Pole by leading him to the head of the government.[176] His hopes could not have outstripped Pole's by too much, lest he lose Pole's patronage. Needless to say, Henry would not have welcomed Starkey's proposal to establish an aristocratic republic, but the point is that Starkey saw an opening for Pole. He was not alone. If Robert Wakefield really taught Pole Hebrew, probably in 1528, this must mean that Henry was grooming him almost immediately after his return to take a leading role in the divorce project, as Wakefield and other Hebraists did.[177] According to Agostino Oldoino, Pole translated Jeremiah's Lamentations from Hebrew, but no manuscript or printed edition is known nor is there much compelling evidence of his facility in the language.[178] Then again, Hebrew characters were displayed on both his tomb and a stained glass window at Lambeth, and he was early credited with the conversion at Viterbo of the Paduan Hebraist Emmanuele Tremelli, a story which probably came from Tremelli himself.[179]

---

[175] *DBI.*

[176] Mayer, *Starkey*, chs. 3–5, and T. F. Mayer, ed., Thomas Starkey, *A dialogue between Pole and Lupset* (Royal Historical Society, Camden fourth series, no. 37, 1989), pp. xiii, 1–2, 142–3.

[177] I owe this suggestion to Richard Rex, and am grateful to him for help with Wakefield. Robert Wakefield *Oratio de laudibus et utilitate trium linguarum* (London: Wynkyn de Worde, n.d.)., fo. Biv for Wakefield's claim; cf. *OEE*, 6, no. 1595, p. 144. The *explicit* of the work says it was read in Cambridge in 1524, but the dates at which Wakefield could have taught some of his other alleged pupils and the way in which he refers to them (especially John Taylor as ambassador to

France) argue for a publication date some time in 1528 or the first half of 1529.

[178] Alfonso Chacón, ed. Agostino Oldoino, *Vitae et res gestae pontificum romanorum et S. R. E. cardinalium ab initio nascentis ecclesiae usque ad Clementem IX P. O. M.* (Rome: P. and A. De Rubeis, 1677), c. 638. There are a few signs of a knowledge of Hebrew in Pole's undated meditations on the Psalms. BAV, Vat. lat. 5969, fos. 1br–48r, e.g. fos. 4v, 18v, and 24v.

[179] For Pole's tomb, see below p. 353 and p. 321 for Lambeth. For Tremelli, [Matthew Parker?], *De antiquitate britannicae ecclesiae* (London: [John Daye], 1572), p. 410 (see below ch. 9 for its authorship). Pastore, *Flaminio*, p. 70 cited the 1605 edition, probably from Wilhelm Becker, *Immanuel*

There was certainly good reason for a crash course in Hebrew, but not only as preparation for a theologian. As Pole would later write, places for royal counsellors were going begging.[180] The reason lay in Henry's wish to escape from Katherine, together with the reluctance of some of his more prominent advisers to further the king's plans. By 1527 Henry had worked out a scheme to gain a divorce.[181] When the original plot miscarried, other proposals were floated, among them the suggestion, probably by Anne's chaplain Thomas Cranmer, that the universities be asked for opinions favourable to Henry's cause.[182] This was in August 1529. One of the universities included was Paris. The assignment fell to Pole, and as I have shown elsewhere he executed it without a trace of hesitation.[183] It also offered him his first opportunity to rework his biography when writing about the episode to Henry in *De unitate*.

In 1530 Pole had yet to do this. Instead, Henry tried to capitalize immediately on Pole's performance. According to Pole later and Chapuys at the time, the king offered him the archbishopric of York.[184] The appointment of a reliable prelate was required by a draft proposal that would have allowed the two archbishops (or any one of them) to resolve the divorce.[185] Pole relatively quickly

---

Tremellius. Ein Proselytenleben im Zeitalter der Reformation (Leipzig: J. C. Hinrich, 1890, 2nd ed.; Schriften des Institutum Judaicum in Berlin, no. 8), p. 7, whom Pastore apparently incorrectly read as saying that Parker's collaborator John Josselyn added the story to the second edition. Pastore thought it more likely that Vermigli bore responsibility for Tremelli's baptism. Tremelli may have stood godson to one of Parker's children, and visited him in 1565 when he could have passed on the story, if not before. John Strype, *The life and acts of Matthew Parker* (Oxford: Clarendon Press, 1821; 3 vols.), 1, p. 59 and *DNB*, 19, p. 1113.

180 *ERP*, 1, p. 119.
181 Virginia M. Murphy, 'The debate over Henry VIII's first divorce: an analysis of the contemporary treatises', unpublished Ph.D. thesis, Cambridge University, 1984, pp. 31–2, 67, 80, 87–90, 181–2, 217, 262.
182 Jasper Ridley, *Thomas Cranmer* (Oxford: Clarendon Press, 1962), pp. 25–9 doubted Cranmer's priority, but the story is generally accepted otherwise.

183 Thomas F. Mayer, 'A mission worse than death: Reginald Pole and the Parisian theologians', *English historical review*, 103 (1988), pp. 870–91 (now in Thomas F. Mayer, *Cardinal Pole in European context: a via media in the reformation* (Aldershot: Ashgate Publishing, 2000)).
184 *L&P*, 5, no. 737 (cf. *CSPSp*, 4:2, no. 888). The accuracy of this report may be reduced by Chapuys's later recollection that Henry had offered Pole Canterbury. *CSPSp*, 5:1, 109, p. 324. Pole referred to Henry's offer in *CRP*, no. 155 and elsewhere.
185 PRO, SP2/N, fos. 155r–60r (*L&P*, 6, 311.4?). The document cannot be dated, but it is certainly later than 1529 and perhaps earlier than 1531. See also G. W. Bernard, 'The pardon of the clergy reconsidered', *Journal of ecclesiastical history*, 37 (1986), pp. 273–5 and his reply to J. A. Guy's criticism in the same issue, pp. 285–6. Similar schemes cropped up frequently after September 1530. J. A. Guy, *The public career of Sir Thomas More* (New Haven: Yale University Press, 1980), pp. 134–5.

disabused Henry of his hopes, through rather mysterious means. Perhaps the only certain action he took – going into retirement at Sheen – turned the trick. Darkest uncertainty surrounds what else he did or said about Henry's policies, and, even more crucially, when in the fluid circumstances of 1530–2. In private, he expressed reservations about the consequences of a divorce, undoubtedly in a written opinion, less probably in an interview with the king. In public, Pole almost certainly acquiesced in the clergy's grant to Henry of the supreme head-ship over the church, and even more certainly did not, as Chapuys incorrectly reported, threaten to speak against the divorce in parliament in order to secure permission to leave England. The signals about Pole's attitude are mixed, their strength weak.

Much of the poor reception arises from Pole twiddling the knobs, with help from Chapuys and Cranmer. Chapuys's report of January 1532 is easiest to dispose of.[186] He must, of course, have been wrong about parliament, where Pole had no business. Even if Chapuys made a mistake for convocation in which Pole sat as dean of Exeter, it is unlikely that he had Pole's intentions right.[187] For one thing, most of those opposed to the new order did not see divorce and headship as distinct issues.[188] Therefore Pole's at least tacit support of the headship in February 1531 would have required him to make a public recantation less than a year later. The evidence for Pole's original attitude is circumstantial, but convincing in aggregate. Most compelling, both lower houses of convocation had strongly resisted the bishops' lead on the headship. As late as May 1531 eighteen members of the lower house of southern convocation issued two blunt official protests on behalf of a majority. Most of these stalwarts were swiftly charged with *praemunire*, and all almost as quickly submitted.[189] Pole was not among them. Punishment of so prominent a figure would have been hard to avoid. He could still have been one of those who merely voted 'present' in February when the headship was accepted, but Bishop Burnet probably argued correctly that Pole, who was certainly in attendance, must have gone along since he lost none of his benefices.[190] For another, a mere threat to speak out does not square very

[186] *L&P*, 5, no. 737 (cf. *CSPSp*, 4:2, no. 888).

[187] Schenk, p. 30 also rejected Chapuys's story, but on the extrinsic grounds of Pole's retiring character.

[188] Walker (pp. 15–21) connects Pole to the opposition group around More and Richard Reynolds, as does S. E. Lehmberg, *The reformation parliament 1529–1536* (Cambridge: Cambridge

University Press, 1970), pp. 28–30.

[189] J. A. Guy, 'Henry VIII and the *praemunire* manoeuvres of 1530–1531', *English historical review*, 97 (1982), pp. 481–503 and Bernard, 'Pardon'.

[190] Gilbert Burnet, *The history of the reformation of the church of England*, ed. Nicholas Pocock (Oxford: Clarendon Press, 1865; 7 vols.), 4, pp. 353 and 191.

well with Pole's repeated insistence that he had told no one other than the king of his scruples before 1539. Finally, the weakest counter-argument. Pole's first biographer said that he had used friends of the king to secure permission to leave.[191] So much for Chapuys.

Pole's written opinion poses stickier problems, mainly because it survives only in Cranmer's synopsis. According to it, Pole had 'written a book much contrary to the king his purpose'.[192] It advanced a number of international and domestic reasons – from Gallic perfidy to popular anti-clericalism – why Henry should commit his case to papal arbitrament. But Pole also tried to explain why 'he had never pleasure to intromit himself in this cause'. Above all, the succession and the dangers of renewed civil war concerned him. As he would do steadfastly in the future, Pole claimed that he could 'never' bring himself to dishonour Henry by helping to condemn his marriage as 'so shameful, so abominable, so bestial and against nature', no matter how just the king's cause. Pole also criticized English reliance on the opinions of the universities, which had been so hard to obtain. He offered another remedy, but Cranmer did not reproduce it.

This is odd, almost as odd as Pole's later distancing of himself from his actions in Paris. There could be no better evidence that Pole's life was a tissue of lies, or at least discontinuities. Alas, the issue is not so straightforward. These are not Pole's words, but Cranmer's, and they cannot be taken at face value.[193] The demands of faction and of his own career gave Cranmer powerful incentives to distort what Pole wrote.[194] He was reporting to his patron Wiltshire, a man sensitive to the smallest sign of resistance to the divorce. Cranmer may have gained access to Pole's writing from the duke of Norfolk, the nearest thing to the head of government in 1531 and Wiltshire's sometime ally.[195] Cranmer's edited version of Pole's opinion would have helped to discredit him with Wiltshire and even more with Norfolk, who probably had fair knowledge of Pole's service in Paris. In addition to partisan motives, Cranmer had personal reasons for giving a particular 'spin' to Pole's words, if not for misrepresentation. Put bluntly, they were rivals for Henry's favour. 1531 was a difficult year for the evangelicals in general, and Pole threatened to make things worse for Cranmer's particular

---

[191] *MMB*, 1:2, p. 287.

[192] BL, Lansdowne 115, fos. 2r–3r, printed in Nicholas Pocock, ed., *Records of the reformation. The divorce, 1527–1533* (Oxford: Clarendon Press, 1870; 2 vols.), 2, pp. 130–1.

[193] This is not the standard assessment. Cf. Ridley's judgment of Cranmer's report as

'obviously an accurate one' (p. 36).

[194] Ridley, p. 29 reached a similar conclusion about the mix of prudential and intellectual reasons which brought Cranmer to his original decision to side with Henry.

[195] *ERP*, 1, p. 182; 4, p. 332; and Guy, *More*, pp. 144–7.

strategy for advancement by questioning one of their key planks.[196] If Cranmer did indeed hatch a plot to outmanoeuvre Pole, it worked. For the moment, both Cranmer and Pole got to keep their gains, Pole an exhibition for study in Italy, Cranmer a royal chaplaincy. Yet in an age in which proximity to the monarch meant power, Cranmer had definitely taken the inside track.

Even the web of conditional language in Cranmer's representation could not conceal Pole's cautious approach to the divorce. He could imagine (although without optimism) circumstances in which Henry might get free of Katherine, he willingly admitted that the king's case could be good, and he concluded only that he could not assist it himself. While this interpretation of Pole's opinion leaves open the possibility that he had begun to change his mind, perhaps convinced in a negative sense by the very opinions he had helped to collect in Paris, this is far from principled opposition. The second of Starkey's letters of 1535 seeking Pole's opinion on the divorce supports this reading of Cranmer's document. Starkey remembered being concerned by Pole's emphasis on the dangers inherent in Henry's plans. More clearly than Cranmer, however, Starkey thought Pole's opinion had contained little else. Adducing the ultimate authority, Starkey noted that Henry too judged that Pole had missed the point by delving into matters of 'policy' rather than sticking to the divorce.[197] Starkey fudged a little by encouraging Pole not to worry about an accusation of 'lightness of mind & changing of sentence'. He was safe because he had 'only put before his [Henry's] eyes the dangers which hanged upon worldly policy', not expressed his view of the divorce.[198] In 1535 Henry and Starkey still thought of Pole as someone who knew a lot about politics, maybe more than was good for him, but not a person who had gone on record about the divorce's substantive issues. Besides, unless Henry were thicker than a post, why would he waste resources in a campaign to get Pole's opinion if he already knew it? Thus Starkey's evidence will probably go further. To stand on its head Pole's sarcastic refutation of Machiavelli's advice to princes to simulate religious behaviour, how could Pole have kept his manifold virtues, chief among them opposition to the divorce, secret from his *domestici* for so many years?[199] From Starkey, or even more from Morison, who would later accuse Pole of nearly everything short of bestiality, but never of concealing his true opinion of Henry's proceedings? Although writing on a tightrope, when Pole assured Charles in 1539 that only the order to give his opinion had forced him out of the silence he had previously maintained

---

[196] E. W. Ives, *Anne Boleyn* (Oxford: Blackwell, 1986), p. 177.

[197] BL, Cleopatra E VI, fo. 375r, repeated on

375v and Mayer, *Starkey*, pp. 209–10.

[198] *Ibid.*, fo. 376r.

[199] *ERP*, 1, pp. 140, 142, 147–8.

between two unacceptable options, he came closer to the truth than in many other of his autobiographical fictions.

Pole appeared to contradict this account in an alternative draft of the 'Apology to Charles V'.[200] In it he claimed to have known exactly what Henry was up to before he left England, having been present at discussions about virtue and the prince's will, apparently held in a royal palace. Among those present was the earl of Sussex, which must date the meeting after December 1529.[201] Pole had told the king that he had to follow Christ and not the philosophers recommended by his advisers. Sussex asked Pole after dinner to repeat his opinion. Pole then realized that he could not change the king's mind and saw no alternative but to pray hard and to leave, hoping that he was wrong about Henry's intentions.

Pole's written opinion, nothing like this direct, made an impact as well. According to Pole, Sir John Russell presented his writing to Henry, who read it.[202] If Henry saw the opinion (and if we accept Cranmer's version of it), the apparent lack of recriminations against Pole would suggest that the king took Pole to mean that he had grappled with the theologians reluctantly and had since concluded that the long list of political considerations his opinion outlined ended the possibility of even limited support for the king's policy. Thus Henry may have treated Pole in the same way he did Lord Chancellor More, allowing him to oppose the divorce in private, provided that he did nothing to hamper the king's pursuit of it. Nevertheless, ambivalence may have begun to turn toward irreconcilable conflict.

It has been a hard slog to get through Chapuys's and Cranmer's documents. When we turn to Pole's alleged interview with Henry, we enter a morass. Errors on closely related points reduce the value of Chapuys's report of Pole's refusal of York, the only external corroboration of that event.[203] The Venetian ambassador's report in August that Henry meant to give Canterbury either to 'Grameldo' (Cranmer?) or to Pole may contain a garbled echo of Chapuys's tale.[204] Of course, if there is any truth to this claim, then Henry had

---

[200] *CRP*, no. 245, fos. 309v–10v.

[201] Lehmberg, p. 47. Sussex was part of the 'inner ring' after Wolsey's fall (Guy, *Public career*, p. 128).

[202] *ERP*, 4, p. 332.

[203] Chapuys further confused things by claiming that Pole immediately wrote Henry against the divorce *after* his arrival in Venice. *CSPSp*, 5:1, no. 109, p. 324. It is

difficult to weigh the value of Hugh Latimer's claim in 1549 that Pole would have been archbishop of York had he not turned on Henry. G. E. Corrie, ed., *Sermons by Hugh Latimer, sometime bishop of Worcester, martyr, 1555* (Cambridge: University Press, 1844), p. 173.

[204] *I diarii di Marino Sanuto* (Venice: Privately Published, 1879–1902; 58 vols.), 57, c. 23.

not permanently turned against Pole yet, which reduces the magnitude of their alleged falling-out earlier in the year, as it magnifies Cranmer's and Pole's rivalry. Every time Pole touched the story of the interview it came out differently, including the sequence of interview and written opinion.[205] The first time around, Pole described the interview carefully, but no writing. On the next run-through a decade later, Pole mentioned writing, but no interview. In his final recounting a few years later, it was interview, then writing. All the versions agree that Pole changed his mind in the course of his meeting with the king, but whereas originally Pole acted alone, upon reflection he decided that God had prevented him from supporting Henry. The impact of his words on the king also changed over time. Sometimes Henry flew into a rage and only prevented himself with difficulty from stabbing Pole to death. Sometimes he calmly asked Pole to give the royal case more thought. Once Henry even agreed with Pole. And although the cast remained fairly stable with Norfolk and Montagu as the principal supporting players, their attitude to the proceedings varied. This leaves us with next to nothing to go on. True, Pole did several times ask Norfolk to bear him out, but I have yet to find any evidence that the duke did; Norfolk probably saw at most only one of these appeals. I shall not even attempt to determine when the interview may have taken place. Only in the second of these writings did Pole date it *mortuo paucis ante diebus Cardinale Eboracense* which would seem to point to December 1530.[206] The range stretches from then through June 1531, a period of singular upheaval.

I lean toward the sceptical conclusion that Pole protested too much and that the interview is mythical, an icon with which to predate his break with Henry and assist Pole's conversion of himself into a seamless saint. The calm report of this moment in the Latin funeral oration for Pole, which simply had him refuse the appointment because he was too young, would support this conclusion.[207] I could also be persuaded to adopt the Pyrrhonist view that it is impossible to know what happened. It at least seems wise to reverse the old hagiographical standard and refuse to trust Pole on any point where his testimony cannot be supported.[208] If we thus discount or discard the interview, accept my reading of Cranmer's summary of Pole's 'divorce opinion', believe Starkey's later report on it (as well as his attitude and aspirations), reject Chapuys's fable, agree that Pole supported the headship, and factor in his behaviour in Paris, we must conclude

---

[205] The versions are *CRP*, nos. 155 and 555 and *CPM*, catalogue, no. 2. I quote *ERP*, 4, p. 327.
[206] *Ibid.*

[207] *ERP*, 5, p. 189. Cf. p. 346 below.
[208] This is the reason I do not here consider the infamous story of Pole's interview with Cromwell (see chapter 2).

that Pole neither came out against Henry's designs nor rejected them in his own mind before he left England in January 1532. And why flee then? The conservatives appeared to have a strong position prior to parliament's reopening, which would not come until two weeks after Chapuys reported Pole's resolution to leave. Pole would have more than borne out the high opinions of his political aptitude had he proved more prescient than the proverbially wily Gardiner and correctly predicted the Submission of the Clergy.[209]

The murk around Pole becomes impenetrable for the next three years, except for the controversy with Sadoleto. With the possible exception of the triennium after 1550, this is the worst documented period of his life after childhood. Starkey and everyone else who knew Pole largely fell silent. Pole later claimed that he had fled to Venice, intent on ignoring England.[210] Perhaps he did. During this time Pole underwent a religious conversion, but one which should if anything have brought him closer to Henry.[211] As in the case of John Calvin, we know few details about this momentous event, aside from Starkey's news to an Avignonese friend in June 1534 that Pole was completely absorbed 'in sacred letters'.[212] But like the newly Protestant Calvin bursting into Geneva, Pole's decision to attack Henry is hard to miss, and in 1537 he got his chance.

---

[209] Ives, *Anne Boleyn*, pp. 188–91.
[210] *ERP*, 1, p. 69.

[211] Fenlon, ch. 2 and Donaldson, pp. 5–6, 30.
[212] BL, Harl. 6989, fos. 43v–4v.

2

The campaign against Henry VIII

The legation of 1537

Once Pole went to Rome, he got the chance to put into action the resistances to Henry VIII adumbrated in *De unitate*. Inspired in part by the Pilgrimage of Grace and the opportunity it presented for papal intervention, Pole drafted for the pope a position paper which laid out the goals for a mission to England. Pole advised subterfuge and suggested that the mission be identified to foreign ambassadors as concerning peace, the Turks, heresy, and the council. Nevertheless, Pole stressed that the legation would be sent 'so innocently'. Its main object had to be restoring 'the accustomed authority' and bringing Henry to penance. Pole proposed to send 'someone confirmed to them [the Pilgrims] in the name of your holiness, to help not only with words, but again with deeds, who would need to have a certain quantity of money' to disburse to 'the so well-deserving' rebels. Pole identified the source of this cash, which must mean that he had help from someone in the papal financial apparatus. The rebels needed the money to protect themselves from the lies Henry would tell, pretending to give them justice, only to seize and execute their leaders.[1] Paul endorsed Pole's suggestions, eventually without reservation.[2] In the first bull of appointment, Paul named Pole 'an angel of peace' who was to bring the English to the council.[3] In the second, dated six weeks later, the pope not only observed that force would probably be required to return Henry to the faith, but also that

---

[1] *CRP*, no. 150. Cf. George B. Parks, 'The Parma letters and the dangers to cardinal Pole', *Catholic historical review*, 46 (1960), pp. 299–317, pp. 310–11, one of the few pieces to get Pole's aims right.

[2] The pope planned in mid-December to send a messenger to the bishops to congratulate them on the rising and offer assistance, but no envoy is known to have gone. ASV, Arm. 41:4, fo. 278, no. 279, cited in Carlo Capasso, *Paolo III (1534–1549)*, 1 (Messina-Rome: G. Principato, 1924; 2 vols.), p. 272.

[3] *CRP*, no. 151.

should force fail, it was better for him and all his supporters to die rather than endanger the salvation of others. Although the Pilgrimage had been put down by the time of the first bull in February 1537, the pope continued to hope that the rebels would rise again, and instructed Pole to encourage them, in part through a crusading indulgence.[4] According to the imperial ambassadors in Rome, Paul had made Pole a cardinal specifically for use against England.[5]

Pole pursued the same double strategy about his aims as the pope did. In the course of a key document in his self-creation Pole wrote the king's council a thoroughly innocuous version of his plans the day after his appointment. The pope had given him the legation because of his zeal for the church. His assignment covered 'three great matters': 'peace with the princes beyond the mountains', 'abolishing of heresies, and resisting against the Turk'. Pole continued in a badly mutilated passage that he had special charge to see 'if God might open any gate [where]by I might enter to do you that good' as he had always hoped. A Latin version is blunter. Pole sought a gate which would allow him to bring England back to the church. Pole concluded by alluding to his prophetic *persona*, declaring that he hoped to give a twist to the old saying about prophets and honour.[6]

I have treated elsewhere Pole's mission and its significance in his religious evolution.[7] Here the degree of planning and the extent to which the pope was prepared to go need emphasis. Amongst the credentials drawn up for Pole in mid-February is a letter of full papal credit to Erard de la Marck, cardinal of Liège, asking him to provide whatever funds Pole needed in order to assist the rebels, beyond those the pope had already given him.[8] Other evidence corroborates this document. Francis I's ambassador to Henry was to tell the king that Pole, if he could not bring Henry back to obedience, was 'to have delivered via the merchants a good sum of money to help the people'.[9] The imperial

---

[4] *CRP*, no. 169.
[5] *CSPSp*, 5:2, nos. 128 and 134.
[6] *CRP*, no. 155.
[7] Thomas F. Mayer, 'A diet for Henry VIII: the failure of Reginald Pole's 1537 legation', *Journal of British studies*, 26 (1987), pp. 305–31 and 'If martyrs are exchanged with martyrs: the kidnappings of William Tyndale and Reginald Pole', *ARG*, 81 (1990), pp. 286–308 (both now in Thomas F. Mayer, *Cardinal Pole in European context: a via media in the reformation* (Aldershot: Ashgate Publishing, 2000)); see also *CRP*,

chapter 3 and my article on Pole in H. C. G. Matthew, ed., *New dictionary of national biography* (Oxford: Oxford University Press, forthcoming).
[8] ASV, Arm 41:5, fo. 169r, no. 152, partially printed in Cesare Baroni, ed. Oderico Raynaldi, *Annales ecclesiastici*, 32 (Paris: Consociatio Sancti Pauli, 1880; 34 vols.), p. 454.
[9] N. Camusat, *Mélanges historiques ou recueil des plusieurs actes, traités et lettres missives depuis l'an 1390 à l'an 1580* (Troyes: N. Moreau, 1619), sig. 13v.

ambassador in Rome sent Charles a similar, if more circumstantial report: Pole had a bill of exchange for 10,000 ducats to be spent on arquebusiers, and was to do all he could in secret to aid the rebels.[10] De la Marck apparently drew on the letter of credit, although I have found no official documents to this effect. According to one source, he gave Pole 15,000 crowns, and Priuli appeared to claim that de la Marck had given Pole 2,000 *scudi*, in addition to another 1,500 sent via him from Rome.[11]

Bishop Giberti was named Pole's number two.[12] Pole could not have asked for more help. Giberti handled all important local negotiations as well as running Pole's household, and brought along experienced men of his own.[13] These included Francesco della Torre, his right-hand man in Verona, Adamo Fumano, canon of the cathedral (both of whose letters add much new information about the legation), and probably also Trifone Benci, butt of many of della Torre's jokes but also scion of a powerful family of notaries and copyists, who would make a distinguished career in the papal bureaucracy.[14] Priuli brought his dependants, but to judge from the comments of della Torre and Fumano, neither he nor they were of much use. At the outset, della Torre reported to Carlo Gualteruzzi that Priuli was 'exactly the reverse of your medal, not only negligent, but very ambitious to be negligent . . . I am sure that we will not leave Italy before he forgets his horse by the side of the road.'[15]

A great deal rode on Pole's mission, as the degree of attention it received in both Rome and England indicates. Letter barrages were exchanged in both directions, and both sides engaged in espionage. In addition to supporting the Pilgrimage, Pole's trump card was Henry's excommunication.[16] The English replied to Pole's cardinalate through Starkey, probably Thomas Wriothesley, the team of Cuthbert Tunstall and John Stokesley, and perhaps Cranmer and John Clerk.[17] But policy remained adrift, despite the urgency of Pole's threat. The

---

[10] *CSPSp*, 5:2, no. 134.

[11] Paul Harsin, *Le règne d'Érard de la Marck 1505–1538* (Liège: Sciences et lettres, 1955), p. 410 and BMIC24, fo. 161r.

[12] *CSPSp*, 5:2, no. 126.

[13] *CRP*, no. 187.

[14] Della Torre's and Fumano's letters to Carlo Gualteruzzi are in Fano, Biblioteca comunale Federiciana, MS Federici 59 and BAV, Barb lat. 5695. For Pole's entourage, see *ERP*, 2, pp. LXXXII–LXXXVIII.

[15] MS Federici 59, fos. 157r–8r. Cf. fos.

158v–9r noting that 'a thousand ridiculous things had happened' to Priuli.

[16] *L&P*, 12:1, no. 34.

[17] The supposition about Cranmer and Clerk comes from a reference by Thomas Master to a note he saw in the Exchequer of Receipt in 1636. Diarmaid MacCulloch, *Thomas Cranmer. A life* (New Haven and London: Yale University Press, 1996), p. 47. PRO, SP 1/111, f. 151r is a letter in Wriothesley's hand. *CRP*, no. 142.

council offered Pole a second chance in the form of a conference in Flanders as Pole was supposed to have suggested in the first place.[18] John Hussey's correspondence manifested the uncertain direction of policy, for example, his report on 18 February that 'some say Mr Pole's promotions [benefices] shall be given, and some nay'.[19] Pole replied to Cromwell and the council, but apparently not to the others. He engaged in more abuse of Cromwell than Cromwell had of him, and insisted that *De unitate* had only one meaning and solely concerned Henry's honour.[20] The letter to the council is much more important, both for the history of his legation and for Pole's image-making.[21] In it Pole maintained that he had written *De unitate* out of duty and conscience, probably meaning that he did not yet conceive of conscience as a personal possession, as Luther did, but rather as a repository of a moral code.[22]

Pole made no effort to veil his hostility to Henry. For example, he sent the nuncio in France a long letter, containing an explicit, if coded, statement of his legation's aims.[23] Pole began with a long attack on Henry's pursuit of a legate, against 'all human commerce' and divine and natural law. At least this meant that Pole was suffering persecution like no one else, other than the apostles, knowledge which consoled him. The body of England suffered from a diseased head, which might be remedied in one of two ways, surgery and diet. The first worked on deep-seated diseases, and the second on problems of more recent standing and was the mode Pole adopted and that he had proposed to Francis. Pole meant that Francis and Charles should cut off commerce with England, a plan he had formed as early as 1531.[24] Further, this plan was directly linked to rebellion, which Pole hoped would again soon break out. Pole's sense of rhetorical occasion did not fail him. A week later in a letter to Cromwell Pole insisted on his love for Henry, and, repeating much of the substance of his letter to the nuncio, tried to get Cromwell at least to admit Giberti to see Henry. Far from being Henry's enemy, Pole wrote that he had helped to protect the king during the Pilgrimage, had prevented the publication of his excommunication, and even sent a servant to offer his help. Indeed, Pole got himself in trouble in Rome by defending the king.[25] Writing to the nuncio, Pole did not protest love for

---

18 *CRP*, no. 145.

19 *L&P*, 12:1, no. 475.

20 *CRP*, no. 154.

21 Priuli thought that Beccadelli might have forwarded a copy of this 'beautiful letter' to Gheri. BMIC25, fo. 149r.

22 Michael G. Baylor, *Action and person: conscience in late scholasticism and the young*

Luther (Leiden: Brill, 1977).

23 *CRP*, no. 174.

24 BL, Lansdowne 115, fos. 2r–3r, printed in Nicholas Pocock, ed., *Records of the reformation. The divorce, 1527–1533* (Oxford: Clarendon Press, 1870; 2 vols.), 2, pp. 130–1.

25 *CRP*, no. 176.

Henry but rather announced that he (Pole) had been declared a traitor, and welcomed the chance to say publicly what kind.[26] Blaming Henry's depravity on his counsellors, Pole recurred to the examples of Fisher and More. Throughout this legation, he urged his satellite Gheri to write Fisher's life, only to have Gheri reply that he was too busy reading Aristotle. (That this seemed an adequate defence may provide further evidence of Pole's own esteem for the Philosopher.) By luck, Gheri replied, 'Giorgio Inglese', once Priuli's familiar, had turned up in Fano, and was ideally suited to the job. He had been in Fisher's household and claimed to know the bishop's ideas. Giorgius Buchareus, as he called himself, was none other than Adam Damplip, eventually executed for treasonable dealings with Pole, and also a sometime famous sacramentarian.[27] Thus Damplip the biographer could have fuelled the worst English fears of Pole.

Aside from plotting propaganda and dodging English attempts to do him in, Pole did not accomplish much. The pope decided to recall him, probably not later than about the middle of April.[28] Pole replied on 18 May, writing almost as if he had not had word of his recall. He considered that it might be best to return immediately, since the end of hopes for a parliament meant there was nothing further to do. Then again, any number of reasons argued that he should stay, above all the vital necessity of encouraging the *populus* and preventing the loss of England.[29] If a safe place could be found from which to await developments, another rebellion would certainly come since the cause still remained. Diet was forgotten. If Pole were to be entrusted to the care of another cardinal, who like himself left all to providence, he would be prepared to risk any danger 'for the honour of the head of the church, and the utility of his church', including martyrdom. Priuli modelled Pole's potential martyrdom on Fisher's, applying to Pole a quotation that must have been derived from Damplip.[30] Pole had the 'living example' of Giberti, who gave up his leisure and safety, and worse, his diocese, depriving a private church to serve the public one. Prudence dictated

---

[26] Pole was attainted on 19 May 1539. S. E. Lehmberg, *The later parliaments of Henry VIII 1536–1547* (Cambridge: Cambridge University Press, 1977), pp. 60–1.

[27] For this see BMIC25, fos. 139r–41r and 146r–9r; *MMB*, 1:2, pp. 286, 293, 300, 306–7, and 319–22. Cf. John Foxe, *Actes and monuments of matters most speciall and memorable* (London: John Daye, 1583; *STC*, no. 11225), pp. 1223–4 and 1228–9

and *L&P*, 15, no. 498.58 for his attainder. No trace of his life of Fisher has surfaced. Gheri claimed that Bucker also wrote a number of shorter pieces about him.

[28] *CRP*, no. 177.

[29] As Priuli well said, this letter was a perfect example of the favourite humanist mode of argument *in utramque partem*. BMIC25, fos. 150r–3v.

[30] BMIC25, fo. 155r.

withdrawal, but both of them left all to Christ, and had ceased to worry about spies, thanks to the courage Christ had given them.[31]

Through various means Pole knew of English moves against him, especially Hugh Holland's news of Cromwell's attempts to have Pole killed or kidnapped. Pole is supposed to have replied, 'Would my Lord Privy Seal so feign kill me? Well, I trust it shall not lie in his power. The king is not contented to bear me malice. He but provokes others against me, and hath written to the French king that he shall not receive me a cardinal or legate, but yet I was received into Paris better than some men would.'[32] In addition to the fact that Pole thus knew what he faced, two other points in Holland's report bear emphasis. First, the last part of Pole's speech evinces his powerful reflex to make examples almost immediately out of experience as he had already done in the case of his honourable reception in France, despite Francis's refusal to receive him, making of it a stick to beat the imperial agents who would not admit him.[33] Second, Pole displayed a keen sense of rhetorical occasion and of English factional politics by blaming Cromwell for his troubles, at the same time as he mocked Henry's ineptitude. When writing Cromwell and the pope, he blamed the king.[34]

After many delays, Pole finally gained permission to come to Liège in imperial territory.[35] This was not much consolation, although it did further Pole's plan to await developments. In the meantime, he returned to studies and above all to scripture. As Priuli told Beccadelli in mid-June, Pole cast all his experiences in biblical terms, and had come to understand that he could not grasp the scriptures without the aid of experience. The key, as Priuli explained, was to persevere in faith and in prayer.[36] Only this could produce the peace that the world could not give. It was up to the believer to seek it, once God had given him grace and taught him the necessary *disciplina*.[37]

The appearance of the fundamental principle of experience, together with the rest of Priuli's vocabulary of *beneficio* and *consolatio*, is of great importance. It is the only major element of 'spiritual' vocabulary not to be found in *De unitate*, or in one of the principal influences on this work, Jan van Kampen.[38] Van Kampen had remained close to Pole's circles after leaving his household, moving first to

---

[31] *CRP*, no. 182.

[32] PRO, SP 1/138, fo. 192v (*L&P*, 13:2, no. 797); cf. Höllger, pp. 51–2.

[33] *CRP*, nos. 173 and 178.

[34] *CRP*, no. 182 and cf. no. 181.

[35] *CRP*, no. 181.

[36] BMIC25, fos. 150r–3v.

[37] BMIC25, fos. [154r–6v].

[38] See above, p. 32–3. Firpo (*Alumbrados*, p. 163n) notes Priuli's stress on experience in 1537 as a Valdesian theme. For a succinct summary of its importance, see Fenlon, p. 68n.

Venice, then to Verona with Giberti and finally to Contarini's household in Rome, and it is possible that he rejoined Pole in Flanders, at least Priuli and all the company eagerly awaited van Kampen's arrival there.[39] Pointing to van Kampen's role is probably unnecessary. Priuli's proximate 'source' was the epistles of Paul, to which he constantly adverted, and on which he congratulated Gheri for having Damplip's explication.[40] *Experientia* had already been a key concept for Petrarch, which may make another bridgehead between 'humanist' and 'spiritual' vocabulary.[41] It is also to be found in Contarini's correspondence with Paolo Giustinian and Pietro Querini, as well as much talk of consolation and benefits (although not of Christ).[42]

More important, experience figured importantly in the Benedictine spirituality that Pole found more important than Valdés.[43] St Bernard placed a great emphasis on experience, along with consolation, for example in his well-known sermon *De conversione*.[44] Like the vast majority of constructs, it is likely that 'Benedictine piety' never existed, at least not in any distinctive form.[45] Nevertheless, large numbers of monks of the congregation of Santa Giustina (later of Montecassino) embraced Paul's view of salvation. Pole knew and depended on members of this order, especially Marco da Cremona, who

---

[39] BMIC25, fos. 155v (Kampen had written Priuli twice), 156r, and 159v.

[40] BMIC25, fos. 146r–9r.

[41] Hans Baron, 'Petrarch: his inner struggle and the humanistic discovery of man's nature', in J. G. Rowe and W. H. Stockdale, eds., *Florilegium historiale: essays presented to Wallace K. Ferguson* (Toronto: University of Toronto Press, 1971), pp. 26–46, p. 27.

[42] Hubert Jedin, 'Contarini und Camaldoli', *Archivio italiano per la storia della pietà*, 2 (1959), pp. 59–118, pp. 12–13, 15, 16, 18, 20, 24, 30 (*beneficio*), 31, 34 (*benefici*), 37–8, 41, 47, 50, 56 ('più con la experientia comprendo il vero'), 58, 59 (both experience and consolation), 60, and 67. Cf. Barry Collett, *Italian Benedictine scholars and the reformation* (Oxford: Clarendon Press, 1985), p. 22.

[43] It is very likely that other kinds of spirituality had an impact on Pole, including that of Bernardino Scotti, one of the earliest Theatines, who was involved in

the writing of *De unitate* (see above), but too little is known of Scotti's or the order's piety this early. For their founder Gaetano da Thiene see William V. Hudon, *Theatine spirituality: selected writings* (New York and Mahwah, NJ: Paulist Press, 1996), pp. 33–42 and 71–111.

[44] J.-P. Migne, *et al.*, eds., *Patrologiae latinae cursus completus*, 182 (Paris: Garnier Frères, 1862), cc. 833–56, cc. 836, 838, 847, 849 (also touching on wisdom hidden from the prudent), 851. For experience as the touchstone of Bernard's piety, see Bernard of Clairvaux, *Selected works*, trans. and foreword by G. R. Evans, intro. by Jean Leclerq, preface by E. H. Cousins (New York and Mahwah, NJ: Paulist Press, 1987), pp. 31, 35, 47.

[45] Gigliola Fragnito, 'Il cardinale Gregorio Cortese (1483?-1548) nella crisi religiosa del Cinquecento', *Benedictina*, 30 (1983), pp. 129–69, 417–59 and 31 (1984), pp. 79–134, 30, p. 130 summarizes the debate.

taught in Padua, and Pole would become its protector.[46] That these two facts establish the 'source' of Pole's beliefs is possible but not very illuminating. That an early sixteenth-century Christian should find Paul his major inspiration after Christ is only surprising to those who still believe Luther's polemics (and too much modern scholarship). *Paulinismo preluterano* pervaded late medieval Europe.[47]

Paul figured in Pole and his household's daily, quasi-monastic discipline, coupled with Bernard.[48] As Priuli described their routine, it began an hour and a half before breakfast when everyone assembled in a little private church (*una giesiola domestica*) where they sang the hours *more theatinico senza canto* (probably meaning without the sort of descants and ornaments to which Starkey had objected in his 'Dialogue'). The appeal of Theatine music was reinforced by Priuli's ardent greetings to Carafa.[49] Giberti sang mass. This emphasized his implicit leadership of the group, which included at least one other priest who could have officiated, and serves as a reminder that the *ecclesia Veronense* had been in being for almost a decade, its impact on Pole increasingly important.[50] During the meal, the company read and discussed Bernard. Then Giberti usually read a chapter of Eusebius's *De demonstratione evangelica*, a work of which he had commissioned a translation shortly before dedicated to Paul III, further emphasizing Giberti's prominence and perhaps setting the frame of interpretation.[51] The group then engaged in elevating conversation for an hour or two. A similar routine occurred in the evening, with vespers and compline and this time Pole reading from Paul, beginning with I Timothy, perhaps because of its injunctions on the form of the church, reinforced by Paul's orders to pray for princes (2:1–2). After the reading, they took a barge on the Meuse or strolled in the garden, a place dear to both Pole and Priuli. They lacked only Gheri and Contarini.[52] The behaviour of Pole and his company made a powerful impression on at least one local religious, Gerard Morinck, who described these

---

[46] Collett, *passim*, esp. chs. 1 and 2 and see p. 78 below for Marco.

[47] Roberto Cessi, 'Paolinismo preluterano', *Atti della Accademica nazionale dei Lincei*, ser. 8, 12 (January–February 1957), pp. 3–30.

[48] Cf. Hubert Jedin, *Girolamo Seripando. Sein Leben und Denken im Geisteskampf des 16. Jahrhunderts* (Würzburg: Augustinus-Verlag, 1984; reprint of 1937 ed.; 2 vols.), 1, p. 266.

[49] BMIC25, fo. 155v.

[50] Adriano Prosperi, *Tra evangelismo e controriforma: G. M. Giberti (1495–1543)* (Rome: Edizioni di Storia e Letteratura, 1969), chs. 5 and 6, especially p. 287, for the summary of the unstable blend of mysticism and disciplinary reform which characterized that church.

[51] Prosperi, p. 231 and note; *ERP*, 2, pp. cvi–cvii.

[52] BMIC25, fos. 158r–9r, partially printed in *ERP*, 2, pp. civ–cv.

devotional exercises in terms of Christ and the disciples and could scarcely say enough in praise of Pole.[53] Pole thought this *otium* God-given, and except for writing letters, little interrupted it.

Pole still took an interest in causing what mischief he could, beyond derailing the English ambassador John Hutton's schemes. In June Pole expected a successful rising in Ireland, apparently because the refugee earl of Kildare, son of the executed tenth earl, had sought him out. The pope entrusted him to Pole, and ordered Pole to arrange for him to come to Rome.[54] By the end of the month even Pole had given up hope, and he was preparing to return.[55] By coincidence, the pope officially recalled him at exactly the same time.[56] The ground was shifting under Pole's feet, both in his entourage and in Rome. Giberti wrote Cardinal Farnese, the cardinal nephew, that he wished to return to his diocese, and Farnese ordered Pole to cut back to spending 300 *scudi* per month.[57] Three weeks later, Pole had the news and said he would leave immediately upon receipt of the safe-conducts; he was understandably loath to trust imperial agents without them.[58] Now in place of either diet or surgery, he could recommend only prayers.

The company returned to Italy in the autumn and reached Verona by the end of September, where Flaminio joined the greeters. Giberti had recommended that he show Pole his paraphrases of thirty-two Psalms, the sort of work with which both (and certainly Pole) were familiar from van Kampen's efforts in the same form.[59] Pole and his party wandered thence to Rome where Pole was solemnly received in consistory on 18 October.[60] The unofficial end of the legation had already come at Ferrara, where Giberti left Pole to return to Verona.[61] His loss was partially compensated by a visit to Vittoria Colonna, then at the

---

[53] Henry de Vocht, *Monumenta humanistica lovaniensia. Texts and studies about Louvain humanists in the first half of the XVIth century* (Louvain: Librairie Universitaire, 1934), pp. 575–8.

[54] *CRP*, no. 191.

[55] *CRP*, nos. 186 and 189.

[56] *CRP*, no. 193.

[57] ASP, Carteggio Farnesiano estero, Paesi Bassi, b. 106, Giberti-Alessandro Farnese, Liège, 29 June.

[58] Cf. *ibid.*, Giberti-Ricalcato, Liège, 21 July.

[59] *ERP*, 2, pp. cix–cxvi. *Paraphrasis in duo et triginta psalmos* was published in Venice in

1538. Alessandro Pastore, *Marcantonio Flaminio. Fortune e sfortune di un chierico nell'Italia del Cinquecento* (Milan: Franco Angeli, 1981), p. 69, who does not mention this visit. For Kampen, see Henry de Vocht, *History of the foundation and rise of the Collegium trilingue lovaniense* (Louvain: Bibliothèque de l'Université, 1951–5; 3 vols.), 3, pp. 191 and 193. An English translation of his work appeared in 1535.

[60] BAV, Vat. lat. 12419, fos. 201v–3r.

[61] *CRP*, no. 206 and cf. MS Federici 59, fo. 163r–v and BAV, Vat. lat. 12419, fo. 201v.

centre of one of the hot spots in the history of the Italian reformation, but perhaps not yet religiously close to Pole.[62]

Pole suffered another loss in September with the death of Bishop Gheri at the age of twenty-four. The cause of his death has been hotly disputed, but it seems likely that it was at least hastened by his rape by Pierluigi Farnese, Paul III's son and captain-general of the church. There are two narratives of the event, the most famous by Benedetto Varchi, writing fifteen years after the fact, the other by Richard Morison.[63] Morison and perhaps Varchi had known Gheri in Padua, so both had reason to be upset by the manner of his demise. Varchi, as a practising homosexual several times accused of and once punished for rape (of a girl), would not have bandied such an allegation. Nevertheless, Farnese has been defended, mainly by the claims that the story is found only in anti-Farnese sources and is not recorded in Beccadelli's brief epistolary life of Gheri written soon after the event.[64] This last is an especially weak argument, since a careerist clergyman like Beccadelli would scarcely risk offending the most powerful patron of his own patron Contarini by accusing the pope's son of such a heinous offence, nor would he have wished to besmirch the angelic reputation he created for Gheri. Beccadelli also stood to gain from his silence, since the pope, at Contarini's behest and with Pole's and Priuli's backing, tried to appoint him as Gheri's successor, as Gheri himself may have hoped.[65] The strongest contemporary

---

[62] Francesco della Torre to Galasso Ariosto in *Delle lettere volgari di diversi huomini, et eccellentissimi ingegni* (Venice: Aldine Press, 1545), cited in Gigliola Fragnito, 'Intorno alla "religione" dell'Ariosto: i dubbi del Bembo e le credenze ereticali del fratello Galasso', *Lettere italiane*, 44 (1992), pp. 208–39, p. 223n. Firpo, 'Colonna', p. 119; but cf. Gigliola Fragnito, 'Vittoria Colonna e l'inquisizione', *Benedictina*, 37 (1990), pp. 157–72 for a counter-view.

[63] Benedetto Varchi, *Storia fiorentina*, ed. G. Milanesi (Florence: Le Monnier, 1857–1858; 3 vols.), 3, pp. 268–73. Richard Morison, *An exhortation to styrre all Englyshe men to the defence of theyr countreye* (London: Berthelet, 1539; STC 18110), sigs. Cvir–CviiiV.

[64] The most sustained criticism of the story is in Raffaello Massignan, *Pier Luigi Farnese e*

il vescovo di Fano (Ascoli Piceno: Cesari, 1905; off-print from *Atti e memorie della R. deputazione di storia patria per le provincie delle Marche*), pp. 249–304. Parks offers similar criticism of Morison's account in 'The Pier Luigi Farnese scandal: an English report' in *Renaissance news*, 15 (1962), pp. 193–200. Beccadelli's letter, written at Donato Rullo's and Priuli's request, is printed in *MMB*, 1:1, pp. 175–82. For the life, see Gigliola Fragnito, *In museo e in villa: Saggi sul Rinascimento perduto* (Venice: Arsenale, 1988), pp. 40–1.

[65] Walter Friedensburg, 'Der Briefwechsel Gasparo Contarini's mit Ercole Gonzaga nebst einem Briefe Giovanni Pietro Carafa's', *Quellen und Forschungen aus italienischen Archiven und Bibliotheken*, 2 (1899), pp. 161–222, pp. 179–80.

confirmation of the truth of the alleged attack is Bembo's refusal to speak of the circumstances surrounding Gheri's end.[66] Contarini, who was then with the pope, did no more than note the event and plunge immediately into negotiations with Cardinal Gonzaga over Gheri's successor, negotiations in which Pole and Priuli, as well as Giberti, participated.[67] Gonzaga knew of the event, at least through a report (in cipher) of printed books about it for sale in Rome.[68] Gualteruzzi noted pasquinades in 1539 which may have referred to it by accusing Farnese of being crueller with his 'member' than Cesare Borgia was with the sword.[69] The significance of Pole's connection to Gheri is manifested in a dream Gheri had shortly before his death in which he saw himself reaching heaven with Contarini, Pole, and Bembo after a difficult mountain climb.[70] In another version of the same dream, now called a 'vision', Beccadelli spelled out the point: human effort was of no use to salvation, as Gheri implicitly learned from his three patrons.[71] And yet Pole never seems to have reacted to Gheri's death. His silence is strange, but perhaps motivated by concerns like Bembo's.

When Pole returned to Rome he apparently brought the Flemish painter Lambert Lombard with him, thereby aiding in the reversal of cultural inspiration from south to north. The thirty-year-old Lombard had been in de la Marck's service for several years, and doubtless met Pole through his patron.[72] According to the first life of Lombard by his student and later Pole's secretary Dominic Lampson, Lombard's work at first sight favourably impressed Pole's major domo Bartolomeo Stella and Priuli. Lampson further claimed that Lombard executed a lost grisaille work, 'The Dialogue of Cebes', for Pole in Rome.[73] Lombard's

---

[66] Gigliola Fragnito, 'Gli "spirituali" e la fuga di Bernardino Ochino', *Rivista storica italiana*, 84 (1972), pp. 777–811, p. 788 n39.

[67] Friedensburg, pp. 173–81.

[68] Edmondo Solmi, 'La fuga di Bernardino Ochino secondo i documenti dell'Archivio Gonzaga di Mantova', *Bollettino senese di storia patria*, 15 (1908), pp. 23–98, p. 33.

[69] BMIC24, fo. 40v.

[70] *MMB*, 1:1, pp. 178–9.

[71] The text is printed in Gigliola Fragnito, 'Aspetti della censura ecclesiastica nell'Europa della controriforma: l'edizione parigina delle opere di Gasparo Contarini', *RSLR*, 21 (1985), pp. 3–48, pp. 47–8 and discussed there pp. 21–3 and in *Museo*, pp. 41–2.

[72] Max J. Friedländer in *Early Netherlandish painting*, 14, *Antonis Mor and his contemporaries*, with comments and notes by H. Pauwels and G. Lemmens (Leyden and Brussels: A. W. Sijthoff and La Conaissance, 1975), pp. 28–33, p. 29.

[73] Dominic Lampson, 'Lamberti Lombardi ... vita', in Alessandro de Vita, ed., *Lo zibaldone di Giorgio Vasari* (Rome: R. Istituto d'Archeologia e Storia dell'Arte, 1938), pp. 209–24, 211–12. For the work see Jöchen Becker, 'Zur niederländischen Kunstliteratur des 16. Jahrhunderts: Domenicus Lampsonius', *Nederlands Kunsthistorisch Jaarboek*, 24 (1973), pp. 45–61, p. 54.

most recent biographer makes much of Pole's patronage. There is room for doubt about how much Pole did for Lombard, especially because he seems to have worked most closely with Baccio Bandinelli, whom he may have met through the painter Francesco Salviati. Bandinelli conducted a famous rivalry with Pole's friend Michelangelo, and was thus perhaps the wrong person to meet through Pole. Nevertheless, Lombard enjoyed success in Rome, and he returned to the Netherlands in 1539 to found the first Italian-style *bottega* which trained most prominent Flemish artists of the second half of the sixteenth century.[74]

Along with Lombard, Pole acquired another Flemish client, the controversialist Albert Pighe. He must have spent much of the summer of 1538 reading Pighe's enormous *Hierarchiae ecclesiasticae assertio*, published in March. Although earlier Pighe had to prod Pole to take action, this time he did not, even though Pole found the reading a 'great burden'.[75] Pole's lack of reaction may provide further evidence that he was not a high papalist. Both Sadoleto and Johannes Cochlaeus criticized Pighe for removing the power of the general council.[76] Pole did not, however, ignore Pighe. When he returned to Rome on 25 October, he found that Pighe had sent a copy of his *Assertio* for presentation to the pope. Pole immediately wrote Pighe and excused himself for not having got the book bound in time and having merely told the pope about it, and also avoided giving his opinion. Pole nevertheless continued to interest himself in Pighe's affairs and his writings.[77]

In addition to his appointment on 7 January 1538 to the commission of cardinals for the council, one of the most telling signs of Pole's standing in general and

---

[74] Godelieve Denhaene, *Lambert Lombard. Renaissance et humanisme à Liège* (Antwerp: Fonds Mercator, 1990), pp. 15–17 for Pole's return trip, and 65–75 for Lombard's time in Rome. Denhaene also claims (pp. 103–4) that Pole's religious ideas influenced Lombard. His *Christ on the cross* (Denhaene, plate 121) does somewhat resemble one of Michelangelo's drawings for Vittoria Colonna which might stand as an icon of their (and Pole's) religious views. For Lombard see also Jules Helbig, *La peinture au pays de Liège et sur les bords de la Meuse* (Liège: Henri Poncelet, 1903), ch. 8 (Pole on p. 152); Jean Yernaux, 'Lambert Lombard', *Bulletin de l'institute archéologique Liègois*, 72 (1957–8), pp.

267–372, p. 290; and the classic summary of Friedländer (see note 72). It is worth noting that Lampson ('Lombardi . . . vita', p. 66) listed both Michelangelo and Bandinelli among Lombard's masters.

[75] *CRP*, no. 226. In one final bit of *doppelgängung*, Starkey spent his summer also reading Pighe's work and preparing notes for a refutation of it. Thomas F. Mayer, *Thomas Starkey and the commonweal: humanist politics and religion in the reign of Henry VIII* (Cambridge: Cambridge University Press, 1989), pp. 265–71.

[76] Hubert Jedin, *Studien über die Schriftstellerartigkeit Albert Pigges* (Münster: Aschendorff, 1931), p. 79.

[77] *CRP*, no. 228.

with the reformers in particular is his co-operation with Carafa and Contarini as intermediaries to the pope from Camillo Orsini.[78] Orsini had sent a long letter of advice, and the three cardinals decided to split it into sections so that they could remember it all. In addition to military recommendations, Orsini had also endorsed the plan to hold a council as a means of curing the church's internal problems. Once the official business was out of the way, Pole kept Orsini's letter for himself and added a passage to his reply which was much longer than his discussion of public matters. Pole's language is about as heated as it got. Calling himself 'a boy in the house of God', he praised Orsini's divine fruits, which gave consolation and salvation to all who read them. Perhaps noting this borderline blasphemy, Pole retracted it a little by assuring Orsini of his salvation. Pole went on about the consolation he derived from Orsini's letters, and called his having missed Orsini at Verona the previous summer one of his greatest troubles. At least he had received 'spiritual food'. This had been crucial in the depths of his legation when he had thought himself completely surrounded by enemies. Orsini's consolation had made Pole feel as if he were walking with the prophets where no one could harm him. Likening himself to Daniel in the lion's den, he cast Orsini as the prophet predicting Pole's rescue. Passing through olfactory and medical metaphors (Pole said he had smelled a soul-restoring odour as soon as he received Orsini's letter), and pointing out Orsini's 'prudence of spirit', he went on to compare Orsini to Abraham bringing strength to Lazarus. Orsini set Pole 'the clearest example of charity and faith', and Pole told him that 'now I experience how your breasts give consolations', such that people far from him can be consoled by words alone. Pole concluded by endorsing the pope's opinion that nothing like Orsini had been seen for centuries.

Two months later Pole wrote Orsini another letter, apparently after they had finally met again.[79] This time the metaphors came even thicker and faster, especially like the one which had implicitly made Pole Orsini's nursling.[80]

---

[78] *CT*, 4, p. 142 and *CRP*, no. 215.

[79] *CRP*, no. 222.

[80] Pole liked the imagery of nursing, even if he sometimes cast himself as a lamb rather than a human baby. Cf. *CRP*, no. 223, telling Contarini that he was taking advantage of 'this good father' (perhaps Marco?) like a 'lamb sucking milk from its mother's breast'. This may be another legacy from Bernard. Such imagery functioned in twelfth-century Cistercian writing as a means of exploring the nature of dependency and allowing men to speak of themselves as nurturing. See Caroline Walker Bynum, 'Jesus as mother and abbot as mother: some themes in twelfth-century Cistercian writing', in *Jesus as mother: studies in the spirituality of the high middle ages* (Berkeley: University of California Press, 1982), pp. 110–69, esp. pp. 121, 147, 154, 163 and 168.

Almost immediately, after calling Orsini a sun among stars, Pole went on to say that having heard Orsini's voice 'the child in the womb of my soul immediately exulted for joy' and he felt 'the fruit of your soul acting on the fruit of the womb of my soul' and Pole wondered why the mother of God should come to him, 'unless you were to gestate the God of consolation in the womb'. Orsini was not only a greater prophet than Isaiah, he was Paul writing the Corinthians on the spiritual and the carnal (a point Pole had made in the first letter when speaking of Orsini's spiritual prudence), man and child. Pole offered another metaphor about Orsini's nurturing powers – he tried to give milk before solid food, apparently like a good mother – and closed by stressing the sun, stars, and light of Orsini's letters. Orsini had a similar effect on others, but on no one more than Pole. Pietro Carnesecchi recalled a conversation in Pole's presence about temptation, during which Orsini talked more than anyone else 'confessing so openly and ingenuously the weakness and fragility which he felt in himself' that Carnesecchi thought he might have scandalized weaker hearers.[81] This story and these two letters testify to a special relationship between Orsini and Pole. Its intensity is highlighted by Pole's contemporary letter to his old mentor Marco the monk that is written in much cooler language.[82]

Pole and Contarini remained in close touch, forming a united front on the score of reform, especially in the wake of the 'exposure' of the *Consilium*, which appeared in a pirated edition in Rome in late 1538. When Colonna asked the two why nothing had been done, they could only shrug their shoulders.[83] Despite this rather cavalier response, Contarini wrote Pole about the same time that a private conversation with Paul III had given him hope of real changes in compositions, although Contarini also advised Pole to keep his opinion close, with only Tommaso Badia and Carafa knowing it.[84] Contarini and Pole constantly discussed their theological beliefs and how to propagate them. One of the most urgent was predestination, especially because of the way it was being preached in Siena by an Augustinian friar whom Contarini attacked

---

[81] *PC*, p. 351. Carnesecchi also recalled another conversation between Pole and Orsini in which Pole, not Orsini, expatiated on temptation. Massimo Firpo and Dario Marcatto, eds., *I processi inquisitoriali di Pietro Carnesecchi (1557–1567)*, 1, *I processi sotto Paolo IV e Pio IV (1557–1561)* (Vatican City: Archivio Segreto Vaticano, 1998), p. 70.

[82] *CRP*, no. 219.

[83] Elisabeth G. Gleason, *Gasparo Contarini: Venice, Rome and reform* (Berkeley and Los Angeles: University of California Press, 1993), pp. 168–9, dating the conversation to November 1538, but that is simply the date of the letter reporting the talk. It could have taken place any time between then and May, when the *Consilium* was printed in Rome. Solmi, p. 32.

[84] *CRP*, no. 230.

anonymously throughout his second letter. Contarini considered the matter at least twice, probably in 1537, and Pole was probably involved both times. The first instance involved an epistolary discussion with Timoteo de' Giusti and Tullio Crispoldi, both Lateran canons and Pole's friends.[85] Contarini concluded that no 'invincible defect' condemned the damned, and this had to be preached. Badia and Pole certainly read Contarini's second set of thoughts on the matter in the form of a letter to Lattanzio Tolomei, friend of Colonna, Michelangelo and Ambrogio Catarino.[86] This much longer and 'theologically unsystematic letter' also combined predestination with the proper mode of preaching.[87] There were presently two groups in the church, wrote Contarini, opponents of the Lutherans who were really Pelagians, and others poorly read in Augustine who incautiously preached his most difficult doctrines (p. 422). Contarini based his discussion on a philosophical disquisition on first causes and God's power and nature, from which he passed to a consideration of 'grace, predestination, and free will' (p. 425). Because of the fall, humans no longer possessed free will capable of willing their proper end. Therefore God gave them written law to make them aware of their failing and grace through which they could daily become sounder and more capable of pursuing their proper end. Thus much for reply to the Pelagians and Lutherans. Next, Contarini turned to the Augustinians who preached 'madness' to the people (p. 428). Contarini took as his text Paul's epistle to the Romans. Its point was to humble the proud and make them aware of the power of grace. Salvation came not through merits but solely through grace 'from Christ through faith' (p. 429). After another complicated consideration of divine causality, Contarini insisted that God chose his elect solely out of His goodness. Christians had no choice but to put their faith in God's promises that they could not hope to understand (p. 431). After an explication of Augustine's criticism of Pelagius, Contarini came to predestination (p. 433). He rejected Augustine's uncompromising view, preferring Aquinas's argument in *Summa*

[85] Hubert Jedin, 'Ein Streit um den Augustinismus vor dem Tridentinum (1537–1543)', *Römische Quartalschrift*, 35 (1927), pp. 351–68, pp. 366–8. Cf. Gleason, pp. 269–70.

[86] Aldo Stella, 'La lettera del cardinale Contarini sulla predestinazione', *Rivista di storia della chiesa in Italia*, 15 (1961), pp. 411–41; p. 421 for Pole's involvement. For Tolomei, see B. Fontana, 'Sommario del processo di Aonio Paleario', *Archivio della R. Società romana di storia patria*, 19 (1896), pp. 151–75, p. 166; and Antonietta Maria Bessone Aurelj, ed. and trans., *I dialoghi michelangioleschi di Francisco d'Olanda* (Rome: Fratelli Palombi, 1953). Priuli called him 'il nostro' when reporting his death in 1543. BMIC25, fos. 268r–9v.

[87] Gleason, pp. 262–3, including parallels to Aquinas, Contarini's favourite schoolman.

contra gentiles that God gave humans a chance to respond to his grace; some took it, some did not. Predestination to evil was thus not ineluctable. Contarini offered several examples to make his point, although he had to admit that he had still not succeeded in explaining divine justice. This was unsurprising, since he continued to maintain that divine causality was beyond human comprehension (p. 436). Only then did Contarini come to the point: were human actions in any sense meritorious (p. 437), or, as the Sienese preachers taught, were they useless in the face of immutable divine degree? Contarini distinguished between necessary and contingent things, especially between God's foreknowledge and predestination, a view like Aquinas's. He concluded that the divine 'is' surpasses any human sense of time, and made it impossible to give a meaningful answer to the question whether so-and-so was reprobate for all eternity. Contarini blithely assured Tolomei that he could give him lots of scriptural passages in support of his view, but forbore for reasons of space. His argument is more complex and philosophical than Pole's usual approach, and the relative de-emphasis of scripture might not have won his approval, yet Contarini told Gonzaga that Pole had 'exhorted' him to send the letter.[88] It is also impossible to say what Pole then thought of Contarini's cautious approach to preaching.[89]

England and his failed legation remained much on Pole's mind. Within two months of the Truce of Nice, Pole wrote the pope a not very subtle request for another mission against Henry.[90] Before the end of the year, it would be granted, but Henry struck faster. Beginning at the end of October 1538, the government furiously investigated the so-called Exeter conspiracy.[91] The inquiry began with Pole's brother Sir Geoffrey, and it quickly caught up both his older brother Lord Montagu and his mother. Sir Geoffrey would be pardoned, but Montagu was executed along with the marquess of Exeter, both in large part for approving of Pole's proceedings. The evidence is too exiguous for much of the plot to be reconstructed, but there was more than enough smoke for Cromwell and his agents to have justly suspected at least a little fire. Pole does not seem to have been too deeply disturbed. He laconically reported to Contarini the news

---

[88] Stella, p. 421.
[89] There is no indication that he shared the 'radical' critique of Contarini's views developed in Verona by Flaminio and Crispoldi, against *Evan. ital.*, pp. 75–84.
[90] *CRP*, no. 225.
[91] The only large-scale study is Madeleine H. and Ruth Dodds, *The pilgrimage of grace*,

1536–1537, and the Exeter conspiracy, 1538 (Cambridge: Cambridge University Press, 1915). According to them, in the case of Pole and his family, the only even vaguely treasonable action was Sir Geoffrey's warning to Pole via Hugh Holland, and only one of his letters could possibly be construed as treasonous (pp. 294 and 305).

of Montagu's condemnation, called his brother's death a message from God to defend His cause more eagerly, and replaced him with Beccadelli and Priuli.[92] Perhaps, like Priuli, Pole was becoming *tutto spirituale*, or perhaps his 'indifference' indicated the depth of the monastic discipline which had begun to make him so.[93]

Other tensions around him may have distracted him, especially with his 'father' Marco the monk.[94] Pole, who earlier in the year had been accused of neglecting Marco, this time had to defend himself for having grieved Marco by his departure. In a letter almost as gnomic as some of Colonna's, Pole confessed that he could not get enough from Marco's letters to heal himself.[95] Nevertheless, Pole advised Marco to continue to convert his tears for Pole into internal ones, God's grace, which would give him 'health of soul'. The tears had sprung from Marco's love for Pole, which could not now be requited. Instead, Marco was to continue to pass on the grace he had received, especially to Pole who needed it 'in the garden of my soul'. But this was not the job, Pole hastened to add, that grace would cause him to discharge. This important statement of the relation between grace and works appears to refer to Marco's role in his monastery, as Pole's closing assured him that Bernardino the priest (Scotti?) and Benedetto da Ferrara would serve as Aaron and Hur to Marco's Moses.

Prudent prophets: Pole and Machiavelli

Phase two of Pole's attack on Henry opened in late 1538. It brought him a second meeting with the emperor, but few other tangible results, at least not immediately. It takes on significance in the slightly longer term because during it Pole began his even higher-stakes' battle with Machiavelli over the nature of prudence and the morality of politics. The occasion of his second failed legation led directly to his 'Apology to Charles V' which in turn launched one of the two

---

[92] *CRP*, nos. 237, 258 and 298.

[93] MS Federici 59, fo. 177v. Cf. fo. 180r, noting that Priuli and Pole had 'the spirit and grace of God' and were much less disturbed than the writer was, apparently by the news from England.

[94] For Marco and Pole, see also Fenlon, pp. 31–5.

[95] *CRP*, no. 229. For Benedetto of Ferrara see the notice in Salvatore Caponetto, ed., *Il 'beneficio di Cristo' con le versione del secolo XVI, documenti e testimonianze* (Florence, DeKalb, IL and Chicago: Sansoni, Northern Illinois University Press and The Newberry Library, 1972), p. 488n.

major traditions of interpreting Machiavelli. It is not impossible that he orchestrated its creation.[96]

The first half of the sixteenth century might be called the great age of prudence. As more and more established pieties, political systems, and cultural icons came under fire, an increasing number of people concerned themselves with how to react to rapidly changing circumstances. They did so across a wide front of possible positions. It has traditionally been said that attitudes to prudence divided in two between those who enthusiastically embraced – even invented – what might be called a 'human-scale' version of this most flexible of virtues and those who decried its prominence as the sign of the disintegration of order. In fact, thinking about prudence was much more variegated. Given that prudence meant successfully reading circumstances, this should hardly surprise. Nevertheless, an essentially dichotomous reading of theorists of prudence continues to dominate scholarship. This was Pole's legacy.

On one side, Machiavelli's advice to princes to imitate both the fox and the lion encapsulates much of his view that the prince should tailor his actions to the needs of the moment and dissimulate as necessary. Religion offered an especially good screen for the exercise of power (*Prince*, ch. 18). On the other side, Pole, focusing almost exclusively on this chapter, replied in horror that treating religion instrumentally heralded the Antichrist. This makes a remarkably tidy picture. It is also seriously misleading, and depends to an even greater degree than many of the other elements of the hagiographic view of Pole on assuming that his stance was the only morally defensible one. Taking this line undermines the saintly Pole, if for no other reason than that it introduces a large degree of variation between his theory and his practice. Where lies the morality in proposing to cut off commerce to England, thereby likely inducing much more suffering among the innocent lower orders than among Henry's courtiers? This tactic, regarded as part of the same processes of history which encompassed

---

[96] Peter S. Donaldson, *Machiavelli and mystery of state* (Cambridge: Cambridge University Press, 1988), pp. 7 and 88 suggests this, and sketches the shape of the tradition. Robert Bireley, *The counter-reformation prince: anti-Machiavellianism or catholic statecraft in early modern Europe* (Chapel Hill and London: University of North Carolina Press, 1990), pp. 14–16 for Pole, Girolamo Osório and Ambrogio Catarino and Machiavelli's anti-Christianity. Both Osório and Catarino knew *The prince* and *Discourses*. Osório's *De nobilitate christiana libri III* (Florence, 1552) made Pole's arguments plus new ones. Catarino's *De libris a Christiano detestandis et a Christianismo penitus eliminandis* (Rome, 1552) attacked Machiavelli's destruction of providence, notion of religion as a means of secular control, and of the ruler as both lion and fox. Bireley does not note Osório's (*CRP*, no. 2052) and Catarino's ties to Pole (see the next chapter).

Machiavelli instead of a superhistorical accomplishment, becomes as instrumental as anything Machiavelli recommended. The only difference is that the transcendent justification on which Pole depended Machiavelli saw as the primary obstacle.

As a few critics have pointed out recently, Pole understood nearly all Machiavelli's threat. More, it was fresh in his mind in 1539, and drawn from more than *The prince*, which he had certainly read. His citation of a 'book *de principe*' and his summary of the content leave no doubt. The work had been in print since 1532, and as Pole revealed in the 'Apology', he had plenty of contacts in Florence who could have loaned him either a copy of one of the first five editions or a manuscript.[97] Or perhaps Pole read Agostino Nifo's Latin plagiarism, *De regnandi peritia* in Padua.[98] But was *The prince* all Pole meant? What about the 'Apology's' reference to 'some things, among others' which Machiavelli had written? Had Pole read other works? The likelihood that he did is closely bound up with the time at which he did, according to the evidence of John Legh. Legh, who implied that Pole had made him a brother of the English hospice in Rome, returned to England very shortly after Pole wrote the 'Apology', only to be imprisoned on suspicion of contacts with him. From the Tower Legh recalled a lengthy conversation with Pole about the matters at the heart of the 'Apology': the desecration of Becket's shrine, the martyrdom of More and Fisher, and the danger of Machiavelli's 'poison'. References to reorganization of the Hospice date the conversation to March 1538, when Becket's shrine was still intact. Other errors reduce the reliability of Legh's testimony.[99] Pole led into the third point by asking Legh what 'stories' he had read in Italian. Legh expressed ignorance, and Pole hurried on to warn him against 'reading of the story of' Machiavelli.[100]

---

[97] Adolph Gerber, *Nicolò Machiavelli: Die Handschriften, Ausgaben und Übersetzungen seiner Werke im 16. und 17. Jahrhundert* (Torino: Bottega d'Erasmo, 1962; reprint of edition of Gotha: Perthes, 1912–13), pp. 23–33 for the editions and 82–3 for the manuscripts. For Pole's circle of Florentine friends, see beow. p. 97. Giberti had seen many important people on their trip through Florence in 1537. ASV, Lettere di principi, 12, fos. 178r–80r mentioned Francesco Guicciardini, Jacopo Salviati, Nicolò Gaddi, and Nicolò Ridolfi, whose principal adviser then was Machiavelli's friend and fellow political thinker, Donato

Giannotti. Randolph Starn, *Donato Giannotti and his Epistolae* (Geneva: Droz, 1968), p. 54 and Mayer, *Starkey*, p. 56.

[98] Gerber, pp. 7–12.

[99] Legh set the discussion at a dinner given by John Borobrig, former master, shortly after Pole had removed him on 8 March. Cf. *CRP*, no. 221, for discussion of the reliability of Legh's recollection.

[100] BL, Cleop. E VI, fos. 394v–5r (*L&P*, 15, no. 721). This confession is undated, but must be soon before or after a report dated 21 May of Legh's imprisonment fifteen days earlier (*L&P*, 15, no. 697).

Unfortunately, Pole gave no further hints about what this 'story' was. Whatever work Pole meant, Legh concluded that Pole intended to obliterate its memory.

Even if we must speculate, 'story' has to mean that Pole had read other works by Machiavelli. It seems unlikely that Pole meant by 'story' Machiavelli's life. Did he refer, taking him literally, to the *Florentine histories*, presented to Clement VII in 1525 and published in 1532?[101] He could have, especially because Machiavelli's new kind of example – to which Pole strenuously objected – appeared in book V: 34. Did Pole also object to Machiavelli's subversion of the classical/humanist canons for good history writing? Perhaps he again thought Machiavelli amoral for revealing the nasty things done by governments, including the papacy (e.g., V: 27, recording the imprisonment of cardinal Vitelleschi by subterfuge), which elsewhere appeared in a bad light (e.g., V: 10, 18) or for revealing the secrets of statecraft. Pole might have attacked these dimensions of the *Histories*, but he would also have overlooked the ironies arising from the work's moral slant, which closely resembled his line in the 'Apology'. Machiavelli harped on the shortcomings of princes (esp. V: 1; cf. Preface, p. 7) and the wisdom derived from experience of them; the dangers of division (Preface, pp. 6–7 and *passim*, esp. VII: 1 on factions; cf. V: 31); and generally unmasked rulers' skullduggery. Pole shared these views. Alternatively, he could have taken *The prince* for history because of its routine employment of the same kind of examples. There remains one highly interesting possibility. Did Pole's 'story' just possibly mean the *Discourses on the first ten books of Titus Livy*, by nearly any standard a work of history?[102]

In any case, Pole did not write out of ignorance of Machiavelli's ideas, no matter how partisan his reading, and he offered a reaction anything but uncomprehending and obscurantist. This was not because he had the angels on his side, but rather because he and Machiavelli inhabited the same humanist universe, and used much the same resources of language and argument, which meant that Pole could clearly see the contrast between their ends. His reaction in defence of the power of example both responded to Machiavelli's claim to be able to do better with a new kind of exemplarity at the same time as it revealed the degree to which they were still engaged in the same operation of appealing to the past to justify the present. Even this somewhat subtle formulation is too simple. Although it is now the mode to emphasize irony in the interpretation of

---

[101] Nicolò Machiavelli, *Florentine Histories*, trans. Laura F. Banfield and Harvey C. Mansfield, Jr. (Princeton: Princeton University Press, 1988), p. 3 and Gerber, pp. 36–43 for editions through 1539; cf. pp. 61–79 for the MSS.

[102] Gerber, pp. 8–17 for the editions through 1540, beginning with the Blado of 1531.

Renaissance literature, Pole's reading of and relationship to Machiavelli's ideas is full of it.[103] Perhaps the master irony, and one almost completely overlooked by historians and literary critics alike until very recently, is that the label 'new literary' now applied to Machiavelli attaches as easily to Pole, in both the sense that he was a literary construction, and that he, like Machiavelli, displayed a strong penchant for reading the world through literary categories, as Pole's labelling of Henry's proceedings as a 'tragicomedy' and then as a comedy made into tragedy through savagery indicates.[104] Pole here revealed his deep interest in the literary and how well he kept up with the latest 'literary criticism', since 'tragicomedy' was a new genre.[105] Even better, Pole's reaction to Cromwell's execution called it an example, as Cromwell ending his life like the thief on the cross begging forgiveness imitated Pole's art.[106] It is further ironic that Machiavelli began from a position on language and reality much like Pole's Platonist one, only to be talked into 'his' allegedly distinctive views by his close friend Francesco Vettori.[107]

Unsurprisingly, therefore, Machiavelli's stress on rhetoric, albeit of a new kind, matched Pole's attitude. Words were power and needed careful handling. Further, they both agreed that words became especially problematic in the hands of princes who were often, if not necessarily, tyrants. Tyrants, they adamantly insisted, were the problem. At one point, both Pole and Machiavelli offered the same solution by stressing the role of the good counsellor. On a fairly crude level, the issue between them came down to a competition over the control and dissemination of political advice. Perhaps Pole's aristocratic prejudices motivated him against the *arriviste* Machiavelli. In an irony which looks truly weird in the light of prevailing interpretations, both also at least sometimes abandoned politics and turned instead to prophecy.[108] Although I do not wish to press the point, there have always been those who argue that Machiavelli was a good Christian who had more than a few reservations about Christianity as

---

[103] Donaldson obliquely pointed to some instances, for example on p. 23n.

[104] *ERP*, 1, p. 144.

[105] Nancy Klein Maguire, ed., *Renaissance tragicomedy: explorations in genre and politics* (New York: AMS Press, 1987), introduction, esp. p. 5.

[106] *CRP*, no. 307.

[107] John M. Najemy, *Between friends: discourses of power and desire in the Machiavelli–Vettori letters of 1513–1515* (Princeton:

Princeton University Press, 1993), ch. 4.

[108] The relation between prudence and allegory absorbs Albert Ascoli in an extended meditation on the neat apparent paradox of the inseparability of pragmatism and prophecy. Albert Russell Ascoli, 'Machiavelli's gift of counsel', in Albert Russell Ascoli and Victoria Kahn, eds., *Machiavelli and the discourse of literature* (Ithaca: Cornell University Press, 1993), pp. 219–57, esp. 253ff.

currently practised. His criticisms of the institutional church, from the papacy's political blundering to the grasping Friar Timoteo of *Mandragola*, move him much closer to Pole's views than Pole admitted. As all good prophets must be, they were doomed to talk past one another.

This was unfortunate, but there is yet another irony in their relationship which had much more serious consequences. Unlike either Erasmus or Pole, both of whom were finally reduced to pious exhortations to rulers whatever the strength of their commitments to one kind of community or another, Machiavelli had a solution to the conundrum of how to protect the community from tyranny, how to resolve the dilemma of republic and prince, or, more generally, how to prevent the damage done by contingency. Machiavelli in *The discourses* and in the space between them and *The prince* invented an immanent solution in a playful dialectic of a prince both absent from and present in the community, part of his more general transformation of *virtù* into the acceptance of historical necessity.[109] Pole responded with a transcendent effort to preserve community and prince within the unchanging order of virtue. His serious reading broke Machiavelli's dialectic. This happened either through the historical accident that Pole did not know the *Discourses* or, perhaps more likely by a deliberate, and costly, choice to ignore them. Two great ironies emerge: Machiavelli could have offered Pole just what he needed at the same time as a more complete understanding of Machiavelli on Pole's part might have undercut the ideological readings of Machiavelli which produced *ragione di stato*.

To take the second point first, Pole's invention of a rhetorical humanist theology led directly to those Christian theologians like Giovanni Botero and John Milton who most deeply understood Machiavelli.[110] They then helped to clear the way through the development of constitutional democracy for the success of Machiavelli's proposed means to defend the community. That Pole had the tools and chose not to use them to forward Machiavelli's solution accentuates the further irony that it and they could have saved Pole in his struggle with Paul IV's tyranny. Instead of a new-style political/rhetorical solution, Pole was reduced to trotting out more biblical *exempla*. Yet there is really no reason why he should have endorsed Machiavelli's views, given that they had not worked for Machiavelli. Both got exile as reward for their pains. Neither of their allegedly dichotomous approaches to politics worked alone, but some combination of the

---

109 Nancy S. Struever, 'Purity as danger: Gramsci's Machiavelli, Croce's Vico', in Ascoli and Kahn, pp. 275–90.

110 Victoria Kahn, *Machiavellian rhetoric from the counter-reformation to Milton* (Princeton: Princeton University Press, 1994), pp. 60–84 and part III.

two very well could have. Thus the final irony: Pole missed the single most important point that Machiavelli never said 'consider the end' prescriptively, as John Najemy has brilliantly demonstrated, never fostered immoral politics. This oversight had nearly fatal consequences both for Pole and for Machiavelli's legacy.[111]

The interpretation sketched above rests on work of the past decade on both Pole and Machiavelli. Peter Donaldson and Victoria Kahn have done the most to revise the interpretation of Pole's anti-Machiavellism. Donaldson argues that Machiavelli's ideas amounted to 'sovereignty'. Thus arose a tradition of political discourse which evaluated his notions in positive terms as a matter requiring careful handling by experts (*periti*), and in negative fashion as dangerous secret knowledge to be brought into the open and destroyed.[112] Although still typological like their medieval predecessors, Pole's interpretations were 'progressive or historicist' and cast in terms of process rather than unchanging repetition, and thus came close to Protestant apocalyptic (p. 14). Pole thought Henry was so nearly the Antichrist that there could be no future (p. 15). This is a major reinterpretation, especially the last point, which moves Pole much closer to Machiavelli and both of them back toward the sixteenth century. Pole's line had changed since *De unitate*, and Donaldson attempts to account for this in part by subtle alterations in Pole's view of himself as a prophet (pp. 21–3), a stimulating line of analysis that will go further. In the earlier work, Pole withheld some of what he knew about Henry in order to give himself more power over the king, and threatened him only with penance, not destruction (as we have seen, this was not the case in the unexpurgated text). In this he acted like Isaiah. By the time of the 'Apology', his model had become Moses and his call for *jihad* (p. 29). Pole had more than merely prophetic strings to his bow (to borrow a metaphor of which he was fond) and meant to do more than unmask Henry and Machiavelli with it.

Kahn offers an interpretation of Machiavelli's legacy similar to Donaldson's, and also makes Pole central to one side of it.[113] She argues that Machiavelli's rhetoric was as subversive as the ideas which have for long improperly been extracted from it, and that his method was dialectical. His emphasis on the importance of rhetoric as both a tool to build (whether in the hands of a new prince or a republic, where it was supposed to work better) and also as a tool to destabilize helped to produce the disjunction in readers' attitudes to him. In addition to the evil Machiavel, purveyor of immoral advice, there was also and more commonly the rhetorical Machiavelli, purveyor of amoral advice. Kahn

---

[111] Najemy, p. 188.

[112] Donaldson, pp. 2, 11–12.

[113] Kahn, *Machiavellian rhetoric.*

argues that Machiavelli the republican was only rarely read apart from Machiavelli the rhetorician, and almost never as Machiavelli, proponent of secular politics. Kahn treats Machiavellism as a phenomenon crystallizing anxieties about representation and the possibility of finding (or making) truth in a deceptive world. Most important, Kahn derives Machiavelli and Machiavellism from humanism, especially its fundamentally rhetorical technique of arguing on both sides of a case (*in utramque partem*), which Machiavelli, in distinction to the humanists themselves, made part of dialectical method. Again like the humanists, Machiavelli insisted on the importance of exemplarity, and offered his work as both a more effective way of reading examples, and as a more carefully assembled collection of them, both of which readings became elements in his reception, including by Pole (cf. esp. *Discourses* I. pref.).[114]

In another essay, Kahn demonstrates how Machiavelli substituted for earlier humanist notions of a pragmatic truth a new idea of truth as power.[115] Developing some of her earlier arguments about humanist ideas of exemplarity, she maintains that Machiavelli, like the humanists, found himself in much difficulty over how to handle examples, a problem he temporarily solved with a nifty twist or two of allegoresis, before he came to use examples as merely one possible rhetorical or 'theatrical' tool in the acquisition of power. Thus again like the humanists, Machiavelli centrally concerned himself with prudence, for which he finally substituted a near equivalence of *virtù* and success. This resolution in turn produced a still essentially unreadable world that left the impassioned prophecy of *The prince*, chapter 26 as the only way out.

Pole provides one of Kahn's chief stalking horses. On her rapid reading, Pole attacked Machiavelli as 'a Machiavel', guilty of emptying politics of virtue and fostering a 'rhetorical politics' founded on dissimulation.[116] Pole made 'simple equivalences between politics, religion, and literary modes of representation: the

---

[114] This heavily rhetorical selling point appears in just about any other historian or political theorist contemporary with Machiavelli whom one would care to mention, as demonstrated by Thomas Maissen's *Von der Legende zum Modell: Das Interesse an Frankreichs Vergangenheit während der italienischen Renaissance* (Basel: Helbing & Lichtenhahn, 1994).

[115] Victoria Kahn, '*Virtù* and the example of Agathocles in Machiavelli's *Prince*, in Ascoli and Kahn, pp. 195–218.

[116] Kahn, *Machiavellian rhetoric*, p. 87. According to Kahn, Pole's criticisms were written in 1539 or maybe in the 1540s (p. 137). She also maintains (p. 271 n1) that the 'Apology' was 'summarized in detail in contemporary diplomatic correspondence' but the only evidence she cites is a resumé of the work in *L&P*, 14:1, no. 200. For the only two manuscripts known, see *CPM*, catalogue no. 4. To be fair, Pole let out most of its central arguments in other diplomatic correspondence, e.g., *CRP*, no. 246.

Machiavel's tyranny, idolatry, and atheism are seen as inseparable from his rhetorical force, fraud, and manipulation of his audience'. Kahn contrasts Pole's interpretation to an alternative which saw Machiavelli's rhetoric as pure technique, lacking any moral or political valence. She nevertheless quite rightly suggests that Pole understood Machiavelli perfectly, but that the choice to reply on Machiavelli's rhetorical terms was dangerous because of rhetoric's inherent critical edge.[117] Questioning means could easily spill over into raising difficulties about ends, those of the attacker as well as the attacked.

Kahn is correct in broad outline, but she stops too soon. One implication of her provocative dialectical, rhetorical argument especially raises problems. As Machiavelli's readers revealed, it was grounding in a *common* tradition which made them receptive to him, and a common tradition which especially in the form of argument on both sides of a point was always already a critical one. Not that any individual humanist had to be a critic in more than a narrowly philological sense, but nearly any humanist could be. Furthermore, Pole sketched both sides of the interpretation of Machiavelli, although he chose to develop only one. Pole's criticism of Machiavelli grasps the nature of his rhetoric and becomes a piece of the 'immanent critique' Kahn pursues, one rhetorician criticizing another. We could hardly hope for more help in reading what Machiavelli meant in context. Kahn and other critics, however, have missed the fact that Pole came up with a new end for *his* rhetorical politics, so seriously did he take the potential in the Machiavellian variety. Although he trotted out many of the obligatory defences of virtuous politics and of religious over temporal authority, they all drew on a new form of transcendence, the blood of the martyrs, as well as the eschatology noted by Donaldson, and both had heavy political overtones.[118] So was and did Pole's rhetoric. After claiming in the 'Apology' to have divine sanction for his words, he continued that 'the voice of so many men's blood' spoke through his writing.[119] Transcendence depended on the most concrete presence Pole could imagine.

Machiavelli's politics were anything but transcendent. They were rooted in biology, especially the humors.[120] More than this, his efforts to bridle the prince

---

[117] Kahn, *Machiavellian rhetoric*, p. 137; cf. p. 84. Höllger (pp. 204–7) argues that Pole wilfully misrepresented Machiavelli by focusing only on what he had to say about religion, but this is far from the case.

[118] Josef Ratzinger, 'The papal primacy and the unity of the people of God', in J. Ratzinger, *Church, ecumenism and politics:*

new essays in ecclesiology (New York: Crossroad, 1988), pp. 36–44, noted this in the case of *De unitate*.

[119] *ERP*, 1, pp. 72–3.

[120] See esp. Antony J. Parel, *The Machiavellian cosmos* (New Haven and London: Yale University Press, 1992).

depended on making him simultaneously present and absent, stripping him just as much of any supernatural or religious aura as Machiavelli did the exercise of his power. Politics was grounded in the human community and nothing else. This sounds like a species of republicanism, and to a degree it is. Much effort has gone into trying to decide whether Machiavelli was really a republican, and if so, to account for the contrast between *The discourses* and *The prince*.[121] There is a simpler, less dichotomous solution: Machiavelli treated both community and prince as equally human, equally necessary to the survival of a biologically inevitably limited society (Discourses I. 39 and cf. Discourses I. pref.). As he explained in *The discourses*, every political order got its institutions from a founder, whether Romulus and Remus (or, better, Numa Pompilius who established Rome's religion) or Cesare Borgia (Discourses I. 1–2, 10, 11). Because of innate appetite for power and steady conflict with the rest of the community, the founder had eventually to be shoved aside and replaced with some kind of a republic (what precise kind probably mattered little more to Machiavelli than to most other early modern theorists of politics; Discourses I. 58). Well and good, but republics were subject to the same humors as individual humans, and, worse, to the cycle of growth and decay described by Aristotle and fleshed out by Polybius (Discourses I. 2 and III. 1). The only way to break this cycle was to invent a form of government which would guarantee that the republic's first principles remained in force. Since those first principles came from the founder who had then proceeded to corrupt them, threatening the very order he had invented, there had further to be found a way to separate the founder from his principles. Machiavelli discussed two possible solutions. One, probably the more dangerous, demanded the periodic intervention of refounders, new princes, who by their *virtù* could reinstate the first principles, however temporarily (Discourses I. 9, 18; III. 1; for the dangers involved Discourses I. 33). The second and more effective plan was to find a mode of government which would break the cycle of decay. This second form, closely resembling the age-old mixed government composed of all the basic Aristotelian components, monarchy, aristocracy, and democracy, tilted in Machiavelli's thinking in such a way that monarchy virtually disappeared except for the principles originally derived from it, leaving a society to work according to a creative competition between nobles and 'people', with the latter holding the upper hand (Discourses I. 2, 4–6; I. 10 stipulates that a prince must live under the laws and I. 34 discusses how a properly elected dictator could play the founder's role; cf. I. 49). The prince was thus present in the form of the principles, but absent as an actual

---

[121] Cf. esp. Mark Hulliung, *Citizen Machiavelli* (Princeton: Princeton University Press, 1983).

ruler, the safest possible remedy to the problem of tyranny. The overriding goal was defence of the community. It had no need of any other sanctions, and the only issues requiring attention were the bluntly practical ones of providing for its needs in the most practical and least threatening fashion possible.

Pole's portrait of evil Machiavel thus went a little wide of the mark. More interesting, although of a piece with his general religious evolution, it marked a departure in his attitude to Machiavelli. His first effort to engage most of the questions with which Machiavelli confronted Pole is an autograph draft that someone entitled 'De prudentia et sapientia humana et ea quam per Christum humano generi misericordia dei sit revelata' ('On human and divine prudence and that which may be revealed to humankind by God's mercy through Christ').[122] To judge from its generally moderate tone, lack of topical references, and use of Gheri as an interlocutor, it probably predates 1537 and perhaps even *De unitate*. Unfortunately fragmentary to a degree that makes it exceptionally difficult to interpret, the work is a dialogue between Gheri, Priuli, and Pole. Since the character Pole acted as moderator, it is even more difficult to tell than in most dialogues what case Pole meant to make. Many of the major points of his thinking received attention. Like the good Aristotelian he showed himself almost at his last moment, Gheri defended the value of prudence to the *respublica*, while Priuli insisted it had no use whatsoever in the economy of salvation, the only thing that mattered.

In contrast to Gheri who introduced all the standard Aristotelian-cum-Ciceronian arguments in favour of civil society, Priuli seems in character as the man remote from the business of life, who instead stressed the value of personal experience, just as he did in 1537. At one point he asks in bad temper what made them different from boys if all they knew came from books or 'an external teacher'? Only with the help of 'the internal master of wisdom' (*sapientiae internum magistrum*) could one be called learned (fo. 4v). Both he and Gheri agreed to demand of Pole 'with all effort and abundance' (*copia*) 'not only what he understood but what could be conceived through the internal senses' about their subject. Pole promised to tell them both what philosophers had learned through 'human ingenuity [*ingenio*]' and also what came from scripture and divine revelation (fo. 5r). Despite what might seem an opening for a discussion in biblical terms, Pole framed the debate as another judgment of Paris, with Gheri assigned to decide to which of three goddesses, including the third, 'human prudence', to give the golden apple.

---

[122] BAV, Vat. lat. 5966, fos. 3r–26v.

Priuli accepted this conceit, but insisted that Gheri abandon all other studies and immerse himself in scripture (fo. 6v). Priuli pursued a line not unlike Pole's own in his correspondence with Sadoleto, putting forward Socrates's circumscription of philosophy's domain to the demonstration that humans could know nothing (fo. 8v). Pole suggested that the only way to resolve the dispute was to seek the judgment of the inventor of all arts, whom they should approach through prayer, confident in His promise to hear whenever two or three assembled in his name (fo. 9r). All agreed that leaving everything to do with salvation to God was the only course (fo. 9v). If they prayed, they could hope to receive illumination and even have God appoint one of them His representative. Pole insisted on human weakness and the absolute necessity of leaving everything to God (fos. 10r–11r). Thus a discussion which began in standard academic terms moved into the mystical realm.

Either Pole or Priuli (the text is ambiguous) quickly received an illumination that Gheri should admit that 'human prudence invented with philosophy by human ingenuity and sent forth in letters should be exploded as useless and impediments rather than aids to the knowledge of felicity'.[123] Gheri recognized human prudence as the enemy, and asked Pole to tell him what else invented by 'human ingenuity' was 'not useless but damnable to that blessed discipline [established] by God through Christ', anticipating another theme of Priuli's lessons in 1537 (fo. 12r). But Gheri was not convinced and attacked Priuli for holding an idiosyncratic position. Priuli responded by invoking the prophet who condemned 'the prudence of the prudent and wisdom of the wise' (*prudentiam prudentum et sapientiam sapientum*). Gheri took offence and Pole attempted to defuse the moment by suggesting that perhaps the prophet had merely condemned the abuse of prudence (fo. 13r). Priuli refused to back down, and although agreeing on a definition of prudence as that which procured those things necessary for life, restricted contemplation only to the wise, not the prudent. This is more or less the point finally put forward. Prudence meant the application of principles determined by philosophers, and it had an exclusively social purpose (fos. 14v; 20r). It originated in the knowledge of good and evil, and, as a function of age, fathers taught it to sons (fo. 15r).

At this point Pole opened a tacit, gentlemanly argument with Machiavelli. It was not enough for a prudent man to gain his ends by whatever means, he must get them 'in a good fashion'. The prudent man had to be a good man, or as Priuli put it, adverting once more to classical history and mythology, he needed both

---

[123] *Ibid.*, fo. 12r.

Achilles's and Minerva's shields. More, a truly prudent man had to have all the virtues. If he lacked even one, he did not qualify as prudent. Not even this was enough. In addition, he had to have *disciplina* through revelation from God which would show him that even all the virtues were 'an impediment' without revelation (fo. 15v). Gheri brought the discussion back to the importance of civil society and the roots of prudence in a natural 'inclination' to preserve what was necessary to life, and to love one's self (fos. 16vff). Prudence concerned supplying the needs of the body, a point which provoked a predictable objection from Priuli that humans had both bodies and souls, and therefore not even the 'royal art' of governing met anything more than human ends (fo. 17v). The soul was all. Bishop Gheri refused to accept this, countering that all human law aimed to make prudent men responsible for cure of souls. Another sharp exchange ensued, which led Pole to endorse Gheri's contention, while saying again that only virtuous means were acceptable. Gheri then laid out at length the nature of the body politic, before likening prudent men to its physicians (fo. 22r). Both Gheri and Pole drifted in Priuli's direction, agreeing that supernature was superior to nature, especially in the argument that nurses were better than mothers (fo. 23r–v). This drift continued in a fully Petrarchan return to the setting and the allegory of the dialogue, as Pole enjoined Gheri to climb the mountain and forget human things (fo. 24r). The dialogue breaks off with another classical analogy in which Pole likened 'the work of prudence' to a Roman triumph, in which human felicity figured as a captive.[124] The emperor, making use of his subordinate officers, apparently stood for God, suppressing (or subsuming?) any human effort toward salvation. It would be safe to say that this analogy is obscure.

The general shape of the argument, its modes and literary form, however, are clear enough, a prayerful meditation on one of the central philosophical problems and all its ramifications, especially, it would appear, as recently recast by Machiavelli. If this interpretation is correct, the moderation of Pole's reply deserves emphasis. I would suggest that it arose both from the relatively placid circumstances in which the dialogue was composed, and its lack of polemical purpose. Its most obvious object is to wean Gheri away from the kind of politics and political theory which would have been second nature to the son of the Florentine politician Goro Gheri. Pole endorsed at least some elements of Gheri's civicism, and corrected Machiavelli in temperate terms as a result.

---

[124] This use of prudence and prudential discourse for educational purposes was also typical of Valdésian language, according to Firpo, as was denigration of human prudence. *Alumbrados*, pp. 28 and 44ff.

By the time of his 'Apology' Pole's attitude to Machiavelli had hardened. The work was at least drafted in the first half of 1539 as a preface to an edition of *De unitate*.[125] One appeared shortly after Pole wrote this preface, but without it. Indeed, he cited the missing preface as proof that he had not wished to have the book published.[126] The preface and the book fit closely together.[127] Pole offered Charles a similar story of his relations with Henry, a similar portrait of the good Henry, and blamed the king's demise once more on unbridled desires. Yet there are differences in Pole's treatment of Henry and especially his motives. These are partly a function of Henry's actions in the nearly three years since *De unitate*, including the dissolution of the monasteries (p. 92) but more largely of Pole's own experience and very important immediate context. As he wrote in the 'Apology', Pole was then in the midst of a legation to the emperor designed to persuade him to take military action against the schismatic Henry VIII.[128] Since 'he who speaks with the voice of the church' (the pope) had declared Henry an 'enemy of the public church', Pole had to expose his tyranny to other princes (p. 78).

The legation of 1539

It took Paul III a while to accept a new legation. The desecration of Becket's shrine at Canterbury in September 1538 decided the issue. Pole put his propaganda machine into high gear, almost single-handedly establishing the 'fact' that Henry had Becket's bones burnt. Whether this story was Pole's work originally or arose elsewhere in Rome, Pole deserves the credit for making it the accepted account.[129] That Pole's later dependant Mariano Vittori repeated the same charge in a marginal note to his edition of *Sancti Hieronymi Stridonensis Opera Omnia* at least clinches the case for Pole's consistency, as in all probability does Nicholas Harpsfield's *Life and death of Sir Thomas More*.[130] MS Bodley 493, a life of Becket by Bishop Grandison of Exeter owned by Pole, underscores

---

125 *CPM*, catalogue, no. 4.

126 *CPM*, catalogue, no. 1 for the date.

127 As Höllger, p. 194 also notes.

128 *ERP*, 1, p. 78, with reference to dissuading the emperor from fighting the Turks instead of Henry. All the verbs in this passage are present tense.

129 A recent account denies this, arguing that Pole did not have reliable news of events in England, but this is untrue. John Butler, *The quest for Becket's bones: the mystery of the relics of St Thomas Becket of Canterbury* (New Haven and London: Yale University Press, 1995), pp. 119–23. See my review in *SCJ*, 27 (1996), pp. 647–8.

130 Paris: No Publisher, 1643, book 2, p. 405, col. 1, D. Harpsfield's account is cited in Butler, pp. 122–3.

his interest.[131] Bishop Burnet could well be correct that activity in Becket's defence turned Henry against Pole.[132] Pole probably but not certainly sat on the commission appointed to find ways to punish Henry, along with Contarini and two other allies.[133] He was certainly supposed to help execute plans against Henry by shuttling between Charles and the French king. At a minimum the pope wanted the two to publish Henry's excommunication, and he assigned Pole the task of inducing them to cut off commerce with England or do whatever else seemed necessary.[134] Pole interpreted his instructions to mean the execution as well as the publication of Henry's excommunication, and this could only have meant military action.[135]

The legation did not go well. The pope, probably acting out of misplaced optimism, fatally handicapped it right at the start by letting the emperor know that Francis would do nothing without Charles.[136] Since imperial diplomats also knew from the first that Francis was contemplating the partition of England, they had two good reasons for dragging their feet.[137] But as in 1537,

---

[131] Bodleian Library, MS Bodl. 493 bears both the notation 'Reginaldi Poole Liber 1539' on fo. 1v and the probably forged signature 'R. Poole' on fo. 55v at the end. It is possible that Pole commissioned the manuscript, if it was indeed written in the first half of the sixteenth century. Then again, the scribe identified himself as Robertus Plenus Amoris and added what seems to be the date 1489. The book is described in *Summary catalogue of western manuscripts in the Bodleian Library* (Oxford: Clarendon Press, 1895; 7 vols.), 2:1, ed. F. Madan, no. 2097 and a little sloppily in Otto Pächt and J. J. G. Alexander, *Illuminated manuscripts in the Bodleian Library* (Oxford: Clarendon Press, 1966–73; 3 vols.), 3, p. 68. For Pole's ownership, see Alessandro Pastore, 'Due biblioteche umanistiche del Cinquecento (I libri del cardinal Pole e di Marcantonio Flaminio)', *Rinascimento*, ser. 2, 19 (1979), pp. 269–90, p. 273n.

[132] Nicholas Pocock, ed., *The history of the reformation of the church of England by Gilbert Burnet* (Oxford: Clarendon Press, 1865; 7 vols.), 1, p. 389.

[133] William E. Wilkie, *The cardinal protectors of England: Rome and the Tudors before the reformation* (Cambridge: Cambridge University Press, 1974), p. 235 cites evidence the balance of which supports Pole's inclusion. Wilkie did not notice Cesare Baroni, ed. Oderico Raynaldi, *Annales ecclesiastici*, 21:1 (Rome: Propaganda fide, 1676), 1538, no. 45, which omitted him.

[134] *CRP*, no. 235.

[135] *CRP*, no. 248. Burnet's conclusion again is reasonable, both that Pole was 'going over all the courts of Christendom, to persuade a league against England, as being of greater necessity and merit than a war against the Turk' and that he was 'barefaced in his treasonable designs'. 1, pp. 551 and 562.

[136] *CSPSp*, 6:1, nos. 33 and 34 and Höllger, p. 145. Cf. the summary in Bernard Barbiche and Ségolène de Dainville-Barbiche, 'Les légats *a latere* en France et leur facultés aus XVIᵉ et XVIIᵉ siècles', *Archivum historiae pontificiae*, 23 (1985), pp. 93–165, p. 154.

[137] *CSPSp*, 6:1, no. 35.

the pope and the papal diplomatic apparatus tried hard, despite the occasional blunder. And as in 1537, most of the line pursued came from Pole. Thus the constant arguments that no one had suffered a greater injury from Henry than Charles and that Henry posed a much greater threat than the Turks were Pole's and neither was new.[138] Pole's poor health and the troubles of his family further dragged on the legation. Pole learned of his elder brother's condemnation almost at the moment he set out.[139] It took him more than a month to reach the emperor's court in Toledo, and almost another two weeks before he had an audience.

If the moment is not invented, one reason for the slowness of Pole's progress was a side trip to a chapel in the Alps, where he was overcome with grief at the thought of Henry's sins and prayed that his tears could be transferred to the king.[140] He seemed to hear the prophet's voice praying for his king, and likened his situation to the *exemplum* of David and Saul. The interpretation Pole applied fifteen years after the fact should not be given undue weight, but it is consistent with the documented evolution of his religion by 1539. Pole asserted that he had learned more theology from Henry's persecution than from any university, God teaching him through the 'pedagogue' of Henry's actions. The more the king attacked him, the more Pole understood the *arcana* of scripture and experienced its meaning.[141]

Pole's first optimistic report from Toledo was far from the truth. The Venetian ambassador's recounting of how Charles rendered his interview with Pole shows the emperor in belligerent mood, taxing Pole with a papal about-face since Nice when Paul III had pronounced the Turks the most serious threat.[142] Pole had replied by drawing a distinction between an internal and an external evil, and demanding a remedy for internal illness first. Charles also pointed to a contradiction in Pole's policy, that is, breaking off trade as a warning did not square with making war, as Pole also apparently wished to do. Pole left Toledo almost at once and his legation ground to a halt. Eventually he moved to Carpentras, where he would spend the next six months with Sadoleto. Pole explained his movements in a long letter to Farnese upon his arrival.[143] He

---

[138] As Höllger, p. 144 argues. See *ibid.* for Charles's injury and *CSPSp*, 6:1, no. 37 for the pope's comparison of Henry to the Turks. Höllger (n35) mistakenly assigns priority in both arguments to the pope, not to Pole, although he notes on p. 192 that the legation of 1537 had 'followed closely' *De unitate*'s programme.

[139] *CRP*, no. 237.

[140] *ERP*, 4, p. 337.

[141] *Ibid.*, pp. 339–40.

[142] Gustav Turba, ed., *Venetianische Depeschen vom Kaiserhofe (Dispacci di Germania)*, Erste Abteilung (Vienna: Tempsky, 1889–1901; 3 vols.), 1, no. 69.

[143] *CRP*, nos. 254 and 255.

admitted that it had been his idea to stop somewhere on the way to France, thinking that a trip there without agreement from the emperor would result in just the fiasco of his first legation. Pole, reflecting on his experience in Toledo, decided that appearances meant more than words. He also inadvertently laid some of the blame where it belonged, on himself. After a minute recitation of Charles's excuses, Pole insisted that he had no idea why Charles had refused to act, unless he thought other princes feared his designs on England![144] Pole noted that he had written a threatening letter to the imperial council, telling them that if they refused to act he would have no choice but to turn to France and to the king of Scotland, who had already expressed their willingness.

More than two weeks later, Pole wrote one of the principal imperial counsellors, Nicholas Perrenot de Granvelle.[145] Pole deployed all the resources of his rich vocabulary, drawing especially on his newer arsenal of religious terms. Thus he told Granvelle that Charles should help 'that afflicted island' which had always expected to be 'consoled' by the emperor. Consolation became a major theme of the letter. Pole traded in family imagery, noting the injury done to Charles's 'most noble' house, and to Pole's own relatives, but went on to claim that family meant nothing against the claims of conscience. The martyrs would serve as Pole's new family. Pole dilated on his concern for Henry's benefit, perhaps already mixing noble with religious overtones. God would pursue a *vendetta* against Henry, rather than allowing Pole to take revenge. Divine providence would none the less use Pole as its instrument, as it had long directed his family's fortunes, from the moment his mother became princess Mary's governess. Turning at the end to autobiography, Pole reminded Granvelle that the imperial ambassador had been behind his promotion as cardinal, and he now asked for repayment of all the damages he had suffered as a result.

Neither this letter nor papal pressure had any effect.[146] Pole wrote Contarini that he had turned to the Psalms for consolation. In them he found 'that prudent simplicity' which a servant of God needed in order to deal with men. His letter to Farnese of the same date has a completely different tone, making it appear that further delay did not concern Pole in the least.[147] Reactions to Sadoleto's current book did worry him.[148] This was 'De christiana ecclesia', modelled on Pighe's *Hierarchiae ecclesiae assertio*. It argued that the church consisted mainly of the bishops and the clergy, both of whom badly needed

---

[144] Charles, for his part, also claimed not to have been able to understand Pole. Höllger, p. 149 n.47.

[145] *CRP*, no. 258.

[146] *CRP*, nos. 260 and 263, and Höllger, p. 171.

[147] *CRP*, no. 266.

[148] *CRP*, nos. 254 and 298.

reform.[149] This engendered violent controversy in Rome, upsetting Pole. He asked Contarini to do what he could to stop the attacks. Pole was also involved in Sadoleto's attempt to woo the Genevans away from Protestantism.[150] Just what he contributed or how he reacted is unknown. No doubt the irenicism of Sadoleto's letter appealed to him, but perhaps Sadoleto's increasingly marked 'pelagian' bent would not have.[151] Sadoleto was reading the 'Apology', either now or shortly afterwards.[152] Pole probably also referred to this work when he told Contarini that anyone wishing to see his book would have to be stalled until it was done.[153] Priuli played the agriculturist in the garden of the Observant Franciscan monastery at Montélimar where they had all been living for about a month.[154] Despite these retired pursuits and his wish for nothing more than *otio* in which to pray, Pole reported a letter from Ireland detailing plans for war and suggesting that 'we' should be involved.[155]

Despite these bellicose sounds, by the time Pole began to write the 'Apology' shortly after his audience of 13 February, he looked likely to fail as badly as he had in 1537.[156] Charles and his advisers had effectively derailed action against Henry that both Francis and Paul III were willing to foment, the pope quite strongly.[157] Imperial recalcitrance is important to understanding the 'Apology'. A mole in Charles's court offered a tip about the real nature of the objections to the mission in general and to Pole in particular: he was a subverter of princes. Henry's efforts to discredit Pole had borne the fruit the king intended. The emperor almost certainly based his conclusion on *De unitate*, particularly its

---

[149] Richard M. Douglas, *Jacopo Sadoleto (1473–1547), humanist and reformer* (Cambridge: Harvard University Press, 1959), pp. 150–4.

[150] Jacopo Sadoleto, *Epistolae quotquot extant proprio nomine scriptae*, ed. V. A. Costanzi (Rome: G. Salomonio, 1760–4; 4 vols.), 3, no. 323 (cf. *L&P*, 14:1, no. 562n).

[151] *Evan. ital.*, p. 111. It seems that Sadoleto's attempt to invoke with Contarini Pole's authority for his letter is a mark of the same irenicism, rather than a sign of a strained relationship with either Contarini or Pole. Sadoleto's increasingly warm relations with Catarino might have been a different story. See the next chapter and *ibid.*, pp. 123–4.

[152] *CRP*, no. 305.

[153] *CRP*, no. 280.

[154] *CRP*, no. 290.

[155] Earlier in March the Council in the North reported having caught two Irish clergymen bearing treasonous letters addressed to the pope and Pole 'moving and exciting them towards some sedition to be made in Ireland'. PRO, SP 1/144, fo. 68r (*L&P*, 14:1, no. 481).

[156] Cf. *CRP*, no. 245, which tied the 'Apology' directly to Pole's audience with Charles.

[157] Höllger (pp. 178–80) notes that Pole and Paul III blamed Charles, but he puts the failure of the legation down to the papal court and regards it as doomed from the start. Pole's skills as a diplomat were not at fault. In favour of Höllger's point, it should be noted that Alessandro Farnese had no more success with Charles in 1540. *Evan. ital.*, p. 236.

appeal to 'the people' of England. Pole's deployment of many earlier hieratic arguments for the superiority of spiritual to temporal power only served to highlight the potential for any prince to be caught in a similar pincer between pope and 'people'.

I should not need to stress that Pole was working in the same gap between prince and republic as Machiavelli had done. It is therefore the more curious that he reacted in identical ways to Henry and to Machiavelli, even without blaming Henry's policies toward the church on Machiavelli, as he did in the 'Apology'.[158] Both were to be countered by the blood of the martyrs, the most immediate, brutally physical presence Pole could find.[159] In the 'Apology', defending his intention in writing De unitate, Pole adduced the martyrs as the principal reason he had decided to comply with Henry's order to give an opinion on the king's proceedings. He likened Fisher and More to 'the finger of God' and in an obvious and highly significant political metaphor called them God's arcana (pp. 69–71). Later, dilating on Henry's monstrous nature, Pole devoted almost six pages to praise of these martyrs and description of their horrible deaths (pp. 93–8). Even worse, Henry had moved on to persecute the dead, a point Pole emphasized with a long insertion on how the devil had treated 'the bodies of the just' (p. 102). These especially included Becket, whose tomb Henry had desecrated and whose bones he had burnt.[160] A contrast between various classical examples and Henry's handling of Becket and his rewriting of history becomes one of the principal arguments of the 'Apology'. Pole did not fail to note the importance of penance, and drew an extended contrast to Henry II's behaviour after Becket's murder which had earned him history's praise (pp. 106–8).

Pole then turned to writing history himself, averring that unlike most historians and writers of dialogues, he would invent nothing (p. 123). His tale concerned Cromwell's rise to power as chief counsellor, and a new version of how

---

[158] Höllger, pp. 195–207 offers an often tendentious reading of the 'Apology', building loosely on Heinrich Lutz's argument that it left politics behind in its unwavering commitment to 'Christian ethics'. *Ragione di stato und christliche Staatsethik im 16. Jahrhundert* (Münster: Aschendorff, 1976; 2nd ed.), p. 33.

[159] Pole evidently hit a major nerve here. Lionel Rothkrug has argued that those parts of Germany that lacked saints'

shrines were much more likely to turn to the reformation. 'Holy shrines, religious dissonance and Satan in the crisis of the German reformation', *Historical reflections*, 14:2 (1987), pp. 143–286.

[160] *ERP*, 1, pp. 101ff. Pole's draft preface, titled 'Qua te tuetur in editione libri ad Henricum viii', intended for an edition of *De unitate* apparently in 1541 (BAV, Vat. lat. 5970, fos. 315r–28v, fos. 321r–6r), treated Becket at length.

Henry's first divorce had come about through his own *concupiscentia* and a Satanic plot laid by one of his advisers (pp. 116–19).[161] It was designed to persuade Henry that his will was law and that he could disregard both natural and positive law (pp. 119–21). The supreme headship resulted, and as the plotter had promised, this solution to the problem of the divorce gave Henry both a great reputation for prudence, as well as great riches (pp. 122–3). Pole gradually revealed this fiend's identity, before recounting a discussion between himself and Cromwell – such was his name – about the best means of 'ruling the republic' and the duty of a 'prudent counsellor' (p. 132). Cromwell told Pole that he was naïve to think a counsellor should always consult the prince's honour and utility according to the law, an idea fit only for airing in the schools or before 'the people'. An effective counsellor worked in secret and always tried to discern what the prince wanted. His job was to make the prince appear virtuous, while yet having his way. Cromwell closed by advising Pole to consult experience rather than abstract speculation and recommending a book by 'a certain modern writer' (p. 135).

Later Pole read this book of secrets, warned of its dangers by those who had already seen it (p. 136). He knew instantly the devil had written it, but only some time later discovered that its author's name was Machiavelli, 'a Florentine unworthy of such a homeland'. Like the son of Satan he was, he had distilled all Satan's malice which 'betrays that noble city' and 'wrote some things, among them a book *De principe*' (p. 137). The book concerned the importance to the prince of bamboozling the populace through manipulating religion (p. 138). Knowing when and how to do this was what Machiavelli called prudence, expressed, as Pole noted, in the simile of the fox and lion (p. 139). According to Machiavelli, as Pole further accurately observed, it was better for a prince to be feared than loved. Dissimulation was the true way to protect 'rule and the principate' (*imperium & principatum*), and only acting in turns like both fox and lion could preserve the *arcana imperii* (p. 140). Henry had adopted Machiavelli's policy of dissimulation, calling it prudence, and used it as a cover for his cruelty, thereby completing Pole's circle to the martyrs (p. 145). Pole had heard last winter in Florence the interpretation of *The prince* according to which it was designed to seduce the Medici into undoing themselves, but dismissed this possibility (pp. 151–2). Pole had the proper ties to various Florentines who had been strong republicans to make this story likely, for example, Piero Vettori (probably son of Machiavelli's patron and collaborator Francesco) and Benedetto Varchi, as well as to others in Florence, above all, Pietro Carnesecchi,

---

[161] There is an echo of this tale in the preface to James V; *ERP*, 1, pp. 176–7.

whom he had known since at least 1536.[162] Pole here turned to his prophetic persona and conjured the charismatically grounded, transcendent protection afforded by Becket's bones (p. 154).

Becket was invoked to defend not just Pole himself, but the whole of the English nobility.[163] More explicitly than in his appeal to 'the people' in De unitate, in the 'Apology' Pole accused Henry of trying to do in the nobles, and set out to guard his class (p. 145).[164] This was in marked contrast to the beginning of Henry's reign, which had ended noble faction 'and joined all and the wills of all in the same man' to a degree never seen in English history (pp. 82–3). This almost sounds as if Pole meant to refer to Henry's accession as an election. Pole focused on the executions of his brother Henry, the marquess of Exeter, and Sir Edward Neville. Their crime, said Pole, was that they were too noble. Henry meant to destroy the flower of virtue in the nobility (pp. 112–13), just as he would the clergy. Pole also noted that he intended to reply to the executions in another work.[165] From this moment he went straight into his discovery that the Machiavellian Cromwell lurked behind Henry. In a nicely dialectical argument like one he had made in De unitate, Pole also blamed the counsellors who had failed to persuade Henry that all was not ruled by his will (p. 119).

As the 'Apology' progressed to its close, Pole became more and more explicit about both Henry's shortcomings and about his likely end, abandoning an earlier, brief opening to the king (p. 75). Henry's fate was out of man's hands. As Jesus had promised, all would be revealed (p. 147). Despite Henry's best efforts to conceal his secrets, divine providence would unmask him (p. 148). Turning to the prophet-model which had become most important in De unitate, Pole invoked Ezekiel, calling down divine vengeance on both Henry and those university doctors who supported his divorce (p. 149). Since he had now exposed all of Henry's sins, there was no choice left but to execute God's judgment (p. 150). Just as Moses had threatened the Israelites with destruction after they built the golden calf, so the pope, Moses's successor, now threatened Henry (p. 153). Pole praised the Levites' indiscriminate destruction of the offending Israelites, and identified himself as one of them (p. 154). And conjured Becket. Safe with him, Pole ripped off Henry's mask and called him Antichrist, or at

---

[162] For Vettori, see below, p. 100. Oddone Ortolani, Per la storia della vita religiosa italiana nel Cinquecento. Pietro Carnesecchi (Florence: Le Monnier, 1963), p. 19. Cf. CRP, nos. 225–6 and 237. The movements of people he may have visited are thinly documented, especially

Carnesecchi (Ortolani, pp. 23–4 skips over 1538).

[163] Cf. a draft preface to De unitate in BAV, Vat. lat. 5970, fos. 326r–7r.

[164] Cf. CRP, no. 241.

[165] Perhaps CRP, no. 290 is a sketch.

least his predecessor. Whichever Henry was, he was acting in Antichrist's and Satan's spirit by changing the laws and punishing those who honoured their fathers (p. 157). Pole lectured Henry on the bounds of his *imperium*, the binding force of laws which not even God could change, and on the sanctity of oaths, while ringing changes on the theme of the real traitor. Would Antichrist reveal Pole as a traitor (p. 159)? Or would Pole expose Henry (p. 160)? It is just another of the manifold ironies in the situation that an anonymous Englishman (perhaps Morison) turned the identification with Antichrist back on Pole.[166] Finally, Pole introduced his peroration by emphasizing the contrast between providence and Henry's prudence, and prophesying the end of the Christian *imperium* if Henry were allowed to keep 'the supreme government of human matters'. Antichrist's *imperium*, drawn from history, would succeed, but he could not avoid the end predicted for him, also in history. Pole called himself one of God's spies (*speculatores*) whose duty it was to hold Henry's sin up to him. Doing this would not effect the king's conversion unless 'the founts of honour, utility, and all good are opened' (p. 171).

Thus did Pole draw together his mission, and thus did he set out the problem of a tyrannous king. He obliquely canvassed a political solution before concluding that only divinely inspired outside intervention, if not by Charles, then by any tyrannicide, could stop Henry (pp. 160–1). Or maybe only God Himself could. Henry was the Antichrist, Machiavelli and Cromwell demons.

Why blame Machiavelli? One answer is that Pole told the truth about a real interview with Cromwell, including the notorious recommendation of *De principe*.[167] The fact that Pole both admitted his *dispositio*, saying he had collected things said at different times 'as at least what I thought up myself, as verisimiliar' and also claimed autobiographical proof that his story was true, raises alarm signals.[168] Pole recast, embroidered, yes, invented episodes as and when needed. This almost certainly happened in this instance. Shortly after their conversation, Pole had fled England, he wrote. The episode supposedly occurred at the time the scheme to consult learned opinion about the divorce arose, that is, in late summer 1529, when Pole was still firmly in the king's

---

[166] PRO, SP 1/155, fo. 57v (*L&P*, 14:2, 613).

[167] This tale has been largely debunked in this century. Paul van Dyke, 'Reginald Pole and Thomas Cromwell: an examination of the *Apologia ad Carolum quintum*', *American historical review*, 9 (1904), pp. 696–724; G. R. Elton, *The Tudor revolution in government: administrative changes in the*

reign of Henry VIII (Cambridge: Cambridge University Press, 1953), pp. 73–4 (although this was not always his line); and Höllger, pp. 197–200 who judged it entirely fictional for largely rhetorical reasons, a promising line of analysis.

[168] *ERP*, 1, pp. 124 and 132.

camp.[169] Pole ran very little risk of having his tale exposed. No one in Charles's entourage was likely to challenge it. In this audience lies a clue to what Pole intended. Pole blamed Machiavelli and his disciple Cromwell for arguing that the prince's will should rule all, despite morality and religion. The counsellor's job was to help his prince get what he wanted.[170] Not by coincidence, the example Pole drew had direct relevance to Charles and his advisers, who were equally guilty of wilful inaction in the face of divine imperatives to deal with Henry.

Pole concluded in his correspondence with Rome that everything had to be left to God, the same point he reached in the 'Apology'.[171] Caught between recalcitrant princes, faced with mounting dangerous and depressing contingencies, Pole had no human recourse, no way to defend the community of the faithful in England from Henry's tyranny, and perhaps himself from Charles's. He desperately needed to innovate to overcome the impasse. He did this in the form of conjoint appeals to martyrs and prophets, including himself, but the martyrs were dead and the prophets unarmed. His variety of prudence had failed once and was about to do so again.[172]

The apocalyptic strain in the 'Apology' undoubtedly had psychological roots, as Donaldson argues, but there was more to it.[173] It seems likely that Pole's apocalypticism, the major change in the 'Apology' from *De unitate*, arose in the same way and at the same time as its central image of the Antichrist, through the catalyst of Pole's experience in Florence in the winter of 1538. Some of the same people who might have been termed followers of Machiavelli, were also and sometimes less circumspectly followers of Savonarola. This was especially true of Vettori, whom Cosimo had just rehabilitated and appointed to a chair at the *studio*.[174] Vettori, although never a Savonarolan, had been among those *arrabbiatti* who had made common cause with the *piagnoni* at the end of the republic.[175] Ten years later he thought Pole would be elected pope and drafted an oration of congratulations.[176] They also corresponded over the death of their

[169] *ERP*, 1, pp. 132–3. Höllger, p. 197, mistakenly assigns it to 1527.

[170] As Höllger (p. 205) correctly observes, Pole here added to Machiavelli's argument. For Machiavelli's ideas about counsel, see Ascoli, 'Gift'.

[171] See, e.g., *CRP*, no. 285.

[172] See, e.g., *CRP*, no. 247.

[173] Donaldson, pp. 3, 5, 26, 29.

[174] Salvatore Caponetto, *Aonio Paleario (1503–1570) e la Riforma protestante in Toscana* (Turin: Claudiana, 1979), p. 41.

[175] Lorenzo Polizzotto, *The elect nation. The Savonarolan movement in Florence 1494–1545* (Oxford: Clarendon Press, 1994), pp. 361–3 and Rudolph von Albertini, *Das florentinisches Staatsbewußtsein in Übergang von der Republik zum Principat* (Bern: Francke, 1955), pp. 418–35. Vettori was among those endorsing capitulation in 1530 (Polizzotto, p. 385) and he later criticized the *piagnoni* (p. 381n).

[176] ASF:AMP, 395, fo. 212r.

mutual friend Flaminio.[177] In 1538 Flaminio had asked Vettori for the *Trattato della santissima carità*.[178] Among those congratulating Vettori on his appointment was Pierfrancesco Gagliano, who had been a Savonarolan and a friend of Contarini.[179] He would later propose to take on a member of Pole's household as vicar in Pistoia.[180] Contarini had a largely favourable attitude to Savonarola as well, as did many other Venetians.[181] Savonarola's memory was exceedingly green in Florence, much beyond Vettori and Gagliano.[182] If Pole knew both Savonarola's legacy, as seems very likely, and the *Discourses*, this marks another suspicious silence in his attitude to Machiavelli, who had accorded Savonarola generally positive treatment.[183] Ignoring Machiavelli and Savonarola would also have suppressed how close his and Machiavelli's ideas on prophecy came.

Contarini remained much in Pole's mind during the writing of the 'Apology'. But just as in the last letter to Contarini quoted with its blend of a wish for withdrawal and war news from Ireland, Pole's frequently expressed longing to escape the world had its limits. Little doubt as there may be that Pole honestly told Contarini that he was confused and that worry about lack of news was ruining his enjoyment of the studies his circle were pursuing in the convent, he yet continued to meditate on England.[184] Even when he wrote that he was both physically and spiritually ill and that he wanted to augment the consolation he felt from solitude, at the same time he still thought something had urgently to be

---

[177] *CRP*, nos. 563–4.

[178] Marcantonio Flaminio, *Lettere*, ed. Alessandro Pastore (Rome: Ateneo & Bizzarri, 1978), no. 14.

[179] Gigliola Fragnito, 'Cultura umanistica e riforma religiosa: Il "De officio viri boni ac probi episcopi"', *Studi veneziani*, 11 (1969), pp. 75–189, p. 111n. Hubert Jedin, 'Contarini und Camaldoli', *Archivio italiano per la storia della pietà*, 2 (1959), pp. 59–118, nos. 17 and note, 19–20 and 28.

[180] *CRP*, no. 1937.

[181] Fragnito, '"De officio"', pp. 119–25. Jedin, 'Contarini und Camaldoli', p. 54n for Venetian publication of some of Savonarola's works.

[182] See especially Donald M. Weinstein, *Savonarola and Florence: prophecy and patriotism in the renaissance* (Princeton: Princeton University Press, 1970) and Polizzotto.

[183] *Discourses*, I. 11 is Machiavelli's famously ambiguous observation that Savonarola had 'persuaded' the Florentines that he conversed with God, but the general evaluation is still positive, since Machiavelli concluded that the quality of Savonarola's life made him believable. I. 45 praised Savonarola as one of the re-founders of Florence in 1494. III. 30 is the most important passage, in which Machiavelli compared Savonarola favourably to the *gonfaloniere* Piero Soderini, and blames his failure on external circumstances, at the same time as Machiavelli once more apparently praised Savonarola's preaching, especially for its attacks on 'the wisemen of the world', which might have proved especially appealing to Pole. *Prince*, ch. 6 is Machiavelli's harshest criticism.

[184] *CRP*, no. 284.

done about England (which would be to *its* consolation, as he wrote Farnese).[185] Pole wished to stay in Carpentras rather than heeding the order to return to Rome, and he also complained that his advice about the succession to the bishopric of Salisbury had been disregarded and the pope had tried to give it to him. In another tense reading cast again in a corporal metaphor, Pole agreed that he had to have a bishopric for the sake of restoring religion in England, but with things as they were it would only give his enemies cause to laugh at him left with the bone while others ate the flesh and blood which should have gone to him.[186]

---

[185] *CRP*, no. 286.   [186] *CRP*, no. 285.

3

The church of Viterbo?

WHATEVER HIS FAILINGS as a diplomat, Pole exercised remarkable power over certain people.[1] Its nature, like the religious faith which undergirded it, is difficult to grasp. Defeated in efforts to define it, later inquisitors called Pole a Lutheran and the 'seducer' of an enormous list of victims, from Priuli to Vittoria Colonna. They and many others comprised the circle of the so-called *ecclesia Viterbiensis*, one of the most famous moments of the Italian reformation. Important as it no doubt was, a caution must be entered. As an increasing number of historians have pointed out of late, especially Gigliola Fragnito, its experience was nothing like as distinctive or as peculiar as earlier generations thought, nor was it a monolith.[2] Possibly still paradigmatic of the experience of the *spirituali*, it was not their only preserve.

It is increasingly common to read the *spirituali* almost as a political movement. Paolo Simoncelli in particular advanced this interpretation. According to him, *evangelismo* had two wings, moderate and radical. Contarini led the moderates defined by his 'De iustificatione' (pp. 101–4). Other moderates included Isidoro Chiari. The radical wing, although it receives much more of Simoncelli's attention, is less easy to understand. Either it had no single leader, or he was Pole. The radicals included Flaminio, Ochino, Brucioli, and so on. Simoncelli's description of a 'leadership contest' among the *spirituali* between Pole and his patron Contarini is most important.[3] They are supposed to have begun to drift apart in 1540, and the gap increased, at least from Pole's side, in

---

[1] *Inq. rom.*, p. 135 calls it a 'charismatic fascination'.

[2] Gigliola Fragnito, 'Ercole Gonzaga, Reginald Pole e il monastero di San Benedetto Polirone', *Benedictina*, 37 (1987), pp. 253–71, p. 266. Cf. *Evan. ital.*, p. 44. Even Firpo who still places it at the centre of

Valdesian spirituality in the 1540s implicitly allows that there were other such circles, proselytized by members of the diaspora from Naples shortly before Valdés's death in 1541. *Alumbrados, passim*.

[3] *Evan. ital.*, pp. 84–100.

the wake of the failed conference at Regensburg in 1541. There Contarini worked out a compromise on justification which Pole did not support in Rome. Thereafter the radicals and Contarini danced a complicated ballet, along with the Dominican provocateur, Ambrogio Catarino Politi, who represents the last alignment in Simoncelli's story, the 'intransigents', most of them associated with the Roman Inquisition.[4] Carafa of course heads this group, along with Marcello Cervini and Dionisio Laurerio.[5] By the time of Contarini's death in August 1542 Pole had become the undisputed head of the *spirituali*, a position he preserved in part by his famous flight from the council of Trent in the summer of 1546. The end of *evangelismo* came in the *Beneficio di Cristo*, conceived as a three-cornered conversation between moderates, radicals, and intransigents (p. 166). Massimo Firpo's parallel analysis stresses doctrine in the development of the *spirituali*, and on this score too finds important differences between Pole and Contarini. Pole and the *ecclesia viterbiensis* were deliberately converted to Valdesianism at just the moment of greatest strain in his relationship to Contarini.[6] Thus both politics and doctrine motivated the establishment of Pole's circle in Viterbo and its differences with Contarini, at the same time as the *spirituali* in general found themselves increasingly suspect in the eyes of the 'intransigents'.[7]

An analysis in political terms takes a step beyond wrangles over orthodoxy and heresy, but Simoncelli and Firpo have thus far followed the Inquisitors' methods. People divide cleanly into two groups, and their differences were doctrinal from the first. Things were not so simple. The intransigents not only deserve the label 'so-called' at least as much as the *spirituali*, but existed as a coherent group to an even smaller degree. Certainly Contarini did not see them as such, speaking of at least two of their supposed members in terms which make them appear to be among those he thought most likely to support him. And as Simoncelli himself brings out, the area of overlap between Catarino and his supposed adversaries was very large.[8] I suggest that the problem lies in a too

---

[4] Cf. esp. *Evan. ital.*, pp. 113–24.
[5] Only Cervini has had an adequate modern study, William V. Hudon, *Marcello Cervini and ecclesiastical government in Tridentine Italy* (DeKalb: Northern Illinois University Press, 1992).
[6] *Alumbrados*, esp. ch. 3. For a caution on the score of the depth of Pole's division from Contarini and consequently within the *spirituali*, see Elisabeth G. Gleason, *Gasparo*

Contarini: Venice, Rome and reform (Berkeley: University of California Press, 1993), p. 293.
[7] Simoncelli, *Caso, passim*.
[8] *Evan. ital.*, pp. 135 and 137. Cf. also Massimo Firpo, *Dal sacco di Roma all'Inquisizione: Studi su Juan de Valdés e la Riforma italiana* (Alessandria: Edizioni dell'Orso, 1998), pp. 139–40 who minimizes the significance of Catarino's agreement.

global interpretation, mainly still developed from positions sympathetic to the perceived losers – the *spirituali* – which greatly reduces the complexity of the original circumstances, and downplays the role of contingency and the vagaries of personality.

The facts are indisputable. Pole did not defend Contarini's formula in Rome, instead deliberately absenting himself, leaving that big job in the hands of Federico Fregoso, Bembo, and Priuli, the last of whom had no standing. Again, Pole undoubtedly left Trent. But the two cases are not like. The difference lies in the fact that in the second, Pole's views were well known, but in the first he revealed them only to Contarini, and they have been partially misunderstood. The strongest similarity between the two moments suggests another interpretation of Pole's actions, one rooted in personality, not politics. It was simply his way to avoid conflict, even if that meant being *hors de combat* at crucial moments. He did that throughout his life, resorting instead to writing, whether in these two instances, in that of *De unitate* or any other of his 'Apologies'. Pole had political skills, but his passivity in the face of crisis constantly negated them. Instead of the confrontational behaviour a high noble should have displayed when encountering opposition, Pole withdrew. Instead of defending his honour publicly against challenge from other men, Pole privately cultivated the congenial members of his household and spiritual relationships with women, above all Colonna.

Pole's friendship with Colonna began to intensify in early 1540.[9] This did not amount to him 'converting' her, because like Pole himself she did not then need conversion. Colonna had been close to Priuli from early 1536, and had probably submitted her religious poetry to his judgment. It is thus not a coincidence that Colonna's and Pole's religious evolution moved on closely parallel tracks from some time in 1537, and that both now strengthened their ties to French evangelicals.[10] Francis I tried to get Pole's patronage for Georges d'Armagnac, a protégé of Marguerite de Navarre whom Pole had known in Venice.[11] At the same time, Pole's standing in Rome began to rise. Of course, he continued as expert on England. The new order of Jesuits carefully consulted Pole about a mission there.[12] Another good sign of Pole's standing was that he was considered, along

---

[9] *Inq. rom.*, p. 124.

[10] Gigliola Fragnito, 'Vittoria Colonna e l'inquisizione', *Benedictina*, 37 (1990), pp. 157–72, pp. 164–6.

[11] *CRP*, no. 304 and Ermanno Ferrero and Giuseppe Müller, eds., *Vittoria Colonna, Marchesa di Pescara, carteggio* (Turin:

Hermanno Loescher, 1892), no. CLXVI.

[12] Thomas M. McCoog, *Monumenta Angliae: English and Welsh Jesuits. Catalogues* (Rome: Institutum Historicum Societatis Iesu, 1992; MHSI, 142–3; 2 vols.), 1 February 1541 and ff.

with Contarini, as legate to Charles V in an effort to prevent him from reaching a unilateral agreement with the Lutherans.[13] Despite being then set on the same level, Pole's and Contarini's relation began subtly to reverse itself. Now Contarini had to ask Pole for help with the pope, and with his responsibilities as protector of the Cassinese Benedictines.[14] Now Contarini was the legate headed north, intended to attend various religious colloquies beginning with Hagenau, Pole his most important contact in the curia.[15] When Contarini finally left Rome in late January 1541 headed for Regensburg, high hopes rode on his legation, for which both Pole and Colonna prayed.[16]

Contarini's instructions would seemingly not have boosted his chances or his friends' optimism. They gave him no power to conclude anything, mainly because the Protestant positions were unknown and perhaps expected to be unacceptable. The instructions spoke in harsh terms of heretics and Protestants, and left both only the option of returning to the church through a general council and submitting disputed points to the pope. And yet, the same document held out the hope that the pope could avoid harsher means, and there can be no question of the emperor's eagerness for a compromise.[17] Again, Contarini, the pope, and Cardinal Farnese may well have had different agendas, but that was only politics as usual in Rome and no cause to expect the worst.[18] Even the substantial distraction of virtually open warfare between the pope and Colonna's brother Ascanio, with whom both Contarini and probably Pole sympathized, likely did not seriously dampen Contarini's chances or his enthusiasm.[19] One final participant, Tommaso Badia, master of the sacred palace, was another intimate of both Pole and Contarini on at least religious grounds.[20] One of Pole's circle, however, refused Contarini's invitation. In a significant sign both of his own leanings and the real meaning of the Valdesians' alleged political design, Flaminio rejected Contarini's intense efforts to secure his services.[21]

Despite all the possible negative indicators, Contarini succeeded at

---

[13] Cf. *Evan. ital.*, pp. 226–81 with Hudon, pp. 36–8.

[14] *CRP*, nos. 320–1.

[15] Franz Dittrich, *Gasparo Contarini, 1483–1542. Eine Monographie* (Nieuwkoop: B. de Graaf, 1972; reprint of 1885 edition), pp. 516–27; cf. Gleason, p. 203. *CRP*, no. 307.

[16] Gleason, p. 203. *CRP*, nos. 314–15 and 318.

[17] Gleason (pp. 204–7) argues that they

doomed his mission from the first.

[18] Gleason, p. 213.

[19] Gleason, pp. 213–15.

[20] *CRP*, no. 318.

[21] Gigliola Fragnito, 'Intervento sulla relazione di Massimo Firpo, "Valdesianesimo ed evangelismo: alle origini dell'*Ecclesia Viterbiensis* (1541)"' in *Libri, idee e sentimenti religiosi nel Cinquecento italiano* (Modena: Panini, 1987), pp. 73–6, pp. 73 and 75.

Regensburg on the most contentious point: the doctrine of justification.[22] Badia, the nuncio Giovanni Poggio, and all the Catholic theologians agreed with the formula drawn up on 2 May. Contarini added that Pighe's unpublished writings supported them, and Johannes Cochlaeus had also endorsed the new formula.[23] Article five offered a new definition of justification as by 'that faith, which is effective through charity' or good works. This was Christ's justice imputed by faith to the sinner. Inherent justice led the sinner to do good works, but without contributing to salvation. These two together produced so-called 'double justification'. Preachers should, however, preach the need for penance and good works, which sounds very much like Contarini's attitude.[24]

As soon as the compromise was adopted, Contarini notified Cardinals Gonzaga, Bembo and Pole.[25] Bembo, although not initially Contarini's choice but rather Badia's, seems to have acted as something of a clearing house, passing on to Fregoso, Laurerio, Rodolfo Pio, Niccolò Ridolfi, and Pole copies of Contarini's *Epistola de iustificatione*.[26] This same list (minus Laurerio) appeared in an earlier letter from Contarini to Pole and Contarini added 'all of whom the same spirit of Christ joins', which makes it appear that he thought them the core of his supporters.[27] Contarini could not have known that almost all would let him down.[28] A month later Contarini had the news that Pole intended to leave Rome.[29] Pole had made up his mind to do this at a time when information from Contarini indicated that little likely would come of the colloquy. The last Pole knew, Contarini was preparing to give up, asking Pole's help securing the pope's

[22] For the controversy about the quality of his compromise, see Basil Hall, 'The colloquies between Catholics and Protestants 1539–1541', in G. J. Cuming and D. Baker, eds., *Studies in church history*, 7 (1971), pp. 235–66; Karl-Heinz zur Mühlen, 'Die Einigung über Rechtfertigungsartikel auf dem Regensburger Religionsgespräch von 1541 – eine verpaßte Chance', *Zeitschrift für Theologie und Kirche*, 76 (1979), pp. 331–59; Gleason, pp. 228–35; and Athina Lexutt, *Rechtfertigung im Gespräch: Das Rechtfertigungsverständnis in den Religionsgesprächen von Hagenau, Worms und Regensburg 1540/41* (Göttingen: Vandenhoeck & Ruprecht, 1996).

[23] Ludwig von Pastor, 'Die Correspondenz des Cardinals Contarini während seiner deutschen Legation (1541)', *Historisches Jahrbuch*, 1 (1880), pp. 321–92 and 473–501, pp. 372–3.

[24] Georg Pfeilschifter, ed., *Acta reformationis catholicae ecclesiam Germaniae concernentia saeculi XVI*, 6 (Regensburg: F. Pustet, 1974), pp. 52–4; cf. Fenlon, pp. 54–5; Gleason, pp. 227–8.

[25] zur Mühlen, p. 341; Gleason, p. 229.

[26] Ernesto Travi, ed., Pietro Bembo, *Lettere* (Bologna: Commissione per i Testi di Lingua, 1987–93; 4 vols.), no. 2253 and Pastor, 'Correspondenz', p. 479. The *Epistola* is in *PM*, 2, pp. 1039–56.

[27] Cf. *Alumbrados*, pp. 178–9.

[28] *CRP*, no. 315.

[29] *CRP*, no. 321 and cf. Pole's reference to Contarini's letter of 3 May regretting his decision (no. 321).

permission to stay in his diocese of Belluno for the summer. Pole even used the argument that Contarini would not accomplish anything when trying to secure Paul's agreement. Pole knew that Contarini would dislike his decision to leave Rome, and defended himself by assuring Contarini that Priuli would take care of business.[30] Bembo wrote Contarini about the 'charges' which Pole left to him on his departure from Rome on 12 May, but it is almost certain that these 'charges' did not refer to Regensburg.[31]

Much has been made of Pole's absence, probably too much.[32] For one thing, Pole was not the only line of defence for Contarini who, although disappointed, quickly nominated Bembo his chief spokesperson in Rome, and redoubled his efforts to satisfy Gonzaga. From the first, Contarini had treated him as one of the major participants, along with at least four or five other cardinals. Both Bembo and Gonzaga had their drawbacks, Bembo his status as a new cardinal and one whose promotion had not met with universal rejoicing, Gonzaga his political aspirations and absence from Rome.[33] According to the political interpretation of this moment, Pole's letter to Contarini of 16 July confirms their alleged distance.[34] Such an interpretation distorts the meaning of this letter, glosses over an earlier one, and discounts a missing letter.

Pole's first reactions to Regensburg came in a letter to Contarini of 17 May, after he received the compromise formula the day before.[35] In it Pole excused himself for not being in Rome and assured Contarini that Priuli held views identical to his, and Priuli told Beccadelli that he would do anything to support Contarini. Unfortunately, Priuli was a poor choice as agent, a fact which Beccadelli and therefore probably Contarini knew. Bernardino Maffei, one of the principal Farnese managers, wrote Beccadelli on 29 May that Priuli 'frequently comes back to Rome to play the merchant, but he does not have much favour here'.[36] He tried hard, and blessed Contarini and Badia 'who suffer persecution on account of the gospel'.[37] Pole went on that Contarini already

---

[30] *CRP*, no. 321.
[31] Travi, no. 2243; Fragnito, 'Intervento', p. 74.
[32] For the most balanced assessment, see Fenlon, pp. 56–61.
[33] Concetta Ranieri, 'Ancora sul carteggio tra Pietro Bembo e Vittoria Colonna', *Giornale italiano di filologia*, n.s., 14 (1983), pp. 133–51, p. 147n.
[34] Gleason, p. 249; Paolo Simoncelli, 'Vom Humanismus zur Gegenreformation: Das

Schicksal des Regensburger Buches in Italien. Versuch einer Rekonstruktion', in Elmar Neuss and J. V. Pollet, eds., *Pflugiana. Studien über Julius Pflug* (Münster: Aschendorff, 1990), pp. 93–114, p. 98; *Alumbrados*, pp. 161–2.
[35] *CRP*, no. 322.
[36] Cited in Fragnito, 'Intervento', p. 75 n5.
[37] BMIC25, fos. 175r–8r (cf. *PM*, 2, pp. 555n, 725n).

knew his thoughts, and there was no need to say more.[38] He judged that on Contarini's efforts 'I saw the great foundation of peace of concord laid . . . truly the foundation of the whole of Christian doctrine'. Although he promised to keep quiet as Contarini had asked, the news deserved to be shouted from the rooftops. Pole's enthusiasm, however short on substance, matched Contarini's own.[39]

Then in July, well after anything of consequence had happened in either Rome or Regensburg, Pole wrote Contarini again.[40] Pole opened by assuring Contarini that he had been extraordinarily affected by Contarini's letter of 20 June (missing).[41] In it Contarini had spelled out how much he wanted Pole's assessment of *De iustificatione*. Pole replied that he judged it as he did all Contarini's writings: Contarini laid a solid foundation, furnished many arguments, dealt charitably with his opponents, and followed a strict logical order. His conclusions were 'as appropriate [*convenientia*] as possible'. Everything Contarini wrote agreed with scripture and the 'sense of the church' and should serve to remove many causes of scandal (*omnia autem scripturis, et Ecclesiae sensui maxime convenientia conclusisse*). Pole did have one criticism, but it has been badly misinterpreted. He had hoped that Contarini would face a sharper adversary who would have given him the opportunity 'of responding to those things which are usually raised from the scriptures against this [position] which you defend, which certainly seem to be very many, and such which need explanation, you [being] the explainer'. Many in Rome had objected to Contarini's opinion, and Pole hoped they would inspire Contarini, as he expected, to offer a clearer explanation.

Thus Contarini's work did not fully satisfy Pole. The problem was not that it was insufficiently scriptural, but that Contarini, with his distinctive qualifications, had not finished the job by laying out how the formula's opponents misread the scriptures they customarily cited.[42] Pole continued that Contarini's objection to his absence annoyed him, since he had already written twice to

---

[38] Might this mean that Pole had already written Contarini, perhaps in the missing letter with several detailed criticisms noted below?

[39] Cf. Gleason, p. 233. Fragnito, 'Intervento', p. 74 argues that Priuli's mission on Pole's behalf means that Pole accepted the formula. As Pole's letter indicates, this judgment is certainly correct.

[40] *CRP*, no. 328.

[41] This may be the letter in which Contarini said that he had written Pole about the article on merit and works, which naturally turned to faith and works. Pastor, 'Correspondenz', p. 494.

[42] Fenlon, pp. 60–1, whose analysis is further misleading in saying that Pole wished that Contarini had 'demonstrate[d] the Scriptural foundation of the doctrine'.

explain his action. He added that his friends had called him away, especially because there was no longer any need of his presence. Or so Pole thought. Nevertheless, he apologized for his blunder. When he had learned that consistory would after all consider the results of Regensburg, he was unbelievably vexed because of 'my private duty to you, and my piety to the cause of Christ, whose glory most shines through the opinion you proposed about justification'. Pole apologized further that when some began to laugh at Contarini and call him an innovator in doctrine, it should have fallen especially to Pole among the cardinals to defend him, since Pole could understand Contarini, both in speech and in writing, better than anyone else. Contarini's opinion unquestionably rested on the oldest foundation of church doctrine. 'But I could not explain this because of my absence, which time, place, duty and piety demanded.'[43] 'This not a little pained me, and the more, because I afterward understood that some . . . had interpreted my absence thus, as to say that I had left in order to avoid a foreseen storm, so they call it, on account of some disagreements among the leading men.'

Pole's defence might seem to make for the political interpretation, since avoiding controversy was one of his favourite generic excuses. By the same token, he used the argument on Contarini the next year in equally delicate circumstances, and it worked (see below). It would have been hypocritical to have deployed the argument on both sides of the fence, to the same person, about the same issue. The possibility of disagreement had inspired Pole to 'fly' to Rome, but the decision was made before he could. Besides, since the matter concerned Contarini's legation, it was up to him to do something about it. Not to worry, Pole concluded, raising difficulties like these was how Christ always inspired the defence of dogma. Thus Contarini should be grateful to divine providence for the chance to defend himself further. Perhaps Contarini's readiness to offer explanations was what Pole most liked about his letter, and Pole congratulated him for it. Now this 'little pearl' (*margarita*) of the true opinion was partially in the open, for many to see, and that too deserved praise.

As the closing again manifested, Pole still had reservations about *De iustificatione*.[44] But the extent to which he went to apologize for having failed to defend it also deserves emphasis, as do Priuli's efforts on its behalf, the more so because Priuli is supposed already to have been a convinced Valdesian. As Priuli put it in July, 'if public matters [including the Regensburg formula] are not

---

[43] *Evan. ital.*, p. 105; *Alumbrados*, p. 160; and Gleason, p. 250, all say that Pole pleaded ill health.

[44] Paolo Simoncelli, 'Pietro Bembo e l'evangelismo italiano', *Critica storica*, 15 (1978), pp. 1–63, pp. 25–6.

going according to the wish [*voto*] of those who desire God's glory and the benefit of Christendom, we must nevertheless trust that His infinite goodness will not abandon his church'.[45] It is also worth noting that Bernardo de' Bartoli, who spent considerable time with Pole in the early 1540s and may have been with both him and Contarini in the immediate aftermath of Regensburg, thought that Pole had agreed with Contarini's formula.[46] Pole was hardly alone in objecting to *De iustificatione*, however mildly, even among the cardinals whom Contarini had singled out. Carafa and Laurerio raised more or less strenuous objections, Laurerio drawing a rebuke from Contarini.[47] Pole was also not the only one to absent himself; Ridolfi did the same.[48] Fregoso vociferously defended Contarini, but left Rome for his diocese before the debate concluded and died shortly thereafter. He passed through Capranica, and many kind words were said about Contarini.[49] Only Bembo refused to keep his head down, and Contarini unburdened himself most to him.[50] Bembo blamed Pole for the outcome, telling Contarini that 'the one among them [the cardinals] who was most in your debt was least willing to pay'.[51] If justification really was the 'foundation' of everything else, the first major contest over it had revealed many possible lines of fracture in the college of cardinals, but not a leadership contest. In the main Pole accepted Contarini's efforts, which must mean that he did believe in 'double justification' (or 'two-stage justification'). And Bembo quickly got over his disappointment, wishing to Colonna in November that he could spend time in Viterbo with Pole.[52]

Pole could have and did sometimes allege the dangers from Henry which kept him in Capranica as another excuse for failing to execute Contarini's mandate. England was much in Pole's thoughts, and he may have tried to approach Stephen Gardiner who joined the English delegation to Regensburg.[53] One piece of evidence undercuts Pole's defence. A minute of a letter to Cristoforo

---

[45] BMIC25, fos. 179r–v.
[46] *PM*, 6, p. 329 (2:1, p. 821); cf. 6, pp. 163 and 298; and 2:2, p. 725.
[47] BMIC25, fos. 169r–74v and Gleason, p. 252.
[48] Travi, no. 2253.
[49] BMIC25, fos. 175r–8v; *PM*, 2:2, p. 725n.
[50] Simoncelli, 'Bembo', pp. 22–5.
[51] Gleason, p. 251, her translation. She thinks Bembo meant Aleandro, Cervini, or Carafa, but Pole's statement about his peculiar qualifications as interpreter of Contarini's mind points at him instead.

See *Alumbrados*, p. 161 for Contarini's regrets about Pole's behaviour expressed to Bembo.
[52] *Colonna Carteggio*, no. CXLI.
[53] Glyn Redworth, *In defence of the church catholic: the life of Stephen Gardiner* (Oxford: Blackwell, 1990), pp. 153–4. Cf. Pierre Janelle, 'An unpublished poem on bishop Stephen Gardiner', *Bulletin of the Institute of Historical Research*, 6 (1928), pp. 12–25, 89–96 and 167–74, 94–5.

Madruzzo is dated from Rome on 22 May 1541 and there is no obvious reason to challenge that date.[54] Pole had been in Capranica as recently as five days earlier. He apparently made at least one more visit to Rome that summer, perhaps in August, when Paul III refused to talk to him for grief at the bad news, probably a reference to his mother's execution.[55] Pole could make a relatively quick trip to Rome if necessary. It was no great distance. The fact that he did not choose to do so in order to defend Contarini may after all intensify their differences about the proper mode in which to discuss justification.

Just about the time Contarini was preparing to leave Regensburg, Pole got the news of his mother's execution on 27 May, relayed thence by Parpaglia.[56] Reports and letters of condolence kept this terrible event before him throughout the summer.[57] He and his biographers tried to make it appear that he was not much affected. Pole emphasized in several letters how quickly he had recovered and how he had converted a private blow into a public gain for the church, but Beccadelli's story of Pole's reaction, offered as an instance of his constancy, in fact must say exactly the opposite.[58]

Beccadelli recounted the episode in the first person, casting himself as Pole's secretary. Pole had summoned him to draft replies to various letters, including one in English. When Beccadelli objected that he could not since he did not know the language, Pole replied that this was too bad, because it contained good news. Beccadelli innocently asked what it was, and Pole replied

> Until now I have believed that the lord God has given me the grace to be the son of one of the best and most honored ladies of England and I have gloried in that and given thanks to His Divine Majesty. But he has wished to honor me more and increase my obligation, for he has also made me the son of a martyr, whom that king, because she was constant in the Catholic faith, has had publicly decapitated, even though she was more than seventy years old and his aunt. Thus he has rewarded the efforts which she took for a long time in raising his daughter. God be praised and thanked.[59]

Beccadelli felt dead at this news, but Pole consoled him that they had one more advocate in heaven, and then withdrew into his oratory. After an hour, he came out with his usual composure securely in place. This would be a signal instance

---

[54] *CRP*, no. 324.
[55] *CRP*, no. 636.
[56] BMIC25, fo. 179r.

[57] BMIC25, fos. 179r–v. Cf. *CRP*, nos. 331–2.
[58] *CRP*, nos. 314, 330, and 332.
[59] *MMB*, p. 329.

of constancy, were the story what Beccadelli represented it as. If Beccadelli witnessed such a scene, it could only have been long after the countess's death, for then he was at Regensburg with Contarini, and only rejoined Pole in Viterbo (not Capranica where he was when the news originally came) in the autumn.[60] Thus a tale of remarkable constancy must in truth reveal Pole's reaction both studied (in his set speech) and uncontrollable (in his hour-long prayer) at least several months after he had first heard of his mother's execution. This, combined with an exchange of letters with Colonna in which they both insisted that no one else had consoled them as much as the other, and in which Pole took Colonna as his mother, a better one than Moses had, suggests that Pole took his mother's death much harder than he or Beccadelli wished posterity to believe.[61] He may further have consoled himself by 'expositions' of some of the Psalms that he had begun earlier in the summer. According to Priuli, he worked through the issues of 'justification, faith, works, [and] law' in them, perhaps as an example to Contarini.[62] These may be the meditations in Vat. lat, 5969 on Psalms 142 and 101, two of the seven penitential psalms, 89–93 and 102.[63] These address the issues Priuli mentioned, along with the importance of experience and God's justice, as they stress Pole's favourite allegorical exegesis and fondness for Paul, especially (as Pole's age thought) the letter to the Hebrews.

'Una certa confabulatione spirituale'

Pole spent the rest of the summer in Capranica and Bagnoregio, some of the time with Colonna.[64] In September he took up residence as legate of the *patrimonium Petri* in Viterbo.[65] His appointment on 13 August may have come almost by chance, an emergency choice, made quickly in order to clear the way for Paul III to leave for Lucca.[66] However that may be, Pole's installation was a major affair. He was formally met at Ronciglione by four notables and at the limits of Viterbo by the *gonfalionere* with one hundred uniformed youths, at the gate of the Dominican monastery of Santa Maria di Gradi by fifteen noble

---

[60] See the introduction to my edition of Beccadelli and *CRP*, no. 339.
[61] See note 58.
[62] BMIC25, fos. 169r–74v.
[63] BAV, Vat. lat. 5969, fos 1br–48r; 55r–118r; 122r–32v; 133 ff., the last of these a dialogue, perhaps with Mary Tudor.

[64] The title of this section comes from Morone. *PM*, 2, pp. 559–60.
[65] *CRP*, nos. 335–6.
[66] Feliciano Bussi, *Istoria della città di Viterbo* (Rome: Bernabò e Lazzarini, 1742), p. 311 and cf. *L&P*, 16, no. 1228.

4 Rocca, Viterbo.

citizens and a large crowd, and then at the San Sisto city gate by all the civil and religious authorities. Thence there was a procession to San Lorenzo, the principal church, and finally to the Rocca (illus. 4), where an artillery salute greeted Pole.[67] Although the legates usually stayed in Palazzo San Sisto, located beside the church of that name, Pole's predecessor Cardinal Corner continued to occupy it until his death in 1543, leaving Pole to stay in the Rocca most of the time.[68]

Although it has been traditional to regard Pole's legation as an officially sanctioned opportunity for withdrawal, he involved himself in the patrimony's

[67] Giuseppe Signorelli, *Viterbo nella storia della chiesa* (Viterbo: 'Unione', 1938–1940; 2 vols.), 2:2, p. 143, from an unknown source.

[68] BMIC25, fos. 186r–7v, 211r–12r and 213r–14r. Cf. *PM*, 3, pp. 149–50n. For Corner's continued presence, AS (BCAV), Riforme 42, fo. 105v. For San Sisto and the Rocca see Andrea Scriattoli, *Viterbo nei suoi monumenti* (Rome: Capuccini, 1915–20),

pp. 224–8 and 306–10. Carnesecchi claimed Pole also stayed at the Dominican convent of Santa Maria in Grado or di Gradi. Massimo Firpo and Dario Marcatto, eds., *I processi inquisitoriali di Pietro Carnesecchi (1557–1567)*, 1, *I processi sotto Paolo IV e Pio IV (1557–1561)* (Vatican City: Archivio Segreto Vaticano, 1998), p. 126.

government, beginning with his *bandi* (ordinances).[69] Some were apparently peculiar to him and all of them display distinctive features.[70] Thus the usual opening prohibition of blasphemy was stricter than in some other regulations, including Paul IV's notoriously draconian ones for Rome.[71] There was to be no work on holidays, nor commerce, nor prohibited games played indoors or out. Many of the regulations concerned measures designed to suppress faction fighting. Only at no. 14 did Pole arrive at the prostitutes which so exercised Pope Paul beginning already in his no. 2. Pole intervened in a number of cases, including a tax dispute with the Apostolic Chamber which he got resolved to the benefit of the Viterbesi, and a major and long-running feud between native shepherds and interlopers, with a similarly positive outcome for the locals.[72] He also took at least some care over the appointment of officials.[73]

Pole did not find his job taxing and left most of the day-to-day business to his vice-legate.[74] As he told Contarini in December, he had to discharge various duties, but not enough 'to cause any impediment to that sweet leisure [*otio*] that I want', to which the administration of justice provided 'a sweet condiment'.[75] Pole guarded his mornings for study, and heard none but extraordinary cases before lunch. There were few of any kind, and they took no more than an hour or two. That left 'the rest of the day [which] I pass with this whole and useful company of Sig. [Pietro] Carnesecchi and our Marcantonio Flaminio. I call it useful, because in the evening Marcantonio feeds me, and the better part of my household, with "that food which does not die", in such manner that I do not know when I have felt greater consolation, nor greater edification.' Only

---

69 The records of the city council (the Riforme) record much activity by Pole. Riforme 40, fo. 114r; 41, fos. 21v, 58v, 69v, 112v; 42, fos 151v, 162v, 165v, 315v–16v; and 43, fo. 199r, a request for Pole's restoration as legate because of the good job he had done. See also *CRP*, nos. 342–3, 346–7, 349, 351–3, 357, 361, 363, 370, 376–7, 380, etc.

70 *CRP*, no. 340. They are discussed briefly in Signorelli, *Viterbo*, p. 153n.

71 ASV, A. A. I–XVIII 6544, fos. 15r–18r.

72 Tax case: AS (BCAV), Riforme 41, fos. 21v, 35v–6r, 47r–52r, etc. Cf. Giuseppe Signorelli, 'Il soggiorno di Vittoria Colonna in Viterbo', *Bolletino storico-archaeologico viterbese*, 1:4 (1908), pp. 118–51, p. 137n and *Viterbo*, p. 153. Sheep: Giuseppe Signorelli, *I diritti d'uso civico nel Viterbese* (Viterbo: Monachi, 1907), but Signorelli there mistook Pole's role and silently corrected his error in 'Colonna', p. 137n.

73 E.g., *CRP*, no. 343.

74 E.g., AS (BCAV), Riforme 40, fo. 122r.

75 Colonna, by contrast, called Pole *occupatissimo* at the same time. *Colonna carteggio*, no. CXLII. Was Pole trying to distance himself from her by feigning pressing business, or was he really 'most busy'?

Contarini was missing.[76] For his part, Contarini faulted Pole and Flaminio for failing to disseminate their goods.[77]

To judge from Pole's words, Flaminio provided spiritual leadership to this assembly. The *Processo Morone*, in which Flaminio was typically called Pole's *cor et anima*, reinforces this impression.[78] The 'cell' Carnesecchi described remained intact for about a year, according to him, with Flaminio taking the lead in reading heretical books, including Calvin's *Institutes*, to which he had introduced Carnesecchi in Florence.[79] Apollonio Merenda emphasized the degree to which Flaminio taught Lutheran doctrine in Viterbo, especially through readings of Matthew, but it was Carnesecchi, not Flaminio, who instructed Merenda in Valdés's ideas.[80] As we have seen, it has been argued that Flaminio was acting as a committed apostle of Valdés, deliberately proselytizing Pole and his household. The chronology of the Valdesian diaspora from Naples at first looks suspicious, even if it is not quite exact.[81] That it began before Valdés's death in July 1541 argues premeditation, but large questions arise whether it resulted from a push or a pull, that is, whether the timing depended on missionary zeal or fear, or whether it reflected a political design.[82] Without having to resolve the question of which set of delations might have touched off the exodus, strong suspicions already swirled around Valdés's Neapolitan circle in 1540 (for Nicolás Bobadilla's accusations, see below). It seems certain that Flaminio's alleged plan had little to do with Contarini's putative isolation after Regensburg.[83]

The argument encounters other difficulties. First, the delay with which two of the principal Valdesians, Flaminio and Carnesecchi, joined Pole undercuts the precision of their 'aim', and Beccadelli claimed that Pole had invited Flaminio to Viterbo (see below). Although they probably left Naples in April, the two did not reach Viterbo until October. In the meantime, they had been in Florence and Flaminio had intended to go to Verona. Perhaps both choices indicate the level of protection sought, in the first case from Cosimo I, in the second from Giberti. Of the group which left Naples together, only Donato Rullo joined Pole some time before May in Rome, although Flaminio and Carnesecchi visited there.[84]

[76] *CRP*, no. 341.
[77] *CRP*, no. 350.
[78] *PM*, 6, p. 290.
[79] *PC*, p. 214; cf. pp. 201, 203, 205. Cf. Carol Maddison, *Marcantonio Flaminio. Poet, humanist, reformer* (London: Routledge and Kegan Paul, 1965), p. 117; Fenlon, p. 91n; Oddone Ortolani, *Per la storia della vita religiosa italiana nel Cinquecento. Pietro*

Carnesecchi (Florence: Le Monnier, 1963), pp. 40–1.
[80] *PM*, 6, pp. 267, 271, 273.
[81] *Alumbrados, passim* but esp. pp. 178–80.
[82] Fragnito, 'Intervento'.
[83] *Ibid.*, p. 73 and see below p. 125.
[84] But they stayed with Gonzaga. Ortolani, p. 31.

Carnesecchi had his suspicions of Rullo's sincerity and took pains to emphasize that he always stood closer to Priuli than to Pole.[85] They were followed by Merenda, formerly Bembo's dependant, and Vettor Soranzo in September and only eventually did Flaminio, together with Carnesecchi, enter Pole's household.[86] Second, other Valdesians targeted Cardinals Gonzaga, Ridolfi, Bembo, and Fregoso, which highlights the breadth and the attractiveness of the whole 'reform tendency', as it dilutes the centrality assigned to Pole.[87] While it seems indisputable that Flaminio was a Valdesian, two more major problems remain for the thesis of planned conversion. One we have already encountered: it explains too much, since Pole had come to hold the central tenets assigned to Valdés some years before coming to Viterbo. This does not necessarily mean that his spirituality was not Valdesian, but even if it were, Flaminio could have done no more than reinforce it in 1541. Pole approved of Flaminio's efforts to translate some of Valdés's works, perhaps already then, but, again, he was more than receptive well before that, and Contarini accepted the same works.[88]

The other objection to Flaminio's hypothetical role in Viterbo is potentially even more important, although it demands unravelling another knotty bit of Pole's self-creation. Placing Flaminio at the head of this circle reverses the relationship that Pole would claim had obtained in the course of his interview with Carafa in 1553. According to Filippo Gheri's report to Beccadelli, Pole told Carafa that 'he [Pole] could not deny that he [Flaminio] could have caused a disturbance when he came into his [Pole's] household, and that he [Pole] in order to remove any scruple, had persuaded him [Flaminio] to read the doctors of the church, and to calm himself with these [or bring himself back calmly to these; *acquetarsi a questi*], seeing [Pole] that [Flaminio] was posing a danger because with his good intellect and judgment that he had in the literary matters in which he was consumed, he could have wished also to make himself master and judge in theological matters, which was dangerous'.[89] Beccadelli may perhaps have drawn on this statement. He certainly made his treatment of Flaminio an instance of Pole's gentle way of dealing with heretics designed to persuade them to re-enter the church.

> If someone by accident found himself in some bad beliefs, he [Pole] sought to retrieve him with charity and not to frighten him with reprehensions and rebukes, saying that sinners [who were] not obstinate nor public were

---

[85] *PC*, pp. 200–1.
[86] *Ibid.*, p. 198.
[87] *Alumbrados*, pp. 177–80.
[88] Firpo, *Sacco*, pp. 99–100; *PC*, p. 535.
[89] *MMB*, 1:2, pp. 349–50.

to be returned with charity to the good road. For example, Messer Marcantonio Flaminio, his old and dear friend, returning from Naples, and having been found coloured with certain not-very-safe beliefs that he had drawn from the conversation of Valdés in Naples, in order to help his friend, whom he knew had a good life and mind, without saying anything about this, he invited him to stay with him in that Viterban leisure, where he then was. Speaking partly of studies of humanities, in which Messer Marcantonio excelled, partly of sacred things, he proceeded with such dexterity that in process of time, making him a member of his household, he made him without dispute understand Catholic truth. He [Flaminio] stayed in healthy and straight doctrine, continuing in which, writing sacred verses, he died a good Christian in the house of his most reverend lordship. He [Pole] used to say that he had done little service for Catholics beyond the benefit of having saved Flaminio, and not let him fall with the heretics, as he might easily have done, among whom he could have done much damage through the easy and beautiful style which he had of writing Latin and the vernacular.[90]

The major difference between these two statements is that Pole did not connect Flaminio's troubles to Valdés as Beccadelli did.[91] This discrepancy makes it likely that Beccadelli based himself not on Pole's talk with Carafa, but on Giovanni Morone's recollection of a conversation with Pole about the alleged heretics in his household. Morone had warned Pole of murmuring about his keeping a disciple of Valdés and Ochino. Pole replied 'I saw this good intellect and good writing of Flaminio, and I feared that he would do a great evil if he became a heretic. I have gone very slowly, pulling him back to the good way, in such fashion that I hope it will have profited the church of God. Therefore those who blame me ought rather to praise me for having done such a deed.'[92] Marie Hallé could be correct that the final lines of Pole's letter to Contarini just cited, in which he noted that everything else was going well, refer to his plans for Flaminio.[93]

Beccadelli's and Morone's stories are probably not independent, and both had motives of self-preservation for putting such a statement into Pole's mouth, as of course did Pole himself. They yet deserve credence, especially given another early visitor to Viterbo, the Jesuit Bobadilla. Pole wrested him away from Ignatius Loyola, Paul III, and Morone. All three had wanted him to go to the

---

[90] Ibid., pp. 326–7.

[91] Pointed out by Fenlon, p. 89, who endorses the argument that Pole was concerned not by Flaminio's adherence to Valdés, but by his Calvinist views of purgatory and penance.

[92] PM, 2, pp. 462–3. Cf. Fenlon, p. 90.

[93] Hallé, p. 289.

Empire, but Pole demanded him for Viterbo where he went for Advent perhaps staying until spring.[94] Pole requested him almost certainly at Colonna's instance.[95] She had met Bobadilla in Ferrara in 1539 and invited him to Naples in 1540 to patch up her brother's failing marriage.[96] While there he may have frequented the same Valdesian circles as Colonna, Flaminio, and Merenda, with whom Bobadilla visited the Neapolitan diocese of Bisignano.[97] If so, they had their differences. According to an anonymous report, Bobadilla attended one meeting at which Valdés himself (called Paolo in the text) lectured on Paul. Bobadilla broke up the gathering by shouting that the speaker lied when he called the pope the Antichrist and then induced the viceroy and the archbishop to chase the heretics.[98] Merenda reported that Bobadilla had preached at Bisignano that works earned salvation, and Carnesecchi had explained that Bobadilla did not understand justification. All the same, Bobadilla had helped to get Merenda his place in Pole's household.[99] Bobadilla specialized at the time in reading the epistles of Paul, and that was what he did in Viterbo, along with preaching and hearing confessions. Pole was very pleased on all scores.[100] The presence of an experienced anti-Valdesian and confessor fits exactly with Beccadelli's story of Pole's rationale. Forty years later Bobadilla claimed that Pole had used him in much that fashion, giving him 'certain suspected books, not his own' to examine before the pope sent him to Germany, that is, probably while in Viterbo.[101] Pole was most annoyed when Loyola reclaimed Bobadilla, writing the general that Bobadilla had just begun to have a positive effect and that 'I would feel great displeasure from it [Bobadilla's withdrawal], when I did not know that, besides obeying our lord [the pope], it were to the greater glory of God, and the greater benefit of his church.'[102] Bobadilla's role, Pole's defence, and Beccadelli's and Morone's statements raise more than a little doubt about who was converting whom. And as Fenlon demonstrates, Flaminio ended up rejecting the more radical implications of his Calvinist reading and came to defend the mass and the church.[103]

The most celebrated product of Pole's and Flaminio's relationship and of the Italian Reformation is the *Tratatto utilissimo del beneficio di Giesù Cristo crocofisso*

[94] Nicolai Alphonsi de Bobadilla, *Gesta et scripta* (Madrid: Lopez del Horno, 1913; MHSI, 46), p. 620, ¶20 and ¶22.

[95] Signorelli, 'Soggiorno', *passim*.

[96] Arthur L. Fisher, 'A study in early Jesuit government: the nature and origins of the dissent of Nicolás Bobadilla', *Viator*, 10 (1979), pp. 397–431, p. 415.

[97] *Alumbrados*, pp. 135ff., 159–62 and 172–3 and *PM*, 1, pp. 241–3.

[98] Bobadilla, *Gesta*, pp. 17–21.

[89] *PM*, 6, p. 273.

[100] *CRP*, no. 344.

[101] Bobadilla, *Gesta*, p. 560.

[102] *CRP*, no. 344.

[103] Fenlon, pp. 90–5.

verso i Cristiani, known as the *Beneficio di Cristo*. Here again the evidence suggests a partnership with Pole in the senior spot. Given the large degree of overlap between *De unitate* and the *Beneficio*, Pole deserves more credit for the work than he has usually received. Firpo obliquely points in this direction by linking its publication (a little conjecturally) to Pole's and Morone's presence in Trent.[104] Boiling the work down to the single point of justification by faith, as Salvatore Caponetto suggests, immediately points to how much it coalesces with Pole's beliefs, although they were scarcely peculiar to him.[105] More indicative is its constant criticism of 'human prudence', one of Pole's principal bugbears.[106] One wonders whether its most extended *exemplum* intended to illustrate 'the whole mystery of the faith' may also have come from Pole. The tale of the king's pardon to his rebels, inspired by the merits of one of the king's kinsmen, seems especially salient to him, whatever it may say about his convoluted relationship with Henry.[107] It will bear remembering that however the *Beneficio* is interpreted – whether as rooted in the possibly heterodox beliefs of Valdés, the certainly heretical ones of John Calvin, traditional Benedictine piety or something else – it ignored institutional religion and the pope, stressing an almost mystical relation between God and the chosen few.[108]

Perhaps the best way to conceive of the process through which the *Beneficio* came into being is to think of it as a collective effort with deep and broad roots.[109] No more than any other of 'Pole's' works does it make sense to attribute it to a single author. Into the summer of 1542 many collaborated in the *Beneficio*'s final revision.[110] At much the same time Flaminio also expounded Matthew and John.[111] The only evidence for his work on the *Beneficio* comes from Priuli's letter of 1 May 1542 to Beccadelli, who along with Galeazzo

---

[104] *Alumbrados*, p. 148 and *Sacco*, pp. 119–45.

[105] Salvatore Caponetto, ed., *Il 'beneficio di Cristo' con le versione del secolo XVI, documenti e testimonianze* (Florence, DeKalb, IL and Chicago: Sansoni, Northern Illinois University Press and The Newberry Library, 1972), p. 475.

[106] *Beneficio*, e.g., pp. 49 and 59.

[107] *Beneficio*, pp. 31–2.

[108] Elisabeth G. Gleason, ed. and trans., *Reform thought in sixteenth-century Italy* (Chico, CA: Scholars Press, 1981), pp. 104–5 provides a concise summary of the work. Carlo Ginzburg and Adriano Prosperi, *Giochi di pazienza. Un seminario*

sul 'Beneficio di Cristo' (Turin: Einaudi, 1975), p. 29 reject hunting for its sources, although they more or less agree about the degree of its coalescence with Benedictine theology and spirituality.

[109] This was Tommaso Bozza's characterization, cited by Ginzburg and Prosperi, p. 40 and then dismissed as 'gratuitous'.

[110] *Beneficio*, p. 471. For the most likely reconstruction of its history, see Ginzburg and Prosperi, pp. 69–70.

[111] BMIC25, fos. 190r–2r and *PC*, pp. 195 and 203; cf. *Alumbrados*, p. 38.

Florimonte had just visited Viterbo.[112] Some of those directly involved besides Pole and Flaminio are known: Carnesecchi and Beccadelli read at least one draft, and Priuli is likely also to have taken a hand.[113] Contarini, who may have meant to refer to the work as one of those 'goods' Pole and Flaminio were hoarding, contributed a major piece. The concern at that moment was Catarino. Pole had sent Contarini a letter about him on 7 April, which raised concerns when it had not yet arrived on the 24th. About the time Priuli learned of its receipt came a suggestion from Contarini that Pole read Bernard on justification. Priuli reported that Flaminio liked the passage so much that he meant to incorporate it in his *libretto* and Priuli judged that it alone would serve as a reply to Catarino.[114] It appeared near the end of the *Beneficio*, the last direct quotation, used to demonstrate the necessity of individual belief in justification.[115] This is crucial information. Not only does it reveal Flaminio's role, but it also highlights Contarini's intervention. The *Beneficio* was attracting a distinguished parentage and work on it served to repair any cracks in the *spirituale* front.[116]

Pole's involvement provides further evidence about the history of the *Beneficio*. For one thing, the timing of his missing letter to Contarini reinforces the supposition that Catarino aimed his criticisms at an earlier version of the *Beneficio* than that published, the work originally of a Benedictine monk, Don Benedetto da Mantova, as revised once already by Flaminio. The work circulated in manuscript, and it may have been through Colonna that a copy came to Catarino's hands.[117] He then launched his first attack on it, which must have followed closely on the heels of his blast against Contarini's actions at Regensburg, *De perfecta iustificatione a fide et operibus liber* (published in both 1541 and 1542).[118] For another thing, Pole's defence may well have been motivated by the fact that he knew both authors, not just Flaminio. He had almost certainly met Benedetto in Venice through Cortese. Benedetto had been Cortese's protégé at San Benedetto Po and followed him when Cortese went to San Giorgio Maggiore, where he may also have met Flaminio.[119] Probably this same Benedetto was in Bologna with Contarini and his nephew Placido as the *Beneficio* underwent final revision.[120] Finally, according to much later testimony,

---

[112] BMIC25, fos. 196r–8r.
[113] Fenlon, pp. 79–80 and *Beneficio*, p. 435.
[114] BMIC25, fo. 197v.
[115] *Beneficio*, pp. 80–1.
[116] *Evan. ital.*, pp. 120 and 139–40 argues that the 'radicals' at Viterbo managed to force Contarini into an accommodation with them in order to end his political isolation, but the evidence suggests much more a process of negotiation between equals.
[117] Ginzburg and Prosperi, p. 69.
[118] *Evan. ital.*, p. 121.
[119] *Beneficio*, pp. 486–7.
[120] BMIC25, fos. 213r–14r (*PM*, 3, pp. 149–50n).

Catarino had aimed his work at Pole, as well as Flaminio, although he had 'suppressed the cardinal's name'.[121] Thus Pole's letter about Catarino suggests that he had gone to the defence of himself, a Benedictine (or two, if we count Cortese who had the very highest opinion of the work), of Flaminio, and of Contarini.[122]

Catarino's criticism marks the cracking of another fault line among the *spirituali*, since he had earlier been an intimate of both Colonna (who attended his thoroughly evangelical sermons in Carafa's company) and of Michelangelo, and had known Contarini in Rome in 1540.[123] Earlier yet, he had been a *piagnone*, another strong link to the *spirituali*.[124] More, Pole would probably have agreed with much of Catarino's attack, from its broadsides against idle speculation in matters theological, to insistence on the distinction between the two kinds of faith that justified. Pole strongly discouraged 'curiosity' in his circle, especially in advice to Colonna warning her to stay away from Luther, Bucer, Calvin and Melanchthon. His further advice to her, remembered by Carnesecchi, that 'she should try to believe as if she should be saved through faith alone, and on the other hand try to act as if her salvation consisted in works' comes close to Catarino's notion of justification, while it stops short of his insistence on the importance of sacramental means of forgiveness.[125] The limits to Catarino's agreement with Pole and the *Beneficio*, the conclusion of which resembles Pole's advice to Colonna, is manifested in Catarino's comment on the end of the *Beneficio*. It is a pure polemic, quite beside the point, motivated by Catarino's emphasis on the penitential system.[126] Other than this, Pole and Catarino differed mainly in style: while the *Beneficio* was written in simple, appealing language, Catarino used the vocabulary of scholastic theology and university debate.[127]

Whatever one makes of the complex spirituality and home-spun theology of

---

[121] *PM*, 6, p. 290.
[122] *Beneficio*, p. 454.
[123] Ulrich Horst, 'Ambrosius Catharinus OP (1484–1553)', in Erwin Iserloh, ed., *Katholische Kontroverstheologen* (Münster: Aschendorff, 1984–8; 5 vols.), 4, p. 111; Romeo De Maio, *Riforme e miti nella chiesa del Cinquecento* (Naples: Guida, 1973), pp. 98 and 107. For Carafa, Colonna and Catarino's preaching, see the documents cited by Fragnito, 'Vittoria Colonna e l'inquisizione', pp. 163–4.
[124] Lorenzo Polizzotto, *The elect nation. The Savonarolan movement in Florence 1494–1545* (Oxford: Clarendon Press, 1994), pp. 165–6, 441–2, and *Evan. ital.*, pp. 19–24 and *passim* for suggestions about the affinities between Savonarola and the *spirituali*.
[125] 'Ella dovesse attendere a credere come se per la fede sola s'havesse a salvare, et d'altra parte attendere ad operare come se la salute sua consistesse nelle opere'. *PC*, p. 268. Cf. Fenlon, pp. 95–6 and 98 where he notes how close Catarino's quotation of Paul's dictate *non plus sapere quam oportet sapere* came to Pole's attitude to curiosity.
[126] *Beneficio*, pp. 83 and 420. Fenlon, p. 96.
[127] This comparison is suggested but not drawn by Fenlon, p. 87.

the *Beneficio*, it was not the only thing Flaminio was writing, nor can Pole's involvement in everything from construction projects to parrying attempted assassinations be ignored. Those other writings reflect a side of Flaminio that the inquisitors overlooked, missing a lead from Catarino. He severely faulted the work's similes, one of the playfully poetic Flaminio's most important contributions.[128] His chosen mode of expression was poetry, pastoral odes and verse epistles, written in Latin. Then again, he also wrote parapharases of scripture, the Psalms above all. Despite the best efforts of serious-minded historians, the fact remains that Flaminio did all these things *at the same time*. To take only one example from near the end of his life, on 4 May 1549 he described a mystical experience of rejuvenation to Caterina Cibò.[129] In another letter of nearly the same date (and certainly before 27 May) Flaminio reported that he had decided to take the advice of Vincenzo Gheri (Cosmo's brother) and finish his collection of verse epistles, including one in which he imagined himself as Pole's lap-dog (see the next chapter). The agonistic dimension of Flaminio's poetry emerges in his resolution to include a *carmen* to Pole's client Marcantonio Faita, who would be annoyed if his companions were honoured with a verse but he was not, as well as one to Trifone Benci out of gratitude for having 'combated' Flaminio's detractors. Besides, Benci could stand to be made fun of.[130] The balance of Flaminio's remaining letters concern his poetry, even if the last surviving letter offered spiritual consolation to Lelio Torelli, an important counsellor of Duke Cosimo.[131] This unstable mix of poetry and piety characterized nearly everyone in Pole's Viterbo circle and the *spirituali* more generally.[132] The case of Priuli's and Carnesecchi's close friend, Francesco Berni, equally notorious as a 'Lutheran' and a writer of scandalous verse, is nearly typical.[133] Perhaps Colonna was the only one of Pole's intimates, with the possible exception of Michelangelo, who fully integrated her religious beliefs and her late poetry. The complexity of the *Beneficio* thus mirrors its authors' complexity. No wonder it has proven so difficult to make sense of a work written by men who thought poetic *lusus* as important as religion.[134]

---

[128] See, e.g., *Compendio d'errori*, in *Beneficio*, pp. 379–80, a criticism of the example of the king who declared an amnesty to rebels. Cf. Maddison, p. 146.

[129] Marcantonio Flaminio, *Lettere*, ed. Alessandro Pastore (Rome: Ateneo & Bizzarri, 1978), no. 59.

[130] *Ibid.*, no. 60.

[131] *Ibid.*, no. 66.

[132] S. Longhi, *Lusus. Il capitolo burlesco nel Cinquecento* (Padua: Antenore, 1983).

[133] T. F. Mayer, 'Nursery of resistance: Reginald Pole and his friends', in Paul A. Fideler and T. F. Mayer, eds., *Political thought and the Tudor commonwealth: deep structure, discourse and disguise* (London: Routledge, 1992), pp. 50–74.

[134] *Ibid.*, p. 55 and see now Anne Reynolds, *Renaissance humanism at the court of Clement VII: Francesco Berni's Dialogue against poets in context* (New York and London: Garland Publishing, 1997).

As Contarini's contribution to the *Beneficio* together with his correspondence with Pole indicates, he gave almost no indication of bad blood between them, not on the personal, political nor theological levels. He continued to send Pole his writings, including a treatise on preaching, and to solicit reaction.[135] Pole, for his part, gave in to Contarini's demands and replied with a treatment of the subject, completely redone after being confronted by Bobadilla's much different ideas. Pole asked for Contarini's assessment.[136] Unfortunately the treatise is lost and little is known of Bobadilla's preaching.[137] At least Colonna once saw the work, but it has otherwise vanished, the only one of Pole's writings of which I have found no trace, not even in the Inquisition's archives in Rome.[138] There may be a clue to Pole's opinion in the *Compendium* of the *Processo Morone*, in which the inquisitors charged that Pole 'wrote a book on the manner and art of preaching' which defended the Lutheran doctrine of justification 'and disapproved scholastic theology and argued that the pure and simple gospel was to be preached'.[139] De' Bartoli's testimony may also help a little. According to him, Pole had frequently had him preach in non-scholastic fashion on justification, saying that he should 'stand on the words of the text'.[140] At another time Pole thought de' Bartoli's Lenten sermons on penance should be jettisoned in favour of the *beneficio di Cristo* and Lutheran justification as the apostles had preached.[141]

Pole and Contarini continued to correspond frequently. Thirteen letters from Pole to Contarini survive from 1542 before Contarini's death in August and Pole referred on 1 May to Contarini's frequent letters. Pole assured Contarini of the pope's goodwill to him in the same letter as he wrote that he had a higher opinion of Cervini, the alleged intransigent, the more he knew him.[142] Even had Pole been reluctant to read Contarini's work, Priuli was not, begging Beccadelli in March 1542 to get a copy of Contarini's 'brief exposition' of Paul as soon as possible. Priuli must have meant the notes published as *Scholia in epistolas Divi Pauli*. As Elisabeth Gleason observes, many of these concerned justification.[143]

---

[135] *CRP*, no. 339, a cover letter for Beccadelli who was to give Pole's opinion orally. *Evan. ital.*, p. 120 and Gleason, pp. 274–5 treat the sending of a messenger as another instance of Pole's refusal to endorse Contarini's views and reluctance to express his opposition, but this was Pole's standard practice from at least 1535.

[136] *CRP*, no. 345.

[137] For the little known about early Jesuit preaching, see John W. O'Malley, *The first Jesuits* (Cambridge: Harvard University Press, 1993), pp. 91–104.

[138] *CPM*, catalogue, no. 11.

[139] *PM*, 1, pp. 197–8.

[140] *PM*, 6, p. 165.

[141] *PM*, 6, p. 202.

[142] *CRP*, no. 354.

[143] Gleason, p. 284.

Did the urgency in acquiring Contarini's work have to do with the polishing of the *Beneficio*? A letter of early May 1542 suggests this, at the same time as it captures Pole's and Contarini's relationship then. This is the letter in which Pole acknowledged Contarini's perhaps unwitting contribution to the *Beneficio*. It opened with praise of Contarini as 'the true image of a servant of Christ in the magistracy'. More important, Pole said he had read Bernard on justification, as Contarini had suggested, and was not surprised that he 'speaks more clearly than the others', since Bernard founded everything on the scriptures, 'which in their interior sense preach nothing other than this justice'. 'Thus if the other adversaries of this truth set themselves to examine [the matter], as it is, that is, through these two rules, of scripture and experience, all controversies would doubtless cease. Now they err, who do not know the scriptures and the power of God which is hidden in Christ' that God was using Contarini as an instrument to reveal.[144] Several points will bear emphasis. First, Contarini suggested Bernard, and second, it does not appear that Pole knew what he had written about justification before this moment. Third, Pole expected Contarini to endorse his hermeneutic, and, finally, he referred to Contarini as God's instrument in terms almost identical to those he used when judging Regensburg. Nothing in Pole's letter indicates any division of opinion. A falling-out might have lain behind the long silence from Bologna in late May and early June, despite several requests from Pole and Priuli to Contarini to let them know what they could do for him on their visit to Rome for Pentecost.[145] In this case the reserve, if such it was, came from Contarini's side, not Pole's.

In mid-year, Contarini and Pole confronted a conflict in Modena between Bishop Morone and the members of its Academy, who increasingly tended toward heresy.[146] Nearly all the important *spirituali* became involved, including Cortese and Sadoleto, both native Modenesi. Once again, Contarini and Pole supposedly took much different positions, and Contarini made this moment a test of his leadership. He drew up a catechism, circulated it widely among the cardinals, and then invited the members of the Academy to sign it. Pole and his circle are said to have sympathized with the Academicians, although both they

---

[144] *CRP*, no. 358. Fenlon, p. 67 quotes Pole's hermeneutic of 'scripture and experience' but implicitly treats the rest of the letter as consistent with Pole's putative negative attitude to Contarini's theology.

[145] *CRP*, no. 359. Cf. BMIC25, fos. 203r–4r and 205r–6r.

[146] The most complete treatment is in *Inq. rom.*, pp. 29–118. Everyone agrees that Modena's heretics put at least a severe strain on Pole's and Contarini's relationship. Cf. even Fragnito, 'Intervento', p. 74.

and Morone tried to make persuasion work.[147] Pole knew many Modenesi, among them Filippo Valentini, and he and Contarini undoubtedly disagreed over tactics.[148] Even before Pole saw the catechism, he had talked to Carafa, Juan Alvarez de Toledo, and Cervini, all 'intransigents', about the situation in Naples and 'the things of Regensburg'.[149] It seemed safer to Pole for Contarini to send the catechism only to the pope who could get Badia's opinion. The other cardinals could then add their private letters to Morone. Pole feared that Sadoleto would be sticky about justification and had suggested that Bembo approach him and ask him to suspend giving his judgment until he could consult Contarini, Cortese, Badia, and Pole, and Sadoleto had apparently agreed.[150] Pole hoped to avoid scandal caused by public disagreements among the cardinals.[151] Had he really wished to contest Contarini's leadership, forcing this issue into the open would have made more sense. Firpo correctly observes that Contarini was trying to avoid fracturing his group, but the nature of that group is much broader than Firpo argues: it included not only the *ala Contariniana*, but three cardinals of the so-called intransigent wing as well. It was Pole, not Contarini, who bent all to hold the *whole* reform tendency together, or at least to avoid a conflict that would tear it apart.

Contarini's was not the only catechism suggested for use in Modena. Morone thought another one was 'written by Messer Flaminio and the Viterbese company'.[152] It has been recently claimed that this represented another initiative by Pole, but there is no evidence for that proposition.[153] Pole certainly stood at the centre of things. Contarini took his advice and sent his catechism only to Badia, perhaps thereby implicitly acknowledging Pole's leadership. Badia in turn

---

[147] *Inq. rom.*, pp. 59 and 67. If Pole were so sympathetic to the Modenesi and so heavily involved in pleading their case, why did none of them know that?

[148] *PM*, 1, p. 331.

[149] The inclusion of Cervini must further reinforce Pole's regard for him, since he was neither an inquisitor nor in any real position to be helpful, except as one of the Farneses' most trusted agents.

[150] Richard M. Douglas, *Jacopo Sadoleto (1473–1547), humanist and reformer* (Cambridge: Harvard University Press, 1959), pp. 158 and 282.

[151] BMIC25, fos. 208r–10r. Cf. *PM*, 3, pp.

146–7n. *Inq. rom.*, p. 70n prints most of Priuli's letter, but gives a somewhat misleading interpretation of Pole's of the same date, saying that he had evaded giving his opinion. Priuli spelled out in great detail how Pole thought the matter should be handled. Pole's suggestion to solicit the most authoritative endorsement possible was also a means to keep the matter 'in house', since Badia was a close ally.

[152] *PM*, 3, p. 145.

[153] Massimo Firpo, 'The Italian reformation and Juan de Valdés', *SCJ*, 27 (1996), pp. 353–64, 361.

passed it to Pole, perhaps further reinforcing his position.[154] Badia's role underwent a major change as well, in which Pole also had a hand. On 12 June he had just been made a cardinal, along with Cortese and Morone.[155] Badia had asked Pole to induce the pope to rescind his appointment, but Pole had done so only as a private person, not as a cardinal, and Paul had replied that the more Badia refused, the more worthy he became. Pole said nothing about Cortese's promotion, although Priuli sounded ecstatic, said it had redoubled Pole's joy, and asked Beccadelli to visit him in Priuli's name. Three weeks later he forwarded Pole's congratulations to Cortese, then with Contarini, apologizing off-handedly that they had grown a little old.[156] Pole's congratulations to Morone got even staler, and his remarks to Contarini at the time of the promotion are puzzling. First, Pole noted a difference of opinion about Morone's candidacy, which meant that it was less easy to see the Holy Spirit at work in his case. Second, he emphasized how easy Badia's selection had been. Finally, Pole reported that Cardinal Farnese had said that the pope had never thought to promote anybody but Badia and Cortese, offering another implicit contrast to Morone.[157] It may be that here is a real political rupture within the *spirituali*, reducing the importance of the great triumph they had just scored. Perhaps Pole blamed Morone for the difficulties the *spirituali* were encountering in Modena, where the Inquisition was about to shoulder aside Pole's cautious approach.[158] Then again, perhaps Morone did not yet belong to the *spirituali*.

Badia held far the most important position among them as a result of the promotion, for he shortly afterwards became a member of the first congregation of the Inquisition, along with Carafa and Alvarez.[159] Pole told Contarini of this development at the same time as he apologized for the delay in sending his comments. It had arisen because Pole had been waiting to use Contarini's

---

[154] *CRP*, no. 369. The catechism is in *PM*, 3, pp. 190–235. Cf. Gleason, pp. 286–90. It may be that Pole passed the catechism to Badia, rather than the other way around, according to an obscure remark of Priuli. BMIC25, fos. 211r–12r.

[155] Simoncelli (*Evan. ital.*, pp. 263–5) could not come up with a political explanation of this promotion, and argued that it surprised the *spirituali*. He claimed this was especially true of Badia's appointment, but this not only does violence to the texts

he cited, but Simoncelli also overlooked Pole's role in Badia's promotion.

[156] BMIC25, fos. 201r–2r and fos. 211r–12r.

[157] *CRP*, no. 360.

[158] *Inq. rom.*, pp. 90–1; cf. Gleason, p. 300.

[159] *Inq. rom.*, p. 89. The other members were Pier Paolo Parisi, Bartolomeo Guidiccione, and Laurerio. See Adriano Prosperi, *Tribunali della coscienza: Inquisitori, confessori, missionari* (Turin: Einaudi, 1996), pp. 39–46.

messenger.[160] Contarini remained calm, and not much put out with Pole. He replied on 22 July with thanks for his reactions. Pole had noted a bad reading, and a misuse of pseudo-Dionysius.[161] Thus Pole must have offered a fairly detailed criticism of Contarini's work, to which Contarini responded jocularly.[162]

Pole's scrutiny apparently focused on article twenty-five covering penance, a subject on which he had made himself an expert while writing *De unitate*.[163] According to Contarini, Pole had said that 'the sinner through Christ is perfectly reconciled with God, and there is no need for our efforts'. If this is an accurate summary, as Contarini protested it was, then Pole did share the 'radical' insistence that justification was by faith *alone*, in contradistinction to double justification. But this was not quite all that Pole had said. He had further spoken of two kinds of offence committed by the sinner, the first against oneself and the second against the church. The first arose from the contravention of 'natural law written in our hearts by God' but unfortunately Contarini did not explain the second.[164] Contarini quickly sent Pole a treatise, 'De poenitentia', asking him to submit it to the judgment of his entire company, including Colonna, and let him know their reactions to his 'imperfect and perhaps strange ideas [*parti*] immediately, making me a participant of the grace that God copiously gives there'.[165]

Pole did not reply at once for any number of good reasons, none of them to do with reservations about Contarini's ideas. Pole told Contarini that he wished he 'could simultaneously play Martha and Mary [that is, live both the active and contemplative lives], as you do through the singular grace of God'.[166] This has been taken to mean that Pole saw insoluble problems in Contarini's ideas, but it is actually the germ of his notion of the ideal magistrate, as spelled out a few years later in *De summo pontifice*, and thus the highest possible praise of Contarini.[167] If they differed over justification, their disagreement did not have political consequences. The most important reason why Pole did not see an urgent imperative to write was the changed situation in Modena, which had

---

[160] *CRP*, no. 369.

[161] *CRP*, no. 372.

[162] Firpo says that Contarini once again took Pole's and Badia's advice in the dénouement, writing Morone the day after his letter to Pole that there was no choice but to hand over to the inquisitors. *Inq. rom.*, p. 90. In fact, Contarini mentioned only Badia. *PM*, 3, p. 136.

[163] *Inq. rom.*, p. 72.

[164] *Evan. ital.*, p. 127 quotes only the first part of Contarini's summary of Pole's views.

[165] Franz Dittrich, *Regesten und Briefen des Cardinals Gasparo Contarini (1483–1542)* (Braunsberg: Huye, 1881), p. 361. For the work, see Gleason, pp. 294–7.

[166] *CRP*, no. 383. Gleason (pp. 297–8) downplays the degree of disagreement between Pole and Contarini, tracing them to personalities rather than politics or doctrine.

[167] *Inq. rom.*, p. 72. See below pp. 177–80.

begun to fade into the background with Contarini's appointment as legate to Spain and Sadoleto's to France.[168] The reform tendency once again held the leading diplomatic posts.[169] Pole also told Contarini the truth when he said that other 'important business had supervened'.[170] There had been two major crises and several minor ones with which he had to deal. The small ones concerned the building of a new prison in Viterbo, as well as the reform of the Franciscan nuns of Santa Rosa, an operation in which Pole asked for and received both Cervini's and Alvarez's co-operation.[171] The first large difficulty arose in the government of the patrimony, where preparations for the defence of Civitavecchia demanded unusual amounts of attention. Pole came up with a creative means of financing the repairs.[172]

The second problem was even more urgent, a concerted effort by English agents to penetrate Pole's household. One Alessandro da Bologna had appeared in Viterbo in company with two youths masquerading as Flemings. Some of Pole's household discovered them to be English and had them imprisoned in the Rocca. Alessandro claimed that he was escorting the two from London to Francesco Casale, brother of Henry's ambassador to Venice. Pole's servants recognized Alessandro as one of the king's couriers, and he gave inconsistent answers when interrogated. Therefore Pole asked Cervini what to do and to investigate Casale's involvement.[173] Cervini replied with information that caught Alessandro in various lies.[174] The pope had told Cervini to tell Pole to keep Alessandro under guard and continue to interrogate him. Pole confessed himself defeated by Alessandro's tergiversations and sent all three to Rome.[175] Alessandro did not stay in prison long. September found him in Venice, and Edmund Harvel, calling him Henry's servant, sent him back to England.[176] This outcome roughly corroborates Beccadelli's and Dudic's story of Pole's

[168] BMIC25, fos. 215r–16r.

[169] *Inq. rom.*, p. 72 regards this as a surprising – and unforeseeable – development.

[170] This claim might seem to be contradicted by Priuli's letter to Beccadelli of 26 June (BMIC25, fos. 211r–12r) which made it sound as if there was nothing more important for Pole to decide than where to spend the summer. This may mean that Priuli, whose incompetence in practical matters we have already seen become the butt of jokes, was not involved in any of Pole's administrative decisions. Surely if Pole had been lying to Contarini, he and Priuli would have concerted their letters, as they almost always did otherwise.

[171] For the prison, BMIC25, fos. 217r–20v; the nuns are discussed in *CRP*, nos. 366 and 382. Cf. Signorelli, *Viterbo*, 2:1, p. 380.

[172] *CRP*, nos. 370 and 376–7.

[173] *CRP*, nos. 374–5.

[174] *CRP*, no. 379.

[175] *CRP*, no. 380.

[176] *L&P*, 17, no. 767.

clemency to three unnamed assassins at Viterbo, although it appears the clemency must have been the pope's or Cervini's. Were Pole clement, this might have represented resistance to the trend to uniform enforcement in the pope's temporal domains, consistent with the views later expressed in *De summo pontifice*.[177]

Pole might naturally have put 'De poenitentia' aside in the face of fears for his safety. He reassured Contarini that he would reply to it as soon as he had time, and had asked the pope not to refrain from making use of or to remove Contarini when he had so much to contribute to the matter.[178] This does sound as if opposition to Contarini's involvement in Modena had arisen, but Pole had done his best to defuse rather than exploit it. When tension arose between Pole and Contarini, it concerned Contarini's request that some of Pole's household staff accompany his legation.[179] At the same time as he rejected Contarini's application in detailed fashion through Priuli, Pole summarily refused it in his own letter, apparently meaning to say that he needed his servants to keep himself safe, and again told Contarini that he needed more time to form an opinion of his work. Besides, it would be better to talk about it, just as Pole hoped soon to talk to Sadoleto, as he did about a week later.[180]

He never had the chance to do that with Contarini, who died on 24 August. Beccadelli sent frequent bulletins on his declining health, which Priuli said grieved Pole more than any similar news ever had. Pole had consoled himself that reports of the deaths of his brother, More, Fisher, and his mother had all proved premature and perhaps that would happen in Contarini's case, and he continued to hope for the best and to try to cheer up Colonna.[181] Colonna wrote Contarini's sister that Pole had been Contarini's 'singular, intimate and truest friend, and more than brother and son' whose usual imperturbable reaction to deaths of those near to him had broken down in this case, so much so as to make it appear that the Holy Spirit had abandoned him.[182] Just now things become murky. For one thing, some of Priuli's letters are missing.[183] One of

---

[177] Paolo Prodi, *Il sovrano pontefice. Un corpo e due anime: la monarchia papale nella prima età moderna* (Bologna: Il Mulino, 1982), translated by Susan Haskins as *The papal prince, one body and two souls: the papal monarchy in early modern Europe* (Cambridge: Cambridge University Press, 1988), p. 148.

[178] *CRP*, no. 383.

[179] BMIC25, fo. 223r–v.

[180] *CRP*, no. 384; BMIC25, fo. 221r. For Sadoleto's movements, see also BMIC25, fo. 227r.

[181] BMIC25, fos. 225r–v and 229r–v.

[182] *Colonna carteggio*, no. CXLVII.

[183] E.g., BMIC25, fo. 223r–v, referring to a letter of the day before, no longer extant. Another letter from Pole to Beccadelli, known in the eighteenth century, has since disappeared. *CRP*, no. 385.

these asked Beccadelli to keep close Pole's and Colonna's last letters to Contarini about the catechism, a request repeated on 27 August.[184] Priuli also began to express concerns about the post.[185] Although they quickly evaporated, more care over messengers was taken in both Bologna and Viterbo.[186] What anyone in Viterbo might finally have said about the catechism can rest only on supposition.

Pole and Priuli stepped into the void left by Contarini's death and did their best to provide for his dependants. They did not succeed with Beccadelli, whom Priuli could not induce to come to Viterbo.[187] He ultimately chose service with Cervini as his vicar in Reggio Emilia, but there is no sign that anyone in Viterbo knew of that option before he told them of his appointment.[188] Beccadelli's hesitations and the new degree of caution in Viterbo both arose from Ochino's flight. Ochino, widely praised by the *spirituali* as a preacher and especially close to Colonna, in mid-August stopped at Bologna to see Contarini on the way to Geneva.[189] According to Ochino, Contarini had admitted to believing in justification by faith, and Ochino claimed that the cardinal had been poisoned in consequence.[190] Giberti was yet more damningly implicated in Ochino's flight.[191] Ochino was preaching in Verona when he received orders to return to Rome. Giberti had informed Gonzaga on 28 August that after Ochino left Verona and went to Florence he had refused those orders but had waited until 1 September to let Cardinal Farnese know. Giberti protested complete innocence of Ochino's intentions. Whatever transpired in Bologna and whatever Giberti knew (and it seems certain that Ochino had told him his plans), Ochino put Colonna and Pole almost as directly on the spot by writing from Florence on 22 August, announcing his decision to leave rather than 'preach Christ in a

---

184 BMIC25, fos. 231r–2r. Cf. *Inq. rom.*, p. 73.

185 BMIC25, fo. 223r–v. Simoncelli, *Caso*, p. 30n treats this letter (with incorrect date and reference) as evidence of a generalized surveillance of the Viterbo circle.

186 See e.g., BMIC25, fos. 213r–14r (cf. *PM*, 3, pp. 149–50n).

187 BMIC25, fos. 249r–v and 251r–4r.

188 Gigliola Fragnito, *In museo e in villa: Saggi sul Rinascimento perduto* (Venice: Arsenale, 1988), pp. 84 and 104 and BMIC25, fos. 263r–5v.

189 For Ochino's relations with Colonna see Ranieri, 'Carteggio Bembo-Colonna',

pp. 141–9 and Emidio Campi, *Michelangelo e Vittoria Colonna: un dialogo artistico-teologico ispirato da Bernardino Ochino* (Turin: Claudiana, 1994), part 1. I am grateful to Dr Campi for sending me a copy of his book.

190 Gigliola Fragnito, 'Gli "spirituali" e la fuga di Bernardino Ochino', *Rivista storica italiana*, 84 (1972), pp. 777–811, pp. 791–3.

191 Adriano Prosperi, *Tra evangelismo e controriforma: G. M. Giberti (1495–1543)* (Rome: Edizioni di Storia e Letteratura, 1969), pp. 312–16 and Fragnito, 'Fuga', pp. 781–2.

masquerade and jargon' and asking for their judgment of his action.[192] The man who persuaded him to leave Italy was Vermigli who shortly afterwards also escaped, writing Pole beforehand.[193] It has been traditional to see the reorganization of the Roman inquisition – in train already for a year and taking a large step in June towards its formalization in July in *Licet ab initio* – as a danger signal of the first magnitude to the *spirituali*.[194] While this may be putting the cart before the horse, its existence undoubtedly intensified the threat posed by Ochino and Vermigli. The *spirituali*, already suffering from the death of one of their most prominent leaders and perhaps from the troubles in Modena, now began to face the Inquisition.

Ochino's and Vermigli's cases produced almost immediate results and helped to refocus the Inquisition's attention from Modena and Lucca to Viterbo, where Flaminio served as pre-eminent attraction. On 2 September the Mantuan ambassador in Rome reported to Gonzaga, who was as much incriminated in Ochino's disobedience as anyone else, that rumours were going around concerning 'some little things [*qualche cosetta*] about Flaminio and the others who are at Viterbo with the cardinal of England, about which the good laugh'. The link to Naples and Valdés had raised suspicions, but there was only 'a good opinion' about 'those of Viterbo'. Nevertheless, the deputies of the Inquisition and Alvarez in particular investigated *minutissimamente*.[195] Colonna was already under surveillance from Rome (not by the Inquisition) because of her brother's misdeeds, and Farnese knew the content of some of her correspondence.[196] Pole

---

192 *Colonna Carteggio*, no. CXLVI.

193 The letter is lost. Martire almost certainly knew Pole in Padua, may have spent some time with him in Rome in late 1536 and had perhaps counted on Pole's protection when he was in trouble for preaching Paul in Naples in 1540. Pole had certainly wished to have Martire in Rome then. He may also have kept in touch with the circle of Viterbo while in Lucca. Philip McNair, *Peter Martyr in Italy. An anatomy of apostasy* (Oxford: Clarendon Press, 1967), pp. 133–7, 166, 171–2, 191, 284–5, and 289.

194 *Inq. rom.*, p. 89n. *Evan. ital.*, pp. 45ff. esp. 51 virtually removes any significance of *Licet ab initio* by the argument that the practices and attitudes it embodied had already been in place for years.

195 Edmondo Solmi, 'La fuga di Bernardino Ochino secondo i documenti dell'Archivio Gonzaga di Mantova', *Bollettino senese di storia patria*, 15 (1908), pp. 23–98, p. 51. Simoncelli (*Caso*, pp. 30–2; the same point in *Evan. ital.*, p. 51) confuses matters by, for example, quoting a dispatch of 2 September after Ochino had fled as if it applied to the situation at the time of *Licet ab initio* six weeks earlier. Cf. Fragnito, 'Fuga', pp. 785–6 and 784–5 for Gonzaga.

196 Simoncelli, *Caso*, p. 31 who greatly magnifies the significance of this episode and tries to make it part of a general plot against the *spirituali*. He also suggests that there could have been spies in Pole's household, and points to Thomas Goldwell because he later became a Theatine. As Fragnito shows, the

advised Colonna to send Cervini whatever she had from Ochino, which she hastened to do as soon as it arrived.[197] Since Cervini was not yet an inquisitor, this simultaneously suggests that Pole was not much worried about the Inquisition (had he been, he might have recommended Badia) and reinforces Pole's earlier high opinion of Cervini.[198] They had co-operated since 1540, had worked especially closely throughout the summer of 1542 on Pole's problems in Viterbo, and continued to operate together in papal service.[199] Given Cervini's high standing in the curia, he was a natural choice. Unfortunately, nothing is known of Cervini's attitude to Pole's advice or how Colonna executed it. It may be that Cervini and Colonna did not get along.[200]

The first session of Trent

Later inquisitors made a coherent story of the sequel to this summer in Viterbo, the next big step in the history of the *spirituali*, the opening of the council of Trent.[201] They linked the two through Pole's and Flaminio's 'seduction' of Morone, which was supposed to have happened as Pole and Morone, both legates to the council, travelled north. The accusation came originally from G. B. Scotti.[202] He called himself a close friend of Catarino, from whom he got some of his information. Catarino in turn had it from Pietro Gelido, who claimed to have got true religion from Pole and to know that Morone had as well. The rest of Scotti's highly circumstantial account came from the 'Lutherans' in Modena. Flaminio had taken the lead, badgering, even 'battling', Morone, throwing him to the ground, until he had finally given in. Pole acted as judge between them and confirmed Flaminio's opinions.[203] The fisticuffs are not the only unlikely part of this tale, which almost certainly over-plays

Theatines were the first to attack Ochino and Vermigli ('Fuga', p. 778), but there is no sign that Goldwell was a spy, nor, if I am correct about Pole's relations to the early Theatines, is there any reason why he or any of them should have been.

[197] *Colonna Carteggio*, no. CXLIX. Cf. Fenlon, p. 73, who does not take note of the time between Ochino's flight and this letter.

[198] He did not join the commission until 1546 at the earliest. Hudon, p. 121.

[199] BMIC25, fos. 268r–9v.

[200] Hudon, pp. 119–20 citing unpublished work of Concetta Bianca.

[201] Fenlon does as well by arguing (pp. 98–9) that Pole thought the only solution to doctrinal disagreements was a general council, but there is little evidence for that proposition before Pole took part in Trent in 1545.

[202] See *PM*, 6, pp. 144–5.

[203] See *PM*, 6, pp. 133–4 (replacing 2:1, p. 245); 6, pp. 221–32 (greatly amplifying 2, pp. 349–51); and 2:2, p. 754.

Flaminio's role and makes the internal situation of the *spirituali* appear more tense than it was. Some later interpretations further downplay the contingency in this moment.[204] While Morone's diplomatic experience and championship of Trent as the council's site made him an easy choice as legate, Pole was a surprise.[205] He had attended a consistory in early October in which Priuli expected that the former jurist Pierpaolo Parisi, Badia, and Morone would be named legates, along with Pietro Bertano, bishop of Fano whom he thought would shortly be named a cardinal. None of that had happened, and Pole had returned to Viterbo with other unnamed cardinals.[206] The news of his appointment came on the 18th, forwarded by Flaminio.[207] Priuli described it a few days later as 'unexpected and unforeseen', and noted that Pole's appointment came a day after the other two.[208]

Parisi and Morone stopped in Viterbo long enough to plan their itinerary. Morone was making his second visit to Viterbo within a month. On both occasions Priuli noted that Pole was very taken with him.[209] This time Priuli reported that Pole 'is more than *affetionato*' to Morone 'for the great grace of God that he has discovered in him in these few days'.[210] They left with Colonna's blessing on 'such a union with the chain of true peace'. Colonna, worried about ambushes, asked Morone to protect Pole, but this time he did not need help.[211] The metaphor Colonna used to describe the pair, Tobias and his guide, would recur in Pole's self-image. Morone recollected more or less accurately that although he and Pole had entered Trent together, they had not travelled in company.[212] They made their ceremonial entrance on 21 November.[213]

On the face of it, nothing much happened in Trent. The prince-bishop Madruzzo greeted the legates, and Pole found his Paduan friend Tommaso Sanfelice in charge of local arrangements.[214] It was probably now that Pole came to know Tommaso Campeggi, a leading curialist, with whom he maintained excellent relations.[215] Pole and most of his party lodged in what Priuli called the 'Rocca', probably the Castello del Buonconsiglio.[216] The most important

---

[204] *Inq. rom.*, p. 114.
[205] Hubert Jedin, *Storia del concilio di Trento*, 1, 3rd ed., trans. G. Cecchi and O. Niccoli (Brescia: Morcelliana, 1987), p. 519.
[206] BMIC25, fos. 251r–4r.
[207] *CRP*, no. 391.
[208] BMIC25, fos. 260r–1r.
[209] BMIC25, fo. 249r–v.
[210] BMIC25, fos. 260r–1r; cf. *Inq. rom.*, p. 114.
[211] Sergio M. Pagano and Concetta Ranieri,

eds., *Nuovi documenti su Vittoria Colonna e Reginald Pole* (Vatican City: Archivio Vaticano, 1989), p. 137 and *PM*, 2, pp. 1066 and 705–6.
[212] *PM*, 2:1, p. 556; cf. for confirmation 4, pp. 402, 407–8, 422–3 and 6, pp. 133–34 (2:1, p. 245).
[213] *CRP*, no. 397.
[214] *Ibid.*
[215] See, e.g., nos. 355, 408 and 413.
[216] BMIC25, fos. 263r–5v.

moment in his public activities came when the legates met the imperial ambassadors, including Granvelle. This may have been when Pole first met Granvelle's son, Antoine, a major figure in the rest of his career.[217] Having fallen ill, Pole left Trent before 20 February for Treville.[218] Farnese summoned him to Bologna to consult about the council on 3 May.[219]

In private things were different. Pole may first have met many persons of evangelical leanings, including Pietro Antonio di Capua, archbishop of Otranto together probably with his secretary, Guido da Fano, who had once been set to spy on Pole but now shared his beliefs.[220] Di Capua may well have been part of Pole's inner circle in Trent. He must have been close to Morone, since they were virtually the only prelates present in Trent who argued in favour of keeping the council in session as a means of preserving Germany for the church.[221] Pole's influence was alleged to have extended through Di Capua to a circle of Neapolitans, including Giovanni Battista Perez and Vincenzo Abate, both Giulia Gonzaga's dependants and thus means of cementing Pole's long-distance links to her, originally fostered by Colonna.[222] More immediately at Trent itself, the preacher Andrea Ghetti da Volterra numbered among Morone's, di Capua's, Madruzzo's, and Pole's clients. Denounced by Dionigi Zannettini (Il Grechetto) in 1543, Volterra had a run-in with him at Morone's table almost as serious as Sanfelice's, which cost him attendance at the council.[223] Morone refused to intervene to prevent Volterra from expressing disrespect to Grechetto's episcopal office. While in Trent, Volterra lectured publicly on the Ten Commandments, according to Merenda, after the fashion of Valdés, Flaminio, and Carnesecchi.[224] It was then rumoured that he 'held the opinion that Cardinal Pole held and those others about justification'.[225] In 1548, Pole

[217] *CRP*, no. 401 and Jedin, *Concilio*, 1, pp. 523–7.

[218] *PM*, 2, p. 1075n and *CT*, 4, p. 328n; cf. J. V. Pollet, ed., *Julius Pflug, Correspondance* (Leiden: Brill, 1969; 5 vols.), 2, p. 436.

[219] *CRP*, no. 349.

[220] Andrea Gardi, 'Pietro Antonio di Capua (1513 – 1578). Primi elementi per una biografia', *RSLR*, 24 (1988), pp. 262–310, p. 272 says nothing specifically about his time with Pole at Trent. For da Fano, see Aldo Stella, 'Guido da Fano eretico del sec. XVI al servizio dei re d'Inghilterra', *Rivista di storia della chiesa in Italia*, 13 (1959), pp. 196–238, p. 204.

[221] Jedin, *Concilio*, 1, pp. 537–9.

[222] *PM*, 6, pp. 428–30.

[223] Gottfried Buschbell, *Reformation und Inquisition in Italien um die Mitte des XVI Jahrhunderts* (Paderborn: F. Schöningh, 1910), p. 97; *PM*, 6, p. 335 (cf. 2, p. 849); 1, pp. 254–6. For Sanfelice, Hubert Jedin, *Storia del concilio di Trento*, 2, 2nd ed., trans. Giulietta Basso and Igino Rogger (Brescia: Morcelliana, 1974), pp. 210 and 220–2; *CT*, 5, p. 240; and *PM*, 1, pp. 317–18.

[224] *PM*, 6, p. 273.

[225] Massimo Firpo, *Gli affreschi di Pontormo a San Lorenzo: Eresia, politica e cultura nella Firenze di Cosimo I* (Turin: Einaudi, 1997), p. 233.

continued to back Volterra, along with Gonzaga, although Volterra rejected their efforts to induce him 'to try hard and to force himself not to give scandal to the multitude'.[226]

Pole's agreement with Morone about Volterra marked only one point of an increasingly profound understanding between them. Whatever may have transpired on the journey to Trent, Pole and Morone spent a great deal of time together once they arrived. Already at the end of December, Colonna replied to a letter from Morone in terms which indicate that he must have praised Pole's spirituality. Colonna contrasted her difficulty in understanding Pole to Morone's 'almost as quick as possible acceptance'. Morone had wished to be recalled from Trent, but without being separated from Pole, which made Colonna especially happy because Pole's and Morone's new relationship would serve to shield her from Priuli's and other's criticism that her 'slavery' to Pole was 'pride, too maternally carnal and such things'.[227] Although it would require more than ordinary historical criticism to get to the bottom of what Colonna meant, it may be that here lies an important tension within the *spirituali* beyond anything yet proposed. At the least, Priuli and Colonna did not get along. Colonna's reference to Priuli as 'Giesi' (or Gehazi, the prophet Elijah's servant) acting under her Elijah's (Pole's), orders, seems to reflect her esteem for him only in so far as he was firmly subordinated to Pole.[228] Two years later she suggested to Morone that he should call Priuli to Bologna for a year 'in order that, uncovering a piece of his so-well concealed flesh, he would be content through his absence to become a little fatter and livelier than he seems now'.[229] No one has succeeded in deciphering this allusion, but its edge seems plain enough, especially since the proposed plan would have separated Priuli from Pole. Morone's explanation of Colonna's strange phrase made it an allegory of the fact that Priuli 'was staying with the cardinal [Pole] demonstrating that he loved him spiritually'.[230] Not very far between the lines it looks as though Colonna and Priuli were at a minimum accusing each other in good Pauline fashion of being carnal rather than spiritual, but this interpretation only scratches the surface. It may be that this all refers to the proceedings at Trent and Priuli's reactions to them, but it is difficult to say.[231] Then again, her letter may have nothing to do with Trent, but rather with the dynamics of her, Pole's, and Priuli's relationship.

---

226 Buschbell, pp. 281 and 97.
227 Pagano-Ranieri, pp. 139–42 and *PM*, 2, pp. 1068–71.
228 Pagano-Ranieri, pp. 155–8. The biblical reference is 2 (or 4) Kings 4:8ff.
229 Pagano-Ranieri, pp. 164–6.

230 *PM*, 2:2, p. 708.
231 Fenlon (pp. 213–16) offers the most detailed reading, but in perhaps too literal and theological terms as a function of Trent's decree on justification.

Thus it may have been over-interpreted and the moment made too fraught on anything other than a personal level.

The next step in this intense tricornered relationship once again concerned Modena. Pole (or perhaps Priuli or Flaminio) recommended the Dominican de' Bartoli to Morone at the end of 1542 as a preacher there.[232] De' Bartoli recalled that Pole had written Colonna, ordering him to go to Modena some time in 1543, perhaps to preach Lent.[233] De' Bartoli was close enough to Pole and Morone to appear as one of the first witnesses to Morone's 'conversion' and to Carnesecchi's talk of justification in Viterbo.[234] He had also been one of a coterie of Dominicans in Viterbo grilling Pole about doctrine. Its leaders were Tommaso de' Rossi and Dionigi Tornaquinci, and the others included de' Bartoli's 'companion', Giovanni Grisostomo (a particular target of Priuli and Flaminio, according to Carnesecchi), Angelo Cattani da Diacceto, and Tommaso Buoninsegna, with 'fratrem Marianum', like Buoninsegna, from Siena.[235] De' Rossi had once told Pole that the Lutheran doctrine of justification (or perhaps of confession) was an error because of its consequences, and Pole had replied that consequences did not matter if the doctrine were true.[236] Pole's works went around this circle as well and De' Bartoli had read one about justification.[237] Perhaps also in Viterbo Pole had objected to another Dominican about scholastic expositions of justification, particularly Aquinas's.[238] This kind of behaviour would in retrospect seem especially incautious, and resonated in certain Dominican circles later.[239] Now it reinforces the strength of Pole's position and his lack of concern about his beliefs.

Before Colonna next wrote Morone, Pole left for Treville. That news greatly worried her, so much that she could not immediately answer Morone, nor even enjoy his 'testimony against Messer Alvise' about her relationship with Pole. As incredible as some of Colonna's earlier statements is her assurance to Morone that whatever he wrote her 'is born from another breath than yours', making of Morone almost Pole's ventriloquist's dummy. This was in part her response to the fact that Morone had raised the stakes in this family romance and told her that he had been 'father, mother, and all the spiritual duties together' during

---

[232] *PM*, 2:1, pp. 469 and 538 and 2:2, p. 725n.

[233] *PM*, 6, p. 293 (2:2, p. 715; cf. 1, p. 193); *PM*, 2:2, p. 647; and *PM*, 1, p. 198. Cf. Pagano-Ranieri, pp. 143–4.

[234] *PM*, 6, pp. 199 and 168 (cf. 2:1, p. 264) for Morone.

[235] *PM*, 1, pp. 343, 187, 194, 196 and 264; Signorelli, *Viterbo*, 2:2, p. 222 n62; *PM*, 6,

pp. 169, 159, 199, 235n. For more on Buoninsegna and Grisostomo, see *Processi ... Carnesecchi*, pp. 126–7.

[236] *PM*, 6, pp. 163–4, 262–5 and 216.

[237] *PM*, 6, pp. 169, 172–3.

[238] *PM*, 6, pp. 163 and 201.

[239] E.g., *PM*, 6, pp. 216 and 263–4.

Pole's illness. Colonna doubted that 'a single subject' could do all this, although she assured Morone that she was not trying to claim a more privileged standing with Pole.[240] From the sound of Colonna's next letter, Pole must have been in Treville at this time. Then, on 20 May, she described a contest in humility between them, with Morone claiming that everything he did for Pole was of no significance, and Pole responding that he could never repay Morone, no matter how minor the service rendered. She consoled Morone for being alone in Trent with the thought that he and Pole were the same, 'heated by the same virtue', while she was literally left out in the cold.[241]

Morone had been left behind when Pole went to Bologna. The day after Pole arrived on 10 May a consistory debated whether to withdraw the other legates.[242] This was the sum total of his official business in Bologna. He quickly turned back to Morone, at the same time taking perhaps the most crucial step on the way to becoming an *inglese italianato*, learning Italian. He first wrote Morone a letter that he considered very crude. When Morone 'honoured' it with a reply, this emboldened Pole to write another. He was still diffident enough to ask Priuli to write a cover letter.[243] Pole apologized and wrote that 'my prudence' – with which he carried on a dialogue throughout the letter – advised him that he had made a big mistake in sending 'that my so badly written, inept and barbarous letter'. He had done it in order to have another chance to 'experience [*experimentare*] your Christian goodness'. Writing in this fashion was behaving as if someone had 'sent a stable-boy, shoeless and without clothes, who at great pains had covered what is not honest to see'. This letter, like his first attempt, still 'did not have such decorum' as was needed. Now Pole was moved to write because discussing with Morone 'the things of God' outweighed prudential reservations. Apologizing again for his crude style, Pole converted his failing in 'the care of letters' (*cultu literarum*) into a remedy against pride. Only at the very end did Pole get to the point of offering advice about Morone's 'internal combats' which led to consolation. That needed another letter, although Pole did say that their incidence varied greatly among 'the servants of God'. Since Morone had so many, this argued not imperfection but 'a more perfect and mature spiritual age'.

In his second letter Pole took up the theme, after a fashion.[244] He reassured Morone that God never deserted any spirit that asked for help, since souls were 'brides of Christ'. Christ had promised 'a glorious company . . . to that soul

---

[240] Pagano-Ranieri, pp. 145–6.
[241] Pagano-Ranieri, pp. 147–8.
[242] Jedin, *Concilio*, 1, p. 534.

[243] *CRP*, no. 403.
[244] *CRP*, no. 405.

which feels the desire for a spouse'. Solitude hid the Spirit, an effect of 'that abyss of our shadows caused by sin'. Sin's effects blocked out not only the sun, but the true light 'that penetrates all'. The Spirit intended this in order to curb 'the infinite malice of our pride', the source of all trouble. Pole feared that his barbarous writing was getting in the way, but continued anyway, since Morone had put up with his wretched Italian in their conversations.

This letter made two highly important points. The first is Pole's implicit view of the church. Instead of the Pauline metaphor of it as the bride of Christ, Pole substituted the individual soul. Granted, that soul would have 'a glorious company' but only once it by itself had become Christ's bride. This seems to mean that the institutional church was of no more importance to Pole than it was to the other framers of the *Beneficio*. The soul's direct relationship with God, cast in the most intimate metaphor Paul could devise, was much more (exclusively?) significant. Second, the intensity of Pole's tie to Morone mirrored this direct relationship with God and was so strong as to bring Pole to communicate with Morone in Italian, despite the fact that they both could have used Latin (Pole still did at crucial moments) and Pole had apparently got along just fine almost exclusively in that language for the better part of his fifteen years in Italy. Was this a sign of the humility Colonna emphasized in their relationship? Was the metaphor of the naked stable boy in part an emblem of both their relationship and also of humility?

Priuli sent the second letter to Colonna, who pronounced it the finest thing Pole had written.[245] Without too much ado, she turned it around and used it as another shot in her feud with Priuli, arguing that her overwhelming temptation to see Pole was a sign that she, like Morone, had 'the spirit of God'. She defended her 'affection' for Pole by likening it to faith, 'receiving absolutely from God as much as he [Pole] does'. In July Colonna wrote Pole another letter, again defending herself for wishing to see him so much, because talking to him brought her closer to Christ. Pole's writings served 'to turn the sword of the word against any of our confidence, and make my soul be on wings, certain to fly to the desired nest'.[246] Colonna closed the first of these letters with news of another member of their circle, Michelangelo, who was then painting the Capella paolina in the Vatican. This part of the letter is corrupted, but according to one reading, Colonna was trying to broker an exchange of two objects, which may have been works of Michelangelo's belonging to Pole and Flaminio.[247]

Colonna's close ties to Michelangelo have recently been traced to religious

---

[245] Pagano-Ranieri, pp. 149–51.
[246] Pagano-Ranieri, pp. 153–5.
[247] I here follow Ranieri's text, p. 151.

roots, embodied in Michelangelo's drawing of the crucifixion for her.[248] This new kind of presentation drawing, intended as a pure gift for which Michelangelo expected nothing in return, has further been connected to the *spirituale* view of gratuitous salvation.[249] The radical difference in Michelangelo's practice at first confused Colonna who did not understand that she was not expected to reciprocate. Eventually she learned her lesson, faulting Pole for the 'strange custom which has him accept any present with the very poorest grace', thus completing the triangle between herself, Michelangelo, and Pole.[250] Colonna's favourite preacher Ochino may have inspired the Christocentric image in Michelangelo's drawing.[251] Pole's involvement in the disposition of another such work suggests a similar degree of intimacy between him and Michelangelo as between Michelangelo and Colonna. Gonzaga asked Pole either to induce Colonna to give up her drawing or to have Michelangelo make another for him.[252] This degreee of influence with Michaelangelo accords with the fact that both Michelangelo's early biographers put Pole high on the list of his friends.[253] Michelangelo's poetry reflects as personal and idiosyncratic a religion as Pole's, and Michelangelo placed a high value on the Bible and had been a Savonarolan.[254] Although a great deal more remains to be done, the general link between Savonarolans and *spirituali* sketched by Simoncelli and the specific one between Michelangelo and the Viterbo circle hypothesized by Maria Calí point to part of the tie between Pole and Michelangelo.[255] Possibly Pole's prominence in curial and *spirituale* circles first drew him to Michelangelo's attention. Then again, they had many friends in common, perhaps especially Bartolomeo Stella, whose ties to Michelangelo went back years, and Carnesecchi and almost certainly Priuli during his days in Rome had been

---

[248] Michael Hirst, *Michelangelo and his drawings* (New Haven: Yale University Press, 1988), pp. 117–18.

[249] Alexander Nagel, 'Gifts for Michelangelo and Vittoria Colonna', *Art bulletin*, 79:4 (1997), pp. 647–8, esp. pp. 647 and 650.

[250] *PM*, 6, p. 430.

[251] Campi, pp. 1–77.

[252] ASM:AG, 1915, fos. 587r–8v (*CT*, 10, p. 584) and *Colonna Carteggio*, no. CMLXVI. It is possible that Pole had earlier been enlisted as broker with Michelangelo by Colonna, but the syntax of her letter is almost impossible to decode. *CRP*, no. 407.

[253] Ruggero Beltarini and Paola Barocchi,

eds., Giorgio Vasari, *Le vite de' più eccellenti pittori scultori e archittetori* (Florence: Sansoni, 1966), 1:1, p. 109 and Ascanio Condivi, *The life of Michelangelo*, in Charles Holroyd, *Michael Angelo Buonarroti . . . with translations of the life of the master by his scholar, Ascanio Condivi* (London: Duckworth, 1903), p. 84.

[254] Giorgio Spini, 'Policità di Michelangelo', *Rivista storica italiana*, 76 (1964), pp. 557–600.

[255] *Evan. ital.*, ch. 1 and Maria Calí, *Da Michelangelo all'Escorial. Momenti del dibattito religioso nell'arte del Cinquecento* (Turin: Einaudi, 1980), esp. ch. 4.

close to Michelangelo, as had Beccadelli, and so on.[256] It may be that Michelangelo introduced Pole to his student and Pole's possible client Marcello Venusti.[257] Even more significant, perhaps through Michelangelo Pole came to know his collaborator Sebastiano del Piombo, who probably painted his portrait of Pole just about now (see chapter 9).

Colonna hoped that Pole would come back to Viterbo from Bologna, but he may not have managed to escape until after Colonna left for Rome in November.[258] Instead of seeing Pole in person, Colonna received another letter of advice. Pole told Colonna that women need have no fixed role, and she was therefore grateful to have been set up at his right hand. She continued to liken Pole to Christ.[259] Christ's vicar on earth had almost as much use for Pole as Colonna did. As Priuli told Beccadelli, Pole's actions depended on the pope's wishes, and neither is very clear for the rest of the year.[260] The pope certainly made good use of Pole as consultant on imperial religious affairs. Once back in Rome, Pole hoped to go to Viterbo, but both ill health and ongoing negotiations with the emperor kept him back, especially over the 'recess' of Speyer, news of which had reached Rome on 4 June.[261] Pole was appointed to a commission to draft the papal response with Marcello Crescenzi and Cortese, by then or shortly thereafter an inquisitor.[262] Various drafts, including a very severe one, were discarded before Flaminio polished the final version. It remained strongly worded, accusing the emperor of both breaking his promise and also trying to settle religious affairs without the pope. The text reached a wide audience in the empire, mainly through unofficial channels, but fortunately for papal policy, it was overtaken by the peace of Crépy, signed on 18 September.[263] Pole helped write a temperate letter of congratulations. In addition, the text rehearsed papal efforts to summon a council, but in the version in Pole's papers, anyway, did not convoke another.[264]

---

[256] For Stella, G. Poggi, P. Barocchi and R. Ristori, eds., *Il carteggio di Michelangelo* (Florence: Sansoni, 1979; 5 vols.), 4, nos. MCLXXIII and MCLXXV; 5, nos. MCCXXIX, MCCXLVII, and MCCLXVIII for Beccadelli. For Carnesecchi, Calì, p. 131.

[257] Giorgio Vasari, 'Di diversi artefici italiani', in *Le Vite dei più eccellenti pittori, scultori e architetti*, ed. Maurizio Marini (Rome: Newton, 1991), p. 1333 and T. F. Mayer, 'Marcello Who? An unknown Italian painter in Cardinal Pole's entourage', *Source*, 15 (1996), pp. 22–6.

[258] Pagano-Ranieri, p. 98.

[259] Pagano-Ranieri, pp. 98–9.

[260] BMIC25, fos. 266r–7r.

[261] BMIC25, fos. 273r–4r. Jedin, *Concilio*, 1, p. 553.

[262] Jedin, *Concilio*, 1, p. 553n. *PM*, 2, p. 466 n58 for Cortese.

[263] Jedin, *Concilio*, 1, pp. 555–7. The editors of the version in *CT*, 4 tried to claim that the breve was never officially dispatched.

[264] *CRP*, no. 414.

Morone remained very much on Pole's mind. Priuli wrote him frequently with news of Pole and Colonna, and advice about more delicate matters. Among points concerning Priuli were some writings that Morone had promised to have copied after di Capua returned them. These may have been by Pole, and may have concerned his opinion of justification.[265] Another was preaching in Modena. Priuli wrote Morone two letters of recommendation for the general of the Franciscan Minims, who wished Morone's help forming his own small community, but whom Priuli (and Pole) thought better suited both to preach in Morone's diocese and also to be made his coadjutor.[266] In fact, Bartolomeo Golfi della Pergola was appointed to preach Lent in 1544, but under whose auspices is much less clear than in De' Bartoli's case.[267] Soranzo played the leading role, but Pole and Priuli are also supposed to have been heavily involved.[268] The evidence shows that they came into the case only after Pergola's preaching had led to denunciations, although De' Bartoli later said that Flaminio and Priuli had taught Pergola to be a Lutheran before he preached in Modena, and claimed that he had also heard in Pole's rooms in the Vatican that Morone intended to defend Pergola.[269] Morone feared that his vicar, Domenico Morando, was over-zealously pursuing these delations, but Priuli advised him through Beccadelli that Morando was only doing a good job and he should conduct his investigation carefully. Soranzo, who had heard Pergola preach Lent in 1543, refused to believe the charges, but Priuli still thought it best to proceed cautiously.[270] Priuli continued to back Gasparo, the general of the Minims, and not Pergola, again telling Morone that he should have given Gasparo a trial as preacher and then made him his coadjutor. Pole endorsed Priuli's plan. In June, Priuli learned that Morone would have accepted his advice had not Gasparo been assigned to Palermo.[271]

---

[265] BMIC25, fos. 273r–4r. Cf. *PM*, 2, p. 460.

[266] BMIC25, fo. 275r and fos. 277r–9r.

[267] *PM*, 1, p. 264 and Cesare Bianco, 'Bartolomeo della Pergola e la sua predicazione eterodossa a Modena nel 1544', *Bollettino della società di studi valdesiani*, 151 (1982), pp. 3–49.

[268] Pio Paschini, *Tre ricerche sulla storia della chiesa nel Cinquecento* (Rome: Edizioni Liturgiche, n.d.), p. 122, corroborated by *PM*, 2:1, pp. 430–1.

[269] *PM*, 2:1, pp. 266 and 282.

[270] BMIC25, fos. 281r–3v and 285r–v.

[271] BMIC25, fos. 287r–8v, 275r and 277r–9r.

4

The council of Trent

De concilio

POLE RETURNED TO Trent in 1545 (illus. 5). The legates were appointed on 22 February, ten days after Pope Paul announced that the council would reassemble.[1] Pole's involvement quickly became a sideshow to the dramatic reconvening as the pope delayed his departure from Rome on 'suspicion of ambushes'.[2] He may have had another reason. According to the preface to *De concilio*, Pole asked for a month free from other responsibilities in order to reflect on the council. The legates failed to notice the assignment, although the work is addressed to them, nor is there any other reference certainly to *De concilio* now, which must arouse hesitation in accepting Pole's claim.[3] No manuscript from Pole's hand has been found, and Girolamo Seripando reworked the text issued by Paolo Manuzio's press.[4] There is another reason to hesitate before reading it as Pole's work. Although the content of the 1562 book overlaps other of his writings of circa 1545, especially the opening sermon discussed below, there are significant differences. Above all, the major point of that sermon – the necessity of the church's leaders doing penance – appears only toward the end of *De concilio*, and did not figure throughout most of the work. For another, the list of the council's functions varies between the two writings. The third role given in the sermon, peace, appears only in the second run-through in *De concilio*, and in a much muted form.[5] Perhaps the biggest reason for thinking the text might yet

---

[1] *CT*, 4, pp. 391 and 393.
[2] *Ibid.*, p. 396.
[3] Fenlon, p. 102 takes the preface at face value, as does Herman Josef Sieben, 'Eine "ökumenische" Auslegung von Apg 15 in der Reformationszeit', *Theologie und Philosophie*, 60 (1985), pp. 16–42, pp. 18 and 34. Cf. *CPM*, catalogue, no. 16.
[4] See *CPM*, pp. 26–7.
[5] And what should be made of a lone citation on fo. 7v to Scotus in the 1562 edition?

5 Duomo, Trent.

go back to 1545 is its handling of faith, the first of the council's tasks, as well as the principal element in justification. Then again, the link between faith and the papacy strongly resembles the argument put forward in *De summo pontifice*, in theory written only in 1549–50. It seems safe to conclude that most of the work belongs to Pole in the same sense that any of 'his' works do, but it cannot be established that the text as we have it reflects his views in the spring of 1545. With all due caution, then, let it be claimed that Pole put forward the following view of the council.

Pole grounded his text almost exclusively in scripture, an approach that has no counterpart in earlier writing. This may be as H. J. Sieben suggests because he intended the work to be 'ecumenical', designed to reach out to the German Protestants he was thought to be concerned to get to the council, and specifically to respond to Luther's *Von den Konziliis und den Kirchen* of 1539.[6] In any case, there can be little doubt of his concern for Luther and his followers.[7] At the conclusion, Pole said that he hoped to contribute to 'reconciling the German people, who are called Lutherans' to the church (fo. 57v). Despite a beginning that resembles Pighe's *Hierarchiae ecclesiasticae assertio* in its architectonic meta-

---

[6] Sieben, pp. 20–1.   [7] *CT*, 11, p. 944 and Fenlon, p. 101.

phors (fo. 1v), and a view of the ecclesiastical constitution almost as monarchical (fo. 4r–v) as Pighe's extreme papalist construction, Pole rejected Pighe's deduction that the pope therefore ruled the church. Pole carefully skirted the question of papal inerrancy, as he did nearly all the big issues in the earlier literature, arguing instead that the council depended on the Holy Spirit and had nothing whatever to do with human concerns or powers. Pole further rejected Pighe's assertion that the council's model was to be found in the Old Testament, and instead used the apostolic council of Jerusalem as his exemplar.[8] As Sieben brings out, Jerusalem was not just *a* model, but the *only* model of a council, and all subsequent meetings were merely interpretations of it.[9] The Bible, together with the history of the martyrs, provided all the evidence Pole needed.

Pole's stress on the centrality of faith in holding the church together marked another departure. Already on fo. 3r he twice identified the *petra* (rock) on which the church was built not with Peter but with 'the stone of faith, that Peter, as the first stone placed in the church, professed', the same faith that all members of the body of the church had to accept. This had been Erasmus's reading.[10] It was this faith, not Peter, that Christ guaranteed would never fail (fo. 3v). Quickly Pole turned to the necessity of the Holy Spirit. A council depended on its *effusio* that would 'illuminate' it with the 'doctrine of faith' (fo. 5v).[11] This was why the council of Jerusalem became the model, since it was the first after the Ascension and Pentecost (fo. 6r). Before that the apostles' meetings and any other potential models were no better than synagogues (one of several points at which Pole excluded the Jews from the council). Without the Spirit, the council would be of men, rather than of the church (fo. 6v). By definition and because of the Spirit's presence, the council dealt only with Christ's and God's honour (fo. 7r–v).

The council handled only the faith, which it was 'to explicate, and confirm, and order with charity' (fo. 7v). This formula recurs a number of times, but before Pole went into further depth on the nature and role of faith, he addressed the role of the 'pastors' who with their flock made up the church. He grounded their position in prophetic authority, especially Ezekiel (fo. 8r). It was their job to be both merciful and judgmental (fos. 8v–11v). Their office guaranteed all else, as Christ was true God and man when he exercised both powers. Because He was both and humans were spirit and body, He needed a vicar, a visible sign

---

[8] Sieben, pp. 24–5.
[9] Sieben, p. 22.
[10] John E. Bigane III, *Faith, Christ or Peter: Matthew 16:18 in sixteenth century Roman* *Catholic exegesis* (Washington: University Press of America, 1981), pp. 15–34.
[11] The last phrase is missing in the manuscript.

like the sacraments. Peter and his successors filled that office. Yet the Spirit governed the church, even if Christ willed his flock to Peter (fo. 12v). The proof that Peter's anything but juridical position arose from providence rested on three kinds of evidence: he was called father, with all the honours that Isaiah enumerated; 'Tu es Petrus' gave him the *potestas principis* of making a new, celestial people; and the role he had in building the church. In short, he was 'father, tutor [or guardian] and shepherd [pastor]' (fo. 15v).

Then came the meat, the explication of a council on the model of Jerusalem. It deserved its priority because in it all three of the functions derived from Christ were exercised. Not, however, by Peter alone. Peter preached the 'word of regeneration', as defined first by James and then by Paul, who said it meant that humans were saved 'not from the works of justice which we do, but according to his [God's] mercy', that is, we are 'justified by grace'. This was the faith Peter preached, and this was the faith the legates to a council had to spread (fo. 17v). The legates may well have had divergent agendas, but not according to Pole. Peter did have powers peculiar to him, including the right to resolve disputes and dismiss the council (fo. 19r), but even there Paul and Barnabas confirmed his power to discipline disturbers of ecclesiastical peace. Again what mattered was not Peter but *Petri fides* (fos. 19v–20r) by whomever represented. It was *Petri fidem* that resolved controversies (fo. 22r). Similarly, Peter had priority in spreading the word, but all the apostles preached (fo. 21r), and therefore so should all the members of the council. 'The word of faith and charity' (fo. 23r) should resolve any disputes in it, which meant that all human considerations should be given up, as when God summoned men to him by faith (fo. 23v). Faith served to abolish all that humans thought important (fo. 24r–v). Here Pole entered a caution, but without reference to Peter. He faulted those 'who so preach *sola fide* that they detract from pious actions of charity, who speaking in this perverse fashion give occasion and license to the lazy of doing nothing, and to the active of doing badly, whom we judge to preach the faith not so much perversely as impiously'. They should take care for the laws and their ancestors rather than hold them in contempt (fo. 24r). Still, 'the first office of faith [was] to strip a man of all human goods' (fo. 24v), after which he had to combine faith and charity in preaching. This echoed Contarini's opinion, as Pole continued to recuperate the losses of Regensburg. Faith without law meant no charity, but justification by the law was worse in its 'intolerable burden' and mixing of law with faith in salvation (fo. 25r). Trust in God and Christ would produce 'ascending faith, descending charity' (*fides ascendens, hunc [?] caritas descendens*; fo. 25v). There was much more of the same, but Pole always made clear that faith came first, and then charity or works of law (fo. 28r). Pole also wrote of both the chirograph which confirmed that sin had been erased (fos. 26v–7r) and of a pact (*foedus*) on which the *ecclesia Romana* was founded (fo. 41r), both terms which recall not so much Luther's notion of salvation as Calvin's. There would not have been much need for Pole to explicate his view of justification, had the other two legates read *De concilio* in anything like this form. Thus it was not just a matter of justification by faith and what Sieben calls papalist ecclesiology being compatible: they were identical.[12]

'Papalist' can be accepted only with extreme caution. Pole had not yet finished. Peter's primacy rested on the blood of the martyrs (fos. 31v–2r) and miracles that 'declared' Peter's faith, above all Constantine's conversion (fos. 32r–8v), not on juridical or political powers.[13] At the same time, martyrs and miracles fulfilled the prophets' predictions that the vicar of Christ would have both honours and afflictions, especially in the form of emperors (fos. 39r–40r). This was the *foedus* behind the papacy. Much of this section was supported from Hegesippus, another sign of Pole's broad knowledge of the Greek fathers, although he seems to have used an unknown translation by Ambrose.[14] Nevertheless, Pole later argued that emperors had a role in the council and certainly had to support it (fos. 45v, 47v) in addition to preserving peace (fo. 47v), and that kings were equally shepherds with the clergy (fo. 48r) even if they needed priestly blessing (fo. 49r). Remedies were up to the pope, but everyone, including princes, had to imitate Christ and pray for God's mercy on his people (fos. 50v–51r).

Having established Peter's pre-eminence in this guarded fashion, Pole spelled out the council's job under three headings: 'explaining the faith', discipline, and charity toward Christ's flock in the form of ecclesiastical canons (fo. 44r–v). The pope should take the lead in confessing his sin and praying for conversion. The rest of the heads should then repent and lead the whole church to penitence (fo. 52v). Their prayers instead of 'fleshly prudence' would lead to solutions, as God had meant when he promised that Peter's faith would never fail (fo. 53v). The legates should imitate Daniel's prayer for repentance and mercy, which Pole treated at length (fos. 54r–56v). Everything depended on confession of sins, a thing no one wished to do (fos. 56v–7r). Pole made that theme the text of his opening sermon.

---

[12] Sieben, p. 20.
[13] For the possibly spurious *De baptismo Constantini* published with *De concilio*, see CPM, p. 91.
[14] Only fragments of Hegesippus survive, mostly in Eusebius's *Ecclesiastical history*,

but Pole seems to have had a complete work, which confirms the supposition that it was extant in the sixteenth century. Cf. the edition by H. J. Lawlor and J. E. L. Oulton (London: SPCK, 1954).

Trent

Pole left Viterbo after Easter and slipped into Trent on 4 May.[15] Once there, he renewed old contacts and made new ones. Among the new was the Dominican Girolamo Muzzarelli, at this time only a 'minor theologian', but later to be one of Pole's most important allies. Again, Pole probably met for the first time another Dominican, Bartolomé Carranza, with whom he would later collaborate closely in England. One of Carranza's oldest friends, another Spaniard and also a member of the conciliar congregation over which Pole presided, was Francisco de Navarra, who would receive some of Pole's most important autobiographical letters in the future, and was one of the stoutest defenders of an approximately conciliarist position.[16] According to a witness against Carranza later, Navarra stayed with Rullo and Priuli, all of them acting suspiciously.[17] Carlo da Sesso, who would later help to lead the Inquisition to Carranza before being executed for heresy, claimed to know Pole in Trent.[18] Nearly all these new friends came like Pole from the upper reaches of the European nobility, not infrequently the displaced reaches, as in Carranza's, Navarra's, or Morone's case.

Some of Pole's most important relations at the council were with three Cassinese Benedictine abbots, Isidoro Chiari, Luciano degli Ottoni, and Crisostomo Calvino, whose right to be admitted and to vote at the council Pole defended.[19] Pole knew Chiari from his days in Padua, although there is no evidence that Chiari taught Pole.[20] As the researches of Barry Collett and Adriano Prosperi and Carlo Ginzburg have shown, all three viewed justification much as Pole did, and engaged in similar biblical scholarship, especially Chiari, who identified the rock of Matthew 16 with faith, not Peter.[21] Pole helped to secure him the see of Foligno.[22] More important yet, Ottoni held a view identical to

---

[15] *CRP*, nos. 424 and 430, and *CT*, 10, p. 74.

[16] Hubert Jedin, *Storia del concilio di Trento*, 2, 2nd ed., trans. Giulietta Basso and Igino Rogger (Brescia: Morcelliana, 1974), p. 37.

[17] *Doc. hist.*, 2, pp. 608–9.

[18] Massimo Firpo, *Dal sacco di Roma all'Inquisizione: Studi su Juan de Valdés e la Riforma italiana* (Alessandria: Edizioni dell'Orso, 1998), p. 212n.

[19] H. O. Evennett, 'Three Benedictine abbots at the council of Trent, 1545–1547', *Studia monastica*, 1 (1959), pp. 343–77; *CT*, 2, p. 371.

[20] As Fenlon, pp. 30 and 145n and Barry

Collett, *Italian Benedictine scholars and the reformation* (Oxford: Clarendon Press, 1985), p. 88 claim.

[21] Collett, p. 151. For Chiari, see pp. 88–94 and chs. 5 and 7 *passim*. For Calvino, pp. 186 and 254. For Ottoni, ch. 6 *passim*. Collett, pp. 136–7 tries to distinguish degli Ottoni's theology of justification from that of the *spirituali* including Pole, but neither of the views of double justification he ascribes to the group adequately characterize Pole's idea.

[22] *CT*, 10, p. 805n.

Pole's of the action of God's providence in history, from which he derived a dislike for speculative theology.[23] Ottoni repeatedly got in trouble with the Inquisition, after having his commentary on the exegesis of Romans by Chrysostom (one of Pole's favourite Fathers) censured at Trent, and Pole helped to defend him, whatever their putative disagreements on doctrine.[24] Gregorio Bornato, another Benedictine of nearby Brescia, and author of the tract *De libero arbitrio* for which he or his editor claimed Pole's endorsement, may also have taken part in these discussions. Bornato's work was a compendium of Benedictine theology and piety.[25] Calvino made little impact at Trent, although his contributions were later called famous in the dedication of Bornato's posthumously published work.[26]

Pole made one last friend at Trent while waiting for the council to open. Marco Girolamo Vida, a survivor of the grandeur of Leonine Rome when he wrote a notable treatise on chess, had since followed Giberti's lead and become a reforming bishop. He may well have met Pole through Cardinal Gonzaga, as one of whose informants from Trent he served. At least one of his reports concerned Pole, who had bemoaned the destruction of trees in and around Treville.[27] Vida later wrote a dialogue dedicated to Pole featuring himself and Flaminio as principal speakers, and set it in Pole's presence during the summer of 1545.[28] It turned on the merits of civilized versus natural life. Flaminio defended nature, often by violent attacks on the mores of humans in cities, but Vida won him over. Flaminio probably held views like those Vida assigned to him, and thus by bringing him around Vida converted him just as much as Pole was alleged to have done, albeit from a civil rather than a religious aberration. That Pole could have attended a discussion *de republica* underlines his interest in politics, and Vida's version of him as a great political sage made another contribution to his image.

Pole had time to talk politics and attend to his friends since he largely stayed in the background during the council, intervening in the debates only a handful

---

[23] Collett, pp. 133–4.

[24] Gigliola Fragnito, 'Ercole Gonzaga, Reginald Pole e il monastero di S. Benedetto Polirone', *Benedictina*, 37 (1987), pp. 253–71, esp. p. 254 for bibliography on degli Ottoni.

[25] For it, see Collett, pp. 114–17 and Carlo Ginzburg and Adriano Prosperi, *Giochi di pazienza. Un seminario sul 'Beneficio di Cristo'* (Turin: Einaudi, 1975), pp. 142ff.

[26] *De libero hominis arbitrio* (Brescia: Giacopo Britannico, 1571), sig. A3v, by Cornelio Francesco.

[27] *CT*, 10, p. 872.

[28] T. F. Mayer, 'Nursery of resistance: Reginald Pole and his friends', in Paul A. Fideler and T. F. Mayer, eds., *Political thought and the Tudor commonwealth: deep structure, discourse and disguise* (London: Routledge, 1992), pp. 50–74, pp. 50–1.

of times. His remarks were always well received, as even a relatively hostile observer like Angelo Massarelli had to admit.[29] He set his imprint firmly on the first meeting through the opening sermon that he wrote and that Massarelli read to the assembly on 7 January 1546.[30] It was an oration worthy of Colet, and included many familiar themes.[31] Pole framed his text on the council's three tasks, 'the extirpation of heresy, the reform of ecclesiastical discipline and morals, and the external peace of the whole church'. Success demanded heeding the prophet's warning to avoid the worst sin of trusting 'our power or prudence' instead of leaving all to Christ, a point Pole made again in the first discussion of the council's title when he chided the members for worrying about such an 'inanity' rather than leaving it to God.[32] Any member of the council could undertake reform only to the degree that he thought himself unworthy. That meant acknowledging our sins, Pole told the council fathers, in several different ways. 'Experience, that cannot lie' demonstrated that evils too numerous to count overwhelmed the church. Even if Pole confined himself only to the council's three tasks, the problems of each were entirely the heads' fault. In the case of heresy, failing to stamp it out was equivalent to having sowed its seeds. The second point required no attention, and the third, peace, received an extended discussion of God's punishment for the clergy's sins, especially the intrusion of laymen into bishoprics and the alienation to the laity of the church's goods, 'which are the goods of the poor'. Had God punished them as they deserved, they would have suffered the fate of Sodom and Gomorrah.

How to avoid the coming divine judgment? Turning again to the prophets, Pole cited Ezekiel's admonition that the sin must first be condemned, and that could only come through the Holy Spirit. Narrowing his focus to the bishops, whom Pole treated as if they were virtually the council, he said they had nearly brought the church to its current sorry state after the disasters of the fourteenth century. They had to listen to the prophets again if they would set the proper example for the people (*populus*) and bring them through confession of their sins to penitence and divine mercy. Turning to the council's deliberation, Pole stressed the need for dispassionate consideration, especially in the case of servants of princes. The council was not a place for praising princes, but God alone, following the prophet Daniel's example. After a long excursus on Ezekiel's exhortation to tears of sorrow, Pole returned to the bishops holding princes' proxies and urged them to serve Christ, not men. There should also be no infighting, but rather all the members should imitate Christ and thereby gain 'the

---

29 *CT*, 2, p. 561.
30 *CT*, 4, p. 548n.

31 *CT*, 4, pp. 548–53.
32 *CT*, 1, p. 19.

spirit of peace, charity and gentleness'. This could only come through prayer. The fathers greeted Pole's speech with a measure of surprise, sitting in silence for some moments, before Cardinal del Monte's leading of the hymn 'Veni creator Spiritus' came close to the right response.

Procedure posed the biggest problem facing the council. Should it deal with doctrine and reform in tandem, or treat them separately? The pope wished the first course, while the emperor, still trying to buy time for negotiations with the Protestants, hoped to begin with reform and defer doctrine. That would also become Pole's preference, but at first he helped to carry the pope's plan to deal with both simultaneously.[33] He supported his case by the necessity of a preaching episcopate.[34] Pole laid out a major principle of his conduct during the debate over the council's title when he declared that conscience must be obeyed until the majority declared otherwise.[35] The first matter of doctrine addressed was the status and text of scripture. Pole lost twice, first when the council endorsed the council of Florence's declaration of the canon rather than examining each book individually as both Pole and Cervini had wished, and then again on the score of new editions of the Hebrew and Greek Bible. This was in part an ecumenical move on Pole's part.[36] He did carry an important point on 26 February when he persuaded the council to separate the discussion of scripture and tradition by the argument that it was a spot at which 'our adversaries' had especially attacked the church.[37] Pole had a little better luck in the inconclusive debates on the reform of bishops and preaching, defending the right of the regulars to preach, and the bishops' need for their help.[38] In this session the council never got around to the highly conflicted issue of episcopal residence, and especially whether the bishop held his diocese by divine right. Later it was alleged that Pole, in common with many other members of the 'Contarinian wing', favoured divine right episcopacy.[39]

Concern for the heretics and careful calculation of polemical advantage might have stood Pole in good stead when the council turned to debates over original sin and justification. Instead, except for one speech, he missed nearly the whole discussion, before withdrawing from the council altogether. Already on 21 May he had missed a session devoted to preaching for reasons of health.[40] A week later Cervini reported that 'a deep and constant pain in his left arm' handicapped Pole.[41] On 14 June he was well enough to intervene in the debate over the draft

---

[33] Fenlon, p. 121; *CT*, 4, pp. 570–1.

[34] Cf. *PM*, 6, p. 335 and 2:2, p. 847.

[35] *CT*, 4, p. 578.

[36] Fenlon, pp. 121–2 and *CT*, 5, p. 65.

[37] *CT*, 5, p. 21.

[38] *CT*, 5, p. 135.

[39] *CT*, 9, p. 349.

[40] *CT*, 5, p. 152.

[41] *CT*, 10, p. 505.

decree on original sin.[42] Pole began by endorsing del Monte's advice to invoke the Holy Spirit. He then implicitly turned to experience. 'We feel in us what original sin is' even if neither we nor any other 'most holy fathers' have been able to define it. We know it means death for us, inherited from Adam. This was what philosophers meant by evil inclination, especially Aristotle who preferred a republic to a monarchy and therefore proposed laws to restrain concupiscence. God in much different fashion drew men to the right way through 'benefits and graces'. Yet not even they were enough. Only the death of God's Son could save the human race. The point was that Pole thought the proposed decree's treatment of baptism left itself open to the interpretation that baptism removed the potential to sin. This speech may represent the moment at which Pole, with the agreement of the other two legates, chose to defend Protestant views in order that they not be condemned unheard.[43] Pole's use of concupiscence, one of Luther's favourite concepts, suggests this interpretation, even if Pole was not interested in such theological niceties.[44] Whether speaking for the Protestants or from his own experience, Pole had openly criticized the council's actions.[45]

A week after his intervention on original sin, Pole spoke again.[46] After Cervini announced that the subject of justification had come to the top of the agenda, Pole pronounced the matter so difficult that prayer was especially needed, and argued that the works of their adversaries needed careful consideration. They should not be read as opponents and dismissed with the judgment 'Luther said that, therefore it is false.'[47] Instead of concluding once a heretic, always a heretic, Pole urged the council to read all books 'in a fair spirit, by whomever written and whomever published, and keep that which is good, refute the bad, nor should we wish immediately to confute everything, but rather admit the truth which we seek'. Pole used the example of Pighe who in his zeal to defeat all

---

[42] *CT*, 1, pp. 75–6 and 5, p. 220.

[43] Fenlon, pp. 127–8 thinks this must have happened in secret before 9 June when a list of Protestant errors was publicly presented.

[44] Fenlon, pp. 130–1 compares Pole's statement to Seripando's commentary on it and distinguishes between Pole's efforts to understand his experience and those of a trained theologian to clarify a concept.

[45] Fenlon, p. 131.

[46] *CT*, 1, pp. 82–3 and 5, p. 257.

[47] Fenlon, p. 134 calls this 'characteristic sleight of hand' intended to cover Pole's real opinions. He is doubtless correct about

Pole's views, but it seems unnecessary to characterize his display of them as somehow devious. For more on this point, see my '"Heretics be not in all things heretics:" cardinal Pole, his circle and the potential for toleration', in J. C. Laursen and C. J. Nederman, eds., *The roots of toleration in Europe, 1100–1700: theory and practice* (Philadelphia: University of Pennsylvania Press, 1997), pp. 107–24.

his opponents fell into Pelagianism. 'Therefore, the middle way is to be held' without fear or favour.

Departure and opinions on justification

Not quite a deathbed speech, it was none the less Pole's last. A few days later, word arrived from Rome that he had been granted licence to leave Trent in order to recover his health, and on 28 June he departed for Treville.[48] His absence was not intended to be permanent.[49] When Massarelli noted Pole's withdrawal, he twice ascribed it to reasons of health and said that Pole had been ill for forty days.[50] Dermot Fenlon thinks that Pole underwent something like a mental breakdown and suffered from psychosomatic illness.[51] Caught between his own innermost beliefs and his almost counter-reformation antagonists, Pole collapsed. But Massarelli's was not the only explanation of his departure.[52] According to Carnesecchi years later, first Colonna and then Priuli and Flaminio had told him that Pole had left in order to avoid signing the decree on justification. Colonna attributed this to God's disposition. Just what Pole's objection had been, alas, no one had told Carnesecchi.[53] One of the members of the committee that drafted the decree endorsed Colonna's analysis, although assigning blame to Pole for having destroyed inherent justice.[54] More recently, this theory has become part of the political interpretation of the *spirituali* and his leaving made into a calculated move intended to preserve his ideological purity and his leadership.[55] These are radically different analyses. On the one hand, a broken man, slinking away in defeat, on the other, a hero, preserving his

---

[48] *CT*, 10, p. 531 and 1, p. 557. Fenlon, p. 134 says Pole's permission arrived on 20 June, but that is actually the date of Maffei's covering letter for it.

[49] *CT*, 10, p. 545 and *CRP*, no. 474.

[50] *CT*, 1, pp. 442 and 557.

[51] Fenlon, p. 135. Fenlon also considers the possibility that Pole left for doctrinal reasons, as Cardinal Guise allegedly charged in 1549 but cf. the next chapter, p. 190.

[52] Nor was it accepted by everyone then, according to Antonio Caracciolo, who claimed that Pole had given great scandal by pretending to be ill. *PM*, 1, pp. 131–2,

checked against the manuscript in BPP MS pal. 638, fo. 134r–v. The master of ceremonies also had his doubts. *CT*, 2, p. 387.

[53] *PC*, pp. 549–50 and Sergio Pagano, ed., *Il processo di Endimio Calandra e l'inquisizione a Mantova nel 1567–1568* (Vatican City: Biblioteca apostolica vaticana, 1991), p. 308.

[54] *PM*, 6, p. 333; cf. 2, p. 835. Deponent claimed that Pole's opinion was printed, but no text in type of his reactions to the decree is known.

[55] Simoncelli, *Caso*, p. 39.

virtue intact. The tendency for Pole's image to bifurcate continues. In this instance it turns out to be fairly easy to choose between the alternatives, while yet allowing that some of Pole's illness was genuine. As his forthright, if delayed, reaction to the debate over justification together with its sequel manifests, whatever was bothering Pole, he did not collapse, and may have withdrawn for just the reason Colonna put forward. A flight in order to avoid face-to-face conflict followed by a writing also fits Pole's pattern.

Undoubtedly Pole was not in good physical condition when he headed to Treville, at least not according to the bulletins he sent del Monte and Cervini. Both of them also complained of ill health, which further complicates the effort to determine what, if anything, was wrong with Pole.[56] Within two weeks, however, his health had improved, or perhaps as soon as he left Trent, in part through exercise, although two Paduan physicians warned him that he still risked paralysis if he did not take it easy. Pole wished to have the opinion of the council's physician, Girolamo Fracastoro, and promised to follow it.[57] About the same time, Colonna gave a detailed summary of Pole's illness, which she had just discussed with the pope.[58] They had heard that the physicians would have preferred to treat it with medicine, but that it was both hard to get and they also expected Pole to resist using it. Instead, they would try a careful regimen and change of air. The pope had once had a similar illness, which began as paralysis 'with twisting of the mouth'. The physicians had ascribed it to catarrh, and prescribed someplace hot. Catarrh was an elastic diagnosis and helps little in identifying Pole's complaint.[59]

Pole stayed in Treville through the summer, missing the crisis which blew up over the suggestion that the council should be moved away from Trent.[60] Pole successfully stalled his return until he was ordered back in late August, at which time he pronounced himself the sickest he had been since arriving in Treville. Now he suffered not only in his arm but in his shoulder and left eye, which he thought might have been related to the season and the moon. Rather than risk permanent disfigurement, Pole proposed to stay in Padua until he was sure what to do.[61] He was needed in Trent because of the decree on justification, and the coincidence between orders to return there and worsening health looks like corroboration of Fenlon's case for psychosomatic illness.[62] Pole tried to escape

---

[56] *CRP*, no. 475; for the legates' poor health, see, e.g., *CT*, 10, p. 655n.

[57] *CRP*, no. 476.

[58] Sergio M. Pagano and Concetta Ranieri, eds., *Nuovi documenti su Vittoria Colonna e Reginald Pole* (Vatican City: Archivio Vaticano, 1989), pp. 104–7.

[59] My thanks to Daniel Brownstein for a discussion of this diagnosis.

[60] *CRP*, no. 481.

[61] *CRP*, no. 484.

[62] *CRP*, no. 485.

the necessity of commenting on the draft decree by sending an agent to Rome.[63] In addition, Pole wrote Morone a brief summary of his position.[64] Pole thought that since no matter of doctrine was independent of the problem of justification, more time was desperately needed, for two reasons. First, the council had no guidance given that the matter had been ignored for 1,500 years. Second, a decree would leave it vulnerable to Protestant attacks fuelled by twenty years of heated controversy. They would discredit the council's authority at a time when authority was desperately needed because of the numbers of people leaving papal obedience. (Was this a tacit admission that the council should rescue the pope?) The only possible basis for a decree had to be scripture, even if this meant appearing to agree with the heretics, and the only possible means to arrive at a decree calmly was for the pope to impose a hiatus until a large number of bishops, representing the church, could approve it. Pole revealed an episcopalist sympathy again when he continued that there had never been a poorer turn-out of bishops at a council, and their small number would undermine the decree further. It is difficult to say to what degree the link between episcopalist sentiment and an unusual quantitative concept of representation reflects Pole's grounded views or a grasping at any and all straws.[65] That Flaminio probably attacked the decree in the same letter in which he strongly urged a reform led by the bishops on the antique model may support the conclusion that Pole's position was genuine.[66] As Fenlon observes, the heart of Pole's objection to issuing the decree was ecclesiological, not theological, a matter of concern to avoid undermining the church's authority, not the pope's alone.[67] Pole apparently intended for Morone to approach the pope on his behalf, but Morone instead gave his letter to Niccolò Cardinal Ardinghelli, the pope's secretary and datary, and no obvious friend of Pole.[68] In any case, neither his agent's mission nor Pole's approach to Morone worked. They bought him another month, but then he had to give his opinion on the decree.

---

[63] *CRP*, no. 486.

[64] *CRP*, no. 489.

[65] See Thomas F. Mayer, *Thomas Starkey and the commonweal: humanist politics and religion in the reign of Henry VIII* (Cambridge: Cambridge University Press, 1989), pp. 135–7.

[66] Adriano Prosperi, *Tra evangelismo e controriforma: G. M. Giberti (1495–1543)* (Rome: Edizioni di Storia e Letteratura, 1969), p. xvii.

[67] Fenlon, p. 167.

[68] *CRP*, no. 495. Cf. Fenlon, pp. 166–70. Ardinghelli had almost certainly known Pole in Padua in the 1520s when he lived with Bembo while attending the university, but left no trace of his presence in Pole's circles. During Contarini's legation to Regensburg, Ardinghelli made his disapproval obvious. He was deeply involved in the pope's correspondence with the legates, which may be why Morone chose him. *DBI*.

Or so the pope ordered, probably some time in the third week of September.[69] Even then, Pole still made excuses, primarily about his health. He had moved to Padua even without waiting for the pope's orders, so urgent was a cure.[70] This claim, along with others about poor health, seems to be contradicted by Pole's assurance to Colonna that he had not had an attack of 'my own infirmity' since arriving in Padua.[71] There he lived in Bembo's house, and had the use of both study and garden, which Pole greatly enjoyed.[72] Not even these surroundings and leisure could bring him willingly to write about justification. Almost as soon as Pole left Trent, the legates had sent him the deliberations over justification for his opinion, and he had apparently ignored their request.[73] Even now he thought of sending a *viva voce*, instead of a written opinion, again pleading ill health. Its onset must have been suspiciously sudden, since this letter is dated the day after that to Colonna just cited.[74]

Pole probably changed his mind about how to respond and sent both a messenger and a written opinion, composed before 9 October.[75] The messenger was Juan Morillo, Pole's theologian whom he 'converted', which may explain Cardinal Mendoza y Bobadilla's later association of him with Pole's heresy.[76] In fact, Pole wrote two opinions, one of them more or less public, to judge from Seripando's commentary on it.[77] Which of the two Massarelli entered as an official document is unknown, since neither fits his identification of it as 'about twofold justification and it is in the opinion of Cardinal Contarini'.[78] One of these is not directly tied to the draft decree, while the other on which Seripando commented is.[79] These distinct rhetorical aims no doubt have much to do with

---

[69] *CRP*, no. 496.

[70] *CRP*, nos. 491–2.

[71] *CRP*, no. 499. For other assertions of ill health, see, e.g., no. 498.

[72] Ernesto Travi, ed., Pietro Bembo, *Lettere* (Bologna: Commissione per i Testi di Lingua, 1987–93; 4 vols.), nos. 2550, 2553, 2556, 2559, 2565, 2569.

[73] *CRP*, no. 475.

[74] *CRP*, no. 500.

[75] Fenlon, p. 172.

[76] *CRP*, no. 501. For Mendoza y Bobadilla, *Carranza y Pole*, p. 297. Firpo maintains that Pole passed to Morillo Valdés's original manuscript of his comments on Paul, which Morillo may have obtained from Carnesecchi in Paris, but there is no evidence for either proposition. Firpo, *Sacco*, pp. 117, 142, 148.

[77] Both versions passed through Seripando's hands. *CT*, 12, pp. 671–4 and 674–6. Alfredo Marranzini, 'Il problema della giustificazione nell'evoluzione del pensiero di Seripando', in Antonio Cestaro, ed., *Geronimo Seripando e la chiesa del suo tempo nel V centenario della nascita* (Rome: Edizioni di Storia e Letteratura, 1997), pp. 227–69 does not discuss Seripando's comments.

[78] *CT*, 1, p. 585 and 12, p. 671.

[79] Fenlon, ch. 11 considers these opinions in reverse order from their sequence in *CT*, and from that followed here. This makes it easier to find ambiguity and confusion in the second text. As Fenlon says on p. 189, there can be no doubt about Pole's views in the first commentary which 'revealed the extent of his commitment to the doctrine of salvation by faith alone'.

the difference in language between the two pieces. The first is written more assertively from its opening 'it can never truly be said that man is justified in the presence of God by works done outside of grace . . .; of ourselves we are always evil, they [our works] can never be good such that they will justify us in the presence of God' through to the virtually identical conclusion 'in ourselves we are unjust and sinners . . . and our blame [*culpa*] is never absent from us'. Much of the argument turns on the prophets, and the need for repentance and trust in Christ through faith. Only once does Pole appear to move away from that case, but when he wrote that true believers did not 'rely on our justice, but rather on His word' this was not a concession that humans might have justice, but a rhetorical sally against anyone who might think they did.[80] Pole rested his case solely on scripture and experience. This opinion is almost entirely consistent with Pole's other writings touching on justification, including *De concilio*.[81]

Pole's second attempt addressed the council's proposed point-by-point refutation of Lutheran doctrine.[82] Only in article seven did the framers slip and appear to endorse Luther's concept according to which Christ's merits imputed to the sinner justified him. In a seeming effort to clear up this problem, the article also insisted that justification was permanent, as against Luther's (and Pole's) insistence that the justified remained sinners. Article seven gave Pole his best opportunity to salvage something from the draft, and he eagerly seized it, in the main quite clearly.[83] After praising 'the form and disposition' of the draft, he observed that he found some sections obscure and passed immediately to article seven's attempt to establish only one kind of justice: 'There is one justice of God through Christ, that is charity or His grace, by which we are not merely reputed justified, but we truly would be called and would be just' ('Una est iustitia Dei per Christum, hoc est caritas ipsa vel gratia, qua iustificati non modo reputamur, sed vere iusti nominemur et simus'). Pole feared that this phrase would appear to contradict the decree's earlier discussion of imputation, and that it did not accord fully with scripture which divided justification into 'various parts', not just charity and the other theological virtues. As Seripando noted, these were Augustine's words. Pole went on to explain that justification consisted of satisfaction through Christ's merits and sanctification which the Holy Spirit gave humans along with charity and the theological virtues. He cited Paul and Peter in his defence.

---

[80] Fenlon, p. 192, takes it as a slip – albeit an insignificant one – and a sign that Pole's belief in imputed righteousness may have been incomplete.

[81] Fenlon, p. 194, who also notes the absence of *De concilio*'s formula of *fides quae per*

caritatem operatur.

[82] *CT*, 12, pp. 674–6.

[83] Fenlon, p. 178 emphasizes the 'inconsistency and vacillation' of Pole's commentary.

Pole continued with an argument implying a view of human nature virtually indistinguishable from Luther's, nor did Seripando object.[84]

> Charity cannot exist with the impiety of sin. It is therefore necessary that first at least our sins be remitted before we have charity, and that the first and most powerful part of justification be this same remission of sins . . . because our sins are remitted to us through another justice, truly that of Christ imputed to us, satisfying for us, and through it, God's anger having been appeased, charity is given to us. For first acknowledging our sins and injustice through repentance, we must placate God's justice, not through our charity, which before this remission of sins we do not have, but embracing as ours and offering the merits and justice of Christ we may satisfy His justice, and so by it, as if we had not sinned, we are absolved from all guilt.

Christ's justice formed the 'essential' part of justification, 'and this is not charity nor because of it'. Charity came only because of 'Christ's justice imputed to us'. But then Pole took a superficially odd turn. Therefore, he concluded, justification did not come solely through charity. Nor did Christ's justice gain us only charity, but also the other virtues, through which we are justified, as the article seemed to deny by stressing charity. This seems to contradict not only his emphasis on charity alone as the outcome of justification, but more importantly the claim that justification depended solely on the imputation of Christ's merits, put forward even more strongly in his next sentence. 'Nor in it [charity] alone is the reason of our justice, nor can it alone make us just.' Seripando, trying to make sense of these two statements together, asked 'therefore what is it, which makes us just intrinsically and in itself?' I would argue that Pole had already answered that question, and was here quibbling in a polemical way with the draft's single-minded focus on charity, while still regarding charity as the outcome of justification, not an essential part of it. His next statement says as much. 'That Christ's justice imputed to us not only has the effect that we are given charity, but indeed that we are absolved from sins, absolved by just satisfaction, which is the essential and necessary part of justification, to which as to its genus it should be referred.'[85] There was thus no question but that justification preceded charity, however ham-fisted Seripando judged Pole's attempt to make a scholastic distinction.

If this was not clear enough, Pole went on to write about the will and make a

---

[84] Fenlon, p. 179.
[85] Fenlon, pp. 180–1, takes this statement as part of Pole's acknowledgment of an intrinsic justice in humans.

similar point. He objected to canon three's statement that free will could 'prepare itself for grace and consent [in justification] with this same grace calling and stirring, as if at least in part justification ought to be attributed to our virtue, and not completely to the grace and virtue of God himself, and so at least in that part we should be able to glorify ourselves'. This had the effect of confirming what the decree had earlier condemned, 'free will to hold itself in justification as from itself [*exanime*]'. Pole proposed instead that the canon reiterate the condemnation in place of its claim that free will could do anything through God's grace. This is an unambiguous statement about the will's powerlessness to accomplish anything toward justification.[86] Seripando saw nothing amiss.

Lest the nature of his objection be left unclear, Pole adduced two further arguments, each cast in scholastic form, and both depending from an argument made by a principal scholastic authority, Aquinas, that there was no such thing as an indifferent, morally neutral, act. The fourth canon said that 'servile fear', the fear of hell, was not sinful in the unregenerate. Pole attempted to construct a syllogism in reply. Since no acts were indifferent, nor did any merit arise except from acts of charity, therefore 'servile fear' had to be sinful, 'because it is not from charity nor love of God, but rather love of self'. The conclusion did not follow, but the point could not be missed: no merit before justification. Fear of hell was only useful as a spur to conversion, a point Seripando endorsed, referring to canon four. Pole's second attempt at a scholastic rejoinder took exception to canon nineteen's (not nine as Pole wrote, thereby confusing Seripando) assertion that not every act of 'the impious' was sinful, leading to the same conclusion

---

[86] Fenlon, p. 183 glosses this passage to say that Pole contradicted himself, 'simultaneously affirming and denying the freedom of the human will', but this seems not to be the case, certainly not in his observations on this canon, and probably not in the text as a whole. Fenlon appears to have split Pole's suggested revision in two, as if he had written 'this [the statement *liberum arbitrium habere se in iustificatione tanquam exanime*, which is not quite an exact quotation] should be put here rather than "to prepare itself and consent", and free will can do all the rest through God's grace', but the comma after consent is not in Pole's text which rather proposes to incorporate the final clause with the first, both together marked for deletion, if Pole had his way. Reading the sentence as Fenlon does yields a contradiction Pole could not have missed, no matter how disturbed or confused he may have been. Since Pole did not propose adding *per gratiam Dei* as Fenlon supposes, the rest of his commentary is beside the point. The whole passage (*CT*, 12, p. 675) reads 'In III. canone libero arbitrio tribuitur facultas et virtus, qua seipsum possit preparare ad gratiam et consentire ipsi cum ipsa gratia vocante et excitante, quasi saltem ex parte iustificatio sit tribuenda virtuti nostre, et non tota gratie Dei et virtuti ipsius, et sic saltem de ea parte possimus gloriari. Idcirco probat quidem, quod superius recte damnatum est, liberum arbitrium habere se in iustificatione tanquam exanime; optaret tamen, ut poneretur hic potius quam preparare se et consentire et alia omnia potest facere liberum arbitrium per gratiam Dei.'

about justification. Pole did not make either deduction explicit, but in light of his previous argument, he probably judged it unnecessary to belabour his point.[87]

Pole closed with two comparatively minor observations, both straightforwardly put. Canon ten's claim that the justified could fulfil God's law needed clarification, since, as Augustine had argued, this could happen only in heaven 'and now it is impossible for us'. The canon's statement amounted to saying that we had no more need of Christ's merits once justified.[88] Finally, the last canon's attribution of eternal life to 'the merits of human works' needed to be modified by the addition of 'by the merit of God's grace and the merits of Christ'. Pole's suggested phrasing was less than elegant, but he made clear the necessity of avoiding Pelagianism. It is perhaps also the only moment in this text when his determination to defend justification by faith blundered, if we read him as saying that God's grace and Christ's merits operated in addition to human effort, rather than giving rise to it. It is much more likely that if Pole slipped he did so not by distinguishing human effort from divine action, but by leaving open the possibility that humans could contribute to their salvation after justification.[89]

At least one of Pole's documents reached Trent, most likely the second, given its form and Seripando's notes. It aroused no response, at least not from the legates, or if they did offer a judgment, Pole kept quiet about it.[90] He merely acknowledged receipt of their letters on 18 October and their kindness to Morillo.[91] Later he claimed to Cervini that 'the lords of the council' (the legates?) had seen his opinion and judged that it did not 'disagree' with the decree, even if its words seemed a little different, and Cervini apparently did not contradict him.[92] Mendoza y Bobadilla later thought that the congregation for the council saw Pole's opinion before the decree was published, but if so, there is no record of its reaction.[93] The only even implicit reaction came from Johannes Cochlaeus, writing to congratulate Cervini on the decree and on the successful defence against 'new fantasies', a comment that has been taken to refer to Pole's ideas. Cochlaeus also expressed great surprise that the decree did not bear Pole's

---

[87] Fenlon, p. 186 points to canon XIX as Pole's target and assigns importance to Pole's failure to spell out the inference in both cases.

[88] Fenlon, p. 187 treats these final two criticisms as hesitantly expressed, rephrasing the first as if it had been a diffident question, not a clear statement of Pole's wishes.

[89] Fenlon, p. 188 interprets this passage as Pole's near acquiescence in the Tridentine decree.

[90] *CRP*, nos. 506–7.

[91] *CRP*, no. 502.

[92] *MMB*, 1:2, p. 347.

[93] *Carranza y Pole*, p. 297.

signature which led him to worry about Pole's health.[94] It may be, however, that Carafa took exception to Pole's behaviour. According to Antonio Caracciolo, the discussion of justification at Trent marked the first disagreement (*disparere*) between them.[95] The notorious Grechetto had already denounced Pole (and nearly everyone else at Trent) as a Lutheran, first in March and then again in August.[96] Others may have known Pole's views. Morone later said Pole had objected to the 'order' of the decree and its jumbling together of points that required separate treatment, not to its 'substance', but this report almost directly contradicts Pole's commentary.[97] No one could miss Pole's ostentatious refusal to associate himself with the decree. Its final text differed considerably from the September draft, marking a defeat not only for Pole but in most respects for Seripando as well.[98] Pole never recorded his judgment of it. As Cochlaeus observed, his signature did not appear on the text printed in early 1547, against the publication of which he had argued. Nor would he attach his seal to two later printed versions of the council's decrees, one of 1548 and another the following year. In at least the first instance, he did not stand alone. Cardinals Crescenzi, Morone and Cortese also tried to dissuade the pope from promulgating the decree, apparently like Pole because they feared it would mean the loss of the Lutherans.[99] Paul stubbornly refused to listen to them in January, but by early February he changed his mind and rejected an official publication, perhaps lest that prejudge his right to approve the council's actions.[100] Pole may also have spoken forthrightly to the pope.[101]

Pole returned to Rome on 17 November 1546.[102] Flaminio wrote a *carmen*

---

[94] Walter Friedensburg, 'Beiträge zum Briefwechsel der katholischen Gelehrten Deutschlands im Reformationszeitalter', *Zeitschrift für Kirchengeschichte*, 18 (1897), pp. 106–31, 233–97, 420–63, and 596–636, p. 621. Jedin (2, p. 359) took Cochlaeus 'certainly' to be referring to Pole, and Fenlon (pp. 195 and 197) agreed, adding that Cochlaeus's later expression of concern for Pole's health 'tends to confirm this judgement'. Cochlaeus's interest in Pole's well-being was probably genuine, since he asked Cervini again in October for news about it (Friedensburg, p. 623). If his interest in Pole's health was sincere, this may indicate that he did not mean Pole had 'fantasies'. If Cochlaeus did mean

Pole, this was not only an uncharitable comment, but a hypocritical one, since it did not prevent him from asking Pole for more help, and it also conflicted with his earlier agreement with the formula on justification at Regensburg, of which Pole probably knew. *CRP*, no. 509.

[95] *PM*, 1, p. 131, checked against BPP MS pal. 638, fo. 134.

[96] *CT*, 10, pp. 586 and 587n.

[97] *PM*, 2, p. 460; cf. Fenlon, p. 196.

[98] Jedin, 2, ch. 8, *passim*.

[99] *Ibid.*, p. 360.

[100] *Ibid.*, pp. 364–5 and cf. Fenlon, p. 197.

[101] Endimio Calandra testified to that effect. *Processo Calandra*, p. 309.

[102] *CRP*, no. 504.

describing the trip and casting their relationship in a peculiar light, especially at such a crisis.[103] It portrays Flaminio as Pole's lap-dog, begging him to be taken along to Rome in Pole's litter. 'Flaminio' cannot understand why Pole refused the trip, since 'good heroes' always have dogs. Flaminio asked for no more than a corner to occupy, and described his appealing physical features, especially a slight frame 'more worthy of girls than of men'. Like a faithful hound, Flaminio could keep Pole's feet warm, and if the way was too difficult, 'your very best client Morilla [sic]' could take care of him like a good mother preparing a bride for her wedding. Were Pole not to take Flaminio, like little dogs (*catelli*) he was likely to fall prey to wolves. Play Flaminio must.

Pole suffered no ill effects in Rome from his behaviour. Cervini, high in the pope's confidence, thought Pole's standing unaffected, continuing to ask for help in forwarding a client's chances for a bishopric and in securing his own

---

[103] *Marci Antonii, Joannis Antonii et Gabrielis Flaminiorum Fornocorneliensium Carmina* (Padua: Giuseppe Comino, 1743), pp. 41–2, 1, no. XXXV: 'Cur me, Pole, tua venire ad urbem/ Lectica prohibes? tuae quid, oro,/ Summae participem benignitatis/ Esse non pateris? Canes bonorum/ Heroum comites fuere semper;/ Et caelum Canis incolit supremum/ Inter sidera; nec polus, beate/ Sedes callicolum, suam Catellam/ Dedignatur habere secum: at ipsa/ Sum despecta tibi, nec unum apud te/ Angulum valeo impetrare. verum/ Si nostram vacet aestimare formam,//Non indigna tuo favore credar./ Est pilus mihi lucidus, venustae/ Pendent auriculae. nigris ocellis,/ Et candae placeo jubis comatae./ Nec sum corpore vasta, nec figura/ Tam brevi, ut videar puellularum/ Comes dignior esse, quam virorum./ Nec turpi scabie laboro; nec sunt/ Invisi pulices mihi molesti./ Nec sum prorsus inutilis futura,/ Si Cassam recreas, vehisque tecum;/ Nam pedes tibi suaviter fovebo,/ Qui jam frigoribus rigent acutis./ Nec vero timeas, luto referta/ Quod via assidue ambularim; amicus/ Et cliens tuus optimus, Morilla/ (42) Me suis manibus pie, ac benigne/ Puro flumine ter quaterque lavit,/ Et munda dedit esse mundiorem/ Sponsa, quam bona mater ad maritum/ Vult deducere nuptiis paratis./ Quod si non satis haec videntur esse/ Ad flectendum animum tuum; catelli,/ (Ah nimis miseri mei catelli!)/ Te, precor, moveant, tenella pleno/ Quos gestans utero, pedes movere/ Vix quae amplius: & tamen necesse est,/ Milliaria singulis diebus/ Multa conficiam misella, ni te/ Volo linquere. Sed prius vel istis/ Optem filiolis meis sepulcrum/ Fiant viscera matris; ipsa praeda/ Optarim prius esse vel luporum,/ Quam te, maxime Pole, derelinquam.' Carol Maddison, *Marcantonio Flaminio. Poet, humanist, reformer* (London: Routledge, 1965), p. 151 guessed that the poem dated from the summer of 1543. George B. Parks, 'Italian tributes to cardinal Pole', in Dale B. J. Randall and G. W. Williams, eds., *Studies in the continental background of renaissance English literature: essays presented to John L. Lievsay* (Durham, N.C.: Duke University Press, 1977), pp. 43–66, 50–1 noticed this poem, but mistakenly said it was 'written by Flaminio for Pole's kitten', apparently as a result of mistranslating *catella* (!) and missing that Flaminio is the speaker.

recall.[104] Pole took a leading role in consistory, and was identified with Morone as spearheading reform efforts. When the pope proposed to give the Datary to his grandson Ranuccio in succession to Cardinal Pucci, although Pole could say nothing because he had already spoken, he made a cross with his fingers, according to one interpretation in order to indicate that Ranuccio should act like the Syrene who carried Christ's cross. This unlikely prospect caused general laughter.[105] It also seems that Pole considered returning to Trent, although Massarelli thought his legation ceased when he left Padua, and Morone may have replaced him in August.[106] Diego Hurtado de Mendoza, the imperial ambassador to Rome, thought in mid-1547 that the emperor should cultivate him, unless his views on justification proved damaging.[107]

January and February 1547 brought a rash of deaths important to Pole. First came Bembo's, then Henry VIII's, and finally Colonna's. Pole left no very strong reactions to either the first or last, although he visited Bembo on his deathbed at which time he reminded him of their joint appearance in what Bembo called Cosmo Gheri's dying vision.[108] Probably Pole adopted the means of consolation he recommended to Madruzzo when his brother died at nearly the same time: prayer.[109] The third death, Henry's at the end of January, left Pole to deal with more pressing matters when the pope decided to appoint legates about England to the emperor, the French king, and the king of Scotland.[110] Pole wrote the pope two letters, arguing that Madruzzo was the best choice for the empire, and offering his own services.[111] Madruzzo may have proposed this to Pole originally, and Cardinal Farnese endorsed the plan. Pole then objected that this would both offend France and leave the emperor lord of England, but he abandoned his reservations.[112] On 25 February, two of the three legates were named, but not Pole, because of Granvelle's opposition.[113] Mendoza y Bobadilla, with whom Pole had a running dispute over a pension on Granada, undermined him with the emperor.[114] By the end of March, any hope of sending Pole was gone, officially because of fear that he would offend the new rulers of England, the

---

[104] *CRP*, no. 512; Jedin, 2, p. 414.

[105] *CT*, 10, p. 924.

[106] *CRP*, no. 509 and *CT*, 1, p. 449 and 10, p. 589.

[107] Fenlon, p. 219.

[108] For Bembo *CRP*, no. 513. For the visit, Beccadelli, 'Vita del cardinale Pietro Bembo', in *MMB*, 1:2, pp. 223–52, pp. 247–8.

[109] *CRP*, no. 516.

[110] *CT*, 10, p. 821. See also A. von Druffel, 'Die Sendung des Card. Sfondrato an den Hof Karls V. 1547–48. 1', *Abhandlungen der historischen Classe der königlichen bayerischen Academie der Wissenschaften*, 20 (1893), pp. 291–362, pp. 312–24.

[111] *CRP*, nos. 514–15.

[112] *CT*, 11, p. 891.

[113] *CT*, 10, pp. 641 n2, 821 and 827.

[114] *CT*, 11, p. 105.

6 *Civita, Bagnoregio.*

excuse Mendoza had suggested.[115] Pole later claimed to have made an approach to England, as well as to the emperor, after Henry died; perhaps he meant in 1548 (see below).[116]

The rumours swirling around Pole may have helped to inspire the appearance of one of the first publications contributing to his myth, Paolo Giovio's *Descriptio Britanniae, Scotiae, Hyberniae, et Orchadum*, which appeared probably in May 1548.[117] Near its end, Giovio recounted Pole's legation of 1537 and its sequel in the Exeter conspiracy, which Giovio described as part of Henry's revenge on Pole. At the conclusion Giovio bemoaned Henry's failure to attend to the call to penance in *De unitate*.[118] Pole probably gave Giovio a summary of his book and the details of recent English history perhaps via Giovio's collaborator and Pole's client George Lily.[119] Even if Pole did not, his prominence in Giovio's work was hard to miss. Giovio may have meant to appeal to both the English nobility and to the emperor, as well as the *spirituali* to take action against England, perhaps under Pole's leadership.[120]

Probably also in January 1547 Pole received the office of perpetual governor of Bagnoregio (illus. 6).[121] About the same time he gave up active involvement in the legation of Viterbo, but was not replaced as legate for another three years.[122] In Bagnoregio he lived in the Augustinian convent of Sant'Agostino (illus. 7), with its nearly new Renaissance cloister by Sanmicheli. Pole enjoyed the place and spent a good deal of time there over the next six years, possibly beginning that summer. Among his guests may have been Morillo and Carnesecchi.[123] Pole did not spend all his time in Bagnoregio on spiritual topics, and actively forwarded the commune's interests. He secured the commitment of its boundary dispute with Bolsena to himself and Cardinal Sforza and produced a compromise.[124] It did not hold and other disputes soon arose. Similarly, he defended Bagnoregio against the governor of Viterbo in a case involving trespassing sheep, and intervened in other ways.[125] Concern for the citizenry of

---

115 *CT*, 11, p. 157.

116 *CRP*, no. 555.

117 Thomas F. Mayer, 'Reginald Pole in Paolo Giovio's *Descriptio*: a strategy for reconversion', *SCJ*, 16 (1985), pp. 431–50, p. 436 (now in Thomas F. Mayer, *Cardinal Pole in European context: a via media in the reformation* (Aldershot: Ashgate Publishing, 2000)).

118 *Ibid.*, p. 433.

119 T. C. Price Zimmermann, *Paolo Giovio: the historian and the crisis of sixteenth-century Italy* (Princeton: Princeton University Press, 1995), p. 216.

120 Mayer, 'Giovio's *Descriptio*', pp. 442–9, mainly endorsed by Zimmermann, p. 216.

121 *CRP*, no. 511.

122 ASVe:APR, 7, fo. 363v (*CSPV*, 5, 670).

123 *PC*, pp. 351 and 514.

124 *CRP*, no. 517.

125 *CRP*, no. 519.

7 *Convent of Sant'Agostino, Bagnoregio.*

Bagnoregio appeared most clearly in a practical piece of patronage. According to Dudic, Pole, finding Bagnoregio's 'men completely dedicated to leisure . . . lent the city money, by which it would be helped to establish a woollen industry, and so in cultivating that art, they would not live poorly, leading leisurely and idle lives'.[126] Like other sixteenth-century biographers, Dudic fictionalized this episode.[127] In fact, probably drawing on the experience of the place gained from spending most of the summer there, Pole originally merely ordered the *Consiglio grande* in November 1550 to establish the mill 'in order to cut out of misery and idleness, the cause and origin of all evils, the unemployed [*disoccupati*] citizens of the city', and made them take out a loan in Rome to pay for it.[128] The next year, Pole was persuaded to loan the comune one hundred *scudi* of his own,

126 *ERP*, 2, p. 60.
127 See the introduction to Thomas F. Mayer and D. R. Woolf, eds., *The rhetorics of life-writing in early-modern Europe* (Ann Arbor: University of Michigan Press, 1995).
128 Eletto Ramacci, Untitled typescript history of the cardinals governor of Bagnoregio, pp. 116 and 114 from destroyed records once in the communal archive, along with ASVT, Archivio notarile di Bagnoregio, protocollo no. 99 (Venturini, Giov. Antonio), fo. 35v. I am most grateful to Sig. Ramacci for allowing me to read his work and for many kindnesses.

advancing the same sum again the following year.[129] Pole may have made another loan along with Cardinal Campeggi in 1554, but all for naught: a flood destroyed the works.[130] This did not prevent Pole from demanding repayment in 1555, but he probably never got his money, and somewhat gracelessly converted a part of the loan into a gift in 1557.[131] That money went into new walls (the commune was already sliding off its precarious perch), and a rehabilitation of Porta Santa Maria.[132] According to local folklore, the eagle over the gate commemorates Pole's largesse.[133] He remained governor until his departure for England in 1553 when he nominated Cardinal Corner his commendatory.[134]

Pole did not get his way over England in 1547, nor did he over the translation of the council to Bologna. He opposed a move on the grounds of his undiminished hope that the Lutherans would still come to Trent, if the council returned.[135] If Pole had thought himself defeated at Trent, this becomes an almost delusional moment. The possibility of moving the council that had arisen in the summer of 1546 had come to the point by April 1547 where ambassador Mendoza had threatened to protest. He did not do so until 23 January 1548, and Pole was deputed to reply.[136] He was one of eight cardinals opposed to moving the council, and perhaps the pope meant to give the reply greater weight with the emperor by assigning him the job, or perhaps he was rubbing Pole's nose in his defeat.[137] Pole did not work alone. On 3 February three other cardinals joined him, Jean du Bellay, Alvarez, and Crescenzi, the last of whom as the only jurist probably had a large hand in the draft.[138] The papal secretary Blosio Palladio polished its style.[139] Its bulk put forward a historical

---

[129] Ramacci, p. 117.

[130] Ramacci, p. 125.

[131] Ramacci, pp. 118 and 138.

[132] Ramacci, p. 142.

[133] Eletto Ramacci, *Bagnoregio e Civita. Guida storico-turistica* (Montefiascone: Graffietti, 1986), p. 77.

[134] Ramacci, 'Cardinals', pp. 119–25.

[135] *CT*, 12, p. 944. Fenlon, p. 101 quotes some of Averardo Serristori's report of 15 December 1547 to Cosimo I, but without a date and in a context which makes it appear to refer only to his expectations before the council met.

[136] *CT*, 11, p. 354; Hubert Jedin, *Storia del concilio di Trento*, 3, 2nd ed., trans. A. Sorsaja, G. Moretto, and Giuseppe Alberigo (Brescia: Morcelliana, 1982), pp.

241–2. The protest is printed in *CT*, 6:3, pp. 717–26, followed by the papal reply on 728–38. The editors noted the version in *ERP*, but did not discover its likely original in BAV, Vat. lat. 5967, fos. 62r–79r, which runs very close to the printed text until it breaks off. Its existence underlines the degree of Pole's involvement.

[137] *CT*, 11, p. 959. Pole continued to be involved in efforts to keep in or return to Trent the council, including serving on a commission of four cardinals which was to judge the validity of its move to Bologna. Jedin, 3, pp. 162, 165, 260, 279n, 291–4.

[138] *CT*, 1, p. 742 and 11, p. 959.

[139] Jedin, 3, p. 241. BAV, Vat. lat. 5967, fos. 62r–79r is not in Palladio's hand.

argument intended to exculpate the pope from the legal charge of negligence and refute Mendoza's assertion that the emperor had shown greater concern for the council, and this may well have come from Pole.[140] If so, it could not have helped his standing with either Mendoza or the emperor.

Madruzzo was usually right in the middle of the negotiations about the suspension or translation of the council, and since the time when they had first become close at Trent, Pole's relationship with him intensified. It now threatened to become as close as that with Morone. Madruzzo was said to trust Pole so much that he would leave the choice of a legate to Charles entirely up to him, and Pole for his part did not hesitate to commend Bartolomeo Spadafora warmly to Madruzzo.[141] Spadafora was in trouble with the Sicilian Inquisition, and Pole asked Madruzzo both to recommend him to the emperor and to take him under his own protection.[142] Carnesecchi had been investigated by the Inquisition in January 1546, and Pole wrote a letter to the pope on his behalf that resulted in the quashing of the *processo*.[143] At least the fringes of his orbit were coming under pressure again, and Pole also wrote Madruzzo on behalf of Cesare Carduino, a Neapolitan for whom Madruzzo had already tried to intercede with the Viceroy.[144] Pole may have come closer to trouble than he knew. His former chaplain Merenda probably first fell foul of the Inquisition in 1548–9.[145] De' Bartoli, not investigated until 1552, said he had last spoken to Pole in 1547 or 1549 (almost certainly the first), when Pole assured him that anyone who knew true religion could live 'among friars, priests and anyone'.[146] If

---

[140] Jedin, 2, pp. 241–3.

[141] Pole remained an expert on imperial affairs, and was consulted when the question of a legate arose again in August 1548. *Nuntiaturberichte aus Deutschland. Erste Abteilung 1533–1559*, 11, *Nuntiatur des Bischoffs Pietro Bertano von Fano 1548–1549*, ed. Walter Friedensburg (Berlin: A. Bath, 1910), pp. 78 and 707.

[142] *CT*, 11, p. 959 and *CRP*, no. 522. For Spadafora (although not this episode), see Salvatore Caponetto, 'Origini e caratteri della Riforma in Sicilia', *Rinascimento*, 7 (1956), pp. 219–341.

[143] *PM*, 6, pp. 233–4n. Cf. ASF:AMP, 3268, fos. 593r–4v for the *processo* of four years earlier.

[144] *CRP*, no. 525.

[145] *PM*, 2, pp. 158–60.

[146] *PM*, 6, p. 166; cf. *PM*, 2, p. 263. In the full version of his testimony, Bartoli specified that he had talked to Pole in the English hospice in Rome on 31 May and recalled the conversation as having taken place 'three or four' years after their previous meeting when Pole had obliquely suggested that Bartoli leave his order, in the context of a discussion of Bartoli's preaching. This first moment probably belongs to 1543, putting the second into 1546 or 1547, and if Bartoli is correct about the day and one of the two years he suggested, the meeting must have taken place in 1547. By 14 May 1549 Pole had moved for the summer to Civitella San Paolo, where he certainly was still on the 30th. *CRP*, nos. 546–7.

de' Bartoli's testimony can be trusted, it underscores Pole's refusal to accept defeat and provides direct confirmation of the thesis that Pole was a Nicodemite (see the conclusion). At the same time the Inquisition may have begun to worry about Pole, his client Thomas Goldwell became a Theatine novice in Naples.[147] Carafa could therefore not have concerned Pole much, or was he deliberately trying to ingratiate himself with the inquisitor?

An opening to Somerset

England once more attracted Pole's interest in late 1548. In October John Yonge wrote Throckmorton that Protector Somerset would receive letters from Pole if he wrote as a private person.[148] Yonge may have been the Catholic controversialist and hopeful client of Pole, to whom he dedicated his 'Enarrationes in Joelis prophetae'.[149] Hugh Latimer's opinion that Pole could have been a good preacher dates from about the same time, and reinforces the possibility that Somerset was negotiating seriously.[150] The English sent at least one mission to Pole, and in reply, Pole dispatched Richard Hilliard and Throckmorton in April bearing credential letters to the earl of Warwick and Domingo de Soto, the emperor's confessor. Warwick did not reply, but that did not deter Pole from sending them again in May. They reached the imperial court by the 14th, but Granvelle and the emperor initially refused to allow them to proceed. Hilliard consulted the English ambassador, Sir Philip Hoby, who did 'not disapprove' his going to England.[151] To judge from the date of Somerset's reply, 4 June, it seems the emperor quickly relented.[152]

Hilliard had detailed instructions. He was to begin by assuring the Protector of Pole's love, and then pass to the dangers threatening both him and the realm.[153] First was a boy king, and Hilliard was to cite numerous examples from both ancient and more recent history. Nor could England depend on its alliances. An even greater threat came from internal dissension between the

[147] T. E. Bridgett and T. F. Knox, *The true story of the Catholic hierarchy deposed by Queen Elizabeth* (London: Burns and Oates, 1889), p. 215.

[148] *CSPDom*, 1, p. 11.

[149] Bodleian Library, Rawlinson MS C 45. For Yonge, see the *DNB* and Diarmaid MacCulloch, *Thomas Cranmer. A life* (New Haven and London: Yale University Press, 1996), p. 535.

[150] G. E. Corrie, ed., *Sermons by Hugh Latimer, sometime bishop of Worcester, martyr, 1555* (Cambridge: Cambridge University Press, 1844), p. 173.

[151] *CRP*, no. 547.

[152] *CRP*, no. 548.

[153] *CRP*, no. 544.

bishops and the clergy, a reference to Gardiner's imprisonment (fo. 23r). Pole also proposed solutions. Since the usual remedy for religious difficulties, an appeal to the pope, was closed, there should be a debate between learned men, with the victory going to the majority. Prayer, offered in 'equity of spirit', was the only way to bring that discussion to the truth. Naturally, it needed a moderator, and who better than him? The English should have no fear of his partisanship for the Roman church, and Pole proposed a meeting on neutral ground. Borrowing a leaf from 1537, he suggested Flanders, even though that would be very inconvenient for him. Above all, the Protector had to act to protect Edward's legitimacy, since a schismatic was automatically deprived.

The council did not delay in its reply, although it seems to have been in two minds about what to write Pole and on what authority. A version in English, which may have been the original draft and is signed only by Somerset, spends more time on specifically English conditions and replies at greater length to Pole's most important proposal, the conference, than does the text in Latin, which must have been the version sent.[154] Whoever drafted the Latin document chose to use language almost identical to Pole's, opening by noting the 'consolation' the council had felt from the thought that Pole still loved his country. The letter quickly came to the point. Instead of sending Pole a royal pardon which would allow him to come home, the council had been forced to treat him as a foreign prince who preferred Rome to England 'on the pretext of piety'. The dangers Pole had cited were invalid, and, besides, the council trusted 'divine providence'. The English had no reason to fear other princes, and were instead expecting them to convert, following the lead of English learned men who had already decided the case. The council held out the possibility that Pole could spend his old age in England, and originally intended to offer a conference in which they would convince Pole on the grounds of scripture. To judge from Pole's response, this proposal did not make it into the version as dispatched.

Pole did not see this letter, dated 6 June 1549, until the end of July.[155] He had already taken a reply in hand, but delayed completing and perhaps posting it until mid-October. The council's letter may have discouraged him along with the emperor's refusal to help.[156] He began to write before news of the Prayer Book rebellion arrived.[157] It broke out in early June and later that month came demands for the restoration of the Act of Six Articles and Pole's return, as well as the first response from London by late June. Fighting commenced in late July

---

[154] *CRP*, no. 548.
[155] *CRP*, no. 553.

[156] *CRP*, no. 552.
[157] *CRP*, no. 555.

and was nearly over by 21 August.[158] All of this news arrived slowly in Rome. On receipt of some of it on 31 August the pope both summoned Pole to consult, and also called a consistory.[159] The pope's expectation that Pole would be sent to restore England to the faith and make it a fief of the holy see sounds as if the information that spurred him to act must have been the by-then superseded rebels' demands. The lost occasion, known to have been missed two weeks later, may have provided a stimulus to Pole to resume writing.[160] He made up in length for the delay.[161] Disappointed by the council's letter, Pole had thought to leave the matter to God's providence, but his messengers convinced him that the letter they had brought from England did not correspond to what they had been told. This gave Pole the rhetorical opening of blaming the discourteous letter on Somerset's secretary and trying one more time with the duke. He registered his objections to the dishonourable treatment he had received at great length, and returned to his annoyance and the question of honour periodically throughout the letter. He made the affront offered to him an indicator of how low the regime in England had sunk, to make fun of his 'simplicity' (sincerity; fo. 4v). Pole dealt with Somerset as one great noble to another who badly needed to be taught manners, as if, Pole wrote not very subtly, he had come from the lowest station (as Somerset more or less had). Pole tried to bring up the proposed conference, expressing relief that he would not have to make such a taxing journey since it was clear it would have had no results, but returned instead to how insulted he felt. Instead of taking him as concerned only for the salvation and honour of England, the council had accused him of malice, and on and on. Pole was especially annoyed that the suggestion that he come in person to consult English representatives had been taken as a sign of pride (even though insisting on how well suited he was might appear to be prideful). Pole was wounded to the quick.

As often in such circumstances, he turned to autobiographical *exempla* drawn from his experiences with Henry VIII, all designed to show Somerset's action to disadvantage and all emphasizing his standing. The first demonstrated that Henry, 'the greatest enemy I have had in the world', faced with an instance of Pole's sincerity, had not mocked him. The moment was Pole's written opinion on Henry's first divorce and its sequel, and has become one of the most famous scenes in Pole's myth. Pole's brother, probably Lord Montagu, was worried that

---

[158] W. K. Jordan, *Edward VI. The young king* (Cambridge: Harvard University Press, 1968), pp. 453–77.

[159] ASVe:APR, 7, fo. 67r (*CSPV*, 5, no. 572)

and fo. 70r.

[160] ASVe:APR, 7, fo. 76v (*CSPV*, 5, no. 577).

[161] *CRP*, no. 555. I cite the text from BAV, Vat. lat. 6754, fos. 3r–27v.

Henry would take strong exception to Pole's opinion, but Pole assured him that the king would recognize the spirit in which he wrote and asked his brother to arrange an interview. This took place in a private garden, and, true to Pole's prediction, Henry objected violently to his opinion, without, however, taking exception to him. Pole tacked on Sir John Russell's assurance to him that he would not fear to give Pole's opinion to the king, whatever it was. Somerset and his secretary were supposed to learn from 'these two examples'. Pole lectured Somerset on a secretary's role, in an ekphrasis with implications for his own composing practice. A secretary should 'express with words the inner sense of his lord, just as it is the duty of a painter to paint the exterior figure of a body' (fo. 6v). Pole may not have stooped to making fun of Somerset, but he certainly treated him with the maximum degree of condescension. The second example reconstructed Pole's life in writing. Trying to induce Somerset to agree to a conference, Pole told him that Henry had ordered learned men to meet him at Liège, especially Doctor (Nicholas) Wilson, but the pope had forced Pole to return to Rome (fo. 14v). As we have seen, this was not quite true. The moral this time was that Somerset's pride had ruined the meeting.

The ease with which both men operated in the same language underscores the degree to which they might have seen eye to eye on the religious beliefs underlying it. The overlap in language is perhaps clearest and of greatest significance for Pole's religious beliefs in his turning Somerset's 'consolation' back on him (fo. 14v). This large area of potential agreement did not arise casually. It was no coincidence that Somerset's monarch owned a manuscript of the *Beneficio*, and Edward Courtenay translated it during his reign.[162] Many of those who had once shared views of justification like Pole's had gravitated to England under Archbishop Cranmer's regime, including the pair that had first made things uncomfortable for Pole, Ochino, and Vermigli, and his convert Tremelli.[163] Pole deliberately treated theological points cursorily, and virtually ignored papal primacy. The basic problem, as neither he nor Somerset seems to have recognized, was that they had two incompatible political agendas. Somerset expected Pole as a private person to sue for pardon, and Pole thought it his role as a public man to advise the government on religious policy. There was no middle ground. Much of the body of Pole's letter is predictable, as he

---

[162] Salvatore Caponetto, ed., *Il 'beneficio di Cristo' con le versione del secolo XVI, documenti e testimonianze* (Florence, DeKalb, IL and Chicago: Sansoni, Northern Illinois University Press and The Newberry Library, 1972), p. 507.

[163] A. G. Dickens, *The English reformation*, 2nd ed. (University Park: Pennsylvania State University Press, 1989), pp. 258–9.

rigorously reversed the allegations Somerset made, as for example, that Edward should beg pardon of him on account of Henry's injuries to Pole and his family, not he of Edward. Edward should pray for the repentance that Henry was denied, and so on.

As Pole always did, he insisted that he did not care about his private interest, and had written out of love of country and concern for its welfare. Besides, fixing the public problem would automatically resolve his private difficulties. He spent much more time on his family's sufferings than he had before, offering a history of the family from Henry VII forward (cf. also fos. 18v–19r where Pole used his family's history as a means to threaten Somerset with the emperor's wrath, an argument that sounds increasingly desperate in light of Charles's utter refusal to have anything to do with avenging the Poles). Pole's private case took up increasing amounts of space, as perhaps imperceptibly the issue became not one of policy at all, but of the perception in England of Pole's inner thoughts. Deprived of the chance to deal with Somerset one-on-one, Pole's forte, he was forced to try to replicate those dynamics in writing, with the result of looking a little pathetic and sounding exceedingly querulous.

Sometimes Pole rose above that level, especially when spelling out once more his objections to the supreme headship. No prince dared presume to be supreme lord, a title which belonged only to God and His Son, and only divine law therefore could be the ultimate standard (fo. 9r–v). Pole was also not convinced that pure religion had been restored in England. 'Spiritual understanding' of scripture came only to those to whom God gave it along with the Holy Spirit, and Somerset's actions in mocking Pole, early identified as the sin against the Holy Spirit, revealed that he did not have it (fo. 10r). Obedience made only a passing appearance. It did not return, either, when Pole accused Somerset of sacrilege through executions and spoliations, which also did not bespeak a 'spiritual understanding' of scripture. Obedience reappeared only much later, and was glossed as obedience to God in heaven (fo. 11r). The pope was never mentioned.

Pole did once or twice get down to brass tacks, as when he faulted Somerset for allowing wild new heresies to have official hearings, especially Trinitarian aberrations that he said had been discussed before the marquis of Dorchester (or Dorset? Henry Grey) (fo. 12v).[164] Just as Pole had feared, these heresies had led to division among the people, which in turn had engendered rebellion. Pole also

---

[164] That there were anti-Trinitarians in England is beyond dispute, but I have been unable to identify this episode. Cf. G. H. Williams, *The radical reformation* (Kirksville, MO: Sixteenth Century Journal Publishers, 1992; 3rd revised ed.), pp. 1196 and 1015 for Jan Laski's embryonic views.

adverted many times to the threat the emperor posed, but because he knew all too well that Charles had refused to do anything, the only way Pole could make that threat look alarming was to refer to Charles's upbraiding of ambassador Hoby, and to talk in generalities about how much Charles should resent his aunt's treatment (e.g., fo. 17v). This was not much. Threats drawn from recent English history might carry more weight, and Pole repeated his earlier examples of the dangers of a boy king, especially Henry VI (fo. 16v). Pole showed that he had learned something from his dealings with the emperor, for when he obliquely referred to the argument of *De unitate* about the people's power over their corrupted head, he carefully assigned the right to act against the king to the emperor alone (fo. 20v). He also insisted that he had never said anything more to the emperor than that he act for the good of both people and king, including at the beginning of the present negotiations with England (fo. 21r). This reduced the emperor's threat, but Pole had one more argument, divine vengeance, reminding Somerset of God's propensity to punish the proud through war, like that the English were then waging against both France and Scotland (fo. 22r). When word of the Prayer Book rebellion reached Pole, he forbore to use it as one last threat, even though he had predicted civil discord. All he wished was the re-establishment of concord. Unfortunately, Somerset's own lack of concord with the council probably helped to make it impossible for him to deal further with Pole. The only sign of a reaction to this initiative came from the duke of Northumberland's instruction in 1552 for a mission to Charles V. It was to carry copies of Pole's letters so that the emperor could see what trouble he was making.[165]

---

[165] C. S. Knighton, ed., *Calendar of state papers domestic series of the reign of Edward VI revised* (London: HMSO, 1992), no. 790. This may mean that the English had intercepted letters, perhaps including *CRP*, no. 596. The mission was Sir Andrew Dudley's. Gary M. Bell, *A handlist of British diplomatic representatives 1509–1688* (London: Royal Historical Society, 1990), p. 54. His instructions in W. H. Turnbull, ed., *Calendar of state papers foreign series of the reign of Edward, 1547–1553* (London: Longman, Green, Longman and Roberts, 1861), no. 599 make no mention of Pole's letters and neither does his slim correspondence.

5

The war of the saints

SHORTLY AFTER HIS letter to Somerset, Paul III's death distracted Pole from England.[1] Almost as soon as it happened on 10 November, Pole found himself called upon to discharge a vital political role when Camillo Orsini asked his advice about whether to reinstate Ottavio Farnese in Parma. The problem arose from one of Paul's most egregious acts of nepotism. He had detached Parma and Piacenza from the states of the church and erected them into a duchy for Ottavio, but in his last days had changed his mind. Orsini was dispatched to take possession, Ottavio raced north from Rome to forestall him, and the pope fired off new orders to Orsini to resist Ottavio's pretensions.[2] In this tense situation, instead of telling Orsini what to do, Pole advised him to have his messenger present the matter to the college of cardinals governing the church during the papal vacancy.[3] This letter went against Pole's own wishes, it appears. It was later said that he endorsed the plan to surrender Parma because he thought the papacy should have no temporal possessions.[4]

Orsini's letter sprang both from his friendship with Pole and from good politics. Many thought Pole most likely to succeed Pope Paul. This did not transpire. Instead, at one of the most important moments of the Italian and European reformations Pole missed election by one vote. After leading on the first ballot by a comfortable margin, on 4 December 1549 Pole gained twenty-four of the twenty-eight votes necessary. Alessandro Farnese then proposed to have Pole elected by adoration, a sort of acclamation. Pole initially agreed, but then changed his mind. Despite this, the bankers placed his odds at 90–95 per

---

[1] The chapter title comes from Matteo Dandolo's dispatch of 18 December (ASVe:APR, 7, fo. 147r).

[2] See Ludwig von Pastor, *Geschichte der Päpste im Zeitalter der katholischen Reformation und Restauration*, 5 (Freiburg: Herder, 1919),

pp. 673–4.

[3] *CRP*, no. 556; cf. ASF:AMP 395, fos. 15r–16r and ASVe:APR, 7, fo. 118r–v (*CSPV*, 5, no. 594).

[4] Archivio di stato, Siena, Archivio del Balia (hereafter ASS:AB), b. 720, no. 57.

cent. On 5 December, Carafa attacked Pole as a heretic. An elaborate scheme to procure Pole's election through an orchestrated series of public vote changes came up four short, thanks to Carafa and the Inquisition, or so runs the current interpretation. The story is much more complex, and because of this I have told it elsewhere.[5] Here the cause of Pole's most important failure matters most. My detailed treatment shows that Carafa does not deserve the blame. For one thing, another inquisitor introduced the most damaging evidence against Pole, while yet a third helped to defend him. This action makes 'the Inquisition' a shibboleth, not an explanation. For another thing and far more important, the principal responsibility rests with Pole and his stubborn if high-minded refusal to campaign. He and Carafa did indeed fight hard throughout the lengthy conclave, but their single combat tells only part of the tale. It is best interpreted as a grand battle between French and imperial factions, with Farnese holding the balance. The sad outcome was that the reform tendency, and with it Pole's candidacy, broke up under political pressure. Despite this, Pole remained the leading candidate until just a day or two before Julius III's election on 7 February 1550.

Pole reacted typically, if with a better than usual sense of occasion. He summed up his non-candidacy along with most of his religious views in the form of perhaps his most important work, 'De summo pontifice', dedicated to one of the lynchpins of the imperial front, the sixteen-year-old Giulio della Rovere. The dedication is dated 20 January 1550, precisely the day on which Carafa pressed hardest for della Rovere's vote.[6]

The papal office and reform

'De summo pontifice' evinces a political impulse that could easily have led to the kind of reform that many of Pole's brother cardinals feared he had in mind.[7] The

---

[5] Thomas F. Mayer, 'Il fallimento di una candidatura: il partito della riforma, Reginald Pole e il conclave di Giulio III', *Annali dell'Istituto storico italo-germanico in Trento*, 21 (1995), pp. 41–67 and 'The conclave of Julius III and Cardinal Pole', in Thomas F. Mayer, *Cardinal Pole in European context: a via media in the reformation* (Aldershot: Ashgate Publishing, 2000).

[6] Mayer, 'Fallimento', pp. 58–9.

[7] The only serious treatment of this text is M. Trimpe, 'Macht aus Gehorsam: Grundmotive der Theologie des päpstlichen Primates im Denken Reginald Poles (1500–1558)', Th.D. thesis, University of Regensburg, 1972. Adriano Prosperi offers some suggestions, particularly that the work was founded in Christian Ciceronian notions of duty, in 'Il principe, il cardinale, il papa. Reginald Pole lettore di Machiavelli',

work's pretext is that della Rovere needed to know the nature of the papal office in order to choose the best candidate. Pole employed humanist argumentation, and his evidence usually came from scripture, almost always from either Paul or the prophets. He did occasionally, especially in several sticky corners, appeal to ecclesiastical custom, but never even to the degree that, say, Thomas More did. His description of the papacy is as evangelical as that in *De concilio*.

Pole's work has been praised for grounding the papacy on the martyrs, but in fact this dimension of the argument is more muted than in *De unitate*, and Pole's major argument took the papacy's justification directly back to Christ (e.g., fos. 32r or 70v) or to the Holy Spirit, as well as to the prophets (e.g., fos. 97rff), whose office the pope (in common with all the other bishops) now exercised (fos. 8v, 19v, and especially 102r).[8] Pole called the papacy the *principatus super humeros* prophesied by Ezekiel (fo. 34v), and contrasted it as a seat of mercy to the judicial tribunals of secular government that served vengeance and punishment (fos. 35vff and 63rff). The pope's chief weapon of excommunication was for healing, not damnation (fo. 76r–v). The papacy grew out of love, first Peter's love for Christ, then Christ's love for his flock, and love became the distinguishing mark of the *principatus super humeros* (e.g, fo. 37r). Although Pole described *principatus* in the language of jurisdiction and *imperium*, he gave those terms unusual content.

The pope had a simple job. All he had to do was imitate Christ, thereby following the 'hidden counsel of God' (fo. 44v and *passim*; cf. fos. 33r and 38v). This meant both imitating Christ's love for his flock as expressed on the cross, and also simultaneously rejecting what human prudence regarded as the virtues necessary for good government (e.g, fos 38v and 32v). Instead of human prudence and fortitude, the pope needed *imbecillitas* and divine *sapientia*. Only once he had experienced them could he arrive at true strength and wisdom.

---

in *Cultura e scrittura di Machiavelli: Atti del convegno di Firenza-Pisa 27–30 ottobre 1997* (Rome: Salerno, 1998), pp. 241–62, pp. 253ff. Trimpe's work suffers especially from its author's failure to locate any of its numerous MSS, in at least three different families and in both Italian and Latin. Prosperi (p. 253) notes that the work exists in several versions that demand proper philological treatment, although his call is muted by his misidentification of Pole's interlocutor as Cardinal del Monte. Cf. pp. 75–80. The near impossibility of establishing a synthetic text has led me reluctantly to use (as does Prosperi) John Fowler's edition printed in Louvain in 1569, which I have checked against the manuscripts as far as possible.

[8] Josef Ratzinger, 'The papal primacy and the unity of the people of God', in *Church, ecumenism and politics: new essays in ecclesiology* (New York: Crossroad, 1988), pp. 36–44 for the martyrs.

Thus, instead of wishing to expand his power as did all those who governed according to the precepts of human prudence, the pope should concern himself only with defending his flock by both celestial and terrestrial means, that is, with the resources of both the angelic and ecclesiastical hierarchies (fos. 79v–87r; cf. also fo. 52r–v). Further, the pope should reject domination and judgment, as a *ratio gubernandi* disapproved by God (fos. 74v–75r). He was also to practice *paupertas*, although Pole did not go so far as to cite the notorious fourteenth-century conflict over apostolic poverty, still alive (if gone underground) in his day (fo. 90r). The *principatus super humeros* entailed contempt for worldly honours (e.g, fo. 43v).

Establishing peace was the most important duty which fell to the pope, a point to which Pole devoted perhaps 10 per cent of his text (esp. fos. 41v–2r and 53v–61r). This meant peace within the church and between rulers and their people, as well as between the pope and secular princes (fos. 44v–5r and 119r–v.) Pole put forward the standard papalist claim that the pope had all power and his unique role in salvation made him superior to princes, but he reduced the impact of this claim in three ways. He maintained, first, that the pope should be a super-confessor to princes, needed because of their belief that they were above the law (fo. 115v); second, that although it was easy to find examples of conflict between popes and emperors, they should strive for co-operation (maybe even co-ordination of powers?; fos. 112r–28v); and third, that the pope should stay out of secular business as far as possible because that would derogate from his superior position on Christ's cross (fos. 130v–132r). If he had to deal with secular matters, he should take the cross with him (fos. 135v–136r).

Popes and bishops could not simply withdraw from intervening in the world because that would be cruel to the flock, failing to protect them from powerful men's depradations (fo. 75v). As a magistrate, the pope could punish, but only after he had tried clemency to the maximum degree (fo. 77r). This is one of several points at which Pole came right to the edge of criticizing past popes. It would be best if the pope and the bishops, following the apostles' example, confined their attention to spiritual cases, leaving secular matters to other experts (fo. 131v). Pole put all of this under the heading of *consolatio*, with special reference to the pope's power of binding and loosing (fos. 24v; also 53r, 73v, 78v, etc.), and *consolatio* and *pax* flowed from the head to the *infima plebs* (fo. 73v). He asserted, however, that this was impossible to understand without the aid of Christ's spirit, who engendered both understanding and right action, a possibly anti-intellectual, certainly 'mystical' stance (fos. 25v, 32v, 41r, etc.).

This could all be like Innocent III's high-minded claim that the pope had oversight of secular rulers' behaviour *ratione peccandi*, but Pole did not endorse anything like high papalist positions. Perhaps most important, he treated the pope as different only in degree from the bishops, all equally the apostles' successors. This was especially important because Pole traced the refounding of the *nova Roma*, the *civitas Dei*, to the apostles together, not to Peter alone, and as he repeatedly wrote, the *prima institutio* as the standard for the present primarily interested him (above all fos. 67r–69r and 141r–146r). In the specific case of the relations between pope and general council Pole argued, first, that the pope never had greater power than when he exercised it as head in the presence of all the bishops representing the body of the church (fos. 95r–v and 100r–v). Second, albeit with some reluctance, he proposed that although the council could only admonish an erring or insane pope, not remove him, the cardinals could withdraw their allegiance and elect a new pope (fos. 102v–107r), which had been the premise behind the *concilabulum* of Pisa.[9] Pole described the church as a narrow oligarchy, or perhaps a mixed monarchy, in another place paralleling the pope's duty of reconciliation and peace-making to the combination of *regium, oeconomicum, & politicum gubernandi genus* in the *civitas* (fo. 72v). Whichever polity Pole would have chosen when and if he lost the luxury of good humanist confusion about political theory, hierarchy need not mean nascent absolutism.

Thus a charismatically grounded, charitative 'principate' that Pole could yet describe in more or less standard terms of probably Aristotelian political discourse.[10] It is not too hard to see how a Farnese could attend only to one side of this unstable blend, and a Carafa to the other. At the same time, the whole of the dialogue reads like a reply to both, and on both levels simultaneously, both spiritual and political. Pole was neither as abstracted as he and his hagiographers later tried to claim, nor a strong papalist (like Carafa), as in more modern views of him. His view of papal monarchy could have severely damaged its bureaucracy, but even there Pole showed some politic flexibility, allowing that dispensations would always be necessary since no written law could cover every case (fos. 109v–110v). This argument, of course, would guarantee the continued existence of the Penitentiary, in whatever reduced form.

After the conclave, Pole continued to think about the papal office and reform in three closely related works. Two, a pair of companions to 'De summo pontifice', are relatively easy to understand. The third, 'De reformatione ecclesiae', is not. In both the companions, originally written in Italian, Priuli joined

---

[9] Francis Oakley, 'Almain and Major: conciliar theory on the eve of the reformation', *American historical review*, 70 (1965), pp. 673–90.

[10] Pole identified the *ars civilis* that the apostles taught as what Aristotle had called *politica* (fo. 137v).

Pole and della Rovere as speakers.[11] Della Rovere's involvement likely means that they were written before Pole left Rome in 1553. The first stressed the pope's responsibility to see that the nobility and other 'rulers of the people' did their job.[12] Sounding like Starkey, Pole argued that rulers had to be shown that the otiose life was 'most pernicious' (fo. 141r). The pope should set an example by never forgetting that he served others' commodity, not his own (fo. 143v). His office concerned solely 'the spiritual architecture of the church' (fo. 145r), and he had to remember as well as show others the necessity of renouncing all government to God (fo. 147r). All had to be governed by the rule of right reason, especially the people (fos. 150r–151r). That meant above all 'circumcising' concupiscence, first for material goods and then of any kind, the root of all trouble (fos. 156rff and 181r). Cupidity quickly became a metaphor for human prudence (fo. 162v), as always Pole's real target. Discussion of human prudence led naturally to reining in human intellect through proper education, including in how to interpret scripture through faith not intellect (fo. 174r). Parents were to educate their children as 'slaves of God' and every father needed a spiritual father to supervise him (fo. 182v). Formal education came next, with grammar schools for all (fos. 187v and 189v). If priests did their job in instructing parishioners, law would need only to fill in the gaps in good observance. Nevertheless, every city required good bishops, and Pole floated a plan for the religious supervision of Rome descending from the cardinals, members of the pope's body, through parish priests acting as bishops (fos. 197v–200r).

The second treatment of the papal office more closely resembles both 'De summo pontifice' and 'De reformatione ecclesiae', although it also contains a good deal of material similar to the work just discussed.[13] In place of an emphasis on structure and office, it roots the papacy in Christ's passion (book II, fo. 5r–v). It also adopts the metaphor of the vicar of Christ as Christ's wife, and all three of the speakers outdid themselves in claiming a knowledge of conjugal love (fos. 28v–31v). The discussion spilled over into the third day in tones increasingly reminiscent of Bernard. The difficulty of finding a good candidate for pope, since he might well look like a humble, unassuming person (fos. 21v–22v), led back to the husband–wife metaphor, the excellence of Christ persuading the reluctant candidate to take the job (fo. 25r).[14] This passage resembles Pole's description of himself in his letter to Navarra (see below). The best example of a good governor was Paul, who learned the best form of government during his rapture.

---

[11] *CPM*, catalogue nos. 12g and l.

[12] BAV, Vat. lat. 5966, fos. 139v and 145v.

[13] ACDFSO, St. st. E 6–a, fasc. 4.

[14] BAV, Vat. lat. 5965, fos. 99vff. also gave much attention to how to recognize a good candidate.

Government was love (fo. 27v). It was also a matter of leading the flock to God's banquet as had Ezekiel (fos. 35r–36v). Priuli took that opportunity to get Pole to talk about reform of the church, which he did in book IV.

The discussion parallels that in 'De reformatione ecclesiae', beginning with the transfiguration as the model of good government (book IV, fo. 1r), even if most of the specifics repeat those in the first dialogue on the pope and therefore deviate from the imprecise designs of 'De reformatione'. The popes had followed the model of the transfiguration from the first, employing the general council (fo. 1v). This point is equally clear in most of the versions of 'De reformatione', but much of the rest of its content is not. This is because Pole's pronounced anti-intellectual strain now almost overwhelmed his arguments, which were as usual cast in the form of dialogues, at least as rhetorical as ever. Pole's withdrawal from the centre of power made him ever more eager to persuade, but through increasingly obscure means. It is never easy to synthesize Pole's ideas, and now as his writing became more and more contemplative, merely grasping them can pose a challenge. To put it simply, Pole was even less interested than he had been in communicating through argument, preferring to instil religious experience in its place.

'De reformatione ecclesiae' exists in a dozen versions, the precise relations between which are almost impossible to sort out.[15] Pole may have worked on it over a period of as much as fifteen years. The council of Trent provided its original occasion, and Pole via Priuli conducted negotiations with Seripando over the work as late as 1556.[16] Pole several times began afresh by discarding (or forgetting) the most recent drafts and going back to an 'original' version. Were it not for the discovery of the latest text in the archives of the Inquisition, the situation would be worse. Thanks to it, we can say with fair confidence where Pole ended up, even if it does not necessarily become much easier to say how he got there.

One main line of evolution is clear. In the earliest versions Pole stressed the role of faith and continued to speak the language of benefit, illumination, and peace. For example, there was once a long disquisition on the impossibility of knowing God which argued that some men could know more of Him than others, a passage redolent of the earlier language of the image of God and his benefits. It concluded emphatically that 'justice is of faith'.[17] Leaders of the church were distinguished from their flock primarily by being more charismatic.

---

[15] *CPM*, catalogue no. 8.
[16] BAV, Vat. lat. 5964, fo. 351r. Carlo De Frede, *La restaurazione cattolica in Inghilterra sotto Maria Tudor nel carteggio di* *Girolamo Seripando* (Naples: Libreria Scientifica, 1971), pp. 73 and 100–2.
[17] Vat. lat. 5964, fos. 427v–8r and 430r.

In the latest drafts, leaders had become office holders, their flock responsible for the deformation of the church, and faith had virtually disappeared.

All versions of the work begin by seeking a definition of reform within the context of the best state of the church as instituted by Christ.[18] Reform meant restoring its original condition. The speaker (the two interlocutors are identified only as 'Q[uaestio].' and 'R[esponsum].') hurls his first incendiary device by saying that any whom Christ had made 'participants of his glory' could undertake reform.[19] Pole offered as his warrant Paul's rapture into the third heaven.[20] The equally 'rapturous' transfiguration became the church's model.[21] This charismatic Christianity was not as dangerous as it first appeared, since the 'enigma' of the transfiguration was interpreted to represent the two aspects of the glorious state of the church on earth. Both thoroughly familiar from Pole's earlier writing, they are penance and law, the first leading to the second.[22] Christ's companions in the transfiguration represented them, Elijah the preacher of penance, Moses the teacher of law, and anyone wishing to preside over the church had to follow one or both examples.[23] Therefore, reform of the church rested on an ancient model, not the synagogue, but rather the 'beauty' (*pulchritudo*) of the Jews, a 'shadow' that Christ revealed in full. Whoever combined penance and law with the faith of Christ would be as beautiful as possible.[24]

In order to explain, Pole had reluctantly to offer a lesson in exegesis. Sounding like Tertullian, he laid down the rule that the parts of scripture that sounded most meaningless to human ears were those that best opened 'the road to contemplating God's wisdom'. Unrepentant on the score of justification, Pole gave as the most obvious example of the power of absurdity the principle that salvation came through faith. Isaiah then appeared proclaiming the *verbum crucis*, the foundation of the church.[25] He also introduced the subject of preachers, who had the principal role in its reform.[26] In earlier versions, these preachers were identified as the bishops, the successors of the apostles.[27]

---

[18] Vat. lat. 5964, fos. 2r/135r/351r and 52r, the latest version which substituted new wording but with the same content. ACDFSO, St. st. E 6-a, fasc. 4, fo. 1r again has similar content with different wording.

[19] Vat. lat. 5964, fos. 2v/135v/165r/351v/ACDFSO, fo. 1v.

[20] Vat. lat. 5964, fos. 3v/54r/136v/165v/352v.

[21] Vat. lat. 5964, fos. 4r/137r/166r/353r.

[22] Vat. lat. 5964, fos. 4v/54v/137v/167r/353v/ACDFSO, fo. 3r.

[23] Vat. lat. 5964, fos. 5r/55r/138r/167v/354r/ACDFSO, fo. 3v.

[24] Vat. lat. 5964, fos. 6v/56r/139r/168v–9r/355r?/ACDFSO, fo. 4v.

[25] Vat. lat. 5964, fos. 8r–v/57r–v/140v–1v/170v–1v/356v–7v/ACDFSO, fos. 5v–6r.

[26] Vat. lat. 5964, fos. 9v/172v/142r/58r/358r/ACDFSO, fo. 6v. This is one of the points that makes me suspect that 'De modo concionandi' bore a close relation to 'De reformatione'.

[27] Cf. Vat. lat. 5964, fos. 358r/172v vs. 9v/58r/ACDFSO, fo. 6v.

The bishops originally bore principal responsibility for restoring all the other ministers and could only do this if they knew God's word.[28] The very earliest versions stressed their importance almost to the exclusion of anyone else and set the council's principal task as their reform.[29] Already at that time, however, Pole had turned his back on a major plank of humanist reformers, preferring that the bishops reside in their dioceses rather than gain an education.[30] If ignorant bishops spent their nights praying for illumination, they would go to school with the angels and learn how to set the example of *viva fides*.[31] All they needed otherwise was God's chastisement, as Ezekiel had once provided. This would lead them to penance and hence to God's spirit.[32] Pole expanded this in an early variant with the Pauline (and Lutheran) notion of *fides ex auditu*, repeated many times, instead of continuing as in the intermediate texts about prayer and its parts.[33] In the variant text, Pole wrote about preaching, to which the intermediate stage also eventually turned in more or less the same terms. Following Moses's example, good preachers would have relied on threats, the only means of keeping the people in the right path.[34] Now, under the new dispensation, faith had replaced the law.[35] John the Baptist's preaching reduced fear and increased joy, as it gave true light and consolation.[36] Accepting Christ's word led to true peace.[37] The law without the *verbum crucis* killed.[38] The first version treats this point at length, introducing levels of faith and the notion of vocation.[39] But just as in *De unitate*, Pole fairly quickly returned to penance, which had to be preached along with the gospel in order to avoid scandal, a point covered at even greater length than faith.[40] Works too put in an appearance as the means by which Christians declared the 'glorious spectacle' of Christ's resurrection. Baptism killed the old man, although his flesh remained unless controlled by the spirit. The hallmark of the passage was faith and its vital importance to redemption.[41]

This discussion did not survive into the later versions, any more than the charismatic bishops did. The later texts instead stressed how much the present

---

[28] Vat. lat. 5964, fos. 10r/58v/143r/ACDFSO, fos. 6v–7r.

[29] Vat. lat. 5964, fos. 411rff./174rff./360rff. These early versions spell out an agenda for a council, laying out canons on episcopal residence (fos. 177r/362v/413v) and the necessity that the bishops pray for spiritual guidance (fos. 181r/366r/415v). This aborted sequence fits neither Pole's plans at Trent nor in London.

[30] There is an independent treatment of the same point on fos. 143r–7v.

[31] Vat. lat. 5964, fos. 178r–v/414r–v/363v–4r.

[32] Vat. lat. 5964, fos. 364v/179v.

[33] Vat. lat. 5964, fos. 182v/367v/417r.

[34] Vat. lat. 5964, fos. 184v/368v/418v.

[35] Vat. lat. 5964, fos. 186r/370r–v/419v.

[36] Vat. lat. 5964, fos. 372r/421r/476r.

[37] Vat. lat. 5964, fo. 476v.

[38] Vat. lat. 5964, fo. 424v.

[39] Vat. lat. 5964, fos. 425r/377r.

[40] Cf. also Vat. lat. 5964, fos. 388r/205v–6r/434v.

[41] Vat. lat. 5964, fos. 195v/379r/426r–v, followed by another section on the importance of law, fos. 196r–9v/379vff.

state of the church had declined from the ancient model that had once under-girded the bishops' status.[42] None the less, the tone had not changed out of recognition. Pole still emphasized the necessity that bishops have divine illumination through *charitas* and the *virtus spiritus Christi*.[43] If anything, he hammered away even more on the necessity of residence, and it was still God's spirit that taught an ignorant bishop what to do.[44] Faith even reappeared, before almost vanishing in the rush to works. Pole came close to making works justify, since they manifested the good will that signified the presence of God's spirit.[45] The intermediate and later texts reconverge at this point and return to the preaching of the gospel, but now as the call to 'the obedience of faith'.[46] Preachers were to cite the prophets in confirmation of the gospel, and to imitate the evangelists themselves. Thereby they imparted to their flocks faith and hope, but also either *amor* or *charitas*, depending on the text.[47] Perhaps most consistently, Pole de-emphasized scripture in favour of illumination.[48] The bishops' office similarly remained *aedificatio*, *exhortatio*, and *consolatio*.[49] *Exhortatio* concerned exclusively 'this doctrine . . . of works'.[50] Although faith could not be entirely excluded, it appeared mainly as a stimulus to works. Works were not useless and rewards piled up in heaven, even if Pole did not quite con-nect the two.[51] There follows in most of the dialogue's versions an extended meditation on human weakness and the necessity of baptism.

This is not the rhetorical conclusion. In the latest versions, Pole inveighed against the *populus*, beginning with its insistence that only written law made 'a true rule' and condemning it as the worst member of the church, before finally blaming it for having let the bishops degenerate.[52] One of the people's principal failings was their avidity for scripture that led to innumerable controversies, a point which sounds as if it could have arisen from Pole's experience in England.[53] The best principle of reform was for the *populus* to obey its superi-ors.[54] The council could not lay the blame where the *populus* wished it, because

---

[42] Vat. lat. 5964, fos. 10v/59r/ACDFSO, fo. 7v.

[43] Vat. lat. 5964, fos. 11v–12r/59v–60v/ACDFSO, fo. 8r.

[44] Vat. lat. 5964, fos. 14v–16r/61v–2r/ACDFSO, fos. 9v–10v.

[45] Vat. lat. 5964, fos. 17r–v/63r/ACDFSO, fo. 12r.

[46] Vat. lat. 5964, fos. 18r/63v/148r/ACDFSO, fo. 12v.

[47] Vat. lat. 5964, fos. 19r/64v/149r.

[48] Vat. lat. 5964, fos. 20r/65v/ACDFSO, fo. 14r.

[49] Vat. lat. 5964, fo. 21r.

[50] Vat. lat. 5964, fos. 22r–v/66v–7r/ACDFSO, fos 14v–15r.

[51] Vat. lat. 5964, fos. 24v/68v/ACDFSO, fo. 16r.

[52] Vat. lat. 5964, fos. 41r–8v/78v–82v/245v–6v/ACDFSO, fos. 25v–9v.

[53] Vat. lat. 5964, fos. 86r/249r/ACDFSO, fo. 32v.

[54] Vat. lat. 5964, fos. 90v/253r/ACDFSO, fo. 35v.

they themselves were the root cause of the church's decline.[55] And so on. It is impossible to miss Pole's rooted hostility to popular action. Just in case one might, he adduced historical examples of its evil consequences for the church, and especially for rulers, and of the *populus*'s aversion to any kind of discipline.[56] Pole seems finally to have learned the lesson of the reactions to *De unitate* and the 'Apology'. But the levelling tendency of Pole's charismatic Christianity won out in the conclusion that every Christian must have an inner 'domestic master', the spirit of God.[57] Nothing but long experience of that spirit's monitions would tame the turbulent *populus*.[58] Only after experiencing the 'supreme evil' would conversion become possible.[59] Returning to a favourite theme, Pole stressed that trust in human wisdom was the greatest foolishness, amounting to another passion for Christ.[60] The last version concludes simply. Until the people acknowledged their fault and begged God for mercy, no reformation could happen.[61] This change of rhetorical aim made irrelevant the extensive treatment not only of the bishops but also of other rulers in earlier versions.

It is a little difficult to account for this change. In nearly all his other writing, including other apparently contemporary treatments of the same issues raised in 'De reformatione', Pole had strongly criticized the nobility. The final form of 'De reformatione' might sound like a preparation for Pole's return to England, and may therefore be connected to Pole's opening to Edward VI in 1552 (see below). If so, his experience of the lords' intransigence on the score of church property would have undercut his attacks on the *populus*. Nor can the point be saved by assuming an Aristotelian definition of this term, since Pole carefully distinguished the *populus* from its rulers. One point is clear. By demolishing both nobility and *populus*, albeit in different texts, Pole left himself no obvious political means of pursuing reform other than the crown, should he ever return to England. It is no surprise that Pole threw himself into Mary's arms.

Aftermath: Inquisition and England

Pole's thoughts may have begun to turn home again not only because of the fiasco in the conclave, but also a grievous loss suffered shortly after when

---

[55] Vat. lat. 5964, fos. 92r/255r/ACDFSO, fo. 36v.

[56] Vat. lat. 5964, fos. 94v/257r/ACDFSO, fo. 38r.

[57] Vat. lat. 5964, fos. 98r–9r/261r–3v/330v–1v/ACDFSO, fo. 41r–v.

[58] Vat. lat. 5964, fos.

101v/264v/333r/ACDFSO, fo. 42v.

[59] Vat. lat. 5964, fos. 105r/268r/336r/ACDFSO, fo. 44v.

[60] Vat. lat. 5964, fos. 106v/269v/337v/ACDFSO, fo. 45r and 129r/292v/ACDFSO, fo. 56v.

[61] Vat. lat. 5964, fos. 131r/ACDFSO, fos. 57r–8r, somewhat rearranged.

Flaminio died in Pole's house on 17 February.[62] This must have made a dramatic scene. Flaminio was attended by the physician Girolamo da Ponte or Pontano, perhaps already one of Pole's clients, and by Egidio Foscarari, soon to replace Morone as bishop of Modena, who heard Flaminio's confession.[63] According to Caracciolo, Carafa also intruded himself, lurking in the shadows, first whispering to the priest administering the last rites to ask Flaminio what he believed about the eucharist and then emerging to express his joy and talk to Flaminio during his last moments.[64] This tale must be invented. Most of it seems unlikely on its face, and it is contradicted by Pole's and Carafa's discussion of Flaminio three years later, during which Pole told Carafa the story of Flaminio's end, citing Foscarari as a witness to Flaminio's orthodoxy, but neither he nor Carafa mentioned Carafa's presence.[65] However odd it might be to include Carafa as such an important participant, it is stranger yet that Pole does not figure in any way.[66] He did in the controversy over how to shape Flaminio for posterity. Pietro Vettori wrote Pole in March offering consolation and praising Flaminio as a great poet and a good Christian.[67] Pole replied somewhat intemperately, asking Vettori to imagine his grief, and advising him to turn to sacred letters if he really wished to follow Flaminio's manner of living.[68] Pole's effort to console himself may have taken the form of a brief writing, 'De passione Christi'.[69]

Not only Flaminio's image attracted Pole's attention shortly after the conclave, but his own as well. Navarra wrote from Trent regretting that Pole had not been elected and praising his *fortitudo* as an 'athlete of Christ'.[70] Pole responded three months later rejecting Navarra's praise and proposing another image of himself, founded in his emotions. Pole thought the accusation of timidity more nearly accurate, since he did not always escape the fear characteristic of strong men. Navarra had heard stories about Pole's behaviour in the conclave, and Pole confirmed that he had never tried for election. Rather than revealing his

---

[62] Alessandro Pastore, *Marcantonio Flaminio. Fortune e sfortune di un chierico nell'Italia del Cinquecento* (Milan: Franco Angeli, 1981), p. 164.

[63] Da Ponte's account of Flaminio's death is in *Marci Antonii, Joannis Antonii et Gabrielis Flaminiorum Fornocorneliensium Carmina* (Padua: Giuseppe Comino, 1743), pp. 342–4 and for Foscarari *PM*, 2, pp. 401–2n and *MMB*, 1:2, p. 350.

[64] Antonio Caracciolo, *De vita Pauli IV*

pontificis maximi (Cologne: Johann Kinck, 1612), p. 54.

[65] *MMB*, 1:2, p. 350.

[66] Even Beccadelli said that Flaminio died in Pole's house. *MMB*, 1:2, p. 326. Dudic omitted any mention of Flaminio.

[67] *CRP*, no. 553.

[68] *CRP*, no. 564.

[69] BAV, Vat. lat. 5969, fos. 333r–50v and 353r–64r.

[70] *CRP*, no 562.

contempt for the office, his behaviour reflected the 'role that God had imposed on me', that of an ass with no use for honours. When Farnese first proposed his election, Pole made no reply. As the heavy reworking of the manuscript here indicates, it took him some effort to get this part of the story right. Sticking with the role of ass, Pole insisted that he, too, had no sense of honour. When Farnese and Madruzzo came to lead him to be adored, he had felt like the ass which bore Christ into Jerusalem. Slipping the ass's bridle, as it were, Pole had changed his mind and said they must wait for the morning. Two more cardinals then once more persuaded him to acquiesce, but he once again changed his mind about acting the ass. Pole had no doubt that God was imposing on him, and felt himself unable to move. Pole then changed metaphors, writing that the duration of his backers' support made him feel like the once barren but now fertile wife, only to revert once more to the immobilized ass. God's treatment of him was a *beneficium*. Then, in a revelation of the depth of his humanist culture, Pole contrasted his (or God's) ass to Apuleius's. He closed by affirming again that his honour was God's.[71]

Pole should have felt himself honoured in the early days of Julius's pontificate. Almost immediately he was appointed to a new commission for the Inquisition.[72] A week later, the pope named him to another for the reform of the Datary, and enlarged its competence to cover the Penitentiary shortly thereafter.[73] Finally, he joined yet another commission for the council.[74] Throughout the year he was added to others, including those for the reform of Rome and its *studio*.[75] In September, Julius assigned Pole, Morone, and Cervini to draw up the bull resummoning the council, and in December he mediated a dispute between Ascanio Colonna and his son Fabrizio, along with Orsini and the imperial ambassador.[76] Pole had nothing to do with Julius's proposed reform of the conclave, perhaps because he was away from Rome when the pope undertook it in the summer of 1550.[77] None of the pope's marks of favour prevented Pole from speaking even more bluntly to Julius than he sometimes had to Paul. When the pope wished to make his 'nephew' Innocenzo del Monte a cardinal, Pole argued with him late into the night and initially induced him to change his mind, thereby incurring the pope's anger.[78] Pole did not back down, and in his

---

[71] *CRP*, no. 573.
[72] *CT*, 2, p. 157.
[73] *CT*, 2, p. 158 and ASVe:APR, 7, fo. 250v (*CSPV*, 5, 652).
[74] *CT*, 2, p. 168.
[75] *CT*, 2, pp. 193 and 198. For the Roman

university, cf. *CRP*, no. 592.
[76] ASVe:APR, 7, fo. 464v (*CSPV*, 5, no. 685) and fos. 525v–6r (*ibid.*, no. 690).
[77] *CT*, 13, pp. 204–32.
[78] ASVe:APR, 7, fo. 300v (*CSPV*, 5, no. 662).

letter of congratulations warned Innocenzo to watch his step.[79] It was not the best of starts with the man whom Julius promoted to head his administration. This liability was partially offset by the appointment of Pole's old friend Romolo Amaseo as secretary of apostolic breves.[80]

Pole might have taken it as less an honour than an affront had he known that Julius wished to appoint Priuli to the see of Brescia.[81] When the Venetian ambassador approached the pope, Julius said he was inclined to Priuli because he had spent so much time with 'such a holy cardinal', even though it would mean taking Priuli away from his studious and solitary life. The ambassador thought Priuli would rather have the right of next appointment, but the pope considered the two equivalent, and the goodwill of the previous occupant, Cardinal Andrea Corner, made Priuli's selection certain.[82] Given that Corner had just succeeded Pole in Viterbo, it looks almost as if he and Pole had made a side deal for Brescia. Carnesecchi later thought that Pole had been behind Julius's plan, and had kept it secret from Priuli.[83] Pole's recollection seven years later instead credited the Venetians with asking Julius to give Priuli the reversion, but he added that he had thought it improper to do anything on behalf of such a close friend.[84] Cardinal Durante instead got the see, and Pole secured Nicolás Bobadilla's services for three months or more to help him.[85] Loyola may have agreed to Pole's request in return for a favour Pole had done him in June 1550.[86]

Securing Bobadilla from Loyola was more success than Pole had with the Cassinese, whose protector he still was, in whose house in Rome, San Paolo-fuori-le-mura he may have lived, and at whose dependency, Civitella San Paolo north of Rome, he perhaps spent some of each summer.[87] Julius gave him authority to reform one of the order's Roman houses immediately after the conclave, and one of Pole's principal agents was appointed papal commissary to investigate an assault on a monk of Subiaco.[88] He was particularly

79 *CRP*, no. 569.
80 *CT*, 2, p. 14.
81 ASVe:APR, 7, fo. 624r–v (*CSPV*, 5, no. 696).
82 Eubel, 3, p. 140.
83 *PC*, p. 431.
84 *CRP*, no. 2211.
85 *Monumenta Ignatiana*, ser. 1, St Ignatius de Loyola, *Epistolae et Instructiones*, 3 (Madrid: Lopez del Horno, 1905; MHSI, 3), pp. 611 and 614 and *Nicolai Alphonsi de Bobadilla, Gesta et Scripta* (Madrid: Lopez

del Horno, 1913; MHSI, 46), p. 167.
86 *CRP*, no. 571.
87 *Inq. rom.*, p. 239, perhaps drawing on Filippo Gheri's letter of 29 April 1553 (*MMB*, 1:2, p. 348), which reported that Pole had been at San Paolo, intending never to return to Rome.
88 *CRP*, no. 560. ASV, Misc. Arm. 41:59, fo. 379r, Vincenzo Parpalee (note on dorse: Vincenzo Parpaglia), *notario & commissario nostro*, Rome, 24 March 1551.

interested in the troubles of the abbey of San Benedetto Po outside Mantua.[89] His ally at Trent Luciano degli Ottoni had been elected abbot the year before, in part through Pole's assistance, but the next annual chapter had deprived him on charges that he had allowed heretical books to circulate and caused havoc in his monastery. Cardinal Gonzaga was trying to find a face-saving solution, with Pole's aid.[90] Pole wrote the monks of San Benedetto, but they refused to listen to him any more than to Gonzaga, and with the roles now reversed, Gonzaga promised to support Pole.[91] Degli Ottoni continued to expect Pole's help in December, asking Gonzaga to arrange for him and Pole to judge Ottoni's case.[92] Gonzaga refused, instead asking the inquisitor of Ferrara to investigate, and pronounced himself convinced of degli Ottoni's guilt.[93] Whether Pole intervened further is unknown. His influence over the Cassinese had gone into decline already with Cortese's death, and was nothing like it had been in 1540 when Cortese described it as second only to Contarini's.[94]

Either at the same time or after the general congregation in one of the next two years, Pole had little better luck. He complained that he had not been informed about the congregation's actions, and had no response to his recommendation of one Sebastiano. More important, Pole tried to induce the prior of San Paolo-fuori-le-mura in Rome to agree to find a new post for Prospero Vallisnieri, formerly prior there, and one of the most famous philosophers among the Cassinese.[95] Pole suggested either that Vallisnieri return as abbot of Civitella San Paolo or go elsewhere outside Rome.[96] Whatever the outcome, Pole resented the fact that others had asked della Rovere to intervene with him for Vallisnieri, because he did not care who the abbot was, and objected to outside interference in principle. One suspects that he was also offended

---

[89] *CRP*, no. 577.

[90] Gigliola Fragnito, 'Ercole Gonzaga, Reginald Pole e il monastero di S. Benedetto Polirone', *Benedictina*, XXXVII (1987), pp. 253–71, p. 257 and Carlo Ginzburg and Adriano Prosperi, 'Le due redazioni del "Beneficio di Cristo"', in *Eresia e Riforma nell'Italia del Cinquecento* (Florence–Chicago: Sansoni–The Newberry Library, 1974), pp. 137–204, pp. 195–7. Fragnito does not include Gonzaga's letter to Pole just cited.

[91] *CRP*, no. 578.

[92] Ginzburg-Prosperi, pp. 196 and 202–4;

Fragnito, 'San Benedetto Polirone', p. 259.

[93] *Ibid.*, pp. 259–60.

[94] *Gregorii Cortesii monachi casinatis S. R. E. cardinalis omnia quae huc usque colligi potuerunt, sive ab eo scripta, sive ad illum spectantia* (Padua: Giuseppe Comino, 1774, 2 vols.), 1, pp. 136–7.

[95] *PM*, 1, p. 338 and 2, pp. 567–8.

[96] Firpo (*PM*, 2, p. 568n) claims that Vallisnieri was in trouble with his superiors over doctrine, and connects that difficulty to this letter, but he gives no evidence for the first point.

that della Rovere would dare to approach him. The master–pupil relationship that Pole had established in the conclave still obtained as far as he was concerned, as attests the letter he wrote in August 1550 sending della Rovere a token of Socrates and urging him to outdo his virtue.[97] Della Rovere thought of their relationship in that light, too. According to Merenda, della Rovere continued to work on translating the *extra conclavi* version of Pole's 'De summo pontifice' into Latin.[98]

Pole could have used the Cassinese as stouter allies. While the pope had made his attitude clear, so increasingly was the tendency for Pole to be caught in the middle. As Pietro Gelido wrote in his sarcastic epitaph for Pole, 'to the Roman church he died a Lutheran, and to the Lutherans he died a papist'.[99] Gelido claimed to know exactly what Pole was as a result of his 'seduction' into Pole's sect that must have occurred about this time.[100] Even before the conclave Vergerio had begun his decade-long attack on Pole as a Nicodemite (a view Gelido shared), Francesco Negri shortly joined the chorus in even more pointed fashion in the 1551 edition of his *Tragedia del libero arbitrio* identifying Pole by name, and just then the Inquisition began to slip its lead and move against people both highly placed and ever closer to Pole.[101] First came Soranzo. In March 1551 he was charged with heresy and taken to Castel Sant'Angelo, to be freed three months later after offering a written confession.[102] Just before his arrest, Celso Martinengo, a Benedictine then preaching Lent in Milan and shortly to become a refugee in Geneva, wrote Ippolito Chizzola that he expected Soranzo to resolve his difficulties over the relations of faith and charity. In the same letter, Martinengo asked Chizzola to greet Morone and Pole.[103] Soranzo was that somewhat unusual case, a nearly fully-fledged Italian Lutheran.[104] The circle was closing and options becoming fewer, for Merenda as well, who was arrested

---

[97] *CRP*, no. 579.

[98] *PM*, 6, p. 274n.

[99] *PM*, 6, p. 406n.

[100] *PM*, 1, p. 201 and 6, pp. 289–90. Gelido had entered Ippolito d'Este's service by 1552, which provides the likely *terminus ad quem* for his association with Pole. *PM*, 1, p. 334.

[101] For Vergerio and Negri see Fenlon, pp. 236–7 and Simoncelli, *Caso, passim*.

[102] Pio Paschini, 'Un vescovo disgraziato nel Cinquecento italiano: Vittore Soranzo', in *Tre ricerche sulla storia della chiesa nel Cinquecento* (Rome: Edizioni Liturgiche,

n.d.), pp. 133–40.

[103] *PM*, 2, pp. 1111–13. Cf. Paschini, p. 143 who dated the letter 1552.

[104] Filippo Tamburini, 'La riforma della Penitenzieria nella prima metà del secolo XVI e i cardinali Pucci in recenti saggi', *Rivista di storia della chiesa in Italia*, 44 (1990), pp. 110–40, pp. 124–6. For his second *processo* see E. Camozzi, 'Le istituzioni monastiche e religiose a Bergamo nel '600. Contributi alla storia della soppressione Innocenziana nella Repubblica Veneta, 2', *Bergomum*, 76 (1982), pp. 47–75.

in Naples in 1551, transferred to Rome, and imprisoned there until his abjuration in 1553. He, too, fled to Geneva.[105]

In the spring of 1552, apparently unbeknownst to Pole, he had his most serious brush yet with the Inquisition when his client De' Bartoli underwent investigation. Serious brush, yes, but Pole had the pope's complete backing. The inquisitors had to hand over to Girolamo Muzzarelli and the general of the Dominicans, Muzzarelli's and Bartoli's order. Muzzarelli, an experienced inquisitor, had been appointed master of the sacred palace or chief papal theologian by Julius. According to Muzzarelli, Julius, 'being constantly irritated by the office of the Holy Inquisition' and its attacks on Pole and Morone, ordered Muzzarelli to prevent it from taking depositions against cardinals and other high church officials.[106] He did even more against Bartoli, whom Julius several times called a *poltrone* who deserved the galleys.[107] Although the content of Bartoli's 1552 deposition is unknown, it incriminated Morone and Pole to such a degree that Julius had Muzzarelli launch 'a real and true campaign of intimidation' against Bartoli.[108]

According to testimony from both Muzzarelli and Bartoli, Muzzarelli took Bartoli into a garden at the Minerva in Rome, and treating their conversation as a confession, asked him why he had calumniated Morone and showed him letters that exonerated the cardinal. Bartoli admitted his mistake. According to Bartoli, Muzzarelli had threatened to torture him if he did not clear Morone, a charge Muzzarelli denied.[109] Bartoli recalled another examination about Pole in front of Muzzarelli and the Dominican vicar general. Bartoli refused to retract what he had heard from another Dominican, particularly about Pole's views of justification and purgatory. Muzzarelli twice accused him of lying, and berated him for thinking that 'such a holy man [could] say this'. He then changed tack and tried to bring Bartoli to modify what he had said about Pole, and Bartoli again refused. Muzzarelli, becoming angry, told Bartoli that he did not know what he was talking about and lacked competence to discuss matters of doctrine, especially in the case of such important persons. Bartoli began to waver, asking Muzzarelli's pardon. The vicar also introduced doubts into Bartoli's mind, sufficient to lead him to withdraw his accusations against Morone. Not, however, against Pole. Bartoli insisted that he had more evidence, because he had spent more time with him. Bartoli's major point remained that Pole had agreed

---

[105] *PM*, 1, p. 242.

[106] *Inq. rom.*, pp. 216–19.

[107] *PM*, 6, pp. 322–3 (2:2, pp. 804 and 807).

[108] *Inq. rom.*, p. 222. Firpo attempts to

reconstruct Bartoli's first *processo* on p. 220.

[109] *PM*, 6, pp. 322–3 and 326–9 (2:2, pp. 804–7 and 815–17).

with Contarini about justification at Regensburg.[110] Bartoli's intransigence may have led to doubts about Pole in the pope's mind.[111]

Bartoli abjured in May, but this did not end either Pole's or Morone's troubles.[112] At nearly the same time, Catarino, perhaps the key figure in this offensive although he kept himself in the shadows, probably invited to Rome another witness against the two cardinals, Giovanni Battista Scotti. Scotti gave an information, the content of which is unknown, except that some of it probably incriminated Soranzo. Carafa personally handled the interrogation.[113] Scotti later claimed to have been close to Catarino, from whom he had learned that Pole had 'seduced' both Morone and Gelido, who had written Catarino with the good news of his conversion.[114] Two other witnesses testified about the same time, but neither Lorenzo Davidico, also led to suspect Priuli and Pole by Catarino, nor Reginaldo de' Nerli, O. P., seems to have said anything directly damaging to Pole, and Davidico merely spoke privately to Cardinal Carpi.[115] Davidico would try to hurt Pole in the future, but not yet, and Nerli, once among Giberti's collaborators, would defend both Pole and Morone.[116]

It will bear emphasis that Pole, appointed to the commission of the Inquisition in 1550, had ceased to attend its meetings by early the next year.[117] Especially in light of Bartoli's *processo*, it might appear that the charge of *ignavia* (idleness) levelled at him over his government of Viterbo might better be raised here. Had Pole remained active, surely he could have affected what the Inquisition did, and easily defended himself and his allies? Two years later he told Carafa that he had objected to the Inquisition's harsh manner of proceeding.[118] Ordinarily, we might suspect that Pole had used that interval to develop an *ex post facto* explanation, but in this case we can probably accept it. For one thing, it accords with his later attitude to heresy.[119] For another, Muzzarelli thought Pole shared his belief that the Inquisition should proceed

---

[110] *Ibid*, pp. 819–21.

[111] Paolo Simoncelli, 'Diplomazia e politica religiosa nella chiesa della Controriforma', *RSLR*, 18 (1982), pp. 415–60, p. 433.

[112] *PM*, 2:2, p. 804n.

[113] *Inq. rom.*, p. 205.

[114] *PM*, 2:1, p. 350 (modified in 6, p. 232) and 2:2, p. 754 (not in 6).

[115] *Inq. rom.*, pp. 206–15. Dario Marcatto, *Il processo inquisitoriale di Lorenzo Davidico (1555–1560). Edizione critica* (Florence: Olschki, 1992), pp. 105–7 for Davidico and Catarino.

[116] The inquisitors thought little of Davidico. *PM*, 6, p. 157.

[117] Fenlon, pp. 234–5. Pole's behaviour as inquisitor makes a contrast to Seripando's. Cf. Adriano Prosperi, 'Evangelismo di Seripando', in Antonio Cestaro, ed., *Geronimo Seripando e la chiesa del suo tempo nel V centenario della nascita* (Rome: Edizioni di Storia e Letteratura, 1997), pp. 33–49, p. 48.

[118] See below, p. 197.

[119] See below, pp. 271–83.

gently.[120] Those two acting in tandem and with Julius's full support could have proved a powerful break – if not more – on Carafa and his allies. Thus Pole's retirement from the Inquisition, another instance of his propensity to avoid conflict in person, had enormous consequences.

In April 1552 war forced the suspension of the recently reconvened council. One consequence was Truchsess's arrival in Rome, where the newly flush Pole presented him with 1,000 gold crowns, promising the same every year that Truchsess remained in exile.[121] Navarra once again wrote Pole, expressing his sorrow and the hope that he would derive consolation from seeing Pole.[122] Pole urged Navarra to come to Rome as the best place to pursue reform, nor did Pole share Navarra's sadness about the state of the church. Rather he thought those now freed from the council could return home and convert their tears over its demise into a river of 'our peace'. Pole urged Navarra to believe that the council's interruption did not mean the end of hopes for reform. This was up to those who had attended the council, and to God, who had taken 'the cloth of reform' to heaven in order to reweave it. Our tears, wrote Pole, were a sign that God was coming, just as He answered the Hebrews' prayers. This first trace of an apocalyptic attitude was reinforced by Pole's expectation that God would bring forth the council's hidden fruits at the end of His time. Pole offered two examples intended to console Navarra: the Israelites' flight from Egypt which at first only made things worse, and the desperation of God's 'new people' before He fulfilled their hopes. Pole himself took hope from the fact that the suspension fell on Good Friday. As soon as he heard, he thought he saw Christ's dead body, like the council 'representing the whole church'.[123] The suspension grieved him terribly, but then he thought of the resurrection. As happened then, tears will bring joy back to life through the bishops, Pole's major rhetorical point. 'This is the kind of reformation that can have no better beginning than from the bishops' tears.' They are like the form of the church that first pleased Him, the new Jerusalem, a line very similar to that in 'De summo pontifice'. The council might have failed, the pope might have neglected his duty, but the bishops could not.

Pole made clear where the pope's duty lay, returning to one of the principal themes of 'De summo pontifice' and sketching the plan for peace that he would follow over the next five years. When the pope's secretary consulted him on Julius's behalf later that summer, Pole replied that the war between the emperor

---

[120] *CRP*, no. 670.

[121] Bernard Duhr, 'Die Quellen zu einer Biographie des Kardinals Otto Truchsess von Waldburg. Zugleich ein Beitrag zu seiner Charakteristik', *Historisches*

Jahrbuch, 7 (1886), pp. 177–209, p. 194.

[122] *CRP*, no. 595.

[123] Fenlon, p. 233 quoted this passage somewhat out of context as a sign of Pole's defeat after the conclave.

and the king of France would cause not only civil damage, but also encourage the enemies of religion.[124] The pope had to do what his piety told him and could not stand as a 'lazy spectator' but rather had to procure peace by whatever means. His office demanded that he concern himself only with trying, whatever the results. Proper fruit could not fail to follow. Pole thought that the major consideration in deciding which agents the pope should use was the war's cause. Its length could only mean that it had arisen from God's anger, and therefore the only way to get at the root was to begin by placating Him. Peace with the princes would follow after 'the certain way' of reform was once more taken. The pope's representatives should have as their object the establishment of a truce followed by a conference. The best agents were those most at peace with God. Anyone could serve, no matter in what hole they were found, provided they had such peace. Alas, no such could be found any longer, so the pope had to come as close as he could. The agents had to know how to isolate the 'hard points', bring them to the princes' attention, and terrify them into taking action before they ruined the world.

From this point almost nothing concrete is known of Pole's movements or activities – other than writing – for nine months.[125] His writing alone may reveal his plans. Pole devoted much attention to a proposed edition of *De unitate*, for which he wrote at least one long preface, and on which he took advice from Navarra and probably others.[126] Working backwards from that preface, addressed to Edward VI, may help to determine what moved Pole to rake over the past. The best indication of its date is Pole's reference to Edward's entering *adolescentia*, which began at fifteen (fo. 24r/p. 346). Since Pole intended the letter to secure the reversal of his attainder, it may have had to do with the opening the nuncio in France thought he saw in England in October 1552.[127] Pole meant to go home.

The letter does not contain much new by way of argument, and is more interesting as another stage in Pole's retrospective self-creation. Now the trigger for *De unitate* became a conflation of his mission to Paris with Henry's order to give his opinion at the time he sent Sampson's book.[128] Pole said that the whole affair

---

[124] *CRP*, no. 596.

[125] Morandi said that Pole had already moved to Maguzzano, whence he sometimes returned to Rome, but on unknown evidence. *MMB*, 1:2, p. 307 n41 and cf. Simoncelli, *Caso*, p. 81.

[126] *CRP*, no. 604.

[127] See *CPM*, catalogue no. 2. References

below are taken from the version in ASAS, 40/76. *Correspondance du nonce en France Prospero Santa Croce (1552–1554)*, intro. by Francesco Giannetto, ed. J. Lestocquoy (Rome: Gregorian University Press, 1972), no. 32.

[128] ASAS, 40/76, fo. 4r–v (*ERP*, 1, p. 312).

in Paris had been entrusted to him alone, with the assistance of Guillaume de Langey, even though divine providence had still rescued him from actually doing anything.[129] Pole telescoped events again, moving directly from Paris to Venice, where he found himself forced to write (fo. 5v/p. 314). Pole assigned himself yet another *persona*, of a priest in confession (fo. 10v/p. 323), as well as a physician (fo. 11r/p. 324). He also likened himself to a virgin preserving her chastity for her husband, whom Henry had by implication attempted to rape (fo. 21r–v/pp. 342–3). The most telling moment in the letter came when Pole appealed to his favourite witness the duke of Norfolk to support his version of what happened when he was offered the archbishopric of York. In the two versions of this letter, this moment is heavily reworked, without much change in substance. Pole's life as written gave him much trouble (fo. 13r/p. 327).[130]

As for the book he wanted to introduce to Edward, Pole claimed that while he was in the conclave persons unknown had printed *De unitate*. Many who got copies would now criticize him if he suppressed it. Chief among them was Truchsess, who begged him to issue the work (fo. 23r/p. 345).[131] Furthermore, Pole had news that someone in 'lower Germany' wished to publish it, a reference to Vergerio's planned edition, which appeared in 1555. There is no trace of an edition of 1549–50, which would have been the second, and Pole's planned version the third.[132] Pole may have worked over this letter after its original moment had passed, as he often did, but then why still address Edward directly?

Pole's effort to republish *De unitate* might have been reinforced by a conversation with Carafa at San Paolo-fuori-le-mura, perhaps on 30 March 1553.[133] At one point, Carafa pressed Pole to write and publish something. Pole objected that he had no need for an apologia, at least not until his accusers revealed themselves. He defended himself by his honour and his conscience, insisting that he did not wish to write. Carafa would not back down, and Pole admitted that he enjoyed writing and worked hard at it, but it was not his duty to publish, nor

---

129 *Tota mihi res est commendata*. ASAS, 40/76, fo. 5r (*ERP*, 1, p. 313).

130 For this episode and its steady reworking by Pole and his biographers, see Thomas F. Mayer, 'A sticking-plaster saint? Autobiography and hagiography in the making of Reginald Pole', in Mayer and D. R. Woolf, eds., *The rhetorics of life-writing in early modern Europe: forms of biography from Cassandra Fedele to Louis XIV* (Ann Arbor: University of Michigan Press, 1995), pp. 205–22.

131 For his interest, see *CRP*, no. 885.

132 Thomas F. Dunn, 'The development of the text of Pole's *De unitate ecclesiae*', *Papers of the Bibliographical Society of America*, 70 (1976), pp. 455–68, pp. 459–60.

133 *MMB*, 1:2, pp. 347–53, a letter dated 29 April. Fenlon (p. 242) suggests the date because Carafa was making the rounds of the seven basilicas when he came to San Paolo. It is curious that Filippo Gheri waited a month after this historic encounter to report on it to Beccadelli.

'writing his vocation, but [rather] faithfully to counsel the pope when asked his opinion'. Not for Pole any notion of authorship.[134] Nevertheless, reworking *De unitate* might have answered Carafa without doing precisely what he asked.

This meeting was reported in the context of three close encounters with the Inquisition within a year. This sounds worrying. First, there had been a recent conversation between Cervini and Pole about the 'calumnies' against him. Cervini raised three problems, probably drawing at least in part on Scotti's testimony of 1552: Flaminio; justification at Trent; and the testimony of a witness under examination (perhaps Matteo Lacchi).[135] Pole told Cervini what he would tell Carafa on the first head, that is, he had taken Flaminio into his household in order to save him from going over to the heretics. Pole could not reply to the third until he knew the specific charges. As for the second, 'those lords of the council' (the legates or the cardinals in commission?) had seen his opinion and judged that 'it did not disagree with the decree', although he might have used different language. Next, Rodolfo Pio had warned one of Pole's men the previous summer that the Inquisition had written evidence against Pole, probably de' Bartoli's deposition.[136] Pole did not learn this until 'about Easter', apparently of 1552. Pole approached Pio and asked for details of the charges and expressed his displeasure over their suppression. Pio swore that he had never said anything about any writings and had only the highest opinion of Pole.

Two inquisitors confronted, and two at least allegedly convinced of Pole's innocence. The third, Carafa, was a tougher nut. He was thought to be Pole's most serious open enemy, including in the Inquisition.[137] Two of his friends had to intervene in order to arrange a meeting with Pole. The first, the bishop of Sagona, Girolamo de Federicis, testified that Carafa had never had anything to do with the attacks on Pole, and helped to persuade Pole over dinner to see Carafa. The other mediator was Bernardino Scotti, who tried repeatedly to reconcile the two and finally succeeded in setting up their meeting, which he attended. His involvement is vital to understanding this much-commented upon event.[138] Federicis's role, together with Muzzarelli's, highlights the degree

---

[134] *MMB*, 1:2, pp. 350–1.

[135] *Inq. rom.*, p. 236, but his first deposition dates only from 1555. For Scotti and Cervini, see *PM*, 6, pp. 144–5.

[136] *Inq. rom.*, p. 237. It is very hard to know what to make of this. Had Pio really spoken to Parpaglia in 1552, why did Parpaglia wait nine months to tell Pole? Why not believe Pio's protestation that he had never told Parpaglia about any evidence against Pole?

[137] *CRP*, no. 636.

[138] Fenlon, pp. 238–50, esp. pp. 247 and 249; Giovanni Miccoli, 'La storia religiosa', in *Storia d'Italia*, 2 (Turin: Einaudi, 1974), pp. 431–1079, pp. 1062–6; Simoncelli, *Caso*, pp. 81–6 and 'Diplomazia', p. 431; and *Inq. rom.*, pp. 242, 245–6, and 248–9.

of Julius's concern, since both had acted as the pope's agents in his effort to restrain the Inquisition.[139] Their standing has been used to make of this encounter a sort of reverse show trial in which Carafa was supposed to more or less publicly abase himself before Pole, but Scotti's role has been overlooked.[140] He was Carafa's right-hand man as well as Pole's old friend, and his intervention gives the meeting much more the cast of a sincere effort to reconcile Pole and Carafa rather than a political display of force. No question that all was not as it seemed. It is unlikely, for a start, that the meeting was a casual affair. Carafa, supposedly setting out to visit the seven basilicas of Rome, began with San Paolo.[141] Pole was in his room with Muzzarelli, and as Carafa's stay lengthened past the ordinary time, finally came out to see him. It looks as if Pole and Muzzarelli had left Carafa to dance attendance, setting the stage for his defeat by causing him to lose a little face.[142] Pole and Carafa spent more than two hours together, punctuated by visits from one of Carafa's servants reminding him of the late hour.

Carafa told Pole that he had nothing against him except Flaminio. This has been called an out-and-out lie, but it is not certain that Carafa would have accused Pole of anything more, since the contents of the *processo* he had in the conclave are not known.[143] Pole replied next to the point, saying that his exile, personal dangers, and deaths of his relatives should have earned him the benefit of the doubt rather than deep distrust over every little point. The story of Flaminio's death recounted above followed and rendered Carafa *consolatissimo*. Next they spoke of Pole's writings, before turning to the subject of the Inquisition. Pole said that he did not like 'the manner it used', preferring 'the way of charity and gentleness', a likely reference to the use of torture.[144] Next, they discussed 'donna Julia', Giulia Gonzaga, and Pole's friendship with her. Pole said he had tried to win her over with 'courtesy'. Still the conversation continued, with Pole telling Carafa that other cardinals had warned him about what Carafa had said of him, and Carafa replying that one must not trust cardinals. They also discussed a moment in the conclave when Carafa had released his voters and Pole had refused to follow suit. Rather than defending himself, Pole said

---

[139] *PM*, 6, pp. 296–7 and 322; Sergio Pagano, ed., *Il processo di Endimio Calandra e l'Inquisizione a Mantova nel 1567–1568* (Vatican City: Biblioteca Apostolica Vaticana, 1991; Studi e Testi, no. 339), p. 242 n2; and *Inq. rom.*, p. 238n.

[140] *Inq. rom.*, p. 239.

[141] Fenlon (p. 242) suggested that the date

was 30 March.

[142] *Inq. rom.*, p. 239.

[143] Miccoli, p. 1063. Cf. *Inq. rom.*, p. 240.

[144] Pastor cited in Fenlon, p. 243, who yet thought Pole was complaining about the investigation of transparently loyal people like Soranzo.

his 'most loving' reaction left open the possibility that God wished Carafa to be pope. Turning to points of personal honour that Pole had earlier insisted meant nothing to him, Pole taxed Carafa first with refusing to discuss any of these matters in consistory, despite often sitting together, and second with a particular snub over the archbishopric of Armagh, probably referring to a dispute about the recent provision of George Dowdall, who may have been in Pole's orbit.[145] Carafa swore up and down that he had never meant any disrespect. Pole's reaction was not recorded. Carafa is supposed to have reported back to his colleagues on the Inquisition that very evening, adding that he thought Pole the best choice for pope when Julius died. In short, Pole 'lived the very best and believed the very best', according to Carafa. As the report summed up, the three inquisitors had done their worst, only to be convinced otherwise, and Pole had been no happier with the result than he was saddened by the attacks. He remained as constant as ever.

It is hard to miss the dislike between Pole and Carafa, but whether this sprang from ideological or personal roots rather than political or social ones is much harder to say, that is, whether Pole and Carafa were not simply behaving to one another as would any two great nobles engaged in a dispute. The two had once been close and they still vied for leadership of the reform tendency. Scotti's intervention strongly suggests this interpretation. No matter how sincerely, for the moment things had been patched up between Pole and Carafa, through papal auspices and personal friendships. Pole stood very high, perhaps almost at the crest of his influence under Julius, and looked likely to rise even higher, since his chief competitor had endorsed him to succeed. At almost the same time as their meeting, too, Cardinal Farnese had asked him to intervene with Orsini who had proposed to cut down some trees in Farnese's garden as part of the refortification of Rome, another sign of Pole's high standing (and of his love of gardens).[146]

Despite signal success at San Paolo and all his support, Pole left Rome, having decided at Easter never to return.[147] His uncharacteristically precipitate departure within two weeks of Carafa's capitulation had the consequence of nearly wrecking the effect Julius and Muzzarelli had worked hard to achieve. This makes it look suspiciously as if Pole's resolve arose from a desire to make himself scarce. Beccadelli offered the only motive. He claimed that Pole wished to avoid the uproar in Rome caused by Julius's war against the Farnese. It began

---

[145] Henry A. Jefferies, *Priests and prelates of Armagh in the age of reformations, 1518–1558* (Dublin: Four Courts Press, 1997), p. 165.

[146] *CRP*, no. 607.

[147] *MMB*, 1:2, p. 348; cf. *CRP*, no. 609.

in April 1551, but had largely blown itself out within a year, which Pole spent in and around Rome.[148] Given that Beccadelli knew a much different story, including when Pole left Rome, his account raises more suspicions than it allays. Perhaps his tale refers not to Pole's departure but the earlier move to San Paolo-fuori-le-mura, which was outside Rome, if barely. In any case, it does not help much to determine why Pole left in 1553. From Pole's letter to Julius announcing his arrival in Maguzzano, however, the move sounds like one of his normal summer retreats, although to a much greater distance from Rome than usual.[149] Peter Vannes reported Pole's intention to summer in the Veneto, stressing that he had no particular mission.[150]

One more piece of evidence may help. It comes from a notoriously unreliable source, Davidico. He claimed that he had a long conversation with Priuli when he and Pole were at Isola del Garda (in September 1553) and Davidico was staying in Salò.[151] Davidico, who alleged long-time intimacy with Pole and Priuli, had begun to distance himself, acting on suspicions communicated to him by Maffei. But when Pole summoned him to Isola, he went. Priuli took him for a long walk and asked him about the troubles that had led Morone to throw Davidico out of his diocese of Novara.[152] Priuli pressed Davidico about what he had said about his and Pole's 'secrets' and whether he had delated either them or two gentlemen in their confidence. When Davidico denied this, Priuli did not believe him, and, according to Davidico, acted frightened. Priuli tried to induce him to come to Germany, since the questions being raised touched on matters such as the lack of a scriptural basis for purgatory, and then asked Davidico to swear to maintain secrecy. Davidico refused. If we could trust this evidence, it reinforces the possibility that Pole fled Rome. Davidico claimed to have known Priuli since about 1550, and to have been introduced by Tullio Crispoldi, Giberti's close collaborator.[153] Despite having his suspicions aroused by Catarino and then being asked to investigate by Tommaso da Vigevano, Davidico at first observed nothing. Nevertheless, he was certain of Priuli's guilt, and offered three other witnesses to support his story.[154] He claimed that Priuli

---

[148] Maria Rodríguez-Salgado, *The changing face of empire: Charles V, Philip II, and Habsburg authority* (Cambridge: Cambridge University Press, 1988), pp. 42–6.

[149] *CRP*, nos. 613 and 610.

[150] W. H. Turnbull, ed., *Calendar of state papers foreign series of the reign of Edward, 1547–1553* (London: Longman, Green,

Longman and Roberts, 1861), no. 678.

[151] *Processo Davidico*, pp. 122–7. Cf. Massimo Firpo, *Nel labirinto del mondo. Lorenzo Davidico tra santi, eretici, inquisitori* (Florence: Olschki, 1992).

[152] *Inq. rom.*, p. 211.

[153] *Ibid.*, p. 125.

[154] *Ibid.*, pp. 110–11.

believed in astrology and had a book of prophecies of an angelic pope, who would, naturally, be Pole.[155] Priuli had regularly badgered Davidico about ceremonies, and Davidico had indirectly accused Priuli of heresy.[156]

None of this made it even to Pio's ear before November at the earliest, and Davidico's *processo* dates only from 1556. Given his unreliability, and the fact that his testimony lacks corroboration, it would be wise to accept his evidence only with great caution. We are therefore left to speculate about what led Pole to leave Rome. Most likely, his ingrained habit of fleeing conflict in person came into play. Backed up by the pope and Muzzarelli, he had bearded Carafa, but he still did not trust to his own resources to keep his antagonist at bay.

Despite Pole's exit, Muzzarelli continued to work on his reconciliation with Carafa throughout the summer. He sent Pole a report on a dinner with Carafa and two other cardinals (perhaps Pio and Cervini?) the day after the meeting at San Paolo.[157] Carafa had said he was prepared to demonstrate his love for Pole and asked Muzzarelli how to do that. Muzzarelli had advised him to write Pole about the meeting and ask him for a copy of *De unitate*, which Carafa had earlier read in part and enjoyed. This not particularly subtle move on Muzzarelli's part to bring Pole to publish seems to have been the main point of his lost letter.[158] Pole instead dwelt at length on his meeting with Carafa, stressing the degree to which neither had expected a good outcome despite the hopes of their mutual friends, and ascribing their new friendship to divine providence. That was Pole's strongest manner of expressing approval, and may indicate that he really was pleased by their relationship. If so, it becomes all the harder to understand why he left Rome. Returning to Muzzarelli's urgings to publish something, Pole told him as he had Carafa that he was not a writer, and left the decision to publish to the pope. Publication was like preaching, and demanded a licence. He could have written an apologia as his friends wished, acting out of 'divine wisdom' rather than human prudence, and according to the law of nature that mandated self-defence, recast by Pole as requiring defence of one's reputation. Letting stand the judgment that he was 'without religion' would have been the worst possible means to damage his reputation. Yet he saw no way to resolve the dilemma that if he wrote, he would simultaneously offend those against whom his friends urged him to act, and harm his friends and his honour. Thus he turned to the 'divine oracle' of the pope, and Julius agreed with Carafa that he should not publish.

---

[155] *Ibid.*, pp. 117–18.
[156] *Ibid.*, pp. 122–5.
[157] *CRP*, no. 636.

[158] Simoncelli, 'Diplomazia', p. 434 thought the impetus came from Julius trying to paint Pole into a corner.

Carafa's change of mind is worth noting, and probably indicates that he realized that Pole's writing posed more danger to him than Pole's silence.[159] Julius had emphasized the threat not so much to Pole's honour as to that of the college of cardinals were such an intestine dispute to become known. The pope ordered Pole not to write and took him under his protection. Pole felt himself immediately bound by a 'divine chain' not to write, and accepted Julius's protection instead of 'indulging in human passions that would rather have inflamed anger and hatred'. Although he would have liked to have written for private reasons, obedience to the church made this impossible. Pole credited Carafa with having shown him the risk in publication, but also thought that he should have recognized the dangers to which silence might give rise among the judges (apparently of the Inquisition). As he had in person with Carafa, Pole offered the vicissitudes of his life as proof of his loyalty to the church, and bemoaned the fact that they had not prevented his being given new *stigmata*. The overtones of saintliness were superseded by fashioning himself as the nearest thing to a martyr.

Next Pole became a victim of Satan, who through the Inquisition had tried to overthrow the Roman church. This is Pole's strongest criticism of that institution, and seems to mean that he thought himself safe from it. Pole levelled an open attack not on its chiefs but on Teofilo Scullica da Tropea, Carafa's theologian and its commissary.[160] Scullica had denounced Contarini, Morone, and finally Pole. All his actions reflected Satan at work, but God had defended the accused by getting rid of Scullica (who died in June 1551). Pole sketched a defence, but put the burden of further action on Carafa, who should try hard to manifest his love for Pole. Suspicions of him had arisen, thought Pole, out of his own 'simplicity' in not realizing that Muzzarelli spreading around the news of Pole's defence would raise suspicions of Carafa. Now Pole wished only for them to become permanent friends. Muzzarelli's reply urged Pole to publish *De unitate* in order to save souls, and assured him that he would continue to lead Carafa to express his high regard for Pole, while Muzzarelli himself would be a 'wall' to protect Pole's faith.[161] Muzzarelli's language, full of the love of Christ and allusions to the prophets, manifests the depth of his ideological agreement with Pole.

The degree of Pole's and Muzzarelli's fellow-feeling highlights the consequences of Pole's failure to act the role the pope and Muzzarelli assigned him. Pole missed his cue and exited stage north at just the wrong moment, undercutting a long-term campaign by Julius to bring the Inquisition to heel and end the government of Rome by dual powers.[162] Had the pope succeeded in controlling

---

[159] *Inq. rom.*, p. 246.

[160] *Inq. rom.*, p. 195.

[161] *CRP*, no. 670.

[162] *Inq. rom.*, p. 234.

the Inquisition, it would have been a much gentler institution, acting towards heretics as Pole and Muzzarelli recommended, at least those holding important positions. That he did not must be put down to a large degree to Pole. Perhaps this is unfair and perhaps Pole was as indifferent to the Inquisition as an institution as he was to the Datary or the Penitentiary. Perhaps his version of Christianity as founded in an intensely individual experience rendered him powerless in the face of a Carafa and his dogmatic and institutional certainties. The facts remain that Muzzarelli was perfectly capable of shouting down de' Bartoli, and that Pole had out-faced Carafa more than once. That he failed to do so now becomes all that much more significant.

6

Temporal and spiritual peace

Legate again

WHEN POLE HEADED north in late spring 1553, he probably intended from the first to go to the Cassinese house of Maguzzano on Lago di Garda.[1] There he found himself once more on Venetian soil, in his *patria*, as he wrote the new doge in July.[2] With the unexpected death of Edward VI on 6 July Pole's career took the turn he had tried to prepare by republishing *De unitate*. Almost as soon as the news reached Rome, Julius wrote to ask Pole's advice and without waiting for a reply appointed him legate to England.[3] Pole proposed to move immediately, but upon reflection decided that the nuncio in Flanders should be consulted first, a move which fit the caution which arose in Rome once the euphoric news had cooled a little.[4] Many cardinals expressed support, including Carafa, which Muzzarelli interpreted as a sign that the reconciliation hammered out at San Paolo-fuori-le-mura was proceeding under God's guidance.[5] In the

---

[1] *CRP*, no. 604. For more on Pole's twin legations in 1553–4, see *CRP*, chs. 8–9.

[2] *CRP*, no. 616.

[3] Or perhaps the bulls of the 5th superseded the breve of 2 August (*CRP*, no. 618). The bulls betray the confusion in both the pope's and Pole's secretariates. No copy of the first (no. 619) has been found in Rome, for example, which may mean that it is only a draft from Pole's chancery or perhaps one of Innocezo del Monte's numerous mistakes. The others are nos. 620–2. On 6 August (no. 623) Julius had the first of many amplifications of Pole's powers drawn up, and it too has no Roman version.

[4] *CRP*, nos. 634, 642–5. Cf. René Ancel, 'La réconciliation de l'Angleterre avec le Saint-Siège sous Marie Tudor', *Revue d'histoire ecclésiastique*, 10 (1909), pp. 521–36 and 744–98, pp. 526, and 651.

[5] *CRP*, no. 670. Paolo Simoncelli ('Diplomazia e politica religiosa nella chiesa della Controriforma', *RSLR*, 18 (1982), pp. 415–60, p. 431), by contrast, thinks that the two inquisitors supported Pole's nomination as a means of forcing him to put his cards on the table and that Julius was playing a similar game by demanding (according to Cardinal Mendoza seven years later) that Pole publish an apologia, as Muzzarelli had suggested.

midst of all this excitement, Pole wrote his attack on the Inquisition and sent it off to Muzzarelli. His confidence, which may have ebbed earlier in the year, had come back in unprecedented force. Unfortunately, his agenda and the emperor's did not mesh. Charles's principal concern at first was with the rights of 'possessioners', those holding ex-monastic property, while Pole inflexibly insisted that obedience had to be restored immediately followed by the property. Pole's stubbornness on any issue increased in proportion to the amount of time he had considered it important, and church property now represented almost a ten-year-old problem. The canonist Niccolò Ormanetto, who probably entered Pole's service at Maguzzano, may have contributed to his intransigence.[6] Ormanetto, however, put principal responsibility on Pole, and he was in Rome at the time Pole displayed greatest inflexibility.[7] When Charles added his son's marriage to Mary, a full-scale impasse resulted.[8]

Pole knew exactly how Mary and the emperor should proceed, and dispatched messengers to both. Since the queen owed her accession entirely to divine providence, 'the principal foundation of our religion', Mary had to re-establish papal obedience. No human assistance, not even the emperor's, had any value.[9] Pole gave Charles a little credit to his face, while spelling out that he had to console the pope for the loss of his authority in England. Speed was necessary before 'the consolation of the benefit received' passed. Pole's messenger was to stress the importance of dealing with obedience in the first parliament of the new reign, refuse to allow Charles to argue from the precedent of the Empire, and to refer to Pole on the score of property.[10] The imperial court thought the mission premature and Charles ordered Pole to come no further than Trent.[11] Lest the point be missed, Charles's chief minister Granvelle wrote

---

[6] Ormanetto's career in the 1540s and early 1550s is very poorly documented. The best study is Paolo Preto, 'Un aspetto della riforma cattolica nel Veneto: l'episcopato padovano di Nicolò Ormaneto', *Studi veneziani*, 11 (1969), pp. 325–63, who hypothesized Ormanetto's presence at Viterbo and Trent, but aside from a *carmen* from Flaminio, there is no sign of any tie to Pole before early 1554 (*CRP*, no. 846). *Marci Antonii, Joannis Antonii et Gabrielis Flaminiorum Fornocorneliensium Carmina* (Padua: Giuseppe Comino, 1743), p. 148.

[7] *CRP*, no. 1047.

[8] Heinrich Lutz, ed., *Nuntiaturberichte aus Deutschland 1533–1559 nebst ergänzenden Aktenstücke*, 14, *Nuntiatur des Girolamo Muzzarelli; Sendung des Antonio Agustín; Legation des Scipione Rebiba* (Tübingen: Niemeyer, 1971), p. 154; Ancel, 'Reconciliation', p. 785.

[9] *CRP*, no. 649.

[10] *CRP*, nos. 653 and 655.

[11] Gustav Turba, ed., *Venetianische Depeschen vom Kaiserhofe (Dispacci di Germania)*, Erste Abteilung (Vienna: Tempsky, 1889–1901; 3 vols.), 2, pp. 624–9 and 629–32.

Pole directly on 6 September that Charles thought the time wrong to send a legate to England.[12]

This did not much deter Pole. In addition to the mission to the emperor, Pole sent off several others, including a couple to Rome, another went north, and the nuncio in Flanders sent one of his men, Gianfrancesco Commendone, to England in secret.[13] The news was not encouraging.[14] Pole reacted by demanding that the first parliament not ignore obedience and that at the least a papal representative be nearby when it met.[15] He again wrote the queen and emphasized that her success depended solely on providence.[16] Everyone in Italy wished to see her re-establish religion, especially by giving up the supreme headship and restoring obedience. Introducing his martyrological theory of the papacy, Pole said he was sent by the rightful holder of the primacy, and Mary could learn what he wanted from the blood of those who had died for *dottrina*. Through the deaths of so many martyrs providence had confirmed that the pope had all power on heaven and earth. Mary had spent much time in the 'school of tribulation', and thus should know exactly what Pole meant. She should have learned how to govern herself so as to produce 'consolation' which she could then pass on to others, a statement of Pole's credo.

Pole next planned to enlist Muzzarelli's help in Rome, and Muzzarelli enthusiastically agreed.[17] Pole also addressed himself directly to England in a long letter to Stephen Gardiner, bishop of Winchester, who had spent much of Edward's reign in the Tower.[18] Pole reiterated his usual interpretation of Mary's success and stressed that providence had also spared Gardiner. Nevertheless, he had not met expectations. Gardiner had luckily not fallen into heresy after he had failed to resist schism. Obedience had once more to be restored at all costs.

Before Commendone reached Rome, Julius sent carte blanche for Pole to act without regard to the emperor, the king of France, or anyone else.[19] Further, he assured Pole that he would listen to no one but him, and had arranged extraordinary financial provision. Despite Julius's support, Pole decided to stay in the Franciscan monastery on Isola del Garda until he had replies to the letters to Rome he had sent via Commendone.[20] While there Pole wrote Cardinal Contarini's nephew Placido, who had recently become cellarer of Santa

---

[12] *CRP*, no. 677.
[13] *CRP*, nos. 659, 661, 671, 663, 678; ASV, Bolognetti 94, fo. 26v; and Turba, pp. 629–32.
[14] *CRP*, nos. 682–3.
[15] *CRP*, no. 678.
[16] *CRP*, no. 664.
[17] *CRP*, nos. 683 and 688–9.
[18] *CRP*, no. 665.
[19] *CRP*, no. 684.
[20] BMIC25, fos. 300r–1v.

Giustina, Padua.[21] The letter was addressed as much to Pole as to Contarini.[22] Its subject was obedience, which Pole explained arose out of the necessity of killing the will and the flesh. Although he did not say so explicitly, he rooted obedience in virtually the same soteriology that Trent had condemned. Pole's opportunity arose from Contarini's request for 'consolation' against the demands of his new job and those disturbing him in it. Contarini complained that he could no longer pursue his sacred studies (which Pole likened to preaching), but Pole told him bluntly that his monastic vow of obedience demanded that he obey his abbot in everything. His will was dead and had to remain so, just as did his flesh lest it lead him to sin again. Spiritual peace could only come from doing one's duty. It was up to Contarini to make the cellarer's profane duties sacred, providing both consolation and sanctification of his will. Pole enjoined Contarini to convert secular business into sacrifice, which would allow him to pray more. The timing of this letter in the midst of the preparations for his return to England helps to explain why he insisted on restoring obedience first.

Julius's change of mind in late September may have tested Pole's obedience. Instead of going to England, Pole was made legate for peace. This would still allow him to move north, although not too quickly, and prevent damage to the papacy.[23] Pole replied that he would observe Julius's instructions to the letter and leave for Trent the next day.[24] On his arrival, Pole received his agent Henry Pyning's report on a secret three-hour interview with Mary.[25] Despite Charles's and Granvelle's flat refusals, Pyning had reached England and immediately saw the queen.[26] Mary said that Pole's letters had pleased her very much, and that she would give half her kingdom to have him there. When Pyning expressed Pole's eagerness to comply, Mary said she feared the heretics and had to go slowly. She wished Pole could be at the coronation, but time did not allow. She intended to swear the same oath as her father had (which of the several Henry wrote she did not specify), and to ask parliament to lift all laws about the headship, which she did not want. The queen wanted a dispensation for the coronation, and Pyning had promised that she would have it at all costs. Pole's reply repeated much of the content of his first two letters to her, and it came much more quickly to the point of the necessity of reunion with Rome.[27]

At the same time, Pole wrote Edward Courtenay, who had just been released from the Tower.[28] Pole expressed his joy at Courtenay's restoration and offered

---

[21] Jacopo Cavacio, *Historiarum coenobii D. Iustinae Patavinae* (Venice: Andrea Muschio, 1606), p. 275.

[22] *CRP*, no. 686.

[23] *CRP*, no. 690.

[24] *CRP*, no. 704.

[25] *CRP*, nos. 707 and 699.

[26] *CRP*, no. 689.

[27] *CRP*, no. 719.

[28] *CRP*, no. 720.

consolation not only for himself but also the 'common benefit'. Calling Courtenay the 'flower of the ancient nobility', Pole dwelt on their kinship and his friendship with Courtenay's father. Noble pride dripped from the tale Pole told Courtenay of his last meeting with the marquess of Exeter, when the marquess had faulted him for leaving England, saying 'Lord cousin Pole, your departure from this kingdom now demonstrates in what a miserable state we find ourselves. This is a common shame for all of us, who are of the nobility, that we let you leave.' Pole concluded by expressing his pleasure that Courtenay had exercised his mind in prison. Whether Pole knew it, among his exercises was the English translation of the *Beneficio di Cristo*.

Pyning remained in London until Mary dispatched him on 8 October with her first letter to Pole, which merely covered an oral report.[29] This looks wise in light of the fact that Granvelle saw it, as he had probably seen all the correspondence back and forth to England. The emperor was not amused. Charles considered the new legation a smokescreen and had dispatched Juan de Mendoza in post to stop Pole.[30] Even the choice of messenger seems to have been intended as an insult.[31] Mendoza brought direct orders from Charles to Pole not to proceed with either of his legations.[32] Pole replied that unless Mendoza had more than his oral presentation contained, he meant to go on, since as a legate he had to obey the pope, however much he would have wished as a private person to accede to the emperor's orders. Mendoza dodged Pole's point and argued that the emperor's proximity to England made him the best judge and that he did not oppose either legation, merely their timing. Pole retorted that Charles had to object either to him or his mission, and warned Mendoza that princes had to withstand closer scrutiny than private men and their reputations suffered if they did not act properly. Mendoza again claimed that Charles had no objections in principle. The two almost reached an agreement about Pole's movements when the question of his agenda entered the discussion. Mendoza said the emperor thought civil matters and his son's marriage had to come first. Pole would say only that 'civil matters' (read: church property), the marriage and religion all needed to be dealt with as quickly as possible. He refused to be drawn on the score of whom Mary should marry, but it was now clear to him that the emperor's opposition sprang from fear that Pole would object to England falling under foreign domination. Thus to the question of obedience and church property marriage had been added. Pole and the emperor had come to a full stop and Pole saw no alternative but to comply with the emperor's wishes and withdraw to Dillingen (illus. 8) with Truchsess, especially since Mary sent him a new letter

---

[29] *CRP*, no. 721.

[30] *CRP*, nos. 724–5.

[31] Turba, pp. 632–4.

[32] *CRP*, no. 743.

8 Episcopal palace, Dillingen.

ordering him to halt because his legation was 'hateful to our subjects'.[33] A few days later, he wrote Charles a strongly worded and unusually brief letter asking for his help in convincing Mary to restore obedience and for permission to come to see him. As was by now becoming usual, Pole also forwarded a packet from Rome containing the pope's concession to the emperor that he could decide when Pole should come.[34]

Julius did not help Pole's difficulties. His orders, once again overtaken by events, both reversed Pole's priorities by saying Mary should start with temporal matters, and also simultaneously told Pole to use his own judgment about how to avoid further harm to Mary and to listen to the emperor's assertion that the peace legation was a cover.[35] On 9 November Cardinal Morone sent Pole more strongly worded and clearer orders, as he took over the direction of papal policy.[36] Pole was to write Mary no more than generalities, possess himself with patience in Dillingen, and avoid opposing the emperor, as he had Mendoza.

---

[33] *CRP*, no. 740.

[34] *CRP*, no. 747.

[35] *CRP*, no. 745.

[36] *CRP*, no. 754.

Despite his contradictory orders, Julius now moved solidly into Pole's camp, if he had ever been as doubtful about him as some have thought.[37]

While some in England continued to make trouble for Pole both on the score of property and the marriage, there were signs that the queen thought Pole should come as far as Brussels.[38] This would have encouraged Pole to send another mission to Brussels by Pedro de Soto.[39] But Pole also had a liability there in the person of Rullo, who not only intrigued with the Venetians but was suspect as a heretic as well. Muzzarelli, by now nuncio at the imperial court, did his best to defuse the situation.[40] The premise for de Soto's mission was a creative construction of Mary's letter of 28 October as agreeing with Pole about both ends and means.[41] Pole asked Charles for permission to come immediately.[42] Making a point to Charles that may not have been completely wise given their differences in 1539, Pole stressed that the people had not benefited from Henry's change of religion, but rather suffered great damages. They did not abhor papal authority, and the tumults when it was abrogated had come from them, not the few. All of them had asked for its restoration, especially at the last and biggest moment, the Prayer Book rebellion. As for the nobles holding church property, providence would lead them to fall into line behind the queen. If that failed to work, Pole had faculties from the pope to accommodate them. That is, of course, if Charles would let him come. Pole added as an afterthought that he was very eager to come to Flanders to talk about peace.

Two weeks after sending de Soto to Charles, Pole replied to Morone's letter of 9 November.[43] After the usual 'spiritual' compliments, Pole told Morone that he did not consider the matter of obedience settled, and, as he had begun to do in the case of the Inquisition, blamed opposition on Satan. Although Pole noted that the best means of fighting him was prayer, he continued by refusing to obey the pope's orders about the emperor. De Soto thought Julius should pressure Charles and he was worried that if Mary saw the pope's letters, he would be discredited. He closed by refusing to dissimulate, lest that cause more trouble. Although it was too late for parliament, Pole was certain that at least Mary could

---

[37] *NB*, 15, p. xxx and Simoncelli, 'Diplomazia', p. 436.

[38] *CRP*, nos. 757 and 763; *CSPSp*, 11, pp. 356–7, 396 and 412–13; *CSPFor*, nos. 95 and 138; and Ancel, 'Reconciliation', p. 764.

[39] *CRP*, no. 758. Venancio D. Carro, *El Maestro Fr. Pedro de Soto, O. P. y las controversias politico-teológicas en el siglo*

XVI, 1, *Actuacion Politico/Religiosa de Soto* (Salamanca: Convento de San Esteban, 1931), p. 106 and chs. 14–15.

[40] Weiss, 4, pp. 173–4 (*CSPSp*, 11, pp. 449–51) and *Nuntiaturberichte*, 14, p. 238n.

[41] *CRP*, no. 746.

[42] *CRP*, no. 759.

[43] *CRP*, no. 764.

not have a quiet conscience. The queen was deluded if she thought parliament's acts of legitimation and the sacraments sufficient to insure her *ragione della corona* or pacify her conscience.

Pyning's return occasioned Pole's letter, which also gave rise to another to the queen.[44] For the first time, Pole used English rather than the 'strange tongue' of Latin, complaining that Mary must have thought him a foreigner to write him in it. Pyning had reported that Mary was suffering new attacks of melancholy. Pole put them down to the burdens of her office, which he almost as much as said overwhelmed Mary 'coming forth out of your virginal chamber'. The only solution was to pray God for counsellors who would serve His honour, and the grace to follow their advice. Writing directly to the queen, Pole gave his straightforward reactions to the two acts. Since they had confirmed Mary's title, it depended only on parliament. That gave her enemies an opening to argue that she was schismatic, and Pole piously opined that 'so it happeneth ever when prudence human will take upon her to order the matters that pertain to conscience and religion in other fashion than God in his church hath ordered them'. The restoration of the mass, done outside the church, constituted a damnable, schismatic offence. Mary did not differ from Northumberland, who said he acted 'to maintain his state and for ambition'. Pole further objected to Mary's styling Henry VIII *regem piissimae memoriae* since Christ's followers had to hate their parents and if Henry was pious, what became of those who resisted him? In another of his complex family romances, Pole faulted Henry for trying to be the supernatural father, protested that he did not hold what the king had done to Pole's family against him, and even mourned his actions as no mother ever had her son's. (A conclusion citing the saw about prophets without honour was mercifully cut.)

This letter, which may have become a set of instructions part way through, was only the first of a mountain of similar texts and myriad schemes for missions to England. Nothing much changed in their content, and there is no trace of Mary's reactions, other than a note or two of missing letters from her.[45] Quite a few reports on English affairs did make it back to Pole once he reached Brussels, including a copy of Mary's articles of 4 March 1554, translated into Latin and corrected by one of Pole's secretaries.[46] Pole sometimes suggested variant tactics,

---

[44] *CRP*, no. 765.
[45] See *CRP*, ch. 10.
[46] ASAS, 40/97, translation of *A copie of a letter wyth articles, sente from the Queenes Majestie unto the Bysshoppe of London, and by him and his officers at her graces* *commaundemente to be putte in spedye execution wyth effecte in the whole diocese, as wel in places exempt, as not exempte* (London: John Cawood, 4 March 1554; *STC* 9182). The other documents are ASAS, 40/98–112.

for example, having Mary ram the restoration of obedience through parliament, or dwelt at length on the injustices done to him and his family, but the main point remained steady. Whenever Mary thought about the 'maintenance of her state', she should remember that she had it only through divine providence which made her crown depend from the holy see, as well as from inheritance. Only papal obedience would insure her title.[47]

In December permission finally came for Pole to leave Dillingen.[48] The decision to ask a dispensation for the marriage triggered the emperor's actions. Morone wrote Pole that it would be granted on the same day Pole left, 1 January.[49] At nearly the same time Julius made it clear that Mary should wed Philip. She needed his power in order to subdue the ferocious English and re-establish Catholicism. Obstructing the marriage therefore harmed religion and the papacy. Julius 'wished' that Pole would hold the same opinion, and Morone assured him that Pole would. This was all top secret.[50] Pole's trip went quickly, but its object had changed. Despite the conclusion of the marriage, there appeared little hope of Pole's going to England soon. Therefore peace became his top priority.[51]

Morone sketched the line that Pole would pursue for the next eighteen months.[52] It combined general principles, Pole's forte, and political observations, at which he showed himself less adept. He was to persuade the emperor of the honourability of peace or a truce, and remind him of the difficulties of war and the ruin of *Christianitas*. With Henry II, Pole should use flattery and shame together with hard political considerations, especially the difficulty of defending Siena. Morone stressed that these were the pope's instructions, not his, and that the pope had approved the letter sight unseen. But as had been the case from the beginning of Julius's pontificate, more than a few confusions arose, even with a cardinal of Morone's eminence and experience.[53] However much Pole made of his actions for peace, and however well they fit his theology, he turned to peace as a result of a political decision taken in the matter of England.

Shortly after Pole reached Brussels, he protested to Morone that he had never spoken against the Spanish match, although he had thought that Mary should remain single because of her age and feared that a foreign entanglement might interfere with his legation.[54] Now he was certain that the marriage would provide 'the greatest arm for establishing matters of religion'. Pole had spoken to

[47] *CRP*, no. 777.
[48] *CRP*, no. 769; *CSPSp*, 11, pp. 433, 437 (Weiss, 4, p. 170), and 471–2.
[49] *CRP*, no. 787.
[50] *CRP*, no. 775.
[51] *CSPSp*, 12, p. 122.
[52] *CRP*, no. 790.
[53] E.g., *CRP*, no. 814.
[54] Weiss, 4, p. 199 and *CRP*, no. 796.

Granvelle about peace, acting especially as an Englishman, since it would allow Philip to be 'planted' to the consolation of the realm. Mary had raised concerns about her bishops, and Pole meant to send someone to advise her and communicate his faculties to receive schismatics.[55] When Pole saw the emperor on 1 February, Charles aborted any talk of England, and turned to peace.[56] Pole was not so easily led, but Wyatt's rebellion put off his plans for another mission to England by Pyning.[57] He began instead to plan for peace negotiations.[58] As soon as he could he wrote Mary a moral lesson about how she had missed the point of Wyatt, which should have been so clear that she had no need of a prophet to interpret it.[59] Pyning's covering instructions took a more narrowly political line, mainly aimed at manoeuvring Mary into the proper position to allow peace talks to go ahead.[60] Two sets of instructions covered Mary's bishops, telling them to seek absolution from Pole, a plan Julius may not have endorsed.[61]

By then Pole was in St Denis, where Henry II had asked him to wait until after Easter.[62] Pole profited from the delay by writing the 'Discorso di pace', together with covering letters to both Henry and Charles. Pole took the occasion of Passion week and Henry's devotions to urge him to reconcile himself not only with Christ, but with the emperor, and told the king that although the 'Discorso' arose from conversations with Charles, it had as much relevance to Henry, who should read it in his 'closet of prayer'.[63] Thus Henry saw the 'Discorso' before its addressee, to whom Pole only dispatched it at the beginning of April, before Pole returned to Brussels but after he had seen the French king.[64] According to Muzzarelli, Granvelle judged the work not to the point, and the nuncio doubted that Charles would see it.[65]

Pole couched the 'Discorso' as a reply to Charles's observations during his audience with Pole, and composed it of fundamental assumptions about consolation and providence, and about the 'benefit' of peace.[66] He asked the emperor to assist in two ways. First, he should join all those fervently praying for peace. Second, he should spell out precisely what he thought was wrong with earlier peace-making (p. 386). This would allow taking advantage of any opportunity to make a better peace than had arisen three times in the past. Either both parties had grown tired of war; one conquered the other; or they decided to con-

---

[55] *CRP*, no. 808.
[56] *CRP*, no. 798.
[57] *CRP*, no. 799.
[58] *CRP*, no. 803.
[59] *CRP*, no. 815.
[60] *CRP*, no. 816.
[61] *CRP*, nos. 817–18.

[62] *CRP*, no. 824.
[63] *CRP*, no. 830.
[64] *CRP*, no. 849 and *Nuntiaturberichte*, 14, p. 43.
[65] *Nuntiaturberichte*, 14, pp. 46–8.
[66] The best text of the Italian version is in *NB*, 15, pp. 381–403.

tend in 'courtesy' rather than arms, as had happened at Nice (in 1538). Pole concluded that all had failed because none had been founded on true agreement and love (p. 387). They had led to constant attempts to undermine the other. That had been God's plan to bring the princes to accept only from Him 'that peace which can console both them and all Christendom together'. Although any time was the proper time to make peace, Pole argued that the present moment was especially well-suited precisely because God's providence had allowed war for so long (p. 388).

A long section followed designed to demonstrate that it was useful and honourable to make peace, especially because of the damage war had done to religion and to the *populi*, who had suffered most (pp. 388–90), a strong echo of Erasmus's *Querela pacis*. Things had become so bad that 'the whole body of Christendom' stood on the brink of ruin. Instead of pursuing 'the public good' or 'the common good', princes sought their private honour, leading to the enslavement of *populi* and 'free states' (p. 391). Yet divine providence had so ordered things that the princes could still have peace, just as God had kept them in power, despite their constant feuding like the daughters of Rebecca. This had served to teach them how to rule in times of both peace and war, and more important that the harder they fought, the less they gained (pp. 392–3). Pole recited a history of their wars to prove that they should follow God's counsel (pp. 394–5). Borrowing a leaf from his idea of the papacy, Pole argued that while God appointed other princes solely as agents of 'His divine justice to punish the *populi* for their sins', Charles and Henry were 'ministers principally of His mercy to the benefit and consolation of His people'. They thus followed the law of charity and love which St James [2.8] had called royal (p. 396).

Pole still drummed on the point that any peace founded on the honourable and useful would not last. It had to arise from mutual love, the inculcation of which divine providence had assigned him (p. 397). There lay Pole's principal rhetorical point. The emperor and the king of France should leave the judgment of their 'differences' to the church, whose body, Christ's body, had suffered from their wars. Pole was certain peace would come if the princes left it to God, as Pole stressed in his peroration that the 'people' had to do. They had no remedy other than prayer (pp. 402–3). In short, the 'Discorso' was thoroughly spiritual. It nevertheless produced practical results in the form of Henry's positive reaction and list of demands, beginning with the restitution of Milan.[67] Otherwise, Pole's discussion with Henry, which took place either at the end of March or early in April, accomplished little, except to raise suspicions of him in both the

---

[67] *CRP*, no. 850.

English and the imperialists.[68] They became so severe in Brussels that Pole fell into disgrace.[69]

On the score of the English church, Pole made more tangible if somewhat irregular progress. Pyning returned to St Denis just about the time Pole wrote Henry with Mary's nominations of a dozen bishops and their proxies seeking absolution.[70] Pole's chancery went to work the next day, producing absolutions for Robert Warton or Parfew (of St Asaph, nominated for Hereford), John White (Lincoln), Gilbert Bourne (Bath and Wells), James Brooks (Gloucester), George Coats (Chester), Henry Morgan (St David's), and Maurice Griffith (Rochester) in one letter and the next day their appointments.[71] Thomas Cothern (or perhaps Chetham), a suffragan bishop, also received absolution on the strength of his autograph letter.[72] Pole absolved Richard Thornden, suffragan bishop of Dover at about the same time, and gave him powers to absolve others, except clerics, who had to approach archdeacon Nicholas Harpsfield.[73] Pole slightly outstripped his powers, and apologized to the pope for having done so.[74] He took a different approach with Gardiner, who apparently asked for absolution, or at least expressed his repentance in a missing letter. Instead of granting absolution, Pole emphasized God's grace to Gardiner which had prevented him from falling into heresy after schism, and unsubtly reminded him of those English persons who had the 'strength of spirit' to resist. Pole also sent Gardiner a description of Julius for dissemination.[75] Perhaps Pole knew of Gardiner's attempt to neutralize him by having him made archbishop of Canterbury, a post Pole did not want.[76] Gardiner replied coolly thanking Pole for his letter and pointedly asking him to write a letter to parliament about unity, without making anything explicit or making it appear that a decision might be taken any time soon, and to provide assurances that the 'reformation' in hand would not touch property.[77]

Pole waited a month to reply to Gardiner's letter. When he did answer, he was

[68] CRP, no. 845. Ancel, 'Reconciliation', p. 765 and note. CSPSp, 12, p. 152.

[69] Nuntiaturberichte, 14, pp. 39n–40; CSPSp, 12, pp. 190 (Weiss, 4, pp. 233–4) and 225–6; CRP, no. 859; Ancel, 'Reconciliation', pp. 766 and 769.

[70] CRP, nos. 831 and 848 (a dozen). Ancel, 'Reconciliation', p. 775 and note said 'a dozen' must be an error, since all the other texts refer to only ten bishops.

[71] CRP, no. 834. In a distressing sign of things to come, both Wharton and Griffith were nominated twice, the second time singly. CRP, nos. 837–8. Christina H. Garrett,

'The legatine register of Cardinal Pole 1554–57', Journal of modern history, 13 (1941), pp. 189–94, p. 194 pointed out that Pole's actions were illegal under English law until 30 November 1554.

[72] CRP, no. 835.

[73] John Foxe, Actes and monuments of matters most speciall and memorable (London: John Day, 1583; STC no. 11225), p. 1669.

[74] CRP, no. 828.

[75] CRP, no. 841.

[76] CSPSp, 11, pp. 201–2.

[77] CRP, no. 847.

blunter than Gardiner.[78] As legate he could not speak 'covertly' about papal authority. It was not and could not be under discussion. Pole would concede that he might use his powers more or less rigorously since Julius was inclined to be indulgent, but obedience had to come first, before anything else, including church property. Pyning carried Pole's letter to Gardiner, as well as a new set of detailed instructions for dealing with Mary.[79] Pole had heard that some powerful persons objected to absolution for the bishops before parliament had restored the whole kingdom, and he was worried that this argument would undo everything. Therefore Pyning had to tell Mary that it scandalized God and handicapped those in high places who ought to serve as examples to their flocks. It was horrible to refuse any schismatic who had God's grace to wish to return.

Perhaps in the spring of 1554 Pole wrote one or possibly two very similar dialogues designed for Mary's instruction.[80] Their content is largely familiar. Cupidity of the great posed the basic problem facing Mary, who had to acknowledge, as her character did, that she owed her throne to God alone. In one of the rhetorical tricks Pole loved, he also had Mary agree that he could best tell her what to do. Legislators could not induce obedience, which depended only on God and contempt of all things human. True penance was the goal, especially in a kingdom like England where the 'civil and ecclesiastical state' lay in ruins. Pole not only confessed that he could not compare himself to John at the cross, where Mary of course represented her original, but also that he had been forced to suffer Christ's new passion from a distance. The point was that Mary could hope for consolation for her deep sorrow, once Pole told her what was written 'in the book of the cross'. This content overlaps Pole's contemporary writing, whether on the papal office or on the reformation of the church (see the last chapter).

Discredited in Brussels (to the degree that he may have requested recall) and facing slow progress in England, as always when frustrated Pole withdrew, this time to the Premonstratensian house at Dilighem, just outside Brussels.[81] It may have been here that Tremelli, exiled from England, approached him for help, only to be brusquely rebuffed, probably out of concern to be seen consorting with a heretic.[82] As usual, Pole spent at least some of his time writing,

---

[78] *CRP*, no. 867.
[79] *CRP*, no. 879.
[80] *CPM*, catalogue nos. 9a-b.
[81] *Nuntiaturberichte*, 14, pp. 49–50, 55, 60, 79 n3 and *CRP*, no. 857. His first letter from Dilighem is *CRP*, no. 871. For Pole's stay, see *Monasticon Belge*, 4:3, *Province de Brabant*, ed. U. Berlière *et al.* (Liège: CNRHR, 1969), p. 709. Cf. Turba,

Venetianische Depeschen, pp. 648–53.
[82] *De antiquitate Britannicae ecclesiae & privilegiis ecclesiae Cantuariensis, cum archiepiscopis eiusdem 70.* (London: privately printed by John Daye, 1572), p. 414. The authors converted Pole's reception of Tremelli into a general reason for English reluctance to recall him out of fear of his harsh treatment of Protestants.

continuing to work on 'De summo pontifice' and sending it to the Louvain theologians Ruard Tapper and Josse Ravesteyn for their comments.[83] He also worked on 'De reformatione ecclesiae' and discussed it with Cardinal Seripando, and probably the Venetian ambassador.[84] These meetings no doubt helped to fuel imperial suspicions that 'certain Venetians' in his household were misleading Pole on the score of peace.[85]

In Rome, matters did not look much cheerier, Pole's attitude to the marriage causing special concern. Morone ordered Pole to express public joy over it, as he had thus far failed to do. Doing this would show him to be *non doppio*, and Morone begged Pole to avoid that.[86] He got a reply that would have reinforced his concerns.[87] Pole thought the reconciliation close, the only remaining difficulty church property. Peace also looked promising. Pole protested vociferously that he had never given anyone cause for suspicion and claimed to have written Mary another letter saying that a second Spanish marriage would fix what an earlier one had broken. A few days later Pole was still annoyed with Morone, answering again his plea openly to approve the marriage.[88] This time Pole added a reply to the further charge that he was too ready to retire from worldly affairs, a point Morone had not raised. The attack would not have surprised Pole, he said, if it came from someone who did not understand what he meant when he assigned the credit for every good action to God, but Morone should have known better. Similarly, Pole's predilection for retirement and avoiding positions that entailed much action might well give rise to accusations of laziness, or that Pole thought more of his private studies than of any public action, or, perhaps worst of all, that he believed like those who, attributing all to God, stood around with their thumbs hooked in their belts waiting for Him to take care of everything. Morone should again have known better. Since it appeared that he had forgotten, Pole recited his political credo. He had never wished to hold any magistracy, but rather to be useful to those in command. The honour of God and the magistrate's true honour were the same. Pole could never recall having left or refused his prince's or anyone else's service unless they had never asked him or they had not allowed him to serve their true honour. Pole then rehearsed his relations with Henry VIII. He had never thrust himself for-

---

[83] *CRP*, no. 1029.

[84] Pio Paschini, *Un amico del Card. Polo: Alvise Priuli* (Rome: Pontificio Seminario Romano Maggiore (*Lateranum*, no. 2), 1921), p. 123 and Carlo De Frede, *La restaurazione cattolica in Inghilterra sotto Maria Tudor nel carteggio di Girolamo Seripando* (Naples: Libreria Scientifica, 1971), p. 73.

[85] *Nuntiaturberichte*, 14, p. 40.

[86] *CRP*, no. 869.

[87] *CRP*, no. 871.

[88] *CRP*, no. 875.

ward, because he followed the prophet's words that it was better to be called, a point which Pole underlined heavily. His favourite 'similitude' of the careful physician then put in an appearance. Pole closed with an expression of his love for Morone. There is no doubt that it had been strained. Julius's attitude concerned Pole as well.[89]

Nor was the news from England good. Church property still worried the queen, who insisted that Pole had to get it taken care of from Rome.[90] Opposition to Pole continued to crop up, and Mary had to prod him to send someone to congratulate her on the marriage.[91] Julius had finally resolved the problem of the property by ordering Pole to allow Mary to decide most cases of alienations.[92] Pole could therefore turn his attention to peace, despite his gloomy forecast that war looked more likely. He tried throughout the summer.[93] Into this reasonably depressing climate came another mark of divine favour, as Pole called it to Morone, that of being criticized from all quarters, including in a letter from Germany.[94] This was an anonymous attack, the work of Vergerio, which concerned Pole enough to write a draft letter about it to Truchsess.[95] The writer had first accused Pole of intending to publish *De unitate* in order to cause trouble. Truchsess above all knew this was not true, since he had read Pole's preface, which may mean his letter to Edward VI. Divine providence had given Pole the chance to defend himself, both his reputation and the doctrine of the church. Since Truchsess had pressed Pole hard to publish, it was only fitting that Pole send him both preface and book, intended in part as a reply.

Vergerio had levelled other charges, especially that Pole, knowing the 'evangelical truth' about justification, had taken great pains to prevent the Italians from learning it. Pole confessed to having held this view, but he had got it straight from Paul, *interprete ecclesia*, not from 'those interpreters ... who arrogate to themselves the true understanding of these words'. He had not fully understood what justification meant until he read James *eadem ecclesia interprete* who said it came by works. Pole thus directly disputed the interpretation of justification *sola fide* as meaning 'without works', and came as close as he could to

---

[89] *CRP*, no. 878 and *Nuntiaturberichte*, 14, pp. 84–5.
[90] *CRP*, no. 881 and Weiss, 4, p. 275 (*CSPSp*, 12, p. 272).
[91] *CRP*, no. 882.
[92] *CRP*, no. 897.
[93] *CSPV*, 5, nos. 907 and 915.
[94] *CRP*, nos. 873 and 883. Lutz, *NB*, 15, p.

202, said the attack came from Vergerio, but did not identify it. It was probably similar to his *Epistolae duae, duorum amicorum* (1555), printed in Simoncelli, *Caso*, pp. 243–52. Cf. Andrew Pettegree, *Marian Protestantism. Six studies* (Aldershot: Scolar Press, 1996), p. 186.
[95] *CRP*, no. 885.

saying that he had never really held that view.[96] Vergerio and his allies took only Paul's interpretation and ignored James's. The church linked the two, and those who did not had separated from it and disturbed its peace. Pole insisted that he always followed the church's interpretation, and was greatly offended with Vergerio. He had no idea what Vergerio was talking about when he claimed to have lots of evidence from eminent Italians of Pole's attempts to inhibit preaching. Pole admitted that he might have warned an unlicensed or intemperate preacher to refrain from preaching without also setting an example of justification through his actions. 'He is just who does justice.' This was the only true faith, infused by the Holy Spirit, which made human hearts love God. Faith without works did not have that effect and was dead. Separating them put all into confusion.

Pole further called Truchsess as a witness that he had never tried to defend himself as a private person when similarly serious charges had been levelled at him, perhaps a reference to the conclave. He had preferred to act like the prophet who said he was deaf to his accusers and dumb in reply. Now, however, since he held a public office, he had to defend himself, using the arms which divine providence had always provided. The best means was his letter replying to Francisco de Navarra's false praise of his behaviour in the conclave, to which Truchsess could also attest. The letter, which few had seen, would demonstrate that he had never sought any honour, much less the papacy. He knew only too well how much responsibility any magistrate had, which would have to be accounted for at the Last Judgment. Truchsess could publish the letter and free Pole from any suspicion of ambition, especially when the circumstances under which the letter had been written were taken into account. Pole had never acted out of any human consideration, and his humility was certainly not hypocritical. Vergerio had attacked him because he was trying to make peace between the empire and France, allowing them to confront the heretics. This was true, but Pole had never condemned anyone without trying hard to cure them first, and hence was not guilty of the savagery Vergerio ascribed to him. At Trent, Pole had argued that paternal love was the proper manner of treating heretics. Only open rebels deserved harsh treatment. Besides, as an Englishman, Pole was especially close to Germans (or Saxons), since they had been converted by the Englishman Boniface, and that some of them tried to induce others to leave papal obedience especially grieved him. Pole closed by

---

[96] Fenlon, pp. 201–4 connected Pole's reinterpretation to Trent, which seems likely enough. He also brings out the selectivity of Pole's memory on this point, and perhaps also on the council's attitude to Protestants.

asking Truchsess to unmask the author of the letter. Perhaps it concerned him more than he admitted.[97]

Immediately after the royal wedding, Pole sent his congratulations.[98] Philip responded by opening direct negotiations.[99] Pole's old friend Carranza had been left in the dark, but Pole assured him that he would gladly have him and De Soto in England.[100] Yet Carranza also reported strong anti-Spanish and anti-Catholic feeling, and the emperor continued to proceed cautiously, dispatching an express courier to consult the new monarchs about Pole's movements, and they thought it still too early for him to come.[101] Philip's confessor, Fresneda, wrote to warn Pole that he might face trouble in the royal council.[102] Perhaps emboldened by Fresneda's support, Pole tried in late September to pressure Philip.[103] He had, he wrote, been waiting for a year, despite coming in the name of Peter and his successor. Many crimes had been committed against them in England, but now that Herod was dead (probably meaning Henry rather than Edward) there was no further reason to deny Peter admission. From offence to Peter, Pole moved on to offence to Christ and his legate who should have been admitted at first. Then Pole threatened Philip: if he did not make obedience the 'foundation stone', Pole predicted with Christ the destruction of the house.

Philip's reluctance hinged on the property. Although both he and Mary had finally sent Simon Renard to Pole in mid-October, even after that they still demanded further changes to Pole's bulls.[104] Sir John Mason, who was stoutly in Pole's corner, thought he found the lack of progress so disappointing that he meant to return to Italy.[105] Granvelle wanted a precise accounting of what Pole would do, but Pole told him this was none of his business.[106] Renard met with Pole and Muzzarelli on 22 October, a week after giving Philip gloomy advice about Pole's mission, and repeated that the possessioners were causing

---

[97] It may be that Pole returned once more to the problem of justification in the *Treatie of Iustification* (Louvain: John Fowler, 1569), but resolving the question of authorship requires greater theological expertise than I possess. See *CPM*, catalogue no. 42.

[98] *CRP*, no. 910 and *CSPSp*, 13, no. 13, pp. 14–15.

[99] *CRP*, nos. 913 and 921. Cf. *CSPV*, 5, nos. 925 and 936.

[100] *CRP*, nos. 912 and 928. *Carranza y Pole*, pp. 39–44 and *Doc. hist.*, 3, pp. 254–62.

[101] *CRP*, no. 917; Weiss, 4, pp. 281–4 and 287–8; *CSPSp*, 13, nos. 13, pp. 14–15 and 26, pp. 22–4.

[102] *CRP*, no. 935 and *Nuntiaturberichte*, 14, p. 125.

[103] *CRP*, no. 939.

[104] *CRP*, nos. 958–60 and *CSPV*, 5, no. 953. For Renard, ASV, Bolognetti 95, fos. 280v–1v. For the changes, see *CRP*, no. 964.

[105] *CSPFor*, no. 268. For Mason's attitude to Pole, see, e.g., no. 280.

[106] *Nuntiaturberichte*, 14, p. 137.

trouble.[107] Renard had to know whether Pole would come as legate, how he meant to use his faculties, and whether the amplification Philip and Mary had asked was certain. If he received satisfactory answers, Pole could come before parliament met. Pole impatiently demanded immediate entrée, and then answered Renard's stipulations. Although it would be best to come as legate, he could lay that person aside. Despite agreeing to come without insignia or using his faculties at first, Pole refused to accept the archbishopric of Canterbury before the restoration of obedience and without the pope's approval.[108] Philip and Mary issued a patent for the exercise of his legatine powers on 10 November, and promised to treat him as legate, even though parliament did not wish him to act as such before it approved.[109] Pole assured Renard both that he would always consult their majesties, and that Julius would do whatever they asked. Renard pronounced everything settled.[110]

Although expressing his thanks to both king and queen, Pole was not reconciled to dealing with church property as agreed, and Muzzarelli had to cut him off in discussion with Renard in order to prevent him ruining the deal.[111] Julius, after consulting a dozen cardinals, decreed that the reconciliation outweighed property, and a bull predated 1 August gave all possessioners free title.[112] It went off in post and Morone urged Pole to abide by it and leave it to God to find a way to restore the property.[113]

The return home

With whatever reservations, Pole nearly met the English desire that he move rapidly because of the parliament called for 12 November. With an escort from Brussels by Sir William Paget, the possessioners' leader, and after a reception in England designed in part to display their power, Pole arrived in London on 24 November.[114] Gardiner, Paget's chief rival, together with the king and queen

---

[107] Weiss, 4, pp. 325–8.
[108] *CRP*, nos. 967 and 975; Turba, pp. 660–4; and *CSPV*, 6, no. 14.
[109] *CRP*, no. 985.
[110] *CRP*, nos. 967 and 970.
[111] *CRP*, nos. 971–2 and 1345.
[112] *CRP*, nos. 979 and 916.
[113] *CRP*, no. 980.
[114] The most detailed account of Pole's trip is *CRP*, no. 998, pp. 306–7, supplemented by Rullo's letter of 29 November in De Frede, pp. 49–55; Dudic, *ERP*, 1, pp. 32–3;

ASM:AG, b. 568 (Fiandra), unfoliated, Guglielmo Cavagliate-duke of Mantua, Brussels, 8 December 1554; Archivio di Stato, Trent, Corrispondenza Madruzziana, busta 4, fasc. 12, fos. 197r–9r; and *CSPSp*, 13, pp. 443–4. Pole's own narrative is in *CRP*, nos. 989–90. See also ASF:CC 3, fos. 173r–80r, together with *CSPSp*, 13, no. 127. For the significance of Pole's reception, see *CRP*, no. 989.

received him. Pole told their majesties that he had come not only as their vassal, but also as 'minister of God's vicar'. A Spanish observer noted his 'most spiritual looks', enhanced by his hood and red cap. Pole excused himself from a banquet the next evening, and made arrangements with Philip and Gardiner to address parliament on 28 November. Perhaps even more important, on Monday Philip intercepted Pole and discussed property for an hour, the king demanding a settlement before the reconciliation, and presenting Pole with Julius's final bull that had just arrived. Mary did not see it until the following day. A later summary of Pole and Philip's encounter laid out a deal by which Pole agreed to a blanket absolution except for property in crown hands, and Philip accepted that the crown would not keep anything it could not in good conscience.[115] In parliament, Gardiner introduced the legate with suitably portentous language, and Pole began to speak, apparently *ex tempore*.[116] He began by thanking the members for having reversed his banishment, which he protested had never affected his love for his country.[117] Although the texts do not perfectly agree, it seems that he likened parliament's restoration of him to the temporal nobility to his 'restitution of this noble realm to the ancient nobility'.[118] The pope, Pole continued, had a special regard for England, since it had been the first realm to accept Christianity. Pole rehearsed the history of Britain's conversion, identifying it as 'a great prerogative of nobility'. Next came the history of England's miseries since it left the unity of the church, and the comparison to the fall of Asia and Greece to the Turks and of Germany to the Lutherans, first made in *De unitate*, together with the accusation of avarice as the root of the problem, also first levelled in *De unitate* against Henry and now extended to all Englishmen.

Even when all seemed darkest, continued Pole, God kept the faith alive in the queen, an oblique likening of her to the Virgin Mary. God and divine providence had 'miraculously' preserved her, and given her a husband, who, although a mighty knight, sought to win England through love. Pole then implicitly observed Charles's failure to regain his own realms for the church, while noting his joy at England's return. Charles was like David whose shedding of blood prevented him from building the temple, which fell instead to Solomon the *rex pacificus*. Thus it might well happen in the case of Charles's son Philip, but he could become the king of peace only if 'universally in all realms

---

[115] *CRP*, nos. 998 and 1345.

[116] John Elder, *Copie of a letter sent into Scotlande* (London: John Wayland, 1555; *STC*, 7552), sigs. Div and Eiir. Cf. *CSPSp*, 13, no. 127.

[117] For the sources of the composite text of Pole's speech given here see *CRP*, no. 991.

[118] The version in ASV, Segreteria di Stato, Inghilterra 3, which is probably in the hand of Pole's principal secretary and has some claim to pride of place as a result, stresses most consistently both England's and Pole's nobility.

we adhere to one head'. It looks as if Pole may have attributed supreme power to the pope, before offering a standard division of power into temporal and spiritual, the one for punishment, the other for 'ministration'. Pole did not adduce the views of 'De summo pontifice'. He made clear only that the pope had the power of the keys and would use them mercifully. Pole closed by exhorting parliament to do away with the rest of the laws which prevented him from doing his office. According to three reports, since Pole had not made himself heard by all, Gardiner summarized his speech, prefacing it by citing scripture to call Pole a prophet.[119]

Two days later, Saint Andrew's Day, upon petition of parliament transmitted via the king and queen, Pole formally reconciled England.[120] Luckily, just an hour before, the final document about the property had arrived.[121] At a special evening session of parliament, Pole appeared by licence with many of his household. Gardiner asked the Houses to confirm their action. After he once more read the petition, Mary asked Pole in English for absolution.[122] Parts of Pole's bulls were then read before Pole began to speak about the reasons the English had for gratitude. Then, everyone kneeling, Pole pronounced the absolution in English. All shouted 'Amen, Amen'.[123] The next day the mayor and aldermen of London came to ask Pole to make a public entry to the city, and it was agreed for the following day, Sunday. Gardiner preached at St Paul's on the text *Tempus est jam de somno surgere* to a large crowd.[124] Formally, the reconciliation was launched.[125] Pole immediately dispatched the news to Rome. Included in his packet was a letter to Carafa.[126]

The act confirming the reconciliation bore the date 30 November.[127] It said not a word about church property. The same silence did not obtain either at St

---

[119] *ERP*, 5, p. 313; 1, p. 35; and *CSPSp*, 13, no. 127.
[120] *ERP*, 5, pp. 317–18.
[121] E. Harris Harbison, *Rival ambassadors at the court of Queen Mary* (Princeton: Princeton University Press, 1940), p. 210.
[122] *CRP*, no. 998.
[123] *ERP*, 5, p. 317; De Frede, p. 57; and Raphael Hollinshead, *Chronicles of England, Scotland and Ireland* (London: J. Johnson *et al.*, 1807–8; 6 vols.), 4, pp. 67–8.
[124] *ERP*, 5, pp. 293–300 and an English version in Glyn Redworth, *In defence of the church catholic: the life of Stephen Gardiner* (Oxford: Blackwell, 1990), pp. 328–9.

There is an Italian summary in Folger Shakespeare Library, W. b. 132/78 (Strozzi transcripts), fos. 72r–3r. Susan Brigden, *London and the reformation* (Oxford: Oxford University Press, 1989), p. 574 has Pole preaching Gardiner's sermon. For Gardiner's sermon and actions in parliament, see also Weiss, 4, pp. 345–7 (*CSPSp*, 13, p. 108) and a brief notice in Hollinshead, 4, pp. 73–4.
[125] Cf. *CRP*, no. 998 and Ancel, 'Reconciliation', pp. 794–6.
[126] *CRP*, no. 997.
[127] *CRP*, no. 995.

Paul's or in parliament. On 25 November, the dean, John Feckenham, preached a sermon saying that holders of church property had a moral obligation to return it. The sermon was taken to reflect Pole's views, and Feckenham found himself hauled before the council.[128] Parliament wrestled with whether to include the pope's dispensation to possessioners in the act ratifying reunion with Rome. After almost a month's debate, a meeting was held between Pole, Mary, Gardiner, other members of the privy council and various specialist advisers.[129] Pole directly challenged both lawyers and privy council. Princes, including Henry VIII, got in trouble, he said, because of their counsellors. Both spiritual and legal ones had approved the church's despoliation. The bishops refused to oppose the lawyers, and told them they had done a good job. Pole began his critique from their understanding of the 'political body', considered first in human terms and then Christian. In the first, England did not differ in any way from other realms, except that some, especially the Romans, had been better governed, acknowledging that religious matters could not be subject to secular jurisdiction. In Christian terms, no kingdom was a 'body', but rather a 'member of the universal church'. It had a supreme head on earth, Christ's vicar, who had disposal not only of all spiritual matters, but of any temporal goods given to the church. Therefore, parliament's consent could not abridge the pope's power. God was angry, and had punished the authors of the expropriations, first Cromwell, then Somerset, and finally Northumberland. After citing the counter-examples of the good counsellors Fisher and More, Pole turned to the nobles and told them he wished them to deal with the property in such a way as to 'show true repentance' and to restore divine worship. Pole then returned to the pope's authority, citing the fourth Lateran council and the dispensation to Cardinal Wolsey allowing him to convert church goods for the support of his new college. If parliament made itself absolute lord of church property, this would be completely contrary to the return to obedience. Mary firmly endorsed Pole's views. This agreed with the queen's general policy, according to the Mantuan ambassador in Brussels. We can rely on his report at least for Pole's views, since they were probably acting in concert as part of a more general scheme to draw on Mantuan support, the centrepiece of which was probably the move of Pole's chief English agent Michael Throckmorton to Mantua instead of accompanying Pole home to England.[130] Many of the ambassador's reports

---

[128] *CSPSp*, 13, p. 108. Cf. Jennifer Loach, *Parliament and the crown in the reign of Mary Tudor* (Oxford: Clarendon Press, 1986), p. 108 and *Carranza y Pole*, p. 44.

[129] *CRP*, no. 1008. Cf. Loach, *Parliament*, pp. 109–11.

[130] *CSPDom*, 1, pp. 67, 75–6.

coincide with Pole's opinions and actions.[131] He claimed that Mary and Philip submitted everything parliament did to Pole's written judgment, and he had been deeply involved throughout its sitting. On the score of church property, the ambassador's remarks read almost like a transcript of two other texts among Pole's papers, headed as addresses to Philip and Mary. Putting them together with the ambassador's evidence makes it appear that Pole had applied heavy pressure to both parliament and the rulers.[132]

Despite these blunt speeches, for the time being Mary gave in to carnal prudence. On 24 December, both Pole and the lawyers lost when the dispensation went into the bill, which passed on 3 January 1555. Pole tried to salvage what he could by demanding at the end of the dispensation that the laity who had movable property remember Belshazzar's example, and those holding goods needed for ministry be 'always mindful' of their salvation.[133] The lawyers carried the larger principle that a papal dispensation governing property was insufficient by itself in England. As Priuli reported in January, Pole had opposed the provisions against ecclesiastical liberty *gagliardissimamente*, but had not been able to fix everything.[134]

The defeat over church property did not seriously affect Pole's energy or optimism about either of his legations. Already before the resolution he fired off a barrage of letters to France and to Brussels intended to restart peace negotiations.[135] French attitudes looked encouraging.[136] Renard, often cool to Pole's undertakings, sounded almost as excited.[137] Sebastiano Gualteri and Antoine de Noailles together revived Pole's original proposal of 1552 for a peace conference, perhaps near Calais, which was at first intended to be a small affair.[138] Pole reported to Morone that the bishops had their full jurisdiction restored, he could exercise all his faculties, and planning for a mission to Rome would begin as soon as parliament ended.[139]

---

[131] ASM:AG, b. 569 (Fiandra), unfoliated, Guglielmo Cavagliate-duke of Mantua, 17 February 1555. Cf. *Nuntiaturberichte*, 14, p. 218.

[132] *CRP*, nos. 1009–10.

[133] *CRP*, no. 1013. The reference is to Belshazzar's use at a drinking party of the temple vessels his father had plundered from Jerusalem, for which he was killed. See Daniel, 5:1–30. Detailed summary of the act's provisions in Felix Makower, *The constitutional history and constitution of the church of England* (New York: Burt Franklin, n.d.; orig. publ. London, 1895),

pp. 63–4n. For the lawyers' involvement, see Lewis Abbott, 'Public office and private profit: the legal establishment in the reign of Mary Tudor', in Jennifer Loach and Robert Tittler, eds., *The Mid-Tudor polity c. 1540–1560* (Totowa, NJ: Rowman and Littlefield, 1980), pp. 137–58, pp. 147–8. Cf. Pogson, p. 150.

[134] *CRP*, no. 1035.

[135] *CRP*, nos. 1003–4.

[136] *CRP*, nos. 1012 and 1015–16.

[137] Weiss, 4, p. 523.

[138] *CRP*, nos. 1026, 1028, and 596.

[139] *CRP*, no. 1030.

In the midst of all this Pole found time to continue to worry about Vergerio's attacks, which he had finally seen.[140] Most of his reaction consisted of personal abuse, beginning with the charge that Vergerio must have been drunk, passing to the assertion that he was no kind of evangelical Christian given the hatred he displayed for Pole. Pole's attack turned on the predictable claim that Vergerio had distorted his words in *De unitate*, singling out the address to the emperor. Pole claimed that he had meant it only for Henry to show him how badly he had behaved, and not for the emperor at all. This had all been explained in the preface to the book written last summer, which Pole now sent Truchsess with permission to publish it. This never happened; instead Vergerio's version of *De unitate* appeared in Strasbourg in 1555 in a volume containing a number of Protestant attacks on the papacy.[141]

Almost immediately after the reconciliation, Pole had consulted the bishops about the needs of their dioceses, and late in January and early February began a period of intense labour on the English church.[142] Pole told all those who had gained office irregularly to supplicate for dispensation, and many received absolution, including his old antagonist Tunstall.[143] More important, Pole sent the clergy away to their cures 'exhorting them to entreat the people and their flock with all gentleness, and to endeavour themselves, to win the people rather by gentleness, than by extremity and rigour', in the words of John Foxe.[144] Pole thus set the tone for the execution of the reconciliation which would carry over into his policy on heresy (see the next chapter). Bishops, among them Gardiner, and some deans and chapters, including at Canterbury, received faculties to reconcile in their dioceses, including one or two not yet absolved themselves.[145]

Pole next turned his attention to an obedience mission to Rome. He could not secure its sending until early March 1555, almost two months after parliament rose.[146] Among other things it delivered a request for archbishop Cranmer's deprivation.[147] The mission found both Julius and Marcellus II, his immediate successor, dead and replaced by Paul IV, the former Carafa. In both conclaves, Pole had been a leading candidate, which may explain why the plan to make him

---

[140] *CRP*, no. 1034.
[141] *CRP*, no. 885.
[142] *CRP*, no. 1000 (3 December 1554).
[143] *CRP*, nos. 1040–3, 1045, 1056, 1069–71.
[144] Foxe, p. 1482, citing no source.
[145] *CRP*, no. 1054. Cf. the supplemental instructions printed in Nicholas Pocock, ed., *The history of the reformation of the church of England by Gilbert Burnet*

(Oxford: Clarendon Press, 1865; 7 vols.), 6, pp. 366–9. At least some bishops further delegated the power to reconcile. Pogson, pp. 187–8.
[146] *CRP*, no. 1108.
[147] Diarmaid MacCulloch, *Thomas Cranmer. A life* (New Haven and London: Yale University Press, 1996), p. 572.

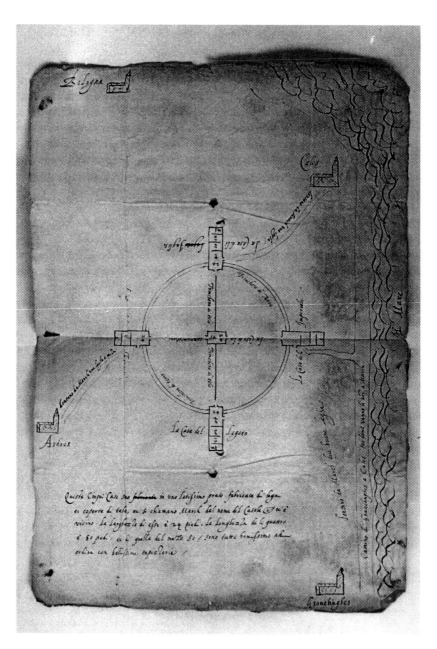

9 *Plan of peace conference at Marcq (Archivio di Stato, Mantua).*

Cranmer's replacement did not go much forward. He was reluctant to take the post in any case, since he refused to hold a bishopric if he could not reside.[148] He was equally reluctant to stand for pope, a feeling shared and perhaps reinforced by Morone.[149] News of Julius's death reached England on 6 April, and Philip asked Pole's views on the conclave.[150] Pole replied that he did not plan to go to Rome because of the peace negotiations, unless expressly ordered to do so by the college of cardinals, and would not stand.[151] Philip's letter to Charles of 8 April repeated Pole's excuses almost verbatim.[152] Although not pressing Pole's candidacy, Philip still induced Charles initially to support him.[153] When Cervini was quickly elected in the first conclave, Pole expressed sincere joy.[154]

This was not the view in Brussels, nor do the imperial planners of the peace conference seem to have thought much of Pole.[155] He reacted as he did to Marcellus's election partly because of his expectation that the new pope would continue to make peace, and Cervini acted as Pole wished, confirming his powers as legate.[156] The conference had grown into a large, three-way affair, with the English to act as neutral mediators.[157] In some quarters, it engendered almost wild optimism, adding to the pressure on Pole.[158] Small wonder that he was in poor health and expected to die in April.[159] Nevertheless, by early May the arrangements had all been made and Pole had recovered.[160] Six delegates from each side were to come to Marcq, not far from Calais, under Pole's presidency.[161] He fell violently ill again about the 6th, but nevertheless managed to adhere to the schedule for departure.[162]

The conference opened on 23 May, Ascension Day, in a setting of wooden buildings, hung with tapestries, surrounded by a fence or palisade (illus. 9).[163]

---

[148] *CRP*, no. 1104. Cf. René Ancel, *Nonciatures de France. Nonciatures de Paul IV. Nonciatures de Sebastiano Gualterio et de Cesare Brancatio* (Paris: Librairie Victor LeCoffre, 1909, 1911; 2 vols.), 1, p. 305 and *CRP*, no. 133.

[149] *CRP*, no. 1153.

[150] *CRP*, no. 1170.

[151] *CRP*, nos. 1179–80.

[152] Manuel Fernandez Alvarez, ed., *Corpus documental de Carlos V*, 4 (Salamanca: CSIC, 1979), p. 203.

[153] *CSPV*, 6:1, nos. 49 and 57.

[154] *CRP*, nos. 1184, and 1193–4. Cf. William V. Hudon, *Marcello Cervini and ecclesiastical government in Tridentine Italy* (DeKalb: Northern Illinois University

Press, 1992), pp. 152–3 for the conclave and 154–5 for Pole's attitude.

[155] E.g., ASM:AG, b. 569, unfoliated, Giovanni Battista Abbadino-Sabino Calandra, 5 June 1555.

[156] *CRP*, no. 1203.

[157] *CRP*, nos. 1120, 1151–2, 1164, and 1187.

[158] ASM:AG, b. 569, unfoliated, to Ferrante Gonzaga, 20 April 1555.

[159] *CSPV*, 6:1, no. 57.

[160] He was well enough on the 8th to write to Loyola (*CRP*, no. 1215).

[161] *CRP*, no. 1204.

[162] *CSPV*, 6:1, no. 57.

[163] For the best treatment of the conference, see Heinrich Lutz, *Christianitas afflicta. Europa, das Reich und die päpstliche Politik*

Each delegation had separate quarters, with a meeting hall at the centre of the circle.[164] The constable and the cardinal of Lorraine led the French delegation, while Granvelle headed the imperialists along with the duke of Medina Celi. Gardiner, Paget and the earl of Arundel seconded Pole.[165] He opened with an oration in Italian thanking God for having sent such worthy ambassadors, promising them all assistance, and concluding with the prophet's words: 'peace is the work of justice'. He proposed to start with the points in contention. Formal replies from each delegation followed, and then separate meetings with Pole and the English delegates which consumed three days. The English as mediators replied on behalf of each side to the other. The English suggestion of a marriage to settle the difficulties was accepted, but the French refused to budge over Milan. Pole then proposed that arbitrators come to Calais to confer with him, probably on 30 May to 1 June. Nothing resulted.[166]

Upon returning to Marcq, Gardiner again suggested the marriage, and that the general council consider the question of rights. The imperialists asked for four days to deliberate. The French, although refusing the second marriage, agreed to the

---

Footnote 163 (cont.)

im Niedergang der Hegemonie Kaiser Karls V. 1552–1556 (Göttingen: Vandenhoeck and Rupprecht, 1964), pp. 384–98. Among Mary's outlays were £1,500 to Pole. CSPV 6:1, no. 75.

[164] There are many descriptions and plans of the arrangements (for the French plan, see Lutz, Christianitas, p. 387), but perhaps the best of both come from Mantuan agents. ASM:AG, b. 569, unfoliated, Guglielmo Cavagliate-duke of Mantua, Brussels, 23 May 1555, describing a wooden house set in un prato grande, round, placed on a small elevation, surrounded by a ditch of a man's height replete with towers. There were four gates, with houses in front of each, wooden, covered with cloths thirty-four passi long and twelve wide. The French were on the west, the imperialists on the east, facing Gravelines, Pole on the north, the English on the south. Another big wooden house lay in the middle of the plain, with gates for each party. Cf. also Muzzarelli's secretary's description in Nuntiaturberichte, 14, p. 259n.

[165] Lutz, Christianitas, pp. 388–9. William Cecil accompanied Pole, as he had joined his escort home in 1554, and Strype claimed that Pole 'seemed to delight in him for his wisdom, policy, learning, and good society' and Burnet that Cecil 'came to have more of his [Pole's] heart than any Englishman'. Pole left Cecil a silver inkstand. Historical Manuscripts Commission, 9th report: 13, Manuscripts of the Marquess of Salisbury (London: HMSO, 1915), p. 142. John Strype, Ecclesiastical memorials relating chiefly to religion, and its reformation, under the reigns of King Henry VIII, King Edward VI, and Queen Mary (Oxford: Clarendon Press, 1816; 3 vols.), 3:1, p. 346. Burnet/Pocock, ed., 2, p. 479. PRO, SP 12/1, fo. 56 (Robert Lemon, ed., Calendar of state papers, domestic series, 1547–1580 (London: Longman, Brown, Green, Longman and Roberts, 1856), 1, no. 24).

[166] CRP, no. 1253.

delay in order not to wreck the conference. Pole probably had to cajole them into staying.[167] Granvelle accepted the proposal about a council, but said it should decide only about points not covered by treaties.[168] Pole praised what he took as 'this pious spirit' equivalent to the ancient piety of Constantine and Charlemagne. For the rest of its life, the conference was a vertiginous affair, at least to judge from the reports of the Mantuan observer which swung from great hope to black despair.[169] Pole tried nearly any tactic, including the shift of having one delegate from each party again meet him at Calais.[170] Despite Marcellus's exhortation to peace, no agreement could be reached about Savoy or Piedmont, and the conference broke up. Pole begged the delegates not to point fingers over its failure, and filed a report with Paul IV, followed a few weeks later by a more detailed one carried by Thomas Goldwell. Pole retired to Canterbury, worn out.[171]

Even as Pole concluded the conference, Henry II had nearly made a deal with the new pope which made further negotiations unnecessary. Carlo Carafa, about to be made cardinal secretary of state and a former soldier, had evolved a pro-French policy which would shortly lead to the truce of Vaucelles with the empire. It excluded the English and led more or less directly to war. It thus looks as if Pole's second refusal to contend for the papacy contributed almost as directly as his failure to advance his chances in 1549 not only to Paul IV's version of the counter-reformation and the end of the *spirituali*, but also to war in Europe.[172] News of Carafa's election reached Pole on 2 June, and he sent his congratulations from Calais on the 6th.[173] Pole stressed the opportunity before the pope to reform the entire church on the Theatine model and confessed his fears for the peace conference. One wonders how Paul read this ingenuous letter. It is hard to say on the basis of his reply of 30 June which dwelt on the chances for peace and on the pope's wish, already expressed in his first letter to Pole, to have Pole in Rome.[174] In the consistory of the same day, Paul expressed himself ready to do anything for him.[175]

Through the summer Pole still hoped for peace, at the same time as he made substantial progress on ecclesiastical property.[176] Paul fired off a flurry of orders about the English church, descending to detailed points of finance, together with at least one injunction to provide more information.[177] Just then Pole had a

---

167 *Nuntiaturberichte*, 14, no. 106.
168 *CSPV*, 6:1, no. 118.
169 ASM:AG, b. 569, unfoliated, Giovanni Battista Abbadino-Calandra, 20 May.
170 *CSPV*, 6:1, nos. 120–1.
171 *CRP*, nos. 1242 and 1250–1.
172 *Inq. rom.*, pp. 309–15.
173 *CRP*, no. 1237.
174 *CRP*, no. 1260.
175 *ERP*, 5, p. 139.
176 *CRP*, nos. 1278 and 1339; *CSPV*, 6:1, nos. 161, 166–7, and 182.
177 *CRP*, nos. 1265, 1279, 1289, and 1381.

great success. After months of keeping the pressure on Mary, he induced her to renounce first fruits and tenths in crown hands. After a meeting with the queen at Hampton Court on 2 August, on the 9th Pole sent a copy of the renunciation to Rome for the pope's approval and reported to Morone his efforts to overcome certain counsellors' resistance.[178] Once he gained Mary's agreement, Pole took up the problem of the church's poverty by reminding the queen of the monasteries, colleges, and chantries, together with pensions for ex-religious and the cathedrals.[179] The resolution of the property question (although still provisional in Pole's eyes) should have come with the bull *Praeclara*, nominally of 20 June, but probably really drawn up considerably later.[180] Even this was not the end. Paul had to send a breve clarifying that his bull of 14 July rescinding all alienations of church property did not apply to England. It did not come until the end of October, just after parliament had met.[181] The bill approving the renunciation encountered difficulties, which Pole had to help to resolve by addressing the commons before it passed in a division on 3 December.[182] The difficulty may well have turned on Pole's continued resistance to adding the clause that the possessioners could hold their property without scruple of conscience.[183] The Venetian ambassador, Giovanni Michiel, said the act made Pole as happy as the reconciliation.[184]

Along with peace and property, Pole found himself in his first major difficulties with Paul. They stemmed from the pope's nomination of Bernardino Scotti to the see of Trani in the kingdom of Naples, a deliberate provocation to Philip.[185] Philip had wanted to know whether Scotti came from the diocese and would reside, and Pole had urged the king to confirm the nomination. Although Philip was willing, he would not contravene his father's decision to appoint only natives. Pole had also twice seen Don Gómez Suárez de Figueroa, who could not produce the policy on natives, but knew it had been drawn up while Cardinal Seripando was in Brussels. Trani turned into a protracted dispute, with Pole caught in the middle.

Thus began a difficult period. Shortly after Pole talked to the king, Philip departed for the Netherlands, leaving Pole as Mary's mainstay. Michiel somewhat confusingly claimed that he lodged at court, left in charge by Philip (but

---

[178] *CSPV*, 6:1, no. 176 and *CRP*, nos. 1344, 1338, and 1346.

[179] *CRP*, no. 1344 and Loach, *Parliament*, p. 130.

[180] For the problem of its date, see *CRP*, no. 1359.

[181] *NB*, 15, p. 280n and Burnet/Pocock, 6, pp. 1–4.

[182] Loach, *Parliament*, pp. 135–7.

[183] *CRP*, no. 1345.

[184] *CSPV*, 6:1, no. 298.

[185] *CRP*, no. 1346.

he had refused because he was the pope's representative), nothing was done without his advice, and that he left business to other counsellors as before.[186] Pole said on 26 September that he had not left Greenwich since Philip departed, Michiel reported on 21 October that Mary would not let Pole out of the palace, and in December Sir Thomas Gargrave sent the earl of Shrewsbury a report that Pole 'lies much at the Court'.[187] Nevertheless, Pole's stay did not prove permanent. His correspondence in September and October is dated from a number of different places in and around London, including but not limited to the court. Philip allowed him to attend the select council's meetings whenever he wished, and he did so regularly until early October, by his own testimony.[188] He once even set the agenda for a meeting during the parliament and the synod![189] Philip complimented Pole on his efforts in September, and Pole provided circumstantial evidence of the kinds of things he and the council had done.[190] In October, he left reporting on the council's work to others, distracted by his recall to Rome, but at almost the same time he assured Cardinal Carafa that Philip had pressed him to join the council and Pole had replied that he would do his best.[191] Again in November, busy with the synod, Pole deferred to others for council news.[192] Even in these cases, Pole always hurried on to write about important business, as well as Mary's health and activities.[193] Pole's role continued through 1556, badly documented as it may be. Thus he was twice present at council meetings, although his name was not recorded on the attendance lists.[194] In September 1556 he wrote Morone that he was constantly caught up in both secular and ecclesiastical business.[195] Michiel's *relazione* of early 1557 minced no words, and should receive special credit because of how

---

[186] *CSPV*, 6:1, nos. 200 and 204. Cf. no. 209 for the council. David Loades, *The reign of Mary Tudor: politics, government and religion in England 1553–1558*, 2nd ed. (London and New York: Longman, 1991), pp. 203 (Pole's failure to take a councillor's oath) and 209 (for his accommodation at court, which Loades makes more or less permanent) and *Mary*, p. 254 for Mary and Pole.

[187] *CSPV*, 6:1, no. 251 and Edmund Lodge, *Illustrations of British history, biography and manners in the reigns of Henry VIII, Edward VI, Mary, Elizabeth, and James I* (London: John Chidley, 1838; 3 vols.), 1, p. 260.

[188] *CRP*, no. 1401. See also Glyn Redworth,

"'Matters impertinent to women:' male and female monarchy under Philip and Mary', *English historical review*, 102, no. 447 (June 1997), pp. 597–613, pp. 601–4.

[189] For the select council, see *CRP*, no. 1418. Loades, *Reign*, p. 195 takes this memo as evidence that Pole did not regularly attend council meetings.

[190] *CRP*, no. 1378.

[191] *CRP*, nos. 1396 and 1401.

[192] *CRP*, no. 1430.

[193] E.g., *CRP*, no. 1441.

[194] J. R. Dasent, ed., *Acts of the privy council* (London: HMSO, 1890–1907; 32 vols.), *1554–56*, p. 282 and *1556–58*, p. 7.

[195] *CRP*, no. 1680.

close Michiel was to Pole.[196] He noted that Pole headed a new small council, was Mary's principal confidant, and had the complete government of the kingdom, both spiritual and temporal. Michiel praised Pole's government by example, which had ended factional politics. Going even further, Michiel averred 'that one could say that really the king and prince was he', although Pole's modesty made it appear otherwise. Similarly, Carlos de Motiloa's later testimony that Philip had left the kingdom to Pole (and Carranza) may not be too far off, at least in the first case.[197] Three years later Pole explained why he spent so much time on secular government. He aimed throughout to get back the expropriated property, which he could not hope to do without the assistance of those 'whose advice and counsel I use everyday'.[198]

The end of Thomas Cranmer

The high-profile proceedings against Nicholas Ridley, Hugh Latimer, and Cranmer opened in September. The trial of the first two was conducted by legatine authority, as Foxe noted, but Pole took no further role.[199] As for Cranmer, Cardinal Puteo, newly named inquisitor general, deputed his authority to try him to James Brooks, bishop of Gloucester.[200] Pole's direct involvement was limited to certifying the notaries' delivery to Cranmer of Puteo's delegation, although he may have intended to confer with Latimer, Ridley, and Cranmer after their condemnations.[201] Pole certainly sent de Soto to reason with the imprisoned Cranmer after his trial in Oxford, and de Soto continued to take part until the end.[202] His authority, however, came directly from the pope, not from Pole.[203] Likewise, the man who finally persuaded Cranmer to produce an acceptable recantation, Juan de Villagarcia, a Spanish Dominican and then Regius professor of theology at Oxford, was Carranza's client.[204]

---

[196] Eugenio Albèri, *Le relazioni degli ambasciatori veneti al Senato* (Florence: Insegna di Clio *et al.*, 1839–63), ser. 1, 2, pp. 349–53 (*CSPV*, 6, no. 888). For Michiel's relations with Pole's circle, cf. BMIC25, fo. 304r, printed in *ERP*, 5, p. 348.

[197] *Doc. hist.*, 3, pp. 109–14.

[198] *CRP*, no. 2252.

[199] *CRP*, no. 1385.

[200] MacCulloch, p. 573.

[201] *CRP*, no. 1384.

[202] Jasper Ridley, *Thomas Cranmer* (Oxford: Clarendon Press, 1962), pp. 379–80 and MacCulloch, pp. 586ff.

[203] His papal licence to absolve and reconcile heretics is ASV, Misc. Arm. 41:67, fo. 178r, dated 23 February 1553.

[204] *Carranza y Pole*, pp. 245ff and James McConica, ed., *The history of the university of Oxford*, 3, *The collegiate university* (Oxford: Oxford University Press, 1986), pp. 145, 325, and 353.

Although keeping his distance from the trial and almost certainly from the execution, Pole took a deep interest in converting Cranmer.[205] On 26 October he reported to Philip the deaths of Ridley and Latimer, along with the news that Cranmer's resolve might be softening.[206] He had wished to speak to Pole, and Pole thought his repentance important, but as he wrote the nuncio Muzzarelli, apparently later on the same day, had he known that de Soto would write 'despairing of the salvation of that miserable man's soul', he would not have sent a letter to him three days earlier.[207] Pole nevertheless wrote this (and at least one other) letter to Cranmer, concentrating on the eucharist and papal supremacy.

The most important of these is not a savage invective, but rather the kind of written substitute for a personal encounter in which Pole specialized.[208] Pole cast himself as Cranmer's physician and friend, following Christ's example (fo. 2r). He also approached Cranmer as legate on behalf of him whom Cranmer had betrayed, sounding a note he would hit consistently in both letters (fo. 3r). The apostles, martyrs, confessors, and all the pious invited Cranmer to their 'common city' as promised in the true sense of scripture that Cranmer had perverted. Pole taxed Cranmer with having thrown over thousand-year-old doctrine, confirmed by Cranmer's predecessor Lanfranc and many general councils.[209] If it were up to him, Pole would call down damnation on Cranmer, but standing in for mother church he invited him to repent (fo. 4v). Pole blamed Cranmer principally for Henry's crimes, likening him to Satan in Eden (fos.

---

[205] Carranza was the principal force behind Cranmer's execution, and used him in a sermon before the queen as an example of the proper punishment of a heretic. *Doc. hist.*, 3, p. 27 and *Carranza y Pole*, pp. 68–9.

[206] *CRP*, no. 1414.

[207] *CRP*, no. 1415.

[208] I quote from the 1584 Cremona edition of *De sacramento*, which has been collated against the copy in the Marciana and the 'originals' in BL, Harl. 417 and BAV, Vat. lat. 5967, fos. 141r–7v. For the history of the text, see *CRP*, no. 1411 and *CPM*, catalogue no. 7. Among those joining the chorus of condemnation, Burnet distinguished himself. According to him, the letter was 'a piece of high-flown rhetoric', and 'only a declamation against heresy and schism, against a married clergy, and separation from the see of

Rome, and the rejecting of *transubstantiation*. In it all he [Pole] proves nothing, but supposes all his own principles to be true and sure: he inveighs against the poor prisoner with seeming tenderness, but with a great acrimony of style, and in an insulting manner, like one that knew he might say what he pleased.' Burnet concluded that 'I do not think it worth the while to put it in the Collection'. Burnet and Pocock, 3, p. 244 (emphasis in original). Loades, by contrast, calls it 'one of Pole's best efforts as a piece of polemic'. *The Oxford martyrs* (London: B. T. Batsford, 1970), p. 223.

[209] General councils did not appear in Harl. 417 either here or later, perhaps because Cranmer had just appealed to one. MacCulloch, p. 583.

5r–6r). Yet some of the strongest writing here does not appear in the version most likely to have gone to Cranmer. True, Pole accused Cranmer of both ambition and covetousness, not to mention lust for his 'concubine' (fo. 7r–v) and called him a thief who got in not through the window but through even stealthier means, *cuniculos* (literally rabbit-holes). Nevertheless, penance could easily atone for these sins (fo. 9v).

Cranmer principally offended in his notion of the eucharist (fo. 11v). Pole opened with a striking simile. If Ezekiel could revivify the dry bones with God's help, why could God not transubstantiate bread and wine (fos. 11v–12r)? A long passage proving Cranmer's peculiarity followed. Then came a similarly long demonstration of Cranmer's ignorance of scripture (fos. 15r–16r) that became an extended meditation on *consilium/sapientia/prudentia/stultitia* like those found in many of Pole's works (fos. 17v–18v). This introduced Pole's theme, the need for childlike faith (fo. 19v). Pole touched on Cranmer's perjury before turning to the absurdity of viewing the eucharist as a sign (fo. 22r–v). Pole modified his emphasis on childlike faith to claim that revelation was a gradual process with three levels of initiation (fos. 25v and 32r), none of which Cranmer had reached. In order to believe in the miracle of transubstantiation, Cranmer had to allow the capture of his intellect and senses, as the disciples' had been by Christ's authority (fos. 35r–36r). Pole treated the equivalence of body and bread mainly as an argument for attributing all to spirit and faith, which became his peroration. He defined faith in the same way Bernard had in his sermons on the *Song of songs*, indicating Pole's continued reliance on Benedictine piety.[210] His strongly anti-intellectual argument, not to mention his opening metaphor, squares oddly with his endorsement at just this time of de Soto's complaint about the neglect of scholastic theology at Oxford and tentative plans to remedy the lack.[211]

We do not know what Cranmer made of this letter, if he ever saw it.[212] He is known only to have written Mary, and she passed the letter to Pole, who replied on 6 November.[213] This letter has been taken as even more vicious than *De sacramento*, and its tone does differ.[214] Perhaps the marked contrast of its

---

[210] Bernard of Clairvaux, *On the love of God*, trans. Edmund Garratt Gardner (London: Dent, 1915), pp. 27, 39, 71.

[211] *CRP*, no. 1414.

[212] Ridley, *Cranmer*, p. 382 says Cranmer thought the pamphlet 'very impressive' and Loades, *Martyrs*, p. 223 says Cranmer 'was

duly impressed', both on unknown evidence.

[213] MacCulloch, pp. 579–80 summarizes Cranmer's letter and on 583 Pole's reply (*CRP*, no. 1421).

[214] Ridley, *Cranmer*, p. 382 and Loades, *Martyrs*, p. 223 ('cold, furious and abusive').

legalism with the fideism of the earlier letter means that Ormanetto or Henry Cole wrote it. Pole opened by assuring Cranmer of his goodwill, and that he prayed for him daily. Cranmer had said that if anyone could convince him that he had erred about papal authority and the eucharist, he would humbly submit. Pole undertook to try reason, as Cranmer wished, but did not expect to succeed because Cranmer had not become a heretic in the normal way through his own reason or appetites. Instead, he had sworn to the truth and then mocked it. Cranmer took his oath to the pope intending to 'crucify' his authority, commit- ting fraud and taking a false oath against the whole realm. God had therefore justly blinded him and entrenched his ignorance. At this point, a large piece of the letter is missing, and it resumes deep in an argument about law. Borrowing a leaf from Starkey, Pole wrote that canon law worked in 'all complexions and form of [politic] body'. When it stopped, so did life and breath.

Turning to the eucharist, Pole branded Cranmer's views as monstrous as those about the pope. Cranmer had no excuse for his ignorance, having read Tunstall's *De veritate corporis et sanguinis Domini nostri Iesu Christi in Eucharistia* (Paris: Michel Vascosan, 1554). Trying to stick to reason, Pole labelled improb- able Cranmer's doctrine that the eucharist was a sign, and even were it probable, the more probable the falser. After another gap, Pole abandoned reason and reverted to the approach used in *De unitate*. He set out to show Cranmer how he had fallen. Above all, he had committed perjury. Unfortunately, this section is also damaged, and breaks off just as Pole said he would not judge Cranmer's intent. Pole returned to the law, lecturing Cranmer on the relations of canon and common law in the condemnation of heretics. He ridiculed Cranmer's defence that only the imperial crown could condemn to death as if that were to say that Cranmer wished for a more rapid execution. He then adduced the metaphor of soul and body, with canon law as soul animating the rest. Pole linked Cranmer's perjury to his failure as a scholar of the eucharist, but without making explicit how simple faith entered in. Pole closed by assuring Cranmer that he would continue to pray for him.

The London synod

Immediately after Cranmer's condemnation, Paul IV appointed Pole his succes- sor on 11 December, and for the next few months the end of Cranmer's career as archbishop and the beginning of Pole's intertwined.[215] For the moment both

---

[215] *CRP*, nos. 1459–61.

were overshadowed by Pole's most important action as legate, the London synod.[216] More than a little confusion surrounded its assembly. Pole's haste may have sprung from eagerness unrestrained by competence, but the same problems had arisen in the first vice-gerential synod in 1537, which was much more carefully managed.[217] Pole had meant to hold such a gathering from the time he returned to England.[218] Although he had made plans for a 'convocation' or a 'synod' earlier in the summer, he only announced to Philip on 26 October that it needed to ratify negotiations over church property, high on parliament's agenda after taxation, and already the subject of discussions in convocation.[219] (The ratification could not go through normal channels, since the archbishop, although an imprisoned heretic, still held office, which prevented the dean and chapter from acting.[220]) Pole added that the synod could deal with all matters related to *reformationem ecclesiae anglicanae*, but the church as property had top priority. The king and queen responded quickly to Pole's suggestion and authorized him to summon the meeting on 2 November.[221] It began informally on 4 November, but the first of the mandates summoning the bishops did not go out until the 8th. There may have been no hurry because those of Canterbury were already in attendance, but the same was not true in the case of northern convocation, summoned on the same day.[222] Perhaps Pole thought the summons to southern convocation applied to both, and that it could therefore simply be converted into a synod, or forgot about the north.[223] It took a further two days for the dissemination of the mandate to the southern bishops, at which point the official opening was fixed for 2 December.[224] Pole also waited until after calling the synod to ask for Roman approval.[225] The conclusion seems inescapable that Pole opened it prematurely.

The synod met in an unsettled atmosphere.[226] Pole may already have known about the Dudley conspiracy, and myriad other distractions confronted him. Peace negotiations continued, and Pole worried that the pope's actions endan-

---

[216] Cf. the summaries of the synod in Dixon, pp. 455–68, especially pp. 455–6 n a chronology and 461–7, allegedly a translation of *Reformatio Angliae* (but very condensed).

[217] MacCulloch, p. 186.

[218] E.g., *CRP*, no. 1040. Cf. Pogson, p. 159.

[219] *CRP*, no. 1414.

[220] *CRP*, no. 1430.

[221] *CRP*, no. 1420.

[222] *CRP*, no. 1426.

[223] *CRP*, no. 1425. For the relative unimportance of northern convocation see S. E. Lehmberg, *The Reformation parliament 1529–1536* (Cambridge: Cambridge University Press, 1970), p. 74, and for the complete lack of information about it at this period, MacCulloch, p. 404.

[224] *CRP*, no. 1426.

[225] *CRP*, no. 1427.

[226] *CRP*, no. 1437.

gered them.[227] Gardiner, the chancellor, lay mortally ill, and Pole would be deeply involved in replacing him and avoiding being given the office.[228] Further, the pope's disagreement with Charles and Philip rapidly escalated, and Pole was forced to mediate, as well as bear the brunt of some of Paul's accusations directed at the king.[229] Pole frequently had news of Paul's actions against both Pole's allies in Rome and members of the pope's own family, and in those cases he also tried to intervene.[230] Moreover, the pope could almost simultaneously praise Pole's plans for the synod and demand that he take care of peace negotiations as soon as possible.[231] His active role in government caused more tension with the pope, who worried that Pole would not discharge his legation properly.[232] As if all this were not enough, Pole's emphasis on church property had intensified. As he explained to Philip, he had opened the synod by making known Philip's reasons for divesting himself of church property, and the synod's first action had been to draft approval of Philip's plans for pensions.[233] One reason for this stress was Mary's wish to deal with property as soon as possible. Although it is very difficult to say how much of this was off Mary's own bat, she also wanted attention to preaching, in consultation with Pole, especially against heresy (which was to be mildly treated), the regulation of books, visitations of churches and universities, and pluralism in benefices. The synod considered most of this agenda.[234]

Rullo's description of Pole giving 'continual exhortations and most beautiful and most Christian orations' probably accurately characterizes his role.[235] Not much is known about Pole's plans, and virtually nothing about the synod's proceedings.[236] An autograph draft of a sermon that has been taken to be Pole's opening address must have been intended for its prorogation.[237] 'De reformatione ecclesiae' and its associated texts (see the last chapter) might serve as a blueprint, especially because of their overlap with several texts discussed here that almost certainly were connected to the synod, for example, on preaching, the bishops, and education. Unfortunately, the degree to which 'De reformatione'

---

227 *CSPV*, 6:1, nos. 269, 297, 307, and 327.

228 *CRP*, nos. 1430, 1441, 1449, and 1478.

229 *CSPV*, 6:1, no. 269.

230 See, e.g., *CRP*, nos. 1401 and 1463, or 1415.

231 *CRP*, nos. 1442, 1458, and 1470.

232 *CSPV*, 6:1, no. 289.

233 *CRP*, no. 1430.

234 *CRP*, no. 1418.

235 De Frede, p. 76.

236 Wilkins printed some sort of abbreviated diary along with Bonner's circular letter of 10 November, reprinted in *ERP*, 5, pp. 229–30. According to Charles Wriothesley, the bishops met twice a week. *A chronicle of England during the reigns of the Tudors*, 2, ed. W. D. Hamilton (Camden Society, n.s., 20, 1877), p. 132.

237 *CPM*, catalogue, no. 10j. See below, p. 243.

changed on the first two of these dimensions destroys its possible value to understanding the synod. That these concerns had been and may have remained on Pole's mind for a long time is still of some use. His circular letter to the bishops asking them to prepare financial reports on their dioceses for convocation documents a glaring motive.[238] One group of fragments may represent his views in late 1555, and one of them could be a draft of his opening remarks.[239] The major reason for hesitation in calling this text Pole's initial sermon is that it says that the bishops, the audience, have already written about the *vulnera* of their dioceses, which sounds like an echo of Pole's orders to them at the prorogation, although it could also reflect the impact of Pole's consultations with them in convocation already in 1554.[240] Aside from this single point, the text reads like a commencement rather than a conclusion. It concerns *reformatio* and *hoc synodo*. The place to start was the deformities of the clergy, which the bishops had to fix through obedience to Pole as legate. The ancient canons, beginning with the apostles', provided the model. The worst wound was episcopal non-residence, the cure the enforcement of the ancient canon *Ne episcopus*.[241] Bishops had to reside in order to lead by both word and example, and to preach. They must begin with repentance and thereafter never depart from 'preaching of the gospel'. Bishops were warned about how to govern their households in order to avoid glorying in the world. 'Glorifying Christ' meant loving their flocks and providing *consolatio* for sinners. Pole exhorted the bishops to pray for grace,

---

[238] *CRP*, no. 1363. Pole's letter (no. 1462) saying that the synod would deal with 'ecclesiastical disorders and needs' does not help very much. *CPM*, catalogue no. 10k also cannot reflect Pole's opening agenda.

[239] BAV, Vat. lat. 5966, fos. 41r probably to 44v, autograph draft. The *incipit* of a letter in English on fo. 39v may help a little to date this sheaf of documents. It is addressed to 'the datary of the pope', Scotti, and replies to his letter brought by Goldwell, who returned to England by 15 December (*CRP*, no. 1462). Cf. *CPM*, p. 73 for the exclusion of another text which appears to concern Pole's aims for the synod.

[240] *CRP*, no. 1000.

[241] I have not been able to identify this canon. It is not in the *Corpus iuris canonici*, at least not under any similar title, nor in Norman

P. Tanner, S. J., ed., *Decrees of the ecumenical councils* (London and Washington: Sheed & Ward and Georgetown University Press, 1990; 2 vols.). It may perhaps have been quoted from memory from the synod of Arles (314 C.E.) which contained a canon beginning 'nullus episcopus' (XVII) and another (XIX) 'De episcopis peregrinis' which is similar to the subject matter Pole recollected. *Sacrorum conciliorum nova et amplissima collectio in qua praeter ea quae Phil. Labbeus, et Gabr. Cossartius S. J. et novissime Nicolaus Coleti in lucem edidere ea omnia ... quae Joannes Dominicus Mansi ... evulgavit* (imprint varies; Florence and Venice: Antonio Zatta, 1759–1927; 54 vols.), 2, col. 473.

peace, piety and chastity, and for the *doctrinam fidei*.[242] Another fragment in this group covers most of these points, emphasizing preaching, the one job peculiar to the bishops (fo. 37r).

This sketch conforms well to the matter of four of the synod's first five canons: no. 2 (fos. 5r–11r) ostensibly about the canon law but including the sacraments; no. 3 on residence in benefices with cure of souls and by bishops together with no. 4 on the necessity of preaching (fos. 11v–14r and 14r–15v); and no. 5 on clerical discipline including households and clerical marriage (fos 15v–17v).[243] Probably the most significant canon, no. 11 (fos. 23r–24v) on the education of the clergy in newly established seminaries, crops up in two other texts among these fragments, although it is impossible to say whether they pre- or postdate the canon.[244] Both begin with the importance of *vocatio*, designed as a speech for the boys' master. All, especially the master, had to pray for grace. The boys were to be taught two kinds of doctrine, celestial and rational (the liberal arts and everything of *humanum ingenium*, including *leges civiles*). All the second were 'handmaids' to the first that gave true wisdom. Once saved from Satan through baptism, the boys were ready to learn it. The master needed another kind of doctrine, that of 'the humility of Christ' as manifested especially through his obedience even to death. Christ's example should be followed in everything the master did. He was to instil it in his pupils by demanding obedience. Just as Pole had written Placido Contarini, obedience meant giving up one's will. The boys' education consisted of three parts. First, drawn from the apostles' creed, concerned faith. The second, modelled on the Lord's prayer, taught prayer as a means of submitting to the divine will. The third, found in the decalogue, taught how the intellect 'submitted to the truth of faith' and the will to God's.

All the synod's canons differ from Pole's drafts in a very important way. They lay down only the law, leaving out the explanation and exhortation at which Pole excelled. For example, the decree on seminaries spelled out in precise detail the division of students into two classes, enacted as a means of financing the schools which had been discussed in the synod on 20 January, but said almost nothing

---

[242] Michiel's reports on the synod focus on reform of the bishops. *CSPV*, 6:1, nos. 269 and 274.

[243] For the texts see *CPM*, catalogue no. 19. Both the MSS are pretty obviously drafts, missing things like Ottobono's canon in decree 1 which is almost certainly of English provenance, but agree well enough in substance with Pole's report to Morone at the synod's conclusion (*CRP*, no. 1497) and with the *Reformatio Angliae*, Manuzio's Roman edition of 1562. I cite the last with due caution.

[244] BAV, Vat. lat. 5966, fos. 27r–31v is the more nearly coherent text, and I have quoted it except as otherwise indicated. Cf. *CPM*, catalogue, no. 21.

about what the boys should learn.[245] Attention to finance could be defended on the general grounds of the impecunious state of the English church and on the specific one that the students were to be poor, but the reduction of the curriculum to 'those books' was exceedingly unhelpful and surprising in one as learned as Pole, much concerned with the proper teaching of philosophy and theology since the 1530s, and credited with having invented a new kind of humanist theology.[246] Even in that short passage, the canon paid more attention to schoolmasters' morals than to the curriculum. Those critics who have emphasized the 'arid legalism' of Marian Catholicism and of Pole's reforms would appear to be half right.[247] The end result might fit that rubric, but it seems wide of Pole's intentions. It also needs emphasis that Pope Paul entirely approved Pole's stress on discipline and the law, and that his breve endorsing the synod hardly qualified as the exhortation Pole had requested.[248] If Pole lacked ardour, he was not alone. The fact that it proved difficult to get the canons drawn up and that Pole managed to avoid sending them to Seripando until at least September 1556 suggests a painful process of converting aspirations into law, and at least some measure of slippage between what Pole thought reform meant in the abstract and what he could endorse in practical terms.[249] Ormanetto, singled out by Dudic for his importance to the synod, or Carranza, a former canonist, must have had a lot to do with the revisions.[250] His testimony that he 'ordenó en forma por mandato del Legado' the decrees may stand.[251]

The rest of the dozen canons touch on an array of topics. The first ratified a decision taken during the synod (or perhaps by convocation acting independently) to declare annual celebrations of the reconciliation. The canon set the tone for the whole collection by predicating its declaration on a thirteenth-century constitution of Cardinal Ottobono. This may well have come from Bonner's

---

[245] *ERP*, 5, p. 230 for the proposals. Pole asked for and received a treatise on the education of boys from his client Girolamo da Ponte, a professor at the university of Rome, but it is brief and generic. The most notable point in 'De recta studiorum philosophiae ratione capita quaedam iussu Reginaldi Poli Cardinallis que scholis Angliae servanda' (BAV, Vat. lat. 12159, fos. 170–72r) is Da Ponte's stress on Aristotle, of whom he thought Aquinas the best Latin interpreter.

[246] Egidio Foscarari judged Pole's *De concilio* to represent a new departure in theological method and Ercole Gonzaga endorsed

Foscarari's opinion. *CT*, 8, pp. 247–8.

[247] A. G. Dickens, *The English reformation*, 2nd ed. (University Park: Pennsylvania State University Press, 1989), p. 309.

[248] *CRP*, nos. 1470 and 1427.

[249] De Frede, p. 105.

[250] *ERP*, 1, p. 42 and *CRP*, no. 1451 for Ormanetto; *Carranza y Pole*, pp. 59–65, but Tellechea Idigoras admits that nothing is precisely known of Carranza's involvement. Cf. J. P. Marmion, 'The London synod of Reginald, Cardinal Pole, 1555–1556' (Keele University MA thesis, 1974), 1, pp. 82, 120 and elsewhere.

[251] *Carranza y Pole*, p. 63.

example in his visitation of London in 1554, which drew heavily on the papal legates Cardinals Otto and Ottobono.[252] The second canon was a grab-bag, sketching the books those with ecclesiastical jurisdiction or cure of souls should own (the constitutions of Otto and Ottobono, a Latin Bible, and such 'other books' as necessary) and establishing rigorous censorship of heretical works, before noting the necessity of education in order to overcome 'the errors of late times'.[253] To that end, it included a definition of the seven sacraments, largely drawn from the council of Florence (fo. 6v), as was much of the rest of the decrees' substance. As John Marmion suggests, Pole may have deliberately bypassed Trent and returned to Florence, a council he knew well from at least the time of *De unitate.*[254] Although the eucharist attracted no particular privilege in this section of the canon, towards its end the whole was said to have been drawn up 'to honour the body of our Lord Jesus Christ' (fo. 10v). To be certain to get the maximum amount into one canon, it concluded with an injunction to attend church.

The third canon mandated episcopal residence, but it actually covered much more. From the topic of residence for cathedral canons in order to assist the bishop, the regulation moved to financial levies for the support of schools, thence to dispensations for those pursuing studies, before concluding with pluralism. Thus no. 3 included points about benefices of any kind, despite canons 7, 8, and 9 specifically on that topic. No. 4 on preaching was the second most important canon after no. 11.[255] Preaching was the principal duty of bishops, modelling themselves on the apostles. Teaching the rudiments of the faith by whatever means was enjoined on all clergy, not just bishops, and extended to the catechesis of children briefly touched on at the end of the canon. In order to help those less able, a simple model was proposed – preaching repentance first and then against 'vices and abuses' – and for those priests even less competent 'certain homilies' were to be written.[256]

Canon no. 8 was one of the most up-to-date in its condemnation of accesses or expectative presentations to benefices (the technical issue on which Paul IV would catch Priuli) while no. 9 inveighed against simony, but perhaps the harshest language in the *Reformatio* came in canon no. 10 on church property. It

---

[252] W. H. Frere and W. M. Kennedy, eds., *Visitation articles & injunctions of the period of the reformation* (London: Alcuin Club, 1910; 3 vols.), 2, p. 330.

[253] *Reformatio Angliae*, fos. 5r–11r. Marmion, 2, pp. 7–21.

[254] Marmion, 1, p. v. Loades endorses this suggestion in 'The piety of the Catholic restoration in England, 1553–8', in

Loades, *Politics, censorship and the English reformation* (London and New York: Pinter Publishers, 1991), pp. 200–12, p. 203 and *Reign*, p. 294.

[255] Loades, 'Piety', p. 204 says the canon was relatively de-emphasized, but he does not say relative to what.

[256] Cf. Marmion, 1, pp. 133–4.

reiterated the bull of Paul II the provisions of which had been specifically suspended for England in Julius's breve of 28 June 1554 (although it later noted that it did not apply to those with dispensations). In order to make the alienation of ecclesiastical goods harder, all administrators and holders of benefices were to inventory their possessions and send a copy to some central depository. Finally, canon 12, the longest, covered visitations and the enforcement of lay discipline.

Not all the synod's discussion found its way into the canons. Perhaps the most important omission was scripture. On 16 December the synod had divided up the New Testament in preparation for an English translation, enjoined careful consideration of the proper words on the 20th, and took up the issue of interpretation almost as soon as it returned from its Christmas recess.[257] Even earlier on 13 December *The institution of a Christian man* was examined, and the apostles' creed was assigned to certain members of the lower house, perhaps for fresh translation or as the basis of a catechism. And there all these matters rested. As in the case of the seminary curriculum, although the canons mandated doctrinal instruction, little was done about its content. Pole asked Carranza to write a catechism, which he corrected and proposed to have published, but it did not appear until 1558 in Antwerp in Latin.[258]

Pope Paul took several moves during the synod which might at first appear worrisome (and did to Morone), including withdrawing all legates and nuncios in Philip's territories, except Pole (see the next chapter). A few days later, Paul named their common friend Scotti a cardinal and shortly thereafter confirmed him as one of a commission for the datary.[259] Scotti, who probably really did not wish to be promoted, wrote Pole and asked his advice.[260] Pole replied that Scotti should do as he did and obey in inverse proportion to how much 'repugnance' he felt.[261] It will bear underlining that Scotti approached Pole and that Pole replied ingenuously. Pole tried to convince Morone that Scotti was a good thing, but Morone was no more easily persuaded than Philip had been. He told Pole he thought Scotti 'a true Israelite, and completely well-inclined to you', but continued that there were frequently new reasons for suspicion (which he reinforced by referring to Scotti as 'Bernardino Alias'!).[262] Pole overlooked Morone's reservations in his response, calling Scotti 'our cardinal Trani'.[263]

After taking a break for Christmas which Pole spent with the queen, the

---

[257] *ERP*, 5, pp. 229–30.

[258] *Doc. hist.*, 3, pp. 301–2 and 1, pp. 347–9, 353, 356. Marmion, p. 265, says on unknown evidence that there was a proposal to translate the catechism into English. Cf. *Carranza y Pole*, pp. 71–2,

75–7 and 136–9 for Priuli's involvement.

[259] *CRP*, no. 1476.

[260] ASVe:APR, 8, fo. 19r.

[261] *CRP*, no. 1467.

[262] *CRP*, no. 1476.

[263] *CRP*, no. 1491.

synod reconvened on 6 or 7 January, addressing the interpretation of the New Testament on the 8th.[264] Three weeks later, Paul's breves approving it finally arrived.[265] As the synod neared its end Pole received two more encouraging pieces of news about the situation in Rome. First, Philip bent and appointed Scotti to Trani, earning Pole's congratulations.[266] At nearly the same time his bulls for Canterbury came, full of praise from Paul. According to Bernardo Navagero, the Venetian ambassador to the pope, Dudic, and Caracciolo, the pope said many laudatory things in the consistory in which Pole received the archbishopric.[267] Pole reciprocated with a congratulatory letter to Scotti a few days later on both his cardinalate and Trani in which he begged Scotti several times to make full use of him.[268] In this promising climate, the synod was prorogued in early February. On the 10th Pole promulgated the canons and had his order read to all the members in 'Lambeth parish church'.[269]

Pole probably preached a sermon near the synod's close.[270] In it he enjoined the clergy to act as his 'undershepherds', and especially to tell the rest of England that he could fix anything amiss. Pole quoted his favourite prophet Ezekiel as saying that was how he had acted for God. The clergy would gain rewards for their suffering, but had to reflect on what a terrible charge they had: God would demand the blood of their flock from them. False teachers threatened them, as they had Paul, and had to be fought off through Christ's doctrine. The worst problems arose through ignorance, which made it that much more important to defend doctrine against heretics. Pole singled out clerical covetousness as the heretics' best opening. Concupiscence was the root problem, and government had to restrain it. Pole thus set up a balance on the issue of church property, simultaneously condemning both the possessioners and also avaricious clerics, who caught the poor between them. Pole's stress on government and discipline sounds like a preface to the 'arid' canons and a thoroughly Augustinian move, but he quickly continued that good religion, the comfort Jesus brought, helped even more.

The canons did not comfort the clergy. Mason wrote that most priests wished Pole back in Rome, and an anonymous report concluded that the synod had deeply upset the bishops and the prelates, because now they had to go and preach without excuse.[271] The summary placed great stress on the synod's

---

[264] *CRP*, nos. 1479–80.

[265] *CRP*, no. 1484.

[266] *CRP*, no. 1482.

[267] ASVe:APR, 8, fo. 64v; *ERP*, 1, p. 42; and *PM*, 1, p. 142. Caracciolo's statement may not be independent of Dudic's.

[268] *CRP*, no. 1490.

[269] *CRP*, no. 1492.

[270] BAV, Vat. lat. 5968, fos. 1ar–4v, 'Ad sacerdotes in synodo'. See *CPM*, catalogue no. 10j.

[271] PRO, SP 11/7 no. 6 and ASP, Carteggio Farnesiano, Inghilterra, b. 103, 1538–1732, fo. 1r.

injunctions about preaching, claiming that 200 sermons were to be prepared, to be preached either in Latin or English as the curate could. Bishops had to reside, 'preaching, setting a good example, and governing their flock'. Pole set the standard by enforcing the new regulations about diet and preparing to go to Canterbury where he would both sing mass and preach. His report to Morone a week later began with how much time the synod had spent on property; the rest of his summary largely agrees with the substance of the other versions of the canons.[272]

The canons represent a reasonably impressive initial effort to deal with the effects of twenty years of schism. Nevertheless, most commentators pronounce the synod a failure, or at least argue that Pole failed to follow through in the implementation of its canons.[273] Indeed, they were never published.[274] Efforts to trace their impact in Pole's conduct of his legation produce mixed results. Some have found echoes in his visitation articles.[275] Then again, canon twelve on visitation left little more than a few weak verbal parallels in the articles of the numerous visitations conducted over the next three years. Canon three on residence might never have been passed, to judge from Pole's legatine register. Its stipulation of a two-month time limit after promulgation within which clerics had to supplicate for dispensation for non-residence remained a dead letter. About one point there is virtually universal agreement: the importance of the seminary legislation. Pole's design had a major effect on the legislation adopted at Trent.[276] Those few schools founded in England probably also arose in part from canon eleven.[277] While the rest of the canons did not have much effect at home, they may have on the continent. Morone thought Scotti meant to imitate them in his diocese, and Seripando may have used them in

---

[272] CRP, no. 1497.

[273] Pogson, pp. 168–9. The rest of his thesis is organized around the canons and their enforcement (or lack thereof). Marmion (pp. 255–6) thinks Pole succeeded on the score of discipline and failed on doctrine. Loades, Reign, pp. 293–4 largely endorses Marmion's interpretation, combined with Canon Dixon's. Dixon (p. 468) was characteristically harsh in his judgment that Pole ran out of energy.

[274] Marmion, 1, p. 161.

[275] Frere and Kennedy, 2, pp. 388n, 389n, 390n, 393n, 394n, 397n, 401n, 402n, 404n and 407n.

[276] Paul V. Brassel, Praeformatio reformationis Tridentinae de seminariis clericorum (Roehampton: Manresana, 1938); J. A. O'Donohoe, Tridentine seminary legislation, its sources and its formation ((Louvain): Publications Universitaires de Louvain, 1957) and Marmion, 1, pp. 165–79, a nice summary of the place of Pole's legislation in the sweep of sixteenth-century efforts. Cf. esp. pp. 177–8 where Marmion ties Pole's ideas to the Reformatio legum drawn up under Cranmer's direction, although the parallels are not very close.

[277] Pogson, p. 352. Pogson says it is significant that Pole failed to mention this canon to Loyola, and perhaps it is.

Salerno.[278] Whichever way the lines of force ran between Pole's canons and Carranza's visitations, they surely had some connection with one another.[279]

While trying to salvage something from the débâcle of Vaucelles, which overshadowed the canons in their immediate context, Pole also prepared for his promotion to Canterbury. It proved to be incautious to tell Fresneda his plans before he had even mentioned them to the queen, much less had her approval.[280] Pole's leave to go to Canterbury hinged in part on the expectation that Philip would return, as he did not. Pole originally planned to go on 23 March and sing his first mass on Passion Sunday following, but a month later had been forced to postpone his arrival to the 25th, and in fact never went.[281] He had apparently always meant to be ordained in London.[282] His patent of possession of the archbishopric came on 17 March, and the see's temporalities were restored the day of Cranmer's burning, the 21st.[283] In between Cranmer had signed his final recantation, after supposedly asking Pole for more time to reflect. The document may well have been drafted in Pole's circles and brought up to Oxford by Cole, who preached the uncharitable sermon at Cranmer's execution.[284] If Mary ever did grant Pole leave to go to Canterbury, the discovery of the Dudley conspiracy cancelled it.[285] Pole had a hand in exposing it, and his hapless brother Sir Geoffrey was tangentially involved.[286] Disappointed of his hopes to go to his cathedral, Pole was ordained on 20 March, consecrated at the Observant Franciscan house at Greenwich on the 22nd and shortly thereafter on Lady Day received the pallium at St Mary Arches, a Canterbury peculiar in London, picked as a compromise when Mary refused to allow him to leave the capital.[287] Perhaps the congratulations which came his way from Italy compensated in small measure.[288]

[278] *CRP*, no. 1531 and Hubert Jedin, *Girolamo Seripando. Sein Leben und Denken im Geisteskampf des 16. Jahrhunderts* (Würzburg: Augustinus-Verlag, 1984; reprint of Würzburg, 1937 ed.), 2, p. 17.

[279] *Carranza y Pole*, pp. 321–31.

[280] *CRP*, no. 1499.

[281] *CRP*, no. 1515.

[282] *CRP*, no. 1508.

[283] *CRP*, no. 1516.

[284] MacCulloch, pp. 594–9 and Dixon, pp. 518–20, for the appeal to Pole. Strype originally suggested that Pole wrote the recantation, and Strype and Dixon also thought Pole had written Cheke's. *Ecclesiastical memorials*, 3:1, p. 395.

[285] *CSPV*, 6:1, no. 434. David Loades, *Two*

Tudor conspiracies (Cambridge: Cambridge University Press, 1965), pp. 176–217.

[286] *CSPV*, 6:1, no. 433 and *CSPDomR*, no. 375.

[287] There are various accounts of Pole's ordination and consecration. I have given priority to Faita's (*CRP*, no. 1557), along with the note of the venue of the consecration and list of those in attendance in LPL, Pole's register, fo. 2r. See also PRO, PROB 11/38, fo. 2r–v; and *The diary of Henry Machyn*, ed. J. G. Nichols (London: Camden Society, 1848, o.s., no. 42), p. 102. Other versions in Hallé, pp. 484–5 and MacCulloch, p. 607. For the pallium, *CRP*, no. 1524.

[288] *CRP*, nos. 1525–6.

Pole and preaching

Much more important to Pole, immediately after receiving the pallium and perhaps celebrating his first mass, he responded to the parishioners' request that he begin his cure of souls with them by preaching a long sermon, given *all'improviso*, according to Pole's secretary Faita.[289] Fortunately, this is either not true or Pole sat down very soon afterwards and wrote out his text, several versions of which survive, in part autograph, in addition to Faita's detailed report.[290] Pole had emphasized preaching for years, especially in 'De reformatione', and now that he finally had a chance he produced a sermon like those he had earlier recommended. It opened with a lament for the famine of spiritual food in England, and Pole probably exhorted his hearers to seek it 'with that simplicity of mind that ... is proper of little children' rather than for the sake of novelty (fo. 402r–v). The meaning of the archiepiscopal pallium then attracted attention, Pole linking it directly to Peter's body and perhaps stressing its symbolism of papal plenitude of power and ecclesiastical unity (fos. 403v–404r). Pole then cited Cyprian to support the claim that all bishops derived their authority from the pope, a possible reversal from his reading in *De unitate*. In a possibly apocalyptic reference, Pole said the pallium represented the Lamb of Revelations (fo. 405r). In typically tortured English syntax, Pole insisted that 'whereas both wisdom and strength of mind which are of divers sorts, one natural and another supernatural, being both necessary to all that have any rule given them & specially to those that in their rule doth represent Christ's person as those do most that have cure of governing any part of the flock of Christ, if other baser governments may with the natural discourse and courage of mind show any semblance of a tolerable form of ruling, yet such a cure as primates & patriarchs have can never make any decent governance exempt [sic] he fetch his wisdom of his that being highest of all abased himself'.

From the simplicity of a prelate, Pole passed to obedience and thence to his powers as legate for reconciliation and peace and the addition of Canterbury jurisdiction (fo. 406r). The last was most important, but lack of time had not allowed Pole to attend properly to it (fo. 407r). Instead, he meant to speak about

---

[289] The mass is from Dudic, who may have been an eye-witness (*ERP*, 1, p. 40). Michiel (*CSPV*, 6:1, no. 434) reported the day before Pole's sermon that his first mass would have to be postponed until after Easter, but plans could have changed overnight. Faita made no mention of a mass. Michiel thought Pole's sermon was even better received than his visit. *CSPV*, 6:1, no. 440. Wriothesley (*Chronicle*, 2, p. 134) noted only the reception of the pallium, but no sermon.

[290] See *CPM*, catalogue no. 10a2, the version I quote.

the peace he brought from the pope, almost as if he had cobbled his sermon together from his writings about that legation. Pole invited all to become 'sons of peace', which meant that they must immediately accept his salutation (fo. 408r). Moses and Jesus on Palm Sunday served as examples of leaders' solicitude for their flocks' peace, and also as a warning to heed his injunction (fos. 408v–9r). No one could have this peace except through fear of God, as the example of Solomon showed (fo. 411r), but anyone could who received it in fear of God and obedience to the commandments (fo. 412r). At about this point, according to Faita, Pole broke into tears, and in a low voice urged his hearers to remember the past.

Perhaps heeding his own injunction and remembering his mother's fate, Pole, in a marked departure from his earlier piety, treated the example of the Virgin Mary at length, intercut with others who had kept covenant with God (fos. 412v–15r; 268v). Her humility was the only way to receive God's word (fo. 415r–v). Mere hearing was not enough. The listener, having taken in the words in a state of reverent fear, then had to reflect on them. Otherwise, he would hear them 'but for a ceremony' which would produce 'a ceremonious fruit ... or rather no fruit but great hurt'. Too much diligence in studying scripture was equally harmful, as present experience showed. God forbid that knowledge of scripture should be suppressed, rather everyone should have it (fo. 416r). The traditional mode of reading scripture suited Pole perfectly. 'Not every man should make himself studier of Scripture to learn it of his own wit & labor, for he that maketh himself a scholar will make himself a master & a teacher' (fo. 416v). 'Therefore of those that by the ordinance of Christ and the church have by their office authority and [are] bound to teach & preach Scripture there must be a moderation found that neither the desire of knowledge . . . be reproved, nor utterly repressed, but rather nourished and encouraged, and yet not permitted to everyone [who] hath this desire to feed himself as he list and as his own wit leadeth him' which would be the 'most perilous state'. Pole returned to the Virgin Mary, telling his audience in more convoluted syntax to go 'to that home that they take for their home & to that work then in their conscience where the spirit of God that loveth no idleness speaketh & showeth them to be the work of God requireth of every one in their vocation working it that with the mind of a virgin & bashfull handmaid & praying that God will vouchsafe to perform his promise . . . for no kind of man is excluded from this peace that will not exclude himself by infidelity' (fos. 417v–18r). He then offered a warning reminiscent of earlier Italian controversies about proper preaching that faith without works was not enough, before concluding with Isaiah's insistence that the regenerate must act like seed.

Pole took a cautious approach to preaching in England, even if it must not be forgotten that 'De reformatione ecclesiae' in its earlier versions had assigned great importance to it as the means to reform (see the last chapter). His caution sprang from two roots, his reluctance to identify himself as an author, likening publication to preaching, and his Italian experience.[291] The polemic between Contarini and Catarino had put the issue of how to preach in high relief, and Pole endorsed Contarini's gradualist pedagogy.[292] He did the same to Truchsess in June 1554. Explaining his views of justification, Pole claimed that he had urged preachers to moderation, even to the extent of concealing key points of doctrine.[293] He also stressed that they had to have the proper authority and to teach as much by their example as by their words. Four years later (to the day) his time in England had partly changed his mind. Writing then to Carranza, who had been very active as a preacher at the English court, and defending himself for not residing at Canterbury and not taking better care of his peculiars in London, Pole admitted that he still had reservations about preaching because of its abuse by 'carnal men'.[294] More preaching was the last thing London needed, but Pole stressed its peculiarity.[295] He cited Ezekiel to demonstrate that preaching needed strong support, especially discipline, if it were to prove effective. Nevertheless, Pole turned the issue around and concluded that discipline also needed the word, and asserted that Bonner was taking good care of preaching at Paul's Cross, while Harpsfield and Cole constantly supervised Pole's parishes. If more preaching should be needed, Pole would not fail to provide it himself. He claimed to have preached as often as he could, and to have ordered that non-resident bishops provide commissaries to preach written sermons for them.[296]

---

[291] *CRP*, no. 636.

[292] The Inquisition would later be highly interested in Pole's ideas about preaching, which three of the eighteen heads making up the 'Disciplina Poli' concerned, and may already have been. Had Pole known, that would only have reinforced his caution. *PM*, 1, pp. 198 (at length, including 'De modo concionandi') and 222 for the *Disciplina*.

[293] *CRP*, no. 885.

[294] *CRP*, no. 2252. For Carranza and other Spanish friars, see *Carranza y Pole*, p. 43 and ASM:AG, 1925–VII, fo. 136.

[295] *Ubi major est verbi copia, ibi minus homines proficere*, wrote Pole, which never happened except in London. Dixon, p. 656 misinterpreted Pole as if he had 'not

without cause' claimed that preaching was 'careful, abundant, and praiseworthy', when this was actually a complaint. Dixon also mistakenly said this passage came from a letter to Paul IV. Pole's jaundiced attitude to the Londoners would not have been helped by incidents like that recorded in August 1555 when he, their majesties and Gardiner were jeered when riding through Cheapside. J. G. Nichols, ed., *Narratives of the days of the reformation chiefly from the manuscripts of John Foxe the martyrologist* (Camden Society, o.s., 77, 1859), p. 209. Cf. Machyn, p. 93.

[296] 'Cum enim in ipsa metropolitana ecclesia et nonnullis illis dioecesis meae locis praedicavi saepius, tum etiam Londini bis, neque posthac, juvante Dei gratia, ut spero,

Following up on the synod, albeit a bit belatedly, Pole reported that Thomas Watson and John Boxall were writing sermons in the vernacular on controverted topics, and seemed to claim that some had been published and others would appear shortly.[297] Pole concluded by saying that he meant to publish soon himself, once he had Carranza's and others' criticisms, and in the context, he must have been talking about sermons.

The provision of preaching in English had occupied Pole almost from the first, as it had Mary.[298] In the wake of the synod, it was much on his mind. When accepting the chancellorship of Cambridge in 1556, he singled out as an inducement to take the post the many famous preachers the university had produced, including the recent Lenten preachers before Mary.[299] Then his niece had complained about a paucity of preachers, and Pole had promised to write her bishop to do what he could.[300] At the same time, Pole wrote Fresneda that the queen was very pleased by his efforts to see that 'the brothers of St Adhemar' preached in Calais and elsewhere overseas.[301] Also in 1556 Leonard Pollard, a prebendary in Pate's diocese of Worcester, published his *Fyve Homilies of late made by . . . Leonard Pollard, prebendary of the Cathedrall Churche of Woster, directed and dedicated to . . . byshoppe of Woster.*[302] Worcester, once evangelized by both Latimer and Hooper, got extra attention from the first, with encouraging results. In August 1555, Richard Vernon, an MA who had preached during the

---

deerit.' This phrase was echoed in Dudic's description of Pole's preaching. Dudic, after noting the sermon at St Mary Arches, continued 'alias quoque concionatus est, & maxime Cantuariae in Ecclesia sua, ac nonnullis in locis, quae sua Dioecesi continebantur' (*ERP*, 1, p. 40).

[297] 'Partim edita sunt, partim brevi edentur.' There is nothing in Jennifer Loach, 'The Marian establishment and the printing press', *English historical review*, 109 (1986), pp. 135–48, p. 140. Perhaps Pole merely meant that they had been completed, rather than committed to print.

[298] Pole's attitude to preaching was largely of a piece with the Spanish line, even if Carranza thought he needed a little prodding. Alfonso de Castro, who preached a famous sermon against executions for heresy to the English court, argued in 1547 that lack of preaching was

the first major cause of heresy. Henry Kamen, 'Toleration and dissent in sixteenth-century Spain: the alternative tradition', *SCJ*, 19 (1988), pp. 3–24, p. 14.

[299] *CRP*, no. 1533.

[300] *CRP*, no. 1516.

[301] *CRP*, no. 1499, which also treats the mystery of these friars' identity.

[302] London: William Griffith, 1556; *STC*, no. 20091. Joseph Gillow, *A literary and biographical history or biographical dictionary of the English Catholics* (London: Burns and Oates, 1885–1905; 6 vols.), 5, p. 341, said Pollard wrote the sermons 'under his [Pate's] direction', but the dedication does not suggest a commission. The five sermons cover (1) the Eucharist; (2) faith and knowledge of God; (3) 'Of the primitive and chief authority' of the pope; (4) confession; and 5) the mass.

schism, publicly retracted and preached his errors.[303] George London, a former Benedictine, was prospectively licensed by Pole to preach there in March 1555, and barely three weeks later got a universal licence based on the good job he had done.[304] This favour to London fit with Pole's encouragement of Feckenham, another former Benedictine and famous preacher, whom he installed as abbot of Westminster.[305] It may be too much to suggest that these two instances indicate a preference on Pole's part for Benedictine preaching, but it is possible. Finally, a handful of other preaching licences survive, one to Thomas Nello in November 1556, another to William Darrell, canon of Canterbury, perhaps from 1555, and the last for Salisbury to Dr Thomas Hardin, Dr Thomas Heskins, and John Fessarde, parson of Donhead St Mary in 1558.[306] Pole may well have required all parish priests to own a copy of Bonner's *Profitable and necessary doctrine*.[307]

Although it took Pole eighteen months to get around to his first public sermon, preaching was important to him, and he put effort into it.[308] While the total of Pole's sermons may seem meagre, it is both impressive by comparison with Matthew Parker's total of nine for the twenty-five years after 1534, for example, and also artificially reduced by the accident of survival and by a problem of definition.[309] The complete disappearance of his treatise 'De modo concionandi' also seriously handicaps our understanding of Pole's preaching. Evidence survives for a total of at least twelve (or perhaps as many as fourteen) sermons, beginning with that to parliament at the reconciliation which

---

[303] *CRP*, no. 1320.

[204] *CRP*, nos. 1096 and 1166.

[305] Dixon, p. 94 for Feckenham's preaching.

[306] *CRP*, nos. 1774, 2328, and 2242.

[307] The injunctions for the diocese of Gloucester required all priests to own a copy. David Wilkins, ed., *Concilia magnae Britanniae et Hiberniae* (London: Gosling et al., 1737; 4 vols.), 4, pp. 145–8, reprinted in Frere and Kennedy, 2, pp. 401–8. Cf. Eamon Duffy, *The stripping of the altars. Traditional religion in England c. 1400–c. 1580* (New Haven: Yale University Press, 1992), pp. 525 and 537, as he tells me, apparently making an inference based on an entry in the Morebath accounts of a payment in 1556 for 'a new boke (of ye homililes) concernyg [*sic*] ye churche'. J. E. Binney, ed., *The accounts of the wardens of the parish of Morebath, Devon,*

1520–1573 (Exeter: James G. Commin, 1904), p. 189.

[308] This goes against the standard interpretation of Pole's reservations about, even fear of, preaching. See as typical Loades, *Reign*, pp. 272 and 293 or Pogson, pp. 59, 77 and *passim*. For a not very appreciative study of his style, see J. W. Blench, *Preaching in England in the late fifteenth and sixteenth centuries: a study of English sermons 1450–c. 1600* (New York: Barnes and Noble, 1964), pp. 164–5, who calls Pole 'not a distinguished vernacular preacher', but discusses only two of his sermons. Blench's dated study was generally unsympathetic to the Marians. Cf. pp. 49–57, 157–68, 277–92.

[309] John Strype, *The life and acts of Matthew Parker* (Oxford: Clarendon Press, 1821; 3 vols.), 3, pp. 22–3.

Beccadelli identified as a sermon.[310] If we accept this identification, then a number of Pole's other texts, whether about church property, or the explication of the meaning of the golden rose and sword (papal gifts to their majesties) might also be labelled sermons, as should his opening address to the council of Trent. This would put the total up to about twenty. Even this sum should probably be hypothetically increased in light of Beccadelli's and Dudic's stress both on the number of sermons Pole gave, including at Canterbury, and also the fact that at least some of them were allegedly delivered ex tempore and may not be recorded.[311] Of those at Canterbury no trace survives. Of the others, a text has been found for twelve.[312] Nor did Pole ignore the power of print, planning three of these sermons, beginning with that at St Mary Arches, as a set for publication. All were originally written in English and translated into Latin by Faita in preparation for wider circulation.[313] It would have cost Pole some part of his self-image to do that. The depth of his resistance to writing for the press must not be forgotten. Finally, Latimer's judgment that Pole could have been a good preacher deserves serious consideration.[314]

---

[310] *MMB*, 1:2, p. 314.

[311] Dudic merely translated Beccadelli's words (*MMB*, p. 316 and *ERP*, 1, p. 40). *CRP*, no. 1370 and Elder, *Letter*, sigs. Dv and Eiir for sermons allegedly given extemporaneously.

[312] *CPM*, catalogue no. 10.

[313] *Ibid.*, catalogue no. 10a-c.

[314] G. E. Corrie, ed., *Sermons by Hugh Latimer, sometime bishop of Worcester, martyr, 1555* (Cambridge: University Press, 1844), p. 173.

7

Reconstructing the English church

L IKE POLE'S CHANCE to provide spiritual guidance to his flock through his preaching, so his opportunity to exercise his legatine powers in England was delayed. He had exceptionally broad extraordinary faculties as legate *a latere*.[1] Julius wished to make the reconciliation as easy as possible, and therefore gave Pole powers to reconcile anyone, even heretics, including cases reserved to the pope, together with the authority to delegate those powers. Clergy could be absolved for celebrating mass, marriage, taking orders, and holding benefices by schismatic authority. In addition, Pole got authority to unite or dissolve benefices as necessary, especially for the support of hospitals and schools. Religious who left their houses without licence could be dispensed and allowed to continue to hold benefices, even in secular habit.[2] Wide ordinary powers over clergy allowed him to dispense for incompatibilia, as well as for illegitimacy, orders, defect of age, and mutilations which should have prevented clerics from celebrating mass. He got virtually unlimited visitation rights, as well as the power to appoint heads of lesser monasteries. In short, Pole could do whatever the Major Penitentiary could. Any legate *a latere* was the pope's alter ego, and as Rex Pogson says, Pole would become Paul IV's 'resident agent in north-western Europe'.[3] It is therefore doubly ironic that despite Pole's powers he constantly consulted Rome and also that Paul IV may have become suspicious of Pole in part because of those powers, rather than the way he used them.[4]

Pogson has studied Pole's legation in most detail demonstrating the centrality of re-establishing the law.[5] In order to defend Pole and Mary against the charge

---

[1] Cervini also sent him a volume of papal claims on England. *Calendar of state papers … Rome, 2, 1572–1578*, ed. J. M. Rigg (London: HMSO, 1926), p. 242.

[2] *CRP*, nos. 619–23.

[3] Pogson, p. 114.

[4] Henri de Sponde, *Annalium emin'mi Cardinalis Caes. Baronii continuatio, ab anno M. C. XCVII … ad finem M. DC.XL* (Paris: Denis de la Noüe, 1641), c. 325 1557 VII.

[5] Pogson, pp. 60, 204–5.

of fostering 'arid legalism', Pogson tried to bring out the merits of his approach and to explain his failure.[6] Both arose from his earlier experience in Italy and from his strengths as a spiritual counsellor. Perhaps most important, his twenty years at the centre of Christendom and in exile from England led him to view it as only a part of the international church, susceptible of restoration to that church with the same tools as Pole's Italian allies had used on their wayward members. This both led Pole to overlook the depth of English national feeling and its peculiarly intense experience of heresy, and also to fail to see the necessity of new methods to deal with them, especially the Jesuits.[7] Thus, for example, Pole distrusted preaching as a tool because he had been 'horror-stricken' when Ochino and Martyr fled.[8] Divergent experience also strained his relations with nearly all of those with whom he would have to co-operate in England. Many Henrician bishops had deep reservations about Pole, and Pole reciprocated.[9]

Another earlier strength now proved both an asset and a debit, according to Pogson. Pole's success in small groups and with individual women carried over into his relationship with Mary and his household, which became the implicitly trusted cog in his administration, at the same time as it fed into perhaps his major weakness, his elitist belief that the English should be treated as children.[10] Similarly, Pole's life-long desire to flee the active life ill-prepared him for running a complex organization, and especially for the politically delicate negotiations necessary to restore its finances.[11] As Pogson stresses, the most serious objective limitation on the possibility of success was the short time Pole had, less than two and a half years.[12] Pole's scrupulous attention to detail made the reconciliation a drawn-out process, as the manifold demands on his energies made it 'extraordinary that he even formulated plans'.[13] He insisted on order and ceremonial, although Pogson does allow that such a low-key approach had value in England's confused state. Yet even with more time, Pole would not have produced results because of his refusal to think about the future, a point almost equivalent to the charge that he failed to discover the counter-reformation.[14]

---

[6] David Loades largely endorses Pogson's interpretation in *The reign of Mary Tudor: politics, government and religion in England 1553–1558*, 2nd ed. (London and New York: Longman, 1991), esp. p. 124.

[7] R. H. Pogson, 'Reginald Pole and the priorities of government in Mary Tudor's church', *HJ*, 18 (1975), pp. 3–20, p. 6.

[8] Pogson, 'Priorities', p. 19.

[9] Pogson, pp. 40, 52, and 308.

[10] Pogson, 'Priorities', pp. 7–9 and Pogson, p. 20.

[11] Pogson, pp. 26–7, but cf. 28.

[12] Pogson, pp. 223, 232, 248, etc.

[13] R. H. Pogson, 'Revival and reform in Mary Tudor's church: a question of money', in Christopher Haigh, ed., *The English reformation revised* (Cambridge: Cambridge University Press, 1987), pp. 139–56, p. 154.

[14] Pogson, pp. 236–57.

I have already dealt with a few objections to Pogson's interpretation, else-where with why Pole refused the Jesuits and above with his preaching.[15] There is a great deal in the rest of Pogson's analysis, especially of Pole as administrator. Unlike earlier years when there is very little evidence of how Pole's administra-tion ran, now we have an invaluable source in the form of an original register, which Pogson was the first historian to use seriously. Bibliothèque municipale, Douai, MS 922 consists of 877 folios in six volumes, and at least two more have been lost.[16] Although Pogson clears Pole of a charge of laziness, his is neither a very extensive register, nor does the number of acts it contains impress one by comparison with other continental legatine registers. Pole's total is less than 1,140 surviving acts, out of an original number of about 1,550. Then again, by comparison to Cardinal Wolsey's dispensations, which come to only about 100 for the one year for which evidence survives, Pole was very busy.[17] The quality of Pole's register does not suffer, either, by comparison with most of its English predecessors. They are almost all badly kept, except for Edmund Bonner's.[18]

That the register was among the first undertaken for a long time by a legate (illus. 10 and 11) with wide powers may explain some of its difficulties. Paul III had avoided giving legates faculties like Pole's in order to keep business in Rome.[19] The indiscriminate mixing of documents, including both supplications and bulls, as well as ordinary correspondence, was probably modelled on the practice of Julius III's not very experienced secretariate.[20] Pole's administration learned by doing and made substantial progress in regularizing its practices by 1557. Progress also came on the judicial front. Pogson sampled appeals to Pole

---

[15] Thomas F. Mayer, 'A test of wills: cardinal Pole, Ignatius Loyola, and the Jesuits in England', in T. M. McCoog, ed., *The reckoned expense: Edmund Campion and the early English Jesuits. Essays in celebration of the first centenary of Campion Hall, Oxford (1896–1996)* (Woodbridge: Boydel and Brewer, 1996), pp. 21–37.

[16] For a fuller discussion of this register and its continental peers, together with the internal workings of Pole's administration, see *CRP*, introduction.

[17] Peter Gwyn, *The king's cardinal. The rise and fall of Thomas Wolsey* (London: Pimlico, 1990), p. 285.

[18] As Nicholas Pocock observed long ago and as Paul Ayris concurs (private correspondence). Nicholas Pocock, ed., *The history of the reformation of the church of England by Gilbert Burnet* (Oxford: Clarendon Press, 1865; 7 vols.), 7, pp. 69–70. Pocock thought Cranmer's the worst.

[19] Bernard Barbiche and Ségolène de Dainville-Barbiche, 'Les légats *a latere* en France et leur facultés aus XVIᵉ et XVIIᵉ siècles', *Archivum historiae pontificiae*, 23 (1985), pp. 93–165, p. 145.

[20] E.g., ASV, Misc. Arm. 41:60, which has a note at its end of a large number of *cameralia* that had been extracted from it. For the inexperience of Julius's secretariate, see *NB*, 15, pp. LXXVII–LXXVIII.

10 Legatine seal. From 'The late Rev. Thomas Streatfeild, of Chart's Edge', Archaeologia Cantiana, 3 (1860), pp. 137–44, pl. 1 opposite p. 141.

from diocesan courts in York, Bath and Wells, Gloucester, Worcester and Hereford and found more appeals than had gone to Rome (he does not say what the period for comparison was), a total of seventy-three of all kinds and from all courts between 1555 and 1557.[21] The first appeal in Pole's register dates from July 1556 and only a handful more came in between then and early 1557. From February of that year until the close of the register in July there are sixteen more cases. Judicial process was on the verge of establishment. In theory Rome directed it, but the fact that Pole stood in directly for the pope did not mean that he quickly executed his orders, especially not after Paul IV became pope. Thus an instruction of August 1556 to curtail certain dispensations was not disseminated until 8 January 1557.[22] Worse, Paul's wishes of July 1555 for a new tax survey of the English church were not executed for more than a year, and the results were not well received in Rome.[23]

These delays arose in part from the inadequacy of the clerical side of the English church. Rebuilding stretched its personnel to the limit. The case of Griffin Williams is illustrative. He was first appointed registrar and notary in the diocese of Oxford in February 1555, then in Salisbury in July, before being given the same position in Worcester in 1556.[24] In all, Pole created only forty-

---

[21] Pogson, pp. 229–30.
[22] *CRP*, nos. 1663 and 1809.
[23] *CRP*, nos. 1265, 1699, 1703–4, 1708, 1624.
[24] *CRP*, no. 1088.

*11 Archiepiscopal/*Legatus natus *seal.* Hasted's history of Kent, corrected,
enlarged and continued to the present time from the manuscript collections
of the late Reverend Thomas Streatfeild and the late Reverend Lambert
Blackwell Larking, *ed. H. H. Drake, pt. I.* The hundred of Blackheath *(London: Mitchell
and Hughes, 1886), p. 284.*

one notaries, including several who would have had limited use in England,
making less than two for each diocese, not including those in Wales.[25] The distribution was even more uneven than that, since Salisbury, a trouble spot, and
Lincoln got five each, Bath and Wells, Norwich and Winchester two, and five
may have been for the University of Cambridge (four of these created after the

---

[25] Pogson, p. 232 gives thirty-nine, twenty-
four of them in 1555. He also includes
Pole's three creations of counts palatine
under the heading of lawyers, but only one
of these, John Goodsalve, might have thus
qualified. The other two, Jean Matal and
Pole's familiar Johan Oudenaghen, were
ceremonial appointments, as was usually
the case with these titles.

visitation). Pole named only one in Ireland.[26] Many of Pole's administrators may not have been entirely reliable. Except for two from members of Canterbury administration, there are no supplications for absolution from carry-over clerical office-holders. Pole may have had a little more success than Cranmer in getting his own or at least sympathetic people in place, beginning with Harpsfield, archdeacon of Canterbury before Pole returned, Henry Cole, or William Pye, convocation's delegate at the Oxford disputation with Cranmer who brought Cranmer Tunstall's book on the eucharist and became one of the hinges of Pole's financial machinery, but it must also be stressed that he inherited the core of his archiepiscopal administration.[27] In addition to Anthony Hussey, principal registrar, William Cooke, whom Pole renewed as commissary of the Prerogative Court of Canterbury, had been one of Cranmer's principal men since 1547.[28]

The archdiocesan machinery probably ran little better than Pole's legatine apparatus, if the chaos in the PCC in 1558 is any indication.[29] Nor did the heavy volume of business coming from sede vacantes help, especially since the archiepiscopal vicar-general of the moment also had to serve as vicar-general for any vacant see as David Pole did for the vast diocese of Lincoln in 1556 or Henry Cole for Hereford in 1557, and the principal archiepiscopal registrar, Hussey, as registrar of the vacant see, for example Oxford.[30] Pole's archiepiscopal administration depended initially on David Pole while two other experienced men, datary Ormanetto and chief secretary Faita, ran his legatine apparatus. All three had to play multiple roles. The learned David Pole, already archdeacon of Derby and until recently (still?) vicar-general of Coventry and Lichfield, is typical in his service as archiepiscopal vicar-general, official principal and dean of the court of arches, and auditor of the court of audience, as well as one of the core members of a royal heresy commission issued about the same time.[31] Nor did

---

26 *CRP*, no. 1649.

27 Diarmaid MacCulloch, *Thomas Cranmer. A life* (New Haven and London: Yale University Press, 1996), p. 204 for Cranmer's administrative problems, and p. 569 for Pye.

28 *CRP*, no. 1062. Cooke's probate register is PRO, PROB 11/38. I owe information about Cooke under Cranmer to Dr Ayris. See his forthcoming edition of Cranmer's register. For Hussey, see *CRP*, introduction.

29 Christopher Kitching, 'The prerogative court of Canterbury from Warham to Whitgift', in F. Heal and R. O'Day, eds., *Continuity and change: personnel and administration of the Church of England, 1500–1642* (Leicester: Leicester University Press, 1976), pp. 191–213, p. 200.

30 LPL, Pole's register, fos. 48r and 59v and *CRP*, no. 2300. A total of 145 acts for various sede vacantes passed through Pole's machinery, together with forty-two institutions or collations to benefices of which he was patron, and the archiepiscopal register contains about forty more miscellaneous acts.

31 See my article on David Pole in H. C. G. Matthew, ed., *New dictionary of national biography* (Oxford: Oxford University Press, forthcoming).

this situation improve much over time. Thus in October 1558 Cole was still dean of St Paul's as well as dean of arches. Harpsfield, still archdeacon, replaced him in the second two posts, only for Cole immediately to be appointed commissary of the PCC.[32] And although legatine and archiepiscopal machineries were supposed to be distinct, they overlapped more than a little, causing confusion and extra work. For example, the successor to Pole's familiar Thomas Rise was first appointed to the Canterbury deanery of Shoreham through legatine authority, at which time he was described as rector of Brasted, but then more than six months later was appointed to Brasted by archiepiscopal authority.[33]

Their workload sometimes overwhelmed Pole's administrators producing inconsistency compounded by clerical errors (or perhaps vice versa). During Lent 1555, 189 supplications to eat meat virtually shut down the administration, forcing Pole to issue a blanket dispensation.[34] He did the same thing again in 1557, when there were only eighty individual supplications, probably reflecting the impact of Pope Paul's strictures.[35] In the case of only a few of those from 1555 did Ormanetto intervene, expediting several dispensations 'for urgent reasons'.[36] While it is true as Pogson says that some of the numerous dispensations to eat meat in Lent appear to have rested on careful investigation and some contained fairly rigid conditions, more did not, perhaps most notably the mass dispensation for reasons of bodily weakness to Philip's pages in 1557.[37] Many others gave as their excuse unspecified *aegritudines*.[38] These cases were probably too numerous and unimportant to merit attention. Otherwise, the almost complete absence of local records makes it appear that very little checking was done. Thus only one marriage dispensation in Pole's register shows evidence of having been investigated and proved false, although it was still allowed to stand.[39] When checking was done, it sometimes happened quickly. William Mason's case was completed between October 1556 and March 1557.[40]

To the degree possible, Ormanetto aimed for precision about the facts alleged in a petition. Relatively infrequently he altered them.[41] Although the facts as presented went straight into dispensations for pluralism, the bishop was usually instructed to investigate the location and value of the benefices in question.[42] In another less common type of clerical dispensation primarily concerned with

---

[32] See my article on Cole in *New dictionary of national biography*.

[33] *CRP*, nos. 1397 and 1548.

[34] *CRP*, no. 1081.

[35] *CRP*, no. 1872.

[36] BMD, MS 922, 1, fos. 126r, 127v–8r, and 2, fos. 21r, 24r, 24r–v.

[37] BMD, MS 922, 5, fo. 92v.

[38] BMD, MS 922, 1, fos. 56v or 58v–9r.

[39] BMD, MS 922, 4, fos. 20v–1r. The original dispensation is 3, fo. 46r–v.

[40] *CRP*, nos. 1738 and 1922.

[41] E.g., *CRP*, no. 1140.

[42] E.g., *CRP*, nos. 1668 and 1687.

schism, the ordinary received instructions to test the candidate's worthiness and the veracity of his penitence, but not the facts alleged.[43] The work thereby generated led to the legatine canon stipulating that the facts on which dispensations rested and their terms were to be checked during visitations, not at the time of supplication, although the form of the dispensations did not change.[44] Discrepancies between allegations and realities in cases of pluralism could be striking. One of the more glaring instances concerns the dispensation to Thomas Walpoole (originally called William), perpetual vicar of Pinchbeck, Lincs., to hold the rectory of Stickney. Walpoole alleged that the two benefices lay not more than three miles apart, but in fact they are better than twenty miles distant, and Ormanetto apparently uncharacteristically took Walpoole's word.[45] Another petitioner claimed that his two benefices were within three miles of one another, but they are more than three times as far apart.[46] Despite Ormanetto's best efforts, procedure regularly broke down. Some dispensations lacked key information, including the value of benefices, and even their names.[47] One of the most puzzling oddities is Bernard Horsham's double appointment to a benefice on the same day, both times by Pole as patron, once by virtue of the sede vacante of Chichester, the second time on his own authority.[48] The treatment of married clergy shows inconsistency in the rigour of the provisions often but not always laid down about the distance a formerly married priest had to live from his ex-wife.[49] Cranmer's dispensations, although condemned as schismatic, were usually accepted.[50] Then again, Ormanetto did not simply pass a dispensation for non-residence while studying requested by John Rastell for the chaplain of New College, without knowing the chaplain's age.[51] And occasionally

---

[43] E.g., *CRP*, no. 1352.

[44] *Reformatio Angliae* (Rome: Manuzio, 1562), fo. 26v (Gerald Bray, ed., *The Anglican canons* (Woodbridge: The Boydell Press and Church of England Record Society in association with The Ecclesiastical Law Society, 1998), pp. 132–3).

[45] *CRP*, no. 1351.

[46] *CRP*, no. 1666.

[47] E.g., *CRP*, nos. 1405; 1297 (value); 1433 (admittedly, an Irish dispensation); 1123 (skipping the number of miles between the benefices, without leaving a blank for the information); nos. 1665 and 1676 (neither value nor distance). A large number of dispensations lacked the petitioner's diocese

or made mistakes about it.

[48] *CRP*, no. 2064.

[49] E.g., *CRP*, nos. 1424 (ten miles) or 1205 (twenty). No. 1291 had no stipulation about distance from petitioner's ex-wife nor the number or type of benefices he might hold. No. 1334, by contrast, demanded that petitioner remain outside the diocese in which he had been married.

[50] E.g., *CRP*, nos. 1448, 1653 and many others (taking the dispensation as proof of the facts alleged). Pogson, p. 320. The only instance of re-checking came in 1557 (*CRP*, no. 1877). One dispensation from Cardinal Wolsey was also taken at face value (no. 1709).

[51] *Carranza y Pole*, p. 258.

Table 1 England and Wales: number of acts by subject

	Schism[1]	Pluralism[2]	Marriage	Admin.[3]	Clergy[4]	Ex-relig.[5]
1554	6			3		1
1555						
January	6			6		2
February	2		12	10		1
March	14	17	1	4	19	10
April	7	5	5	2	10[6]	4
May	5	15	12	3	3	3
June	3	9	13			
July	9	24	31	6	10	4
August	5	13	8	3	8	4[7]
September	3	6	14	2	8	
October	9	5	17	1	4	
November	8	2	17	1	20	1
December	1	1	7	2	9	
1556						
January–June missing						
July	1	17	18	4	8	2
August	2	15	21	1	5	1
September	7	11		22		
October	6	30	16	1	7	2
November			3			
December missing						
1557						
January		5	3		2	
February	2	18	24	1	11	5
March	4	13	15	3	9	
April		3	8		4	2
May	2	12	19		14	2
June	1	5	9		13	
July				6		
Totals:	96	224	286[8]	53	166[9]	45
Percentage	10.0	23.5	30.0	5.5	17.0	4.7

Notes:
Statistics are based on the 938 surviving English and Welsh acts. Percentages are not exactly comparable to those for Ireland, since the English and Welsh acts may be entered in more than category. Figures do not equal monthly total because some acts were not tallied because they fit none of these categories, and some are counted under two.
[1] Schism does not include schismatic marriage, but does include clergy who married during the schism, and some dispensations to clergy which also show up under pluralism.

Table 1 *Notes (cont.)*

[2] Includes dispensations which also cover other irregularities, including schism.

[3] Administration. Indicates primarily appointments of notaries, but also of bishops, auditors, etc.

[4] Includes dispensations to take orders, hold benefice while studying, etc.

[5] Ex-religious. Numbers here not included under schism. Total includes nineteen acts dealing with Augustinians, plus one Bonhomme and one Austin friar; six Dominican; three Franciscan (including one mass dispensation for Ireland, covering a Carmelite house as well); two for Syon; six Cistercian; one Carthusian; four Benedictine; two Gilbertine.

[6] Includes one mass dispensation to four Irish clerics.

[7] Includes one peculiar mass dispensation to eleven Irish monks from two different houses of two different orders!

[8] Pogson, p. 212n gives a total of 307 marriage dispensations.

[9] Pogson, p. 320n found 18 more dispensations in local archives, eight of which are also in the legatine register.

scrupulously correct procedure was followed, which suggests that some of the breakdowns discussed here may be an artifact of the sources. Thomas Pentland, MA, first supplicated for a legatine dispensation to hold two benefices and then six days later used it to secure presentation to the second from Pole as archbishop; he came away with an income of £44 p.a. Then again, Pentland was also one of Pole's chaplains and thus perhaps especially careful.[52]

Although it is not easy to find them, several patterns emerge in Pole's dispensations.[53] Perhaps the most striking is the relatively large number of acts connected to the schism still coming up in 1557, including a number of petitions from ex-religious. In the first two years there is a marked seasonal rhythm to incoming business, with July and August the busiest months. By 1557 this had begun to flatten out. It is not surprising that almost a third of the dispensations should be for marriage (nearly all of them retrospective), but it is that such a small percentage (4.7 per cent) should have concerned the ex-religious. This number obviously does not represent anything like the total number of survivors, but I have found only two cases in the register of men who did not seek absolution for having left religion but rather for pluralism, both canons of Durham.[54] The case of John Mylles, one of the canons of Canterbury, who did

---

[52] *CRP*, nos. 1998 and 2003.

[53] Pogson thought the numbers too small to be statistically significant and he is, of course, correct, but a few interesting points emerge.

[54] *CRP*, nos. 1269–70.

Table 2 Number of acts by month[1]

1554	17
1555	
January	13
February	100
March	189 (Lent)[2]
April	36
May	40
June	15
July	86
August	41
September	37
October	42
November	53
December	26
1556	
January–June missing (except for one act of 12 May)[3]	
July	60
August	46
September	32
October	65
November missing, except for three acts of 19 November (BMD, MS 922, VI, fos. 127v–8r, 143v–4r, 144r–v)	
December missing	
c. 80 acts missing for these two months	
1557	
January	1
February	41
March	80
April	23
May	60
June	30
July	1
Total January 1555–July 1557:	
	1,133 (1120 in register)
Acts dated only by year	5
Total surviving acts	1,138
Estimated missing acts	410
Original grand total	1,550 (rounded)

Table 2 (*cont.*)

Notes:
[1] Including those merely noted under an act given in full; 1,554 total for year.
[2] Cf. Pogson, who assigns the dispensations for Lent to the period 31 January–5 April, and says that they tailed off dramatically by Lent 1557.
[3] About thirteen acts known for this and the later gap in 1556 from other sources; original total for the year was probably around 270 acts taking average of two other six-month runs known.

not bother to supplicate for absolution for schism, suggests that there must have been substantial numbers of ex-religious who did not, at least as far as we know from the surviving records.[55]

As many of the dispensations indicate, a great deal of Pole's administrative energy went into repairing finances.[56] He began with the new bishops, most of whom received commendams to supplement the income of their sees, often temporarily, a policy which continued throughout the reign.[57] Pole was woefully ill-prepared to deal with money. Since he had never had much income until just a few years earlier, his household was little better equipped. Pyning handled both the legation's finances, and some of the church's, but most of his records have been lost making it difficult to tell how well he did.[58] Ormanetto served as papal collector beginning in August 1555, but his records are also missing.[59] Pole immediately exposed his naïveté by expecting in September 1555 that the bishops could provide full details of diocesan revenues and expenditures within two or three months, yet perhaps he was not entirely callow, since some financial

---

[55] John LeNeve, *Fasti ecclesiae anglicanae*, 3, ed. J. M. Horn (London: Athlone Press, 1963), p. 34.

[56] See esp. Pogson, 'Money'.

[57] Pogson, 'Money', p. 152 and note, with several errors and some corrections from the treatment in Pogson, p. 301. He lists Griffith (*CRP*, no. 837), Brooks (no. 1159), Oglethorpe (no. 2036), Stanley (no. 1080), and Turberville (no. 1285), but missed Morgan (no. 1134), Curwin (no. 1201), Hopton (no. 937), Robert Parfew/Parfoye/Wharton called James in the register and mistakenly identified as Brooks by Pogson (no. 835; cf. E. B. Fryde, D. E. Greenway, S. Porter, and I. Roy, eds.,

Handbook of British chronology (London: Royal Historical Society, 1986), p. 251), Scot (no. 1562), and Goldwell (no. 2023). Many of these commendams were of small value, e.g., Parfew's of £28.

[58] An account of money paid in February 1558 as the last instalment of the clerical subsidy voted in 1555 (PRO, SP 11/11, no. 53 (*CSPDomR*, no. 723)) is in Pyning's hand. For Pyning's role in Pole's finances, see my 'Cardinal Pole's finances: the property of a reformer', in T. F. Mayer, *Cardinal Pole in European context* (Aldershot: Ashgate, 2000).

[59] ASV, Arm. 42:6, fos. 265r–6v, no. 182.

reporting had already reached Rome.[60] It may have been connected to efforts in the parliament of November 1554 to protect the lands of various bishoprics, and collected between the rising of parliament in January and the assembly of a new one in October.[61]

Even with this head start, the work on pensions to ex-religious took until February 1556, and outlying areas were still not included.[62] Once this survey was finished, a confused, halting effort to collect other financial data began. For instance, of the three bishops known to have had legatine authority to visit their dioceses after the synod's prorogation, only one was ordered to report on finances as well. One of the others was so instructed ten days later, only to have the procedure he was to follow changed six weeks after that.[63] Shortly thereafter, Pole finally implemented the pope's year-old order for an accounting of ecclesiastical income over the last ten years.[64] It was therefore unsurprising that the work was nothing like finished until 1558, and Pole could not send so much as an interim report until May 1556.[65] Central auditing of accounts began only in 1557, followed by an effort to even out disparities in episcopal revenues.[66] War then and in 1558 drew some £8,000 out of the church, and largely undid the benefit of the forgiveness of clerical tenths that Pole instituted in 1557.[67] Undoing the depredations committed earlier proved an intractable problem. Thus in February 1557 Pole sent the bishop of Coventry and Lichfield additional faculties to use against his canons in an effort to recover cathedral plate.[68] Even worse, Pole issued a commission to his suffragan Thomas Chetham in March 1558 for the restoration of proper divine worship (proper utensils, altars, etc.) in his own diocese![69]

Redistribution of revenue proved almost as complicated as the accounting which made it possible, nor is it entirely clear how the crown divested itself of ecclesiastical property. First fruits and tenths were given up by act of parliament (which luckily gave Pole or his successors authority to continue reforms absent his legatine powers).[70] Even with these revenues in hand, when Pole sent out his

---

[60] CRP, nos. 1363 and 1379.

[61] Jennifer Loach, Parliament and the crown in the reign of Mary Tudor (Oxford: Clarendon Press, 1986), pp. 114–15.

[62] Pogson, p. 291 and CRP, no. 1685 for Sodor.

[63] CRP, nos. 1493–5, 1509, and 1534.

[64] CRP, no. 1265.

[65] CRP, no. 1567.

[66] CRP, no. 1829; cf. Loades, Reign, p. 292.

[67] CRP, nos. 2312, fo. 257r and 2271. Pogson observes the slow pace of financial reform in

1558, but does not connect it to the war. 'Money', p. 152.

[68] CRP, no. 1834.

[69] CRP, no. 2191.

[70] Pogson, p. 297, without identifying the act. It was 2 & 3 Philip & Mary, c. 4, ¶ XV. Statutes of the realm (London: Eyre and Strahan, 1810; 12 vols.), 4:1, pp. 275–9. The deal was not finally sealed until February 1556. CRP, no. 1505.

Table 3 The balance of the English church, April 1558[1]

Deficit	Surplus
Canterbury and Rochester £168 16s. 1 1/4d.	Salisbury £226 2s. 9d. (to pay annuities of £146 13s. 4d.)
London £856 8s. 8d.[2]	Norwich £400 (surplus of £506 19s. 8d. [?]) and Exeter £456 8s. 8d. (surplus of £512 17s. 11d.)
Chester [or Ely] £33. 12s. 2d. Lincoln £48 18s. 4d. Bath £107 3d. Gloucester £130. 16s. 6d. Oxford £115 16s. Total of £435 8s. 9d.	Peterborough (£452 12s. 4d.)
Worcester £124 5s. 8d.	Hereford (£200 16s.)
Winchester £129 3s. 7d.	Chichester £124 11s. 17d.
Coventry and Lichfield £604 2s. 6d.	St David's £641.

Notes:
[1] Source: *CRP*, no. 2212 (with variants, most minor).
[2] In addition to the £236 14s. owing to the abbot of Westminster.

first orders about balancing ecclesiastical incomes in April 1558, he admitted that he still lacked information. He knew enough to order Exeter and Chichester to send up their surpluses, but he still did not have a full picture of the state of the ex-religious and their pensions. Transfers of surpluses none the less were worked out to cover the supposed obligations.[71] Thus Salisbury's surplus of £226 went to pay the deficit of £166 in Canterbury and Rochester.[72] London's enormous shortfall of £856 was to come from Norwich and Exeter's overplus of £1,018.[73] As these figures indicate, this accounting was approximate, and Pole did not say what was to happen to the balance. This result arose from a burst of activity in the previous year, when some surpluses were already being reported. In February, Pole ordered Bonner and his assistants to see to the payment of pensions, but at that stage any surplus was to be locked up, nor

[71] *CRP*, no. 2212. All figures given are approximate.
[72] Pogson, p. 297, gives £266. He also cites the version of this table in BL, Lansdowne MS. 989, fos. 57v–9r, a compilation by White Kennet, rather than from a contemporary source, including *CRP*, no. 2212.
[73] Pogson, p. 298 and 'Money' p. 151 mistakenly makes London's shortfall apply to Syon alone.

would Pole allow Bonner to pay any extraordinary expenses without his permission.[74] A month later Cuthbert Scot, newly installed at Chester, got similar orders, while being allowed to spend his surplus.[75] Bonner seems to have finished his work by April, when one of his assistants, Pye, was deputed to collect in Hereford (his surplus also to be locked up).[76] The same day, the archdeacon of Llandaff was instructed to collect the clerical tenth in his diocese, lock the surplus up and send it to the bishop of St David's.[77] At this stage, Pole moved cautiously, granting the authority to spend money only to a favoured few whom he knew he could trust. While money slowly came in, Pole still sought information, thanking James Turberville for his report from Exeter, and then immediately ordering him to continue investigating a number of points.[78] He sent Chichester very similar orders more than a year later.[79] Chichester caused special trouble, its collections still not having been paid in July 1558 and not even by 21 January 1559.[80] The problem may have had to do with the new bishop, John Christopherson.[81]

In addition to the most immediately pressing concern of the pensions, Pole tried to deal with the twin problems of pluralism and absenteeism, and here, too, inconsistency resulted.[82] Sometimes the acts were carefully drawn. That for William Hunt, a former Augustinian canon, could have been a model.[83] It not only set precise limits to the distance between his benefices and to their combined value, but also stipulated that Hunt be virtuous and learned, and provide a substitute in whichever cure he did not reside. Many other dispensations did not rise to this level. Some pluralists were allowed a large income. Benedict Lethen, for example, kept two benefices worth together £53.[84] John Dangarde, BA, got £47 in combined income.[85] Edward Collon in the diocese of Exeter was allowed £60.[86] Even more egregious, Hugh Turnbull, who had greeted Pole's return to England with an extraordinarily obsequious letter from Padua, came back to

---

[74] *CRP*, nos. 1829 and 1833.

[75] *CRP*, no. 1932.

[76] *CRP*, no. 1945.

[77] *CRP*, no. 1946. Pogson incorrectly says Pole had already begun transferring surpluses.

[78] *CRP*, no. 1927.

[79] *CRP*, no. 2243.

[80] *CRP*, no. 2267 and J. R. Dasent, ed. *Acts of the privy council* (London: HMSO, 1890–1907; 32 vols.), *1558–1570*, p. 47.

[81] *Hand. Brit. chron.*, p. 240.

[82] R. H. Pogson, 'The legacy of the schism:

confusion, continuity and change in the Marian clergy', in Jennifer Loach and Robert Tittler, eds., *The mid-Tudor polity c. 1540–1560* (Totowa, NJ: Rowman and Littlefield, 1980), p. 129 claims that Pole scrutinized extraordinarily closely some 200 surviving cases of pluralism.

[83] *CRP*, no. 1161.

[84] *CRP*, no. 1824.

[85] *CRP*, no. 1121.

[86] *CRP*, no. 1313.

hold a number of important benefices, among them treasurer and prebendary of Christ Church, Oxford and prebendary of Canterbury, where Pole used him as his proctor and a commissioner for heresy.[87] Arthur Seintleger, another canon and prebendary of Canterbury, did not too much worse.[88] The chancellor of Waterford was allowed to hold five benefices, although their value was pegged at only £40.[89] The champion pluralist dispensed by Pole was probably Robert Willianton. He held two prebends of St Paul's, as well as two city parishes, they alone worth £48.[90] The average pluralist income seems to have been around £30, although many priests got much less. Pole may have tried to follow Cranmer's standard of a minimum of £8 for a first benefice, but there is only one instance of his explicitly applying that yardstick.[91] There are also only a couple of examples of Pole's use of his related powers to amalgamate benefices, although in summer 1555 he had announced his plans to do that and his orders to Turberville in 1557 told him to send a list of possibilities.[92]

Pole did try to ensure that the clergy's quality improved, as in the dispensation to Hunt, but he did not make much progress.[93] Only about a half-dozen dispensations allowed non-residence for reasons of study. One went to William Darrell, another canon of Canterbury.[94] George Savage got a very generous dispensation to hold a benefice requiring major orders while only a subdeacon and to be absent to study in Louvain or elsewhere. He was required to reside, should he take priest's orders.[95] Thomas Crew received similar treatment.[96] Robert Jones was allowed to hold his rectory while studying at Cambridge.[97] Nicholas Wendon, an MA of Cambridge who was probably studying overseas, got a licence to study while holding a benefice to which Pole duly appointed him a few months later.[98] Ralph Colur got a two-year dispensation to draw the income of a benefice while studying and had to provide a curate.[99] Thomas Key, who had failed to take orders within the time stipulated in his original dispensation, could still keep his benefice on the strength of his educational progress.[100] Key's

---

[87] See *CRP*, no. 1103.
[88] *CRP*, no. 1183.
[89] *CRP*, no. 1138.
[90] *CRP*, no. 1923.
[91] *CRP*, no. 1830. I also take this as a typical instance, because the petition was carefully gone over and it very nearly matches the average I calculated. Pogson, p. 322, gives £22.
[92] *CRP*, nos. 1933 and 2082 for the amalgamations; 1345 (intention); and 1927 (orders to Turberville).
[93] This was also announced in summer 1555. *CRP*, no. 1345.
[94] *CRP*, no. 1312.
[95] *CRP*, no. 1365.
[96] *CRP*, no. 1369.
[97] *CRP*, no. 1985.
[98] *CRP*, nos. 1949 and 2102.
[99] *CRP*, no. 1367.
[100] *CRP*, no. 1368.

dispensation is highly revealing of the carelessness with which many of them were granted. His advancement in learning apparently meant his BA and MA of 1526 and 1531, respectively. Key was also far more than a humble parish priest, rather a substantial pluralist, a fixture in the University of Oxford since the 1520s, and a noted collector of manuscripts.[101] All of this seems to have passed by Pole's officials. A few other students, mostly at Cambridge, got dispensations to take orders *extra tempora*.[102] Pole was also involved in the foundation or refoundation of several schools, including at York (grammar, new foundation), Manchester (college, refoundation), Basingstoke (refoundation), and Northampton (grammar, new foundation), all in early 1557.[103] At his death, he left directions that the almonry in the Mintyard at Canterbury was to be conveyed to the dean and chapter for 500 years as premises for a boys' school.[104] The 'bargain' Pole had been forced to strike with the possessioners presented the biggest obstacle to success on all these counts. Without the lands and revenues in lay hands, big plans for renewal proved impossible to execute.[105]

Ireland too attracted Pole's attention, taking a disproportionate part of his effort, yielding 175 acts, or about 15 per cent of the total.[106] There he was able to insert several bishops who had once been among his dependants, especially William Walsh at Meath and Thomas Leverous briefly at Leighlin and then at Kildare. Walsh probably joined the Irish privy council immediately, and Leverous served beginning in 1558.[107] The restored primate, George Dowdall, depended heavily on both, and it may be that all three, not just Walsh and Leverous, had been in Pole's orbit in exile.[108] This was more of an impact than

---

[101] Cf. Anthony à Wood, *Athenae oxonienses*, ed. Philip Bliss (London: F. C. and J. Rivington *et al.*, 1815; originally published in 1668; 4 vols.), 1, cols. 397–400 for his many offices and works and A. B. Emden, *A biographical register of the university of Oxford A.D. 1501 to 1540* (Oxford: Clarendon Press, 1974), pp. 325–6 and appendix for his MSS.

[102] *CRP*, nos. 1997–99.

[103] *CRP*, nos. 1893, 1901, and 1924. Pogson's account needs correction on the score of the first two, and he does not notice the third.

[104] *CRP*, no. 2286.

[105] Pogson, p. 306 and 'Money', p. 140.

[106] Pogson does not consider Ireland, except occasionally, as when he incorrectly says (p. 233) that Faita and Ormanetto were involved in surveying the value of the Irish sees. The document he cites (ASV, Armaria 64:28, fos. 316r–18r) is the record of Christopher Bodykyn's suitability hearing as archbishop of Tuam. Cf. *CRP*, no. 1393.

[107] Historical manuscripts commission, *Fifteenth report, appendix 3* (1897), pp. 2, 36, 49, and 55; cf. also Flannan Hogan, 'William Walsh, bishop of Meath, 1554–1577', *Ríocht na Mídhe*, 6 (1977), pp. 3–18, pp. 6–7.

[108] Henry A. Jefferies, *Priests and prelates of Armagh in the age of reformations, 1518–1558* (Dublin: Four Courts Press, 1997), pp. 165–9 and see above p. 198.

Table 4 Number of acts by place and subject: Ireland

By diocese (totals):	
Annaghdown (Enachdun)	1
Cashel	11
Clonfert	2
Clonmacnoise	2
Cork and Cloyne	11
Down-Connor	1
Dublin	11
Emly	6
Ferns	3
Kildare	14
Killala	5
Killaloe	1
Kilmacduagh	11[1]
Leighlin	3
Limerick	34
Lismore–Waterford	24
and Waterford	2
	[26]
Meath	23
Ossory	8
Not given	1
Total	175

Notes:

[1] And Tuam, since all the dispensations to Kilamcduagh addressed Christopher Bodykyn as bishop of both; only one dispensation went exclusively to Tuam.

Pole had on the mainland episcopate, where his only client to be elevated was Goldwell, in Wales (perhaps it is another sign of Pole's pride in his Welsh origins that he would send such a valued companion there).[109] Walsh was provided almost immediately, although his provision did not go through consistory until May 1557.[110] Leverous had to wait for his initial appointment until August 1555, despite the fact that his schismatic predecessor was deprived in 1554.[111]

---

[109] At a lower level, Pole also had some success in appointing trusted administrators to key posts, for example, Hugh Turnbull as Dean of Chichester in 1558 probably as an attempt to remedy the see's persistent financial problems. *CRP*, nos. 2267 and 1103 for Turnbull.

[110] *CRP*, no. 962.

[111] BMD, MS 922, 3, fo. 93r–v is a single act dated 18 July 1555 almost certainly addressed to Leverous as bishop of Leighlin. See *CRP*, no. 1951.

Table 5 Types of acts: Ireland

	Schism[1]	Pluralism[2]	Marriage	Admin.[3]	Clergy[4]	Ex-relig.[5]	Lent[6]	Misc.
1555								
March	3		1				1	
April	1	1	1		11	1		
May	1		4	1	6			
June			4		1			
July	4		11		7	1		
August					3	4		
September			5		1			1
October	8		12	1	2			
November	3	1	4		5			
December			1		1			1
1556								
January–June missing								
July	1	1	15		4			
August			6	1	2			
September			1					
October		1	3					
November			3					
1557								
February	1							
March	1		2		3	1		
April		1	4		2	4		
May			1		3			
June					1			
Total	23	5	78	3	52	11	1	2
Percentage:	13.0	2.8	45.0	1.6	29.0	6.4	–	1.0

Notes:

These are not double-counted; the figures equal the monthly total.

[1-5] See notes to Table 1.

[6] *i.e.*, for eating milk and meat.

These two dioceses ranked third and fourth in number of supplications directed to Pole. Limerick, in the lands of the earl of Desmond who himself had several supplications granted, came first by a wide margin, followed by Lismore–Waterford (sometimes Waterford was treated separately). Limerick's prominence may also have to do with the fact that the see was apparently vacant for a good while, necessitating approaches to Pole. Then again, its new bishop, Hugh Lacy, produced some nineteen petitions in the final year of Pole's legation. Cashel, Cork and Cloyne (which Pole's secretaries also sometimes treated as two separate sees), Dublin, and Kilmacduagh had ten or eleven supplications each. Ossory, formerly John Bale's diocese, had eight. In addition to the fact that all these fell within the English obedience, the bishops of Cashel, Dublin and Ossory were Marian appointments, and the other two, Dominic Tyrry and Christopher Bodykyn along with Patrick Walsh at Lismore, supplicated for absolution or dispensation.[112] Bodykyn, the Henrician bishop of Kilmacduagh, although properly consecrated, had to be absolved from schism, and then became archbishop of Tuam after an investigation, one of only three such suitability hearings extant.[113] The burst of dispensations for his dioceses ceased as soon as he received powers to absolve for schism, the only one of these bishops known to have had such powers.[114]

No more than in the case of England does an obvious chronological pattern appear in the dispensations, except for the large number of clergy petitioning to correct irregularities early on, and the proportionately large number of ex-religious who waited until almost the end to seek absolution and dispensation. Again as in England, the total number of clerical acts is tiny, numbering about eighty-six. Several major differences in the English and Irish acts appear. While they both show similar amounts of concern with clearing up the schism (10 and 13 per cent) and with the ex-religious, English supplications about pluralism ran better than eight times higher than in Ireland, while the Irish sent in proportionately half-again as many petitions about marriage, and nearly twice as many for the clergy. For what it is worth, the only petitions for absolution for murder came from Ireland, mostly from clerics.

Did Pole ever visit the Irish church? From July 1555 he had the authority to

---

[112] *CRP*, nos. 1443 and 1229. Whether the bishop supplicated for absolution is not a certain indicator of a high volume of petitions. The bishop of Ferns did so, but his diocese produced only three supplications. *CRP*, no. 1236. Nevertheless, the bishops of all the other dioceses with low totals apparently did not supplicate. *Hand. Brit. chron.*, p. 440n says Pole confirmed John Tonory's appointment at Ossory, on unknown evidence.

[113] ASV, Armaria 64:28, fos. 316r–18r.

[114] *CRP*, no. 1398. The petitions are in BMD, MS 922, 4, fos. 59v–64r and 87r–v.

do so.[115] In April 1556, the deputy was informed that Pole meant to.[116] Unfortunately, the gap in Pole's register covering the first half of 1556 makes it impossible to say whether he did. There is no mention of a visitation in the records of the Irish privy council, and the most recent student of the reformation in Armagh says Pole did not conduct one. It may yet be that the fairy story of Cole's aborted mission to Ireland in late 1558 echoed some kind of visitation; if it is not an invention, it would have followed on Archbishop Dowdall's visit to Mary in August.[117] The marked rise in July 1556 in supplications for marriage dispensations to the highest monthly total, together with the third highest number of acts about the clergy, may indicate either that visitors arrived, or that at least some Irishmen and women thought that they would. Nevertheless, it was not until May 1557 that Ireland got the kind of absolution and mass dispensation that England received in 1554.[118]

Heresy

> Pole: There lie two ways to every end,
> A better and a worse – the worse is here to
> persecute, because to persecute
> Makes a faith hated, and is furthermore
> No perfect witness of a perfect faith
> In him who persecutes.
>
> TENNYSON, QUEEN MARY, ACT III, SCENE IV

As Pogson stresses, the hallmark of Pole's administration was the restoration of obedience.[119] Instead of attacking heresy head-on, Pole expected that Englishmen would docilely return to Rome. Pogson blames this on Pole's experience of Italian reform in the 1520s. This probably entered in, but much more

---

[115] CRP, no. 1376.

[116] J. S. Brewer and William Bullen, eds., Calendar of the Carew manuscripts preserved in the archiepiscopal library at Lambeth 1515–1574 (London: Longman, Green, Reader and Dyer, 1867), pp. 252–3.

[117] Robert Ware, The reformation of the church of Ireland in the life and death of George Browne, sometime archbishop of Dublin (London: Randal Taylor, 1681), pp. 22–3;

Jefferies, p. 170. Historical Manuscripts Commission, Fifteenth report, appendix 3 (1897); Jefferies, p. 168.

[118] CRP, no. 1971. As a result of this act, the Irish parliament placed various impropriations in Pole's control. CPRPM, 4, p. 116.

[119] 'Legacy', pp. 127 and 136; Pogson, pp. 174, 194, 204. Cf. Loades, Reign, pp. 272, 275, and 285.

important was Pole's personal interpretation of heresy and obedience from the time of *De unitate* forward. Accused of heresy several times, more often frustrated in his political designs, Pole usually fairly quickly bowed to pressure and relied on simple obedience. He could not see that others might not find the matter quite so straightforward.

Pole also did not worry much about heresy, because it did not seem an insuperable problem. His visitation articles of 1556 do not even mention it. Famous schismatics and heretics like Cranmer were one thing, but other heretics got off lightly. Two well-known ones appear in the register. Robert Holgate, formerly master general of the Gilbertines who had become archbishop of York in 1545 and married under Edward, was nevertheless absolved, and although denied reappointment as bishop, allowed to exercise his orders, provided only that he stay away from his wife.[120] Edward Crome, the Henrician and Edwardian preacher, approached Pole directly, and after acknowledging his fault in public, was also allowed to use his orders.[121] Crome had got himself in trouble under Mary for preaching without a licence, and had been summoned in January 1555 before commissioners apparently appointed by Pole, including Stephen Gardiner, who probably played the principal role.[122] Crome asked for and got a respite of either one or two months, and also read a book that may have induced him to make his submission.[123] At about the same time as Crome, an Irish layman, John Haklott, received unconditional absolution.[124] And that is the sum total of absolutions for heresy alone in Pole's register. All the rest that mentioned it primarily covered schism. Many of them were as lenient as these three for heresy, especially to high-ranking clerics. Hugh Corey or Curwin, soon to be archbishop of Dublin, received absolution without having specified any particulars of his offence.[125] He might have received favouritism because of his standing with the queen, but that can hardly explain the not much more rigorous treatment of the notorious schismatic Nicholas Shaxton, who was faulted only for having associated with heretics (which came last in the list of his offences), not for having been one himself! He was allowed to exercise his

---

120 *CRP*, no. 1167. Holgate's relatively lenient treatment is especially noteworthy since he had deeply offended Pole at the time of his appointment. *CRP*, no. 467.

121 *CRP*, no. 1435.

122 John Foxe, *Actes and monuments of matters most speciall and memorable* (London: John Daye, 1583; *STC* no. 11225), p. 1483 and Loades, *Reign*, p. 273.

123 Foxe, *ibid.* and John Strype, *Ecclesiastical memorials relating chiefly to religion, and its reformation, under the reigns of King Henry VIII, King Edward VI, and Queen Mary* (Oxford: Clarendon Press, 1816; 3 vols.), 3:1, p. 165.

124 *CRP*, no. 1445.

125 *CRP*, no. 1099.

orders because of a shortage of clergy, hold a benefice, and serve as a suffragan.[126] Paul Bush, the Henrician bishop of Bristol who had resigned his see, received treatment like Holgate's, and the suffragan of Hull, Robert Silvester, did as well as Shaxton.[127] Bush may have repaid Pole for his treatment by writing *A brefe exhortation set fourthe by the unprofitable servant of Jesu christ, Paule Bushe, late bishop of Brystowe, to one Margarete Burges, wyfe to Jhon Burges, clotheare of kyngeswode in the Countie of wilshere*, which has been called 'one of the most effective defenses of the Roman Catholic doctrine of the Eucharist for a lay public'.[128] Patrick Walsh, Edwardian bishop of Lismore and Waterford, was first duly absolved for schism, and on the same day regranted his sees because of his devotion to the pope.[129] Similarly, Alexander Devereux, an ex-abbot whom Henry made bishop of Ferns, was absolved and dispensed to continue as bishop because of his Catholic faith.[130] Even reading heretical books did not disturb Pole. A Neapolitan layman, Mario Cardoino, who claimed to have read such 'more out of curiosity than another cause' was condemned only to confess and do unspecified penance.[131] Even odder, authors of heretical books did not receive immediate condemnation, at least if we can trust Bale, who had every reason to portray Pole as an ogre. He told a story of Bishop Hooper writing Pole from prison, asking for an opportunity to argue his case before parliament, or perhaps in writing. According to Bale, Pole agreed that the request was 'licit and just . . . but it is not proper to respond' to it.[132] Of course, sacramentaries needed very careful handling, and Pole urged special attention to those in Salisbury.[133]

Heresy was usually dealt with through commissioners sometimes acting with authority delegated by Pole, but much more often by the crown, nor did Pole necessarily control his agents. I have found three delegations in his diocese, in

---

[126] *CRP*, no. 1137.

[127] *CRP*, no. 1225; *Hand. Brit. chron.*, p. 230.

[128] Printed *cum privilegio* by the royal printer John Cawood in 1556 (*STC*, 4184). It has no preface. Ellen A. Macek, *The loyal opposition: Tudor traditionalist polemics, 1535–1558* (New York: Peter Lang, 1996), p. 246.

[129] *CRP*, nos. 1229–30.

[130] *CRP*, no. 1236.

[131] *CRP*, no. 1163.

[132] John Bale, *De scriptoribus illustris* (Basel: Oporinus, 1559), p. 680: 'licitam ac iustam . . . sed voto illius respondere non est dignatus'. For the rest of this episode, see *CRP*, no. 992. The case of Bishop Ferrar at St Davids is not an exception to Pole's general leniency. Burnet made it appear that Pole had refused to hear Ferrar's appeal, writing that Ferrar 'put in an appeal to cardinal Pole, but it was not received', while according to Foxe Ferrar had told his successor, Henry Morgan, that he appealed 'as from an incompetent judge, to Cardinal Pole, etc [*sic*]' and Morgan 'in his rage' had ignored him. Burnet/Pocock, 2, p. 494 and Foxe, p. 1555.

[133] *CRP*, no. 1306.

1555, 1556, and 1558. Only the first of these drew on his legatine powers.[134] The second two come from Pole's archiepiscopal register, and thus were probably granted by that authority. The basic core of staff had been established before Pole returned. Thornden, Pole's suffragan, Harpsfield, Richard Fawcet and Hugh Glasier, both canons of Canterbury and probably all lawyers, had been appointed by the dean and chapter of Canterbury in 1554.[135] There was considerable overlap between the first and third of Pole's panels, except for Thornden who had died, and the addition of Turnbull, Mylles (or Warham) and John Warren, all canons of the cathedral. Robert Collins, another lawyer and canon who also appeared in the other two commissions, received one alone as general commissary, including responsibility for heresy.[136] In addition, a heresy commission may have been issued for Cambridge at the same time as the visitation, and the visitors and the commissioners may have overlapped to some degree.[137]

These commissions in part produced a situation that led Canon Dixon to burst out 'Canterbury was now [1557] become the hottest diocese in England, next after London.' He also accused Pole of losing control of his see while embroiled with Paul IV, leaving it to 'reckless subalterns, shutting his eyes to their rigours, willing not to know what was done by them, though feeling himself bound not to forbid it'.[138] Despite Foxe being 'kind' to him, Pogson too made Pole a supporter of 'persecution'. He admits Mary's much greater prominence, but claims that Pole's legatine powers were always available, including in Cranmer's case, and takes the number of executions in Canterbury diocese as evidence of Pole's 'support for the persecution'.[139] A. G. Dickens assigned much of the blame to Pole for executions in Kent, all but six of them in Canterbury.[140] Dickens gives fifty-eight victims, while Patrick Collinson has both sixty-one and forty-one, citing two *significavits* that Dickens may not have used.[141]

[134] *CRP*, nos. 1228, 1529, and 2207.
[135] CCA, Dcc, Reg. V1, fo. 62v.
[136] Foxe, p. 1672 and *CRP*, no. 1643.
[137] The commission is missing but is known from John Lamb, ed., *A collection of letters, statutes and other documents from the MS Library of Corpus Christi College, illustrative of the history of the university of Cambridge* (London: John W. Parker, 1838), p. 203 and Foxe, p. 1960.
[138] Richard Watson Dixon, *History of the church of England from the abolition of the Roman jurisdiction*, 4, Mary-A. D.

1553–1558 (London: George Routledge and Sons, 1891), pp. 631 and 629.
[139] Pogson, pp. 83–7.
[140] A. G. Dickens, *The English reformation*, 2nd ed. (University Park: Pennsylvania State University Press, 1989), pp. 294–5.
[141] Patrick Collinson, Nigel Ramsay, and Margaret Sparks, eds., *A history of Canterbury cathedral* (Oxford: Oxford University Press, 1995), pp. 164–5, citing PRO, C 85/27/20 and 85/144/33–6. Loades, *Reign*, p. 274n gives forty-nine.

Strype's list numbers fifty-four.[142] The total in Foxe is thirty-seven, of whom three might have fallen under Bonner's jurisdiction, plus six more judged by Bishop Griffith in Rochester.[143] By comparison, Bonner burned 113 people in London.[144] If we take a round figure of 300 for the total of burnings, those directly or indirectly attributable to Pole amount to at most 10 per cent (taking Foxe's figures) or 18 per cent (using Strype). In fact, the numbers are probably substantially smaller. The first set of Kentish victims including John Bland can have had nothing to do with Pole, since their case began in May 1554.[145] All the others could have depended on Pole's powers, but royal intervention could have undergirded some of them as well.[146] The mass burning of 31 January 1556 was conducted by a panel that included a judge Pole is never known to have used.[147] By contrast, Thornden and Harpsfield certainly presided in the following January.[148] As Foxe concluded, 'under these [Thornden, Collins, and Harpsfield] a great sort of innocent lambs of Christ were cruelly entreated and slain at Canterbury'.[149] Foxe may not have been fair to Collins, conveniently forgetting his own evidence of Collins's lenient treatment of Bland.[150] He singled out Harpsfield, whose decision to burn the final five victims just before Mary died showed that 'the tyranny of this archdeacon seemeth to exceed the cruelty of Bonner'.[151] This case also provides the only specific link between Pole and the commissioners. In July 1558, he handed in a *significavit* that his commissioners had proceeded against John Cornford, Christopher Browne, John Hurst, Catherine Knight, and Alice (or Alicia) Snoth.[152]

---

142 Strype, *Eccl. mem.*, 3:3, pp. 554–6.

143 Foxe, pp. 1688, and 1909 for Griffith.

144 Gina Alexander, 'Bonner and the Marian persecutions', *History*, 60 (1975), pp. 374–91, p. 391.

145 Foxe, p. 1665. The chronology of burnings together with what is known of the judges further reduces the degree of Pole's involvement. The others are the end of August 1555 (Foxe, p. 1688); unknown time in 1555, apparently entrusted to Thornden, Harpsfield or their deputies, but perhaps really Bonner's work (p. 1669); 31 January 1556, perhaps nothing to do with Pole (p. 1859); January 1557 (p. 1970); 19 June 1557, a case begun perhaps in October 1556 (p. 1977); 'anno 1557' (*ibid.*) and 'about six days before the death of queen Mary' (p. 2053). The third,

fourth, and fifth could have been done under authority of *CRP*, no. 1228; the next two perhaps under no. 1811; and the last under no. 2207.

146 At least three royal commissions are known, of 25 April 1556 (*CRP*, no. 1549a), February 1556 (Alexander, 'Bonner', p. 378), and 8 February 1557 (Foxe, pp. 1970–1 and *CPRPM*, 3, pp. 281–2).

147 Foxe, p. 1859.

148 Foxe, p. 1970.

149 Foxe, p. 1672. Pogson, p. 86n glosses this to say 'Pole thus chose formidable men for these commissions, singly or in groups, and used them repeatedly.'

150 Foxe, p. 1667.

151 Foxe, p. 2055.

152 *CRP*, no. 2262.

Statistical exercises with such small numbers are not very helpful, and modern western sensibilities abhor any execution for religion. Dixon and Dickens seconded by Pogson may even have the moral right since Pole had overall charge.[153] Yet Dixon's earlier assertion that Pole was 'averse from extremity' well illustrates the difficulty of the question.[154] Three points make against assigning Pole responsibility. One, there is little evidence that he used his powers in any way other than to issue general commissions.[155] Two, Pole instructed the commissioners to proceed in remarkably lenient fashion.[156] Merely holding a heretical opinion was not enough, unless one adopted it of one's own judgment, defended it obstinately, and after being better informed. Pole wished that heretics would blame their fault on their leaders, which might well mean that they could avoid the consequences after the condemnation of those leaders. Confidence in their reasoning powers got heretics into trouble, but any who blamed their beliefs on their bishop were to be spared. Instead of appealing to reason, Pole clung to the test of 'paternity', or tradition. Pole did not have much patience – heretics were to be admonished only once or twice before being condemned – but they had at least some chance to come around.[157] In all this, including the stress on 'paternity', his attitude was identical to Cranmer's.[158]

Three, these instructions do not offer the only indication of Pole's attitude. In June 1554 he wrote Cardinal Truchsess, defending his right belief. Although Bishop Burnet claimed that Pole played up his opposition to heresy in order to defend himself to the pope, in this letter Pole did the opposite.[159] Agreeing that those who subverted others' faith deserved death, Pole continued that even in those cases all efforts should first be made to cure 'the putrid member'. Pole appealed to his behaviour at Trent, when he had said that the fathers of the council had to treat those who had left the church like errant children. Even although they were rebels, they were still 'rebel sons and for that reason were to be treated as sons'.[160] Pole wrote with reference to Lutherans in Germany, but he should not have had a more hostile attitude to his fellow Englishmen. Muzzarelli thought Pole favoured gentleness as policy for the Inquisition.[161] Finally, Dudic testified that Pole 'had to work hard on account of heretics. . . .

---

[153] Pogson, pp. 81–4, 86–7.

[154] Dixon, p. 326.

[155] Pogson, p. 86 says Pole issued authority to try Cranmer, but the text he cites (*CRP*, no. 1385) is not about Cranmer at all, but the trial of Latimer and Ridley.

[156] *CPM*, catalogue no. 7e.

[157] BAV, Vat. lat. 5968, fos. 227r–9v.

[158] MacCulloch, pp. 476 and 481.

[159] Burnet/Pocock, 2, p. 479.

[160] *CRP*, no. 885: 'rebelles quidem, sed filios rebelles, et ob eam causam ut filios esse tractandos'.

[161] *CRP*, no. 670.

Nor truly did he omit anything, in order that he might deal with them more mildly, and in order that it not come to the fire or the sword. . . . [N]othing sharper could befall him, than to be forced to punish more harshly those whose salvation he was seeking by so great an effort; and he thought, as he also often used to say, that he and the rest of the bishops were established not only as judges against them, but as fathers. Meanwhile he talked with some of them, and tried either to convince them by disputing, or chiding, or warning, or asking besides, and also exhorting, to lead them into the way again.'[162]

Thus Pole's stance might be described as potentially tolerant, and may have been a legacy from Erasmus who had argued for gentle treatment of heretics in his *Inquisitio de fide*.[163] It was certainly consistent with the imperial attitude, reflected by ambassador Renard and in a court sermon preached by Phillip's confessor Alfonso de Castro, perhaps on the king's orders, reflecting his father's views.[164] As often happened, near-contemporary opinion about Pole's attitude divided, but in more interesting ways than usual. Foxe could not avoid noting that Pole was a papist, but 'none of the bloody and cruel sort of papists', not only because he restrained 'Bloody' Bonner, but also because of his 'solici- tous writings' to Cranmer, not to mention his own difficulties with Paul IV. All this 'notwithstanding, the pomp and glory of the world carried him away to play the papist thus as he did'.[165] Foxe implicitly concluded that only circum- stances prevented Pole from at least practical toleration. This opinion deserves special attention, especially because of Foxe's almost unique objection to execu- tions *causa religionis*.[166] Burnet largely endorsed Foxe's view, despite Strype's best efforts to convince him otherwise.[167] Strype was following Matthew Parker (or perhaps John Joscelyn or George Acworth), who had branded Pole

---

[162] *ERP*, 1, pp. 42–3.

[163] Thomas F. Mayer, '"Heretics be not in all things heretics": Cardinal Pole and the potential for toleration', in J. C. Laursen and C. J. Nederman, eds., *The roots of toleration in Europe, 1100–1700: theory and practice* (Philadelphia: University of Pennsylvania Press, 1997), pp. 107–24 (now in Mayer, *Pole in European context:*) and Desiderius Erasmus, *Opera Omnia*, 1:3 (Amsterdam: North-Holland Publishing Company, 1972), pp. 371–4.

[164] Weiss, 4, pp. 397 and 404, blaming the urge to persecute on the bishops, especially Bonner. Cf. Henry Kamen, 'Toleration and dissent in sixteenth-century Spain: the alternative tradition', *SCJ*, 19 (1988), pp. 3–24, pp. 12–15.

[165] Foxe, p. 1973.

[166] G. R. Elton, 'Persecution and toleration in the English reformation', in W. J. Sheils, ed., *Persecution and toleration* (Studies in church history, 21, 1984), pp. 163–87, pp. 171–80, and MacCulloch, p. 475.

[167] Burnet/Pocock, 2, pp. 479–80. Cf. 3, p. 451 for Strype.

ecclesiae Anglicanae carnifex ac flagellum.[168] Pole is once again caught in the middle.

Parker set the tone for many discussions of Pole's practice, but he rested his judgment almost exclusively on the neuralgic point of Pole's allegedly heartless treatment of Cranmer. Such a narrow focus seriously distorts. A comparison to Pole's handling of Sir John Cheke demonstrates the point. In the midst of an escalating international crisis, Pole might have been forgiven if he had distanced himself from Cheke as he had Cranmer, but this time he intervened actively. Cheke, who had been kidnapped on the continent and brought back to England by force, formally submitted himself to Pole in July 1556, and a few days later asked to speak to him. With Feckenham as intermediary, Pole induced Cheke to recant publicly, which in turn produced the 'conversion' of a number of his supporters.[169] Just before he dealt with Cheke, Pole absolved three other heretics.[170] Others may have worked on Cheke over longer periods of time, including Carranza, and Priuli credited his recantation to Feckenham, dean of St Paul's and newly installed abbot of Westminster.[171] Pole yet figured prominently in the finale, rejecting Cheke's first recantation as insufficient, and perhaps drafting the one he finally signed.[172] As in Pole's instructions, heretics who admitted their fault could expect lenient treatment.

Who deserves responsibility for the repression? To start with the allegedly clearest indicator of Pole's attitude, in Cranmer's case Mary insisted on death, with Carranza pressuring Philip heavily to the same end.[173] As Foxe's stories demonstrate, the leading figure in the prosecutions in Canterbury was Sir John Baker, ably abetted by his servant Cyriac Petit.[174] (Roper, domiciled in Kent, was probably also very active; we have seen that he was twice appointed to royal heresy commissions.) Baker was one of the leaders of a conservative oligarchy that had dominated Kent in the 1530s and 1540s, only to see its power sharply curtailed by an evangelical ascendancy under Edward. The prosecution of Bland

---

[168] [Matthew Parker?], *De antiquitate britannicae ecclesiae* (London: (John Daye), 1572), p. 414.

[169] *CRP*, no. 1616; *CSPV*, 6:1, no. 554; BMIC25, fo. 302v; and Historical Manuscripts Commission, *Third report* (1872), p. 239.

[170] *CRP*, no. 1593.

[171] *Doc. hist.*, 3, pp. 194–201 and BMIC25, fo. 302v.

[172] Dixon, pp. 609–16.

[173] Foxe, pp. 1885–6 and MacCulloch, p. 597.

Cf. *Carranza y Pole*, p. 68 and *Doc. hist.*, 3, p. 27. For what it is worth, Cranmer had wished Pole's death in his reply to the Prayer Book Rebellion. Jasper Ridley, *Thomas Cranmer* (Oxford: Clarendon Press, 1962), p. 295.

[174] Foxe, pp. 1667, 1669, and *passim*; MacCulloch, p. 312; and S. T. Bindoff, ed., *The house of commons 1509–1558* (London: Secker and Warburg, 1982; 3 vols.), 1, pp. 366–8 and 3, pp. 96–8.

reasserted their power.[175] Baker was a member of the original royal heresy commission on which Pole also served, and twice received licences to eat meat from Pole, once in late 1556 and again in early 1557.[176] That is not a great deal to link the two. Yet Baker may well point us in the right direction, since he was one of Mary's most trusted privy councillors and senior financial officials.[177] The balance of present opinion inclines to saddle Mary or the Spanish with responsibility.[178] At least two persons in a position to know objected to Pole's lenient manner of proceeding. Bonner found Pole's practice disappointing, and Pole twice restrained his excesses.[179] Even more tell-tale, Carranza faulted Pole's fervour in dealing with heresy.[180] Pole may even have resisted official policy. He and many of his officers were at the core of a royal commission against heresy of 1556, but the only survivor of that cadre in the following year was William Roper.[181] It similarly indicates Pole's attitude and the source of the main thrust against heresy that after one of his rebukes of Bonner, the council sharply ordered the bishop to reinstate proceedings against two of the accused.[182] If this speculation is correct, it takes on greater significance in view of Pole's possible attempt to defend himself in Rome by his persecution of heretics in England.[183]

---

[175] Peter Clark, *English provincial society from the reformation to the revolution: religion, politics and society in Kent 1500–1640* (Hassocks: Harvester Press, 1977), pp. 54, 62, 65, 81, 98, 100. That most of the JPs were unenthusiastic about enforcing repression highlights the importance of those like Baker who were. David Loades, 'The enforcement of reaction, 1553–1558', *Journal of ecclesiastical history*, 16 (1965), pp. 54–66, pp. 60–1, reprinted with a few additions in Loades, *Politics, censorship and the English reformation* (London and New York: Pinter Publishers, 1991), pp. 27–38.

[176] *CRP*, nos. 1787 and 1897.

[177] Loades, *Reign*, pp. 200 and 360 and Christopher Coleman, 'Artifice or accident? The reorganization of the Exchequer of receipt c. 1554–1572', in Christopher Coleman and David Starkey, *Revolution reassessed: revisions in the history of Tudor government and administration* (Oxford: Clarendon Press, 1986), pp. 163–98, pp. 168, 173, 176–9, 181.

[178] Pogson, pp. 84–6. Loades, 'Enforcement', pp. 56–7; *Reign*, pp. 174–5 and 273; *Mary*, pp. 325–7; Robert Tittler, *The reign of Mary I*, 2nd ed. (London and New York: Longman, 1991), pp. 27–8; and *Philip of Spain* (New Haven: Yale University Press, 1997), pp. 11, 41, 62, 75, 96, and esp. 79–86.

[179] *CRP*, nos. 1593 and 1675.

[180] *Doc. hist.*, 4, pp. 163–7 and *Carranza y Pole*, pp. 30, 47ff, 51–2 and 139.

[181] See above note 146.

[182] Alexander, 'Bonner and persecutions', p. 378.

[183] The evidence on this point comes at fourth-hand from Bernardo Navagero quoting Bartolomeo Spadafora quoting Pole, via an informant. Pole had allegedly written Spadafora in his defence 'come [Pole] perseguita li heretici, se potranno chiarir se è lutherano, o non'. ASVe:APR, 11, fo. 123v (*CSPV*, 6:2, no. 933; partially printed in *PM*, 5, p. 261n).

Given Pole's small concern with heresy, it makes more sense that he did not take full advantage of the opportunities to combat it provided by printing.[184] He has been criticized for the slow publication of new sermons, but Cranmer had the same problem. The homilies he projected in 1542 did not appear until five years later.[185] It is not known whether Pole had anything to do with the bungled opportunity presented by Cranmer's first recantations.[186] According to James Gairdner, he was behind *Bishop Cranmer's Recantacyons*, dated 1556 by Gairdner and assigned to Alan Cope, but almost certainly Harpsfield's work.[187] He gave several licences to read heretical books in order to confute them, one to Carlos 'a Mutilea' or de Motiloa, a servant of Pedro de Castro, the bishop of Cuenca, one to George London, and one to Cole.[188] None of these produced results. Pole, the reluctant author, did not embrace the domestic press as enthusiastically as Bonner did, even if he did not ignore its potential in disseminating preaching, as we have seen.[189] One of the most surprising instances of his overlooking its power was the laborious distribution in manuscript in early 1555 of the faculties for reconciliation. Pole never thought of having either them or his broader faculties disseminated in print as Carlo Carafa did in 1558.[190] This does not mean that he refused to employ the press, but that historians have looked for the wrong kind of printing. Within six months of his return, Pole authorized a new edition of the Sarum Use including a good deal of catechetical material; the text went through numerous editions, although these did not bear Pole's imprimatur for some reason.[191]

Nevertheless, Pole keenly saw the necessity to influence opinion on the

---

[184] Loades makes a similar point in *Reign*, p. 285, but blames the relative inferiority of Catholic polemic on Pole's legalism in pursuing heresy, rather than on his relative lack of concern. Cf. also Tittler, *Reign*, pp. 43–7.

[185] MacCulloch, p. 372.

[186] MacCulloch, pp. 596 and 606.

[187] James Gairdner, ed., *Bishop Cranmer's Recantacyons* (London: Privately Printed, 1877), pp. viii–ix and *CPM*, p. 58.

[188] *CRP*, nos. 1066, 1166 and 1299. For Motiloa, see *Carranza y Pole*, pp. 40–1. Pole may not have had powers to grant such licences, at least they do not appear in any of his bulls.

[189] Jennifer Loach, 'The Marian establishment and the printing press', *English historical review*, 109 (1986), pp. 135–48, p. 141.

[190] Camille Tihon, 'Suppliques originales addressées au cardinal-légat Carlo Carafa (1557–1558)', *Miscellanea archivistica Angelo Mercati* (Vatican City: Biblioteca Apostolica Vaticana, 1952), pp. 159–68, p. 161.

[191] See *CPM*, p. 99. The work received its royal licence before Pole's return. Jennifer Loach, 'Mary Tudor and the re-catholicisation of England', *History today*, 44 (1994), pp. 16–22, p. 21 notes the importance of catechesis, but not in this form.

continent (and learned opinion at home). He was consulted on that score almost from the first. The duke of Northumberland's change of heart on the scaffold provided one of the Marian regime's most important propaganda coups. His speech was immediately printed and translated into French, Dutch, Italian, and Spanish, as well as Latin.[192] Pole may have been centrally involved, and almost certainly was in its diffusion in manuscript. Two copies of Northumberland's statement in Italian appear among papers related to Pole, the first in the main collection of original documents from Pole's legations, ASV, Segr. Stato Inghilterra, 3, fos. 206r–7v, whence it was recopied numerous times, and the second in the Stella papers in Bergamo. Perhaps even more significant, there are both a draft (perhaps in Bartolomeo Stella's hand) and a fair copy of the Latin text among the Stella papers, in the midst of a number of other reports of English affairs which must have been sent to Pole before he returned to the country.[193] Thus he may have forwarded the statement to Rome. Antonio Fiordibello could have taken a copy with him on his mission to the emperor in 1553, during which he cited Northumberland as an example of God's power.[194] Probably numerous other letters and orations from England published in Rome came from materials Pole supplied.[195] For example, *Copia delle lettere del Sereniss. Re d'Inghilterra, & del Reverendiss. Card. Polo Legato . . . alla Santità di N. S. Iulio Papa III*, published in 1555, contained both Philip's and Pole's letters to Julius of 30 November announcing the reconciliation.[196] Similarly, a fragment of the letter which became *Il felicissimo ritorno del Regno d'Inghilterra alla Catholica unione, & alla obedientia della Sede Apostolica* (Rome: Antonio Blado, 1555) is found in Inghilterra, 3, fos. 174r–75v.[197] The supplication from parliament, which survives in numerous manuscript copies and was printed in at least one form, is also

---

192 W. K. Jordan and M. R. Gleason, 'The saying of John, late duke of Northumberland on the scaffold 1553', *Harvard library bulletin*, 23 (1975), pp. 139–79 and 324–55. They did not find any of the following manuscripts.

193 ASAS, 40/88, unfoliated. 40/86–7, for example, are various *avvisi* from England of August 1553.

194 *CRP*, nos. 655, 671, 677, 681.

195 Cf. Loach, 'Press', p. 145 for a partial list.

196 The BAV catalogue dates this 1554?, but it must be early 1555 from the date of Pole's letter's arrival in Rome (see *CRP*, no. 1019). Querini cited what must be a Latin

edition of this book, unless he inadvertently translated the title, *Exemplum literarum Reverendissimi & Illustris. D. Cardinalis Poli Legati Apostolici de latere in Regno Angliae ad Sanctis. D. N. Julium III super eadem reductione, & obedientia*, which I have been unable to find, nor have I located another Italian edition of Milan cited by Loach, 'Press', p. 145.

197 Conversely, there are numerous manuscript copies taken from the printed text of *Il felicissimo ritorno*. See *CRP*, no. 998.

in that file (fos. 162–3v).[198] Sebald Mayer's press in Dillingen became involved, almost certainly through Pole's connections to Truchsess.[199] Pole and members of his household kept up a steady stream of letters to Italy, many of which became anonymous newsletters, perhaps in preparation for publication.[200] Pole showed his awareness of the importance of image-making when he responded to Juan Ginés Sepulveda's request to check his treatment of the reconciliation in *De rebus gestisque Caroli Quinti* by at least sending a copy of his oration to parliament, which Sepulveda summarized at length.[201]

Monasticism

Pole had big plans for the restoration of the monasteries. Dispensations to ex-religious allowing them to live outside their dissolved houses contained the proviso that the dispensation held only until those houses were restored.[202] *Praeclara's* extinction of the religious houses provided further incentive to act. Technically speaking, it made all Pole's acts new foundations, not restorations, although Pole and Mary thought of them in the second way.[203] He began with the Benedictines, and in late 1555 tried to get Cassinese visitors.[204] He did not succeed, and the monks were still in Spain at least a year later.[205] In May 1557, the abbot of San Paolo reported that he had sent a licence for them to leave for England, but they still did not appear.[206] At the same time, Pole meant to revive one of two houses at Canterbury, probably Christ Church priory, and early in 1556 he sent Morone word of plans for the revival of a Benedictine house, almost certainly Westminster.[207] Even without the visitors, it took a long time for Pole's and Mary's intentions to be fulfilled there. Much of the delay arose from the resistance of the dean of the cathedral chapter that had replaced the

---

[198] Again, I have not been able to locate the printed copy to which Loach referred only as *Copia supplicationis*, which may be that cited by Querini (in *Exemplum*).

[199] Loach, 'Press', pp. 145 and 146, citing especially Mayer's publication of *Brevis narratio eorum quae in proximo anglicano conventu . . . acta sunt . . . ex variis literis bona fide excerpta*. I have not been able to confirm this edition.

[200] E.g., *CRP*, nos. 1000 and 1051.

[201] *CRP*, no. 1389.

[202] E.g., *CRP*, nos. 1147 and 1160.

[203] Cf. David Knowles, *The religious orders in England*, 3, *The Tudor age* (Cambridge: Cambridge University Press, 1959), pp. 423–6 and 438–40 for a brief survey of Pole's efforts.

[204] *CRP*, no. 1436.

[205] BMIC25, fo. 303r, printed in *ERP*, 5, pp. 345–50. Cf. Paul's letter to them of 14 July 1556 in ASV, Arm. 42:8, fos. 47r–8r.

[206] *CRP*, no. 2020.

[207] *CRP*, no. 1582.

house, Hugh Weston.[208] In September 1556, Pole approved the financial arrangements for the surrender, endorsed it and licensed the dean and chapter to draw other subventions for the time being, and at the end of the month the monks moved back, although they had to wait until November for official possession.[209] They had given up a great deal, none of them previously having an income of less than 500 *scudi* (about £133), and some more than 1,500. And although Pole never got his visitors and did not get very far establishing Cassinese observance, he did succeed in having the abbot elected for three years. One of the new abbot Feckenham's principal qualifications was his skill as a preacher.[210] Unquestionably, Pole involved himself most closely with this house. Giovanni Michiel counted this as the third restoration, not including one of nuns (Syon) nor the Carthusians at Sheen, who were restored on 16 November, Pole participating actively.[211]

As in the case of the Benedictines, Pole generally worked hand in glove with the crown. The clearest instance is provided by the Knights of St John of Jerusalem, the Hospitallers, in whom the pope also took an interest.[212] Already in summer 1555 they had been promised the restoration of their property, and by late 1556 acted as patrons of benefices, although the order was still regarded as legally dissolved.[213] Clerkenwell, their headquarters in London, had been granted to Mary in 1547 and she had used it as her London residence, so it looked as if it would be easy to accommodate the knights.[214] In response to this news, Paul sent a messenger to Mary and Pole in order to thank the queen and tell them what was needed to bring the order back to its *pristinum statum.* Paul ordered Pole to

---

[208] *Carranza y Pole*, p. 260.

[209] The dean and chapter surrendered on 26 September. C. S. Knighton, ed., *Acts of the dean and chapter of Westminster, 1543–1609* (Woodbridge, Suffolk: Boydell Press, 1997), p. 99; cf. *CRP*, nos. 1681–2, 1698; *CSPV*, 6, nos. 634 and 723; C. S. Knighton, 'Collegiate foundations, 1540–1570, with special reference to St Peter in Westminster', Cambridge University Ph.D. thesis, 1975, pp. 156–7; and *CRP*, no. 1799.

[210] BMIC25, fo. 302r.

[211] *CSPV*, 6, nos. 634 and 794. For the date and process of refoundation, see Maurice Chauncy's contemporary narrative, 'Martyrum carthusianorum in Anglia.

Passio minor', ed. François van Ortroy, *Analecta bollandiana*, 22 (1903), pp. 51–78, pp. 71–4, which stresses not only the degree of Pole's involvement, but also the refoundation's success, together with the royal patent of 26 January 1557 closely paraphrased in Margaret E. Thompson, *The Carthusian order in England* (London: SPCK, 1930), pp. 505–6 (not in *CPRPM*).

[212] See the brief summary in H. J. A. Sire, *The knights of Malta* (New Haven: Yale University Press, 1994), pp. 186–7.

[213] *CSPV*, 6:1, no. 32 and *CRP*, no. 1345. LPL, Pole's register, fo. 44r.

[214] Loades, *Mary*, pp. xi and 142.

assist to the maximum degree.[215] But despite this high-powered attention, it took a long time to put the Priory of England back together. In May 1557 Pole restored Clerkenwell along with its commanderies, and announced that he would nominate the brothers by royal command. At the same time Kilmainham was re-erected in Ireland, and Oswald Massingberd was immediately re-installed as prior.[216] In England for some reason the installation of Sir Thomas Tresham and the nomination of brothers did not take place until December, while in Ireland a delegation of three bishops, including the primate, handled Massingberd's installation, Pole assigned Tresham's to a less impressive panel. The witnesses, too, were ordinary clerics, including two of Pole's dependants.[217] Pole himself preached, however.[218] Only in early 1558 was the royal patent restoring the order's property finally issued.[219] Ireland once again got better service, Massingberd receiving his patent on 8 March.[220] The explanation of Pole's less-than-enthusiastic handling of the Hospitallers may be that they were Philip's and the pope's pet cause, and not Mary's nor his.[221] Carafa, before he became a cardinal, had given military orders high praise.[222] Antonio de Toledo, one of Philip's most senior advisers, was Grand Prior of Leon in the order. Toledo, for his part, claimed that Carranza was the major force behind the Hospitallers' restoration.[223] Carranza thought that Toledo and Pole were good friends *because* Toledo was prior, and that Pole had a high opinion of the order.[224] Tresham may have been in part Pole's choice, since they were close enough that Luigi Schiffanoia, once one of Pole's (or Priuli's) chaplains, could move to Tresham's service.[225] According to Francis Thynne, Pole's device was once to be seen over the door of the Hospitallers' church in Smithfield, meaning that Pole repaired it.[226]

At the same time as the Hospitallers had originally been promised restoration, Mary recalled both Dominicans and Franciscans from Flanders.[227] Pole presented one or the other in a group to her.[228] Sixteen of the Dominicans

---

[215] *CRP*, no. 1392.

[216] *CRP*, nos. 1968–70.

[217] *CRP*, nos. 2131–3.

[218] Dixon, p. 681n called it 'Pole's best performance'.

[219] *CPRPM*, 4, pp. 313–22.

[220] *CPRPM*, 4, p. 43.

[221] *CRP*, no. 2189.

[222] Elisabeth G. Gleason, *Reform thought in sixteenth-century Italy* (Chico, CA: Scholars Press, 1981), p. 78.

[223] *Doc. hist.*, 3, pp. 204–10.

[224] *Doc. hist.*, 5, p. 147. I am grateful to James Boyden for help with Toledo.

[225] ASAS, 40/138 (Bonelli, no. 160) and ASM:AG, b. 578, fos. 243r–4v.

[226] Francis Thynne, 'Reginald Pole', in Raphael Hollinshead, *Chronicles of England, Scotland and Ireland* (London: J. Johnson *et al.*, 1807–8; 6 vols.), 4, pp. 745–60, pp. 759–60.

[227] Dixon, pp. 358–9.

[228] BAV, Ottob. lat. 2418, fo. 259v.

immediately resumed their habits, and eventually a few Dominican nuns, formerly at Dartford, set up at Kings Langley.[229] The Franciscans were especially close to the queen's heart, and Pole would be consecrated archbishop in their house at Greenwich. According to Carranza, he used the 'guardian' of the house as his confessor.[230] There is otherwise not much sign of his interest, except for a petition directed to him from Ireland.[231] Pole's ally William Peto together probably with the Dominican William Perrin made strenuous efforts to get back Greyfriars in London which had been converted into Christ's Hospital under Edward, but the Dominican Villagarcia prevented them.[232] It is not surprising that his action had such powerful effect. Not only did Pole think highly of him, but he also showed much greater interest in Villagarcia's order than in the Franciscans. After all, his soul-mate Carranza was in England to see to his order's re-establishment, and again according to Toledo, he had taken the principal role not only in getting Smithfield set up, but also the Carthusians and Westminster.[233] Another of Pole's most powerful backers was the Dominican Muzzarelli. Villagarcia was Carranza's former student and became one of Pole's collaborators, especially in Oxford, where he was a member of Seth Holland's All Souls'.[234] Pole was involved in re-establishing the Dominicans there, and plans were at least begun, and possibly executed, for one of nuns. The friars' house in Littlegate street had become the mayor's property.[235] Pole, going so far as to summon him to London, worked out a financial settlement that allowed repairs to begin.[236] Only about four months later Villagarcia took possession in August or September 1557. At the same time, a quickly abortive scheme was floated for another house in Cambridge, which became a Franciscan establishment instead.[237] Villagarcia, one friar Richard, and probably at least one more former friar occupied the Oxford house, and Villagarcia had authority from Pole to receive more brothers. (This must mean that Carranza, anyway, still regarded Pole as legate as late as September 1557.)[238]

[229] CSPV, 6:1, no. 32; Dixon, p. 682 and Loades, Reign, p. 300 for Dartford.
[230] Doc. hist., 4, pp. 163–7.
[231] CRP, no. 1020.
[232] William Lempriere, ed., John Howes' MS, 1582 (London: Privately Published, 1904), pp. 66 and 69–70.
[233] Doc. hist., 3, pp. 204–10 and 280–7. The material in the Carranza processo makes it easier to assess Carranza's role than Loades feared (Reign, p. 297n).
[234] Doc. hist., 5, p. 150; 2, pp. 501–11, and p. 513.
[235] 'Survey of the antiquities of the city of Oxford', composed in 1661–6 by Anthony Wood, 3 (Oxford Historical Society, 37, 1899), p. 31; David Knowles and R. N. Hadcock, Medieval religious houses England and Wales (London: Longman, 1971; 2d ed.), p. 218 and Carranza y Pole, p. 258.
[236] Carranza y Pole, pp. 258, 260–1, 261–2.
[237] Ibid., p. 264.
[238] Ibid., pp. 265–6. The house had ceased to exist by the time Priuli donated some of Pole's books to New College, but on

Two other hoped-for restorations did not come to fruition. First, the Augustinian friars sought Pole's help through their general Seripando. At an unknown date, Seripando approached him about restoring the order's property as well as sending some brothers.[239] Neither happened. Second, there were plans to restore a house of regular canons, but of which rule is not known.[240] This may have had to do with Giacomo Chizzola, a member of Pole's household, whose brother Ippolito was a regular canon and famous preacher.[241] Alternatively, the canons may have been Augustinians, who were by far the most numerous religious asking Pole for absolution and dispensation.[242] Of the forty-three supplications, fifteen came from them, ten of thirty-two in England and an even more preponderant five of eleven for Ireland. These numbers are probably not explained simply by the relatively large numbers of Augustinian canons at the dissolution, perhaps as many as 1,964, or about 22 per cent of the total in England, and by far the most numerous by house in Ireland. The Benedictines numbered almost exactly as many in England, and yet they produced only two supplications.[243] Further, the relatively small pensions the canons got would not have maximized their chances of survival.[244] Weak geographical regularities emerge, as do links between brothers of the same houses. The clearest instance

---

condition that should a Dominican convent be re-established, the books should go there instead. New College, Oxford, Register of Leases (Reg. Dim. ad Firmam, 4, according to Emden in P. S. Allen, H. M. Allen and H. W. Garrod, eds., *Opus epistolarum Desiderii Erasmi roterodami* (Oxford: Clarendon Press, 1905–58), 11, p. 380), fo. 88.

[239] Hubert Jedin, *Girolamo Seripando. Sein Leben und Denken im Geisteskampf des 16. Jahrhunderts* (Würzburg: Augustinus-Verlag, 1984; reprint of Würzburg, 1937 ed.), 1, p. 289.

[240] BMIC25, fo. 303r and *CSPV*, 6, no. 771. For the Lateran canons and Cardinal Gonzaga their protector, see Philip McNair, *Peter Martyr in Italy: an anatomy of apostasy* (Oxford: Clarendon Press, 1967), pp. 70–85 and 180–205.

[241] *PM*, 1, pp. 199 and 289; 5, 287–8; ASM:CEG, b. 1945, no. 5, fos. 3v–4v and no. 14, fo. 10r–v.

[242] Only one of the 194 Austin friars known

to have received capacities came to Pole. *CRP*, no. 1160. D. S. Chambers, *Faculty office registers 1534–1549* (Oxford: Clarendon Press, 1966), p. 50 and Francis Roth, *The English Austin friars 1249–1538*, 2, *Sources* (New York: Augustinian Historical Institute, 1961), p. 517.

[243] *CRP*, nos. 1096 and 1864. Aubrey Gwynn and R. Neville Hadcock, *Medieval religious houses Ireland* (London: Longman, 1970), pp. 146–201 for the Augustinians, while the Benedictines cover only eight pages, the Cistercians thirty-two, and the Dominicans and Franciscans seventeen and eighteen respectively.

[244] I have used the maximum figures in Knowles and Hadcock, pp. 488–95. They give a range of 1,568–1,969 Benedictines and 1,672–1,964 Augustinians, out of a total of 6,929–8,781 male religious. I am grateful to Peter Cunich for some additional provisional calculations, pending the completion of his database of the ex-religious.

of the second is Guisborough in Yorkshire, whose ex-prior had become suffragan bishop of Hull. Perhaps Pole's lenient treatment of him (see above) encouraged one of his former brothers to supplicate.[245] Otherwise, with the exception of one other from the diocese of York, the rest originate in southern England, including two from Kent, one from a prebendary of Canterbury cathedral.[246] Nevertheless, despite these relatively large numbers, no houses of Augustinian canons were re-established. Instead, Pole helped in the restoration of the Brigittine (or Augustinian) house of nuns at Syon.[247]

The Cistercians take pride of place for proportional representation in the supplications. Their five English and one Irish supplications mean that between 0.004 per cent and 0.005 per cent of their members at the dissolution asked for absolution and dispensation. As that last silly statistic indicates, only a tiny proportion of the ex-religious approached Pole. It is not known how many were still alive. Pole thought only a few, and although his committee appointed to determine the validity of pensions never reported, it seems likely that the percentage supplicating represented a small minority even of the survivors.[248]

Despite this bleak picture, efforts to restore monasticism were a little more successful and more important than has been thought. Granted, the totals of either number of houses restored or of supplicating religious are trivial by comparison to the numbers at the dissolution: approximately 840 houses and as many as almost 11,000 religious.[249] Nevertheless, the total usually given of seven houses refounded must be increased by at least one and perhaps five or more, assuming that something came of the plans for the Augustinian friars and regular canons, for a total of as many as a dozen.[250] There also seem to have been at least two spontaneous refoundations by ex-religious, both in the North and perhaps undertaken without official approval.[251] A member of Pole's household noted efforts to restore twelve houses already in January 1555, including three each of Franciscans and Dominicans. As he also admitted, the problem lay in finding monks and friars.[252] Thus the number of perhaps 100 religious occupying the houses may be reliable.[253] This is not a vast host, and David Loades must be right that there was no 'backlog

[245] CRP, no. 1335.
[246] CRP, nos. 1182, 1209.
[247] CRP, nos. 1790 and 1797.
[248] Pogson, pp. 291–3.
[249] Knowles and Hadcock, p. 494.
[250] Priuli added the intention to restore one to the total of six given by Loades, *Reign*, pp. 300–1, and Loades there overlooks the Franciscans at Southampton, provided for

in Mary's will, *ibid.*, p. 387.
[251] Claire Cross, 'The reconstitution of northern monastic communities in the reign of Mary Tudor', *Northern history*, 29 (1993), pp. 200–4.
[252] CRP, no. 1051.
[253] David Knowles, *The religious orders in England*, 3, *The Tudor age* (Cambridge: Cambridge University Press, 1961), p. 440.

of unsatisfied religious vocations'.[254] Loades may also be correct that neither Pole nor Mary regarded monasteries as agencies of spiritual renewal, although this is more likely to be true of the queen than of the cardinal.[255]

Visitations

Within two months of the synod's prorogation in February 1556 Pole issued orders to visit at least the dioceses of Winchester, Exeter, Salisbury, Chichester and Peterborough, probably along with Hereford.[256] Ely's turn came in August.[257] Metropolitical visitations of Lincoln, Gloucester, Worcester (at least the cathedral), St Asaph, and Durham probably came at the same time, although York had to wait until 1557.[258] This is enough dioceses to suggest visitation on a national scale, allowing for loss of records. Yet these visitations were not co-ordinated from the centre, at least not on the evidence of the articles and the injunctions. Article XII of the synodical decrees was originally too vestigial to have provided much guidance, and as we have seen there is little overlap between its elaborated form and Pole's visitation articles. It principally served to underscore the archdeacon's role.[259] This, together with much of the rest of the visitations, came from Bonner's model in 1554.[260] The visitor of Lincoln,

[254] Loades, *Reign*, p. 300.
[255] Loades, *Mary*, p. 330.
[256] *CRP*, nos. 1493–4, 1540, 1542 and 2190; Anne Whiteman, 'The church of England 1542–1837', in R. B. Pugh and Elizabeth Crittall, eds., *VCH: A history of Wiltshire*, 3 (London: Oxford University Press, 1956), pp. 28–56, pp. 31–2. The Hereford Act book records an agreement dated 30 June 1556 to pay the costs of the visitation. I owe this information to S. E. Lehmberg.
[257] *CRP*, no. 1655.
[258] The articles and the comperta for Lincoln are printed in Strype, *Eccl. mem.*, 3:2, pp. 389–410 and the articles only in W. H. Frere and W. M. Kennedy, eds., *Visitation articles & injunctions of the period of the reformation* (London: Alcuin Club, 1910; 3 vols.), 2, pp. 397–8, followed by those for the Minster, also issued in Pole's name. The injunctions for Gloucester are in David Wilkins, ed., *Concilia magnae Britanniae et*

Hiberniae (London: Gosling *et al.*, 1737; 4 vols.), 4, pp. 145–8, reprinted in Frere and Kennedy, 2, pp. 401–8. They date from after the publication of Bonner's *Profitable and necessary doctrine* in 1555. See also Dixon's summary, pp. 595–7, with some omissions. For Worcester cathedral, Frere and Kennedy, 2, pp. 392–6 and Wilkins, 4, p. 145; Frere and Kennedy, 2, pp. 409–11 for St Asaph and pp. 412–14 for Tunstall's injunctions for Durham, from a document dated 17 June. *CRP*, no. 1875 for York.
[259] Bray, pp. 160 and 130–7 for the elaborated version.
[260] Frere and Kennedy, 2, p. 330 for the archdeacon's role, and the marginalia citing seventeen precedents from Bonner in Brooks' injunctions (pp. 401–8). By contrast, White drew on Bonner only five times, more frequently on Pole's articles of 1556 (pp. 397–8).

Bishop John White, got only twelve questions, while the list of injunctions for Gloucester is almost as long as Harpsfield's articles for Canterbury.[261] There is also virtually no overlap between the articles and the injunctions, and their tone is substantially different. While White's questions and Goldwell's injunctions are almost exclusively negative, concerned with heresy, unlicensed preaching, and decayed churches (Tunstall's brief injunctions cover only church fabric), and Goldwell's in particular with death and dying, James Brooks's order in more positive fashion plenty of preaching, or at least reading of homilies, teaching of the Paternoster, and study of scripture by unlearned clergy. Some of the problems of the laity are the same in the various articles, but almost the only common point about the clergy was marriage. The comperta of the Lincoln visitation underlined how much responsibility Pole bore for fixing the church, if in no other way than the number of parishes impropriated to him.

Less than a month after his consecration as archbishop Pole undertook a visitation of his diocese, relying on Archdeacon Harpsfield and the maxim 'the archdeacon is called the eye of the bishop' ('Archidiaconus oculus Episcopi voceretur').[262] The questions for the clergy begin with divine service and the sacraments, but quickly divert to frequenting ale-houses, to midwives and keeping a book of reconciliations.[263] The main concerns stand out. Doctrine and education was one, but absent any overt worry about heresy, until the laity were asked whether they had any schismatic or heretical books that the synod had just banned (article XXIX). Did the clergy teach their parishioners articles of faith and the Ten Commandments? Was English used in services? There was no mention of preaching, one of the most serious deviations between Pole's articles and the revised form of article XII. Similarly, the laity were simply asked whether they 'believe the articles of the faith'. Proper lay behaviour caused more concern, from fornication through gaming, to evil-livers. The fabric of the church also drew a good deal of attention, including whether there was a crucifix with the image of Mary and John, as well as another of the patron saint, matters which Pole had already ordered investigated.[264] Were there any uncanonically married, who did not attend the mass, or who frequented *conventicula, conciliabula, lectiones et professiones clandestinas*?

---

[261] Strype, *Eccl. mem.*, pp. 411–12, reprinted in Frere and Kennedy, 2, pp. 397–8.

[262] *CRP*, nos. 2252, 1541, 1550–1, 1564–5, 1598, 1568, and 1578–9.

[263] LPL, Pole's register, fos. 34v–5v, 'Articuli inquirendi in visitatione', printed in

Strype, *Eccl. mem.*, 3:1, pp. 291–3; Frere and Kennedy, 2, pp. 385–91; and slightly imperfectly in *Carranza y Pole*, pp. 350–1. The comperta book is LPL, VG 4/2 (VC III/1/2).

[264] Frere and Kennedy, 2, p. 388.

The following year Harpsfield again visited the diocese (or perhaps this was an extension of the original visitation), this time inquiring about fifty-four articles, including twenty-one covering the clergy.[265] Most of the 1556 articles reappeared, often with new emphasis, and several new areas of inquiry were introduced, among them a question whether erroneous doctrine was taught, especially about the unity of the church. Clerical behaviour drew more attention than it had the year before, from concerns about chastity (repeated twice), to observance of canon law and proper trimming of beards and tonsures. Whether the clergy followed correct procedures also took up much time. Heresy became the number one concern about the laity. One of the questions once more touched on secret preaching, and others concerned false doctrine, especially about the eucharist, which also had to be properly conducted and venerated. Various behaviours came in for censure, in addition to open heresy, and the parish's role in providing social services, including hospitals, was highlighted. Inquiry was also made into the physical state of the church. Schoolmasters were examined about their belief, marriages were to be regularized, and regulations about Sundays and holy days were to be strictly enforced.

During the summer of 1556 the visitation of the universities began. While it has been suggested on the strength of the agenda of 1554 that Mary originally inspired them, the wishes of the London synod provided the rationale for the visitation of Cambridge.[266] Legatine authority undergirded both visitations and both are fairly poorly documented. There is room for confusion even about

---

[265] Frere and Kennedy, 2, pp. 422–6, and 1, p. 145. The articles were printed in Foxe, pp. 1969–70; Hollinshead, *Chronicles*, 4, pp. 141–4; Wilkins, 4, pp. 169–70; and L. E. Whatmore, ed., *Archdeacon Harpsfield's visitation, 1557*, 1 (Catholic Record Society, 45, 1950), pp. 5–6. Eamon Duffy's judgment that this was 'surely the most searching' visitation in Tudor England seems exaggerated, overlooking Bishop Hooper's of Gloucester in 1551, Bonner's of London in 1554 and Harpsfield's own of 1556. *The stripping of the altars. Traditional religion in England c. 1400–c. 1580* (New Haven: Yale University Press, 1992), p. 524. Hooper's articles run to eighteen pages in Frere and Kennedy (2, pp. 291–309) and include eighty-nine interrogatories, and Bonner's to twenty-eight (124), while Harpsfield-Pole's cover only five pages and number fifty-four. Cf. Caroline Litzenberger, *The English reformation and the laity: Gloucestershire, 1540–1580* (Cambridge: Cambridge University Press, 1997), p. 68.

[266] Elizabeth Russell, 'Marian Oxford and the counter reformation', in Caroline M. Barron *et al.*, eds., *The church in pre-reformation society: essays in honour of F. R. H. Du Boulay* (Woodbridge: Boydell, 1985), pp. 212–27, p. 216; *CRP*, nos. 1418 and 1781.

when they took place.[267] Nevertheless, Oxford certainly came first, probably in July and August 1556, although the visitation of Cambridge had been announced by this time as well.[268] Perhaps its priority arose from an effort to drive home the lesson of Cranmer's burning, but more likely both because Oxford was 'safer' than Cambridge, and also because Pole already had trusted men on site, among them de Soto and Carranza. De Soto, who would leave England shortly after the visitation costing Pole one of his closest collaborators, had been lecturing in Oxford along with Villagarcia.[269] Carranza later claimed to have been a visitor, joining a team led by Ormanetto which included Brooks, Cole, William Wright, Brooks's successor as master of Balliol, and Robert Morwent, president of Corpus Christi.[270] The temperaments of at least two of the most important visitors, Ormanetto and Cole, might have caused

---

[267] E. S. Roberts, ed., *The works of John Caius, M. D., second founder of Gonville and Caius College and master of the college, 1559–1573, with a memoir of his life by John Venn* (Cambridge; Cambridge University Press, 1912), *The first book of the annals of the Royal College of Physicians* (1911), separately paginated, p. 27. Cf. esp. Claire Cross, 'Oxford and the Tudor state from the accession of Henry VIII to the death of Mary', in T. H. Aston, ed., *The history of the university of Oxford*, 3, *The collegiate university*, ed. James McConica (Oxford: Clarendon Press, 1986), pp. 117–49, pp. 145–6, who reverses the order of the visitations. Short summary of both visitations in *Eccl. mem.*, 3:2, pp. 28–9 with reference to Foxe. Cf. pp. 1956–64 for Cambridge, dated 1557.

[268] Russell, p. 216 and Cross, p. 146 say in July on unknown evidence, but perhaps the visitation articles in Bodleian Library, MS Twyne 7, fos. 155r–7r and Twyne 2, fos. 84r–5r which I have not been able to see. The best evidence otherwise for the date may be Rullo's presence in Oxford in July and August, before his return to London probably about 25 August. Carlo De Frede, *La restaurazione cattolica in Inghilterra sotto Maria Tudor nel carteggio di Girolamo Seripando* (Naples: Libreria

Scientifica, 1971), pp. 101–2. This date coincides fairly well with a clue in the legatine register, which Faita kept from 9 July to 1 September, probably because of Ormanetto's absence. Another gap in it from December 1555 to early July 1556, with coverage thereafter fairly thick, may mean that the *citatio* to Oxford came before July. For the sequence of visitations, see also *De antiquitate britannicae ecclesiae*, p. 420.

[269] *CSPV*, 6:1, no. 594. Venancio D. Carro, *El maestro Fr. Pedro de Soto, O. P. y las controversias politico-teológicas en el siglo XVI*, 1, *Actuacion politico/religiosa de Soto* (Salamanca: Convento de San Esteban, 1931), p. 250.

[270] *Doc. hist.*, 3, pp. 25–6 and *Pole y Carranza*, p. 72, followed by Jennifer Loach, 'Reformation controversies', in McConica, *Oxford*, pp. 363–96, p. 378. Tellechea Idigoras also listed John Christopherson on unknown authority. Nicholas Sander's welcoming oration named the visitors, not including Carranza (Strype, *Eccl. mem.*, 3:2, p. 473). Cf. Cross, p. 146, who says others were involved. Pogson, p. 346n gives a shorter list, with John White in place of Wright, but this must be an error since Sander identified Wright by surname.

difficulty.[271] To judge from one of Foxe's stories of Ormanetto's behaviour at Cambridge and another told by James Calfhill of his indignant refusal to consider a charge preferred against a priest, he could be extremely arrogant, and Cole could as well.[272] The visitors had about thirty articles covering the observance of foundation statutes, lectures, public ceremonies, governance, finances, books, especially heretical ones, and discipline.[273] All Souls' College came in for particular scrutiny both then and later.[274] This was probably because of its role as nursery of civilians and senior clerical administrators, together with the archbishop's status as founder. It also had strong particular links to Pole through Holland, who had been a fellow until at least 1542 before being appointed warden in April 1556, and Villagarcia, who lived there, and Carranza may have as well.[275] Pole also took a special interest in New College, Cole's college, and left it some books.[276] Carranza knew virtually the whole cadre of its Fellows who would become leading recusants, including Rastell, Nicholas Sander, and John Fowler.[277]

As a result of the visitation, the university's statutes came under review. Meanwhile, Pole issued temporary injunctions.[278] These focused on administration, beginning with the vice-chancellor. He was to oversee the officers, and ensure that heresy and heretics were purged, useful public lectures given and much more of the same, including relations between town and university. The regent masters were cursorily reminded of their duties and the proctors received detailed attention. Pole laid down rules for their accounting and handling of finances, specifying exactly how they were to spend the income from impropriated rectories. Like the vice-chancellor, they were also vigilantly to enforce the statutes, especially against heresy, as well as against an enormous list of other problems. Heads of houses were to reside and bring their students to services every morning, but most of this section concerned law students, who were to be kept rigorously separated from those of arts. Returning to the public lecturers, Pole laid down that they lecture daily for at least an hour, and should not contravene Catholic belief. Philosophers were to do the best they could on that score, following whatever opinions 'dissent the least from Christian truth'. In cases of disagreement, they were to dwell on the weakness of human reason.

---

[271] *CRP*, no. 1776.
[272] Foxe, p. 1960 and James Calfhill, *An answer to John Martiall's Treatise of the cross* (Cambridge: Cambridge University Press, 1846; Parker Society, volume 11), p. 331.
[273] Cross, p. 146 and Russell, pp. 219–20.
[274] *CRP*, nos. 1779, 2249, 2263–5, and 2300.

[275] Emden. *Doc. hist.*, 2, p. 513.
[276] Emden and E. Lobel, 'Cardinal Pole's MSS', *Proceedings of the British Academy*, 17 (1931), pp. 97–101.
[277] *Doc. hist.*, 2, p. 513 and *Carranza y Pole*, pp. 264, 269, and 270.
[278] *CRP*, no. 1768.

Lectures were to explicate texts, not offer forced interpretations. Both of these points fit Pole's philosophical and pedagogical inclinations. That he did not provide more detailed instructions about how to avoid vain disputes is also consistent with his principles, however little it may have helped to inculcate the new modes.

Just a little later, the *citatio* for Cambridge was issued.[279] This time we can say considerably more, thanks to the survival of the bedel John Mere's diary along with Foxe's sometimes more detailed treatment.[280] If anything, Pole got more enthusiastic local co-operation at Cambridge than at Oxford in the person first of the former vice-chancellor, John Yonge, who had handled Somerset's negotiations with Pole. He had preached on the previous St Andrew's Day about the restoration of the primacy, and disputed with Cranmer, Latimer, and Ridley. In addition, he may have written one of the earliest lives of John Fisher.[281]

Heresy was much on the minds of both visitors and members of the university, beginning with a sermon condemning Cranmer, Latimer, and Ridley preached at the visitors' arrival.[282] Preaching and heresy went hand in glove during the visitation, most notoriously in the posthumous condemnation, exhumation, and burning of Martin Bucer and Paul Fagius. According to Mere, the initiative came from the university, and Foxe's account agrees, although he claimed that the vice-chancellor and congregation acted on the visitors' written instructions.[283] Ormanetto duly gave judgment, according to Foxe writing it out himself.[284] Further process involved testimony against the two, with Yonge as lead witness.[285] His reward was appointment to preach at Paul's Cross on 14 and 21 February, even though he was in trouble over his professorship and mastership of Pembroke Hall.[286] The final condemnation occurred on 26 January. Scot and Andrew Perne preached. On Candelmas, Thomas Watson preached against

---

[279] *CRP*, no. 1781. See the brief summary in J. B. Mullinger, *The university of Cambridge from the royal injunctions of 1535 to the accession of Charles the first* (Cambridge: University Press, 1884), pp. 156–7.

[280] Lamb, pp. xxxii–xxxvii and 189–236. The original is CCCC, MS 106, no. 330. There are frequently discrepancies between the two accounts, for example, about which college was visited when. For Foxe's labelling the visitation an 'inquisition', see e.g., p. 1960. Mere's calm tone is remarkable, since he was examined for

heresy during the visitation. Lamb, p. 221.

[281] Lamb, p. 185. Leslie Stephen and Sidney Lee, eds., *Dictionary of national biography* (Oxford: Oxford University Press, 1917), 21, p. 1294 and F. van Ortroy, 'Vie du bienhereux Martyr Jean Fisher', *Analecta Bollandiana*, 12 (1893), pp. 97–287, pp. 200–1.

[282] Lamb, p. 200; Foxe, p. 1958.

[283] Foxe, p. 1959.

[284] Lamb, pp. 201–2; Foxe, p. 1959.

[285] Foxe, p. 1960; Lamb, p. 206.

[286] Lamb, pp. 220, 222, and 226.

Bucer, as he did again when the bodies were burnt on 6 February.[287] On the 7th and 8th Scot preached two more sermons, the first at the hallowing of Great St Mary's.[288] The visitation's other keynote was the search for prohibited books, many being destroyed.[289]

The visitors left injunctions, probably issued by Ormanetto without reference to Pole, and Ormanetto wrote Perne already on 27 February accusing him of lax enforcement.[290] After about the same delay as in the case of Oxford, new statutes arrived in mid-May, along with more injunctions (if Mere did not confuse one with the other).[291] Again, they began with the vice-chancellor, but otherwise the Cambridge statutes diverge substantially from those for Oxford.[292] The second point concerned selection of lecturers, followed by rules for admission to degrees, graces, and lecturers (which received a great deal of attention later in the text), before returning to the vice-chancellor and the university officers. The vice-chancellor had to see to it that 'sound doctrine, honest behaviour and letters' increase. The proctors, assimilated to archdeacons in episcopal administration, were to assist him. Chapter six concerned heresy, offering remission of penalties for repentant first offenders. Stringent regulations governed mass and public processions, including the taking of names of those absent. The injunctions then turned to more substantive matters, beginning with preaching. No one could proceed bachelor of theology without having preached in Great St Mary's, doctors of theology were obliged to preach at Paul's once they had begun to read the Sentences and hold themselves ready to preach whenever the bishop of London wished. In Cambridge, members of the university were to attend all sermons *ad cleros*. Disputations were carefully scrutinized, and a swingeing fine of £1 was laid down for anyone holding a disputation in theology without the approval of the vice-chancellor and two senior doctors. The rest of the long document contained minute rules about the mode of instruction, although not its content. The injunctions caused trouble, especially those covering lectures and attendance at them, and Pole had to order the vice-chancellor to comply with them in November.[293]

The final corporate phase of Pole's governance of the English church came in

---

[287] Lamb, pp. 213 and 215. Cf. J. W. Blench, *Preaching in England in the late fifteenth and sixteenth centuries: a study of English sermons 1450–c. 1600* (New York: Barnes and Noble, 1964), pp. 283–4 for a brief summary of his sermons.

[288] Lamb, pp. 217–18.

[289] Lamb, pp. 208, 212, 215, 217, 218, 219, 220, 221.

[290] Lamb, p. 228.

[291] Lamb, pp. 231–3.

[292] *CRP*, no. 1911.

[293] *CRP*, no. 2128.

the convocation of January 1558. Although it was called in December 1557 for 21 January 1558, it did not meet until a week later.[294] John Harpsfield made plain in his opening address that it was to contribute to the recovery of Calais.[295] It would also capitalize on the opportunity to investigate further the defects of the church, as well as how to dispose of Mary's grants to it. This point was entrusted to a committee of bishops, including Bonner, Griffith, Henry Morgan, David Pole, and Brooks. Pole also wished to see examination of the statutes of newly erected churches or those changed from regular to secular establishments, and White, Christopherson, and D. Pole, along with the deans of Canterbury, Winchester, and Worcester received this task. The next day Bonner brought in a report about problems in the dioceses, but the matter was postponed since not all the bishops were ready. Cole then read the plan to transfer surpluses, and it went to Pole. The lower house was ordered to send up points needing reform by 4 February.[296] On the 9th a subvention of £8,000 was agreed. A week later Goldwell, acting on Pole's instructions, asked the members to leave proxies 'so that things urgently requiring reformation' could be dealt with by Bonner, Thomas Thirlby, Griffith, and other bishops after convocation had risen, thereby anticipating the Whig supersession of convocation by the bishops more than a century later. On the 18th four articles were presented to Cole for exhibition to Pole, two touching on benefices, one on clerical exemption from military service, and one about conferring orders outside canonical times. Finally, convocation had another discussion about fighting, this time the Scots, and then an abortive consideration of tithes, before its prorogation on 8 March.

An extensive list of articles was prepared during this convocation, although not passed. They are more concerned with heresy than earlier plans, and at least as much with clerical discipline. They began with preaching, and ordered the preparation of four kinds of sermons in English: on the eucharist and the other sacraments attacked by heretics; articles of the faith; saints; and ceremonies, along with virtues and vices. This medieval-sounding scheme was to be supplemented by a short catechism in English and documents for the priest to use in

---

[294] *CRP*, nos. 2147 and 2186 which refers to the opening of convocation on the 21st, but this may be a clerical error, based on one of the summons. Christopherson's mandate of compliance is dated 16 January (noted in *CRP*, no. 2147) and Bonner's the 19th (no. 2162), so there may very well have been delay. CCCC, MS 121, no. 12, headed 'Convocatio seu sacra synodus

advocata authoritate brevis regis ... celebrata per dominum Reginaldum Polum cardinalum ... A. D. 1557 primo Januarii' is a *disiectum membrum* of no importance.

[295] Wilkins, 4, pp. 155–68, the first part reprinted in *ERP*, 5, pp. 233–6.

[296] Action like that ordered in *CRP*, nos. 2190–1 resulted.

confession. After enjoining the archdeacons to examine clerical failings, the articles turned to the cathedrals, including their prebendaries. They were to preach, and sixty or more boys were to be taught grammar in each cathedral. Only learned clerics could be pluralists. The universities got separate attention, including their curriculum. Dialectic was to be learned from Porphyry, Aristotle, and Rudolf Agricola, and no others. The significant inclusion of Agricola may well reflect Pole's own education, in which the Frisian could have figured.[297] Aristotle provided the only text for philosophy, and theology had a similarly limited syllabus: the Bible, Peter Lombard, and the other schoolmen. Scholars were to be forced to attend public lectures every day. Fellows had to be poor, and founders' wishes had to be observed. No one could hold a benefice worth more than £20 without studying three years beyond his BA. There was to be no gaming, nor lengthy disputation, and no one could attend school without his ordinary's permission. Much of this sounds like the canons of the London synod.

Another set of articles was proposed for the bishops, mainly concerning benefices and quality of clergy. Here again preaching and heresy figured importantly. Bishops had primary responsibility for the defence against heresy, but they needed help and must therefore appoint licensed preachers. In order to help them, convocation proposed a rudimentary Index, which included the Tyndale Bible and anything against Becket, and a list of prohibited authors. After a long section on clerical discipline, the articles returned to heresy and the importance of inquisitors, especially in the universities. The bishops of Lincoln for Oxford and Ely for Cambridge were to visit them on the score of heresy as soon as possible, and every year thereafter. Although not enacted, this comprehensive effort testifies to the degree to which the English church under Pole had come to understand its circumstances.

Pole and the counter-reformation in England

Pole's legation will never be the stuff of popular fiction. It did not excite his contemporaries, any more than it has stimulated historians. Aridly legalistic it may not have been, but it is not much more thrilling to be told that Pole's greatest administrative success lay in finance.[298] Nevertheless, he deserves credit for his

---

[297] Thomas F. Mayer, *Thomas Starkey and the commonweal: humanist politics and religion in the reign of Henry VIII* (Cambridge: Cambridge University Press, 1989), pp. 39–41.

[298] Pogson, 'Money', p. 305.

accomplishments as administrator, or at least director of administrators.[299] Even those who willingly allow this point usually turn around to fault Pole for failing to discover the counter-reformation.[300] Those who criticize Pole for having refused to admit the Jesuits implicitly endorse a similar view. These assessments encounter two problems. First, as Eamon Duffy points out, they are anachronistic.[301] Second, on John O'Malley's showing, the Jesuits had nothing to do with the counter-reformation.[302] This concept is undergoing reconsideration, and the story of Pole's legation can contribute to the process.[303] Historians have long had a major clue to the real link between Pole and the 'counter-reformation', but have missed its full significance. This is the model for 'counter-reformation' education set in the London synod.[304] As this single point indicates, the antithesis between counter-reformation and whatever it was that Pole stood for is false. Of late this antithesis has begun to break down. Duffy neatly describes Pole's (and Mary's) efforts as parallel to the counter-reformation. They tried and in large part succeeded in restoring traditional Catholicism, incorporating the 'positive' in earlier reforms. Their policy was 'not one of reaction but of creative reconstruction'.[305] Disputation was avoided wherever possible, Pole preferring 'the beauty of holiness' as a means to instil the proper faith. This would prepare Englishmen to read the Bible. Liturgy first, then scripture. Duffy concludes that Pole and Mary needed a 'long-term process of catechesis' in order to entrench their reforms.

This, of course, they did not have, and in this Duffy agrees with Pogson, Loades, and Philip Hughes.[306] Yet Hughes concluded that Pole's emphasis on the papacy rescued English Catholicism, and it is in Elizabethan recusancy that its impact can be found.[307] The matter of time is not so crucial, after all.

---

[299] Loades, *Reign*, p. 297.

[300] The classic statement of this view is Dickens, pp. 309–11. Pogson (p. 357) repeats it, but with a subtly dialectical twist. The most polemical rejoinder is Loach, 'Mary Tudor', which flatly concludes that the Marian church invented the counter-reformation, anticipating some of the arguments made here.

[301] Duffy, p. 525.

[302] John W. O'Malley, *The first Jesuits* (Cambridge: Harvard University Press, 1993).

[303] E.g., William V. Hudon, 'Religion and society in early modern Italy – old questions, new insights', *American historical review*, 101 (1996), pp. 783–804 or R. Hsia, *The world of Catholic renewal* (Cambridge: Cambridge University Press, 1998), ch. 1.

[304] See above, p. 239ff.

[305] Duffy, p. 526.

[306] Philip Hughes, *Rome and the counter-reformation in England* (London: Burns & Oates, 1944), p. 76. Loades, *Reign*, p. 292.

[307] *Ibid.*, p. 119.

Loades disagrees and stresses contingency in his explanation of Mary's fail-ure.[308] Much the same kind of argument could apply to Pole. To indicate the degree to which developments over which he had no control determined the outcome of his efforts, it is useful to begin with a comparison of his administra-tion to that of three other important heads of the late medieval and sixteenth-century church, Cardinals Morton and Wolsey and Archbishop Cranmer. In no case does Pole show to disadvantage. Cardinal Morton met very little suc-cess in his efforts at reform despite being both archbishop and lord chancellor and Wolsey's only legatine synod accomplished virtually nothing.[309] Cranmer had much less success over a much longer period of time in defending the assets of his bishopric and the English church, and his principal reforms made not a great deal more headway than Pole's, especially Cranmer's pet project of reform of canon law.[310] The implicit judgment 'if catholic, therefore incompe-tent' must be set aside.

The ground of assessment has been shifting of late, and after a phase stressing the comparative success of Marian printing and propaganda, emphasis falls on spirituality.[311] But here again the conclusion comes perilously close to Dickens's, provocatively restated as recently as 1987.[312] Referring in obligatory fashion to the Jesuits, together with Dermot Fenlon's argument that Trent trau-matized Pole, Loades concludes that Pole lacked 'theological self-confidence'. He failed to introduce any new devotions, among them to the rosary or the holy sacrament.[313] These are fair criticisms, but lay perhaps too much emphasis on the new again. Devotion to the holy sacrament was important in Italy so Pole might have been expected to know of it, but given the importance of the euchar-ist to him, and Carranza's involvement in efforts to revive Corpus Christi in England, in part at Bonner's urging, it is not surprising to find that Pole took part in at least one Corpus Christi procession, in 1555 at Canterbury, paying for the candles borne by his servants, and in his 1556 articles enquired whether the

---

[308] Loades, *Reign*, p. 395 and 'The piety of the Catholic restoration in England, 1553–8', in *Politics*, pp. 200–12, p. 203. Cf. also *Reign*, p. 293.

[309] Christopher Harper-Bill, 'Dean Colet's convocation sermon and the pre-reformation church in England', *History*, 32 (1988), pp. 191–210, p. 210 and Gwyn, pp. 285–9.

[310] MacCulloch, pp. 166–7, 202, 359, 366, and *passim* for canon law.

[311] Beginning with Loades, *Reign*, p. 292.

[312] A. G. Dickens, 'The early expansion of Protestantism in England, 1520–1558', *ARG*, 78 (1987), pp. 187–221, p. 221: Mary's reign is still 'not merely a huge failure, but one likely to have become more monumental with every succeeding year'.

[313] *Ibid.*, p. 208.

sacrament was borne in procession to the dying.[314] On balance, Loades offers a reasonably positive view, noting that although reactionary (as in the case of Corpus Christi, perhaps), Pole's and Mary's religion was not 'excessively' so.[315] Pole's bishops did a good job of 'thoughtful and sensitive spiritual counselling', and 'represented an indigenous strain of intellect and spirituality'.[316] This spirituality was not monastic, says Loades, although the London Carthusians who had formed Pole stuck him in an earlier generation and gave him a bent for 'contemplation and withdrawal'.[317] In short, Pole fostered a 'distinctively English type of reformed Catholicism' based on an 'ideal of order, discipline and peace' (p. 209). This was, however, 'unrealistic'. 'Judicial persecution on its own was not enough, and neither the habit-forming ceremonialism upon which Pole was so keen nor the sensible humanist theology of Watson and Bonner could provide adequate support. Paradoxically, it was the insularity of the Marian church, not its ultramontanism, or even its association with Spain, which was its fundamental weakness.' In other words, once again no counter-reformation.

Pole's attitude to ordinary Christians has a lot to do with the extent of his failure. As has been repeatedly observed, Pole did not trust simple believers. Hence his policy of law and obedience. As Pogson puts it, Pole had the instincts of a confessor, which meant great success one-on-one and slow progress with any group. As Pogson also says, Pole saw no distinction between spiritual counsel in private and in public, and his very consistency as confessor therefore became a weakness.[318] Once back in England he did not abandon his own intensely spiri-

---

[314] For Italy, Thomas Worthen, 'Tintoretto's paintings for the *Banco del Sacramento* in S. Margherita', *Art bulletin*, 78 (1996), pp. 707–32, pp. 709–10 and in general Miri Rubin, *Corpus Christi: the eucharist in late medieval culture* (Cambridge: Cambridge University Press, 1991). *Carranza y Pole*, pp. 66–7. Rubin downplays the importance of Corpus Christi in England, and argues that there were comparatively few guilds devoted to it, but cf. Mervyn James, 'Ritual, drama and social body in the late medieval English town', in *Society, politics and culture: studies in early modern England* (Cambridge: Cambridge University Press, 1986), pp. 16–47 and Duffy pp. 92, 101, and 566 (for its final celebration at Canterbury which was supposed to have drawn 3000 people).

Historical Manuscripts Commission, *Fifth report* (London: HMSO, 1876), p. 434 for the procession which Pole attended on the way back from Marcq and for 1556, Frere and Kennedy, 2, p. 389, article 43, echoing *Reformatio Angliae*, fo. 25v (Bray, pp. 130–1).

[315] 'Piety', p. 209.

[316] *Ibid.*, p. 208. This point is somewhat modified from *Reign*, p. 292, where Loades judged that none of the bishops was 'an outstanding personality'.

[317] *Reign*, p. 293. There is room for doubt about Pole's ties to Sheen. See above, ch. 1, p. 48.

[318] Pogson, pp. 29 and 46. On p. 43 he describes Pole's failure as a charismatic leader, because he had no feeling for the masses.

tual, even charismatic, religion, as his 'reasonings' with Cranmer or his intensely personal relations with Mary manifest, or, we might add, his almost equally intensely personal preaching. All this was aimed at the elite. Pole, a natural elitist, had his hands further tied in dealing with the English laity by the impossibility of employing the means which had once worked so well in Italy, and for which Pole had been very largely responsible, that is, devotional literature like the *Beneficio di Cristo*. One of the deepest mysteries about Pole's attempt to restore the English church is what became of Courtenay's 1548 translation.[319] Not for England any 40,000 copies sold. The answer could be precisely that the work would have been popular. Pole's intensely personal religion presented another drawback, as it had throughout his life. If one sympathized with his beliefs, all was well. If one did not, mutual incomprehension likely resulted. Pole's continuing stress on the limitations (or worse) of human prudence was certain to annoy Mary's more politically inclined counsellors.[320] Thus Pole failed both with the common people and too many of the political classes.

And yet. Whatever Pole's inherent weaknesses, at least to modern eyes, Loades obliquely put his finger on the major problem limiting Pole's success, the contingent factor of the occupant of Peter's chair.[321] Under Julius III, Pole had carte blanche and but for imperial politics and his own stubbornness, might have largely accomplished his reformation within the first year of Mary's reign. Despite a late start, he did lay an extensive groundwork within a year of his return. Momentum then lagged, but the fault here did not immediately lie with Pole. The irony is not that he failed to discover the counter-reformation, but that he did and Paul IV refused to give him credit.

---

[319] Salvatore Caponetto, ed., *Il 'beneficio di Cristo' con le versione del secolo XVI, documenti e testimonianze* (Florence, DeKalb, IL and Chicago: Sansoni, Northern Illinois University Press and The Newberry Library, 1972), pp. 155–206.

[320] Pogson, pp. 32 and 34.

[321] 'Piety', p. 203. But cf. *Reign*, p. 303 where Loades says that Philip's quarrel with Paul IV did not wreck Pole's work, 'but it was severely damaged because he had made so much contingent upon correct legal and administrative procedures'.

8

Temporal and spiritual war

Aᴛᴛᴇʀ ᴛʜᴇ ʙᴜʀsᴛ of effort on his preaching in 1556, Pole had little time to write, and during the remaining two years of his life produced only one more discursive work other than sermons.[1] As a wealthy man he could afford to engage in other kinds of work, including the building of a new wing at Lambeth Palace. Both his writing and probably his building were intended as responses to Paul IV. Lambeth emphasized his archiepiscopal status as a counterweight to the pope, the writing, an 'Apologia', his role as a cardinal in correcting him. Throughout the final eighteen months of his life, despite the demands of trying to implement the synod's decrees and administer the English church, all the while taking an important role in the government, relations with Rome dominated Pole's life. They were largely determined by war between Philip and the pope. Whatever Paul's differences with Pole in the past, this brought the two to open rupture.[2] The war helped to trigger an investigation of Pole by the Inquisition that led to the withdrawal of his legation and severely damaged his efforts to restore the English church.

This story turns on the pope's behaviour. Characterized by one of the twenti-eth-century's leading historians as 'to all intents insane during his pontificate' and nearly universally as an 'intransigent' and violently anti-Spanish, the pope is

---

[1] The chapter title is derived from Carnesecchi's witty if bitter *bon mot* that 'Così finita la guerra temporale, pare che si dia principio a una spirituale, acciò che il mondo non habbia a stare otioso'. *PC*, p. 217.

[2] Heinrich Lutz, *Christianitas afflicta. Europa, das Reich und die päpstliche Politik im Niedergang der Hegemonie Kaiser Karls V. 1552–1556* (Göttingen: Vandenhoeck and Rupprecht, 1964), p. 380; *ERP*, 1, p. 44;

[Matthew Parker?], *De antiquitate britannicae ecclesiae* (London: [John Daye], 1572), p. 421; and Nicholas Pocock, ed., *The history of the reformation of the church of England by Gilbert Burnet* (Oxford: Clarendon Press, 1865; 7 vols.), 2, p. 565. Cf. also David Loades, *The reign of Mary Tudor: politics, government and religion in England 1553–1558*, 2nd ed. (London and New York: Longman, 1991), p. 365.

usually regarded as inflexible, rigorous, and certain from the first of what he meant to do.[3] As we have seen, at least that last point does not apply to his earlier relations to Pole. As I shall argue here, it is not adequate even when Paul was trying to drag Pole to Rome to try him as a heretic. The Venetian ambassador in Rome, Bernardo Navagero, observed the pope carefully for many years and his description deserves careful consideration.[4] Although he began by noting both that Paul had been elected 'against the will of all the cardinals, who feared his nature' and also that he was 'choleric and scorching hot', Navagero continued with a major contradiction by saying that there was 'an incredible gravity and grandeur in all his actions, and truly he seems born to rule [*signoreggiare*]'. He handled all matters 'vehemently' and did not brook contradiction. Navagero repeated how 'vehement' the pope was before observing that he was *veementissimo* in the Inquisition. The worst offence anyone could cause him was to recommend a suspect. He had to be dealt with very delicately, because once he had been 'sweetened', then it was difficult for him to deny the request. As ambassador, Navagero had constantly to adjust to the moment and could never go in with a fixed agenda. In other words, the pope could be manipulated and made to change his mind. Cardinal Carafa, thought Navagero, had mastered this trick. But even after all his evidence of the pope's changeability, Navagero still noted that he was determined to prevent Morone or Pole from succeeding him. This may be true, but the path Paul followed took many deviations.

At the moment of the new pope's election, such an outcome looked hard to predict, at least Pole sounded almost as optimistic about Paul's reign as he had about Marcellus's. As he wrote the new pope in April 1556, he was pleased with his efforts at reform and encouragement for Pole's work in England. Both in Rome and in England, he faced daunting problems, but like the pope beginning with the curia, he had progress to report at the top.[5] With the help of Bernardino Scotti's prayers, for which he thanked the pope's right-hand man, he expected success.[6] Paul IV's reaction is not recorded, and in a possibly ominous sign for the future, the synod's statutes aroused little response in Rome. More disquieting was the momentum towards war. Since at least the previous October Cardinal Carafa had been trying to bring the pope to attack the emperor, whose son Philip was making increasingly threatening gestures towards

[3] G. R. Elton, *Reformation Europe 1517–1559* (New York: Harper, 1963), p. 207.

[4] Eugenio Albèri, *Le relazioni degli ambasciatori veneti al Senato* (Florence: Insegna di Clio and others, 1839–63; 15

vols.), ser. 2, 3, pp. 369–416, pp. 379–80, 382, 384, and 414.

[5] *CRP*, no. 1544.

[6] *CRP*, no. 1545.

papal territory.[7] The pope had begun by insisting that he wanted peace, but that Charles and Philip had to acknowledge themselves his subjects.[8] When he called the imperial, English, and Venetian ambassadors in on 8 October, he treated them to a harangue on the horrors of the Sack of Rome, the prerogatives of the holy see, and a history of those who had dared to attack the first city of the world.[9] The Sack loomed large in Paul's imagination, even as his intentions changed almost daily.[10] A week after this audience he called Spaniards Marranos and threatened to punish them all. His nephew the count of Montorio persuaded him to calm down and have a reconciliation dinner with a Spanish cardinal he had offended, but at the same time Cardinal Capodiferro, one of the leading members of the imperial party, left Rome, annoyed that Paul had taken away the legation of Romagna and begun an investigation of him.[11]

In November the pope took his first overt action and revoked the legations of all nuncios and legates in Charles's and Philip's territories, with one exception.[12] This was Pole's, and Paul explicitly confirmed it.[13] Was this a mark of signal favour or a not very subtle warning that Pole came next? I am inclined to the first view, especially since Paul had several times tried to get Pole back to Rome and this would seem the perfect opportunity. At the same time, he told the emperor's new ambassador that although he wished peace, 'God's secrets are most inscrutable and one cannot resist his providence and inspiration, and we always allow ourselves to be conducted by what His divine majesty is pleased to inspire us [to do].'[14] A week later he assured Navagero that peace was certain. The pope's statement probably failed to reassure anyone, since Paul said he meant real peace, and found none of the imperial proposals acceptable.[15] Two weeks later the pope's hopes had increased and he intended to send peace nuncios to the monarchs as soon as possible. The pope put the threat of war down to Italians with too much ambition, probably meaning especially Alessandro Farnese, one of the targets of another measure Paul took at the same time when he proposed to revoke regresses to benefices.[16]

---

[7] ASVe:APR, 8, fos. 4r and 24v. All references to this source are to Bernardo Navagero's dispatches, including some to the Dieci, many of which do not appear in *CSPV*. See also the summary in Maria Rodríguez-Salgado, *The changing face of empire: Charles V, Philip II, and Habsburg authority* (Cambridge: Cambridge University Press, 1988), pp. 139–51.

[8] ASVe:APR, 8, fo. 7r.

[9] ASVe:APR, 8, fo. 9v (*CSPV*, 6:1, no. 242).

[10] ASVe:APR, 8, fo. 24v.

[11] ASVe:APR, 8, fo. 19r.

[12] ASVe:APR, 8, fo. 35v.

[13] *CRP*, no. 1471.

[14] ASVe:APR, 8, fo. 45v.

[15] ASVe:APR, 8, fos. 47r and 48r.

[16] ASVe:APR, 8, fos. 62r–3r and 58v for regresses.

The pope eventually sent his nephew Carlo as peace legate. This might have proved an advantage to the imperialists and the proponents of peace in Rome, principally the Venetians, had Philip not pursued a strategy extremely danger-ous to Pole. In an attempt to end the crisis, Philip had announced in February 1556 that he would settle for a truce, which he thought Pole's efforts and those of Philip's ambassador in Rome could make the pope accept.[17] This conjunction reduced Pole to the status of one of Philip's agents, an obvious provocation. Worse, the pope strongly objected to Philip's ambassador in Rome, and Morone asked Pole several times to have him replaced. Pole tried, including sending the king a strongly worded letter against going to war.[18] Morone wrote infrequently, but when he did, the news was usually disturbing. On one occasion, Paul had just treated him to a long disquisition on Milanese tyranny against 'ecclesiastical liberty' in interfering with the Inquisition. Morone admitted the truth of the charge, but tried his best to stay out of the affair while still asking Pole to inter-vene with Philip, as he once again energetically did, and on the pope's behalf.[19] Nevertheless, Morone assured Pole that he would continue to work for peace, however dangerous that might be. The times were strange.[20]

One sign of just how strange was the opening of the Inquisition's formal investigation of Davidico.[21] He claimed intimacy with Pole and his household, one of whom joked with him that Davidico was a spy.[22] He may have been. If so, he targeted Priuli. All he could say of Pole was that he had once twitted Davidico about constantly putting points of doctrine to him. Davidico offered three other witnesses to support his testimony, among them Pole's client Girolamo da Ponte. About Priuli Davidico had shocking revelations, especially his dependence on astrology and prophecy to predict who would be pope. Davidico claimed that Priuli had a century-old prophecy of the angelic pope who would be Pole. He provided a highly circumstantial description of another book of similar prophecies, decorated with a miniature of a consistory presided over by Pole, surrounded by doves and angels and various inscriptions, including one identifying him as 'the true Israelite' of John 1:47. Davidico alleged that Priuli several times expected Julius to die and be replaced effortlessly by Pole.[23]

Davidico's testimony may in part have arisen from sour grapes after his dedication to Pole of *Gioiello del vero Christiano* in 1552 failed to gain a reward.

---

[17] ASVe:APR, 8, fo. 132r.
[18] *CRP*, nos. 1531, 1582, and 1589.
[19] *CRP*, no. 1615.
[20] *CRP*, no. 1582.
[21] Dario Marcatto, *Il processo inquisitoriale di Lorenzo Davidico (1555–1560). Edizione*

critica (Florence: Olschki, 1992) and Massimo Firpo, *Nel labirinto del mondo. Lorenzo Davidico tra santi, eretici, inquisitori* (Florence: Olschki, 1992).
[22] *Processo Davidico*, pp. 105–7.
[23] *Ibid.*, pp. 122–7 and 130–1.

The inquisitors thought little of him.[24] It is possible none the less that an effort was then underway to plant spies around Pole. Although the 'Messer Mariano' Davidico called as witness to his efforts to bring his concerns to Paul IV cannot be Pole's dependant Mariano Vittori, Vittori may have been a spy all the same.[25] This supposition rests on his likely identification with Mariano Pier Vettori da Rieti, leader of the *giovanelli* in Siena in 1539 and principal attacker of Aonio Paleario.[26] The summary of Paleario's *processo* included information from 'Marianus Petrus Victorius de Riete, priest . . . (he was alive in 1560 and in Cardinal Morone's service)'.[27] Vittori's transfer to Morone's service from Pole's probably clinches the identity.[28] If Heinrich Lutz's supposition is correct that the register of Pole's correspondence once in the archives of the Roman Inquisition came from a spy, Vittori could have been he.[29]

While the diplomatic situation worsened almost by the day, Pole sat without worthwhile orders from Rome. Paul grumbled through Morone about the arrangements for clerical taxation that Pole had made, and ordered that in the future they be remitted to Rome, but said little about how Pole should deal with Philip.[30] Pole congratulated his replacement as peace legate, Carlo Carafa's man Scipione Rebiba, but Rebiba barely went through the motions before his mission failed (nor did Pole ever know what it was).[31] Dark and dim though things might look, Pole planned a mission to Rome. Instead he sent a mildly worded letter, assuring Paul that he had once more spoken to the king.[32] Mary tried to

---

[24] *PM*, 6, p. 157. Firpo, *Labirinto*, pp. 106 and 240.

[25] *Processo Davidico*, p. 75. Vittori arrived in Rome too late for Davidico to have spoken to him *questo maggio*, unless he made such a stealthy entrance that Morone did not know of it. He wrote Pole of Mariano's arrival only on 13 June. *CRP*, no. 1615.

[26] Salvatore Caponetto, *Aonio Paleario e la riforma protestante in Toscana* (Turin: Claudiana, 1979), pp. 62–3.

[27] Benedetto Fontana, 'Sommario del processo di Aonio Paleario', *Archivio della R. società romana di storia patria*, 19 (1896), pp. 151–75, p. 163.

[28] See the interrogation of Nicolò Franco, a member of Morone's household along with Pole's former servants Faita and Michele Fachetto. Angelo Mercati, *I costituti di Nicolò Franco* (Vatican City: Biblioteca

Apostolica Vaticana, 1955), p. 179; cf. *PC*, p. 411. See also Angelo Sacchetti Sassetti, *La vita e gli scritti di M. Vittori* (Rieti: Trinchi, 1917), pp. 14–16 and 30ff.

[29] *NB*, 15, pp. XC–XCII.

[30] *CRP*, no. 1624.

[31] *CRP*, no. 1629; cf. *NB*, 15, p. 328n. The only certainty to emerge from Rebiba's mission was his deep distrust of Muzzarelli, which cannot have helped Pole in Rome. ACDFSO, St. st. Q 4-ff, e.g., fo. xiiv a cypher to Cardinal Carafa, 5 August 1556, the following letter to Carafa's brother the duke of Paliano, and other letters to Muzzarelli himself complaining of a lack of response. Cf. *NB*, 15, p. 319n for the question of whether the appointments on 10 April of Rebiba and Carafa meant a tacit cancellation of Pole's powers for peace.

[32] *CRP*, no. 1654.

mediate, although Morone thought it inexpedient to present her letter.[33] Pole knew that fortifications were going up in Rome under the direction of Orsini, Paul IV's leading general.[34] He also knew only too well that an open rupture between king and pope would leave him in an impossible position, the more so in that Mary had left the government in his hands.[35] Michiel even reported in his *relazione* that Mary hoped Pole could fix the country's finances.[36]

Pole's concern increased throughout the autumn, until the outbreak of open war left no alternative but prayer.[37] Philip continued to promise that he would come to England as soon as he could.[38] Paul did not approve of Pole's contacts with Philip. Although he endorsed the way in which Pole had conducted himself, he told Morone that he could not see how any Christian could stay on good terms with a heretic. Pole should break off any discussions and return to Rome at once. Morone had known what the pope would say, and had tried to avoid having it written to England. Throughout he consulted Scotti. Paul refused to climb down as long as he thought his honour threatened.[39] Finally, still without instructions from Rome, Pole dispatched Pyning as his representative in early December.[40] In addition to prodding the pope to write, Pyning was to arrange for the expedition of the English bishoprics and attend to the English hospice, of which Pole was still protector.[41] He probably carried a long letter exhorting the pope to make peace.[42] On the way he diverted to Venice, where he saw Cardinal Carafa.[43] This led to Carafa's recall to Rome, where Pyning had an audience on 1 January.[44] As the war in Italy escalated Morone's bulletins became more and more depressing, even when he reported diplomatic initiatives.[45] Paul's attitude to Mary was also changing, since he had been informed that she neither regretted the war nor refused financial assistance to Philip, and as a result the pope had almost resolved not to do anything more for England. Pole insisted that Paul was acting on rumours and his actions threatened to destroy the church.[46]

Since August the event that would lead to Pole's undoing had been in train: Philip's return. Pole was originally to meet the king at Canterbury, where he had meant already in June 1556 to go for as long as possible after Philip's return, but

---

[33] *CSPV*, 6:1, nos. 525 and 538; *CRP*, no. 1658.

[34] ASVe:APR, 9, fo. 10r (*CSPV*, 6:1, no. 599) and *CRP*, no. 1658.

[35] *CRP*, no. 1680 and *CSPV*, 6:1, no. 525.

[36] *CSPV*, 6:2, p. 1057.

[37] *CRP*, nos. 1729–30.

[38] *CRP*, no. 1764.

[39] *CRP*, no. 1778.

[40] *CRP*, no. 1783.

[41] *CSPV*, 6, no. 752.

[42] *CRP*, no. 1784.

[43] *CRP*, nos. 1804 and 1856.

[44] ASVe:APR, 9, fo. 107v (*CSPV*, 6, no. 781).

[45] *CRP*, no. 1789.

[46] *CRP*, no. 1794.

Philip vetoed that suggestion.[47] Pole tried hard to hold the mean between Philip and Cardinal Carafa.[48] In February 1557, he assured the cardinal that Philip wished nothing more than to obey the pope, and perhaps more important to the cardinal, that the Carafa family could expect good things from him.[49] About a month later Philip arrived in England, after Pole had offered to work on Philip for peace if the pope wished. Paul evidently did not.[50] Instead of following through on his offer, Pole went to Canterbury for Lent, after absenting himself from court on Philip's arrival.[51] Pole informed Rome of his scrupulosity.[52] He stayed in Canterbury as long as he could before being ordered back to court on pain of disgrace, and continued to stay away as much as possible.[53] It was well that he did, as Ferrante Gonzaga's arrival plainly indicated that Philip's war council was assembling.[54] Pole withdrew in order to avoid as papal legate meeting Philip, but this removed him from the leadership of the peace group at the crucial moment.[55]

This was not the only unfortunate result of Pole's painstakingly correct behaviour. Probably in early April he wrote Paul admitting that while he had avoided seeing Philip officially, he had met him in private.[56] According to the Venetian ambassador in France, not the most reliable source, because of his fear of Paul IV, Pole snuck into Philip's chamber at night and proposed a new peace plan.[57] Probably at the same time, Pole drafted a letter from Mary to the pope, defending Philip's help in restoring obedience and hoping that Paul would find a way 'to console the whole Christian people along with me'.[58] It has been thought that Pole's actions formed part of the Venetian campaign for peace, but Venetian dispatches from England reveal that Pole knew nothing of

---

[47] *CSPV*, 6, nos. 505, 580, and 594.

[48] Alberto Aubert, *Paolo IV Carafa nel guidizio della età della controriforma* (Città di Castello: Tiferno Grafica, 1990), p. 112 argues that Carafa, Morone, and Pole were all after peace in the second half of 1556, and that only the pope stood for war.

[49] *CRP*, no. 1856.

[50] *CSPV*, 6, no. 843n and ASVe:APR, 9, fo. 152r.

[51] ASP, Carteggio Farnese Estero, Paesi Bassi, b. 106, fasc. 1550–5, fo. 3r says Pole left on 12 April, but E. Harris Harbison, *Rival ambassadors at the court of Queen Mary* (Princeton: Princeton University Press, 1940), p. 322 gave the date of 29 March; cf. ASVe:Dispacci degli ambasciatori al

senato, Inghilterra, 1, fo. 230r (hereafter ASVe:DASI; *CSPV*, 6, no. 847).

[52] BAV, Barb. lat. 5806, fo. 141r.

[53] ASVe:APR, 10, fo. 30v (*CSPV*, 6:2, no. 910). Pole was certainly still in Canterbury the first part of May. *CRP*, no. 1956. ASVe:DASI, 1, fo. 264r (*CSPV*, 6, no. 924).

[54] *CSPV*, 6, no. 852.

[55] Harbison, p. 322 and David Loades, *Mary Tudor. A life* (Oxford: Blackwell, 1989), p. 276.

[56] This letter is missing, but referred to on 8 May as having been written about a month earlier. ASVe:APR, 9, fo. 168r (*CSPV*, 6:2, no. 880).

[57] *CSPV*, 6, no. 858, p. 1015 and no. 862.

[58] *CRP*, no. 1939.

it.[59] Indeed, after the decision for war was taken, the Venetians repeatedly approached Pole without success.[60] Pole endorsed the war, even though he had to be recalled from Croydon for the discussions.[61] He justified himself in part by the arrest of Morone, whom Philip had charged to handle peace negotiations in Rome, although the Venetian ambassador tried to assure Pole that Morone's arrest happened before he received Philip's commission.[62] Far from being involved in the Venetian mediation, Pole needed it himself.

The crisis came to a head in April 1557. At the very time that Pole met Philip, Paul IV withdrew Pole's legation. It came as part of another general revocation of legates in Philip's territory, but this time Pole was singled out to lose his powers, including those of *legatus natus*.[63] The English ambassador in Rome, Edward Carne, reacted by approaching Morone through Pyning, and Morone advised him that Mary should write on his behalf rather than leaving it to Pole's agents.[64] Whether he knew it, Morone was deeply compromised, and his troubles were becoming Pole's, if it is possible to resolve this particular chicken-and-egg problem. On 24 April, Angelo Cattani da Diacceto deposed before the Inquisition, nominally against Morone, but his most damaging points concerned Pole, even though it sounds as if he was trying to defend him.[65] Cattani testified that he had never understood what Pole believed about works, despite numerous attempts to sound him out. Given the pace of the Inquisition's activities it is a little surprising that the revocation was delayed, but not that the Inquisition took charge of it.[66] It met on unusual days and under tight secrecy, Navagero thought because it was working on Philip's deprivation. It had achieved nearly all-inclusive competence, since it also concerned itself with a dispensation for the remarriage of Constable Montmorency's son.[67] Still, English business involving the legation proceeded, several bishoprics going through consistory.[68]

Although Paul IV has never been described as mercurial, this seems the only

---

[59] Hypothesized by Lutz, *Christianitas*, p. 465. *CSPV*, 6, no. 681 and ASVe:DASI, 1, fo. 238r (*CSPV*, 6, no. 863). For the Venetian campaign, in addition to Lutz, see ASM:AG, b. 1929, fo. 761 and b. 571 (Fiandra), unfoliated, Annibale Litolfi-Sabino Calandra, London, 7 and 16 June 1557, etc.

[60] ASM:AG, b. 571, unfoliated, Annibale Litolfi-duke of Mantua, London, 17, 19, 24 June, and 1 July.

[61] ASVe:DASI, 1, fo. 264r (*CSPV*, 6:2, no. 924).

[62] ASVe:DASI, 1, fo. 282r (*CSPV*, 6:2, no. 952; partially printed in *PM*, 5, p. 277 from a different source in the ASVe).

[63] *CT*, 2, p. 306; *CSPFor*, p. 292; ASVe:APR, 9, fo. 158r (*CSPV*, 6:2, no. 855); *ibid.*, fo. 159r (no. 856).

[64] *CSPFor*, no. 589.

[65] *PM*, 6, pp. 262–5.

[66] *CSPFor*, pp. 301 and 304.

[67] ASVe:APR, 9, fo. 167r (*CSPV*, 6:2, no. 879).

[68] *CRP*, no. 1974.

adjective adequate to his behaviour now. As strange as it may seem to suggest that Paul did not have his mind entirely made up about Pole, it may seem even stranger to allege that Cardinal Carafa tried to prevent the revocation, but he told Navagero just that.[69] On 12 May, Carne, again on Morone's advice and at the cardinals' direction, had audience with the pope.[70] Before Carne could say much, Paul referred to a letter from Pole about peace, and blamed the revocation directly on Philip. (Paul made even more out of Pole's letter in Navagero's rendering. It cannot be certainly identified, but is probably that of December 1556.[71] Paul must have objected to it because it passed beyond exhortation to telling the pope his job.) If Mary would write on Pole's behalf, Paul would restore the legation. Carne begged the pope not to publish the revocation, but Paul replied that what was done was done. Carne then tried to induce him to modify it and exclude England, but the pope countered that nothing proposed in full consistory could be changed. There was yet hope. Paul directed Carne to ask Cardinal Alvarez to propose the matter in the Congregation of the Inquisition, to meet the next day. Discussion took up the whole sitting, and the cardinals left Paul to answer Carne. On the 15th Carne returned to find the pope refusing to revoke his decree while saying he would wait to hear from Mary, ordering the secretary of the breves not to issue the revocation without an express order. Navagero filed two similar reports, adding that the writing of the decree was in Cardinal de' Medici's hands, Cardinal Puteo being ill. When de' Medici asked the pope how to draw up the document, the pope told him to exclude the *legatus natus* attached to Canterbury and to keep the matter secret.[72]

On 22 May Morone's *maestro di casa*, Domenico Morando, was arrested.[73] Three days later, Pole wrote the pope another ill-advised letter that like his December lecture manifests a condescending attitude, but he may never have sent it, substituting a tamer one to Cardinal Carafa.[74] After recounting the reaction of the bishops and the council to the revocation, Pole said he had assured them that Paul would restore his legation. Pole consoled others by telling them that God was testing their obedience. He closed by promising the pope to co-operate with a new legate, but a new legate there must be. Pole wrote Carafa

---

[69] ASVe:APR, 10, fo. 19r (*CSPV*, 6:2, no. 894, pp. 1101–2). At the same time, Carafa claimed to be trying to help Carnesecchi. Massimo Firpo and Dario Marcatto, eds., *I processi inquisitoriali di Pietro Carnesecchi (1557–1567)*, 1, *I processi sotto Paolo IV e Pio IV (1557–1561)* (Vatican City: Archivio Segreto Vaticano, 1998),

pp. XX, XXV, XXIX.
[70] *CSPFor*, no. 606.
[71] *CRP*, no. 1783.
[72] ASVe:APR, 10, fo. 11r (*CSPV*, 6:2, no. 889) and fo. 12r (no. 890).
[73] ASVe:APR, 10, fo. 22v (*CSPV*, 6:2, no. 898; partially printed in *PM*, 5, p. 227).
[74] *CRP*, no. 2010.

thanking him for news of the pope's goodwill, and reported that he had persuaded Philip to send a new representative as soon as he knew the substitute was acceptable. Mary would also be an excellent instrument for patching things up. Then Pole descended to flattery. The restoration of obedience was to the house of Carafa's credit, and the pope should add to it a stable peace. Pole told Carafa of his letter to the pope, and also that the council had concluded that, since Pyning had brought no orders for Pole in late May, Paul had decided not to remove the legation.[75] The lack of any breves Pole put down to God's goodness. All the same, he would have obeyed immediately, had they come. The closing struck a different note than the letter to Paul. The legation, wrote Pole, was not something he wanted, causing nothing but work and expense, and the only thing motivating him was 'the zeal that I am obligated to have for religion, and his holiness's authority and of that holy see'. Instead of veiled threats, Pole tried disabling. Whatever his strategy, he thought the moment of greatest danger had almost passed. Pole, allegedly the non-political animal, included in the same packet for Rome letters to Cardinal Pacheco, head of the imperial party, reporting that he had done the favour asked, and to Cardinal de' Medici, another leading imperialist and number two in the congregation of the Inquisition, as well as to Cardinal Vitelli, congratulating him on his promotion.[76] Pole covered all his bases. Vitelli would become almost as important to Cardinal Carafa as Scotti was to his uncle.

Others in England displayed less optimism. The queen, the parliament, and the nobility all wrote on Pole's behalf. Unfortunately, we do not know exactly what they said. The only surviving texts were found among Foxe's manuscripts and must therefore be drafts. This is certainly the case with Philip and Mary's letter dated 21 May, since the versions that made it to Rome were dated at least five days later.[77] The king and queen began by emphasizing their restoration of religion. The holy see's support had been a great consolation, and Pole's legation crucial. News of the revocation, still not confirmed, had greatly saddened them. They could not believe that the pope would take away even the *legatus natus*, a prerogative of the kings of England. They begged the pope not to embarrass them and cripple the cause of religion. The other two much longer letters hit the same notes of sadness and damage done.[78]

---

[75] *CRP*, no. 2011.

[76] *CRP*, nos. 2012–14.

[77] John Strype, *Ecclesiastical memorials relating chiefly to religion, and its reformation, under the reigns of King Henry VIII, King Edward VI, and Queen Mary* (Oxford: Clarendon Press, 1816; 3 vols.), 3:2, pp. 474–6 and ASVe:APR, 10, fo. 43r (*CSPV*, 6:2, no. 928) for the date of the letters as received.

[78] Strype, pp. 476–80 and 480ff.

Morone's arrest and the outbreak of war

The damage threatened to worsen with Morone's arrest on 31 May at the same time as Tommaso Sanfelice, one of Pole's allies at Trent.[79] In consistory the next day Paul averred that 'the cause of God' demanded that he no longer put up with a case of heresy notorious since the time of Paul III which he had reopened immediately upon his election.[80] Had the problem been anything else, even a matter of state, he would have continued to tolerate it.[81] The pope also named Pole as a suspect, but made it clear that no one was safe.[82] He intended to make certain that no heretic could become pope nor take part in a council, which Paul sincerely wanted once there was peace.[83] It was quickly thought that Pole was his real target, partly for political reasons.[84] Undoubtedly Morone's arrest marked a major turning point, whether it meant that Paul had really been forced to change his mind again about Pole, as Carraciolo later wrote.[85] But as Navagero said, Paul outdid himself in praising those he had formerly vituperated, and vice versa. The pope could indeed change his mind. Understanding Paul presented real difficulties to many of the cardinals, perhaps most notably Rodolfo Pio, who thought him 'as extravagant and bizarre as any man I had ever known'.[86] Small wonder that those with much less experience of Paul had trouble figuring out what was happening to Pole's legation.

Few had any trouble discerning by early June that the end was imminent. Nevertheless, Paul continued to dither about the legation, or at least pretend to.[87] Although approaching the Inquisition first, the pope insisted on following protocol and making the decision in consistory. This sounds like a classic instance of a ruler looking for an out, and it encouraged Carne.[88] The Inquisition continued to gather evidence, examining Pole's old client Spadafora about his correspondence with Pole in England. Spadafora had allegedly informed Pole frequently about moves against him in Rome, and Pole had

---

[79] ASVe:APR, 10, fo. 30v (*CSPV*, 6:2, no. 910; partially printed in *PM*, 5, p. 229).

[80] Simoncelli, *Caso*, p. 177.

[81] ASVe:APR, 10, fo. 31v (*CSPV*, 6:2, no. 913; partially printed in *PM*, 5, pp. 231–3). Cf. *PM*, 2, pp. 29–30 for a similar report, apparently from a broadsheet.

[82] ASVe:APR, 11, fo. 122r (*CSPV*, 6:2, no. 914).

[83] ASVe:APR, 10, fo. 36r (*CSPV*, 6:2, no. 915; partially printed in *PM*, 5, pp. 241–2).

[84] *PM*, 5, p. 251. Aubert (pp. 100–1) argues

that Paul had used Pole's legation 'instrumentally' in order to mask his rapprochement with France, and from the beginning of his reign had kept Julius's agents in place for the same reason.

[85] *PM*, 1, p. 143.

[86] Aubert, p. 77.

[87] ASVe:APR, 10, fo. 45r (*CSPV*, 6:2, no. 930).

[88] ASVe:APR, 10, fo. 50r (*CSPV*, 6:2, no. 932).

replied that matters had to wait until results appeared in England 'and how [Pole] persecutes heretics, if that could clear up whether he was a Lutheran, or not'. Spadafora was an old suspect, but new ones were not lacking, including Pio's vicar in Loreto.[89] Finally, Paul hit on a way to solve his problem, making use of the opportunity Pole had presented him by his promise to co-operate with a new legate. On 14 June Paul named William Peto to replace Pole. The news so astounded Carne that he refused to report it to Mary, telling the pope he would have to do it himself. The pope stubbornly refused to listen to any of Carne's objections, rejecting even the point of fact that Peto was not Mary's confessor. Paul especially praised him for his help about heresy, joining a select group that had assembled at his house every day (at an unknown time). In the same consistory a coadjutor for Brescia was appointed, the pope scorning Priuli's *accesso*.[90] Observers concluded that the pope wished to proceed against 'this sect of England', and Navagero alleged solid evidence that Priuli was one of the pope's main targets. Pole's Roman agent Antonio Giberti told him that a *processo* was being prepared.[91]

The pace of events accelerated. On the day of the consistory, Morone presented his 'Apologia' to the inquisitors. Part of it addressed what he knew of Pole's views on justification.[92] He remembered having been given a writing of Pole's by Marcantonio Flaminio or Priuli, but whether before Trent's decree or after he could not remember. He knew that Pole had wished to reduce the decree's bulk. In conversation Pole emphasized the nothingness of humans which arose from original sin. In order to 'mortify the old man', it was necessary to become dead and buried with Christ. 'Newness of life' came principally from

---

[89] ASVe:APR, 11, fo. 123v (*CSPV*, 6:2, no. 933; partially printed in *PM*, 5, p. 261); cf. ASVe:APR, 14:2, fo. 7r?

[90] For the persistent Venetian efforts to defend Priuli's claim, see ASVe:APR, 10, fo. 71v (*CSPV*, 6:2, no. 954); ASVe:APR, 11, fos. 124v, 125r (*CSPV*, 6:2, no. 973; orig. in Capi dei Dieci, Dispacci degli ambasciatori, b. 24, no. 57 notwithstanding marginal note on APR 11 that not found amongst original dispatches in Capi del Consiglio dei Dieci, busta 24); ASVe:APR, 11, fo. 44r; and ASVe:APR, 11, fo. 46r. Cardinal Durante thanked Carlo Carafa for his nephew's appointment on 22 June. BAV, Barb. lat. 5710, fo. 18r–v. The legate cardinal Trivulzio reported the Venetians'

annoyance. BAV, Barb. lat. 5713, fo. 37r–v.

[91] ASVe:APR, 10, fo. 52r (*CSPV*, 6:2, no. 937) and fo. 54v (no. 938), together with ASVe:APR, 10, fo. 124r (no. 939). Cf. also *CT*, 2, p. 311; *CSPFor*, no. 637; *CSPSp*, 13, no. 311; *PM*, 5, pp. 266–7. But not all reports were pessimistic. On 19 June Filippo Carnesecchi in Venice wrote his brother Antonio not only that Morone had nothing to worry about, but also that the pope was about to change his mind about Pole, thanks to the letters on his behalf from the king and queen. BAV, Barb. lat. 5805, fos. 203r–5r; partially printed (not including this information) in *PM*, 5, p. 268.

[92] *PM*, 2:1, pp. 460–4.

God's 'charity and grace' through the sacrifice of his son, about which Pole never tired of talking. When Pole discussed secular affairs, he placed so much confidence in divine providence that it amazed Morone. Morone claimed not to know much about Pole's particular beliefs, except that he did not deny purgatory. Unavoidably, Flaminio came up, and Morone remembered that Pole had defended himself by claiming that he was trying to convert Flaminio lest his literary skills serve the wrong ends. Priuli and Seripando knew much more of Pole's doctrine than Morone, he wrote, especially Seripando who had read and revised many of Pole's works. Two of them were found among Morone's papers, *De sacramento*, and *De bonis ecclesiasticis*, both containing important passages on free will, predestination, and purgatory.[93]

Even without that harmful discovery, Morone had probably said enough, and the pope's mind was finally made up, or nearly so. On 20 June the breve recalling Pole and replacing him with Peto was written.[94] The pope alleged that Pole was included in the general recall of cardinals to Rome, nothing more. The breve was not dispatched until the 28th, and Paul made unknown changes in the interval.[95] The news had already reached England. Pole later said that Mary had received Carne's dispatch while escorting Philip to Dover, between 3 and 5 July.[96] Pole would never see the breve, since first Philip and then Mary prevented its delivery.[97] Instead, the queen again wrote the pope telling him that she knew the state of England better than he and that Peto did not want the job.[98] Mary bluntly charged that the revocation proceeded from ignorance or at least lack of consultation. If it were confirmed, 'we will for just causes regret our piety toward the apostolic see' (*[d]olemus iustis de causis pietatem nostram erga sedem Apostolicam*). Since Mary continued that the bishops would take the same attitude, she not very subtly threatened another schism. The letter chiefly consisted of an encomium of Pole's unique virtues that made him far

---

[93] Giberti in conversation with Navagero. ASVe:APR, 10, fo. 61r (*CSPV*, 6:2, no. 945; partially printed in *PM*, 5, p. 275). For the works, see *CPM*.

[94] *CRP*, no. 2048.

[95] *CSPFor*, no. 641.

[96] *CRP*, no. 2076, fo. 396r and Loades, *Mary*, p. 291.

[97] *PC*, p. 219; *ERP*, 1, p. 45; *CRP*, no. 2076, fo. 397r.

[98] ASM:AG, b. 571 (Fiandra), unfoliated, Annibale Litolfi–duke of Mantua, Brussels, 29 July 1557, which reads like a summary of the queen's letter. The English were again co-ordinating their efforts with the Mantuans, as the copies of both Mary's and Peto's July letters amongst Cardinal Gonzaga's correspondence indicate. ASM:AG, b. 1929, fo. 781 and fos. 783r–4v. Mary's letter was received in Rome by 3 August. ASVe:APR, 10, fo. 107r–v (*CSPV*, 6:2, no. 981, misdated 5 August). Cf. Loades, *Reign*, p. 366 and *CSPFor*, no. 655, p. 327.

the best legate. Despite her hard-line attitude, Mary did break down and give Pole the news.[99] When he found out, he begged the queen to let him go, showing due obedience to the pope.[100]

Carne continued to badger Paul, but made little progress even after presenting Mary's letter on 7 August.[101] Three weeks later he still awaited an answer.[102] The English had become nervous enough to make contingency plans. Mary ordered Carne to assure the pope that were Pole a heretic, she would be his worst enemy, but the trial had to be conducted in England. The queen doubted Pole's guilt, while again insisting on an English venue for a trial. If her demands were rejected, Carne was to be recalled, making a public protest if possible before he left Rome. Cardinal Alvarez tried to pressure the pope into meeting Mary's demands, but Paul refused to be cowed and cut him off. Other cardinals suggested strongly to Carne that he employ finesse in the hopes that things would improve, especially in the case of an eighty-one-year-old pope.[103] The next meeting of the Congregation of the Inquisition did nothing, either, since four cardinals, three of them imperialists, absented themselves, giving Paul another excuse for delay.[104]

The pope did not drag his feet on the score of arrests, skipping the usual August lull in Rome. Cardinal du Bellay's theologian, Cardinal Bertano's secretary, and one of Farnese's servants were all incarcerated.[105] Their cases were not exactly alike. Bertano's secretary was charged either with heresy or with sodomy, and Farnese's man certainly with sodomy, his 'ganimede' being picked up as well.[106] These two arrests probably had no political overtones, since Bertano and Farnese were enemies. Rather, they were part of Paul's campaign against sodomy and sexual sins in general. Whores and sodomy came second and third in Paul's *bandi* for 1555, preceded only by blasphemy.[107] Carne thought Bertano likely to follow his secretary, since he was 'imperial for the life, as men say commonly', although this may only have represented how little Carne knew.[108] These arrests could have struck close to home for Pole when Giberti was delated

[99] *CRP*, no. 2076, fo. 396v.
[100] *PC*, p. 219.
[101] ASVe:APR, 10, fo. 113v (*CSPV*, 6:2, no. 983).
[102] ASVe:APR, 10, fo. 134r (*CSPV*, 6:2, no. 1003).
[103] ASVe:APR, 10, fo. 117v (*CSPV*, 6:2, no. 991).
[104] ASVe:APR, 10, fo. 124v (*CSPV*, 6:2, no. 996) and fo. 132v (no. 1002).
[105] *PM*, 5, p. 295. For du Bellay's theologian, see Gladys Dickinson, *Du Bellay en Rome* (Leiden: Brill, 1960), p. 148.
[106] *PM*, 5, pp. 295 and 349.
[107] ASV, A. A. I–XVIII 6544, fos. 15r–18r. Cf. Simoncelli, *Caso*, p. 151.
[108] *PM*, 5, p. 296.

to him in February 1558 in terms which make it appear that his behaviour may have drawn similar attention to him as to Bertano's and Farnese's men. A now unfortunately anonymous correspondent writing from Venice claimed to have been asked by Cardinals de' Medici, Morone, and Scotti to warn Pole, and Cardinals Ranuccio Farnese and Puteo alleged that all Pole's troubles arose 'from the life and evil customs of his friends and servants and from those who still practice in his house'.[109] 'Now this new persecution could also be born from the evil handling and evil living of this young man, malignantly arguing from the servant to the master.' He was acting like a student in Padua, not a cardinal's agent in Rome. The writer claimed that he and Ormanetto (to whom he referred Pole for details) had many times admonished Giberti, and that other named individuals joined him in regretting 'that so dissolute life of Messer Antonio'. Whoever the writer was, he knew Pole's circles well, and this should have been a worrying denunciation. Yet Giberti remained in Pole's service, at least handling his finances, although even Priuli, whom the writer called Giberti's *fautor*, came to distrust him.[110]

The 'Apologia'

While Paul filled his prisons, Pole sent Ormanetto to the pope. He reached Rome by 23 August.[111] He had arrived in post in Brussels on 5 August with instructions to tell the pope that Pole would face prison in Rome in order to do what he was ordered, but Ormanetto also had a statement intended to induce the pope to leave him alone.[112] Ormanetto's mission and the 'Apologia' represented a simultaneously submissive and aggressive strategy in Pole's mind, reflected in the divergent statements of Ormanetto's objectives by Beccadelli and Dudic.[113] Almost as soon as Ormanetto reached Rome he saw Cardinal Carafa and executed his instructions by telling him that Pole wanted to show the obedience of a child to its father.[114] Ormanetto had to wait until 4 September to see the pope. On that day the Congregation of the Inquisition

[109] *CRP*, no. 2184.
[110] ASAS, 40/123 (Bonelli, no. 141); 40/131 (no. 153); and 40/135 (no. 157).
[111] *CSPV*, 6:2, no. 999.
[112] ASM:AG, b. 571 (Fiandra), unfoliated, Annibale Litolfi-duke of Mantua, Brussels, 5 August 1557.
[113] *MMB*, 1:2, p. 319; *ERP*, 1, p. 47.
[114] *CSPV*, 6:2, no. 999 and ASVe:APR, 10, fo. 132v (*CSPV*, 6:2, no. 1002). Carne noted his arrival much later, which seems to mean that Ormanetto had not been ordered to co-operate with the English ambassador (*CSPFor*, no. 662).

met at nearly full strength, and Paul was back on bad behaviour. The cardinals favourable to Pole managed to get him to delay taking action until he had heard Ormanetto. Cardinal Scotti invited Ormanetto to see him the following morning, and Carne reported that Scotti expected that the pope would satisfy Mary.[115] In the interval, the pope grudgingly granted Ormanetto audience, breaking his policy of refusing to receive anyone in the evening.[116] Navagero filed a detailed report three days later. Ormanetto, who was very ill, began by telling the pope that Pole had tried to get the pope's messenger to Peto admitted to England.[117] There was great need of a legate, and great danger in any change. Reference to Pole's efforts for religion prefaced what Navagero called a humble complaint about the revocation. Ormanetto did not say anything about Pole's recall, since Pole had not received the breve. The pope began to reply in political terms, blaming the revocation on Philip, but Ormanetto's illness forced him to leave before Paul could say more.[118] The interval between Ormanetto's arrival and his audience was filled up by the fall-out from the battle of St-Quentin, heightened by the duke of Alva's advance on Rome that led Paul IV to think the end of Italy at hand.[119] Pole took advantage of the victory to urge Philip to make peace. Paul was said to have taken this very well.[120] By the same token, Dudic recorded that 'as Ormanetto himself told me, he [the pope] removed all suspicion of depraved religion from Pole, as he said these were evil words of evil men, whose tongues could by no means be contained'.[121] Ormanetto did not take so rosy a view. Two years later he dated the beginning of Pole's troubles now.[122]

If Dudic did not invent his commentary, the pope's positive view, representing another change of mind, must mean that Ormanetto never delivered the 'Apologia'.[123] It opened with a succinct statement of Pole's position. In fully rhetorical fashion Pole asserted that he always based his behaviour on an exemplum except in this case, so novelly did the pope treat him as a cardinal. Contradicting his instructions to Ormanetto, Pole stated that he did not wish

---

[115] *Ibid.*

[116] ASVe:APR, 10, fo. 154r (*CSPV*, 6:2, no. 1018); fo. 168r (no. 1024); and *CSPV*, 6:1, no. 424.

[117] The messenger's travails make a comic opera subplot. In February 1558 he finally left Flanders for Paris, at a loss what to do. BAV, Barb. lat. 5713, fo. 61r–v and Barb. lat. 5717, fos. 28r–9v.

[118] ASVe:APR, 10, fo. 168r–v (*CSPV*, 6:2, no. 1024).

[119] *CSPV*, 6:2, no. 1012.

[120] ASVe:DAS, Spagna, 2, fo. 234r (*CSPV*, 6, no. 998) and *PC*, p. 223.

[121] *ERP*, 1, p. 47.

[122] ASAS, 40/131 (Bonelli, no. 153).

[123] *CRP*, no. 2076. References to the MS given in the text.

to be imprisoned like Morone, whose defence he linked to his own. His only recourse was conscience, on which he relied throughout (fo. 391r–v). Pole did, after all, come up with any number of models, beginning with Adam, but his favourite was St Paul to the pope's Peter, except that Pole did not attack the pope in public (fo. 393v). Pole's first substantive point was that the pope had condemned him unheard, coupled with the injury done to Pole's flock. Although admitting that he had offered to step down on the appointment of a new legate, Pole went on to say that he would have refused to listen to the pope's messenger (fo. 395r–v). He defended himself from having interfered with or ignored Paul's orders, shrugging off the queen and council when they tried to persuade him to pretend he had not been recalled (fos. 396v–98r). At that point he thought to send Ormanetto. Although protesting that the legation was nothing but a burden and he would gladly be rid of it, Pole could not accept the way the pope had treated him (fos. 399r–400r). The ultimate persona then appeared as Pole wrote that he had borne Christ's stigmata and been wounded fighting the heretics. Then it was back to Morone and the offensive discussion of Pole's legation in the Inquisition, rather than consistory (fos. 400v–1v).[124] This reminded Pole of his meeting with Paul at San Paolo-fuori-le-mura and their discussion of Flaminio, which spurred him on to defend himself, as he had threatened to do then (fo. 402r). A story of Carafa's actions in the conclave of Julius III followed, including the tale-within-a-tale of how Pole had saved Carafa's appointment as cardinal (fos. 402v–7v). The original tight organization unravelled further as Pole returned to San Paolo and quoted Carafa's closing words back at him: 'If God grants both of us long enough life to take part in another conclave, you must understand that here this old man (and you pointed at yourself) will make your cause' (fo. 408r). Pole protested that he had given his whole life for the unity of the church and would not suffer in silence mistreatment meted out to a hero of the faith (fos. 409r–10v). He called on God to respond for him (fos. 410bisr–410terr) and accused the pope of being instigated by the devil (fo. 413r–v). Pole was still obligated to obey him, whom no

---

[124] Both Fenlon, p. 269 n6 and Simoncelli, *Caso*, p. 171n put this moment at the beginning of Paul's reign. They support their interpretation with Paul's letter to Philip and Mary of 30 June 1555 in *ERP*, 5, pp. 136–9, but on p. 139 where Pole's legation was confirmed, there is nothing but praise of Pole, and no mention of an inquiry, certainly not by the Inquisition. The moment to which Pole referred must be the consistory of 14 June 1557, when both the *abroganda vel confirmanda* of his legation (as Pole put it, the first of which was never in question in 1555) were discussed in the immediate aftermath of Morone's arrest, as well as the question of Priuli's reversion to Brescia, which Pole said was handled in the same consistory.

one might dare to criticize (fo. 414r–v). But Pole meant the papal office, not the occupant, again turning to Paul's criticism of Peter and adverting to the same collective headship of the church that he had discussed in 'De summo pontifice'.

> Since therefore the cardinals hold the same place with the supreme pontiff in governing the universal church as the apostles did with Peter and the bishops bear the same person in governing individual churches, they ought to obey him as both brothers and servants in Christ and because of Christ, but when they see anything against Christ's honour, they must first admonish him with all humility, and spell out the matter in open words. If he persists, they should criticize him more freely, nor should they agree in such a matter, but resist him to his face. For this establishment of God for his vicar was foreseen, and by his supreme providence.

The cardinals above all are to correct him 'and to advise him permanently, for they are given to him as the keepers of his soul and spies against all ambushes of Satan.... From all this it not only follows that cardinals may freely admonish the pope whenever they know his actions are not of God but of men, but they must also use open words in doing this, for if they do not, his sin will become more serious to Christ' (fos. 415r–16r). Papal inerrancy inhered in the college of cardinals, not the pope. 'Wherefore, for the honour of this college, which Christ's prayer conferred on it, I beg your holiness diligently to consider what is this spirit that has kept that college inviolate for so many centuries through the grace of Christ, in which no one has ever been found to follow any heretical opinion, and pertinaciously defend it' (fo. 418r).

This oligarchical notion of the ecclesiastical constitution did not provide Pole's trump card. This was his faith, the only guarantee of England's restoration, an oblique likening of himself alone, rather than the whole college, to Peter (fo. 419r–v). The two were virtually interchangeable, for after another reference to Paul's rebuke of Peter, Pole said he was no less certain that resistance would be justified. Instead he merely asked the pope whether his actions were inspired by God and what would happen when he impugned the college. Pole concluded that he had used 'the liberty and power' of a cardinal to criticize the pope's human weakness and warn him of dangers to the church. He exhorted the pope to handle his and Morone's innocence charitably.

This is a remarkable document that fits all too well Pole's pattern of writing in place of direct confrontation, and then discarding the writing. In fact, that was the story Beccadelli told about this work, claiming that Pole had burnt it out of 'sweetness of spirit, nothing desirous of vendetta'.[125] Although Pole may have withheld his broadside, he incorporated much of it into the instructions for subsequent missions to Rome, indicating how deeply he felt the pope's injustices.[126] Nor, unlike some of his works, did he try very hard to keep the 'Apologia' itself secret. Carranza, on the point of leaving England when it was written, Villagarcia, and perhaps de Soto all knew of it, although it is not clear how much they knew, or would admit.[127] Villagarcia said most under interrogation, and he claimed that the work was likely about Pole's non-residence at Canterbury 'more than about matters of the faith'. It is no wonder that Philip's ministers displayed such eagerness to lay hands on the 'Apologia' once their opinion of Pole had changed for the worse.[128]

Lambeth Palace

Perhaps Pole composed the 'Apologia' in his new apartments at Lambeth, probably built in 1556 and 1557. He spent the largest part of his disposable income here, at least £1,000.[129] In his negotiations with English officials over the execution of Pole's will, Priuli twice referred to 'great costs' for building and specified that he had to pay £300 to Pole's successor Matthew Parker, one assumes for dilapidations.[130] The marquess of Winchester reported to Sir William Cecil in August 1559 that Priuli expected shortly to be discharged of the £700 demanded of 'the house of Canterbury', probably meaning Lambeth.[131] Pyning's monthly accounts from January 1556 to March 1557 indicate that the work was divided about equally between those two years, with perhaps the majority done

---

[125] *MMB*, 1:2, p. 326.

[126] Cf. Loades, *Reign*, p. 368.

[127] *Doc. hist.*, 2, pp. 511–13 (Villagarcia) and 883–4 (Fresneda adding de Soto, and therefore perhaps to be taken with a grain of salt).

[128] *Doc. hist.*, 2, pp. 883–4 and 897–8.

[129] The figure specified in Pole's will, *CRP*, no. 2286. Other than perhaps at Clerkenwell priory, the only other building Pole is supposed to have undertaken was the conversion of the almonry chapel at Canterbury into his oratory. E. Eveleigh Woodruff and William Danks, *Memorials of the cathedral and priory of Christ in Canterbury* (London: Chapman and Hall, 1912), p. 302.

[130] ASAS, 40/139 (Bonelli, no. 161); 40/152 (Bonelli no. 175); and LPL, MS 737, fo. 140. A. C. Ducarel, *The history and antiquities of the archiepiscopal palace of Lambeth from its foundation to the present time* (London: J. Nichols, 1785), p. 20, said Parker got either £400 or £600.

[131] *CSPDom*, 1 no. 136.

in 1557, judging from costs.[132] A detailed accounting of the building work to which he referred does not survive. Pole's total came nowhere near the expenditure on Hampton Court, where the annual outlay in the 1530s (before serious inflation) averaged nearly £5,000.[133] It did, however, represent between about 5 and 20 per cent of his gross annual income, and provided the greatest exception to his otherwise 'spiritual' patronage.[134] The account in *De antiquitate Britannicae ecclesiae* claimed that Pole meant to spend much more money *in reficiendo Cantuariensis Palatio* had he not died.[135] To some degree, social class won out over religious principle here, but Pole's display had at least one precedent in his fellow ascetic reformer Egidio da Viterbo's construction of the cloister of Santa Trinità in Viterbo, although that was not exactly his own residence.[136]

De antiquitate described Pole's building as 'that long extension to the east joined to Lambeth palace, and a residence constructed to the east with lower and connected upper stories' ('Illa longa ad orientem extensa ad Lamethanas aedes adiuncta, & ad ortum posita statione cum inferioribus & connexis caenaculis extruenda').[137] Francis Thynne translated this as 'the long gallery of Lambeth on the east side, with the inferior buildings and parlor joined to the same', and Francis Godwin in the final edition of *De praesulibus Angliae commentarius* in the early seventeenth century rephrased *De antiquitate* to say that Pole 'erected a certain "solarium" towards the east at Lambeth and some other nearby buildings' ('solarium quoddam orientem versus Lamethae extruxit, et aedificia nonnulla vicina').[138] Another contemporary said that Pole had built a

---

132 PRO, SP 11/10, fos. 13r–16v shows a total of about £600 for the full year 1556, with bursts of activity in March and November.

133 H. M. Colvin *et al.*, eds., *The history of the king's works*, 4:2, *1485–1660* (London: HMSO, 1982), p. 129.

134 Thomas F. Mayer, 'When Maecenas was broke: Cardinal Pole's "spiritual" patronage', *SCJ*, 27 (1996), pp. 419–35 (now in Thomas F. Mayer, *Cardinal Pole in European context: a via media in the reformation* (Aldershot: Ashgate Publishing, 2000)), and 'Cardinal Pole's finances: the property of a reformer', *ibid.*

135 *De antiquitate Britannicae ecclesiae*, p. 419. For the question of its authorship, see the next chapter, p. 363.

136 Andrea Scriattoli, *Viterbo nei suoi monumenti* (Rome: F.lli Capuccini, 1915–20), p. 314.

137 *De antiquitate*, p. 419.

138 Francis Thynne, 'The cardinals of England' added to Raphael Hollinshead, *Chronicles of England, Scotland and Ireland* (London: J. Johnson, *et al.*, 1807–8; 6 vols., 4, p. 756; Francis Godwin, *De praesulibus Angliae commentarius*, continued and annotated by William Richardson (Cambridge: Joseph Bentham, 1743, 2 vols.; originally published in 1616), p. 151. Louis Dony d'Attichy, *Flores historiae sacri collegii S. R. E. cardinalium*, 3 (Paris: Sebastian Cramoisy, 1660), p. 244 made Godwin's version canonical on the continent.

'new gallery' and put at least one stained-glass window in it.[139] We might therefore safely assume that the 'Gallery' referred to in Parker's will of 1574 was Pole's work.[140] The most likely source to spell out precisely what Pole built – suits in the Court of Arches for dilapidations brought by Pole's successors, especially Parker – have been lost. An inventory of Thomas Cranmer's chattels of 1553 does not treat Lambeth Palace room by room and therefore cannot provide a base-line for determining the extent of Pole's construction.[141]

Between Pole's time and the eighteenth century, I have found no discussion of his work. John Hinton in 1749 faithfully if briefly reflected *De antiquitate*.[142] Francis Grose more or less reproduced its description in 1773, amplifying it slightly to say that Pole built 'the whole site of brick buildings fronting the West, between the Lollards' Tower and the Great Court', and adding the vital information that Pole's motto, 'Estote prudentes sicut serpens et innocentes sicut columbae' was 'painted on some of the windows with the representation of a dove and a serpent'.[143] Grose's claim about the brick-built sections of the Palace cannot be true, since this would have included the medieval chapel and the vestry next to it, which was probably Cranmer's construction. Coltee Ducarel's slightly later history of Lambeth Palace noted Pole's building in the context of the difficulties it caused his successors, but except for citing John Aubrey's certainly mistaken assertion that Pole had built the Gate House (really Cardinal Morton's work), Ducarel did not identify which parts of the Palace Pole erected.[144] Thomas Pennant's guidebooks assigned only the gallery to Pole.[145] Edward Blore in an 1828 report on the state of the Palace contemptu-

[139] James Calfhill, *An answer to John Martiall's Treatise of the cross* (Cambridge: Cambridge University Press, 1846), p. 105.

[140] LPL, MS 737, fo. 142.

[141] PRO, E154/2/39, 41.

[142] *The Universal Magazine of Knowledge and Pleasure... and other Arts and Sciences*, 5 (1749), p. 171.

[143] Francis Grose, *The antiquities of England and Wales* (London: S. Hooper, 1773; 4 vols.), 3, unpaginated, Lambeth Palace, plate II. Cf. also BCQ, MS F. III. 7 m. 1, fo. 44rff for the motto. The representation at Lambeth was the work of Pole's client Marcello (see below p. 352), probably either Fogolino or Venusti. See Thomas F. Mayer, 'Marcello who? An unknown Italian painter in Cardinal Pole's entourage', *Source*, 15 (1996), pp. 22–6.

[144] Ducarel, p. 20. His description of the Long Gallery on pp. 43–4 also says nothing of Pole's involvement.

[145] Thomas Pennant, *Some account of London, Westminster and Southwark* (London: J. C. Stadler (1796); the first edition of 1790 is virtually identical), p. 22 and John Wallis, *London: being a complete guide to the British capital... faithfully abridged from Mr. Pennant's London, and brought down to the present year* (London: Sherwood, Neely and Jones, 1810; 3rd ed.), p. 49.

ously dismissed as 'imaginary' the Long Gallery's connection to Pole, and maintained in any case that subsequent alterations had 'almost entirely obliterated' the room's original character.[146] Since Blore won the contract to replace the old wing and do other work at Lambeth that cost in total better than £50,000, we might suspect a base motive for his summary evaluation. All the same, it looks as if he was right that no documents support Pole's connection to the old wing, at least nothing which specifically identifies what he built. By the twentieth century, even what Blore knew, not to mention the sixteenth-century evidence, had been forgotten and replaced with a mere tradition assigning to Pole the wing east of the Chapel that housed the Long Gallery on its first floor and an open 'verandah' on the ground floor, a description which perhaps by coincidence almost exactly matched that in *De antiquitate*.[147] Despite this collective amnesia, the sixteenth-century descriptions are convincing, and graphic evidence fills them out.

Beginning with the panoramic view of London taken from just above Lambeth Palace attributed to Wenceslaus Hollar, through to a watercolour by Blore, reproductions and plans make it possible to get a good idea of what Pole got for his outlay. Hollar's engraving (illus. 12) helps greatly with the working areas of the Palace, normally left out of account, and also gives an important angle on Pole's wing. The print shows a double building, lodgings sited behind the gallery, with a separate peaked roof. An engraving of the Palace from the northeast by Sparrow dated 1773 (illus. 13), apparently based on an earlier print by the Bucks which I have not been able to see, shows the double building, with a single large round-headed window in the gallery and a pair of what appear to be sash windows in the apartment block behind it. It is unclear whether Pole also built the tower shown in both 'Hollar' and Sparrow. Unfortunately, Sparrow's print does not show the garden front, blocked by a wall. Possibly the earliest view of it is another probably eighteenth-century pen and wash drawing (illus. 14) which may have been part of Blore's dossier. It showed a symmetrical façade, with two pair of windows on the first floor above four arches in a ground floor loggia, flanking a central bay, with seven windows on the first floor and three smaller ones in the ground floor.[148]

---

[146] LPL, MS 3563, fos. 26r–7v.

[147] Dorothy Gardiner, *The story of Lambeth Palace. A historic survey* (London: Constable, 1930), pp. 104–7 and Howard Roberts and W. H. Godfrey, eds., *The parish of St Mary, Lambeth, The survey of London*, 23 (London: LCC, 1951), pp. 88 and 97–9.

[148] Gardiner, p. 101.

12 *After Wenceslaus Hollar: 'Prospect of London and Westminster Taken from Lambeth'. This print must have been touched up by another engraver from Hollar's original since new St Paul's shows up in at least an advanced state of construction and Hollar died in 1677. By permission of the Folger Shakespeare Library.*

LAMBETH PALACE, SURRY.

13 *Engraving of Lambeth Palace from the northeast by Sparrow, 1773. Francis Grose, The antiquities of England and Wales (London: S. Hooper, 1773; 4 vols.), 3, Lambeth Palace, plate II.*

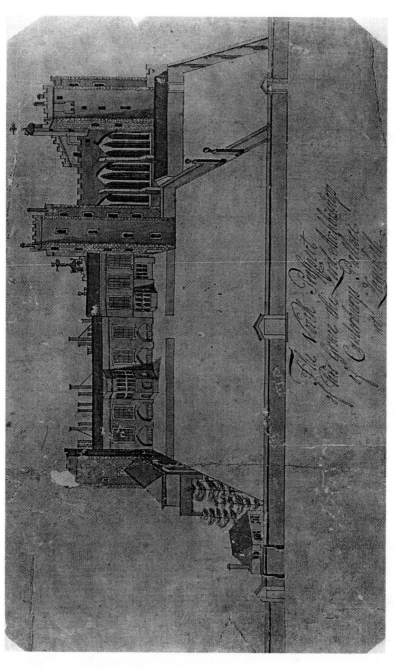

14 Eighteenth-century pen and wash drawing of North Front of Lambeth Palace. LPL, MS 3563, fo. 12. His Grace the Archbishop of Canterbury and the Trustees of Lambeth Palace Library.

15 *Engraving of North Front of Lambeth Palace by Sparrow, 1775. Francis Grose, The antiquities of England and Wales (London: S. Hooper, 1773; 4 vols.), 3, Lambeth Palace, plate III.*

16 *Edward Blore. Watercolour of North Front of Lambeth Palace. LPL, MS 2949/2. His Grace the Archbishop of Canterbury and the Trustees of Lambeth Palace Library.*

The arches are of some importance to assessing the significance of Pole's building. If the loggia were fully Italianate, then they should be round, although hybrid arches were built about the time of Pole's loggia.[149] In the drawing they are four-centred Tudor arches like those for which even Henry VIII had to settle.[150] Probably later if still in the eighteenth century, an engraving of the garden front by Sparrow, published several times by S. Hooper, shows the arches as round (illust. 15). Next, Blore's watercolour (illus. 16) depicted a new structure, a semi-circular bay on the first floor extending from the edges of the innermost windows, with three sash windows in it and two open arches under them, about half the width of the original arches – a less than happy effect – and twin peaked roofs over the Gallery and the lodgings behind, but this time the arches are as distinctly four-centred as they were round in Sparrow's engraving. The central bay was newly built by Archbishop Moore, who had demolished the one seen in the earlier views and replaced it with a 'bow window'.[151] Finally, in the lithograph apparently made from Blore's picture, the arches are nicely pointed.[152]

As Dorothy Gardiner pointed out, this loggia (and by implication its arches) was the most Italianate aspect of Pole's building, one of, if not the first, such loggias in England, and knocks on the head the claim that Italianate taste was a function of Protestant ideology.[153] One of its most Italianate features is its northern orientation, a good idea when shade is at a premium in *bel tempo*, not such a good one when the wind blows straight from the Orkneys. It is possible that Pole derived the inspiration for the loggia from Leon Battista Alberti's *De re aedificatoria*, a copy of which he owned.[154] Alberti said a great deal about

[149] Paula Henderson, 'The loggia in Tudor and early Stuart England: the adaptation and function of classical form', in Lucy Gent, ed., *Albion's classicism: the visual arts in Britain, 1550–1660* (New Haven and London: Yale University Press, 1995), pp. 109–45, e.g., fig. 67.

[150] Colvin, p. 22.

[151] Pennant, p. 22.

[152] LPL, Print XIII/9.

[153] Thomas Wolsey's Long Gallery added to Hampton Court by 1517 may be a precedent. Simon Thurley, 'The domestic building of Cardinal Wolsey', in S. J. Gunn and Philip Lindley, eds., *Cardinal Wolsey. Church, state and art* (Cambridge: Cambridge University Press, 1991),

pp. 76–102, p. 88 and fig. 6. Malcolm Airs alleged that Protestants beginning with Protector Somerset monopolized Italianate style, e.g., in his piece 'Architecture', in Boris Ford, ed., *The Cambridge guide to the arts in Britain*, 3, *Renaissance and reformation* (Cambridge: Cambridge University Press, 1989), pp. 46–97, p. 65.

[154] Bodleian Library, MS Broxbourne 84.11, unfoliated, printed in Alessandro Pastore, 'Due biblioteche umanistiche del Cinquecento (I libri del cardinal Pole e di Marcantonio Flaminio)', *Rinascimento*, ser. 2, 19 (1979), pp. 269–90, p. 287.

loggias on public buildings, especially theatres, and mentioned in passing that a private building should also have one, opening on to a garden, as Pole's did.[155] The Long Gallery above might well have had proximate Italian roots, although they had become a common part of English palaces by his time, transplanted to both Italy and England from France.[156] Unlike its nearest competitors in time, especially Dingley Hall, Northamptonshire finished between 1558 and 1560, Pole's builders did not make the mistake of using an even number of bays and windows.[157] Pole's loggia anticipated later developments by its site on the garden front, instead of in a courtyard.[158] Loggias elsewhere sheltered a 'banquet' of delicacies during or after meals.[159] At Lambeth it was more probably used as an exercise area, and as a bridge between the house and Pole's beloved gardens and trees, including the two fig trees, one still alive, which legend says he planted.

The Inquisition unleashed

Pole could enjoy his arches more in the temporary mood of euphoria brought on both by Ormanetto's success and the outbreak of peace. The treaty was signed on 12 September, the secret articles, the bulk of the document, two days later.[160] One of them promised the restoration of Pole's legation, according to Carne, who thought it the only hope.[161] The clause had no immediate impact on Pole

---

[155] Leon Battista Alberti, *On the art of building in ten books*, trans. Joseph Rykwert, Neil Leach, and Robert Tavernor (Cambridge and London: MIT Press, 1988), p. 300.

[156] For example, the archiepiscopal palace at Croydon had a probably late fifteenth-century Long Gallery. P. Faulkner, 'Some medieval archiepiscopal palaces', *Archeological journal*, 127 (1970), pp. 130–46, p. 134. Bridget Cherry and Nikolaus Pevsner call it sixteenth-century in *The buildings of England: London*, 2 (Harmondsworth: Penguin, 1983), p. 214. In addition, at least the royal palaces of Bridewell (c. 1516) and Hampton Court (1533–7) also did. On their importance as models see Colvin,

pp. 20 and 56 and pl. 10 for Hampton Court.

[157] Henderson, pp. 112–13 for Colvin's suggestion that there was one at Whitehall, and Henderson's own candidate, Dingley Hall, as the first surviving loggia.

[158] Henderson, p. 120.

[159] Henderson, p. 134.

[160] Simoncelli, *Caso*, p. 169; Rodríguez-Salgado, pp. 160–1.

[161] *CSPFor*, nos. 672, p. 339 and 678, p. 341. Carne appears to have meant the article of the treaty of Cave promising pardon 'a tutte le comunità, e persone particulari ecclesiastici o secolari' and 'restituendoli tutti gli honori, gradi, dignità, Iurisdittioni, fortezze, terre, Castelli, offici,

or on English representations on his behalf, and the situation quickly deteriorated. Mary's courier, who had been waiting for seven weeks, would just have to wait longer, said Paul, who barely spoke to Carne when the ambassador finally got access.[162] Two weeks later the duke of Alva tried to pressure the pope about both Pole and Morone, and got a similar answer, as did Carne once more.[163] The next time he saw Paul, he met with bad news. The pope was more opposed to Pole than before the peace.[164] Although never saying as much, Paul's reason for stonewalling was doubtless the state of Morone's investigation that reached the point of formal charges on 4 October. Nos. 2 and 3 alleged that he objected to Trent's decree on justification, no. 7 that the pope was to be obeyed only as a temporal ruler, not the vicar of Christ, and no. 15 that war should not be made on fellow Christians.[165] The political-cum-theological nature of Morone's troubles could scarcely be clearer. At nearly the same time, the net moved another step closer to Pole with Carnesecchi's summons to Rome.[166] The testimony against Morone taken on 12 October of Gabriel Martinet, O. P. looked severely damaging to Pole.[167] Martinet gave Michele Ghislieri, the commissary of the Inquisition, the confession of a former Dominican, Ioannes Arnesius. In addition to the usual laundry list of suspects, Arnesius (or this may now be Martinet) offered the more substantial but still hearsay claim that Pole actively recruited to the *schola Angelica*, especially the clever and inexperienced, if necessary by paying them with Vittoria Colonna's cash. This scandalous information came from Gelido and Orazio Ragnoni, who took the money. Pole's *fama* as heretic was widespread, and Arnesius/Martinet claimed to have heard Cardinal Cervini accuse him.[168] It must have been Martinet's own testimony that Robert Wauchope and Ambrogio Catarino had attacked Pole, along with the Jesuits Diego Laínez and Alfonso Salmerón. All in all, a damaging deposition under the Inquisition's rules of evidence. Bertano may have sent Cardinal Gonzaga a list of the *oppositioni* against Pole and Morone about the same time. Its main

benefici, facultà, crediti, et altri beni immobili'. BAV, Barb. lat. 5115, fos. 96v–7r (cf. the inferior text in Barb. lat. 5121, fos. 328v–9r). It is article six not seven, nor is it secret. The only such article found with these two copies of the treaty concerned Palliano.

[162] *CSPFor*, pp. 334 and 337.

[163] ASVe:APR, 10, fo. 188r (*CSPV*, 6:2, no. 1042) and fos. 189v–90r (*CSPV*, 6:2, no. 1043, misdated the 25th).

[164] *CSPFor*, no. 672, p. 339.

[165] *PM*, 2:2, pp. 590–1 and 593.

[166] BMIC24, fo. 81r (cf. Fenlon, p. 279) and *PM*, 5, p. 314.

[167] *PM*, 6, pp. 287–92 superseding 2, pp. 639–42.

[168] Firpo (*PM*, 6, p. 290n) says this refers to the events of 1553, leading up to the interview at San Paolo, but this may go beyond the evidence. Cf. *PM*, 2, p. 461.

point rested on guilt by association, the inquisitors' favourite device. Pole was charged with having 'too familiar conversation with suspect persons', especially Flaminio. Flaminio allegedly said unCatholic things about the eucharist and Pole did not contradict him. Priuli was suspect for similar reasons, and all were accused of having read heretical books, above all the *Beneficio*. The pope allegedly thought that Pole 'was a saint and an angel in his life, but did not have sound doctrine'.[169]

The most extensive list of accusations against Pole comes from the *Compendium processuum Sancti Officii Romae*.[170] It contained a section titled *Disciplina Poli* with eighteen heads. They included the charges that he was 'averse from the right faith', preached on heresy, tried to get others so to do, sent out heretical preachers, ejected Catholic ones, subvented heretics, read and disseminated heretical books, kept heretical familiars, neglected to punish heretics, had pretended to reform in this regard but had not, before concluding with a pair of charges against which defence would be almost impossible. He was thought suspect by 'grave men', and he had been defamed among both heretics and Catholics, as evidenced by the letters of Celso Martinengo and Vergerio.[171]

Another reason for Paul's delaying tactics was that he had decided on a legation for Cardinal Carafa to Brussels, nominally about peace, but largely dealing with Pole (as well as the aggrandizement of the Carafa family).[172] Before Carafa could leave Rome, the matter of Brescia came up in consistory again, and this time the pope held back none of his hatred of Priuli. He began by whispering to Navagero that Priuli was a heretic. When Navagero objected, Paul spelled out his accusation. 'He is of that damned school and that apostate house of the Cardinal of England', which was why the pope had removed Pole's legation. 'Pole has been the master, and cardinal Morone ... is the disciple, except that the disciple has become worse. Priuli is their equal, and of Flaminio, who, were he not dead, would need to be burned, and we have burned at the Minerva in public his brother Cesare Flaminio, companion of Priuli.' The same held for their friend Galeazzo Caracciolo. 'Were our father a heretic, we would carry the faggots to burn him', fulminated the pope.[173]

---

[169] *PM*, 5, p. 307n.
[170] For the status of this text, see *PM*, 1, pp. 15–90.
[171] *PM*, 1, pp. 222–3.
[172] *CSPV*, 6:2, no. 1058.
[173] ASVe:APR, 10, fos. 204v–6r (*CSPV*, 6:2, no. 1067; partially printed in *PM*, 5,

pp. 309–12). Firpo, p. 311 notes that Cesare was actually Marcantonio's first cousin. Navagero repeated Paul's determination, confirmed by Ghislieri, on 5 November. ASVe:APR, 11, fo. 131r (*CSPV*, 6:3, no. 1075).

Priuli came up in Morone's eighth interrogation on 12 November, which was mainly based on Vittoria Colonna's correspondence. Morone was questioned about her letter to him of 30 November (1546) in which Colonna had suggested that Morone should bring Priuli to Bologna.[174] By so doing, 'uncovering a piece of his [Priuli's] so well-concealed flesh . . . he would seem a little fatter and more alive with this absence' from Pole. Colonna concluded that a visit to Bologna would also force Priuli to 'speak in pelagian fashion'. Both of these phrases attracted the inquisitors' attention. Morone thought that the first was a joke at Priuli's expense, since he was suffering so much from Pole's absence *in Germania*, as Morone recalled, apparently meaning at Trent, although Pole had returned two weeks before this letter was written. Revealing Priuli's flesh meant that Priuli 'loved Pole spiritually as friends do'. In light of the earlier arrests of Bertano's and Farnese's men, it is easy to see how the inquisitors might have put a different interpretation on Colonna's words, and perhaps on Morone's explication. Over the course of the next two weeks one of the star witnesses against Morone, Bernardo de' Bartoli, gave his *repetitio*, which included the assertion that Morone had told him that he had found Christ through Pole.[175]

In what might at first seem to be another delaying tactic, on 1 December the pope suggested to Carne that Cardinal Carafa could settle the matter of Pole's legation with Philip.[176] In fact the pope was engaging in a little black humour at the expense of the unsuspecting Carne. Carafa's mission would indeed settle Pole's fate by securing his condemnation. Whatever Carafa may have done about peace or about the dossiers of Sicilian heretics that Paul wanted sent to Rome where all cases of heresy should go, he also carried with him a dossier against Pole.[177] As Carafa reported back to Rome, 'I told his majesty [Philip] the just and pious reasons that moved his holiness not to fail to see that his majesty was not misguided, and that I had with me part of the examinations and *processi*.' Carafa offered to show them to the king, who agreed to set a date, and Carafa had later presented everything he had to the king's confessor

---

[174] The letter is printed in Sergio M. Pagano and Concetta Ranieri, eds., *Nuovi documenti su Vittoria Colonna e Reginald Pole* (Vatican City: Archivio Segreto Vaticano, 1989), pp. 164–6 and *PM*, 2, pp. 1103–6. *PM*, 2:2, pp. 705ff. for Morone's interrogation. See p. 136 above.

[175] *PM*, 6, pp. 293–5 superseding 2:2, pp. 713–15.

[176] *CSPFor*, no. 688, p. 347 and ASVe:APR, 11, fo. 39r (*CSPV*, 6:3, no. 1117).

[177] *CSPV*, 6, no. 1119.

Fresneda.[178] Fresneda later claimed to have seen the *processo*, but his testimony is a little ambiguous.[179] Originally, it sounded as if he meant a *processo* against Priuli, while in his ratification he said it concerned Pole and Morone, and there is room for doubt about how far the proceedings had advanced. The solidest evidence that they had reached the state of a *processo* may come from Pole himself. In March 1558 he wrote the pope that he knew (1) a record had been opened against him and (2) the object of Carafa's mission.[180] One document in the archives of the Holy Office seems to hint strongly at the existence of a *processo* in the sixteenth century, the 'Sommario delle prove d'eresia contro Vittoria Colonna, Marcantonio Flaminio, Alvise Priuli, Pietro Carnesecchi e Reginald Pole', except that it is found among the papers of the *processo* Morone.[181]

As Paolo Simoncelli asks, how many dossiers did Carafa have?[182] Fresneda's original statement and his ratification both agree that he had seen *el processo, one* dossier. One thing is certain. However many there once were, now that the archives of the Holy Office are open, I can say that there is no *processo* against Pole in them. There are two possible explanations. The open conclusion arrived at by the most careful previous student, Sergio Pagano, illustrates the difficulty of choosing between them. After laying out the compelling evidence in favour of a record's existence, he noted a number of oddities making for the opposite conclusion, especially the fact that an inventory of the Inquisition's archives from the seventeenth century says nothing of it.[183] Some might therefore argue that we should never have expected one, because the proceedings against Pole were nominally directed at Morone. That the printed edition of those

---

178 BAV, Barb. lat. 5115, fo. 145r; 5302, fo. 93v; 5211, fos. 168–70, an almost illegible copy; 5333, fo. 58v; a slightly different text in Barb. lat. 4960 printed in *PM*, 5, p. 320n3; and Simoncelli, *Caso*, p. 172 taken from the printed version of Pietro Nores. Sforza Pallavicino, *Istoria del concilio di Trento*, ed. F. A. Zaccaria (Faenza: Gioseffantonio Archi, 1792–7; 5 vols.), 2, p. 333 characterized Carafa's mission as defending a *processo* against Pole, and Henri de Sponde, a very thorough historian, wrote of a *formato processo* in *Annalium emin'mi Cardinalis Caes. Baronii continuatio, ab anno M. C.* *XCVII … ad finem M. DC.XL* (Paris: Denis de la Noüe, 1641), p. 325 1557 VII.

179 *Doc. hist.*, 2, pp. 560–2 and 563–4.
180 *CRP*, no. 2211.
181 ACDFSO, St. st. R. 5-b, among 'fascicoli restituiti dal conte Luigi Manzoni di Lugo', fos. 73r (or 72v, *PM*, 6, p. 128)-74v (6, p. 113) of second part of 'Summarium processus originalis', printed in *PM*, 6, pp. 425–31.
182 Simoncelli, *Caso*, p. 228.
183 Pagano-Ranieri, p. 30n, referring to ACDFSO, St. st. P-1-a.

proceedings runs to seven fat volumes while the single file in the Holy Office is much smaller points to the second explanation that the records have been destroyed.[184] The Inquisition's archives were several times heavily damaged, first by the rioters who sacked the Tor di Ripetta at Paul's death, next by the French who transported a large part of the remainder to Paris in 1810 where much of it was sold as scrap paper or otherwise ruined, last by the Roman republicans of the mid-nineteenth century who sometimes helped themselves to Inquisition documents.[185]

The second seems to me the more likely hypothesis, but even it cannot be endorsed without confronting another mystery. In 1954 and again with John XXIII's permission Giuseppe De Luca had access to the Inquisition's archives.[186] He was permitted to take notes, although not to remove them. Later, the rumour ran about that he had seen a trial record.[187] Very recently, some have still thought that De Luca may have said he had.[188] Others report having seen De Luca with a file that he apparently meant to imply contained correspondence damaging to Pole and Vittoria Colonna, which may not be the documents recently published.[189] He probably saw the only surviving file against Pole (ACDFSO, Stanza storica E 6-a), but what else may never be known.[190] Unfortunately, De Luca's notes, which would probably resolve the issue, together with his original request for admission, are in the closed current section of the Archive of the Congregation for the Doctrine of the Faith.[191] To judge from his first request for admission, he may not have had

[184] The file is ACDFSO, St. st. N 4-d. In the seventeenth century it consisted of three boxes. Pagano-Ranieri, p. 30n.

[185] John A. Tedeschi, 'The dispersed archives of the Roman inquisition', in *The prosecution of heresy: collected studies on the inquisition in early modern Italy* (Binghamton, NY: MRTS, 1991), pp. 23–45 and Sergio M. Pagano, ed., *I documenti del processo di Galileo Galilei*, with Antonio G. Luciani (Vatican City: Archivio Segreto Vaticano, 1984), pp. 19–22 and 38.

[186] Pagano-Ranieri, pp. 26–7n prints De Luca's original request for admission.

[187] Simoncelli, *Caso*, p. 15n. Pagano discounts Simoncelli's report on the basis of an interview with his source, De Luca's

collaborator and biographer Romana Guarnieri, who denied that she had ever heard De Luca mention a *processo*. Pagano-Ranieri, p. 28.

[188] E-mail from Donald Weinstein.

[189] E-mail from Elisabeth Gleason.

[190] Pagano (Pagano-Ranieri, p. 52n) claims that De Luca saw this *busta*, but in conversation with me, he did not remember why he thought that. For the contents of this file, see *CPM*.

[191] Gigliola Fragnito in her review of Pagano-Ranieri ('Vittoria Colonna e l'Inquisizione', *Benedictina*, 37 (1990), pp. 157–72, pp. 158–9), pointed out the value of De Luca's notes and implicitly faulted Pagano for failing to publish them. That decision, of course, was not up to him.

the archival and other skills necessary to recognize a *processo*.[192] Still, the absence of the original records would seem to mean that the first hypothesis cannot be excluded.[193]

Whatever he knew about the investigation and whatever its state at the time, Pole chose to take Carne's report about a possible settlement at face value, immediately planning to dispatch Gianfrancesco Stella to see Philip and Carafa in Brussels.[194] The longer of two letters to Carafa thanked him for his help with Ormanetto's mission and most of the rest of it sounded like the 'Apologia', including its reference to resistance based on Paul's example and the story of Pole's defence of Carafa's promotion. The letter is almost as aggressive as the 'Apologia', and may have been a smart political move designed in part to undercut Carafa in Brussels.[195] The problem is that there is no evidence that the letter was sent, although Stella went to Brussels in mid-December. Pole undoubtedly intended to act politically, recommending to Philip that he give pensions to Cardinals Puteo and Cicada, both members of the Inquisition.[196]

Stella returned to see Cardinal Carafa again in the wrenching context of the loss of Calais on 7 January. Pole was distracted from his own troubles by the need to support the queen and by new demands placed on him both in council and as head of the English church, including the distasteful necessity of collecting money and arms for war.[197] Stella arrived in Brussels by 20 January, and may have stayed at least until the end of April.[198] He carried instructions almost as assertive as Pole's December letter. Stella was to tell Carafa that Pole would have to defend his honour against the pope's evil opinions, and that he could not do that without 'telling and giving a particular account of his whole life and actions and of all that which had passed at various moments between him and the pope, from the beginning, nor did he [Pole] see how to do that without laying a grave

---

[192] Among the documents De Luca thought should be in the Inquisition's files were all those actually in the Vatican Library (Pagano-Ranieri, pp. 26–7n; see below). It is the more curious that De Luca accurately described the mode of transmission of those codices, but made a large mistake about where to find them.

[193] For the fate of Pole's papers once in the inquisitors' hands, see *CPM*, pp. 29–40.

[194] *CRP*, nos. 2144–6. Whether because of Carne's news or secretarial incompetence, at least one of the documents completing the restoration of the Knights of St John on 1 December is sealed with Pole's legatine seal. *CRP*, no. 2131.

[195] Loades, *Reign*, p. 369 says Pole was 'desperate for vindication' in this letter, but it sounds much more aggressive than desperate. Simoncelli, *Caso*, p. 174 for it as a political move.

[196] *CRP*, no. 2137.

[197] *CRP*, nos. 2153, 2155, 2163, 2186, 2205, 2211, 2233. See also PRO, SP 11/12, no. 66 (*CSPDom*, no. 748).

[198] *Carranza y Pole*, pp. 268 and 271–2.

charge against' Paul, for whose honour he would willingly lose everything.[199] This was why Ormanetto had gone to Rome, as well as to warn the pope of the 'inconveniences' that would follow his actions. Pole found it odd that proceedings in England so pleased the pope, if he had such a low opinion of Pole. This must mean that he had been dissimulating, 'which could not come but from extreme impiety joined to extreme ambition'. The pope had also not shown the proper regard for Mary. Perhaps he was misinformed. There may have been more, but the instructions break off.

Before Stella reached Brussels, much of the damage had been done. Ottaviano Raverta, who had travelled with Carafa, had raced back to Rome, where he arrived on 20 January.[200] The pace of the pope's offensive against heretics had increased, Ghislieri ordering all suspects to Rome, including even dead cardinals, and the situation intensified on Raverta's return.[201] Raverta gave his report on the 22nd; Navagero thought it concerned what Carafa had done against Pole.[202] This was not certain, since secrecy shrouded Raverta's presentations. Philip allegedly had offered to allow an inquisition in Florence on the model of the Roman one, a major climb-down, if true. Cardinals Bertano and Guido Ascanio Sforza told Navagero again that Pole and Morone were Raverta's principal concern.[203] Navagero noted circumstantial evidence in support of that contention, including a meeting the day before of the deputies in Morone's case, now including Cardinal Clemente Dolera, a Franciscan, said to have been co-opted in order to keep Fresneda informed, since Philip deferred to his confessor.[204] At the same time, Soranzo's case moved quickly as well.[205]

Meanwhile in Brussels, Cardinal Carafa amused himself, 'gaming and banqueting', perhaps losing 30,000 *scudi* at cards.[206] More serious matters also transpired, including an attempt by the Jesuits to defend Morone and Pole. This is an odd moment.[207] The Jesuits given the job were Pedro de Ribadeneira

---

[199] *CRP*, no. 2157.
[200] *PM*, 5, p. 319; ASVe:APR, 11, fos. 49r and 52r–v (both partially printed in *PM*, 5, p. 318n).
[201] ASVe:APR, 11, fos. 61v–2r (*CSPV*, 6:3, no. 1155).
[202] ASVe:APR, 11, fo. 69v (*CSPV*, 6:3, no. 1148; partially printed in *PM*, 5, p. 319n).
[203] ASVe:APR, 11, fo. 143r (*CSPV*, 6:3, no. 1156). Why Philip should have had anything to do with an inquisition for Florence

is difficult to say. True, Cosimo was a Spanish client, but the problem previously had been the inquisition in Milan, over which Philip had direct control.
[204] ASVe:APR, 11, fos. 61v–2r (*CSPV*, 6:3, no. 1155, but only a tiny snippet of text calendared). Cf. *PM*, 5, p. 320.
[205] ASVe:APR, 11, fo. 143r (*CSPV*, 6:3, no. 1156).
[206] *PM*, 5, p. 320.
[207] Cf. Simoncelli, *Caso*, pp. 188–91.

and Salmerón.[208] The first was in charge of securing Philip's permission for the order to enter England, a matter requiring Pole's approval, and Salmerón had already deposed twice against Morone.[209] The new general, Laínez, would write in September 1558 that Pole could not stand in God's way by preventing a Jesuit mission to England.[210] Nevertheless, the two talked to Carranza and gave him Morone's self-defence, before deciding that it might do harm to see Fresneda.[211]

About the same time Carafa answered Stella's representations, and Pole thanked Carafa.[212] Unfortunately, Carafa's answer has not been found. He seems to have begun already to play a double game, executing the pope's increasingly fanatical orders and simultaneously trying to mitigate their consequences. Thus in addition to aiding Pole, he promised Philip that he would help Morone, and tried to intervene for Carnesecchi.[213] His behaviour no doubt arose from his desire to forward his family's interests.[214] Stella's intervention may also have had an impact. His mission probably produced additional support for Pole (as well as Morone) from Philip. The king dispatched the count of Feria as high-level envoy to England, where he arrived on 27 January. Although Feria immediately reported that Pole seemed a nice enough fellow with whom the council had their way, subsequent dispatches belie this second claim as they underline Pole's importance in its deliberations.[215] Similarly, in the same dispatch in which Feria famously called Pole 'a dead man', and expressed his disappointment that 'although I have been able to warm him up a little by talking to him every day, and what he has heard from Italy since the fall of Calais has stirred him somewhat, the result is not all I could wish', he noted that the committee on finance was to report to him and Pole.[216] Feria and Pole differed in temperament and principle. Feria, again conceding Pole's goodness, had no doubt of the need for Jesuits in England, and since Pole would not admit them, he became 'lukewarm', a species that Feria thought would not go to heaven 'even if they are called moderates'.[217] Philip approved of Feria's attentions to Pole including expressions of the king's

---

[208] *Carranza y Pole*, p. 161.
[209] *PM*, 5, p. 321; 6, pp. 218–20 and 283–6.
[210] Simoncelli, *Caso*, pp. 190–1.
[211] *Inq. rom.*, pp. 274–5.
[212] *CRP*, no. 2174.
[213] *PC*, p. 230.
[214] *CSPV*, 6, nos. 1175 and 1199. The

Venetian ambassador in Brussels never picked up any news about Pole's *processo*.
[215] *CSPSp*, 13, nos. 397, 402, 404, 406, 435, and 444.
[216] *CSPSp*, 13, no. 413.
[217] *CSPSp*, 13, no. 415.

esteem.[218] His public support may have led some people to think that Pole's legation was being restored.[219]

Pole was not among them. While rumours of new *processi* against him and Morone flew around Rome, and two more witnesses against Morone named Pole, having learned of the *processo* Carafa carried, Pole launched a double defence in both Rome and Brussels.[220] The strategy hinged on Fresneda, to whom Pole sent draft letters to Scotti and the pope, asking Fresneda to forward them if they met with his approval and to talk to Philip. Either utter naïveté or subtle political calculation inspired this plan.[221] Pole adopted a tone of injured surprise in the short letter to Scotti. How could Scotti think him guilty after knowing him for so long? He was blunt that he wanted the pope to treat him as Gregory the Great had Augustine of Canterbury.[222] Pole had much more to say directly to Paul IV, although he masked his main point behind a defence of Priuli's *accesso* to Brescia.[223] Who was he, who was also delated to the Inquisition, to give testimony on behalf of another suspect? Paul should trust Pole, who had never said or done anything blameworthy. He had accepted the pope's explanation for the withdrawal of his legation, but became suspicious when all the other nuncios were restored and Carne was always fobbed off with some excuse. Now came a *processo*. What was he to think? Should he not be satisfied with Paul's answer to Carne that this was God's work? That would mean that God was ordering the father to kill his son, as he had once done with Abraham and Isaac. 'I truly see Your Holiness prepare to rip my life away; what else did you do, when you tried to tear away my reputation for sound faith? What would be the shepherd's life among his flock, once his reputation for sound faith had been removed?' Pole knew better than Isaac what his father the pope planned. The pope had acted on false suspicions, and Pole protested how much he had done for the church, expressing joy at Carafa's election and restoring England. Returning to his biblical analogy, Pole hoped that God would free Pole as he had found a ram to substitute for Isaac. Pole hoped this would happen in Priuli's and Morone's cases as well, in fact, he knew that Philip and Mary and many other pious men, 'like a legion of angels [were] coming to interpose

---

[218] *CSPSp*, 13, no. 403.

[219] H. C. Hamilton, ed., *Calendar of state papers relating to Ireland ... 1509–1573*, 1 (London: Longman, Green, Longman and Roberts, 1860), p. 143.

[220] *PM*, 5, p. 326 and 2:2, pp. 744 and 754.

[221] Simoncelli (*Caso*, p. 175) opted for calculation, calling the plan a 'mossa davvero astuta' and saying that 'la lettera [to the pope] è un capolavoro d'astuzia'. All three letters are dated 30 March.

[222] *CRP*, no. 2209.

[223] *CRP*, no. 2211.

themselves between us and the sword, in order to prevent our being killed'. Nevertheless, unless the pope defended them, the devil would overcome the angels' power. Doubts about Pole's faith meant that the devil was gaining ground in England. Pole asked the pope to restore his and Morone's reputations once the matter was examined, conceding legitimacy to the investigation then in progress, and the letter is much less forthright than either the 'Apologia' or Stella's instructions.

It is uncertain whether this letter made it to Rome. The two surviving copies raise some doubts. One bearing Pole's signature is in Vat. lat. 5967, which must mean that it was held back. By contrast, the copy once in one of Pole's registers is not signed, which seems to point to the same conclusion. This is the opposite of what one would expect, had the letter been sent. The strongest evidence that the letter did get to Rome comes from Carlo Gualteruzzi, reporting on developments in Brussels.[224] According to a letter from the court to the Venetian signory, Pole had (1) ordered Stella to tell the Venetian ambassador in Brussels that Carafa and the king had agreed that the king would exert maximum effort on Priuli's behalf and Carafa had promised to do the same, and (2) sent his own letter to the pope by express courier. Finally, Pole had agreed to dismiss Donato Rullo from his household, as Carafa had suggested, making it appear that Pole had done this of his own volition as a means of placating the pope. Pole, however, apparently did not get rid of Rullo, which raises questions about the rest of Gualteruzzi's second- or third-hand information.[225] The only point that can be confirmed is Stella's presence in Brussels. Rome did not react, although there was less talk of proceeding against Pole, as Morone and Carnesecchi held centre-stage for the rest of the year.[226]

The strongest argument against the letter having been received hinges on Fresneda's role in changing attitudes to Pole in Brussels.[227] The problem was rooted in Fresneda's inveterate hostility to Carranza.[228] It went back at least to 1555, and had flared up again when Carranza was made Archbishop of Toledo in 1557.[229] One of Carranza's defence witnesses alleged that Fresneda had then

---

[224] BMIC24, fos. 82r–90v, fo. 86r (partially printed in *PM*, 5, pp. 350–2).

[225] BL, Add. MS. 35830, fo. 24r and PRO, SP 12/1, fos. 20r–9r.

[226] Lessened attention to Pole may be an artefact of Navagero's departure, probably in March.

[227] Cf. Simoncelli, *Caso*, p. 222 and *passim* and

Inq. rom., p. 272.

[228] *Doc. hist.*, 3, pp. 507, 510, 511, 521.

[229] *Carranza y Pole*, pp. 166–8 and Bartolomé de las Casas, *De regia potestate o derecho de autodeterminacion*, ed. Luciano Pereña, J. M. Pérez-Prendes, Vidal Abril, and Joaquin Azcarraga (Madrid: CSIC, 1969; Corpus hispanorum de pace, 8), p. xlix.

said that it would have been better not to promote Carranza, because of his contacts with Pole and an important member of his household, a chamberlain or secretary, who were 'not very Catholic'.[230] Fresneda later singled out Pole and Priuli as suspects, but if this witness can be believed, he was already the last person to whom Pole should have sent his letters. Fresneda's own testimony that seeing the *processo* had confirmed his suspicion that Pole was 'vehemently suspected in the matter of justification' seems to clinch the point.[231] The dispute between Fresneda's ally Ruard Tapper and de Soto, whom Tapper apparently suspected enough to delate to the Inquisition for his ties to Pole, exacerbated the situation.[232] Tapper, we recall, had read 'De summo pontifice', which might have given rise to his worries.

Fresneda based some of his beliefs on first-hand observation, but he probably derived more evidence from a spy he set in Pole's household. The spy, Francisco Delgado, arrived with credentials from Loyola. Loyola had still not given up on Pole and England, suggesting in June 1556 to Ribadeneira that he might yet go.[233] Perhaps Loyola hoped to curry favour with the powerful Franciscan Fresneda and win him over to a Jesuit mission to England. But there is another, more sinister, interpretation. According to testimony given in Carranza's trial, Fresneda had planted Delgado in Pole's household in order to spy on Carranza, and everyone knew that as Fresneda's client Delgado was Carranza's enemy.[234] Loyola might have helped to 'plant' Delgado since he was said to have suspicions about members of Pole's household, in particular Flaminio.[235] It looks suspicious that Delgado went from Pole's household to Rome.[236] The unassuming Delgado made an effective agent, and none of Pole's familiars suspected him.[237] Rather, they expected after Pole's death that he would help in Spain with several of their cases.[238] Pole helped to have him made a royal chaplain.[239] Even Carranza was taken in, and Villagarcia praised his efforts with the sick.[240] But Delgado spied with extreme reluctance. He testified later that he had sought

---

[230] *Doc. hist.*, 3, p. 237.

[231] *Doc. hist.*, 2, pp. 560–2.

[232] *Doc. hist.*, 2, pp. 560–2 and 563–4.

[233] Thomas M. McCoog, *Monumenta Angliae: English and Welsh Jesuits. Catalogues* (Rome: Institutum Historicum Societatis Iesu, 1992; MHSI, 142–3; 2 vols.), no. 131.

[234] *Doc. hist.*, 2, pp. 560–2 and 563–4 and 3, pp. 505–7. Cf. Simoncelli, *Caso*, pp. 227–9.

[235] *Epistolae Paschasii Broëti, Claudii Jaji,*

Joannis Codurii et Simonis Roderici (Madrid: Lopez del Horno, 1903; MHSI, 24), pp. 681–2.

[236] BL, Add. MS 35830, fo. 30r.

[237] *Doc. hist.*, 3, pp. 507–10.

[238] ASAS, 40/135 (Bonelli, no. 157) and 40/139 (Bonelli, no. 161).

[239] ASP, Carteggio Farnesiano Estero, Inghilterra, b. 103, 1538–1732, fo. 23r–v.

[240] *Carranza y Pole*, p. 264 and BL, Add. MS 35830, fos. 32r–3v.

Ghislieri's advice about whether to stay in Pole's service and another witness against Carranza said Delgado had told him he had seen nothing scandalous in Pole's house and had tried to avoid the assignment.[241] All the same, Delgado would testify against Carranza, and he gave at least as damning testimony against Pole and several members of his household.

Evidence continued to mount in Rome.[242] Some of the most damaging came from one of Pole's strongest allies, Muzzarelli, testifying about how he had suppressed the Inquisition's investigation of Pole under Julius III.[243] Two days later, De' Bartoli confirmed Muzzarelli's story, including details of threats of torture against him if he did not withdraw his evidence against Morone.[244] Muzzarelli's questioning of Bartoli had quickly slid in Pole's direction, and Muzzarelli had lost his temper, calling Bartoli a liar in calumniating 'such a holy man'. Muzzarelli and the general of the Dominicans had tried to get their confrère to change his testimony about Pole's views on justification, but he had stubbornly refused. Any inquisitor who had not known the story of the earlier *processo* and how it was quashed did now. Small wonder that Cardinal Carafa made little progress in his schemes to placate Philip.[245]

Another link in the net around Pole was forged in June with the arrest of Carlo da Sesso. Carranza knew or feared the consequences, informing Villagarcia in Lambeth.[246] Villagarcia later testified that members of Pole's household knew Da Sesso, perhaps already at Trent, especially Rullo and even more Ormanetto since he and Da Sesso were both Veronese.[247] Carranza tried to downplay both his and their contacts with the suspect. Asked to comment on his letter to Villagarcia, he claimed that he was suspicious of Da Sesso as a foreigner, but could learn nothing about him from Pole's household.[248] Da Sesso, the corregidor of Toro, would undergo an auto-da-fé in Philip's presence the following year.[249] Heresy in his kingdoms already concerned Philip, and dis-

---

[241] *Doc. hist.*, 2, pp. 944–50 and 3, pp. 493–8.

[242] Even during the darkest days in Rome, Pole still had friends there, especially Bernardino Cirillo, described by Carlo Gualteruzzi as his old friend and *creatura*, who was Paul's maggior domo. BMIC24, fo. 91v. His ties to Gualteruzzi and Pole's circles went back to at least 1544, and he was especially close to Pole's sometime collaborator Gianfrancesco Bini, one of Paul's secretaries. BMIC24, fo. 274r–v and *DBI*, 25, pp. 786–9. He disapproved of the harsh repressive policies of 'riformatori . . .

che caverebbero un morto dalla sepoltura, per appiccarlo et farne prospettive su le forche' (*DBI*).

[243] *PM*, 6, pp. 322–3 and 326–9 (2:2, pp. 804–7 and 815–17).

[244] *PM*, 6, pp. 326ff superseding 2:2, p. 815.

[245] *CSPFor*, p. 380.

[246] *Doc. hist.*, 2, pp. 499–501.

[247] *Ibid.*, p. 510.

[248] *Doc. hist.*, 3, p. 295 and 5, p. 223.

[249] Henry Kamen, *Philip of Spain* (New Haven: Yale University Press, 1997), p. 81.

coveries of groups of heretics just now did nothing to reassure him. Fresneda, reporting to Cardinal Carafa the news of the arrest of one of the first to implicate Carranza, piously hoped that 'such close and familiar friendship with Pole and Priuli and other men who are there in that household [Pole's] does not contain any evil mystery'.[250] That might be how Fresneda would have characterized Carranza's catechism. It had been printed just a little before in Antwerp and quickly came under suspicion.[251]

Fresneda's campaign, combined with the state of Pole's health, may have led to a major reversal in Philip's policy. In late summer when it was thought that the pope was dying, Philip sent Fresneda his list of candidates to replace him. It did not include Pole. Philip's choice fell on Carpi, Morone, Puteo, De' Medici, and Dolera, the last three inquisitors.[252] The king may have excluded Pole this time because Philip knew Fresneda's views, although he may not yet have agreed with them. According to ambassador Michiel reporting Ruy Gomez's version of Philip's wishes, Philip had refused to accept Filippo Gheri's advice to avoid openly backing Pole, 'who for doctrine and example of life has few equals and no superior, and he has a spirit so calm and stable in the good that he cannot fail to be taken as *confidente* of both Henry II and Philip'.[253] Fresneda and Ruy Gomez belonged to opposite factions of Philip's court, and which had the upper hand at this moment is unclear.

The end

Pole's final illness began in September. Early in the month he reported the state of his health to the king and by the 23rd thought it necessary to recommend the Italians in his household to Philip's protection as his end approached.[254] Pole's illness was part of the epidemic that devastated England in 1558, hitting the rulers and the highly placed especially hard.[255] The queen and Pole fell ill in tandem. Philip responded by dispatching Feria again.[256] His sending was delayed, in part because Pole had made trouble over the most important part of his mission, ensuring the succession for Princess Elizabeth.[257] The two had never got along, and she was thought to intend revenge.[258] Fresneda, continuing to make life difficult for

---

[250] *PM*, 5, pp. 361–2.
[251] Cf. *CRP*, no. 2252.
[252] *PM*, 5, pp. 387–8 (*CSPSp*, 13, no. 469).
[253] ASVe:DAS, Spagna, 2, fo. 108r (partially printed in *PM*, 5, pp. 387–8n).
[254] *CRP*, nos. 2276 and 2287.
[255] Loades, *Reign*, p. 389.
[256] *CRP*, no. 2293.
[257] ASVe:DAS, Spagna, 3, fo. 92, almost

completely in cipher; text taken from *CSPV*, 6, no. 1274.
[258] 'The Count of Feria's dispatch to Philip II of 14 November 1558', ed. M. J. Rodríguez Salgado and Simon Adams, *Camden miscellany*, 28 (Camden 4th ser., 29; London: Royal Historical Society, 1984), pp. 303–62, pp. 322/332.

Pole, blamed him for the failure of Philip's plan. Carnesecchi wrote Giulia Gonzaga that Pole was rumoured to be in trouble with Philip and his ministers, who faulted him for all of Philip's difficulties in England.[259] This letter is probably later, since Feria was ordered to try to protect Pole from Elizabeth and he did his best.[260] Elizabeth complained that Pole had never visited her, and only one or at most two meetings between them are recorded.[261] Near the end Pole wrote his last letter to her, a note saying that he thought it best to 'leave all persons satisfied of me', especially her, and sending Seth Holland to visit in his name.[262] Feria arrived before 13 November and helped to persuade Mary to agree to Elizabeth's succession.[263]

The succession in Rome was also much under discussion, and as both queen and cardinal lay dying, Morone's trial entered a phase of intense activity intended to prevent either him or Pole from following Pope Paul.[264] Just after Pole died, Fresneda grumbled that England needed a 'more ardent pastor' and confided to Cardinal Carafa that he was very doubtful about Carranza's orthodoxy.[265] Between developments in Rome and Brussels, Pole died just in time.

Pole's passion, as George Lily called it, ended on 17 November.[266] Priuli wrote several detailed reports of his last hours, and Dudic's account reads like a transcription.[267] Mary died first and the news was kept from Pole. When he found out he offered Priuli and Goldwell a meditation. Although worried about the consequences of the queen's death, Pole consoled himself with his faith and confidence in providence. Feeling his last paroxysm coming on, Pole ordered the book of prayers for the dying brought and managed to hear the hours. At the moment when he would have communicated had he been able, he asked to be assisted out of bed and, supported by two of his attendants, bowed his head almost to the floor. The scene reminded Priuli of a deposition of Christ, the body being supported by the two Marys. (Priuli was careful to emphasize that Pole had frequently heard mass during his final days.) He died as if going to sleep. Priuli also candidly described sharp disagreements between the two long-time friends during Pole's final days about the disposition of his property.

---

[259] *PC*, p. 301.

[260] 'Feria's dispatch', pp. 322/332 and 324–5/334.

[261] *CSPV*, 6, no. 743. Pole did not see Elizabeth on her secret visit to Hampton Court from Woodstock in 1555 (*CSPV*, 6:1, p. xvi) nor later that year when both were lodged in the same royal palace (*ibid.*, no. 251).

[262] *CRP*, no. 2308.

[263] *CSPV*, 6, no. 1285.

[264] *PM*, 5, p. 398; ed. in Paolo Simoncelli, 'Diplomazia e politica religiosa nella chiesa della Controriforma', *RSLR*, 18 (1982), pp. 415–60, p. 454.

[265] *PM*, 5, p. 361.

[266] BL, Add. MS 35830, fo. 24r.

[267] *CRP*, nos. 2311–12. *ERP*, 1, p. 50.

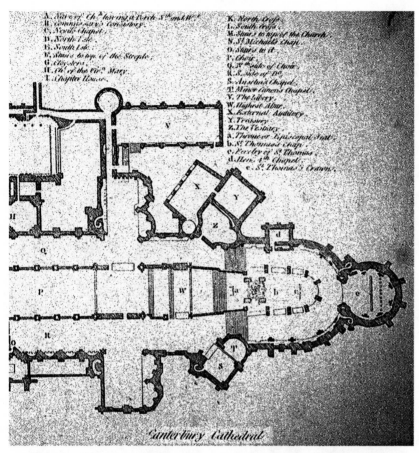

17 *Plan of Canterbury Cathedral. Francis Grose,* The antiquities of England and Wales *(London: S. Hooper, 1773; 4 vols.), 2, frontispiece.* Pole's tomb is in the northwest corner of the Corona.

Not much is known of Pole's funeral.[268] Henry Machyn, a professional undertaker, recorded that the council set the time and place of the burial.[269] Pole's wishes to be buried in Becket's Corona of Canterbury cathedral were respected (see illus. 17).[270] Beccadelli and Dudic both agreed that his body had been kept on a

---

[268] Of records there seems only to be a painter's account in the College of Arms, MS R. 20, fo. 485.

[269] *The diary of Henry Machyn*, ed. J. G. Nichols (London: Camden Society, 1848,

o.s., 42), p. 178.

[270] Pole asked to be buried where Becket's head was, and I infer that means the Corona. *CRP*, no. 2286. Such a tradition is not discussed in John Butler, *The quest for*

catafalque in Lambeth for forty days before being taken by road to Canterbury, but Machyn gave the date of 10 December for its removal.[271] The 'chariot' was decorated with bannerolles worked in gold, banners of Pole's arms, and four of saints in oil.[272] Francis Thynne added a few eye-witness details, such as the casket's conveyance into Rochester cathedral through the disused west door, and the fact that a black cloth with a huge white cross in satin on top of it covered the coffin and Pole's cardinal's hat in the centre.[273] The funeral took place on 15 December, the day after the queen's.[274] According to Dudic there were eulogies in both Latin and English, given on successive days (Thynne said over three days), only the first of which survives. It amounts to the first biography.[275] The speaker knew Pole well, which points perhaps to either Pate or Goldwell, who were granted permission to attend the funeral, or more likely Lily, to judge from a reference at the very end to 'us Cantuarians', which Lily had become by virtue of his new prebend.[276] Lily was also the most experienced life-writer in Pole's circle.[277] The oration was meant for those who did not understand English, which may mean that European dissemination was in view.[278] The speaker began by emphasizing

---

Footnote 270 (*cont.*)

    Becket's bones: the mystery of the relics of St Thomas Becket of Canterbury (New Haven: Yale University Press, 1995).

[271] *MMB*, 1:2, p. 322; *ERP*, 1, p. 51; Machyn, p. 181.

[272] Machyn, p. 181. Could the banner(s) of saints be the 'Four doctors' in Lambeth Palace and traditionally said to have belonged to Pole? According to F. G. Lee, it was hanging in the chapel when Pole arrived. *Reginald Pole cardinal archbishop of Canterbury, an historical sketch* (London and New York: John C. Nimmo and G. P. Putnam's Sons, 1888), p. 127. BL, Add. MS 37146, fo. 68r is a nineteenth-century drawing of Pole's funeral escutcheon, which is like the cartouche over his sarcophagus. On fo. 69r is a reference to 'Vincent, 152, p. 97, banner of cardinal Pole' that I have not been able to identify.

[273] Francis Thynne, 'Reginald Pole', in 'The cardinals of England' added to Raphael Hollinshead, *Chronicles of England, Scotland and Ireland* (London: J. Johnson *et al.*, 1807–8; 6 vols.), 4, pp. 745–60, p. 759.

[274] *CRP*, no. 2315.

[275] For funeral orations as a mode of biography, see Robert Kolb, 'Burying the brethren: Lutheran funeral sermons as life-writing', in Thomas F. Mayer and D. R. Woolf, eds., *The rhetorics of life-writing in early modern Europe: forms of biography from Cassandra Fedele to Louis XIV* (Ann Arbor: University of Michigan Press, 1995), pp. 97–113.

[276] J. R. Dasent, ed., *Acts of the privy council* (London: HMSO, 1890–1907; 32 vols.), *1558–1570*, p. 9.

[277] See Thomas F. Mayer, 'George Lily', in H. C. G. Matthew, ed., *New dictionary of national biography* (Oxford University Press, forthcoming).

[278] BAV, Vat. lat. 5967, fos. 494r–500v, in an unknown hand, possibly that of Priuli's dependant Luca Michelonio. It is probably the same as that in the following copies of Priuli's early letters. The text contains several bone-headed errors of transcription, e.g., 'constituente' for 'conscientiae' (fo. 499v), and there may possibly be a few corrections in Gianbattista Binardi's hand, esp. on fo. 500r–v. The text as printed in *ERP*, 5, pp. 188–97 is almost exact.

the seamless quality of Pole's life. From Pole's parents, he turned to his study of philosophy at Oxford, and then to Padua, where he was taken to be *Cicero Christianus renatus* (perhaps another point in favour of Lily as author), although the speaker hurried on to say that Pole always told his familiars that 'one word dictated by the Holy Spirit was worth more than all of Cicero'. His fame led Henry VIII to recall him to England, where the king wished to make him archbishop, but Pole refused because of his youth. He returned to Italy until he reached the age at which Christ was baptized, spending five years in Venice and Padua, this time chiefly in 'ecclesiastical studies' and withdrawing into a nearby monastery during vacations. He wished nothing more than to flee the world, but God inspired Paul III to call him to Rome in order to find means to make peace among the sects and heretics of the Christian world. Had he succeeded, observed the speaker, we would not have the troubles we do today.

Pole was reluctant to be made a cardinal, and cried among his friends over the prospect, 'as I certainly have understood', noted the speaker. This proved that Pole lacked ambition. His first assignment was the legation of Viterbo where he brought the citizens, who always quarrelled with their governors and one another, to live in peace. The speaker admitted that he left out Pole's other legations, although he mentioned Trent, as he did another mission to make peace during one of Pole's recesses. Because of his success, Pole was offered various bishoprics, which he always refused because he could not reside. His modesty made him the unanimous choice to succeed Paul III. He resisted and tried to force the cardinals to choose someone else. Some blamed him for too much modesty in such a crisis, but God was saving him for England. What a day it was when he restored us as legate! His faith was like Augustine's, making him the second apostle of the English, who may have faced the harder job of the two. The speaker praised Pole's actions on his final legation without descending to particulars. The list of virtues Pole displayed began with prudence, and extended to taciturnity. It also included generosity, as an example of which the speaker cited his gift of Vittoria Colonna's legacy to her daughter. Pole's household was implicitly likened to a monastery that turned away all 'dissolute men'. Pole carefully observed divine worship, and had refused for years to be made a priest because he felt himself unworthy. He was simply a saint: *Sancte educatus, sanctus vixit, sancitissime mortuus est.* As he often told his familiars, if one lived in expectation of death, one could hope for nothing more. His serene expectation of the future testified to his 'sincere and peaceful conscience'. It was divine providence that he and the queen died so close together and could have their divine reward at the same time. The speaker closed with a long set of Old Testament parallels to other liberators of their countries.

Much of this would go into the cult of Pole, but the eulogy's particular 'spin' on Pole's life deserves emphasis. It is a blend of the circumstantial and the sanitized. The brief *curriculum vitae* is scrubbed clean of any of the difficulties that

Pole faced. There is no trouble with Henry, Trent might almost not have happened, and Paul IV is not so much as mentioned. Nor were there any particulars of Pole's restoration of England. There *was* room for the reference to Colonna's *scudi*, which highlights the sometimes narrow focus on those around Pole, perhaps meant to claim a special privilege for the speaker. Nevertheless, despite such implied intimacy, the speaker said nothing of Pole's writing, except under the oblique reference to him as 'the reborn Christian Cicero'. Both of these expurgations did not reflect Pole's own image of himself, unlike the comparison of him to St Augustine of Canterbury and to Old Testament heroes.

The funeral oration is cast in good classical Latin, and emphasized the quality of Pole's Latinity, making him the embodiment of antiquity. His tomb portrayed him in much the same way, with classical windows its most prominent feature.[279] Its importance has been recognized, albeit in garbled fashion. It is the most important *English* religious wall painting of the sixteenth century only in the sense that it happened to be in an English cathedral.[280] As Katherine Eustace noted recently, the 'sophisticated Italianate architectural composition ... symbolic of the Resurrection' contained many of the elements (two-storeys, coffered ceiling, allegorical figures) that would become standard in English sculptural monuments within fifty years.[281] It was the work of Dominic

---

[279] Most of Pole's monument does not survive. His tomb proper was restored at the end of the nineteenth century at the suggestion of the dean and chapter but the expense of the Catholic Truth Society, which put up about £90. The dean, apparently on his own initiative, wished to pay the artist who painted Pole's escutcheon, Edward Frampton, £100 as well, but the CTS balked. See *The Tablet*, 90 (1897), 16 October, p. 622; 95 (1900), 5 May, p. 696; 5 May 1900, p. 700. Frampton seems to have picked up part of Lampson's original design, although the two angels could be fortuitous. Pole's motto is inscribed around the frame. Cf. Katherine Eustace, 'The post-reformation monuments', in Patrick Collinson, Nigel Ramsay, and Margaret Sparks, eds., *A history of Canterbury cathedral* (Oxford: Oxford University Press, 1995), pp. 511–52, p. 513, citing the chapter act books. Eustace also cites the notebooks of M. Bardwell and E. W. Tristram (Victoria and Albert Museum, National Art Library, Box II 213. G.) as recording that the monument had 'suffered from over-zealous antiquarianism'.

[280] Francis Woodman, *The architectural history of Canterbury cathedral* (London: Routledge and Kegan Paul, 1981), pp. 256 and 261. D. Ingram Hill produced a fantastic account of the monument in his *Canterbury cathedral* (London: Bell, 1986), p. 132 and it was overlooked in the most recent guide, which took the present state of Pole's tomb as its original form, inferring that the cartouche reproduced what had been 'painted on the wall' when Pole was buried. Jonathan Keates and Angelo Hornak, *Canterbury cathedral* (London: Scala, 1991; reprint of 1980 edition), pp. 70–1.

[281] Eustace, pp. 512–13 and pl. 130.

Lampson, a Flemish artist who hoped to get training in Italy much more than did his master Lambert Lombard, but he never did.[282]

Lampson produced a striking monument. The 200 *scudi* he claimed Pole left him in his will may have been payment. He and Stella probably collaborated on the *invenzione*.[283] This collaboration emphasizes the Italian inspiration behind the monument, direct in Stella's case, mediated through Lombard and three years' experience in Pole's household in Lampson's. Lampson left a detailed description of his work that accords reasonably well with Thynne's incomplete thumbnail sketch. Thynne was not impressed, describing the tomb as 'yet [c. 1580] to be seen so plain and base as may be, the same being only a heap of brick mortised together, with the top like to the ridge or cover of a house only plastered over with lime, besides which is set his arms and this devise of his: A globe, round about which a snake did spirally wind herself, upon whose head did stand a white "doone" [*sic*; ?dove] and besides the same this poesy written, Prudens simplicitas', Lampson's *symbolo* (see below).[284] James Cole's early eighteenth-century engraving from his own drawing comes closer to Lampson's text (illus. 18).[285] Another engraving of an oblique view into Becket's corona made about fifty years later largely agrees with Cole (illus. 19).[286] Cole's representation makes it difficult to pick out the perspective effects on which Lampson prided himself, but that could also have been Lampson's failure. His two surviving paintings are not very skilful.[287] Then again, an attempt to map Lampson's work onto the present site may demonstrate that he deserves great credit. The wall behind Pole's tomb is flat and the arch at its top approximately twenty-eight feet above the floor is not canted, as are those above all the windows in the Corona.

[282] ASAS, 40/153 (Bonelli, no. 176). The most complete biography is Jean Puraye, *Dominique Lampson, humaniste 1532–1599* (Bruges: Desclée de Brouwer, 1950). See also Jöchen Becker, 'Zur niederländischen Kunstliteratur des 16. Jahrhunderts: Domenicus Lampsonius', *Nederlands Kunsthistorisch Jaarboek*, 24 (1973), pp. 45–61. For Lombard and Pole see above, p. 72.

[283] ASAS, 40/153 (Bonelli, no. 176).

[284] Thynne, p. 759. It may be that Thynne was drawing on his recollections of almost twenty-five years before since he left so much out of the monument, which may well have been in an incomplete state at the time of Pole's interment.

[285] John Dart, *The history and antiquities of the cathedral church of Canterbury* (London: J. Cole, 1726), p. 170. James Cole, who signed the dedication of Dart's book, was also the chief engraver of Dart's *Westmonasterium* (1723). Bernard Adams, *London illustrated 1604–1881. A survey and index of topographical books and their plates* (London: Library Association, 1983), p. 59. Eustace, 'Post-reformation monuments', p. 513 claims Cole's engraving is the only evidence for the appearance of the tomb.

[286] William Gostling, *A walk in and about the city of Canterbury* (Canterbury: W. Blackley, 1825; 2nd ed.), plate facing p. 272.

[287] Puraye, *Lampson*, plates 3 and 8.

18 J. Cole, Engraving of Pole's Tomb. John Dart, The history and antiquities of the cathedral church of Canterbury *(London: J. Cole, 1726), p. 170.*

19 *Becket's Corona, Canterbury Cathedral. By John Raymond from a drawing by R. Godfrey*
in William Gostling, A Walk in and about the City of Canterbury *(Canterbury: W.*
Blackley, 1825, 2nd ed.), plate facing p. 272.

Lampson worked in oils – *colori d'olio* – on the plastered wall. This procedure sprang from haste, which seems to have arisen from his powerful desire to find new patronage after Pole's death. Oils on walls have little staying power, especially when, as here, the artist works over another painting which could scarcely have been dry. The partial St Christopher that appears above Lampson's work, together with the fish which had come through his grisaille by the time of Cole's engraving, belonged to a work probably done under Mary, and certainly not earlier than the last part of Henry's reign, when it could have been meant as an acceptable alternative to the discredited Becket, and the sort of mythological religious element that would have appealed to the king. Lampson's monument superimposed on St Christopher produced an almost animated history of the mid-Tudor reformation, and a powerful indication of the pace of change under Mary.

Lampson began with the architectural elements, a 'vanishing perspective' of Ionic columns done in white marble to match the tomb, designed to make it appear that it sat behind them. 'Twisted porphyries and touchstones' (*paragoni*, a very dark quartz) in appropriate places relieved all this white (none of these is visible, unless on the bases of the columns, or perhaps Lampson meant to take credit for the existing columns?). These columns were arranged with two square pilasters in front, resting on the floor, or the columns were grouped around the pilasters, to judge from the engraving. They must have been painted on the square edges of the recess. Above them was an architrave, 'with a frieze or dentillated zoophorus, frame and pointed pediment, that is in half the shape of a rhombus, as is used, and on that three pedestals [*acroterii*] with three copper balls *contrafatto*, with flames of fire coming from those'.[288] These flames do not show up in the engraving. Contrariwise, Lampson's description does not include the object in it just above the architrave in the same kind of circular frame as Pole's device. It may perhaps have been a profile of Pole, added later, which Cole misunderstood.[289]

On the side walls, also in proper perspective, Lampson painted two niches containing a pair of boy angels, half life-size, with bare arms, one dressed in red, the other in *paonazzo* (the purplish colour of the habits cardinals wore in conclave, for example). One held the arms of Canterbury, and the other of Pole. In the end wall of his perspective gallery Lampson put two barred, prison windows, however elegant in design. The roof (*solaro*) was covered with separate squares moving to the vanishing point, each containing a golden rose. In the middle of the ceiling, hanging from a red silk cord shot with gold was a large glass lamp, the light of which pushed back the shadows 'made against the perspective

---

[288] '[F]risa o Zophoro, dentigli, Cornice et fastigio puntato, cioè di mezza forma di rhombo sicome s'usa, et su quello tre acroterii con tre palle di rame contrafatto, con fiamme di fuochi che uscivan fuor di quelle' (ASAS, 40/153; Bonelli, no. 176).

[289] I owe this suggestion to Pamela Lady Wedgwood.

[*contrafatte dentro alla prospettiva*]'. Under it flew two naked little sprites (*spiritelli*) bearing the cardinal's device (*symbolo*), 'the size of that painted in the house by Marcello'. Alas, this is much too small to be sure what it is, but it might be a heart surrounded by what is almost certainly a serpent, as Thynne said.

On the frieze Lampson wrote in gold letters *Depositum Reginaldi Poli Cardinalis Archiepiscopi Cantuariensis* (missing in the engraving, although noted in Dart's text as being on the tomb, where part of the phrase now appears; Cole must have mistakenly placed the letters 'S. Archie').[290] There was a hole 'like a small open door' (*come un'usciolo aperto*) down to the ground on top of the tomb, probably the blocked-up door visible on the wall at present, so Lampson painted a small architrave, frieze and cornice with a small, round pediment, another pedestal and yet another copper ball, thereby approximately doubling the second tier. (Where this came out in the finished work is difficult to say. Lampson's letter may be more of an *invenzione* than he made it seem, or he may have meant to refer to the two false doors on either side of the tomb.) The whole thing was painted to take advantage of the shadowed state of the recess, an effect Cole apparently attempted to reproduce by lightening his shading from right to left. All this worked splendidly, if Lampson did say so.

Above the perspective gallery, to give it greater relief, Lampson added a larger painting with a false wooden frame, which appears at the top of Cole's engraving. It represented two other naked *spiritelli* flying up into the air, singing. Both had their hands raised, pointing at the scripture verse painted on the frame: *Beati mortui qui in Domino moriuntur.*[291] Above them was a great light, like a full moon, that illuminated the whole painting, and shown through the windows

---

[290] Many lives of Pole note the epitaph on the tomb *Depositum Reginaldi Poli*, but none mention the painting. See, e.g., Godwin, p. 151. According to Gostling (first published in 1777), p. 278 the 'beautiful paintings on the wall [had] sadly gone to decay', and a note to the posthumous edition of 1825 said 'they have lately been entirely obliterated'. Opinions varied about their quality. In the interval between editions of Gostling's book, one William Woolnoth pontificated that the whole of Pole's monument was of 'extreme rudeness', including 'some rude paintings', which he admitted were 'nearly obliterated'. *A graphical illustration of the metropolitan cathedral church of Canterbury* (London: T. Cadell and W. Davies, 1816).

[291] Gregorio Leti claimed that Elizabeth had a – probably entirely fanciful – epitaph added. 'Qui giace il Cardinal Reginaldo Polo, huomo dotto, tranquillo, grave, modesto ne' suoi costumi, non meno prudente che destro ne' maggiori affari; & di cui errori sarebbono restati ignoti agli huomini, se non si fosse mostrato con troppo smoderata passione attaccato agli interessi di Roma, e del Papa, che fu la ragione che lo precipitò in un abisso di Crudeltà, & a far violenza al suo naturale, per avanzare più tosto l'intiera destruttione de' Protestanti alla quale sempre aspirò.' *Historia overo Vita di Elisabetta, Regina d'Inghilterra, detta per sopranome la Comediante politica* (Amsterdam: Abraham Wolfgang, 1693), p. 334.

painted above the tomb. As a final touch, Lampson added what he called the tetragrammaton, dimly visible through the light. He did not explain the significance of most of this, but the general scheme refers clearly enough to the translation of Pole's soul from the earthly, barred prison to heaven. That would square with Pole's own increasingly both resigned and apocalyptic attitude in his late years. Then again, Dart described the ensemble as consisting of 'the resurrection, a sephulchre, twelve angels (were these right up against the ceiling, cut off in Cole's engraving?) and God in Hebrew written, and angels supporting the cardinal's arms'.[292]

Pole's tomb was in advance of funerary decoration in both northern and southern Europe, perhaps following Gianmatteo Giberti's injunction that large tombs posed an obstacle to worship. Just as Pole's household observed standards that would become those of counter-reformation cardinals, so did his tomb 'anticipate' counter-reformation funerary monuments.[293] It seems again truer to say that Pole invented than failed to discover the counter-reformation.

Carnesecchi's deep disillusionment with the ideological content of Pole's will makes much the same point. He heartily approved Giulia Gonzaga's objection to its preamble as 'superfluous, not to say scandalous, especially at that time'. God be thanked that our faith did not depend on men, he continued.[294] Later he reported a malicious rumour that Pole had died 'desperate', although Carnesecchi refused to believe it.[295] The point that upset Carnesecchi in Pole's will was its protestation of loyalty to the papacy.

> First, through the grace of God in the sincerity [purity] of whose faith I was taught by my elders and accepted from the holy Roman church, integral and undoubted mistress of all churches, with all humility I commend my soul to omnipotent God . . . in whose one holy and catholic church and in obedience to the Roman pontiff . . . I have always lived and wish to die. From our most holy father and lord Pope Paul IV, who before his pontificate I always loved like a father and whose honour after God I have always faithfully served during his pontificate, just as in all my actions and legations which I have undertaken for the apostolic see I am conscious that

---

[292] Dart, *Canterbury*, p. 171.

[293] Gigliola Fragnito, 'Cardinals' courts in sixteenth-century Rome', *Journal of modern history*, 65 (1993), pp. 26–56, p. 45 and Kathryn B. Hiesinger, 'The Fregoso monument: a study in sixteenth-century tomb monuments and Catholic reform', *Burlington magazine*, 118/878 (May 1976), pp. 283–93.

[294] *PC*, p. 294.

[295] *PC*, p. 386.

I have never sought anything but God's honour and the dignity and utility of his church . . . I ask benediction with all reverence, wishing him peace, safety and all true consolation.[296]

Carnesecchi, working from hearsay, badly misinterpreted this passage as acknowledging the pope as Peter's successor whom Pole had always obeyed as such.[297] This reading got Carnesecchi into trouble. One of the charges against him became not only that he had denied papal primacy, but also had tried to make it appear that Pole had as well. Defence of hierarchy could have odd results, the inquisitors closing ranks with the prime suspect against another heretic.[298] This was not to be the only peculiar twist in the contest for Pole's reputation.

---

[296] Machyn, p. 49; *ERP*, 5, p. 182. Simoncelli (*Caso*, pp. 215–16) claims that Pole's style in the title of the printed copies of his will, including as its last element *apostolicae sedis legati*, was meant to defend him against Paul IV, but this is his normal style after the legation *a latere* was withdrawn. For it see, e.g., *CRP*, no. 2069.

[297] *PC*, p. 277.

[298] *Ibid.*, p. 558.

9

The making of a saint

THE BIFURCATION IN Pole's image that arose already during his lifetime intensified after his death. In an attempt to launch a pre-emptive strike on his detractors, Beccadelli and Priuli immediately planned an edition of Pole's works. Hostility in Rome provided much of the motive. Paul IV went out of his way to criticize Pole, and Morone remained in prison, perhaps in more trouble than before, both happening because of Philip II's metamorphosis from staunch supporter into leading attacker.[1] The imperial cardinals defended the two, but the Spaniards, led by Pedro Pacheco with Francisco de Mendoza not far behind, joined the critics.[2] In this threatening climate, a worried Beccadelli wrote Priuli in March 1559 that he could not wait to see Pole's writings, in addition to his will which Beccadelli had already read.[3] This rapid dissemination testifies to its importance as a defensive document.[4] Priuli replied in June that he would like nothing more than to visit him in Ragusa,

> bringing with me a goodly quantity of relics and most precious monuments of the talent and piety which that holy spirit [Pole] has left which I have, and which are and will be preserved with all due diligence with the hope that from them may come not only true and perpetual praise to him with the glory of God and the edification not only of his country . . . but of the rest of Christendom, and who knows that God will not one day open a way to put my plan into execution.[5]

In December, Priuli announced the same intention.[6] His death prevented the proposed edition's completion. Instead, Morone and Gonzaga took over the initiative during the last session of Trent, with the burden of the work falling to

---

[1] E.g., *PM*, 5, pp. 414–16.

[2] *PM*, 5, pp. 474 and 503 and *Inq. rom.*, pp. 261–325.

[3] *PM*, 5, p. 430n and BPP, MS. pal. 1010, fos.

298v–9r.

[4] Cf. *CPM*, pp. 25 and 86–9.

[5] BMIC24, fo. 306v.

[6] BPP, MS pal. 1019/3, 8N.

Seripando. Their collaboration produced *De concilio* in 1562.[7] This, the first book to appear from Paolo Manuzio's Roman press, was the only one of Pole's works to be published, despite a comprehensive plan including his correspondence, at least some of which Seripando had also seen.[8]

At the same time, a major effort to write Pole's biography got under way. Manuzio's preface to *De concilio* became the first published biography, albeit more in the nature of an *elogium*.[9] About the same time two other biographies were in preparation, by Beccadelli and Dudic, both written at Trent, and both substantially indebted to Pole's view of himself. The second of these would contribute most to the development of his image. The two texts have frequently been taken as mirror images, a perception their authors encouraged.[10] In fact, they differ quite a bit on points of fact, and their Poles are not at all the same.[11] Nevertheless, they were plainly intended as hagiography. Beccadelli's opening sentence promised his readers 'an image . . . adorned with all the virtues and excellencies that today might come together in a Christian gentleman'.[12] Dudic made his aim equally explicit: he had set out not only to translate Beccadelli's original, but also to modify it in order to demonstrate that Pole was on a par for sanctity with the martyred More and Fisher. Dudic adopted Beccadelli's conclusion that Pole belonged in the company of martyrs, and this became a constant of historiography.[13] Both men intended to paint Pole as an example of constancy, especially through their treatment of the conclave of Julius III.

---

[7] ASV, Concilio tridentino, 42, fos. 177r–8v and 205r–6v. Gigliola Fragnito, *Memoria individuale e costruzione biografica* (Urbino: Argalia, 1978), p. 17. Cf. *CPM*, pp. 26–7.

[8] Ester Pastorello, *L'epistolario manuziano. Inventario cronologico-analitico 1483–1597* (Florence: Olschki, 1957), no. 1040; A. Renouard, *Annales de l'imprimerie des Aldes*, 3rd ed. (Paris: Jules Renouard, 1834), pp. 528–30. For the priority of *De concilio*, see Paul F. Grendler, 'The adages of Paolo Manuzio: Erasmus and the Roman censors', in James V. Mehl, ed., *In laudem Caroli: renaissance and reformation studies for Charles G. Nauert* (Kirksville, MO: Thomas Jefferson University Press, 1998), pp. 1–21, p. 7.

[9] This campaign was the second effort to defend Pole in print. The first came in 1556 with Bernardino Tomitano's *Clonicus* and the dedication of book IV of Pierio

Valeriano's *Hieroglyphica seu de sacris aegyptiorum aliarumque gentium literis commentarii* (Basel: Palma Ising[?], 1556; reprinted Louvain: Bart. Honoratus, 1586). See also George B. Parks, 'Italian tributes to cardinal Pole', in Dale B. J. Randall and G. W. Williams, eds., *Studies in the continental background of renaissance English literature: essays presented to John L. Lievsay* (Durham, N.C.: Duke University Press, 1977), pp. 43–66, which must be used with care.

[10] Fragnito, *Memoria*, pp. 64n and 161.

[11] For more on these two texts, see the introduction to my forthcoming edition.

[12] Ludovico Beccadelli, 'Vita del cardinale Reginaldo Polo', in *MMB*, 1:2, p. 277.

[13] Andras Dudic, *Vita Reginaldi Poli* (Venice: Domenico and Giovanni Battista Guerrei, 1563), sig. 3v; *Vita*, in *ERP*, 1, p. 65 repeating Beccadelli, 'Vita', *MMB*, 1:2, p. 333.

The motives behind these intentions need more work, especially in the case of Dudic, who collaborated with the shadowy Gianbattista Binardi. Dudic had asked Binardi's help because of his own artistic failings, and Dudic went on to emphasize how much substance Binardi had contributed, in addition to having 'polished' 'this whole portrait [*effigiem*] of Pole'.[14] In addition to Binardi's relative obscurity, Dudic's later conversion to Calvinism has cast a shadow over his work. G. B. Morandi argued that Dudic attacked Pole from a crypto-Protestant position, and although this is anachronistic, one of the co-authors of Dudic's life may have included a number of subtle criticisms of Pole.[15] In addition to the possibly negative comparison to other heroes who had died for the faith, for example, it was similarly noted that two of the four men created cardinal with Pole had become pope. 'Dudic' noted this again when discussing the same two serving with Pole as legates to the first session of Trent.[16] But in 1556 Dudic had extravagantly praised Pole (together with their mutual friend Manuzio) for their 'true religion of Christ, by whom I was confirmed in the faith and by whose examples I was invited to spend life piously and holily'.[17] Near the end of his life, Dudic expressed a similar opinion in offering his study of Pole as a model for a series of biographies of men 'which our age and our fathers' consider eminent'.[18] Thus the theory of Dudic the crypto-critic may not work. Likewise, the meaning of Beccadelli's ties to Pole's allies the *spirituali*, in whose defence Beccadelli is generally agreed to have written, requires further attention.[19]

---

[14] *Vita*, sig. 4r.

[15] *MMB*, 1:2, p. 274 and Morandi's notes. Domenico Caccamo, *Eretici italiani in Moravia, Polonia e Transilvania (1558–1611). Studi e documenti* (Florence–Chicago: Sansoni–The Newberry Library, 1970), pp. 112–13; Gigliola Fragnito, 'Aspetti della censura ecclesiastica nell'Europa della Controriforma: l'edizione parigina delle opere di Gasparo Contarini', *RSLR*, 21 (1985), pp. 3–48, p. 39; and Lech Szczucki, 'Miedzy ortodoksja a nikodemizmem (Andrzej Dudycz na soborze trydenckim)', *Odrodzenie i Reformacja w Polsce*, 19 (1984), pp. 49–90, p. 90 (the English summary) all reject Morandi's thesis.

[16] *ERP*, 1, pp. 14 and 19.

[17] Caccamo, pp. 112–13. For Manuzio's religion, see Fragnito, 'Censura ecclesiastica', pp. 26–8; Simoncelli, *Caso*, pp. 40–2; and A. J. Schutte, 'The *Lettere volgari* and the crisis of evangelism in Italy', *Renaissance quarterly*, 28 (1975), pp. 639–88.

[18] Pierre Costil, *André Dudith, humaniste hongrois 1533–1589. Sa vie, son ouevre et ses manuscrits grecs* (Paris: Belles Lettres, 1935), p. 448.

[19] Hubert Jedin, *Il tipo ideale del vescovo secondo la riforma cattolica* (Brescia: Morcelliana, 1950), pp. 49, 54–5 and Simoncelli, *Caso*, pp. 191–2; but see Fragnito, *Memoria*, pp. 157–9 and 'Per lo studio dell'epistographia volgare del Cinquecento: le lettere di Ludovico Beccadelli', *Bibliothèque d'humanisme et renaissance*, 43 (1981), pp. 61–87, pp. 64 and 87.

The accident of print denied Beccadelli much immediate impact, for Dudic alone achieved the honour of publication in the sixteenth century. His biography quickly assumed a dominant position in Pole historiography.[20] For example, his story of the interview with Henry VIII in which Pole refused the archbishopric of York went into the revised edition of Nicholas Sander's *De origine ac progressu schismatis anglicani* (Rome: Bonfadini, 1586) and thence into nearly all continental historiography, beginning with Pedro de Ribadeneira's and Girolamo Pollini's adaptations.[21] Earlier in *De visibili monarchia ecclesiae* (1571), Sander had quoted Dudic verbatim on the reconciliation.[22] Pole could be regarded as the revised *De origine*'s hero. It drew heavily on *De unitate* and book II concluded with Pole's death rather than Mary's. Whoever compiled it, perhaps William Allen with some assistance from Robert Persons, had access to at least some of Pole's manuscripts in Rome.[23] The book, and hence the image of Pole conveyed in it, became 'the basis of every Roman Catholic history of the English Reformation'.[24] Among these was Persons's unpublished 'Certamen ecclesiae anglicanae', which drew on both Sander and Dudic and featured Pole prominently.[25] Undoubtedly the most important of the later adaptations and translations of *De origine* was François Maucroix's (1676, with at least three more editions by 1715, including one of s'Gravenhage). From it descends

---

[20] Lack of evidence about many of the authors discussed below makes it impossible to sketch their motives and the discussion is therefore usually limited only to their texts' intentions. Except for a few crucially important works, coverage ends in 1950, since subsequent research has been treated elsewhere in the text.

[21] Thomas F. Mayer, 'A sticking-plaster saint? Autobiography and hagiography in the making of Reginald Pole', in Mayer and D. R. Woolf, eds., *The rhetorics of life-writing in early modern Europe: forms of biography from Cassandra Fedele to Louis XIV* (Ann Arbor: University of Michigan Press, 1995), pp. 205–22, pp. 211–12, especially for William Allen's possible role in the revision of *De origine*. It also figured prominently in Girolamo Ghilini, *Teatro d'huomini letterati* (Venice: Guerigli, 1647), pp. 203–4.

[22] *De visibili monarchia ecclesiae* (Louvain: John Fowler, 1571), pp. 678–80.

[23] On pp. 308–9 the editor noted that Pole had added a fifth book to *De unitate*, probably meaning the preface to Edward VI, which the editor had probably seen in Vat. lat. 5971, or just possibly the copy in the Inquisition archives. Cf. *CPM*, pp. 48–50. For the editor's identity, see Joseph S. F. Simons, ed., Robert Persons, *Certamen ecclesiae anglicanae* (Assen: Van Gorcum, 1964), pp. 301–4.

[24] Thomas Law in his *DNB* article on Nicholas Sander. Cf. J. H. Pollen, 'Dr Nicholas Sander', *EHR*, 6 (1891), pp. 36–47, pp. 41–7. See in general the pioneering articles of Jenny Wormald, 'The historiography of the English reformation', *Historical studies*, ed. T. D. Williams, 2 (1958), pp. 50–9 and W. Brown Patterson, 'The recusant view of the English past', in Derek Baker, ed., *The materials, sources and methods of ecclesiastical history* (Oxford: Blackwell, 1975), pp. 249–62.

[25] Simons, *Certamen, passim*.

modern historiography of the English reformation. Maucroix's work served as 'the proximate cause' (Law) of Gilbert Burnet's *History of the reformation*, the first volume of which, published in 1679, in turn led to Joachim LeGrand's *Histoire du divorce de Henry VIII* (Paris: E. Martin, *et al.*, 1688) and thence straight to the great burst of interest in church history in the first half of the eighteenth century.[26] Even though Maucroix had apologized for Sander's partisanship in his preface, his translation of the equally partisan Dudic in 1677 manifested intentions as blatantly hagiographical as most of his predecessors'.[27] He wrote in his brief preface that everything Dudic had written was *la verité* and that although he did not wish to give a eulogy of Pole, 'I would only say that it would be difficult to find in the same man such nobility, piety and learning [or doctrine] as in the famous Cardinal POLE.'[28] Why either work should have interested a protector of the Jansenists and a 'convinced Gallican' is puzzling.[29] Perhaps this evidences both the reception of Pole's tolerant attitude to Protestantism and also that he was read as other than a staunch papalist.

Equally as important to *De origine* (but not independent of it) Pole appeared in a very favourable light in the continuations of Cesare Baronio's *Annales ecclesiastici*. The first of these by Abraham Bzowski or Bzovius praised Pole's fearlessness in 1537 and when treating his fellow Dominican Carranza's later troubles, gave a glowing report on Pole's restoration of the church in England, drawing a veil of silence over his problems with Pope Paul.[30] Henri de Sponde (1568–1643), incorporating Bzowski's work into his *Annalium emin'mi Cardinalis Caes. Baronii continuatio, ab anno M. C. XCVII... ad finem M. DC.XL* (Paris: Denis de la Noüe, 1641) made Pole one of his heroes. He dutifully adopted the salient parts of Pole's story of Henry VIII, including the burning of Becket's bones, and Pole emerged as Beccadelli's constant model of virtue.[31] De Sponde concluded with an *elogium* of Pole firmly within the already dominant tradition.[32]

---

[26] See the sketchy treatments in Rosemary O'Day, *The debate on the English reformation* (London: Methuen, 1986), pp. 38–55 and A. G. Dickens, J. M. Tonkin, and Kenneth Powell, *The reformation in historical thought* (Cambridge, Mass.: Harvard University Press, 1985), pp. 105ff.

[27] *Histoire du schisme d'Angleterre de Sanderus*, 1 (Lyon: Guillimin, 1685), sig. aiiiiv.

[28] F. Maucroix, *Suite du schisme d'Angleterre, ou les vies des cardinaux Polus et Campege* (Lyon: Guillimin, 1685; added to vol. 2 of his translation of Sander), sig. Aiir–v.

[29] Renée Kohn, ed., *Lettres de Maucroix* (Paris:

PUF, 1962), pp. 17–35, esp. p. 27.

[30] *Annalium R. P. F. Abrahami Bzovii... continuatio*, 20 (Cologne: Johann Munich, 1641), 1537, no. VI. For the Dominican Bzowski (1567–1637), see Alfred Baudrillart *et al.*, eds., *Dictionnaire d'histoire et de géographie ecclésiastique* (Paris: Letouzey et Ane, 1912–), 2, p. 1518.

[31] *Annalium*, p. 173 1538 XIII for Becket. E.g., p. 269 1549 XIII for the conclave, drawn from Sander and p. 101 for another adaptation of his text.

[32] *Ibid.*, pp. 333–4 1558 VI.

Outside the mainstream running through *De origine* and Baronio, many other writers eulogized Pole in the sixteenth century, beginning with Paolo Giovio.[33] Seripando could not write enough praise.[34] Onofrio Panvinio lauded the 'most pure and holy Pole' in his manuscript biographies originally written for Pius IV, who helped to sponsor the campaign to rehabilitate Pole and his allies.[35] This image was so powerful that when Antonio Carafa, one of Paul IV's nephews, revised Panvinio's biographies Pole emerged largely unscathed.[36] Likewise, Caracciolo's life of Paul tied itself in impressive knots trying to preserve both Pole's sanctity and Paul's vendetta.[37] Caracciolo's seventeenth-century successor as historian of the Theatines, Giuseppe Silos, did even better. Not only was Pole an avatar of Christian virtue, but also association with him raised Bernardino Scotti's status.[38] Perhaps unconsciously, Giovanni Botero both captured and reduced the ambiguities in Pole's career at the same time as he summed up his predecessor's biographies when he made Pole into 'the perfect exponent of the counter-reformation', as Simoncelli says.[39]

Pole became a standard feature of the new genre of bio-bibliographical compendia from the first, especially those of cardinals. Girolamo Garimberto (1506–75) including him in his treatment of the 'good and holy life', illustrated by several invented tales, applied the adjectives 'prudent and constant' to Pole.[40] A little later André Thevet in his *Les vrais pourtraits et vies des hommes illustres* defended him against the charge of Lutheranism and used him, a little

---

[33] See above, p. 165.

[34] E.g., *CT*, 2, pp. 404 and 406.

[35] Alberto Aubert, *Paolo IV Carafa nel guidizio della età della Controriforma* (Città di Castello: Tiferno Grafica, 1990), pp. 195 and 198. See also Giovanni Antonio Petramellario, *Ad librum O. Panvinii de summis pontificis et S. R. E. Cardinalibus a Paulo Quarto ad Clementis VIII annum pontificatus octavum continuatio* (Bologna: Heirs of Giovanni Rossi, 1599), pp. 47–50.

[36] Aubert, pp. 206 and 208.

[37] *Ibid.*, pp. 233–51, esp. pp. 239 and 241.

[38] Giuseppe Silos, *Historiarum clericorum regularium* [*libri*] (Rome: Mascardi, 1650; 2 vols.), 1, encomium on p. 314.

[39] Paolo Simoncelli, 'Diplomazia e politica religiosa nella chiesa della Controriforma', *RSLR*, 18 (1982), pp. 415–60, pp. 442–3.

[40] Girolamo Garimberto, *La prima parte delle vite, overo fatti memorabili d'alcuni papi, et di*

tutti i cardinali passati (Venice: Gioliti, 1667), pp. 39–46. Clifford M. Brown with Anna Maria Lorenzoni, *Our accustomed discourse on the antique: Cesare Gonzaga and Gerolamo Garimberti, two renaissance collectors of Greco-Roman art* (New York: Garland, 1993), esp. pp. 40–6. In the 1540s Garimberto may have been in Cardinal Farnese's service (pp. 42–3). In 1558 he was Nicolò Gaddi's familiar (BAV, Barb. lat. 5710, fos. 45r–v and 47r–v) and his famous collection of antiquities was housed in the Gaddi palace (Brown, pp. 47–61). He wrote five other books, including *Concetti di Girolamo Garimberti, et d'altri autori, raccolti da lui per scriver e ragionar famigliarmente*, new ed. (Venice: N. Bevil'acqua, 1564) and *Il capitano generale di m. Girolamo Garimberto* (Venice: Giordano Ziletti, 1556).

inconclusively, to illustrate how fortune's plaything can yet triumph through constancy.[41] Antonio Maria Graziani's *De casibus virorum illustrium* included a strongly positive portrait, featuring the claim that Pole in *De unitate* 'discussed the whole matter accurately, lucidly, and equally moderately and freely'.[42] One of the stranger guises under which Pole appeared came in Cornelius à Lapide's very popular *Commentaria in quatuor prophetas maiores* (first edition 1633) where his behaviour in 1537 figured as a specimen of the constancy represented by Ezekiel's hyacinth.[43] These portraits quickly became potted lives.[44] Giovanni Imperialie, a physician from Vicenza, produced a more distinctive biography in his *Museum historicum*, vociferously defending Pole against Paul IV and quoting Flaminio's carmen that appeared on one of Pole's portraits (see Catalogue below).[45] In one case Pole was divided into his virtues, rather than left as a composite exemplar of them.[46] He also increasingly became a writer, sometimes remembered merely as lists of works that varied a good deal in their completeness.[47] Louis Dony d'Attichy wrote the most thorough seventeenth-century life, portraying Pole as a prophet and martyr, deservingly buried in Becket's tomb.[48]

---

[41] Paris: I. Kervert et Guillaume Chaudiere, 1584, pp. 571–5.

[42] Antonio Maria Graziani, *De casibus virorum illustrium* (Paris: Cellier, 1680), pp. 209–28. This is the earliest printed edition I have found, but Graziani died in 1611.

[43] Cornelius à Lapide, *Commentaria in quatuor prophetas maiores* (Antwerp: H. Verdussen, 1728), pp. 1039–40.

[44] They began with the second edition of Antoine du Verdier, *Prosopographie, ou description des hommes illustres, et autres renommez* (Lyon: Paul Frelon, 1605, pp. 2392–7; 1st ed., Lyon: Antoine Gryphius, 1573). The 2nd ed. was much augmented. Henri Albi (1590–1658), *Eloges historiques des cardinaux illustres, françois et etrangers, mis en parallele avec leurs pourtraits au naturel* (Paris: A. de Cay, 1644), pp. 242–52 contained an equally uninspired representation of Pole as *un homme parfait* and there is a very brief notice in Paul Freher (1611–82), *Theatrum virorum eruditione singulari clarorum* (Nürnberg: J. Hofmann, 1688), p. 30. Another, which drew on unpublished materials, appeared in Olivier de Coste (Hilarion de Coste),

Histoire catholique ... où sont descrites les vies, faicts, et actions ... dans les Xvi et Xvii siecles (Paris: Pierre Chevalier, 1625), pp. 284–92.

[45] Giovanni Imperiale, *Museum historicum et physicum* (Venice: Giunta, 1640), pp. 32ff.

[46] Jacques Rho, SJ, *Variae virtutum historiae* (Louvain: Heirs of Pierre Prost, Philippe Borde and Laurent Arnaud, 1644), pp. 490 and 617–18.

[47] See for example Antonio Possevino, *Apparatus sacri* (Venice: Society of Jesus in Venice, 1606), 3, p. 123; *Nomenclator SRE Cardinalium* (Tolosae (Toulouse?): Domingo de la Case, 1614), p. 132; John Pitts, *De illustris Angliae scriptoribus* in *Relationum historicarum de rebus Anglicis*, 1 (Paris: Rolin Thierry and Sebastian Cramory, 1619), pp. 757–9; Francesco Maria Torrigi, *De eminentissimis S.R.E. scriptoribus cardinalibus* (Rome: Stefano Paolinio, 1641), pp. 46–7; and Louis Jacob, *Biblioteca pontificia* (Lyon: Heirs of Gabriel Boissat and Laurent Anisson, 1643), p. 430.

[48] Louis Dony d'Attichy, *Flores historiae sacri collegii S. R. E. cardinalium*, 3 (Paris: Sebastian Cramoisy, 1660), pp. 225–48.

Just as the initial impulse to create the constant Pole arose from accusations of heresy, so later defences drew from similar fuel, now assembled not just by 'Catholic' detractors, but also by Protestants. One of the most important of these was Johann Sleidan who did not write very much about Pole beyond calling him a liar once or twice, but that was plenty for Pole's defenders, first among them probably the Carthusian Lorenzo Surio.[49] Vergerio's sarcastic commentary on the appeal to Charles V in *De unitate* was published in English in 1560.[50] It joined in the vilification of Pole in England that began in December 1558 with an attack on him from the pulpit, evidently designed for an international audience.[51] Matthew Parker may well have had a hand in this sermonizing. He (or perhaps his collaborators John Joscelyn and George Acworth) later almost topped Vergerio's negative view of Pole in *De antiquitate Britannicae ecclesiae*, certainly meant for the continent.[52] Parker, like most of his contemporaries, made his historiographical judgments on ideological grounds, dismissing virtually all Italian history as devoid of truth because written by papists; the work opened with sneering remarks about all the encomia Pole had received from 'the academy of Venice' (p. 405). Nevertheless, Parker and his collaborators put a good deal of research into their life, the Padua-trained Acworth probably contributing the information just cited along with other Italian sources, among them in all likelihood one of Manuzio's editions of *Epistolae clarorum virorum selectae . . . ad indicandam nostrorum temporum eloquentiam*, probably Dudic (especially for Pole's friends in Padua who were converted into a veritable Camorra), a pasquinade accusing Pole of having fathered two children with the

---

49 Lorenzo Surio, *Commentarius brevis rerum in orbe gestarum ab . . . [anno] MD usque in annum MDCLXXIII* (Cologne: Gervinus Calenius and heirs of Johannes Quentel, 1568), pp. 376, 385, 671–2, 680, 682.

50 *The seditious and blasphemous oration of Cardinal Pole, translated into English by Fabian Wythers* (London: O. Rogers, 1560) (earliest ed.; *STC*, 20087). Wythers is known otherwise only to have translated Johannes ab Indagine, *Briefe introduction . . . unto the art of chiromancy* (London: J. Daye, 1558; *STC*, 14075) and Claude Dariot, *A breefe and most easie introduction to the astrologicall iudgement of the starres* (T. Purfoote, 1583; STC, *6275*). John Strype, *Ecclesiastical memorials relating chiefly to religion, and its reformation, under the reigns of King Henry VIII, King Edward VI, and*

Queen Mary (Oxford: Clarendon Press, 1816; 3 vols.), p. 257 asserted that Wythers made his translation 'about the year 1547, or 1548'.

51 ASM:AG, b. 578, fos. 210r–11v (*CSPV*, 7, no. 2).

52 [Matthew Parker?], *De antiquitate britannicae ecclesiae* (London: (John Daye), 1572), pp. 405–24. For Joscelyn's role in at least the research, see John Strype, *The life and acts of Matthew Parker* (Oxford: Clarendon Press, 1821; 3 vols.), 2, pp. 244–52 and May McKisack, *Medieval history in the Tudor age* (Oxford: Clarendon Press, 1971), pp. 44 and 47–8. I am grateful to Fritz Levy for help on this point. The book does not acknowledge either Joscelyn's or Acworth's involvement.

Abbess of Santa Clara at Viterbo (p. 410), as well as Manuzio's preface to *De concilio* and *De concilio* itself (pp. 406 and 410). From Acworth the University orator too could well have come the stress on Pole's training in rhetoric and philosophy, and the condemnation of his style as 'redundant', although the work did concede that Pole had the better of Sadoleto in their correspondence over Bonamico (doubtless known from *Epistolae selectae*) (p. 407). In his later reply to Nicholas Sander's *De visibili monarchia*, punningly titled *De visibili Rom'anarchia* (London: John Daye, 1573; *STC*, no. 99.5), Acworth praised the sanctity of Pole's life, and blamed the 'butchery' of Mary's reign on Bonner, while yet faulting Pole, the holiest legate, for defrauding the clergy of first fruits and tenths (pp. 55, 67, 126–8). Parker cast his net for information widely, including among the Marian exiles. One of them who had been in Frankfurt must have given him the story of Juan Morillo's conversion by Pole (p. 411) which Parker's informant must have had from Morillo.[53] One marginal note refers to unidentified archival sources for the allegedly simoniacal contract Pole made with John White at his translation to Winchester (p. 418). Although the story of this transaction together with its alleged bribery of the pope must have arisen from a misunderstanding of the pension on Winchester reserved to Pole by the queen, *De antiquitate* otherwise made good use of Pole's archiepiscopal register, for example, for the details of his ordination and installation as archbishop (pp. 417–18).[54]

Much of Parker's interpretation descended from Henrician polemic against Pole, especially one of Tunstall's and Stokesley's letters printed by Foxe. It was introduced out of chronological sequence to support the case that Pole chose Italian degeneracy over his country and gratitude to his prince (p. 406), although Parker emphasized how much this had literally cost Pole (p. 407). This point was elaborated into Pole's 'monstrous metamorphosis' as he fulfilled the adage *inglese italianato, diavolo incarnato* (pp. 406 and 408). As a result, Parker could simply reverse the central value of Dudic's biography. Thus instead of constancy, inconstancy characterized Pole (pp. 410–11), Acworth probably providing the term *dapocagine* and its definition to describe Pole as one who tailored his opinions to those around him (p. 411). At the same time, Parker emphasized Pole's isolation between papists and evangelicals, endorsing Vergerio's basic point (p. 410). But not even 'Parker' was immune to the attractive side of Pole's personality. In his peroration he observed that Pole would have been outstanding 'in all

---

[53] A. Gordon Kinder, 'Juan Morillo – Catholic theologian at Trent, Calvinist elder in Frankfurt', *Bibliothèque*   *d'humanisme et renaissance*, 38 (1976), pp. 345–50, p. 349.

[54] CCCC, MS 127, no. 1 for the pension.

his excellent gifts of learning and singular ornaments of virtues' had he not been seduced 'by pontifical mores' (p. 423), before concluding that he was a 'tyrant' for burning Cranmer (p. 423).

Parker's views dominated English Protestant historiography, reappearing in the *Chronicle* that appeared under Holinshead's name and in Thynne's appended lives of the archbishops of Canterbury (written by 1585), a near translation of Parker, but without most of the overtly ideological commentary or personal abuse, for example the 'timidity, idleness or hypocrisy' that prevented Pole being elected pope (p. 411).[55] 'Holinshead' also drew a good deal of material from the major exception to the main direction of English Protestant writing, Foxe, and apparently by force of his authority, perhaps accidentally reproduced his balanced attitude by writing that although Pole's nature was 'malignant', he was 'of more lenity than many other popelings'.[56] Foxe's mature view represented a change of heart. In the first edition of the *Acts and monuments* (1563), in the course of the story of Adam Damplip, once in Pole's circle, Foxe vilified Pole parenthetically as 'a man of noble birth, but yet an archenemy unto God, and to Christ's true religion, yea, altogether given to papistry, ambition and hypocrisy'.[57] This judgment disappeared from the 1570 edition in which Foxe first reflected on Pole's attitude to heresy, rather than reproducing the party line as he had done in 1563. The change seems to have been induced by the discovery of new evidence, especially Bonner's letter to Pole acknowledging Pole's orders to exercise restraint in the treatment of heretics.[58] But Foxe also suppressed evidence favourable to Pole that he had printed in 1563, especially his pardon to three penitent heretics, although the episode was still mentioned.[59] It would be safe to say that Foxe's handling of Pole was much more nuanced than most of his Protestant contemporaries (or successors). Francis Godwin, whose *Catalogue of the bishops of England* first appeared in 1601, in a second edition in 1615 and in

---

[55] For the date, see Francis Thynne, *Animadversions upon… Chaucers workes*, ed. F. J. Furnivall (Early English Text Society, o.s., 9 (1875), revised ed.), p. lxxv. David Carlson, 'The writings and manuscript collections of the Elizabethan alchemist, antiquary, and herald Francis Thynne', *Huntington library quarterly*, 52 (1989), pp. 203–72, p. 228 thought that Thynne's lives of the archbishops might be based on BL, Cleop. C III, fos. 184v–93r.

[56] Raphael Hollinshead, *Chronicles of England, Scotland and Ireland* (London: J. Johnson et al., 1807–8; 6 vols.), 4, p. 144. For Pole and heresy, see above ch. 7, pp. 271–83.

[57] John Foxe, *Actes and monuments of these latter and perillous days* (London: John Daye, 1563; STC, no. 11222), p. 656.

[58] *The first (second–) volume of the Ecclesiastical History* (London: John Daye, 1570; STC, no. 11223), pp. 2157–8; *CRP*, no. 1675.

[59] *Actes and monuments* (1563), pp. 1525–6.

an expanded Latin translation in 1616, relied on Parker, more as the revisions progressed, and mainly reproduced his attitude to Pole.[60] Not all English historiography took even as negative a stand as this. Antony à Wood's biography was almost entirely favourable.[61]

Very early a canonical set of high points in Pole's life was established, with a few variations. *De unitate* almost always appeared. Most often the episodes focused on the crises of his diplomatic career, especially 1537 (the single most commonly cited example of Pole's constancy) and 1554, the reconciliation, and, usually, his death. Writers faithfully following Dudic regularly included his interview with Henry VIII in addition, and many thought Becket's fate needed mentioning. Andre Duchesne's treatment in *Histoire generale d'Angleterre, d'Escosse, et d'Irlande* was typical.[62] Undoubtedly the summit of sixteenth- and seventeenth-century historiography was the third edition of Alfonso Chacón's *Vitae et res gestae pontificum romanorum et S. R. E. cardinalium* as edited by Agostino Oldoino, S. J. He drew on the additions to the second edition (1630) by Andrea Vittorelli and Francesco Ughelli as well as Dony.[63] The more than forty sources cited by Oldino (better than quadrupled from Vittorelli's nine and the life as a whole is proportionately even longer) reflect Oldino's thoroughness and provide the best guide to that epoch's writing about Pole. All of Chacón's editors also typify how denatured Pole had become, stripped of most of his political and religious context, although Oldino did openly defend him against a charge of heresy. His activity at Trent was barely mentioned.

Seventeenth-century study of the council did not overlook Pole. Paolo Sarpi

---

[60] [Francis Godwin], *A catalogue of the Bishops of England, since the first planting of Christian religion in this Island, together with a brief history of their lives and memorable actions, so near as can be gathered out of antiquity* (London: George Bishop, 1601; STC 11937; London: Thomas Adams, 1615; STC 11938); and *De praesulibus Angliae commentarius* first published in 1616, continued and annotated by William Richardson (Cambridge: Joseph Bentham, 1743, 2 vols.).

[61] Anthony à Wood, *Athenae oxonienses*, ed. Philip Bliss (London: F. C. and J. Rivington *et al.*, 1815; 4 vols.; originally published 1668), 1, cols. 277–95.

[62] Paris: Jean Petitpas, 1614, pp. 1294–5 (*De unitate*); 1305 (cardinalate and first

legation, with attack on Sleidan's veracity); 1307 (Becket); 1357–68 (legations of 1553 through to his death). The smallest appearance of Pole as virtuous Christian probably came in Florimond de Raemond (Remond), *Histoire de la naissance, progrez, et decadence de l'heresie de ce siècle*, 6 (Paris: Chas. Chastellain, 1605), fo. 25r–v.

[63] *Vitae et res gestae pontificum romanorum et S. R. E. cardinalium*, 3, ed. Agostino Oldoino (Rome: Filippo and Antonio De Rubeis, 1678), cols. 627–38. For Chacón (1540–99), cf. Cochrane, pp. 427–8, who does not mention this work. Unfortunately, I have not been able to see the first edition of 1601, and therefore cannot say which parts are certainly to be attributed to Chacón.

and Sforza Pallavicino both gave him a good deal of attention. Sarpi noted Pole's actions where relevant, but refrained from any characterization except to note once the 'goodness of his nature'.[64] Various refutations of Sarpi preceded Pallavicino's which proved to be the most successful.[65] His *Istoria del concilio di Trento* (first edition 1655) reported Pole's activities from 1537 onward, all under the rubric of 'an angel of mercy and a composite of all the virtues'.[66] Pallavicino carefully followed the sequence of canonical events, including Becket's burnt bones (1, p. 216). Pallavicino's Pole rested solidly on the sources, especially the now missing register of his correspondence in 1553–4.[67]

After a brief treatment by Thomas Fuller that dwelt mainly on pasquinades, near the end of the seventeenth century Pole made his first extended appearance in English in William Joyner's preface to the reading of Maucroix's translation of Dudic.[68] Joyner (or Lyde) intended in his *Some observations upon the life of Reginaldus Polus cardinal of the royal blood of England. Sent in a pacquet out of Wales, by G. L. gentleman and servant to the late majesty of Henrietta Maria* 'to reduce this noble offspring of the royal family into favor again among his compatriots'.[69] Joyner admitted the difficulty caused by Pole's many facets, but singled out his opening oration to Trent as his brightest moment (pp. 10–11). Pole was supremely virtuous, his life 'like a well-contrived poem' (pp. 17 and 13). In place of constancy, Joyner praised Pole's 'serenity' (p. 25). Taking a swipe at Bishop Burnet as one of the 'mechanic spirits' who had undermined noble men (p. 36), Joyner turned to extracts from Manuzio's preface to *De concilio* (pp. 37–46), Sadoleto's letters (pp. 47–54), and Giovanni della Casa's and Bembo's opinions (pp. 54–5). Joyner praised Pole above all for his eloquence, 'which was very noble in all [his contemporaries], though only royal in Polus'. It was a great loss that Pole had left no treatise on preaching, on the shortcomings of the Puritan brand of which (especially Hugh Peter) Joyner spent the next dozen

---

[64] Paolo Sarpi, *Istoria del concilio tridentino*, ed. Giovanni Gambarin (Bari: Laterza, 1935; 3 vols.), 2, p. 51. See also 1, pp. 164, 177, 206ff; 2, pp. 189–91, 208, 214, 221.

[65] Hubert Jedin, *Das Konzil von Trient. Ein Überblick über die Erforschung seiner Geschichte* (Rome: Edizioni di Storia e Letteratura, 1948) and *Der Quellenaparat der Konzilsgeschichte Pallavicinos.* (Rome: Casa Editrice S. A. L. E. R., 1940). For Pallavicino, see Josef Höfer and Karl Rahner, eds., *Lexikon für Theologie und Kirche* (Freiburg: Herder, 1957–68), *s. n.*

[66] Sforza Pallavicino, SJ, *Istoria del concilio di Trento* (Naples: Vaglio, 1853–6; 3 vols.), 1, p. 216.

[67] *Ibid.*, 2, pp. 230–9 and 260–6.

[68] Thomas Fuller, *The history of the worthies of England*, ed. P. Austin Nuttall (reprinted New York: AMS Press, 1965; first published 1662; 3 vols.), 3, pp. 128–30.

[69] London: Matthew Turner, 1686, p. 7. For Joyner see Leslie Stephen and Sidney Lee, eds., *Dictionary of national biography* (Oxford: Oxford University Press, 1917) (hereafter *DNB*).

pages (pp. 63–75), before concluding with another fifty pages of odds and ends. A peculiar work, but the grandfather of modern English scholarship on Pole.

The object of Joyner's particular animus, Gilbert Burnet, did not deserve such treatment, any more than did LeGrand, the butt of Burnet's own criticism.[70] Burnet mainly treated Pole even-handedly. Although decrying the cardinal as 'barefaced in his treasonable designs' during the Exeter conspiracy, and describing him as 'indeed a man of an easy and generous temper, but much in the power of those whom he loved and trusted' during the conclave of Julius III, Burnet somehow drew on one of Pole's letters to Truchsess for the conclusion that he

> professed himself an enemy to extreme proceedings. He said, pastors ought to have bowels, even to their straying sheep: bishops were fathers, and ought to look on those that erred as their sick children, and not for that to kill them: he had seen, that severe proceedings did rather inflame than cure disease: there was a great difference to be made between a nation uninfected, where some few teachers came to spread errors; and a nation that had been overrun with them.[71]

Burnet went further and praised most of Pole's synodal legislation, 'above all, that design of his, to have seminaries in every cathedral for the planting of the diocese, [that] shews what a wise prospect he had to the right methods of recovering a church, which was overrun, as he judged, with heresy. It was the same that Cranmer had formerly designed, but never took effect.'[72] Readers would not have missed the unflattering comparison. Nevertheless, Burnet adhered to the party line that Pole had 'hastened the execution of Cranmer', although qualifying even that demerit as 'the only personal blemish I find laid on him'. John Strype, following Parker, later persuaded him 'that Pole was not so mild as I had represented him'.[73] Even under that kind of pressure, Burnet backtracked and blamed Mary for the persecution.[74] His final character of Pole could almost have come from Dudic.[75] 'He was a learned, modest, humble, and good-natured man; and had indeed such qualities, and such a temper, that, if he could have

---

[70] For Burnet's relations with LeGrand, see Nicholas Pocock, ed., *The history of the reformation of the church of England by Gilbert Burnet* (Oxford: Clarendon Press, 1865; 7 vols.), 3, pp. 4 and 22 and J. P. Nicéron, *Mémoires pour servir a l'histoire des hommes illustres dans la republique des lettres* (Paris: Briasson, 1728–41; 42 vols.), 26, pp. 126–31.

[71] Burnet/Pocock, 1, p. 562; 2, 255–6 (conclave, done from Jacques-Auguste de Thou's treatment, which is largely derived from Dudic); and pp. 479–80.

[72] *Ibid.*, 2, p. 524.

[73] *Ibid.*, 2, p. 525 and 3, p. 451.

[74] *Ibid.*, 3, p. 462.

[75] *Ibid.*, 2, pp. 590–1.

brought the other bishops to follow his measures, or the pope and queen to approve of them, he might have probably done much to have reduced this nation to popery again.' This was a back-handed compliment, and Burnet justified it by declaring Pole 'the only man of that whole party, of whom I found any reason to say much good' and he had therefore treated Pole's virtues in order 'to let the world see how little I am biased'. Of course, Pole's greatest failing was 'a vast superstition to the see of Rome'.

Pole's handling of the 'possessioners' greatly concerned Burnet. He wrote an anonymous pamphlet, *A letter written to Dr. Burnet, giving an account of Cardinal Pool's secret powers* (London, 1685), published by the well-known Whig Richard Baldwin. It included Pole's bulls of 1553.[76] Nathaniel Johnston touched off a minor controversy with an indirect response. His *The assurance of abbey and other church-lands in England to the possessors* (London: Henry Hills, 1687), pp. 90ff replied to *How the members of the Church of England ought to behave themselves under a Roman Catholic King* (London: Randall Taylor, 1687; Wing H 2961). Neither it nor a rejoinder to Johnston by John Willes, *Abby and other Church-Lands, not yet assured to such possessors as are Roman Catholicks; Dedicated to the Nobility and Gentry of that Religion* (London, 1688), said much about Pole. The issue of 'assurance of abbey lands' remained alive into at least the next century.[77]

Reformation controversies continued to dominate the image of Pole in the enlightened eighteenth century. Joyner's fears of Pole's obscurity would have evaporated. He was commonplace enough for John Hinton to include a capsule biography in his *Universal magazine* for 1749, along with a portrait (catalogue no. 34). Hinton claimed to have used Beccadelli and based his judgments on Burnet, although he rejected Burnet's defence of Pole's treatment of heresy, perhaps originating the claim that Pole bore responsibility because of his failure to restrain his agents.[78] By the time Hinton wrote, a good deal of new source material had come into play and more was about to be made available. One of the most important contributions was Thomas Tanner's list of Pole's works in *Bibliotheca britannico-hibernica: sive de scriptoribus qui in Anglia, Scotia, et Hibernia ad saeculi XVII initium floruerunt*, together with a biographical sketch

[76] For Burnet's authorship of *A letter*, see J. E. S. Clarke and H. C. Foxcroft, *A life of Gilbert Burnet* (Cambridge: Cambridge University Press, 1907), p. 532. For Baldwin, Mark Goldie, 'The revolution of 1689 and the structure of political argument: an essay and an annotated bibliography of pamphlets on the allegiance controversy', *Bulletin of research in the humanities*, 83 (1980), pp. 473–564, pp. 494–5.

[77] LPL, MS 1998, fo. 131, A. C. Ducarel to Archbishop Secker on that head in 1765.

[78] *The Universal Magazine of Knowledge and Pleasure ... and other Arts and Sciences*, 5 (1749), pp. 169–71.

and list of sources.[79] As one might expect, the work of Catholic exiles like Hugh
Tootel and the non-juror Jeremy Collier continued to reflect Pole's positive reputation.[80] Both recognized the importance of manuscript sources, chief among
them the legatine register in Douai that Tootel rediscovered, although he failed
to use it.[81] Neither did the greatest editor of Pole's manuscripts, Cardinal
Angelo Maria Querini, who knew of it.[82] Querini's five volume *Epistolarum
Reginaldi Poli [libri]* marked the greatest breakthrough in Pole scholarship
before this century. Querini is a fascinating figure, Jansenist sympathizer,
Vatican Librarian, indefatigable collector of materials and historian of the
Cassinese Benedictines, founder of the imposing Biblioteca Queriniana in his
native Brescia.[83] He was not an easy man to work with, as he drove even the
most good-humoured of popes and his sometime patron Benedict XIV to

[79] London: G. Bowyer, 1748; reprinted
Tucson: Audax Press, 1963, pp. 602–3.

[80] Charles Dodd (pseudonym of Hugh
Tootel), *The church history of England from
the year 1500 to the year 1688, chiefly with
regard to Catholicks*, 1 (Brussels (but
London, no publisher), 1737). Jeremy
Collier, *An ecclesiastical history of Great
Britain, chiefly of England* (London: Keble *et
al.*, 1708–14; 2 vols.), 2, pp. 135–7, 286,
351–3, 372–4, 377, 388–90, 393, 402, and
406–7.

[81] I have not been able to confirm that most of
the indexing to the register is in Tootel's
hand. *Catalogue des manuscrits de la
bibliothèque municipale de Douai, par M.
L'abbe Deshaines* (Paris: Imprimerie
nationale, 1878). Collier's citations of
manuscript sources seem often to have been
taken from Burnet rather than the originals;
how he used the Douai register (p. 388) is
unknown.

[82] BCQ, MS F. III. 7 m. 1, fo. 49r, Thomas
Philippe Cardinal d'Alsace-Boussu,
probably to Querini, Malines, 7 March
1748.

[83] Still the best biography is Alfred
Baudrillart, *De cardinale Quirini vita et
operibus* (Paris: Firmin-Didot, 1889),
supplemented by Paolo Guerrini, 'Il

cardinale Angelo Maria Quirini nel
bicentenario della sua biblioteca', *Memorie
storiche della diocesi di Brescia*, 17 (1950), pp.
57–84 and especially *Miscellanea
Queriniana. A ricordo del II centenario della
morte del cardinale Angelo Maria Querini*
(Brescia: Fratelli Geroldi, 1961). Arnaldo
Momigliano, *Essays in ancient and modern
historiography* (Middletown, CT: Wesleyan
University Press, 1977), p. 293 for Querini's
Jansenist sympathies. Querini was a noted
ecumenist, at least for his century, making a
trip to England where he met Burnet, and
corresponding extensively with German
protestants. See Friedrich Lauchert, 'Die
irenischen Bestrebungen des Kardinals
Angelo Maria Quirini (O. S. B.) speziell in
seinem literarischen Verkehr mit deutschen
Protestantischen Gelehrten', *Studien und
Mitteilungen aus dem Benediktiner- und
Zisterziensorden bzw. zur Geschichte des
Benediktinerordens und seiner Zweige*, 24
(1903), pp. 243–75. For the trip, see
Querini, *Commentarii de rebus pertinentibus
ad Angelum Mariam S. R. E. Cardinalem
Quirinum* (Brescia: Giovanni Maria
Rizzardi, 1749), pp. 51–7. The list of
Querini's MSS in the BCQ runs to a dozen
folio pages.

admit.[84] Nevertheless, Querini made good use of such auspices in assembling about 400 of Pole's letters (less than 20 per cent of those now known), both Beccadelli's and Dudic's lives and a mass of other materials, as frequently as possible taken from manuscripts. These were often uncritically handled and the editing leaves a great deal to be desired, because of the incompetence of one of Querini's principal amanuenses and deliberate expurgation or amelioration.[85] The 'diatribes' Querini added to the four volumes published during his lifetime constitute a detailed biography. Querini also set himself to write a formal life, but it amounted to only twelve folios plus a preface.[86] Querini's motive was polemical. His volumes were to defend Pole against Johann Georg Schelhorn's aspersions, including the Vergerian implication that Pole was really a Protestant.[87] Despite all his energy and erudition, Querini's image of Pole came straight out of the sixteenth century.

Much the same is true of an impressive plagiarism of Querini's work published about twenty years later by Thomas Phillips (1708–74). The book was

---

[84] The pope frequently described Querini in unflattering terms, and tried to have the Inquisition ban his publications. 'Il suo [Querini's] mestiere è di far note ai libri degli altri, per esempio, alle lettere di card. Polo, ma non è in grado di comporre da sè, non avendo fondamento di sapere, ed essendo affatto senza logica.' *Le lettere di Benedetto XIV al Card. [sic] de Tencin*, ed. Emilia Morelli (Rome: Edizioni di Storia e Letteratura, 1955–84; 4 vols.), 1, p. 412. Cf. also R. Haynes, *Prospero Lambertini. The humanist pope Benedict XIV* (London: Weidenfeld and Nicolson, 1970), p. 156. This attitude represented second thoughts for the pope, who had given Querini authority to assemble materials for *ERP*, including from the Beccadelli family archive in Bologna. Ludovico Beccadelli–Benedict XIV, Bologna, 21 December 1743 (BAV, Vat. lat. 12909, fo. 27v).

[85] See the introduction to *CRP*.

[86] BCQ, MS F. III. 7 m. 1, fos. 57r–68r (with separate foliation 1r-12r) is the life and the preface is Venice, Biblioteca Querini-Stampalia, Cod. Cl. VI, XXXV, filza 6. The roughly equal proportion between the two gives a good idea of the length of Querini's suite in bombast. The life is largely drawn from Beccadelli and Dudic, but Querini made good use of his four years in England (1710–14) to incorporate à Wood, Collier, and Laurence Echard's *History of England*, especially on the question of the apostolic succession of Marian bishops and Anglican orders. See Guerrini, p. 62 and unpublished work of my former student Sarah Hingtgen on Querini's sources.

[87] Johann Georg Schelhorn, *Amoenitates historiae ecclesiasticae et literariae* (Frankfurt–Leipzig: Daniel Bartholomäus, 1737–8; 2 vols.), 1, pp. 1–179 (on Flaminio) and 180–209 (Carnesecchi). Schelhorn also sent Querini two letters. The first, containing his reactions to *ERP*, offered some criticisms of Pole mainly for his diplomacy. Querini printed them with extensive annotations (*ERP*, 1, pp. II-LXXX and I-XXIV). For the exchange, see Lauchert, pp. 248–53 and Simoncelli, *Caso*, pp. 234ff.

originally printed in Oxford, where Pole was in remarkably good odour. In addition to à Wood, in 1730 and 1758 images of him graced the *Oxford Almanac* (Catalogue nos. 35 and 36).[88] Phillips, as Joyner's grand-nephew, had Pole in his blood.[89] He, like Joyner, also had a chequered career as a sometime Jesuit. Even more than Joyner, Phillips meant to defend Pole and the Catholic church. It would be charitable to say that Phillips immersed himself deeply in his sources. His opening sentence is a grandiose paraphrase of Beccadelli's. 'The Author's design is to place Cardinal Pole in a true, distinct, and conspicuous light, and show his whole conduct to have been one uniform system of the most exalted, and, at the same time, the most amiable virtues, which can adorn a man of letters, a patriot, a Christian, and a prelate.' For Phillips a mere saint was inadequate.[90] He expected trouble from his proposed transvaluation of values, and also feared that Pole's life would prove boring, since his character never varied, no matter the circumstances (pp. vii–viii). Previous lives failed to raise Pole to the proper 'altitude' (p. xi). His character showed all the virtues of the English, raised to the highest degree: 'piety and zeal in his Maker's cause . . . ; simplicity of mind and manners joined to elevation of genius, and consummate knowledge; magnanimity and freedom of speech and sentiment; humanity and disinterestedness; modest worth, void of vanity and ostentation, and all the milder virtues of the heart' of the bluff Englishman (p. xii). If this overheated passage does not make the point that Phillips still inhabited Pole's universe, despite his worries that his contemporaries found the sixteenth century closed, the rhetorical way in which he treated some of the major episodes of his hero's life will. For example, Pole's first confrontation with Henry was introduced thus: '[A] scene was now opening, and such a part assigned him, as required all the firmness and generosity of a soul superior to hope and fear, and every tender feeling of nature' (I, p. 34).

Phillips claimed to write nothing but facts, keeping Pole's virtues separate from his narrative, but the balance was unstable. At the opening of part II, he set out Pole's virtues in a passage taken almost verbatim from Dudic, with embellishments (pp. 217–33). Pole was still the constant saint combined with

---

[88] Thomas Phillips, *The history of the life of Reginald Pole* (London: Thomas Payne *et al.*, 1767, 2nd ed.; 2 vols.; originally published Oxford: William Jackson, 1764–5). There was also a Dublin edition by J. A. Husband in 1765. W. F. Hook's judgment is exact: 'Phillips has simply translated and re-arranged Quirini.' Walter Farquhar Hook, *Lives of the archbishops of Canterbury*, 8 (London: Richard Bentley, 1869; 2nd ed. 1884), p. 4n.

[89] *DNB*. See also his autobiographical essay, *Philemon* (privately printed, 1761). The British Library copy was presented to William Cole by Phillips.

[90] I quote from the 2nd ed.; p. v.

the man of affairs, who should be such an object of admiration that 'his life [was] like a gentle stream, which does not only glide through lonely vales, but visits, in its course, populous cities, and is, at once, their wealth and ornament'. This rhetorical flourish consorts oddly with Phillips' reverence for the facts, as we might expect of a writer caught on the cusp of the conversion of salvation history into its scientific cousin. Phillips's work marks the moment at which Pole's highly rhetorical self-creation became fact, absent its original persuasive purposes. As a Catholic writing in the wake of the '45, Phillips no longer had a political motive like Pole's when he attacked Henry VIII. In place of the active life, Phillips could offer only objectivity.

This move did not persuade his critics, including some high Tories, justifiably concerned that Phillips might blacken them by association.[91] Some of this barrage of works had no importance, except for the level of vituperation they reached in attacking Pole.[92] One of the others was a respectable biography (despite its author's bad reputation), another a serious work of scholarship, and Phillips's book helped to inspire the only English translation of Beccadelli, not Dudic, perhaps because the translator, Benjamin Pye, was illaterate. Pye's notes amount almost to a biography. Gloucester Ridley's *A review of Mr Phillips's History of the life of Reginald Pole* (London: J. Whiston *et al.*, 1766) set out both to defend the Church of England and also to judge Pole by the standards of the Gospel (pp. iii and 3). The blanket condemnation of Phillips's work as 'false or misrepresented' resulted (p. 4). Ridley made the excellent point that it was hard to see Pole's life whole because it was divided between England and Italy (p. 5). His accomplishments in Italy were little known in England, while the Italians did not regard his 'ingratitude, resentment, and treason' as of much significance. Similarly,

> that milder merit of the heart, which distinguished him among his favorites at Padua, is lost to us amidst that most illiberal abuse, with which he foams against his King and benefactor: the appearance of humanity and disinterestedness, which he put on at Rome, drop off when we look at him travelling from court to court, to rouse up the princes of Europe to invade his country.

---

[91] This inference follows from the dedication of several of these works to Richard Trevor, bishop of Durham, for whom see Norman Sykes, *Church and state in England in the XVIIIth century* (Cambridge: Cambridge University Press, 1934), p. 39.

[92] Edward Stone, *Remarks upon the history of the life of Reginald Pole* (Oxford: William Jackson, 1766) and Richard Tillard, *A letter to Mr Phillips, containing some observations on his history of the life of Reginald Pole* (London, privately printed) are typical.

Ridley, a collateral descendant of the Edwardian bishop, scorned what the Italians thought of Pole, and dutifully quoted the proverb 'Parker' had made his speaking text (p. 92). In short, 'his glosses to deceive, and then, especially when he calls God to witness, are notorious proofs of his falsehood: indeed his own cowardice was too great to permit him to act with truth and simplicity.... [F]ear and design kept him always on his guard, and he never talked, but from behind a mask' (p. 350). Ridley's youthful experience as an actor lay behind his Italianate Pole.[93]

Ridley referred (p. 357) to a more imposing work whose author orchestrated the campaign against Phillips: Timothy Neve's *Animadversions upon Mr Phillips's History of the life of Reginald Pole* (Oxford: Clarendon Press, 1766), dedicated to the archbishop of Canterbury.[94] Neve had the help of the respected antiquaries Thomas Birch and John Jortin as well as the politician Charles Townshend, which gave his work the status almost of an official rejoinder.[95] Neve accused Phillips of insulting England and took him up on his proposal to rely only on facts rather 'than the gaudy declarations of affected eloquence' to which Phillips had resorted (preface). The only way to understand Pole was to put him in context (p. 5). Neve agreed, too, that the best means of doing that was through Pole's writings, but differed radically from Phillips over their nature. 'We shall find his writings . . . dictated with this sole view, of blazing out the splendor of his own actions; and aggravating the defects, and depreciating the merits, of those he looked upon as his enemies.' Under no circumstances could such 'a violent, partial man' be heard as sole witness in his own cause (p. 90). Not inaccurately, Neve similarly judged *De unitate* (p. 127). The 'Apology' to Charles expressed Pole's 'implacable, revengeful malignity . . . in still stronger terms' (p. 150) and seemed to Neve 'that most inflammatory and scurrilous address . . . where all the vile and bitter expressions, which a fruitful and malicious imagination could invent, are in the coarsest language, without any regard to decency or religion, applied to his sovereign' (p. 322). Therefore Pole got what he deserved as a result of challenging Henry (p. 244). Neve's opinion of Pole's style extended

---

[93] *DNB.*

[94] Neve also gave Pye a copy of *ERP. The life of Cardinal Reginald Pole, written originally by Lodovico Beccadelli . . . translated by Benjamin Pye* (London: Bathurst, 1766), p. 167. Pye (pp. 172–3) offered a summary judgment of Pole much like Neve's. Pye and Neve knew Querini's work well, and both accused Phillips of plagiarism (Pye, Appendix, pp. 179–92; Neve, pp. 93ff, 140–1).

[95] Neve's copy with autograph corrections is British Library, shelf mark 4868.g.6. It contains correspondence with all the persons mentioned in the text. For Neve see *DNB.*

to his use of metaphors on which he expatiated at such length 'as to bewilder his reader almost as much as himself' (p. 553). Neve might have claimed to have put Pole in context, but this remark alone belies the point. Pole's worst offence, as usual, was Cranmer's burning. David Hume disagreed, making Pole a pillar of toleration, his personality moderating his principles. Hume's view had a long afterlife.[96]

The fate of Pole's story of his refusal of the archbishopric of York illustrates the transition in historiography occurring during this controversy. Both Phillips and his critics took the once rhetorical story as fact. Ridley insisted that he would 'never rely on Pole's testimony when not supported by others', but he yet blithely assessed the York interview as an instance of 'the common weakness of irresolute men [who] fluctuating between the choice of a present and future advantage, and, loath to quit either, lose both'.[97] Pye offers an even more egregious instance. He argued in his preface that 'a biographer seems to be by profession a writer of panegyric' who therefore 'often makes a sacrifice of truth without scruple', before concluding that 'it would be absurd . . . to make such effusion of the fancy . . . the basis and ground-work of real history'. Despite a few doubts about the documentary record, Pye nevertheless accorded Beccadelli's story enough credence to judge that it showed Pole in a bad light: 'he prevaricated with his prince; he deceived his friends; he acted disingenuously with himself'.[98]

Edward Hasted closed out the eighteenth century with a laudatory brief life in his *History of Kent*. He paraphrased Burnet's judgment of Pole before concluding that 'he [Pole] was a man of as great probity and virtue, and of as excellent endowments of mind, as any of his predecessors who had sat in this see [of Canterbury] before, had ever been, and have since, to the present time'.[99] By this time, despite Querini's labours, writing about Pole was largely confined to England. It would remain so until late in the next century when some of Schelhorn's countrymen adopted Pole as an ally in the wake of Vatican I. Nothing much happened to his image in the nineteenth century, no matter in

---

[96] David Hume, *The history of England from the invasion of Julius Caesar to the revolution in 1688* (New York: Harper & Brothers, 1879; 1st ed. 1759; 6 vols.), 3, pp. 359–66 and, e.g., S. Hubert Burke, *Historical portraits of the Tudor dynasty and the reformation period* (London: John Hodges, 1883; 4 vols.), 3, p. 56.

[97] Gloucester Ridley, *A review of Mr. Phillips's History of the life of Reginald Pole* (London: J. Whiston et al., 1766), pp. 24 and 20.

[98] Pye, pp. ix, 27–8.

[99] Edward Hasted, *The history and topographical survey of the county of Kent* (Canterbury: W. Bristow, 1797–1801, 2nd ed.; reprinted Menston, Yorks.: Scolar Press, 1972; 12 vols.), 12, pp. 444–51.

what country, despite the steady accumulation of new sources. He remained either a saint or a chief sinner, depending on the religion (or the politics) of the writer. The Tory Edmund Lodge wrote one of the most widely disseminated lives, in which, to be fair, he introduced one new interpretation.[100] His first paragraph is as pregnant as Beccadelli's.

> Reginald Pole, a noble example to the age in which he lived, stood almost alone, without acquiring the degrees of distinction which he justly merited. ...Thus in his own time more admired than understood; respected, but not imitated; and of habits too widely dissimilar from those of others of his own station to admit easily of comparison; it is rather his character than his history that has been transmitted to posterity. It is the common fate of good counsels that have been rejected, and of worthy examples that have been contemned to pass in a great measure unrewarded.[101]

In other words, although peculiarly eminent, Pole failed. All the same, Lodge continued in Beccadelli's and Dudic's tradition by treating Pole as an example, while filling out his ten pages with material from à Wood and Godwin's history of Mary's reign and closing with a list of Pole's writings from à Wood (pp. 262–3).

Pole appeared in other standard biographical compendia, including the Coopers' *Athenae Cantabrigienses*, which cited but apparently did not use a few new MS sources and joined the ranks of those praising Pole.[102] Gaetano Moroni summarized Pole as having 'eminently the talents of a statesman and a great bishop'.[103] The most important such article was James Gairdner's in the *Dictionary of national biography*, originally published in 1896, which included a few notes on iconography by Sir George Scharf, director of the National Portrait Gallery. Gairdner produced a temperate and largely unobjectionable account. He concluded like Lodge that Pole failed through no fault of his own (p. 45).[104] Joseph Gillow included an article on Pole in his *Biographical dictionary*,

---

[100] *DNB*.

[101] Edmund Lodge, *Portraits of illustrious personages of Great Britain, with biographical and historical memoirs of their lives and actions* (London: Henry Bohn, 1849; 8 vols.), 1, p. 253. For the editions of this popular work, see below p. 435.

[102] C. H. Cooper and Thompson Cooper, *Athenae Cantabrigienses* (Cambridge:

Deighton and Bell, 1858–61; 2 vols.), 1, pp. 183–5 and 2, p. 551.

[103] Gaetano Moroni, *Dizionario di erudizione storico-ecclesiastica* (Venice: Tipografia Emiliana, 1851; 103 vols. in 53), 53, pp. 40–2.

[104] Gairdner summarized his article in S. L. Ollard, ed., *A dictionary of English church history* (London: A. R. Mowbray, 1912), pp. 467–70.

in which he quoted Hume on Pole's opinion of religious persecution as his conclusion.[105]

Gillow's assertion that 'all writers unite in their praise for Pole's piety, learning and integrity of life' was not quite accurate, especially not for his own century that saw the publication of the most sustained attack on Pole, W. F. Hook's in his massive *Lives of the archbishops of Canterbury*.[106] Hook began by noting that Pole was distinguished by numbers of 'advocates' and 'adversaries', making it relatively easy for a biographer to judge him. Hook certainly made his judgment easily. Pole's 'besetting sin . . . was his abhorrence and detestation of Henry VIII' (pp. 2–3). '[R]emembering that Pole was unconscious of the evil that was in him' served to explain 'the many and sometimes the astonishing inconsistencies that perplexed his career' (p. 5). His beliefs were all Protestant, but he became a papist out of hatred for Henry. He went overboard in his zeal for the papacy, despite 'his better self', and for all his efforts still did not achieve popularity in Rome. This is a nicely paradoxical characterization. Hook judged Pole on religious rather than political grounds, or better religious and psychological. Having exposed the story of the interview with Henry over York, Hook observed that Pole 'first deceived himself' on the basis of 'an imagination, that he had suffered in the cause he was at that time supporting. . . . Exaggeration sometimes approaches so nearly to fabrication, as to render the one undistinguishable [*sic*] from the other' (p. 44). The same judgment applied to Pole's conduct during and after the Pilgrimage of Grace. Hook tried to allow that Pole had a right as a nobleman to lead an insurrection once it had already begun, but still judged his actions 'base in the extreme', arising from self-deception and a mind 'unconsciously dishonest' (pp. 74–5). Such a disordered intellect could only produce a work like *De unitate* in which '[i]n some whole paragraphs we find nothing but a diarrhoea of meaningless words' (p. 83). At other times, Pole's mind was 'vacillating and sensitive' until he had decided what to do, at which time he became 'a man of determined will'. Hook, despite more than a little animus against Pole (he accused him of both ambition and covetousness), offered the path-breaking assessment that 'Pole had many faults, but he had also many virtues. He was neither a hero nor a saint' (pp. 186–7). He was, however, an unmitigated blackguard when it came to the persecution under Mary, acting out of 'selfishness awfully criminal', a point Hook drove into the ground (pp. 371–95).

---

[105] Joseph Gillow, *A literary and biographical history or biographical dictionary of the English Catholics* (London: Burns and Oates, 1885–1905; 6 vols.), 5, pp. 336–41, including a list of works and a brief iconography.

[106] Above note 88. For Hook, see *DNB*.

Hook not only quoted extensively from Pole's writings, but also made much use of new sources. For example, he reached the accurate conclusion that Pole had assisted Henry willingly in gaining the opinions of the University of Paris on the basis of several of his letters among the State Papers (pp. 37–9). He was also first to discuss Pole's letter to the emperor of 1535 (pp. 70–2). In this case he relied on the collaboration of Thomas Duffus Hardy and Gustav Bergenroth, neither of whose memories or transcriptions could be fully trusted.[107] One of the worst howlers thus introduced concerned a letter in which Pole allegedly proposed to Mary (p. 12). After Hook wrote, Rawdon Brown, a strong admirer of Pole, added substantially to the corpus of documentary evidence in his summaries from an inferior copy in the Biblioteca Marciana in Venice of one of Pole's registers.[108] One of the most important sources, which regrettably took the longest time to make an impact, came into play about the same time. As in Hook's case, the validity of Anglican orders exercised many Anglicans (and their Catholic opponents), and in the course of the controversy that continued throughout the century until the publication of the bull *Apostolicae curae* (1896) Edgar Estcourt first seriously used Pole's register in Douai.[109] F. A. Gasquet and his collaborators published a few pieces from it in a collection intended to document the problem of orders.[110] Lord Acton apparently meant to include

---

[107] T. D. Hardy, *Report . . . upon the documents in the archives and public libraries of Venice* (London: Longman, Green, Reader and Dyer, 1866), p. 69 done by Bergenroth from memory (*ibid.*, p. 68).

[108] 'As compiler of a calendar, I have merely to register documents, without commending or vituperating the individuals to whom they relate but from the day Pole entered himself as a student at Padua, in 1521, until his final departure from the Lake of Garda towards England in 1553, my belief is, that he did more to maintain the repute of his country for high breeding, scholarship, integrity, and consistency, than any other Englishman I ever heard of.' *CSPV*, 6:1, p. xi. Much of the rest of the preface is a summary of Pole's great deeds, especially in the conclave.

[109] E. E. Estcourt, *The question of Anglican ordinations discussed* (London: Burns &

Oates, 1873). He worked in Douai with the assistance of the Benedictine Austin O'Neill (p. vii). Neither the *DNB* nor Gillow say when. Pencil notes on the register indicate the documents he published. Some of Estcourt's texts were translated, sometimes after collation to other copies, in Arthur Lowndes, *Vindication of Anglican orders* (New York: James Pott and London: Rivingtons, 1897–1900; 2 vols.), appendix to vol. 2, pp. lxx–xcii.

[110] J. Moyes, F. A. Gasquet and D. Fleming, *Documenta ad legationem Cardinalis Poli spectantia* (Rome: Privately Printed, 1896). For more on this critical moment in Anglo-Roman relations, see T. A. Lacey, *A Roman diary and other documents relating to the papal inquiry into English ordinations MDCCCXCVI* (London: Longman, Green, 1910), pp. 171–84.

excerpts among his many aborted publication projects. There is a partial, randomly selected, and not always accurate transcript in the Cambridge University Library, Add. MS 4841. Acton conducted more extensive archival searches for Pole materials, although it is not clear why, perhaps as a cover for a projected book on the Index. He used the volume in the Marciana and apparently collaborated with Brown, investigated the holdings in the Archivio segreto vaticano (which he most inaccurately characterized as 'few'), and visited at least Parma and Madrid as well.[111] But in his published writings Acton made little more mention of Pole than did John Lingard in his mammoth *A history of England from the first invasion by the Romans to the revolution of 1688* (1819–30).

One of the oddest semi-biographical treatments of Pole is F. G. Lee's.[112] Dedicated to both the archbishops of Canterbury and Westminster, the Anglo-Catholic Lee hoped his book would contribute to the reunification of the Church of England with Rome.[113] Lee's first chapter sketched Pole's career up to 1539, with the object of casting as evil a light as possible on Henry and Cromwell. The rest of the book jumped ahead to Mary's reign and the restoration of Catholicism. The moral was the continued relevance of Pole's legatine synod. English Protestants regarded it as a dangerous precedent as is clear from Henry Raikes's translation of its decrees published in 1839.[114] Otherwise, Lee's work has comparatively little to do with Pole despite its title and chiefly has value for its contributions to Pole's iconography, although Lee did do some basic research, e.g., on the sources for the synod (p. 160).

Lee unabashedly offered Pole as an example, and this continued to be his fate. Ethelred Taunton and his circle saw Pole as the patron of their brand of Catholic revival. Taunton meant to write a biography, but got no further than an entry in the eleventh edition of the *Encyclopedia britannica*, appearing by coincidence in the same year as *The Catholic encyclopedia* in which Herbert Thurston had a big article on Pole. Thurston, like Taunton, claimed to know something of Pole's correspondence beyond what Querini published but I have been unable to establish how they found it or what they meant to do with it. Before Taunton

---

[111] Damian McElrath, *Lord Acton: the decisive decade, 1864–1874. Essays and documents* (Louvain: Bureaux de la R. H. E.; Bibliothèque de l'Université; & Publications Universitaires de Louvain, 1970, pp. 11, 53, 69, 129, 137–8.

[112] *Reginald Pole cardinal archbishop of Canterbury, an historical sketch* (London

and New York: John C. Nimmo and G. P. Putnam's Sons, 1888).

[113] See the 'Prologue', pp. xi–xxxviii and 'Practical epilogue' on the Order of Corporate Reunion, pp. 261–303.

[114] *The reformation of England, by the decrees of Cardinal Pole* (Chester: R. H. Spence, 1839).

could hand over to his protégé Marie Hallé (writing as Martin Haile), a German biography appeared by Athanasius Zimmermann, S. J.[115] Unlike most of his predecessors, Zimmermann began his biography in down-beat fashion, bemoaning the neglect of Pole's life. Querini and his follower Phillips were 'too eulogistic' and had omitted too much. Hook and Canon Dixon were mere *Parteigänger*, and Hook was abusive in addition (p. 5). Zimmermann's method marked a change of direction. The problem was not sufficient material, but its selection and arrangement (p. 6). More, he promised strict neutrality (p. 7). Nevertheless, Pole still served as an example (p. 8). Zimmermann's conclusion came close to Gairdner's: Pole failed through no fault of his own (p. 378). With these two authoritative students behind it, failure became the almost universal judgment in this century.[116]

Zimmermann's interpretation relied heavily on supposition, and his style on hyperbole. The description of the 'pious and well-educated teacher' Niccolò Leonico and his student Pole, 'conscientious and responsive to all good', is typical (p. 19). For Zimmermann, Pole was a religious man from the first (pp. 22–3; cf. 379). This sort of extrinsic argument got Zimmermann into trouble, since he found it therefore surprising that Pole should have waited a long time to visit Rome (p. 24). Similarly, he wrote that Pole's liberal arts training should have left him feeling deficient in theology (p. 25). He 'must have' felt the contrast between the virtuous churchmen he knew in Italy and Cardinal Wolsey or been saddened as he saw Cromwell rise (pp. 31 and 34), and so on.

Zimmermann's allegedly critical handling of sources foundered on his rever-

---

[115] Athanasius Zimmermann, *Kardinal Pole, sein Leben und seine Schriften. Ein Beitrag zur Kirchengeschichte des 16. Jahrhunderts* (Regensburg: Friedrich Pustet, 1893). Pole was an object of interest in Germany earlier in the nineteenth century, especially with his inclusion in a series of little biographies of famous churchmen. Moritz Kerker, *Reginald Pole, Cardinal der hl. römischen Kirche und Erzbischof von Canterbury: ein Lebensbild* (Freiburg/Breisgau: Herder, 1874). Kerker also wrote the article on Pole in the 1st ed. of *Wetzer und Welte's Kirchenlexikon* (French translation by Jacques Goschler (Paris: Gaume Frères and J. Duprey, 1868–1870; 26 vols.), 18, pp. 419–21),

which was replaced in the 2nd ed. of Joseph Hergenröther and Franz Kaulen (Freiburg/Breisgau: Herder, 1882–1903; 12 vols.), 10, cols 125–31 by an article by Alphons Bellesheim, historian of the Catholic church in Ireland and Scotland. Pole also appeared in H. Hurter, *Nomenclator literarius theologiae catholicae*, 3rd ed. (Innsbruck: Wagner, 1906; 3 vols.), 2, cols. 1466–8.

[116] See, for example, Gerald G. Walsh, 'Cardinal Pole and the problem of Chrisitan unity', *Catholic historical review*, 15 (1930), pp. 389–407, or Harold Child's denial in Katharine Garvin, ed., *The great Tudors* (London: Nicholson and Watson, 1935), pp. 241–50.

ence for Pole. Thus the story Pole told of Paris in the preface to Edward VI was found more reliable than the hard evidence of his contemporary correspondence with Henry VIII. Zimmermann saw the problem: 'The question, whether Pole unintentionally spoke untruth or had already forgotten after a few years preceding events which he must certainly have known, is very important. . . . Had Pole veiled or forgotten the true state of affairs, then his letters and writings are not authentic sources, then must all of his statements, which are not supported by other sources, be doubted' (p. 36). Zimmermann dismissed most of the evidence in favour of Pole's enthusiastic co-operation with Henry's design before quoting Pole's letter of July 1530 and dropping the issue, except for a footnote explaining that Pole must have been eager to get back to England not to collect his reward but because he feared that Cromwell would get up to something worse than he already had!

Hallé's biography contains a remarkable echo of Zimmermann's words. Also writing of Pole in Paris, she asserted that '[t]he point is important, as it would prove either an extraordinary laxity of memory as to past events, or such a carelessness of statement, that Pole would have to be given up as a reliable authority on any subject, at any time'.[117] Hallé outdid Zimmermann in purple prose, but she took the same attitude to him that Phillips did to Querini.[118] Whatever the degree of her indebtedness, Hallé, the daughter of a German concert pianist and conductor and a mother from Louisiana, went beyond any of her predecessors in the range of manuscripts she consulted.[119] She worked (or at least drew on

---

[117] Marie Hallé (writing as Martin Haile), *Life of Reginald Pole* (London: Pitman, 1911, 2nd ed.; 1st ed. 1910), p. 72. She was not the only author to depend heavily on Zimmermann, without full acknowledgment. The French life by Reginald Biron and Jean Barennes, *Un prince anglais, cardinal-légat au XVIe siècle, Reginald Pole* (Paris: Librairie Générale Catholique, 1922) is equally guilty, although the authors identify Zimmermann's book as a 'vie de grande valeur', and were even more slavish in following Pole's versions of events. The Benedictine Biron had published on Pole earlier, but Barenne proposed the biography (p. 2). I have not been able to see an earlier French study, J. F. Martin, 'Le cardinal Pole', *Bulletin de*

l'archiconfraternité de N. D. de Compassion, 4 (1903), pp. 335–52; 5 (1904), pp. 92–118; 6 (1905), pp. 43–59.

[118] Hallé also made free use of Phillips and through him of Querini. For example on p. 131, citing Phillips, 1, p. 111, her text of Pierre Bunel's letter about Pole's controversy with Sadoleto over Bonamico reads like a translation of Querini.

[119] Beyond her extensive bibliography, I have not found much information about Hallé. Among her works is a *Life and letters* of her father (London: Smith, Elder, 1896), but it is almost no use for her life (or her father's, beyond its external events, and the bald – if obvious – claim that he was Catholic). With Edwin Bonney she wrote on Lingard (1911), as well as biographies of Mary of Modena (1905), James Francis

sources) in Rome, Modena, Mantua, and Padua, and had access to René Ancel's researches in Parma, Naples, and Brussels (p. vii). She also made it appear (Appendix F, pp. 542–3) that she had seen the Douai register, but her references are inexact enough to raise doubts whether she was working from first-hand observation. In any case, she made no use of the information. Despite all her erudition, she frequently missed sources and cited those she did use sloppily.[120] Worse, her Pole could do less wrong than almost any previous biographer's. Once more her first paragraph tells the tale.

> Few figures stand out from among the shadows of the past more clearly, or with a friendlier aspect, than does that of Reginald Pole – learned, simple-minded, pious, endowed with intellectual gifts of the highest order, wise and prudent in counsel, ardently zealous, and yet patient and long-suffering in the extreme, and with a rectitude of mind as true to its conscience as the needle to the pole. Of a jocund humour, which many waters could not quench, and delightful in conversation, he was endeared to his contemporaries by qualities that have left a memory and fragrance which time does not stale, but carries from age to age. (p. 1)

Pole was 'the greatest Englishman of his time' (p. 2). As this opening manifests, Hallé had a long suite in hyperbole, too.[121] Hers was the last but one biography

---

Footnote 119 (*cont.*)
Edward (1907), and William Allen (1914). For Sir Charles Hallé see *DNB*. Marie Hallé was very well-connected in the circles of Catholic historians, acknowledging the assistance of J. H. Pollen (in both *James Francis Edward* and *Lingard*) and Gillow (who drew up the bibliography for *James Francis Edward*, for example), as well as various religious, mostly Benedictines, whom I have not been able to identify.

[120] Cf. Georges Constant, 'Á propos d'une nouvelle vie de Reginald Pole', *Revue des questions historiques*, 90 (1911), pp. 498–514. Constant's criticisms were often wide of the mark, especially the assertion that Hallé cited no published calendars. Hallé's book was received rapturously in the Anglo-American Catholic press. See,

for example, the lengthy review by Walter F. Desterre, 'Reginald Pole, prince of the church', *American Catholic quarterly review*, 37 (January–July, 1912), pp. 95–110, 227–42, 449–62.

[121] Hallé was only one of a number of women to be attracted to Pole at the turn of the century. Among others were Harriet W. Preston and Louise Dodge in the *Atlantic monthly*, 74 (November–December, 1894), pp. 641–57, and C. M. Antony (possibly a pseudonym), the title of whose *The angelical cardinal, Reginald Pole* (London: Macdonald and Evans, 1909) needs no commentary. I have not considered fiction about Pole, which included a popular novel by William Ainsworth in the last century and several books by Hugh Ross Williamson in this.

of Pole in English.[122] K. B. McFarlane produced a brief essay in 1924 which concluded that Pole became 'an ineffectual cardinal at the expense of losing a capable editor of Cicero', and Philip Hughes gave Pole a great deal of mainly sympathetic attention, beginning in his *Rome and the counter-reformation in England* first published in 1942.[123]

It might have been thought that Hallé's mixed German and American ancestry might have given her a relatively dispassionate attitude to Pole. It did to some degree in the case of her only successor writing at full length in English, the German Wilhelm Schenk. In his posthumous book and an earlier article, Schenk suggested as much. He proposed to go beyond any earlier work by treating Pole in an almost dialectical fashion. As he put it at the conclusion of an article on Pole's early education 'Pole's disposition, early formation and experience were to enable him to combine some of the positive achievements of Renaissance humanism with the serious concerns of a Catholic reformer.'[124] Since Schenk appended this conclusion to a condemnation of Bembo's playful brand of humanism for its 'nihilism', he unintentionally set up the tension between serious and playful that has proved fruitful in the study of Renaissance humanism ever since.

Despite this promising beginning, and some impressive auspices (both Hubert Jedin and Hughes read the typescript), Schenk offered his book as yet another tract for the times.

> Through a sympathetic consideration of his [Pole's] life we may be able to gain a closer insight into the tensions of the past; we may be able to re-live the fateful decisions of the sixteenth century.... Then it will appear of course that the tensions of the past are not really dead and gone but are still with us.

---

[122] And the last but two in any language. The most recent is Maria Teresa Dainotti, *La via media. Reginald Pole 1500–1558* (Bologna: EMI, 1987), which has no serious value except for printing the text of a marble memorial to Pole placed in the inner court of Maguzzano in 1958 (p. 211). It reads 'Reginaldo Polo Beatae Margaritae Martiris Filio cardinalis Angliae clarissimo generi Eboracensis heredi qui heic [sic] A. D. MDVIII "Vere Angelus pacis" ut patriam dilectam unitati restitueret ecclesiae summopere adlaboravit IV ab eius obitu saec. a. MCMLVIII positum in spem.' Dainotti gives no information about the auspices under which it was erected.

[123] K. B. McFarlane, *Cardinal Pole* (Oxford: Basil Blackwell, 1924). Philip Hughes, *Rome and the counter-reformation in England* (London: Burns and Oates, 1944; first published 1942), ch. 2.

[124] Wilhelm Schenk, 'The student days of Cardinal Pole', *History*, n.s., 23 (1948), pp. 211–25, p. 225.

…The vitality of religion – the unity of Christendom – the relation between politics and religion – the problem of Christian humanism – the conflicting claims of action and contemplation: all these, to name only the most dominant themes in Pole's life, are our concerns as much as Pole's. (p. viii)

Despite this aim, or perhaps because it required that Pole's life be made more problematic than artificially pious if it were to serve as an example 'to the common run of us' (p. 30), Schenk moved a good way towards an interpretation in which ideology would not consistently overwhelm the sources. Thus he was the first sympathetic historian to get Pole's involvement in Paris right (p. 24). The momentum of this start could not be sustained. On the next page, the power of Pole's words led Schenk to treat his story of his confrontation with Henry over York as the purest truth (the same thing happened with the interview with Cromwell, despite Paul Van Dyke's demolition of it in 1904; p. 37).[125] Then again, Starkey, flatly dismissed as a spy by Zimmermann and Hallé, had his reports of Pole's beliefs entered into evidence (p. 36), no doubt again in order to heighten the 'tensions' and the 'evolution' of Pole's career. Schenk's description of *De unitate* is also refreshingly candid (p. 70), even if the interpretation of the work in the context of the question of Pole's treason is made to serve the 'fundamental conflict of his early life: "vita activa" against a *soi-disant* "vita contemplativa"'. Schenk's book is nothing if not tightly organized.

Its greatest value lies in increasing the corpus of Pole's writing taken seriously. Although forced to work from microfilm, Schenk tried to use Pole's papers in the Vatican Library, and was the first to consider 'De reformatione ecclesiae', however briefly (pp. 97–8). He also rediscovered, and apparently would have published had he lived, the 'Apologia' to Paul IV. Nevertheless, the story of Pole's image is not one of 'the sovereignty of the sources', the positivist triumph of evidence over bias.[126] In Schenk's case, his preconceptions led him largely to ignore the insight that 'De reformatione' set up an opposition between faith and reason all to the advantage of faith, perhaps because of his own vaguely Thomist leanings. Extrinsic categories often get in the way. 'Catholic reform', the label Jedin invented, becomes in Schenk's hands the opposite of 'Renaissance' (pp. 49–61), as well as the motivation behind Pole's final choice of a career (p. 68). Curiously, too, Valdés overwhelms the evidence of *De unitate* on the score of Pole's idea of faith and justification (p. 95). Naturally, while Pole remained a

---

[125] Paul van Dyke, 'Reginald Pole and Thomas Cromwell: an examination of the *Apologia ad Carolum quintum*', *American historical review*, 9 (1904), pp. 696–724.

[126] I borrow this phrase from Robert Finlay, '*AHR* forum: *The return of Martin Guerre*', *American historical review*, 93 (1988), pp. 553–71, p. 571.

Catholic reformer, Carafa had to be 'the first leader of the Counter-Reformation' (p. 105). Schenk could operate between categories if need be, especially when he found Pole guilty of weakness arising from confusion about which principle to endorse in failing to stop the persecution despite his personal opposition (pp. 153–4). '[T]his was a wrong' (p. 167). Yet in the next paragraph the categories return, placing Pole as proponent of Catholic reform in the path of 'the modern State . . . the insatiable Leviathan'. Schenk concluded that

> [i]t is this stand that should secure Pole a hearing in our time. There is no other refuge . . . except religion, but that refuge can become a veritable fortress if it is built with the seriousness and care of men like More and Pole. . . . No one would claim that Pole was always successful in this resistance, but there can be no doubt that he tried to perform this task to the best of his ability.

Schenk's point captures the rest of twentieth-century historiography. Heinrich Lutz, like Schenk a German-speaking Catholic, saw Pole's fate in similar terms, while G. R. Elton re-read Pole's career in the same way, except with the positives on the side of the state, while Elton's student Rex Pogson was caught somewhere in between.[127] Schenk's emphasis on the importance to Pole of 'the sphere of inwardness' could be the premise of Dermot Fenlon's work on the spiritual Pole.

In 1977 appeared a radically 'deconstructive' study of Pole and his historiography. Paolo Simoncelli's, *Il caso Reginald Pole: eresia e santità nelle polemiche religiose del Cinquecento* set out to uncover how Pole became an icon intended to defend the *spirituali*. Gigliola Fragnito had already suggested that there was such a campaign, developing the point in passing about the same time as Simoncelli and then at greater length in an article of 1985.[128] Simoncelli set up a contrast between Pole and his opponents based on the 'emblematic' opposition between Pole and Carafa, 'the one active, the other passive', the one certain of his election as pope, the other unwilling to forward his chances (p. 147). Although this structure is much too stark, it began Pole's historicization. Pirandello could have written Simoncelli's final sentences. 'Who in reality was Pole? At bottom, not that one who was, but that one who appeared or who was wished to appear; that is, Pole was destined to *really be* that one who should have appeared. This at

---

127 Heinrich Lutz, *Christianitas afflicta. Europa, das Reich und die päpstliche Politik im Niedergang der Hegemonie Kaiser Karls V. 1552–1556* (Göttingen: Vandenhoeck and Rupprecht, 1964), *passim*, and the preface to *NB*, 15. See esp. G. R. Elton, *The Tudor revolution in government: administrative changes in the reign of Henry VIII* (Cambridge: Cambridge University Press, 1953), pp. 7, 72–4, 76–7.

128 *Memoria*, p. 17 and 'Censura', pp. 17–26.

bottom [was] his tragic – or fortunate – destiny' (p. 241; emphasis in original). Surpassed in gnomic portent only by grammatical complexity, these words led to the pessimistic conclusion that Pole could never be untangled from his 'myth of sanctity'.

It was appropriate that Edizioni di storia e letteratura, published Simoncelli's volume, even if it may not have been quite the book the editors had hoped to get. The founder Giuseppe De Luca, one of the most important twentieth-century students of Pole, had been hard at work well before Schenk wrote, although he never produced most of his projected studies. De Luca, indefatigable scholar and priest, collected references to Pole, combed the Vatican, both archives and libraries, and fostered interest in him. His reverence for Pole cooled after he was admitted to the Inquisition's archives, but a book translated into English about that time still bore the marks of his former attitude.[129] De Luca's friend and correspondent Giovanni Papini devoted a chapter to Pole in his study of Michelangelo, correctly noting that it was strange that Michelangelo's biographers had not made more of his friendship with Pole.[130]

'Il volto del Salvatore': Pole's graphic images

Even if sources alone do not shape history, their steady accumulation has helped to produce a more historicist view of Pole. Nothing similar can be said for his graphic image, which Schenk read literally at face value (p. 115). This is as dangerous a way to treat Renaissance portraits as it is Renaissance biographies.[131] A portrait and a life were much more than representations of superficial reality, they concerned the 'fabrication of identity'.[132] Both were

---

[129] Romana Guarnieri, *Don Giuseppe De Luca tra cronaca e storia (1898–1962)* (Bologna: Il Mulino, 1974), p. 52. Elisabeth Gleason reports that De Luca told her after his visit to the Inquisition's archives that Pole and Vittoria Colonna were not 'as holy as one thinks'. For De Luca, see Giovanni Miccoli, 'Don Giuseppe De Luca, testimone di una stagione della chiesa e della cultura italiana', *RSLR*, 25 (1989), pp. 476–99, a review of Luisa Mangoni, *In partibus infidelium. Don Giuseppe De Luca: il mondo cattolico e la cultura italiana del Novecento* (Turin: Einaudi, 1989), and Giovanni Antonazzi, *Don Giuseppe De Luca, uomo cristiano e prete (1898–1962)* (Brescia: Morcelliana, 1992).

[130] Giovanni Papini, *Michelangelo, his life and his era* (New York: Dutton, 1952), pp. 379–82. For Papini and De Luca, see Antonazzi, *passim*.

[131] Richard Brilliant, *Portraiture* (Cambridge: Harvard University Press, 1991), p. 11 in general. Cf. Richard Wendorf, *The elements of life: biography and portrait-painting in Stuart and Georgian England* (Oxford: Clarendon Press, 1990), especially ch. 1.

[132] Brilliant, pp. 14 and 88.

intended to capture and idealize the sitter's virtues and to substitute for or replace his or her physical absence. Both were relics.[133] Painted portraits, despite all the advances of the fifteenth century, including the invention of the 'autonomous' portrait, still retained iconic force. As Leonardo da Vinci put it, they represented 'the motions of the mind', but as Leon Battista Alberti (and then supposedly Vittoria Colonna) maintained 'the face of a man who is already dead certainly lives a long life through painting'.[134] Alberti posited that portraits could not sacrifice truth to beauty, and others therefore ranked portraiture below 'history' painting which lacked this constraint.[135]

Despite powerful imperatives to idealization, sixteenth-century artists had to provide an 'accurate' likeness, setting ideal and real in tension.[136] These twin demands led to complicated negotiations between artist and sitter about how to represent the subject.[137] The combination of technical advance and ideological and sociopolitical demands for representation of inner worth made a portrait an 'indexical icon' that 'purports to denote by resemblance the act of portrayal that produced it'.[138] This level of sophistication in the interpretation of portraiture is

---

[133] Luba Freedman, 'The concept of portraiture in art theory of the Cinquecento', *Zeitschrift für Ästhetik und allgemeine Kunstwissenschaft*, 32 (1987), pp. 63–82, pp. 74–7; Clark Hulse, 'Dead man's treasure: the cult of Thomas More', in David Lee Miller, Sharon O'Dair, and Harold Weber, eds., *The production of English renaissance culture* (Ithaca: Cornell University Press, 1994), pp. 190–225, pp. 208–9, and 217; Brilliant, p. 67.

[134] Leon Battista Alberti, *On painting*, ed. and trans. J. R. Spencer (New Haven: Yale University Press, 1966; rev. ed.), p. 63; John Pope-Hennessy, *The portrait in the renaissance* (Princeton: Princeton University Press, 1966), p. 101 for Da Vinci; and David Rosand, 'The portrait, the courtier, and death', in Robert W. Hanning and David Rosand, eds., *Castiglione. The ideal and the real in renaissance culture* (New Haven: Yale University Press, 1983), pp. 91–129 on 'Castiglione's generation' and 'the revelation of an inner (or at least, a completer) life' (p. 117) and for Francisco de Hollanda allegedly quoting Colonna (p. 126).

[135] Freedman, pp. 66 and 70.

[136] Brilliant, p. 32 on the relative ease of recognizing 'the individual in the type', rather than the other way around. Cf. also p. 37 for E. H. Gombrich's notion of a schema, or a type of a head, which the artist brings with him and modifies to suit each sitter. His strictures on the study of renaissance portraiture on p. 127.

[137] Freedman, pp. 63, 67–8, 78, 80–1; Giuseppe Bertini, 'Il ritrovato ritratto di Fino Fini (1431–1519) proveniente dalla quadreria di Palazzo Farnese di Roma', *Mélanges de l'Ecole française de Rome, Italie et Méditerranée*, 108 (1996), 1, pp. 377–9; Brilliant, p. 18.

[138] Harry Berger, 'Fictions of the pose: facing the gaze of early modern portraiture', *Representations*, 46 (Spring 1994), pp. 87–120, pp. 93–5. Francis Haskell does not think the idea that a portrait reflected character became established until 'well into the sixteenth century'. *History and its images: art and the interpretation of the past* (New Haven: Yale University Press, 1993), p. 28.

*20 Sebastiano del Piombo (Sebastiano Veneziano). The Hermitage, St Petersburg,
Russia. Catalogue, no. 1.*

a recent development, and much work remains to be done merely in assembling
the corpus of Renaissance portraits.[139] Given the first situation, what follows is
little more than an interpretive sketch. I hope the Catalogue at least responds to

---

[139] The most comprehensive effort thus far is Lorne Campbell, *Renaissance portraits: European
portrait-painting in the 14th, 15th and 16th centuries* (New Haven: Yale University Press, 1990).
Cf. also Angelika Dülberg, *Privatporträts. Geschichte und Ikonologie einer Gattung im 15. und 16.
Jahrhundert* (Berlin: Mann, 1990).

the second and is reasonably complete. I have divided the treatment of graphic representations into painted and printed portraits of Pole, although that distinction is not always easy to maintain when trying to determine how the images came into and remained in existence.

Rather like the case of Dante and Italian epic poetry, the first portrait of Pole is by far the best. Although both the sitter's identity and the attribution have been contested, the portrait now in the Hermitage in St Petersburg is probably both of Pole and by Sebastiano del Piombo (illus. 20; no. 1).[140] It is one of only two even vaguely documented portraits. There are textual references to several others, but of those one has been destroyed and the rest remain unidentified.[141] It seems likely that Vittoria Colonna commissioned Sebastiano's portrait.[142] Even before Pole's promotion, she and Pope Paul created the demand, describing Pole similarly as either an 'angel of God' (Paul) or as having 'the face of the Saviour' ('il volto del Salvatore'; Colonna).[143] In early 1546 Cardinal Madruzzo's secretary Aurelio Cattaneo wrote that Colonna was trying to get a portrait *a ogni modo*, and she had portraits of Contarini and Pole.[144] Sebastiano was an obvious choice given his numerous ties to Pole's circles, not least through Michelangelo.[145] One of their most important collaborations was the *Pietà* for San Francesco in Viterbo, where Sebastiano did a good deal of other work, including a *Dead Christ* now in the Museo civico.[146] Thus Pole, familiar with Sebastiano's work, could have contributed to his selection. He may have sat for

---

[140] See the catalogue below for support for this and any other statements left undocumented in this section.

[141] Gigliola Fragnito, *In museo e in villa: saggi sul rinascimento perduto* (Venice: Arsenale, 1988), pp. 111–12 notes a fresco commissioned by Beccadelli from Pellegrino Brocardo in the villa of Šipan, now destroyed (p. 21). He also made a copy of Morone's portrait of Pole, but neither copy nor original has been identified. The portrait which Paolo Manuzio proposed to send 'nostro compar Ramusio' in 1573 likewise has not been identified. Pastorello, nos. 1616 and 1621 (pp. 281 and 283).

[142] It is just possible that the portrait ascribed to Pietro Labruzzi is a copy of the one done by Colonna's commission, according to a probably unreliable provenance. See

catalogue no. 11.

[143] BPP, MS pal. 1026/1.

[144] *CT*, 10, p. 863 and Franz Dittrich, *Regesten und Briefen des Cardinals Gasparo Contarini (1483–1542)* (Braunsberg: Huye, 1881), p. 246n. Madruzzo used Cattaneo to communicate with Pole. *CRP*, no. 516.

[145] In 1530 Soranzo described Sebastiano as *nostro* in a letter to Bembo. Pio Paschini, *Tre ricerche sulla storia della chiesa nel Cinquecento* (Rome: Edizioni Liturgiche, n.d.), 'Un Vescovo disgraziato nel Cinquecento italiano: Vittore Soranzo', p. 102. Cf. Maria Calí, *Da Michelangelo all'Escorial. Momenti del dibattito religioso nell'arte del Cinquecento* (Turin: Einaudi, 1980), ch. 3 and Hirst, *passim* for Sebastiano's collaboration with Michelangelo.

[146] Hirst, ch. 3 and Calí, p. 161.

Sebastiano on the occasion of his return from Trent when Colonna lionized him for refusing to agree to the decree on justification.[147]

In Sebastiano's portrait self-presentation and artistic representation almost coincide.[148] That is, although Sebastiano did not necessarily recreate the image Pole intended, he did create one similar to those Pole and his biographers constructed. His portrait thus mediated Pole's identity, rather than merely reflecting it, as Linda Klinger Aleci suggests of Renaissance portraiture in general.[149] Sebastiano's work fits Aleci's description of how a portrait provided 'the occasion for a rhetorical enactment of the experience of friendship', just as its function as example would allow it to move out of context. As Colonna gazed on the portrait, her 'contemplation . . . serv[ed] in a process of introspection and self-transformation' that may have led her both to see Christ in Pole and to transform herself into his/their servant.[150] Sebastiano's accomplishment, perhaps together with Pole's own hopes for the portrait, is encapsulated in a letter from another sitter wishing a portrait by him. Claudio Tolomei hoped in 1543 that 'seeing myself vividly portrayed by your art will provide me with a continual stimulus to purge my soul of its many defects, and seeing therein the illuminating rays of your genius [*virtù*] will kindle in my soul a noble longing for glory and honour'.[151] Glory and honour may not have been Pole's aim, but Sebastiano's portrait projected onto him an image he wished to project outward. It is one sign of their success that it is almost impossible to recover the painting's 'occasionality'.[152] It refers to no time or place. Aside from Pole's dress, almost

---

[147] The moment cannot be much more precisely pinned down. Pole was away from Rome from late June 1542 until May 1543 (but in its environs, as he was later when legate of Viterbo); again from April 1545 to November 1546 (in Trent and the north); and back from the moment of his return through the time of Sebastiano's death in 1547.

[148] Brilliant, p. 46 with cautions on pp. 59 and 90 about the relationship between the sitter and 'his' portrait and Oscar Wilde's opinion (p. 82) that portraits revealed the painter. But cf. also p. 122 for the case of Goethe, in which artist and subject co-operated as 'compatible friends'.

[149] Linda Klinger Aleci, 'Images of identity: Italian portrait collections of the fifteenth and sixteenth centuries', in Nicholas Mann

and Luke Syson, eds., *The image of the individual: portraits in the renaissance* (London: British Museum Press, 1998), pp. 67–79.

[150] Aleci, p. 69. Cf. Brilliant, pp. 112–13 on the necessity of masks in order to 'sanitiz[e] facial expression' which permitted 'the wearer to impersonate someone, even himself'.

[151] Quoted in Brilliant, p. 129.

[152] Elizabeth Honig, 'In memory: Lady Dacre and pairing by Hans Eworth', in Lucy Gent and Nigel Llewellyn, eds., *Renaissance bodies: the human figure in English culture c. 1540–1660* (London: Reaktion Books, 1990), pp. 60–85, p. 62, borrowing a term from Hans-Georg Gadamer.

nothing ties him to a station, a position, or an office.[153] While the portrait typifies Sebastiano, especially its fingers, a few characteristics suggest a more distinctive meaning.[154] This is especially true of the design. Pole's pose seems modelled on Raphael's portrait of Juanna of Aragon (1518).[155] The palette also comes closer to that in Sebastiano's female portraits, not just because of the colour of Pole's garb. In earlier portraits of cardinals (e.g., *Ferry of Carondelet* or *Antonio del Monte*) Sebastiano had used mostly grey and black tones.[156] These two points combined with Sebastiano's likely homosexuality and at least one known homoerotic portrait by him suggest more than spiritual affinity between sitter and artist.[157] The directness of Pole's gaze, while not uncommon, yet fixes both artist and viewer exceptionally strongly, suggesting a powerful bond with Sebastiano. Sebastiano got his man.

His man may not have been male, or not exclusively so. Colonna's reading of Sebastiano's portrait offers a classic case of what Elizabeth Cropper has called the 'subjective, or affective (that is to say, passionate or emotional) beholding' characteristic of high Renaissance art that was closely bound up with the 'Petrarchan culture of desire' in which Colonna had been immersed.[158] Sebastiano's image reflects Cropper's assertion that 'beauty . . . is *the* problem of the high Renaissance'.[159] Cropper continues that 'the emergence of the affective beholder' produced 'discursive gendering' of images, which shifted into cross-gendered beauty inextricably mixing masculine and feminine.[160] This ideal of beauty and mode of beholding defined a new relationship between artist and subject, 'whether gendered, ungendered, or bigendered: . . . possession'.[161] Her

---

[153] Contrast Gerhard Flicke's portrait of Cranmer, which portrays him as bishop and student of scripture. Diarmaid MacCulloch, *Thomas Cranmer. A life* (New Haven: Yale University Press, 1996), pp. 338ff.

[154] E. H. Ramsden, *Come, take this lute: a quest for identities in Italian renaissance portraiture* (Salisbury: Element Books), pp. 152–3.

[155] Campbell, no. 71 and p. 61.

[156] Ramsden, p. 151.

[157] For the *Portrait of a man in armor* in the Wadsworth Atheneum, Hartford, CT see Wendy Steadman Sheard, 'Giorgione's portrait inventions c. 1500: transfixing the viewer' in M. A. Di Cesare, ed.,

Reconsidering the renaissance. Papers from the 21st annual conference (Binghamton, NY: MRTS, 1992), pp. 141–76, p. 149; Hirst, pl. 65. The portrait seems not unrelated to Sebastiano's *Salome* (Hirst, pl. 30).

[158] Elizabeth Cropper, 'The place of beauty in the high renaissance and its displacement in the history of art', in Alvin Vos, ed., *Place and displacement in the renaissance* (Binghamton, NY: MRTS, 1995), pp. 159–205, p. 161.

[159] *Ibid.*, pp. 170 (emphasis in original) and 175.

[160] *Ibid.*, pp. 185–7.

[161] *Ibid.*, p. 191.

remarks on Michelangelo's presentation drawings, particularly those for Colonna, as instances of the 'desire for the impossible object' characteristic of the early *Cinquecento* apply to Sebastiano's portrait.[162] Colonna was the 'beholder not necessarily gendered as male', while Sebastiano, like Michelangelo, may well have been a beholder 'in whom questions of sex and gender are not elided'.[163] Cropper concludes that Michelangelo's subjectivity, which has been reified as homosexual, was more complex, encapsulating a universal poetics (in the broadest sense) of desire manifested in his art (or perhaps the other way around).[164] Sebastiano's work may have had less universal appeal, but his portrait of Pole expressed both his and Colonna's subjectivity at the same time as it represented Pole's, all three profoundly linked in a necessarily ungendered way.

Achille Bocchi's emblem for Pole (illus. 21), which to a degree best captures Pole's relationship with Michelangelo, functioned in much the same way. Begun during the conclave of 1549–50, it was published in *Symbolicae quaestiones* five years later.[165] It came from one of Michelangelo's most famous drawings, a *Rape of Ganymede* he had presented to his beloved Tommaso de' Cavalieri.[166] True, Pole's Ganymede was clothed, but the original nude version appeared as an emblem on the previous page. The meaning of Pole's emblem is at least as obscure as that of any other, but one wonders whether a sixteenth-century viewer could have missed the resonances of the central image. Bocchi drew on the Neoplatonic interpretation of the myth of Ganymede, raped by Zeus and put into service as cup-bearer to the gods, according to which the myth represented transcendence, the direct opposite of its surface content.[167] No doubt Bocchi's accompanying verse was meant to control the reading of Pole's emblem and point it in a religious direction, but separating the two could have been difficult.[168] For one thing, the dogs in the emblem could refer to Flaminio's lap-

---

[162] *Ibid.*, pp. 192–6.

[163] *Ibid.*, p. 201.

[164] *Ibid.*, p. 203.

[165] Karen E. Pinkus, 'The "Symbolicae Quaestiones" of Achille Bocchi: humanist emblems and counter-reformation communication', Ph.D. thesis, City University of New York, 1990, p. 12. The work was published by Bocchi's own press in 1555.

[166] James M. Saslow, *Ganymede in the renaissance: homosexuality in art and society* (New Haven: Yale University Press, 1985), pp. 17–18. Saslow discusses Bocchi's

emblem for Pole on p. 69, emphasizing its religious appeal to Neoplatonists.

[167] Leonard Barkan, *Transuming passion: Ganymede and the erotics of humanism* (Stanford: Stanford University Press, 1991), p. 100.

[168] Eugenio Battisti, 'Michelangelo o dell'ambiguità iconografica' in J. Adolph Eisenwerth, Marcell Restle and Herbert Weiermann, eds., *Festschrift Luitpolt Dussler* (Munich: Deutscher Kunstverlag, 1972), pp. 209–22, p. 215. The verse read 'Aspice quam sentit magni Iovis armiger ales/ Quid rapit, & cui fert in Ganymede

dog carmen, although their manifest content comes from the myth.[169] For another, Sebastiano's assimilation of Ganymede to St John erased the line between religion and sexuality.[170] One commentator who suggests that the other emblem symbolized pederasty insists that Pole's could not, and may have implied that his reforming ideals could do something about the vice.[171] Yet there is no obvious reason why Bocchi could not have shared Sebastiano's attitude. Michelangelo certainly discussed his sexual desires in Neoplatonic idiom.[172]

Sebastiano may have painted his portrait almost literally in a race with Giorgio Vasari, who included Pole in *La rimunerazione delle virtù* in the Cancelleria palace in August 1546 at Cardinal Farnese's behest (illus. 22; no. 2).[173] No love was lost between the two artists, and Sebastiano might have known Vasari's low opinion of his portraits.[174] The two likenesses are closely related, especially through the subject's gaze: Pole is one of only a handful of figures in Vasari's work to engage the viewer (illus. 23). Giovio's plan for the fresco dictated Pole's inclusion.[175] In a possibly homosexual joke, Giovio substituted for three eunuchs next to himself a group of Pole, Bembo and Sadoleto. Giovio probably meant to indicate religious sympathies as well.[176] Giovio thus helped to fix an image of Pole in two media, painting and writing. Through his *museo* he also contributed to its appearance in a third, prints.

It may have been now that Giovio secured a portrait of Pole for his collection.

---

suo./ Unguibus en etiam per vestem parcit aduncis,/ Ne quid pacatis sensibus officiat./ Sic olim expressit mire otia laeta Leocras/ Sculptor compositi corporis, atque animi:/ Tota mente Deum, ac pura nosce, & cole, presto/ Laeta domi, atque foris pax erit usque tibi.'

169 Above p. 162.

170 Barkan, p. 100; Saslow, p. 42.

171 Annette Kruszynski, *Der Ganymed-Mythos in Emblematik und mythographischer Literatur des 16. Jahrhunderts* (Worms: Wernersche Verlagsgesellschaft, 1985), pp. 46–50.

172 Barkan, p. 103 and Alexander Nagel, 'Gifts for Michaelangelo and Vittoria Colonna', *Art bulletin*, 79:4 (1997), pp. 647–68, 653.

173 To Cardinal Farnese, 15 August 1546. Armando Schiavo, *Il palazzo della Cancelleria* (Rome: Staderini, 1963), p. 162.

174 Freedman, p. 73.

175 It is printed in A. F. Doni, *Disegno*, ed. M. Pepe (Milan: Electa, 1970), p. 107. See Clare Robertson, '*Il gran cardinale': Alessandro Farnese, patron of the arts* (New Haven: Yale University Press, 1992), pp. 64–5; Ernst Steinmann, 'Frezkenzyklen der Spätrenaissance in Rome', *Monatshefte für Kunstwissenschaft*, 3 (1910), pp. 45–58, p. 56; Julian Kliemann, 'Il pensiero di Paolo Giovio nelle pitture eseguite sulle sue "invenzioni"', in *Paolo Giovio, il Rinascimento e la memoria (Como, 3–5 giugno 1983)* (Como: Società Storica Comense, 1985), pp. 197–223; and Schiavo, pp. 155–64.

176 Gigliola Fragnito, 'Evangelismo e intransigenti nei difficili equilibri del pontificato farnesiano', *RSLR*, 25 (1989), pp. 20–47, p. 47 thinks that the three cardinals represented a dialogue between doctrinal positions.

21 *Emblem in Achille Bocchi,* Symbolicae quaestiones *(1555).*

22 *Giorgio Vasari.* Rimunerazione delle Virtù. *Sala dei Cento Giorni, Cancelleria Palace, Rome.*

23 Detail: Giovio, Pole, Sadoleto, and Bembo.

It was done at an uncertain time by an unknown Roman artist and is known only in a copy by Antonio Maria Crespi now in the Biblioteca Ambrosiana (cat. no. 4) and a woodblock by Tobias Stimmer (see below). The artist of Crespi's original may have been Jacopino del Conte, who moved in Perin del Vaga's orbit (cat. no. 5).[177] Given Giovio's passion for accurate likenesses, the original's loss is a great pity.[178] There was an industry producing portraits of Pole in Rome in the mid-to-late 1540s, with Sebastiano right at the centre of it, even posthumously.[179] In addition to his competition with Vasari, he had ties to Perin, who may have painted a portrait of Pole about the same time as they did (cat. no. 3).[180] The pose

[177] Linda Wolk-Simon, review of Elena Parma Armani, *Perin del Vaga, l'anello mancante: Studi sul manierismo, Art bulletin,* 71 (1989), pp. 515–23, p. 522.

[178] T. C. Price Zimmermann, *Paolo Giovio: the historian and the crisis of sixteenth-century Italy* (Princeton: Princeton University Press, 1995), pp. 160–1. For Giovio's collection, see also Haskell, *History and images,* pp. 45–8 and Aleci.

[179] For example, Della Torre hoped to get copies of Colonna's portraits of Contarini and Pole for himself. Dittrich, *Regesten,* p. 246n.

[180] Wolk-Simon, p. 523n.

of the suppositious image closely resembles Sebastiano's, except that the seated Pole's left hand is turned up rather than hanging down over the arm of his chair. The pose of all the early portraits is similar, including Giovio's. The major variation is whether Pole holds a letter and in which hand. The two best-known portraits, one in Lambeth Palace (cat. no. 6) and the other in the collection of Lord Talbot of Malahide (cat. no. 12), belong in the same group. The first of these, of which at least three copies exist, is closely related to Sebastiano's, although less fluidly executed. It is distinguished as one of only two portraits with a titulus other than Pole's identity, a variant of another carmen to Pole by Flaminio: 'Si sic Pole Tu/Ac Potuisset/mentis imago/pingi/nis oculi/pulcrius aspicerent'. In the early 1560s Pole made his last appearance so far as I know in Italian painting, in another group scene, commissioned once again by Cardinal Farnese. Taddeo Zuccaro placed him on the extreme right of *Julius III restoring Parma to Ottavio Farnese* along with two other cardinals (cat. no. 10). Like Giovio, the authors of the programme, Panvinio and Manuzio, moved Pole's image between media.[181]

As in Italy, so in England series of famous men incorporated Pole's portrait. Unlike the uniformity of Margaret Beaufort's portraits, all of which descended from a single original, Pole's image varied considerably between these.[182] This category includes the picture at Hardwick Hall (cat. no. 12) and probably that once in the possession of Earl Granard (cat. no. 13). The English portraits are all much inferior as representations *al naturale*, but like the Italian versions, many of the English pictures may have had public purposes.[183] The panel painting at Lambeth inscribed with the date of Pole's election as a fellow of Corpus Christi College, Oxford (cat. no. 7) could have been done in preparation for or commemoration of the university visitations, or in order to curry favour with an important alumnus. It is unrelated to the portrait now in Corpus (cat. no. 8). The occasion of the National Portrait Gallery portrait (cat. no. 9) is unknown, but it may have been Pole's funeral. The final group of English portraits, including the Talbot of Malahide and probably that once at Oxburgh Hall, Norfolk (cat. no. 15) fall into the class of devotional images, preserved by recusant families. They are far fewer in number than portraits of More.[184]

[181] Loren W. Partridge, 'Divinity and dynasty at Caprarola: perfect history in the room of Farnese deeds', *Art bulletin*, 60 (1978), pp. 494–530, pp. 494–6. Panvinio was a noted expert on portraiture. For his written image of Pole, see above p. 361.

[182] Frederick Hepburn, 'The portraiture of Lady Margaret Beaufort', *Antiquaries journal*, 72 (1992), pp. 118–40.

[183] For the difficulties of determining private or public function, see also Roberto Zapperi, *Tiziano, Paolo III e i suoi nipoti: nepotismo e ritratto di Stato* (Turin: Bollati Boringheri, 1990).

[184] Hulse, p. 211.

Later in the sixteenth century prints began to appear, often in biographical encyclopedias, and often in company which made Pole other than an orthodox Catholic. The first of these, a woodblock by Stimmer (cat. no. 20), is more important for its appearance in a collection by the Protestant Nikolaus Reusner than for its resemblance to any other image of Pole, although it almost certainly came from Giovio's *museo*. Given the popularity of Pietro Perna's copiously illustrated editions of the two volumes of Giovio's *Elogia* (1575 and 1577; see catalogue), it is a little surprising that Stimmer's image had no afterlife. All these points also hold for the engraving in Thevet's *Les vrais pourtraits* (1584; cat. no. 19). At first sight it might appear fanciful, but it may derive from Giovanni Cavino's medal celebrating the restoration of England (cat. no. 40). Thevet frequently worked from medals, and although he took many of his images from Giovio's *museo* doubtless via Perna's editions or translations of them, he could not have done in this case.[185] On Cavino's medal Pole appears at the extreme left, wearing similar headgear to Thevet's cardinal, probably a *galerus rubeus*.[186] Otherwise, aside from his prominent nose, there is little to identify Cavino's figure as Pole. To judge from its frequent plagiarisms, one of the most successful engravings appeared in 1598, the work of Théodore de Galle (cat. nos. 21–32). The inscriptions were never repeated from one plagiarism to the next, although they nearly always emphasized his virtues and royal rank. From Richard Chiswell's version for Burnet's *History of the reformation* (cat. no. 28) it became one of the better known images in England. Doubtless its quality contributed to the remarkable stability of Pole's appearance in print. That stability was further enhanced by an excellent engraving of Sebastiano's portrait by Nicholas de Larmessin dated 1729 (cat. no. 33). From it descended the frontispiece to Phillip's biography (cat. no. 37). Its career was aborted thereafter by the first engraving of the Talbot portrait in 1816. It was redone at least three times thereafter, most successfully by H. T. Ryall (cat. nos. 38 and 39).

The history of Pole's graphic representation falls into three periods. In the first, dominated by Sebastiano's portrait, he appeared as a magnetic, albeit ethereal, figure. Once Sebastiano's portrait was copied, especially in the versions in which Pole holds a letter, he temporarily became a man of affairs, an appearance enhanced by his inclusion in Giovio's *museo* and in the Farnese portraits, whatever other purposes may have motivated Giovio's and Farnese's choice. The

---

[185] Jean Adhémar, 'André Thevet collectionneur de portraits', *Revue archéologique*, ser. 6, 20 (July–September, 1942-3), pp. 41–54, pp. 45–6.

[186] John Hunter, 'Who is Jan van Eyck's "Cardinal Nicolò Albergati"?', *Art bulletin*, 75 (1993), pp. 207–18, p. 215.

ethereal Pole cropped up again in the first period of prints, running down to the reappearance of Sebastiano's portrait via de Larmessin. Immediately challenged by the Talbot Pole, a gaunt figure virtually indistinguishable from the NPG portrait, since then the ethereal and the gaunt Pole have wobbled unstably back and forth. It is probably not an accident that the most positive biography, Hallé, had Sebastiano as its frontispiece, and the most critical, Schenk, Talbot. In art as in prose, Pole's image has stubbornly remained bifurcated. Nevertheless, the fact that the two most important twentieth-century lives were written by a woman and a man makes plain that Pole's universal, ungendered appeal captured in the first portrait continues to hold.

Catalogue of images

ABBREVIATIONS:

BL   British Library, London
CIA   Courtauld Institute of Art, London
NPG   National Portrait Gallery, London
NPGA   Archives of same
        Pole file of illustrations (notes probably by John Kerslake,
        doing research for Sir Roy Strong)
Scharf   Sir George Scharf, sometime curator of NPG

N.B.: Information not otherwise attributed is drawn from
notes in NPGA.

I. Painted portraits[1]

1. Sebastiano del Piombo. The Hermitage, St Petersburg, Russia. 112 × 94.5 cm (c. 44 × 37.2″).[2] Mid-1540s? Michael Hirst and Carlo Volpe also note a poor copy at Budapest, identified as of cardinal Robert de Lenoncourt, dated 1550. Hirst accepts that both sitter and artist are probably Pole and

---

[1] As the rankest amateur of art history, I beg the indulgence of experts for mistakes in technical vocabulary. I especially regret that I did not realize the importance of knowing the size of art works until too late to cover all the entries.

[2] Dimensions given in Carlo Volpe, *L'opera completa di Sebastiano del Piombo* (Milan: Rizzoli, 1980), catalogue no. 181 and Sylvia Ferino-Pagden, ed., *Vittoria Colonna, Dichterin und Muse Michelangelos* (Vienna:

Kunsthistorisches Museum and Skira Editore, 1997), p. 251. Michael Hirst, *Sebastiano del Piombo* (Oxford: Clarendon Press, 1981), p. 121 gave 113 × 95 cm. Cf. T. Fomicheva, *The Hermitage: catalogue of western European paintings*, 2, *Venetian painting, fourteenth to eighteenth centuries* (Moscow and Florence: Giunti, 1992), pp. 294f. Cf. no. 33 below for a sale catalogue engraving.

Sebastiano.[3] To the few doubters about the sitter's identity should be added Sir Roy Strong.[4] Most recently, Christian G. Arseni has raised doubts about the attribution on stylistic grounds.[5] The identification of the sitter goes back at least to 1729 (cf. no. 33 below) when the artist was given as either Raphael or Sebastiano, and it was still assigned to Raphael in a sale catalogue of 1755.[6] P.-J. Mariette noted that the work could not be by Raphael on chronological grounds and first cautiously attributed it without argument to Sebastiano.[7]

Provenance: documented in collection of Joseph Antoine Crozat in the early eighteenth century, although it may actually have been in his brother Pierre's.[8] Horace Walpole saw the remaining pictures in the collection in 1771 when they were still in Louis-Antoine Crozat's hands, including the Sebastiano, which he tried to acquire without success.[9] Where the portrait went at that time is slightly obscure, but there appears to have been at least one copy made which came to England while the original certainly went to Catherine the Great.[10] Scharf's somewhat confusing note to the catalogue of an 1890 exhibition said it was in

---

[3] *Tudor and Jacobean portraits* (London: HMSO, 1969; 2 vols.), 1, pp. 252–3.

[4] Hirst, p. 120.

[5] *Vittoria Colonna*, pp. 252–4.

[6] Hirst, p. 120n, who incorrectly cited *Catalogue des tableaux du cabinet de M. Crozat, Baron de Thiers* (Paris: De Bure l'Aîné, 1755), p. 25 both as the first identification of the sitter and also the first attribution to Sebastiano. I am grateful to J. D. Alsop for checking this reference, which gives the dimensions of the work as 'haut de 3. pieds 5. pouces, large de 2 pieds 10½ pouces' (cf. the same information on no. 33 below). For this book, Mariette's sale catalogue of the Crozat collection, in which he was the first to use provenance to verify attribution, see the articles 'Pierre-Jean Mariette' and 'Louis-Antoine Crozat' in Jane Turner, ed., *Dictionary of art* (London: Macmillan, 1996; 34 vols.), 20, pp. 416–18, pp. 416 and 418 and 8, pp. 208–10, p. 210.

[7] *Abecedario de P. J. Mariette et autres notes inedites de cet amateur sur les arts et les artistes* (Paris: J. B. Dumoulin, 1851–60; 6 vols.), ed. Philippe de Chennevieres and Anatole de Montaiglon, 5, pp. 201–2.

[8] Hirst, p. 120, against *Dictionary of art*, 8, p. 210. Schenk, p. xvi said the picture was previously in the Clerville and d'Armagnac collections, on unknown evidence, but perhaps K. Rathe and K. Lanckoronska, who helped him with the illustrations (p. ix). There were once three separate Crozat collections, of which Joseph-Antoine's is now thought to have been the least significant.

[9] W. S. Lewis and W. H. Smith, eds., *Horace Walpole's correspondence with Madame du Deffand*, 3, pp. 178 and 184 and 5, p. 372 (both New Haven: Yale University Press, 1939).

[10] James Granger, *A biographical history of England, from Egbert the Great to the revolution*, 5th ed. (London: W. Baynes and Son, 1824; 6 vols.), 1, p. 192, a note dated 1772; cf. the 1769 edition. Lee, p. 257 says in 1771, without source, although it may be Granger. Pierre Crozat's collection, inherited by his nephew (perhaps Joseph-Antoine's son), Louis-Antoine, was pared down by a sale in 1751, and the residue was sold to Catherine the Great after Louis-Antoine's death in 1770. *Dictionary of art*, 20, pp. 208–10, p. 208.

24 After Perin del Vaga or Bartolomeo Cancellieri. Carlton Towers. Reproduced by kind permission of His Grace the Duke of Norfolk.

REGINAL
DVS.

POLVS.

25 *Antonio Maria Crespi, called il Busto or il Bustino. Property of the Biblioteca Ambrosiana. All rights reserved. Reproduction prohibited.*

26 Unknown. Lambeth Palace, London. c. 1550? His Grace the Archbishop of Canterbury and the Church Commissioners.

27 Unknown. Lambeth Palace, London. Panel painting. His Grace the Archbishop of Canterbury and the Church Commissioners.

Reginald Pole, 1500–1558.
Fellow of C·C·C·, later Cardinal.

28 Unknown. Corpus Christi College, Oxford, Senior Common Room.
Photo: Studio Edmark.

29 Unknown. By courtesy of the National Portrait Gallery, London.

30 *Taddeo Zuccaro. Julius III restoring the duchy of Parma to Ottavio Farnese. Sala dei Fasti farnesiani, Villa Farnese, Caprarola.*

31 Detail.

*32   Pietro Labruzzi. Collection of Lord Talbot of Malahide, formerly collection of
Lord Arundel of Wardour.*

33 Unknown Flemish engraver. André Thevet, Les vrais pourtraits et vies des hommes
illustres *(Paris: I. Kervert et Guillaume Chaudière, 1584). Clements Historical Library,
University of Michigan.*

34 Tobias Stimmer. Nikolaus Reusner, Icones sive imagines vivae, literis cl. variorum, Italiae, Graeciae, Germaniae, Galliae, Angliae, Ungariae *(Basel: Conrad Waldkirch, 1589). Special Collections Library, University of Michigan.*

REGINALDVS POLVS BRITANNVS CARD.

Tu quoque, POLE, decus patriæ, vindexꝗ Britanniæ,
Quem genitrix, frater, morte obita decorant.
MORVS item, atꝗ æui FISCHERVS flos, et ocellus:
Quos et transcripsit mors violenta polo.

35 *Théodore de Galle. Pl. X of* XII *Cardinalium . . .* imagines et elogia
(Antwerp: Philippe Galle, 1598). Department of Printing and Graphic Arts,
The Houghton Library, Harvard University.

REGINALDVS POLVS
Cardinalis.

36 *Giovanni Imperiale,* Museum historicum et physicum *(Venice: Giunta, 1640), p. 32.*
Hardin Rare Books Room, The University of Iowa.

Vol. 2   Pag. 292.

CARDINALIS POLI ETFIGIES REGINALDI

R. White Sculp.

Natus Anno
1500. May. 22.
Cardinalis S. Mariæ
in Cosmedin 1536. May 23.

Consecr. Archiepisc.
Cantuariensis,
1555. Mar: 22.
Obijt 1558. Nov. 17.

Printed for Rich. Chiswell at the Rose and Crown in St Pauls Church yard.

37 *Engraved by R. White. Printed for Richard Chiswell at the Rose and Crown in St Paul's Churchyard. Gilbert Burnet,* The history of the reformation of the Church of England *(London: Printed by T. H. for Richard Chiswell, 1681–3; 2 vols.)*

38 Nicholas de Larmessin the younger. Isaac Bullart, Académie des Sciences et des Artes *(Brussels: F. Foppolas, 1695), 2, pp. 55–60, pl. 9.*

39 Drawn by Adrian van der Werff, engraved by P. van Gunst. No. 16 of fifty plates for Isaac De Larrey, Histoire d'Angleterre, d'Ecosse et d'Irlande *(Amsterdam: Jan Cusens and Cornelis Mortier, 1723 [?]). Special Collections Library, University of Michigan.*

Portrait du Cardinal Polus

D'apres le Tableau de Raphael, ou de Fra Sebastien del Piombo, qui est dans le Cabinet de M. Crozat

haut de 3 pieds 5 pouces, large de 2 pieds 10 pouces, peint sur toile, gravé par Nicolas de Larmessin

40 Nicholas de Larmessin IV. Portrait du Cardinal Polus d'après le Tableau de Raphaël, ou de Fra Sebastien del Piombo, qui est dans le Cabinet de M. Crozat.

41 *'Painted by Raphael, engraved by Major'. Frontispiece to Thomas Phillips,* The history of the life of Reginald Pole *(London: Thomas Payne et al., 1767, 2nd ed.; 2 vols.; originally published Oxford: William Jackson, 1764–5).*

CARDINAL POLE

OB. 1557

FROM THE ORIGINAL OF TITIAN IN THE COLLECTION OF

THE RT HONBLE LORD ARUNDEL OF WARDOUR

42 *Engraved by H. T. Ryall.*

43 Giovanni Cavino, medal.

St Petersburg, which must refer to the original, not the portrait lent to the exhibition. The original must have been there before 1864 when it was included in Gustav Waagen's catalogue.[11] According to NPGA notes citing a 1788 inventory, p. 21, what must be a copy inscribed 'REGINALDUS POLE CARDINALIS LEGATUS 1555' entered the collection of the Marquess of Hastings at Donington Park, Leics., where it (or another portrait of Pole) was when G. P. Harding made his inventory a few years later, and was still in 1890 when Lord Donington lent it to the Tudor Exhibition.[12] The copy differs from the original in the inscription and in size (49 × 39"). Nos. 34 and 37 may have been taken from this copy, which could mean it was in England by mid-century, although no. 34 probably derives from no. 33. Present whereabouts unknown.

---

[11] *Die Gemäldesammlungen in der kaiserlichen Ermitage zu St. Petersburg* (Munich: F. Bruckmann, 1864; 2nd ed., St Petersburg, 1870). Cf. the photo by Hanfstängl of Munich, probably Franz or one of his successors, from an unidentified book *Petrograd*, detached copy in CIA. Cf. Scharf (notes on *Tudor exhibition*, no. 216) who in his discussion of the de Larmessin engraving cited 'Petrograd', p. 249, but actually no.

249. Reversed from Sebastiano.

[12] NPGA, George Perfect Harding, 'List of portraits, pictures in various mansions of the United Kingdom', three MS vols., 3, p. 25. For Harding, see *DNB*, 8, pp. 1219–20. Hastings's portrait may have come to him through his mother, the daughter of the ninth earl of Huntingdon, and thus a direct descendant of Pole through his niece's marriage to the third earl. *DNB*, 9, p. 117.

Donington's gallery also included the portrait of the Countess of Salisbury in the NPG.[13]

2. Giorgio Vasari. *Rimunerazione delle Virtù*. Sala dei Cento Giorni, Cancelleria palace, Rome. August 1546.[14]

3. After Perin del Vaga (?) (1501–47) or Bartolomeo Cancellieri (sixteenth-century).[15] Carlton Towers, Yorkshire. Inscribed: 'Cardinal Polu[s] Anglus'. Undated.

Provenance: Aleci thinks this is the portrait which once belonged to Giovio, but this seems unlikely on grounds of size, and it also does not resemble either of the copies known to have been taken from his *museo*, nos. 4 and 20 below.[16] Then again, the inscription suggests that it was originally part of a series. See NPGA, *The New Gallery, Regent Street. Exhibition of the Royal House of Tudor*, 1890, with Scharf's notes, no. 207, when it belonged to Sir Charles H. Tempest, Bart. The catalogue ascribes it to Perin and dates it Rome, 1535; formerly in Strozzi collection. If the dating and attribution are correct, this could just be the 'original' of no. 6, both of which are closely related to no. 11, except for size.

4. Antonio Maria Crespi, called il Busto or il Bustino (1712–81). Biblioteca Ambrosiana, Milan.[17] Another copy in an unidentified English collection.

Provenance: Carlo Marcora puts it on the list from Giovio's *museo*.[18] It is thought to be copied from Giovio's original, which was by a Roman artist who also did Bembo, Sadoleto and Contarini and came to Giovio via Camillo Bosio, according to Antonio Olgiati, librarian of the Ambrosiana.[19] It is not in its 1686 inventory, but that includes less than half the items Marcora thinks were in

13 J. R. Green, *A short history of the English people, illustrated edition*, ed. Mrs J. R. Green and Kate Norgate (London: Macmillan, 1893; 4 vols.), 2, p. 686.

14 Robertson, pp. 62–8.

15 Linda S. Klinger, 'The portrait collection of Paolo Giovio', Ph.D. thesis, Princeton University, 1991, cat. no. 290.

16 *Ibid.* and cf. Carlo Marcora, 'Ritratti conservati all'Ambrosiano copiati dal Museo Giovio di Como', *Periodico della società storica Comense*, 48 (1981), pp. 89–122, p. 122.

17 *The Ambrosiana gallery* (Vicenza: Neri Pozza, 1986), p. 35. Klinger, illus. no. 79a.

18 Marcora, p. 122. See also Bruno Fasola, 'Per un nuovo catalogo della collezione gioviana', in *Giovio*, pp. 169–80, p. 178.

19 Marcora, pp. 119 and 122. For Bosio, see a letter to him from Carlo Sigonio, dated either 1545 or 1575 and another of 1584, both in Antonio Ceruti, ed., *Lettere inedite di dotti italiani del secolo XVI tratte dagli autografi della Biblioteca Ambrosiana* (Milan: Boniardi-Pogliani, 1867), pp. 103–4, 112. The originals are in Ambrosiana MS S 108 sup., according to William McCuaig, whom I thank for help.

Como.[20] It is similar to Uffizi Gallery, Florence, no. 3021, supposedly copied by Cristofano dell'Altissimo from Giovio's collection and in the Uffizi by 1557.[21] Altissimo's copy, however, seems much closer to no. 6 than to Giovio's, the two known copies of which are almost identical.

5. Jacopino del Conte (1510–96), according to Aleci. English private collection. Undated. Pole holds a letter addressed 'Al Ill.mo Cardinal Reginaldo Polo in Roma' (To Card. Reginald Pole, Rome). 25 × 18". Probably a copy of the portrait in the Ambrosiana. It could be linked to nos. 12–13.

6. Unknown. Lambeth Palace; unidentified Oxford College; private collection, Milan. c. 1550 or earlier?
Provenance: Both the Lambeth copy (measuring 44 × 35"; the Oxford copy is 43.5 × 34") and the next number were in the Palace as of 1575, but not in 1784.[22] It reappeared by 1806, when it was distinguished from no. 7.[23] According to J. Cave-Brown, Archbishop Moore (archbishop 1783–1805) donated it.[24] Scharf said that it was copied for him from an original in Italy, which conflicts with Strong's information.[25] If the painting were in the Palace already, why would Moore have had to donate it? The explanation may be that the painting was removed during the Civil War and only recovered by him. In 1888, it hung in the dining room at Lambeth.[26] The Milan copy was bought on the antique market there in the 1960s. It has a notation on the back in English that it had hung *in alto in biblioteca* ('high in the library').[27] Were it not for the language of the notation, it might perhaps be the portrait that Joyner said was in Palazzo Farnese as of 1686.[28] The Biblioteca grande of Palazzo Farnese held

---

[20] Marcora, p. 117.

[21] Fasola, pp. 170–1 and no. 313; *Gli Uffizi. Catalogo generale* (Florence: Centro Di, 1979), Ic380 (serie Giovio, identified as 'Veneziano, canonista'), 6 × 43 cm.

[22] Strong, 2, p. 252, citing *Archaeologia*, 30 (1844), p. 11, the inventory of Archbishop Parker's paintings and BL, Add. MS. 6391, fos. 194v or 195v. The painting does not appear in the inventory in Ducarel, p. 86 dated August 1784, which noted only one portrait of Pole, which must be no. 7.

[23] *A concise account, historical and descriptive, of Lambeth palace* (London: Herbert and Brayley, 1806), p. 47.

[24] J. Cave-Brown, *Lambeth palace and its associations*, special edition with extra plates in 3 vols. (London: no publisher, 1882; otherwise Edinburgh: Blackwood, 1882), p. 130.

[25] Cf. NPGA, Scharf's notes to *A series of historical portraits selected from the national portrait exhibition of 1866* (London: Arundell Soc., n.d.), no. 185.

[26] Lee, p. 256.

[27] I am grateful to Sig.a Anna Malatesta for her courteous assistance with this painting.

[28] William Joyner, *Some observations upon the life of Reginaldus Polus cardinal of the royal blood of England. Sent in a pacquet out of Wales, by G. L. gentleman and servant to the late majesty of Henrietta Maria* (London: Matthew Turner, 1686), p. 123.

forty-five portraits, according to the inventory of 1653.[29] Joyner gave as the titulus the whole of Flaminio's carmen, 'De Imagine Reginaldi Poli': 'Si velut egregia pictura, maxime Pole,/ Est expressa tui corporis effigies,/ Sic divina tuae potuisset mentis imago/ Pingi, nil oculi pulchrius aspicerent', while on the Oxford and Lambeth versions the titulus is an adaptation of the carmen, and reads 'Si sic Pole. tuae potuisset mentis imago pingi nil oculi pulcrius aspicerent'.[30] The titulus could not have been on the painting in toto, although it does appear beneath the engraving reproduced in Christopher Hare, Men and women of the Italian reformation (London: Stanley Paul, 1914), opposite p. 48, which is a version of no. 32 below. One wonders whether Joyner actually saw a portrait. The painting once in Palazzo Farnese is not in Naples or Parma and Giuseppe Bertini kindly informs me that he has found no trace of it elsewhere. Strong cited Joyner and tentatively identified the Farnese portrait as the large Lambeth Palace type on the strength of the titulus, and further identified this type as that engraved by Reusner (actually Stimmer; see no. 20) and then in no. 25.[31] Aleci dated this type between 1536 and 1545 because Vasari's portrait was supposedly derived from it, and argues against Strong that this portrait and no. 3 are not Venetian, but close to Vasari, and that there is no reason to think that Lambeth is a copy.[32] According to Scharf's SSB 73, p. 40, a copy by Harding, dated 1807 was in the collection of the earl of Derby and illustrated in Knowsley, Lambeth palace illustrated, p. 39 (a mistake for Brayley, Lambeth palace illustrated [London: published for Herbert and Brayley, 1806]?). It is closely related to no. 11, which seems more likely to be the copy, than the other way around, since it is much smaller. If the provenance for no. 11 is correct, this must mean that the large Lambeth was indeed an Italian portrait, which Pole brought with him.

7. Unknown. Lambeth Palace, London. Panel painting. Probably after March 1556 because Pole's arms are quartered with those of the archbishop of Canterbury, and perhaps prepared for the visitation of Oxford in the summer of 1556. It was probably originally on cloth. The inscription, now largely illegible,

---

[29] Pierre Bourdon and Robert Laurent-Vibert, 'Le palais Farnèse d'après l'inventaire de 1653', Mélanges d'archéologie et d'histoire, 29 (1909), pp. 145–98, pp. 163–4.

[30] Marci Antonii, Joannis Antonii et Gabrielis Flaminiorum Fornocorneliensium Carmina (Padua: Giuseppe Comino, 1743), pp. 78–9. Mrs R. L. Poole, Catalogue of portraits in the possession of the university, colleges, city and county of Oxford, 2 (Oxford Historical Society, 81, 1926), p. 213. Cf. the plate in G. M. Bevan, Portraits of the archbishops of Canterbury (London: Mowbray, 1908), opposite p. 49, which looks as if the titulus was still legible.

[31] Tudor portraits, 2, p. 252.

[32] Klinger, p. 151.

is supplied from an engraving by W. Maddocks: 'Reginaldus Polus R. Cardinalis Collegii Corporis Christi oxon. olim socius electus in dictum Collegium – 14 Feb. [1523]'.[33] A second inscription in a box beneath the portrait, nearly illegible already in Maddocks's engraving, was expanded by Cave-Brown from Ducarel's transcription (p. 86) to read 'Natalis probitas doctrinae salvaque virtus te juvene inclarent totum . . . alta per orbem'. According to Daniel Lyson the painting was copied from a portrait once in the Barberini Gallery, but this is probably a mistake for no. 6, and may be a mistake about its provenance as well.[34] I have not been able to confirm a portrait presently in the Barberini collection (see also no. 11 bel.). Lee noted a portrait formerly in Casa Grimani, Venice, 'now in private hands' and thought it 'possibly a reproduction of the ancient one on panel at Lambeth, though the hair and beard are darker; or possibly it is another original by the same artist'.[35]

Might this be a knock-off of no. 5? Was it the more recently arrived of the two portraits at Lambeth, since it was so often reproduced early in the nineteenth century? Cf. no. 9.

8. Unknown. Corpus Christi College, Oxford, Senior Common Room.[36] It appeared in *Royal House of Tudor*, no. 219, small bust to left, 10 × 10", lent by Dr Fowler. He acquired it from the collection at Clopton Hall, Warwickshire.[37] Probably related to the last no.

9. Unknown. NPG. After March 1556 because Pole's arms are quartered with those of the archbishop of Canterbury. It is fairly closely related to no. 7, and may perhaps be a funeral portrait. Fifteenth-century Italian portraits were often

---

[33] *A concise account*, colour plate facing p. 47. Cf. also Thomas Allen, *History and antiquities of the parish of Lambeth* (London, 1827), p. 207, quoted in Lee, p. 257. Even Allen's reading is a little corrupt, since he must have missed the initial 'S' before 'R. E.'. Maddocks's engraving appears in British Museum, Department of Prints and Drawings, *Catalogue of engraved British portraits preserved in the Department of Prints and Drawings in the British Museum*, 3 (London: British Museum, 1912), pp. 483–4 (hereafter *BM catalogue*); two versions of 1810 and 1817 in Lee, p. 258; and in Cave-Brown, facing p. 130.

Granger (1824), 1, p. 193. The entry recording Pole's admission is printed in Lee, pp. 6–7n.

[34] *Environs of London* (London: Cadell, 1795; 6 vols.), 1, p. 264 and 4, p. 595. Cave-Brown (p. 130) repeated Lyson's provenance.

[35] Lee, pp. 247–8. What Lee meant by the panel portrait is a little confusing, since the sister portrait in Milan to the large Lambeth was transferred from panel to canvas. Private communication from Anna Malatesta.

[36] My thanks to Sir Keith Thomas and S. J. Harrison for their help with this picture.

[37] Poole, p. 267.

created posthumously, but according to Sydney Anglo, 'picture' in descriptions of funerals in England meant an effigy of the deceased, not a portrait.[38]

10. Taddeo Zuccaro (1524–66). *Julius III restoring the duchy of Parma to Ottavio Farnese*. Sala dei Fasti farnesiani, Villa Farnese, Caprarola. 1562–3.[39] Pole appears on the extreme right of the painting in a group of three cardinals.[40]

11. Pietro Labruzzi (1739–1805), according to Harding, Labruzzi's contemporary, followed by Scharf. Lord Talbot of Malahide, formerly in the collection of Lord Arundell of Wardour.[41] Undated; Schenk guessed 1543 (p. xv). 11.5 × 8.5". There are numerous copies, usually ascribed to Titian, and it was engraved at least three times (nos. 38–9 below).

Provenance: Scharf thought it may have been listed in BL, Add. Ms. 6391, fo. 234v, no. 17, dated 1796. According to *A series of historical portraits selected from the National Portrait Exhibition of 1866* (London: Arundell Soc., n.d.), no. 195, it belonged to the Rocci family, who bought it from the Colonna.[42] This seems unlikely if the attribution to Labruzzi is correct; it may instead refer to the genealogy of no. 6. Scharf's notes on *Royal House of Tudor*, no. 234, p. 74, call it similar to no. 207 (no. 3 above). His 'Iconographical notes' said it was taken from another copy 'in the Barberini Gallery (see also no. 7 above) which is an ancient copy from the original in the Florentine Gallery', but in his NPGA notes to *National portrait exhibition of 1866*, no. 185 he called it a copy by Labruzzi of the original in Italy of the large Lambeth. The first claim appears to mean that this

---

[38] Corinne Mandel, review of Paolo Tinagli, *Women in Italian renaissance art: gender, representation, identity* (New York: St Martin's Press, 1997), *SCJ*, 29 (1998), p. 596. Sydney Anglo, 'Image-making: the means and the limitations', in John Guy, ed., *The Tudor monarchy* (London: Arnold, 1997), pp. 16–41, pp. 18–22.

[39] Robertson, p. 96. J. A. Gere dates the preparatory drawing to the same years. *Taddeo Zuccaro. His development studied in his drawings* (Chicago: University of Chicago Press, 1969), pp. 180–1 and 199–200.

[40] Of the large bibliography on Caprarola, see especially Robertson, pp. 95–102; Loren W. Partridge, 'Divinity and dynasty at Caprarola: perfect history in the room of Farnese deeds', *Art bulletin*, 60 (1978), pp. 494–530, pp. 509–10, who probably has Pole in the wrong painting (I am nevertheless grateful to him for assistance on this point); I. Faldi, *Il palazzo Farnese di Caprarola* (Turin: SEAT, 1981); and best on the portraits Giuseppe Bertini, 'I ritratti al naturale nella Sala dei Fasti di Caprarola', in *Bulletin de l'institute historique belge de Rome*, 63 (1993), pp. 33–77, p. 73. I have profited from many consultations with Bertini about Pole and Caprarola.

[41] 2, pp. 319 and 320 (1804). Phillips (1, p. xv) claimed that the Wardour of Arundell family were related to Pole.

[42] Cf. Lee, p. 257.

portrait descends from Dell'Altissimo's copy (see above no. 4) from Giovio's gallery via another copy, suspected by several writers in the NPGA notes to be by Moroni, probably meaning Giovanni Battista (1524–78).[43] It is closely related to, and probably derived from, no. 6. The nineteenth-century copy in the Venerable English College, Rome, may have been taken from its 'original'. The fact that the first engraving dates only from 1816 (below no. 38) may argue in favour of the attribution to Labruzzi. The photograph in A. F. Pollard, *Thomas Cranmer and the English reformation 1489–1556* (New York and London: Putnam, 1904), p. 362 shows the frame as it then was and gives an acknowledgment to Cassells.

12. Unknown. Hardwick Hall, Derbyshire, where it was from at least 1865.[44] Undated, but late sixteenth-century. 21 × 17.25". It formed part of a series of famous men. This and the next no. are closely related, and Strong tied both to nos. 6, 8, and 9, a loose grouping.[45] Scharf made a similar list, omitting the next no. and without lumping the images together (*DNB*).

13. Unknown. Formerly in collection of Earl Granard.[46] 1557? Auctioned at Sotheby's, 14 July 1993. 15.5 × 11.5". Identified by Scharf as part of a series of famous men like the last no. Sotheby's catalogue description includes inscription 'Anno Domini 1557/ Aetatis sua [*sic?*] 57'. This may be the painting listed by Harding (3, p. 25) as at Donington Park, at least the inscriptions match.

14. Unknown. Trinity College, Cambridge, picture store.[47] 19 × 16" according to Scharf. It once hung in the Master's Lodge, and was first listed in Harding (3, p. 104).[48] Description: 'Half life size seen to waist. Head slightly left, grey hair, grey moustache and beard. Body to front. Hands in front of waist resting on a table – left hand holding glove. Wears a white surplice showing black at wrists, scarlet amice[49] and square red cap'. The pose does not precisely resemble any known portrait.

---

[43] There is no such portrait in Mina Gregori, *Giovanni Battista Moroni. Tutte le opere* (Bergamo: Bolis, 1979).

[44] CIA, neg. no. B72/38, with note to E. St John Gore, *NT Index* (1963).

[45] *Tudor portraits*, 2, p. 252, pl. 498.

[46] Cf. photo in NPGA dated 1935 and correspondence with Granard from the following year.

[47] I am grateful to Mrs Alison Sproston for information about this painting, especially the description in her letter of 1 May 1996 and to Patrick Collinson for assistance.

[48] Scharf's notes in Trustees' Sketch Book no. 30, p. 56 and SSB, 106, p. 58a.

[49] Either a sort of stole or a hood worn around the neck. It is just one of the elements that does not describe cardinal's dress.

15. Follower of Robert Peake (died 1626).[50] Formerly in the Bedingfield collection at Oxburgh Hall, Norfolk, present whereabouts unknown. According to H. E. P. Bedingfield (private communication), it was sold in 1951 or 1952 to David Trappes-Lomax, from whose estate it was sold again, at which time Bedingfield and the National Trust tried to acquire it. It was resold at Bonhams on 4 July 1996 as Lot 5.[51] 'Body nearly full, face and small eyes turned towards the sinister, white round beard and moustache, crimson cap on the head with a white edge. Dress: pink cape, high collar with white edge, with indented V-shaped opening to sleeves, scarlet under-sleeves, brown fur cuffs, two buttons fastened, opening under neck; the hands are forward holding a book in the centre.... Age 60. Date c. 1550.'[52]

II. Spurious and Supposititious Painted Portraits

16. Jacopino del Conte. *Paul III and a Prelate*. Santa Francesca Romana (Santa Maria Nova), Rome.[53] The *Touring Club Italiano* guide attributes the painting to Perin del Vaga or Sermoneta.[54] Mario Armellini identified the sitter as Pole, but his baldness excludes that possibility.[55] Cf. the fringe of hair in, e.g., no. 11.

---

[50] Roy Strong, *The English icon: Elizabethan and Jacobean portraiture* (London and New Haven: Paul Mellon Foundation for British Art and Routledge and Kegan Paul and Yale University Press, 1969), pp. 225–54 for Peake. On pp. 233–5 he notes a follower of Peake active in the reign of Charles I.

[51] J. R. S. Guiness first brought this information to my attention, and I am grateful to Andrew Moore for confirming it.

[52] Frederick Duleep Singh, *Portraits in Norfolk houses* (Norwich: Jarrold, 1927), 2, p. 128. Although portraits of Pole were assiduously acquired in England, at least one collector declined to include an image of him in his gallery. Despite John Evelyn's recommendation that Lord Clarendon add Pole (listed among the 'Politicians', the other five being Walsingham, Leicester, Raleigh, Wolsey and Sir Thomas Smith), Clarendon failed to do so, at least Evelyn listed no portrait in his inventory drawn up twenty years later. *The diary of John Evelyn with an introduction and notes by Austin Dobson* (London: Macmillan, 1906; 3 vols.), p. 293 and E. S. de Beer, ed., *The diary of John Evelyn*, 3 (Oxford: Clarendon Press, 1955), p. 520n. Maria Theresa Lewis, *Lives of the friends and contemporaries of... Clarendon, illustrative of portraits in his gallery* (London: John Murray, 1852); 3 vols.), descriptive catalogue, 3, pp. 250–435, expanding Evelyn's list, also does not mention Pole.

[53] Cf. Zapperi for Jacopino and this portrait.

[54] *Guida d'Italia, Roma* (Milan: TCI, 1993), p. 261.

[55] *Le chiese di Roma dal secolo IV al XIX* (Rome: Tipografo Vaticano, 1891), p. 892. He was followed by Livio Iannattoni, *Roma e gli inglesi* (Roma: Atlantica Editrice, 1945), pl. facing p. 80, and *Enciclopedia italiana* (Rome: Istituto dell'Enciclopedia Italiana, 1949), 27, p. 616.

17. Perin del Vaga (died 1547). Collection of Earl Spencer, Althorp. Photograph in *National portrait exhibition of 1866*, no. 206, 45 × 36". Also in Manchester Exhibition of 1857, cat. no. 199, where it was ascribed to Perin del Vaga (NPGA notes). There is supposed to be an illustration of it in Gustav Waagen, *Treasures of art in Great Britain* (London: John Murray, 1854), but the version in NPGA has only blank pages where the illustrations should have been, and the only other copy I have been able to see (at Bowdoin College) has no illustrations.[56] Waagen's description (3, p. 455) of a portrait in the collection of Earl Spencer at Althorp, which he could visit only rapidly, appears to fit this no.: Perin del Vaga, 'Portrait of the celebrated Cardinal Pole, at a very advanced age, with a long white beard, in a white dress, with a black collar and cap. He is represented sitting, and seen nearly in front. To the knees. The expressive character is strongly conceived; the brownish glowing colouring appears exaggerated in the hands.' Cf. K. J. Garlick, *A catalogue of pictures at Althorp* (Walpole Society XLV, 1976), no. 295 (formerly 315): *A prelate* ('Card. Pole'). Canvas mounted on wood. 45 × 38". Roman portrait by follower of Sebastiano, influenced by del Conte. It was in the Sunderland collection in 1746, no. 102, and noted by Horace Walpole in 1760 (Walpole Society, XVI, p. 32), and was identified in 1802 as an unknown churchman by Perin and in Harding's inventory (3, p. 200) as Pole.

18. Strong, *Tudor portraits*, p. 252 says Pole's letter to Francisco de Navarra of 17 May 1550 concerned a portrait, but the letter itself was meant.

III. Prints

19. Unknown Flemish engraver. In André Thevet, *Les vrais pourtraits et vies des hommes illustres* (Paris: I. Kervert et Guillaume Chaudière, 1584), Livre VI, chapitre 117, 'Regnaud Pol, Cardinal, Anglois'. Copper-plate engraving.[57] Copy in BM. Detached copy in Pierpont Morgan Library with document MA

---

[56] Algernon Graves, *Summary and index to Waagen* (London: Privately Printed, 1912), lists all the illustrations.

[57] Cf. Roger Schlesinger, ed., *Portraits from the age of exploration: selections from André Thevet's Les vrais pourtraits et vies des hommes illustres*, trans. Edward Benson (Urbana: University of Illinois Press, 1993), pp. 11, 14, and 15. Thevet tried for accuracy, and Jean Adhémar and Jean Baudry think he achieved it. Haskell, pp. 51–2 (with reference to Adhémar). Jean Adhémar, *Inventaire des fonds français: graveurs du seizième siècle* (Paris, 1938), pp. 114–19 is supposed by Schlesinger to give the provenance of Thevet's illustrations, but it merely lists them.

548. A copy in LPL was reproduced in *British Magazine* (no date given), and said to be taken from one for 'De Thouanus, 1584, chap. 117, Regnaud Pol, Cardinal Anglois'. This identification arises from a confusion of Thevet with Jacques-Auguste de Thou, *Les éloges des hommes scavans tirez de l'histoire de M. de Thou*.[58] According to NPGA notes, this print also exists in small versions, reversed, and in the cut and paste books of A. M. Broadley and Thomas Hayes, *Eccl. Iconography* [*sic*], 16, p. 176 (1904).

The strange attire resembles that of Pierre d'Ailly (Livre VI, chapitre 94), but not that of other cardinals contemporary with Pole, e.g., Fisher (Livre III, chapt. 81); Hosius (ibid., chapt. 82); Bembo (Livre VI, chapt. 98); Georges d'Amboise (ibid., chapt. 104); and Charles de Lorraine (ibid., chapt. 120). Granger flatly said that the print was 'fictious' [*sic*].[59] Nevertheless, the garb appears to be derived from that shown on the reverse of a medal commemorating the reconciliation of England (below no. 40), although Pole's beard is longer on the medal.

20. Tobias Stimmer (1539–84). In Nikolaus Reusner, *Icones sive imagines vivae, literis cl. variorum, Italiae, Graeciae, Germaniae, Galliae, Angliae, Ungariae* (Basel: Conrad Waldkirch, 1589), sig. Dd 4.[60] Woodblock. Stimmer is identified as the artist in the preface. Copy also in BN, Madrid.[61] Almost certainly derived from Giovio's portrait (above no. 4). Stimmer, or perhaps an assistant, probably made the drawing when he was sent by Perna to Como in order to prepare the illustrations for two editions of Giovio's *Elogia* (1575 and 1577).[62] It does not meet Stimmer's usual standard. Accompanied by verses from Flaminio ('Si velut egregia pictura'; above) and Blosio Palladio:

Foedarunt miseras passim scelera impia terras:
    Nec quo se virtus iam tueretur, erat.
Cum Deus aeterna impulsus pietate ruinas
    Despexit, nostras indoluitque vices.

---

58 Cf. Haskell, p. 69 for De Thou's 134 portraits, which he never used in writing. I have checked the 2nd ed. of Utrecht: F. Halma, 1696.

59 Granger (1824), 1, p. 192n. The painting is illustrated in the sale catalogue.

60 Paul Ortwin Rave, 'Paolo Giovio und die Bildnisvitenbücher des Humanismus', *Jahrbuch der Berliner Museen*, 1 (1959), pp. 119–54, pp. 153–4.

61 Elena Páez Ríos, ed., *Iconografía britana: Catálogo de los retratos grabados de personajes ingleses del Biblioteca nacional* (Madrid: No Publisher, 1948), p. 534, where said to be de Galle type. Cf. Fasola, p. 170; Klinger, fig. no. 79, said to be from Reusner and connected to Giovio's portrait; and *DNB* (one of only two engravings noticed).

62 Rave, pp. 149–51.

Sicque Polum aetherea iuvenem demisit ab arce:
Dixit & [*sic*]; Hic nostri pignus amoris erit.
Vindice quo priscos virtus retinebit honores:
Qui vitia in fausto [sic] comprimet exilio.
Ergo cum hic adsit coelestum munere, in illum
Iure oculos cuncti fiximus, atque animos.[63]

21. Théodore de Galle (1571–1633). Pl. X (sig. D1r) of *XII Cardinalium* . . .
imagines et elogia (Antwerp: Philippe Galle, 1598). Copy in BM, identified as
Dutch print. Reproduced in Godelieve Denhaene, *Lambert Lombard.*
Renaissance et humanisme à Liège (Antwerp: Fonds Mercator, 1990), p. 15, illus.
no. 11. Two copies in BN, Madrid, and another in Houghton Library, Harvard
(Typ 530.98.415).[64]
Verse below reads: 'Tu quoque Pole, decus patriae, vindexque Britanniae, /
Quem genitrix, frater, morte obita decorant. / Morus item, atque Fischerus flos,
et ocellus: / Quos et transcripsit mors violenta polo'.
Image taken from original in Fulvio Orsini's gallery in Rome. *Elogium* probably by André Schott, SJ. (J. Fabri, 'G415', *Biblioteca belgica*, ser. 3, vol. 6 (n.d.),
p. 7.)
Referred to: John Hutchins, *The history and antiquities of the county of Dorset*,
ed. W. Shipp and J. W. Hodson (Westminster: J. B. Nichols and sons, 1861–74;
reprinted EP Publishing, 1973; first published 1774; 4 vols.), 3, p. 188; Granger
(1824), I, p. 193.

22. Version of last no. Sold in Paris by F. Desroches, rue du Foin près la rue St
Jacques. Undated. Inscription: 'Polus issu du Sang Royal/ Eut toutes les vertus
royales:/ Et comme sage cardinal/ toutes les vertus cardinales'. NPGA. There is
perhaps another copy in BN, Madrid, with inscription 'Renard Polus Cardinal
et Archeveque de Contorbie [sic] en Angleterre Cousin germain du Roy Henry
7 [sic], mort en 1558'.[65]

23. Related to no. 21, reversed, closely related to no. 30. Undated. Titled 'Den
Cardinael Reginaldus Polus, engraving, fol? 179 in upper right'. NPGA.

---

[63] For the verses, see also Guido Battelli, 'Un
umanista romano del Cinquecento: Blosio
Palladio', *La bibliofilia*, 43 (1941),
pp. 16–23, p. 17n.

[64] *Iconografía britana*, p. 533.
[65] *Iconografía britana*, p. 534.

24. No. 21, reproduced in *Herωologia* (1620). Inscription: 'Reginaldus Polus. Principis e stirpe et magni cognominis haeres. Exul, amat patrios Romae mutare penates'. LPL print 151a. Illustrated (from BM copy) in A. M. Hind, *Engraving in England in the 16th and 17th centuries*, 2, *The reign of James I* (Cambridge: Cambridge University Press, 1955), pl. 70a, where it is said to be taken from no. 6; cf. pp. 159–62 for a catalogue of locations. This interpretation descends from Granger, who based himself on Ducarel.[66] The claim is repeated in NPGA notes, and at least once it is identified as the earliest engraving. Scharf corrected this mistake in the *DNB*, which cites only it and no. 20 above. Another copy in BN, Madrid.[67] Reversed in Paulus Freher (1611–82), *Theatrum virorum eruditione singulari clarorum* (Nürnberg: J. Hofmann, 1688), pl. 3 facing p. 30.

Referred to: Hutchins.

25. Unknown. In Claude Pernet (b. ca. 1589), *Illustrissimorum, omnique virtutis, et scientiarum laude praestantissimorum virorum icones* (Rome: no publisher, 1621; BAV: Capponi IV 97), p. 5. Resembles a copy in NPGA from the MacDonnell collection, two sides of the same sheet, with manuscript biography in French, and reference to *Herowlogia* at the end.[68]

Referred to: Hutchins.

26. Unknown. In Giovanni Imperiale, *Museum historicum et physicum* (Venice: Giunti, 1640), p. 32. De Galle type. BM.

Referred to: Hutchins; Granger (1824; cf. 1769), 1, p. 192.

27. F. Wyngard or van den Wyngaerde (1614–79). In Henri Albi, *Eloges historiques des cardinaux illustres, françois et étrangers, mis en parallele avec leurs pourtraits au naturel* (Paris: Antoine de Cay, 1644), p. 242. De Galle reversed; almost identical otherwise. Sommervogel gives a second ed. of Paris (Jean-Baptiste Loyson, 1653) with forty-one portraits instead of the forty of the original.[69] Copy in BN, Madrid.[70]

Referred to: Hutchins.

---

[66] Granger (1824; cf. 1769), 1, p. 192n.

[67] *Iconografía britana*, p. 533.

[68] Also reproduced in Rodolfo Lanciani, *The golden days of the renaissance in Rome* (Boston: Houghton, Mifflin, 1906), p. 211. Mentioned in Lee, p. 258 and Granger (1824), 1, p. 193.

[69] Augustin de Becker, *Bibliothèque de la Compagnie de Jesus*, ed. Carlos Sommervogel (Paris: A. Picard et fils, 1890–1909; 10 vols.), 1, cols. 134–6.

[70] *Iconografía britana*, p. 534, also taken from Albi and identified as de Galle type. Mentioned in Lee, p. 258 and Granger (1824), 1, p. 193.

28. Engraved by R[obert] White (1645–1703). Printed for Richard Chiswell at the Rose and Crown in St Paul's Churchyard. Surrounded by 'Effigies Reginaldi Poli Cardinalis'. Inscription on plinth, on both sides of Pole's arms surmounted by cardinal's hat, reads 'Natus anno 1500. Maii cc. Cardinalis S. Mariae in Cosmedin 1536 Maii 22. Consecr. Archiepic: Cantuariensis, 1555/6 Mar: 22. Obijt 1558. Nov: 17'. In Gilbert Burnet, *The history of the reformation of the Church of England* (London: Printed by T. H. for Richard Chiswell, 1681–3; 2 vols.), vol. 2, facing p. 292. LPL print 150. *BM catalogue* lists an 'exact copy' by P. Simms (cf. Lee, p. 259, without connection to White), together with two Dutch copies (cf. the next entry, and perhaps NPGA print 4c, reversed, which lacks inscriptions and arms and is simply titled 'Cardinal Pole') and a modern version. Lee, p. 257, says it derives from no. 26, which may be possible, although direct from no. 21 seems more likely.

Referred to: Hutchins; Granger (1824; cf. 1769), 1, pp. 192–3.

29. Unknown; pirated copy of White. In Gregorio Leti, *Historia ovvero Vita di Elisabetta* (Amsterdam: Abraham Wolfgang, 1693; 2 vols.), 1, facing p. 137. Lee, p. 257 cites the edition of 1703, 1, fig. 9, which is probably a mistaken reference to the source of the next no. Same surround and inscription on plinth as White. Cf. copy in NPGA (4b), without inscription on plinth, and Lee, pp. 258–9, citing a copy in 'Tweede Deel, fol. 477' of an unknown work.

30. De Larmessin, one of a large family of engravers in seventeenth–eighteenth centuries, probably Nicholas le jeune (1640–1725). In Isaac Bullart, *Academie des Sciences et des Artes* (Brussels: F. Foppolas, 1695; two vols.), 1, pp. 55–60, pl. 9. NPGA. LPL Prints XV 246. It and the NPGA copy are two different pulls. It is derived from no. 21, but perhaps also from no. 26.

Referred to: Hutchins; Granger (1824), 1, p. 192.

31. NPGA, one of three similar small prints. It is initialled TG (?) in lower left corner as if supposedly derived from a reversed no. 21 (?), but it comes almost directly from the last no. Headed 'Cardinal Pool', and ringed by 'Le Cardinal Polus'. Unknown source. Undated.

32. Adrian van der Werff (1659–1722), engraved by P. à [van] Gunst.[71] No. 16 of fifty plates for Isaac de Larrey, *Histoire d'Angleterre, d'Ecosse et d'Irlande*

---

[71] Barbara Gaehtgens, *Adriaen van der Werff 1659–1722* (Munich: Deutscher Kunstverlag, 1987), pp. 37–82.

(Amsterdam: Jan Cusens and Cornelis Mortier, 1723 [?]). First edition Rotterdam, 1697–1713, printed by R. Leers, dedicated to William of Orange; also Dutch ed. 1728–30. According to Barbara Gaethgens, the originals are bound in two volumes, now in s'Gravenhage, Koninklijk Huisarchief.[72] LPL, Print 151b. Copy in BN, Madrid.[73] *BM catalogue*, from a Dutch plate. Inscription by de Larrey: 'Testois du sang royal mais mauvais politique/ J'avertivai [possibly 'invectivai' as Paez Rios reads] le Roi, qui mit ma tête à prix!/ Le Pape cependant n'eut pour moi que meprie/ Et par tout ma vertu n'eut qu'une fin tragique'. De Larrey: 'Ce celebre peintre [van der Werff], qui les a dessinées a voulu encore historier chaque portrait et par des figures qui lui donnent un agréable relief, donner an même temps une juste idée de la personne don't j'ai achevé d'exprimer les principeaux caractères per un quadrin au dessous de chaque estampe'. Probably derived from White (no. 28), perhaps via the BL Dutch plate (not seen, but it appears to be no. 23 above). Another version with different cartouche, archiepiscopal arms and Flaminio *carmen* illustrated in Hare, *Italian reformation*, opposite p. 48. Perhaps the version cited in Lee, p. 258, which 'differs slightly' from the BM copy. Cf. no. 6 above.

Referred to: Hutchins; Granger (1824; cf. 1769), 1, p. 193.

33. Nicholas de Larmessin [IV (1684–1753)]. Engaged by Crozat to engrave part of his collection, plates published in *Recueil d'estampes d'après les plus beaux tableaux et d'après les plus beaux desseins qui sont en France* (*Recueil Crozat*) (Paris: Imprimerie royale, 1729 and 1742; 2 vols.), 1, p. 32. 'Portrait du Cardinal Polus d'apres le Tableau de Raphaël, ou de Fra Sebastien del Piombo, qui est dans le Cabinet de M. Crozat'. NPGA. CIA (Witt Library). Better pull in J. Pierpont Morgan Library, New York, acquired with MS MA 841. BM. J. R. Green, *A short history of the English people, illustrated edition*, ed. Mrs J. R. Green and Kate Norgate (London: Macmillan, 1893; 4 vols.), 2, p. 722. Other prints derived from it in the NPGA and listed in *BM catalogue* are supposed to include one by R. Graves (undated), attributed to Sebastiano. NPGA has a tracing by Scharf dated 4 February 1865, 'dans le Cabinet de Mr. Crozat', from a large version. Its original should be in NPGA, Large portfolios, but cannot be located. Lee (p. 258) said it was copied as Phillips's frontispiece, which may be true in a loose sense, although the image is reversed, itself reversed from no. 1.

---

[72] Gaethgens, pp. 131 and 391–4 (catalogue). For them see E. Pelinck, 'De ontwerpen van Adriaen van der Werff voor de Larrey's "Historie d'Angleterre, d'Ecosse et d'Irlande"', *Oud Holland*, 81 (1966), pp. 52ff.

[73] *Iconografía britana*, p. 534.

[74] I have found no information about Hinton.

34. John Hinton.[74] *The Universal Magazine of Knowledge and Pleasure . . . and other Arts and Sciences*, 5 (1749), opposite p. 169. Probably reversed version of last no., although it could have been taken from the copy of the Sebastiano, if it was then in England. Perhaps the original of Phillips's frontispiece (no. 37 bel.). Cartouche: 'Cardinal Pole The Popes Legate & Archbishop of Canterbury'. Engraved for the *Universal Magazine* 1749 for J. Hinton at the Kings Arms in St Paul's Church Yard London.

35. George Vertue (1684–1756). Engraving in *Oxford Almanac*, 1730 (Bodl. G. A. Oxon. a. 88, fo. 141r), showing Magdalen College, Pole in a group with Wolsey and Waynfleete.

36. John Green (c. 1729–c. 1757). Engraving in *Oxford Almanac*, 1758 (Bodl. G. A. Oxon. a. 88 [239]), of Corpus Christi College, Pole at the centre, with other members, including John Jewel and Richard Hooker, according to a probably eighteenth-century annotation, a remarkably ecumenical line-up.

37. 'Painted by Raphael, engraved by Major'. ?Derived from no. 1, but perhaps more likely from no. 34. Frontispiece to Phillips. Resemblance to Sebastiano noted by Strong, p. 253, my colleague Roman Bonzon, and Lee (p. 258) who claimed it was copied from no. 33.
   Referred to: Hutchins; Granger (1824), 1, p. 193.

38. C[harles] Picart (1780–c. 1837), from drawing by Harold Crease. London: Lackington, Allen & Co., 1816. Engraving of Talbot. LPL Print 149b. Separately printed from the engraving in the first edition of Edmund Lodge, *Portraits of illustrious personages of Great Britain, with biographical and historical memoirs of their lives and actions* (1814, according to the *DNB*, which I have not been able to see). It appeared in the collective edition in four volumes (London: Lackington, Hughes, Harding, Mavor and Lepard; and Longman, Hurst, Rees, Orme and Brown, 1821–34), 1, each biography paginated separately, the engraving dated 20 July 1816. It was replaced by an engraving dated 1 August 1824 by W. Holl in the 1824 ed. (London: Harding, Triphook and Lepard), 2, each biography separately paginated; a slightly different print in the popular edition in eight volumes (London: Henry Bohn, 1849), 1, opposite p. 253; and in the 1904 ed. by the next no.; also in Cave-Brown, facing p. 130. Lee, p. 258, 'from the original by Titian, in the Collection of Lord Arundell of Wardour'.
   Referred to: Hutchins; Granger (1824), 1, p. 193.

39. H. T. Ryall (1811–67). Engraving of Talbot. Printed in *The history of the*

reformation of the church of England by Gilbert Burnet, D. D.; a new edition . . . embellished with forty-seven portraits (London: William Smith, 1841; 2 vols.), 1, facing p. 164; Edmund Lodge, *Portraits of illustrious persons* (London: Charles Black, 1904), 2, each biography separately paginated; frontispiece to Lee. It also appeared as a card, published in London and New York by John Tallis and Co., undated (LPL Prints 149c and Lee, p. 258).

Medal

40. Giovanni Cavino (1500–70).[75] BM Medals Department. Vienna, Kunsthistorisches Museum, Münzkabinett, Inv.-Nr. 5.147 bß [sic].[76] The die is in the collection of the Paris mint.[77] Struck to commemorate the reconciliation of England, it featured a bust of Julius III on the obverse, and a kneeling England, Pole, Julius, Charles V, Philip and Mary on the reverse.[78] It is possible that this medal is connected to Marco Mantova Benavides, one of Cavino's most prominent patrons, and among Pole's acquaintance in Padua.[79]

Unconfirmed or untraced portraits and prints

41. Unknown. In Antoine du Verdier (1544–1600), *Prosopographie, ou description des hommes illustres, et autres renommez . . .* (Lyon: Paul Frelon, 1605) and *La prosopographie, ou, description des personnes insignes, enrichie de plusieurs effigies, & reduite en quatre livres* (Lyon: Antoine Gryphius, 1573). The print is known from Sommervogel, who said it was borrowed from Albi, but that is impossible on chronological grounds.[80] There is no entry for Pole in the first edition, and the only copy of the second I have been able to see (in the BAV Stamp. Barb. Z. II 31–3) has no plate.[81] The 1573 edition had 528 pages and the 1605 edition was greatly expanded. A standard potted life of Pole appeared on pp. 2392–7.

[75] *DBI.*

[76] *Vittoria Colonna*, III.23, p. 256, illus.

[77] Francesco Cessi in collaboration with Bruno Caon, *Giovanni da Cavino, medaglista padovano del Cinquecento* (Padua: Lions Club di Padova, 1969), pp. 50–1, unnumbered pl. facing p. 80 and pl. 19.

[78] Alfred Armand, *Les médailleurs italiens des quinzième et seizième siècles* (Paris: Plon, 1883, 2nd ed.; reprinted Bologna: Forni,

1966; 3 vols.), 1, p. 183 mistakenly said it was struck for the royal wedding.

[79] For Mantova and Cavino, see the correspondence in Padua, Biblioteca del seminario, cod. DCXIX, v. 5.

[80] Sommervogel, cols. 134–6.

[81] I am grateful to Ms Jennie Rathbun of the Houghton Library for assistance with the 1st ed.

42. Lee (p. 248) claimed to know of several oil portraits in Rome, two in the Vatican, one in the English College (see above), and three others in private hands. One formerly belonged to Cardinal Aldobrandini and another 'a large, three-quarter length portrait in *cappa magna*'[82] to Henry Stuart, Cardinal Duke of York. The garb and pose make this yet another otherwise unknown image. I have not been able to locate any portraits now in the Vatican.

43. Musée Impériale de Versailles 1859–61 (from Collège de Sorbonne). Seventeenth-century. 0.68 × 048 m.[83]

44. J. Fougeron, according to *BM catalogue*, n.d.

45. Rodd's priced Sale Cat. 1824, p. 29 no. 92: 'Changed with Dr Barrett for Spelman'.[84]

46. NPGA, SSB 110, p. 17: Duke of Bedford, Woburn Abbey, modern copy, of which original not indicated.[85]

47. Lumley Inventory 1590.[86] John, Lord Lumley was a Catholic, some of whose collection passed to his son-in-law the earl of Arundel, and some probably to his wife. Those pictures remaining at Lumley Castle went to the earls of Scarborough before being dispersed in the eighteenth and early nineteenth centuries. From its place in the inventory, Pole's portrait seems to have been part of another series of famous men.

48. Barrington Hall, Essex, according to BL, Add. MS 6391, fo. 43, no. 6.

---

[82] Clare Constans, *Catalogue des peintures, Versailles* (Paris: Editions de la Réunion des Musées, 1980), p. 144, no. 5093.

[83] 'A jurisdictional garment reserved for the use of an ordinary.' It was fur-lined (ermine for cardinals) and fifteen feet long. James-Charles Noonan, Jr, *The church visible: the ceremonial life and protocol of the Roman Catholic church* (New York: Viking, 1996), pp. 317–18.

[84] *A catalogue of authentic portraits painted in oil, on panel and canvas ... the whole of which are now offered for sale, at the prices affixed by H. Rodd, 9 Great Newport Street, Long Acre* (London, 1824). Rodd was probably Horatio, who was also a bookseller of 23 Little Newport St. See A. N. L. Munby, *Phillips studies* (Cambridge: Cambridge University Press, 1951–60; 5 vols.), 3, p. 47.

[85] Perhaps cf. A. M. B. and E. M. S. Russell, *Biographical catalogue of the pictures at Woburn Abbey* (London: E. Stock, 1890 and 1892; 2 vols.), which I have not been able to see.

[86] Lionel Cust, 'The Lumley inventories', *Volume of the Walpole society*, 6 (1918), pp. 15–35, pp. 23 and 18–19.

49. Nether Hall, Lot 384, 5–6 May 1987.

50. Mrs Eyre Huddleston, Sawston Hall, Stonor, Cambs., after 1968, p. 10.

51. Cardinal Pole, chancellor of Oxford and Cambridge A. D. 1557. Postcard by Day and Haghe, n.d.

52. Garlano? and C. Turner, *Portraits of Illus. Persons*, p. 26: crayon drawing after Sebastiano by R. Dunkarton (or Dunkerton). Also in R. J. Colman, *Catalogue of engraved Norwich and Norfolk portraits*, 1911, p. 131. I have not been able to see either. This citation may refer to no. 15 above.

53. Cardinal Poole. Small oval. London: printed for R. Chiswell. Lee, p. 258. This must be either a knock-off of, or a mistake for, no. 28.

54. An etching in the BM from Cracherode collection, 'without title or lettering'. Lee, p. 258.

55. Apparently N. de Larmessin, reversed, by 'J. S'. Lee, p. 258.

56. Coloured engraving, reproduced in *The King*, 30 September 1905. Inscription: 'The scion of an ancient Dorset family'. Ducarel noted that the Poole family of Dorset had a portrait as of 1784.[87]

---

[87] Ducarel, p. 86.

Conclusion:
'Ein Kämpfer gegen seine Zeit'?[1]

NIETZSCHE MIGHT HAVE coined his tag for Pole so well does it fit him. Pole opposed efforts to upset the balance in the Christian republic to the advantage of monarchs, whether secular or ecclesiastical, and thereby became one of the mid-sixteenth century's most important figures.[2] And failures. Pole had greatness thrust upon him and it missed. Superlatively well educated and repeatedly given opportunities to use his rhetorical skills as a diplomat and administrator, Pole never fulfilled his potential. He failed to change the course of the Henrician reformation managing so to offend the emperor in the process that it took him a dozen years to recover, missed the papacy by one vote, refused to stop the Inquisition in its tracks, fumbled a major chance to regain lost ground from Edward VI, could not make peace in Europe, missed the best opportunity to restore the English church under Mary, and then largely destroyed it and himself through conflict with Paul IV. Or at least so the story could be written. Doing so highlights the role of Pole's personality, especially his inflexibility, at the same time as it overlooks the role of circumstances and contingency, and more important, of his reactions to them, above all in writing.

Pole's faulty sense of rhetorical occasion as much as anything else caused his failure. Nowhere is this truer than in the protracted campaign against Henry that captures Pole entire, language and man, as it suggests the necessity of the kind of approach taken in this book. Pole's and Henry's relationship seems simple when told in the serious terms of motive and event. Up to a point it must be. Their similarity gave Pole and Henry great potential for conflict. Sprung of

---

[1] The chapter title ('A fighter against his time') comes from Friedrich Nietzsche, 'Vom Nutzen und Nachteil der Historie für das Leben', *Unzeitgemäße Betrachtungen* (Munich: Wilhelm Goldmann, 1964), p. 112.

[2] Cary J. Nederman, 'The puzzling case of Christianity and republicanism: a comment on Black', *American political science review*, 92 (1998), pp. 913–18.

similarly lofty families, they shared many characteristics. Most important, they were utterly self-willed. If ever an issue should divide them, that would mean a conflagration. Their resemblances meant that when they fell out, they fought over the same ground. The right to decide who could say what was best for the people of England. The right to determine the succession, a question in which both had a vested interest. The right to appeal to the Old Testament's providential history for justification. Above all, the right to claim that God was on his side. At an even more fundamental level, they contended over honour, a concept whose meaning and practice neither could control. This naturally made them struggle more fiercely.

Although neither stayed within the rules, Henry and Pole chose to pretend that they were playing the game of chivalry. This masked the confrontation with power which embraced them both, whether originally political power, or in the long run the power of the pen. The stresses produced are immediately apparent in the physical behaviour of the protagonists, whether Pole's exile, or Henry's attempts to drag him home. Henry seems perfectly in character as a late-feudal monarch.[3] Seeing Pole in chain mail, rather than his familiar cardinal's habit, is much harder.

The reason lies in another dimension of their only partially metaphorical duel, language and literary behaviour. Talk of honour from Pole's side and loyalty from Henry's did not contain the dispute. Pole turned against Henry an arsenal of acts incorporated in texts, created by his skill in playing with language. Henry and his supporters responded with other acts incorporated in other texts, those of parliament and of propaganda. Here we come to the crux, and perhaps the breaking of the framework. Taking into full consideration Pole's consummate rhetorical prowess threatens the enterprise of this book. As Richard Lanham has argued, a rhetorical history would mock the serious, motivated, eventful kind.[4] Lanham's description of the Renaissance 'rhetorical man' fits Pole perfectly.[5] The 'rhetorical ideal of life' meant that 'words not ideas' mat-

---

[3] S. J. Gunn, 'The French wars of Henry VIII', in J. Black, ed., *The origins of war in early modern Europe* (Edinburgh: John Donald, 1987), pp. 35–7.

[4] Taking full account of 'the rhetorical, playful range of motive' requires that history be recast as 'essentially literary, as animated by dramatic motive, play instead of purpose'. Better yet, it must include 'the symbiotic relationship' between serious and playful epistemology, style, and reality, and be

'rewritten as the quarrel between the central and the social self, between society as drama and society as highly serious, one-time sublimity'. Richard A. Lanham, *The motives of eloquence: literary rhetoric in the Renaissance* (New Haven: Yale University Press, 1976), p. 34. Even 'fully serious history' must incorporate both 'purposive and playful' notions of events. *Ibid.*, p. 20.

[5] *Ibid.*, pp. 3–5.

tered, and winning the game was the main object. Playing gave pleasure, not merely advantage. Pole may have been a dour, taciturn, even grimly intent personality (I do not say he was), but his *personae* revelled in the delights and beauties of language. As his first biographer put it, his style was 'more Asiatic than Attic'.[6] He could not stop the tumble of words and the pleasure they produced. Even if his style did not match Cicero's, Pole took as much 'pleasure in impersonation' as Cicero did.[7]

As rhetorical man, Pole constantly ran the risk of being misread, taken as serious when he was playing, as playful when deadly in earnest. By never putting an idea the same way twice, he could no more satisfy an inquisitor's demand for consistency than he could transmit a stable image to the future without severe editing of the original. Pole's play was his downfall.

It was also the essence of the Renaissance, according to Lanham. This gives us a clue to explain Pole's transition from Renaissance to counter-reformation figure. Of course, we could make the problem disappear by insisting that these categories have either outlived their usefulness or, however valuable in the abstract, do not work in any individual instance. Since it seems unlikely that historians will ever abandon periodization, it would be as well to reject the radical alternative and return to a dialectical reading. By insisting on the centrality of play, by constantly replicating his *personae* while simultaneously reiterating his preference for withdrawal in the face of demands for seriousness and engagement, Pole misread changing circumstances and missed the chance to preserve a safe haven for play within a new universe. His failure is emblematically captured by his inability to do any more than sympathize with the fate of Alessandro Farnese's trees, buffer between his Roman gardens and the world. Once Pole realized his mistake, he tried to be serious, or at least act seriously, and not by coincidence helped to invent the counter-reformation, alas, just when it was about to be upset in his native country. Paradoxically, Paul IV refused to see that Pole had given up some of his playfulness, in no small part because Pole continued to insist on dealing with Paul in playful fashion, sending him letters and messengers replete with more *personae*, more exempla. It may be only in his highly rhetorical sermons that Pole successfully played in public and might have accomplished much more than he did as administrator. While more play in person would also have made Pole a better courtier and thus have forwarded his agenda in England, less play would have stood him in better stead with the pope. His sense of occasion proved almost unerringly defective. Small wonder that he insisted constantly in writing that he wished to withdraw, and that his favourite

---

[6] *MMB*, p. 331. [7] Lanham, pp. 13–14.

personae left him the victim of circumstances. These *personae* went straight into historiography and writer in spite of himself, Pole succeeded wildly at transcending his original context. Thus originally private writings came to compensate for public failure.

This may be unfair to Pole, and a public standard the wrong one to apply in order properly to assess his significance. Pole succeeded best in private away from the public stage. Neither of these points is new, nor is the suggestion that he deliberately defended privacy (or at least some internal space) against the intrusions of tyrants. His withdrawal has almost always been read as resistance, but its precise nature has not been grasped. The private realm was to Pole not merely a political and religious haven, but perhaps even more important a gender refuge, to the degree that these three can be distinguished.

The last chapter's discussion of Pole's image pointed towards this conclusion, and I now argue explicitly that its ungendered nature may reflect Pole's reality more than many elements of his myth. This reality, too, was ungendered. But how to characterize it? With all due caution, I shall identify Pole as homosexual, at the same time as I hasten to add that I agree with those critics who insist there was no such thing in the sixteenth century.[8] This formulation is more than another paradox, desperately framed around the 'hamletic' Pole. On one level the point is deceptively simple: Pole 'identified' with men. On another, it is complex, since this identification did not mean, and probably could not have meant, what it does now. Nevertheless, as Keith Thomas argues, the matter of gender identity and power 'deserves to be placed high on the agenda, not just of "queer historians", but of historians *tout court*'.[9]

Let us defer the problem of characterization and first consider the evidence. Some of it has already been discussed, especially Bocchi's emblem and, most convincing, Sebastiano's portrait. Other indications come from Pole's intensely felt correspondence with Camillo Orsini, his relationship with Flaminio encapsulated in Flaminio's lap-dog *carmen*, or with Cosmo Gheri who died after a homosexual rape, or very likely with Morone, to whom Pole described himself as a naked stable boy. Morone's tortured attempt to explain away Priuli's longing to see Pole during an extended separation skated around any talk of Priuli's 'flesh' and narrowly made it to the relatively safe ground of his spiritual love for Pole.[10] Priuli, of whom it was said that he 'worshippeth and observeth him

---

[8] As defined by Leonard Barkan in *Transuming passion: Ganymede and the erotics of humanism* (Stanford: Stanford University Press, 1991), p. 24.

[9] Keith Thomas, 'Review of Jonathan Goldberg, ed., *Queering the renaissance*' in *The New York review of books*, 41:15 (22 September 1994), pp. 9–12, p. 12.

[10] *PM*, 2:2, pp. 706–8 and see above pp. 136 and 139.

[Pole] for a god', and with whom Pole lived for more than twenty years, was certainly homosexual.[11] The best evidence comes from his relationship with Francesco Berni, a self-confessed homosexual and sometime dependant of Giberti (whom Pietro Aretino accused of being sodomized by Berni).[12] In early March 1533, Berni drafted a poem to Priuli saying 'you know that I love you more than a bear does honey'.[13] Berni included the verse in a letter to Marco Corner, one of the youthful *signori abbati* he and Priuli frequented, and with whom Berni several times said he wished to sleep in a *capitolo* addressed to both him and his brother.[14] Probably in 1534, Berni wrote Priuli a passionate letter that seems difficult to read as anything other than an expression of love.[15] It concluded with an apostrophe to Contarini and another to *i signori virtuosi* whom Priuli had called 'my true friends', perhaps including Pole.[16] Berni was close to at least one more man whose gender orientation is significant to Pole: Pietro Carnesecchi. Carnesecchi appeared in Berni's very important *Capitolo a fra Bastiano dal Piombo* (written about the time of Berni's letter to Priuli), which describes a homosexual agape, with Carnesecchi's 'fried gourds' (*zucche fritte*) as one of the dishes.[17] Carnesecchi was famously beautiful as a youth and young man, as several portraits manifest.[18] Benedetto Varchi, a virtually public homosexual, praised both his beauty and his spiritual elevation.[19] The combination typifies Berni's and Priuli's (and Pole's) circles. Carnesecchi – who also may have

[11] PRO, SP 1/242, fo. 96r, printed in Henry Ellis, ed., *Original letters illustrative of English history*, 3rd series, 2 (London: Richard Bentley, 1846), p. 127.

[12] Francesco Berni, *Rime*, ed. Danilo Romei (Milan: Mursia, 1985), p. 6 for his 'impudent and aggressive homosexuality'. Anne Reynolds, *Renaissance humanism at the court of Clement VII: Francesco Berni's Dialogue against poets in context* (New York and London: Garland Publishing, 1997), p. 137 for Aretino's attack that might ordinarily be taken with a grain of salt, but for Berni's self-revelation.

[13] Antonio Virgili, *Francesco Berni* (Florence: Le Monnier, 1881), pp. 303–4. Also quoted in embarrassed fashion in Pio Paschini, *Un amico del Cardinale Polo: Alvise Priuli* (Rome: Pontificio Seminario Romano Maggiore (Lateranum no. 2), 1921), p. 17.

[14] Romei, ed., pp. 123–5 (comment on p. 16), written in March 1531.

[15] Antonio Virgili, ed., Francesco Berni, *Rime, poesie latine e lettere edite e inedite* (Florence: Le Monnier, 1885), pp. 329–32. For the context and a brief treament of Berni's relations with Priuli see Virgili, *Berni*, pp. 471–3. Paschini (p. 18) labelled the letter 'curious'.

[16] Virgili, *Berni*, p. 471.

[17] Romei, ed., p. 185.

[18] Bernard Berenson, *Italian pictures of the Renaissance, Florentine school*, 2 (London: Phaidon Press, 1963), pls. 1404–6. There is another in the Uffizi.

[19] Oddone Ortolani, *Per la storia della vita religiosa italiana nel Cinquecento. Pietro Carnesecchi* (Florence: Le Monnier, 1963), pp. 20–1 and Umberto Pirotti, *Benedetto Varchi e la cultura del suo tempo* (Florence: Olschki, 1971), *passim*, esp. pp. 47–8.

had a reputation for passive sodomy – in turn leads both to Giovio and to Rullo, whom Giovio coupled in a letter to Carnesecchi asking him to kiss Rullo with the same affection that he (Giovio) would Priuli.[20] Rullo followed Priuli to England, and became as great a suspect heretic, but there is no other evidence of his gender orientation. There is for Giovio. Like Giberti, he was several times accused of sodomy, and there is a probably inauthentic epigram by Aretino calling him a 'hermaphrodite'. Most telling, Giovio chose as his *impresa* a beaver, which when caught, gnawed off its own testicles, leaving them as the hunter's prey. Giovio was lucky, however, in that he had three, according to another pasquinade.[21] It will be remembered that Giovio replaced three eunuchs with a group of Bembo, Sadoleto, Pole, and himself in Vasari's *Rimunerazione delle virtù*.

It could be argued that Priuli, like many early modern Italian men, 'went through a phase' of homosexuality as a youth before 'getting over it'.[22] Priuli's description of Pole's final moments (perhaps significantly addressed to Carranza) belies this possibility. 'When he [Pole] was about to communicate, in saying confession, being supported by two [attendants] . . . he bowed his head almost to the ground . . . in which he seemed to me to represent the holy mother of our Lord, painted beneath the cross sustained by the two Marys'.[23] The joint epitaph for Pole and Priuli among Morone's papers points to the same conclusion: the two were and remained a couple, although they were denied burial together like that accorded Giovanni Pico della Mirandola and Girolamo Benivieni.[24]

---

[20] Massimo Firpo and Dario Marcatto, eds., *I processi inquisitoriali di Pietro Carnesecchi (1557–1567)*, 1, *I processi sotto Paolo IV e Pio IV (1557–1561)* (Vatican City: Archivio Segreto Vaticano, 1998), p. 123, the hostile testimony of Bernardo de' Bartoli. No other witness, pro or con, reported this rumour. Paolo Giovio, *Lettere*, 2, ed. Giuseppe Guido Ferrero (Rome: Tipografo dello Stato, 1958), p. 12.

[21] BAV, Vat. lat. 5225, vol. 4, fo. 903v speaking of Giovio's 'mentulis trabalibus'. I owe knowledge of this text to Kenneth Gouwens and Price Zimmermann, with whom I have also had many helpful discussions of Giovio's gender identification. See T. C. Price Zimmermann, *Paolo Giovio: the historian and the crisis of sixteenth-century Italy*

(Princeton: Princeton University Press, 1995), pp. 324, 9–10 (the *impresa* and Giovio's explanation of it), and 114 (sodomy).

[22] Michael Rocke, 'Gender and sexual culture in renaissance Italy', in Judith C. Brown and Robert C. Davis, *Gender and society in renaissance Italy* (London and New York: Longman, 1998), pp. 150–70, p. 166.

[23] *CRP*, no. 2315.

[24] ASV, Armaria 64:28, fo. 250r and James Saslow, 'Homosexuality in the renaissance: behavior, identity, and artistic expression', in M. B. Duberman, M. Vicinus, and G. Chauncey, eds., *Hidden from history: reclaiming the gay and lesbian past* (New York: New American Library, 1989), pp. 90–105, p. 97.

Pole never expressed himself as unequivocally about Priuli as Priuli did about him, never calling him anything more than 'another Achates' (Aeneas's inseparable companion in the *Aeneid*), but his behaviour speaks volumes.[25] It is not too much to say that he and Priuli were married.[26] This should be a less surprising claim now than it might have been twenty years ago. The nature of early modern homosexuality has become a serious topic of debate, and Pole and Priuli can shed light on the two most contentious issues, whether homosexuality existed and, if so, the nature of relations between homosexuals. The evidence does not allow me to say anything on the score of their sexuality as opposed to gender identification, and the question may be strictly irrelevant given the strong tendency to spiritualize the kind of love Pole and Priuli shared.[27] The majority position on the first point, usually called social constructionism (or more pejoratively 'new inventionism'), holds that the concept of homosexuality is a nineteenth-century invention and absent the label, absent the thing, although a few historians, usually called 'essentialists', maintain that there have always been gays.[28] Instead, there was a 'conceptual plasticity of gender' or 'what we would call bisexuality'.[29] Two major points separate sixteenth-century and modern sexuality and gender identification. First, no one then defined him or herself in

---

[25] *CRP*, no. 206. Feliciano Speranza, 'Acate', *Enciclopedia virgiliana*, 1 (Rome: Enciclopedia Italiana, 1984), pp. 8–9. There seems to be no erotic dimension to this relationship.

[26] Cf. John Boswell, *Same-sex unions in premodern Europe* (New York: Vintage Books, 1995), pp. 10–11 and 191, allowing that despite the fact that neither modern understandings of homosexuality nor marriage obtained, premodern 'same-sex unions' may still be called marriages.

[27] Giovanni Dall'Orto, '"Socratic love" as a disguise for same-sex love in the Italian renaissance', *Journal of homosexuality*, 16:1 & 2 (1988), pp. 33–65, pp. 37–8 and Saslow, p. 97 for Marsilio Ficino's condemnation both of genital sexual relations between men of the same age and also of pederasty.

[28] Two of the leading proponents of social constructionism are David Halperin and Robert Padgug. See their representative

essays in *Hidden from history*, pp. 37–64. Joseph Cady roundly attacks 'new inventionism' in '"Masculine love", renaissance writing, and the "new invention" of homosexuality', in Claude J. Summers, ed., *Homosexuality in renaissance and enlightenment England: literary representations in historical context* (London: Haworth Press, 1992), pp. 9–40. I am grateful to Cady for sending me a copy of his article and discussions of the topic. Boswell was the leading 'essentialist'. Much of the debate smacks of the dreaded historical conundrum of 'originology'.

[29] Stanley Chojnacki '"The most serious duty": motherhood, gender, and patrician culture in renaissance Venice', in Marilyn Migiel and Juliana Shiesari, eds., *Refiguring woman: perspectives on gender and the Italian renaissance* (Ithaca: Cornell University Press, 1991), pp. 133–54, p. 153 and Saslow, p. 91.

terms of sexuality and, second, as already suggested, one of the principal differences lay in the sixteenth-century separation of emotion and sexuality, in the distinction between 'Socratic love' and pederasty.[30] What to call the phenomenon is much less interesting than trying to describe it, and here the second point arises. Again, the majority position holds that homosexual relations were almost exclusively pederastic and therefore asymmetrical in terms of age, power, and, sometimes class.[31] A minority view finds companionate, egalitarian, 'modern' relationships, or at least their possibility; they may or may not have been modelled on the Greeks, especially Aristophanes' speech in *Symposium* 191e.[32] Pole's case complicates the picture. On the one hand, his marriage to Priuli supports the minority view, but on the other, it looks as if both he and Priuli also shared pederastic inclinations.

Naturally, not much can be made of the young boys brought into Pole's household. This was normal for any noble's entourage. The dialogues Pole wrote for two much younger men, Cosmo Gheri and Giulio della Rovere, suggest something more, although neither makes explicit Pole's interest in other than the dedicatees' education. The 'physical culture' opening of 'De humana prudentia', enjoining Gheri to be sure to get enough exercise, may come as close as Pole ever did to expressing an interest in physical beauty.[33] The master–pupil relation Pole established with Della Rovere in 'De summo pontifice' he expected to continue, sending Della Rovere a medal of Socrates as a token. I have not been able to discover whether there was more than superficial significance to this medal, but I do suspect more meaning, especially since it could have been the same token that Cardinal Gianangelo de' Medici (the future Pius IV) sent Pole in 1557, perhaps as a covert sign of a triangular relationship, of de' Medici's success in separating Della Rovere from Pole.[34]

Treating Pole as a pederast may be to get him exactly wrong, as it opens questions about another rooted position in most modern scholarship on Renaissance homosexuality. It is usually argued that the active partner was treated more

---

[30] Bruce R. Smith, *Homosexual desire in Shakespeare's England: a cultural poetics* (Chicago: University of Chicago Press, 1991), p. 11 and Saslow, p. 97.

[31] Rocke, pp. 153 and 167, above all, based on his *Forbidden friendships: homosexuality and male culture in renaissance Florence* (New York and Oxford: Oxford University Press, 1996). Cf. also Guido Ruggiero, *The boundaries of Eros: sex crime and sexuality in renaissance Venice* (New York and Oxford: Oxford University Press, 1985), p. 118.

[32] Boswell, pp. 58–60; cf. pp. 65–7, 75–91 (especially good on the concept of 'friend', concluding with Ganymede), pp. 178ff., 264–5 and *passim*. Cf. also Barkan, p. 23 and Saslow, p. 93.

[33] BAV, Vat. lat. 5966, fo. 1r.

[34] *CRP*, nos. 579 and 2014 and *DBI*, 37, p. 356.

leniently than the passive, since he did not seriously infringe standards of male behaviour.[35] This may be, but such evidence as there is casts Pole in the passive role (in terms of concept, not practice), not at all what would be expected of such a grand noble and prince of the church. He may therefore have bent gender rules in the same way he did many others.[36] The most compelling case comes from his portraiture, especially Sebastiano's painting which cast Pole in the classic female position of the object to be possessed by the beholder (that the original beholder was probably a woman is just the sort of reversal we should expect in Pole's case). The second most important piece of evidence is Pole's letters to Morone and Navarra, in both of which he cast himself in a subordinate role, indeed, in the second in an absolutely passive position as a beast of burden without will or even more significantly honour. If there is anything to my suggestion that this *persona* (if that is the correct word for an animal figure) has gender overtones, then it also has serious implications for notions of honour that Pole's gender identification threatened to undermine.

Thus Pole's experience of gender falls somewhere between both positions on the nature of male same-sex desire, social constructionist and 'essentialist'. This calls once again for a dialectical resolution, as has almost happened in the treatment of sexuality.[37] There seems no obvious reason not to treat gender in the same fashion and to conclude that Pole and his circles fall under the

---

[35] Ruggiero, p. 121 and Rocke, p. 168.

[36] Against Rocke who stresses both that 'sex between males thus always embodied oppositions' (p. 167) and also that gender roles constrained everyone (p. 170).

[37] Such an approach was suggested fifteen years ago by Eve Kosofsky Sedgwick, who defined a continuum of male desire for other men from 'homosocial' at one end to homosexual at the other. She argued that in modern Western culture this continuum has been broken, producing homophobia, but this was not a necessary consequence of patriarchy since the ancient Greeks, as patriarchal a society as the West has known, were not homophobic. *Between men: English literature and male homosocial desire* (New York: Columbia University Press, 1985), pp. 2–5. Thus sexuality must be culturally conditioned, according to Sedgwick by the workings of power (p. 1).

There has been other movement in this direction. Social constructionists almost inevitably tended towards a dialectical interpretation. Alan Bray somewhat hesitantly offered a dialectic between male friend and sodomite, and took an even more cultural relativist position than Sedgwick, but the key factor in making friendship acceptable and sodomy a heinous offence was still power. Alan Bray, 'Homosexuality and the signs of male friendship in Elizabethan England', *History workshop*, 29 (1990), pp. 1–19. Bruce Smith more confidently asserted the same paradox and sketched a way to steer between (or out of) constructionism and essentialism. *Homosexual desire*, pp. 13–14 and p. 18. Randolph Trumbach argued for the existence of a third or possibly a fourth gender in seventeenth-century England. 'London's Sapphists: from three sexes to

rubric of 'homosocial desire' which embraced just about any form of love between men, from the officially sanctioned 'man's man' to the man 'interested in men'.[38]

By its very nature, Pole's gender identification led to resistance, not only in the gross sense that homosexuality had come to be regarded as one of the worst of sins and homosexuals therefore had no choice but to buck the current merely to preserve their existence, but also in much more interesting and empowering ways outlined by Leonard Barkan.[39] According to him, humanism and homosexuality were closely linked, and both were intrinsically subversive.[40] Barkan bases his discussion on the myth of Ganymede, the subject of Bocchi's emblem for Pole, arguing that it 'may express the *identity* or *sameness* that is a condition of the meeting of two apparently distinct selves', a meeting that Barkan argues was fundamental to the challenge humanism presented. Sustained efforts to sanitize the myth by removing its erotic connotations failed, thereby pointing to the problem of interpretation, and highlighting its failure as well. Awareness of these conjoint failures stimulated the humanists to a new kind of creativity and self-awareness, engendered through their encounter with the classical past but only possible in the way it actually happened because of the mediating term of gender identification (pp. 21–6). The particular fate of Ganymede is especially relevant to Pole, apart from Bocchi's emblem, since the interpretation of the myth turned on precisely the opposition between carnal and spiritual that lay at

---

Footnote 37 (*cont.*)

four genders in the making of modern culture' in Gilbert Herdt, ed., *Third sex, third gender: beyond sexual dimorphism in culture and history* (New York: Zone Books, 1994), pp. 111–36. Even the 'essentialist' John Boswell sketched a 'sexual taxonomy', the first position of which overlaps almost exactly with Sedgwick's schema. Type A posits that all people are 'polymorphously sexual'. John Boswell, 'Revolutions, universals, and sexual categories', in *Hidden from history*, pp. 17–36, p. 23. Perhaps most suggestively, F. T. Stevens claimed to have 'dissolve[d] the terms of the debate [between constructionists and essentialists]' and with them 'homo/hetero binarism' in early modern Europe. Quoted in Thomas, review of Goldberg, p. 10.

[38] Thus did Thomas (review of Goldberg) recast Sedgwick's formulation. The resulting double bind seems not to have pinched Pole.

[39] For homosexuality as empowering, see also Smith, p. 12.

[40] Saslow (p. 100) took a first step in this direction with the suggestion that some taken as 'deviants will . . . become "conceptual traitors" capable of deconstructing the official symbols and values that deny their worth and wholeness'. For humanism and homosexuality, see also Ruggiero, p. 137. Ludovico Ariosto notoriously linked the two in *Satire* 6.31–33. Peter DeSa Wiggins, trans., *The satires of Ludovico Ariosto: a renaissance autobiography* (Athens, Ohio: Ohio University Press, 1976), p. 152.

the heart of Pole's religious identity (p. 34). According to Barkan, efforts to make sense of Ganymede, as of humanist understandings of the classical past in general, depended on the trope of transumption which by 'accumulating, juxtaposing, and even betraying tropic meaning [succeeded] in calling attention to its own figural activity' and hence both to hermeneutics and to processes of cultural change (pp. 44 and 48).

The attempt to suppress the homosexual content of the Ganymede myth, pervasive in ancient culture, led to evasion that in turn engendered literary and artistic representation in which rhetoric, 'a belief in the beauties of this world, [and] the desire for fame', were all hopelessly tangled up together, as they were for Pole (p. 55). But the sexual side of the myth would not be quieted, especially not for Michelangelo who drew 'about as explicit an image of anal penetration' as was possible in the sixteenth century. Bocchi's emblem for Pole descended from this drawing. Zeus and Ganymede are simultaneously both two lovers and also body and soul, both pairs inextricably linked to the other (p. 89). Moving back and forth between them represents the 'movement between typological thinking and the representation of repressed desire' (p. 92). In Barkan's interpretation, Bocchi's emblem is 'about' both suppressed carnality and the nature of art. That the image should have been dedicated to Pole makes of him an object on which Bocchi (and behind him Michelangelo) could inscribe their art (and their desire, if Barkan is right; pp. 98–103).

This love was known as *amicitia*, the 'lunga amicitia' that Beccadelli assigned to Pole and Priuli, and the framework within which Beccadelli characterized Pole as 'truly a sincere friend', as it was a Ciceronian friendship that Starkey portrayed between Pole and Lupset.[41] This takes us from Plato to Cicero, and embraces two of the three pagan classical figures of greatest importance to Pole (the third was Aristotle).[42] Cicero's notion of *amicitia* has apparently never been interpreted as having anything to do with gender or sexuality, perhaps because Cicero was 'notoriously straightlaced' or perhaps because *De amicitia*, unlike the *Symposium*, does not blatantly declare its subject to be either love or sex, as well as because of Cicero's public prominence.[43] Nevertheless, the lack of a reading in queer key is surprising. The dialogue does, after all, root *amicitia* in *amor* and in

---

41 *MMB*, pp. 320 and 325; Lorna Hutson, *The usurer's daughter: male friendship and fictions of women in sixteenth-century England* (London: Routledge, 1994), p. 75.

42 For the opening a more intimate early modern 'homosociality' allowed to

'friendship', see Dall'Orto, p. 36.

43 Quotation from Boswell, p. 80. Hutson comes closest to making *amicitia* about affectivity, but her stress on its instrumental side and its displacement into texts mutes its emotional component.

its near relative *caritas*.[44] The essence of friendship (to translate literally) is the discovery of another self such as 'almost to make one of two' (pp. 81, 80, and 23). This point alone raises overtones of Plato's argument in the *Symposium* that all humans had originally been double beings and once Zeus separated them, spent their lives seeking reunion with their other half (*Symposium*, 189d–192a), a metaphor that has often been read as a defence of Socratic love. Just as in the *Symposium*, the corollary of this duality is mutuality and equality, although both Plato and Cicero also allow for a relationship of friendship (or love; *caritas* in Cicero) between partners of different ages (*Amic.*, 101). In Cicero, this is almost an afterthought. In the early discussion of *amor*, he had stipulated that friends were 'equals in love' (32) and also laid down that friends should only be chosen once one had reached the age of judgment (74), and immediately before that there should be no superiors nor inferiors among friends (69–73). Just prior to the late passage, Cicero defined *amor* as 'nothing else than to desire him whom you love' (100).[45] Such love/friendship depended on the friend's virtues, the object to be loved, which sounds like Ficino's commentary on Plato (49–50 and 100). Friendship also demanded *fides*, just one of the many points at which Ciceronian terminology overlapped with Pole's religious vocabulary and may indeed have prepared the way for it (65). The nature of Pole's friendship may best be captured in Cicero's commandment that friends should be wise counsellors, since it was in one-on-one encounters that Pole met his greatest successes (44).

Amicitia was also about political patronage and certainly included the instrumental side of friendship, but read literally Cicero's dialogue describes the other life Pole chose for himself.[46] Although more active in public than earlier biographers sometimes allowed, his preferred sphere was private where he and a small group of friends could love one another without intrusions from politics or other public domains.[47] Valuing private life represents a recent historiographical shift

---

[44] T. E. Page, E. Capps, and W. H. D. Rouse, eds., Cicero, *De senectute, de amicitia, de divinatione*, with an English translation by W. A. Falconer (London: William Heinemann and Cambridge: Harvard University Press, 1938), sections 26–32, 100 and 20 (*caritas*).

[45] I translate *diligere* as 'to desire' since 'value highly' seems inadequate and 'to love' here produces a circular definition. Falconer usually rendered the term as 'to love'.

[46] Neal Wood, *Cicero's social and political*

thought (Berkeley: University of California Press, 1988), pp. 78 and 171. Wood's 'Cicero and the political thought of the early English renaissance', *Modern language quarterly*, 51 (1990), pp. 185–207 focuses on the impact of *De officiis*.

[47] This is not to say that Pole's network of (possibly homosexual) friends did not also function in public. I am thinking in particular of his close ties to Morone or Muzzarelli, and perhaps Carranza, the second two of whom Pole said he 'loved

that gives a new meaning to his resistance.[48] Faced with increasing tyranny in the public spaces he inhabited, Pole withdrew whenever possible, just as his myth had it. Unlike the myth, his motive depended on gender and represented a deliberate choice of *amicitia* over both tyranny and hierarchy of whatever sort. He would much rather have spent time with Priuli and their small circle of friends than served either Henry VIII or the papacy. Not by coincidence, this coterie put much of its energy into Pole's sometimes private, affective, and playful writing.[49] This produced power, not least through its participation in the redefinition of nobility as not so much about virtue as discursive facility.[50] It was Pole's misfortune that writing himself happened not to coalesce with exterior circumstances to the degree that Cicero's self-invention usually did, and that temporarily the sword was mightier than the pen.[51] The wrong-headed serious-minded reading of the myth that arose from his written image gave him a different kind of power, but lost both the play and the friendship. I hope I have restored some of both.

---

uniquely in Christ' (*CRP*, nos. 636 and 951). If so, this suggestion contributes a little to Robert Oresko's quest to uncover the ways in which homosexual sodalities of courtiers contributed to resistance to 'absolutism' ('Homosexuality and the court elites of early modern France: some problems, some suggestions, and an example', *Journal of homosexuality*, 16:1 & 2 (1988), pp. 105–28, p. 124), as it twists slightly Thomas's injunction (review of Goldberg, p. 11) to study the intersection between Judaeo-Christian condemnation of sodomy and ancient acceptance of pederasty. Judaism and Christianity also contained rich resources that could foster homosexual relationships. For some others,

see Boswell, *Same-sex unions, passim.*

[48] E.g., Roger Chartier, ed., *Passions of the renaissance* (Cambridge: Harvard University Press, 1989; A history of private life, 3).

[49] This, too, was a gendered move, as Hutson argues. The ideal of *amicitia* encapsulated the English humanist educational programme which displaced affectivity into discourse, just as Pole did. Unlike Pole, Hutson argues that the object was 'persuading bachelors to marry'. *Usurer's daughter*, pp. 2–3, 62–4.

[50] Hutson, p. 90.

[51] Robert Hariman, 'Political style in Cicero's letters to Atticus', *Rhetorica*, 7 (1989), pp. 145–58, p. 158.

Index

Pole is not indexed, except for an entry covering his works. Popes appear under their papal names.

Printed in the United States
83565LV00007B/40-45/A